ALL IN ONE

Security+™
Certification

EXAM GUIDE

ALL · IN · ONE

Security+™
Certification

EXAM GUIDE

Greg White, Art Conklin, Chuck Cothren, Roger Davis, Dwayne Williams

McGraw-Hill/Osborne

New York • Chicago • San Francisco • Lisbon
London • Madrid • Mexico City • Milan • New Delhi
San Juan • Seoul • Singapore • Sydney • Toronto

The McGraw·Hill Companies

McGraw-Hill/Osborne
2100 Powell Street, 10th Floor
Emeryville, CA 94608
U.S.A.

To arrange bulk purchase discounts for sales promotions, premiums, or fund-raisers, please contact **McGraw-Hill**/Osborne at the above address. For information on translations or book distributors outside the U.S.A., please see the International Contact Information page immediately following the index of this book.

Security+™ Certification All-in-One Exam Guide

90 DOC DOC 0198

Book p/n 0-07-222634-X and CD p/n 0-07-222635-8
parts of
ISBN 0-07-222633-1

Publisher
Brandon A. Nordin

Vice President & Associate Publisher
Scott Rogers

Acquisitions Editor
Tim Green

Senior Project Editor
Betsy Manini

Executive Project Editor
Mark Karmendy

Acquisitions Coordinator
Jessica Wilson

Technical Editors
Eric Jacksh
Larry Passo
Marc Light

Contributor
Mark Huson

Copy Editors
Andy Carroll, Bob Campbell

Proofreader
Stefany Otis

Indexer
Valerie Perry

Computer Designers
Tabitha M. Cagan, Tara A. Davis,
John Patrus

Illustrators
Kathleen Fay Edwards, Melinda Moore Lytle,
Jackie Sieben, Lyssa Wald

Series Designer
Peter F. Hancik

This book was composed with Corel VENTURA™ Publisher.

Dedication

This book is dedicated to the many security professionals
who daily work to ensure the safety of our nation's critical infrastructures.
We want to recognize the thousands of dedicated individuals
who strive to protect our national assets but who seldom receive praise
and often are only noticed when an incident occurs.
To you we say thank you for a job well done!

ABOUT THE AUTHORS

Dr. Gregory White has been involved in computer and network security since 1986. He spent 19 years on active duty with the United States Air Force and is currently in the Air Force Reserves assigned to the Air Force Information Warfare Center. He obtained his Ph.D. in computer science from Texas A&M University in 1995. His dissertation topic was in the area of computer network intrusion detection, and he continues to conduct research in this area today. He is currently the technical director for the Center for Infrastructure Assurance and Security (CIAS) and is an associate professor of information systems at the University of Texas at San Antonio (UTSA). Dr. White has written and presented numerous articles and conference papers on security. He is also the coauthor for three textbooks on computer and network security and has written chapters for two other security books. Dr. White continues to be active in security research. His current research initiatives include efforts in high-speed intrusion detection, infrastructure protection, and methods to calculate a return on investment and the total cost of ownership from security products.

Art Conklin is a research scientist at the Center for Infrastructure Assurance and Security at the University of Texas at San Antonio. He has been a lecturer at the Graduate School of Business at UTSA for the past five years, and is currently working on a Ph.D. specializing in security. Mr. Conklin has an MBA from UTSA, and two graduate degrees in electrical engineering from the Naval Postgraduate School in Monterey, California. His current research interests are in steganography and in security implications of distributed computing. Mr. Conklin is a 10-year veteran of the U.S. Navy, serving as a surface warfare officer and engineering duty officer, and has 10 years experience in software engineering and project management.

Chuck Cothren, CISSP, is a senior network analyst at UTSA CIAS, and has a wide array of security experience including performing controlled penetration testing, network security policies, computer intrusion forensics, and telephony sweeps. He is also well-versed in wireless networking and wireless security assessments. Cothren joined UTSA CIAS in February 2003. He was previously employed as a senior network security engineer working with Fortune 100 clients to provide them with vulnerability assessments and other security services. Prior to that he was employed as a network administrator, and also has experience training and consulting. Cothren is a certified information systems security professional (CISSP) and a coauthor of *Voice and Data Security*. Cothren also holds a B.S. in industrial distribution from Texas A&M University.

Roger L. Davis, CISSP, CISA, is senior internal audit manager at Nu Skin International, evaluating global business operations in over 35 countries. He currently serves as president of the Utah chapter of the Information Systems Security Association (ISSA) and is director of seminars and education for the Utah chapter of the Information Systems Audit and Control Association (ISACA). He is a retired Air Force lieutenant colonel with over 20 years of military and information security experience. Mr. Davis served on the faculty of Brigham Young University and the Air Force Institute of Technology. He coauthored *Voice and Data Security*, which was also translated into Chinese. He holds a master's degree in computer science from George Washington University, a bachelor's degree in computer science from Brigham Young University, and performed post-graduate studies in electrical engineering and computer science at the University of Colorado.

Dwayne Williams joined the UTSA CIAS in 2002 as a senior researcher and has over ten years' experience in information systems and network security. Mr. Williams' experience includes six years of commissioned military service as a communications computer information systems officer in the United States Air Force specializing in network security, corporate information protection, intrusion detection systems, incident response, and VPN technology. Prior to joining the CIAS, he served as director of consulting for SecureLogix Corporation where he directed and provided security assessment and integration services to Fortune 100, government, public utility, oil and gas, financial, and technology clients. Mr. Williams graduated in May 1993 from Baylor University with a bachelor of arts in computer science. Mr. Williams is a certified information systems security professional (CISSP) and coauthor of *Voice and Data Security*.

CONTENTS AT A GLANCE

CONTENTS

ACKNOWLEDGMENTS

We, the authors of *Security+ Certification All-in-One Exam Guide,* have so many individuals that we need to acknowledge—individuals without whom this effort would not have been successful.

The list needs to start with those folks at **McGraw-Hill**/Osborne who worked tirelessly with the project's multiple authors and contributors and lead us successfully through the minefield that is schedule, who took our rough chapters and drawings and turned them into a final, professional product we can be proud of. We thank all the good people from the Acquisitions team, Tim Green, Jessica Wilson, and Gareth Hancock; from the Editorial Services team, Betsy Manini, Mark Karmendy, and David Zielonka; from the Illustration and Production teams, Jim Kussow, Jean Butterfield, Lyssa Wald, Kathleen Edwards, Melinda Moore Lytle, Jackie Sieben, Tabitha Cagan, Tara Davis, John Patrus, George Charbak, Elizabeth Jang, and Lisa Bandini. We also thank the technical editors Eric Jacksh, Larry Passo, and Marc Light; the copyeditors, Andy Carroll and Bob Campbell; the proofreader, Stefany Otis; and the indexer, Valerie Perry for all their attention to detail that made this a finer work after they finished with it.

We also need to acknowledge our current employers who, to our great delight, have seen fit to pay us to work in a career field that we all find exciting and rewarding. There is never a dull moment in security because it is constantly changing.

We would like to thank Mark Huson for his chapter contributions.

Finally, we would each like to individually thank those people who—on a personal basis—have provided the core support for us individually. Without these special people in our lives, none of us could have put this work together.

I would like to thank my wife, Charlan, for the tremendous support she has always given me. It doesn't matter how many times I have sworn that I'll never get involved with another book project only to return within months to yet another one; through it all, she has remained supportive.

I would also like to publicly thank the United States Air Force which provided me numerous opportunities since 1986 to learn more about security than I ever knew existed.

To whoever it was who decided to send me as a young captain—fresh from completing my master's degree in artificial intelligence—to my first assignment in computer security: thank you, it has been a great adventure!

Gregory B. White, Ph.D.

I would like to thank Dr. Glenn Dietrich, who five years ago nudged me to think out of the box and look at an academic career. His guidance and wisdom have acted as the steady influence of a lighthouse for this old sailor as I navigated new shores—thank you for the faith and guidance.

Art Conklin

Josie, I would like to thank you for all the support you have given me to write this book, and the countless other projects I take on.

Chuck Cothren

Uncountable thank yous to my best friend and wife Geena, and to my kids, Angee, Adam, and Reed.

Roger L. Davis

I would like to thank my wife Leah and my family for all the support and love they've shown me on this and every other project I've undertaken.

Dwayne E. Williams

PREFACE

Information and computer security has moved from the confines of academia to mainstream America in the last decade. The CodeRed, Nimda, and Slammer attacks were heavily covered in the media and broadcast into the average American's home. It has increasingly become obvious to everybody that something needs to be done in order to secure not only our nation's critical infrastructure but the businesses we deal with on a daily basis. The question is, "Where do we begin?" What can the average information technology professional do in order to secure the systems that they are hired to maintain? One immediate answer is education and training. If we want to secure our computer systems and networks, our IT professionals need to know how to do this, and what security entails.

Complacency is not an option in today's hostile network environment. While we once considered the insider to be the major threat to corporate networks, and the "script kiddie" to be the standard external threat (often thought of as only a nuisance), the highly interconnected network world of today is a much different place. The U.S. government identified eight critical infrastructures a few years ago that were thought to be so critical to the nation's daily operation that if one were to be lost, it would have a catastrophic impact on the nation. To this original set of eight sectors, more have recently been added. A common thread throughout all of these, however, is technology—especially technology related to computers and communication. Thus, if an individual, organization, or nation wanted to cause damage to this nation, it could attack it not just with traditional weapons but with computers through the Internet. It is not surprising to hear that among the other information seized in raids on terrorist organizations, computers and information about the Internet are present. While the insider can certainly still do tremendous damage to an organization, the external threat is again becoming the chief concern among many.

So, where do you, the IT professional seeking more knowledge on security, start your studies? The IT world is overflowing with certifications that can be obtained by those attempting to learn more about their chosen profession. The security sector is no different, and the Security+ exam offers a basic level of certification for security. In the pages of this exam guide can be found not only material that can help you prepare for taking the examination but also the basic information that you will need in order to understand the issues involved in securing our computer systems and networks today. In no way is this exam guide the final source you will need in order to learn all about protecting your organization's systems, but it serves as a point from which to launch your security studies and career.

One thing is certainly true about this field of study—it never gets boring. It constantly changes as technology itself advances. Something else you will find as you progress in your security studies is that no matter how much technology advances and no matter how many new security devices are developed, at its most basic level, the human is still the weak link in the security chain. If you are looking for an exciting area to delve into, then you have certainly chosen wisely. Security offers a challenging blend of technology and people issues. We, the authors of this exam guide, wish you luck as you embark on an exciting and challenging career path.

Gregory B. White, Ph.D.

INTRODUCTION

Computer security is becoming increasingly important today as the number of security incidents steadily climbs. Many corporations are now spending significant portions of their budget on security hardware, software, services, and personnel. They are spending this money not because it increases sales or enhances the product they provide, but because of the possible consequences should they not take protective actions.

Why Focus on Security?

Security is not something that we want to have to pay for, it would be nice if we didn't have to worry about protecting our data from disclosure, modification, or destruction from unauthorized individuals, but that is not the environment that we find ourselves in. Instead, we have seen the cost of recovering from security incidents steadily rise along with the rise in the number of incidents themselves. Since September 11, 2001 this has taken on an even greater sense of urgency as we now face securing our systems not just from attack by disgruntled employees, juvenile hackers, organized crime, or competitors. We now have to also consider the possibility of attacks on our systems from terrorist organizations. If nothing else, the events of September 11, 2001 showed that anybody is a potential target, you do not have to be part of the government or a government contractor, being an American is sufficient reason to make you a target to some and with the global nature of the Internet, collateral damage from cyber attacks on one organization could have a worldwide impact.

A Growing Need for Security Specialists

In order to protect our computer systems and networks, we will need a significant number of new security professionals trained in the many aspects of computer and network security. This is not an easy task for the systems we connect to the Internet are becoming increasingly complex with software whose lines of codes number in the millions. It is not hard to understand why this is such a difficult problem to solve if one considers just how many errors might be present in a piece of software that is several million lines long. When you add the additional factor of how fast software is being developed, out of necessity as the market is constantly moving, it is easy to understand how errors occur.

Not every "bug" in the software will result in a security hole, but it doesn't take many to have a drastic affect on the Internet community. We can't just blame the vendors for this situation, because they are reacting to the demands of government and industry. Most vendors are fairly adept at developing patches for flaws found in their software and patches are constantly issued to protect systems from bugs that may introduce security problems. This introduces a whole new problem for managers and administrators to be concerned with—patch management. How important this has become is easily illustrated by how many of the most recent security events have been as a result of a security bug that had been discovered months prior to the security incident, and for which a patch has been available, but the community has not correctly installed the patch making the incident possible. One of the reasons for this is that many of the individuals who would be responsible for installing the patches are not trained to understand the security implications surrounding the hole or the ramifications of not installing the patch. Many of these individuals simply lack the necessary training.

It is for this reason, the need for an increasing number of security professionals who are trained to some minimum level of understanding, that certifications such as the Security+ certification have been developed. Prospective employers want to know that the individual they are considering hiring knows what to do in terms of security. The prospective employees in turn want to have a way to demonstrate their level of understanding, which can enhance their chances of being hired. The community as a whole just wants more trained security professionals.

Preparing Yourself for the Security+ Exam

Security+ Certification All-in-One Exam Guide is designed to help prepare you to take the Security+ certification exam. When you pass it, you will demonstrate that you have that basic understanding of security that employers are looking for. Passing this certification exam will not be an easy task for there are many things that you will need to learn to acquire that basic understanding of computer and network security.

How This Book is Organized

The book is divided into sections and chapters to correspond with the objectives of the exam itself. Some of the chapters are more technical than others—reflecting the nature of the security environment where you will be forced to deal with not only technical details but other issues such as security policies and procedures as well as training and education. While there are many individuals involved in computer and network security that have advanced degrees in math, computer science, information systems, or computer or electrical engineering, you do not need to be this technical to effectively address security in your organization. You do not need to develop your own cryptographic algorithm, for example, you simply need to be able to understand how cryptography is used along with its strengths and weaknesses. As you progress in your studies, you will learn that many of the problems in security are a result of the human element. The best technology in the world still ends up being placed in an environment where humans have the opportunity to foul things up—and they all too often do.

Part I: Authentication   The book begins with an introduction of some of the basic elements of security.

Part II: Malware and Attacks   The types of attacks that we are attempting to protect our systems against are presented next.

Part III: Security in Transmissions   This is followed by a discussion of communications security. This is an important aspect of security since we have for years connected our computers together into a vast array of networks. Various protocols are discussed that are in use today and that the security practitioner needs to be aware of.

Part V: Security for the Infrastructure   The next section concerns infrastructure issues. In this case we are not referring to the critical infrastructures identified by the White House several years ago (identifying sectors such as telecommunications, banking and finance, oil and gas, and so forth) but instead the various components that form the backbone of an organization's security structure.

Part V: Cryptography and Applications   Cryptography is an important part of security and the next section covers this topic in detail. The purpose is not to make cryptographers out of the readers but to instead provide a basic understanding of how cryptography works and what goes into a basic cryptographic scheme. An important subject in cryptography, and one that is essential for the reader to understand, is the creation of Public Key Infrastructures and this topic is covered in the section as well.

Part VI: Operational Security   This section addresses operational and organizational issues. This is where we depart from a discussion of technology again and will instead discuss how security is accomplished in an organization. Since we know that we will not be absolutely successful in our security efforts, attackers are always finding new holes and ways around our security defenses, one of the most important topics we will address is the subject of responses to security incidents and how to recover from them.

Part VII: Administrative Controls   The final section of the text concludes with a discussion of change management (addressing the subject we alluded to earlier when discussing the problems with patch management) and security awareness and training. Since we recognize that people are one of our biggest problems in security it only makes sense to attempt to address this problem by educating them on what everybody can do to help with security. Security is not only the responsibility of security administrators, all users must take a certain amount of responsibility and address security in their own environments. An excellent example of this is the subject of e-mail viruses where users must be made aware of the possible ramifications of running programs of unknown origin.

Part VIII: Appendixes   There are two appendixes in *Security+ Certification All-in-One Exam Guide*. Appendix A explains how best to use the CD-ROM bound into this book, and Appendix B provides an additional in-depth explanation of the OSI Model and Internet Protocols, should this information be new to you.

The Glossary   Located just before the Index of the book, you will find a useful glossary of security terminology, including many related acronyms and their meanings. We hope that you use the Glossary frequently and find it to be a useful study aid as you work your way through the various topics in this exam guide.

Special Features of the All-in-One Certification Series

To make our exam guides more useful and a pleasure to read, we have designed the All-in-One Certification series to include several conventions.

Icons

To alert you to an important bit of advice, a shortcut, or a pitfall, you'll occasionally see Notes, Tips, Cautions, and Study Tips peppered throughout the text.

 NOTE   Notes offer nuggets of especially helpful stuff, background explanations and information, and they occasionally define terms.

 TIP   Tips provide suggestions and nuances to help you learn to finesse your job. Take a tip from me and read the Tips carefully.

 CAUTION   When you see a Caution, pay special attention. Cautions appear when you have to make a crucial choice or when you are about to undertake something that may have ramifications you might not immediately anticipate. Read them now so you don't have regrets later.

 STUDY TIP   Study Tips give you special advice or may provide information specifically relating to preparing for the exam itself.

Sidebars

From time to time you will find sidebars in this book. They may present information that is tangential to the main discussion, or may serve to highlight an important concept. Sidebars appear in screened boxes like this one.

End-of-Chapter Reviews and Chapter Tests

An important part of this book comes at the end of each chapter where you will find a brief review of the high points of the chapter along with a series of questions followed by the answers to those questions. Each question is of a multiple-choice format. The answers provided also include a small discussion for each explaining why the correct answer actually is the correct answer.

The questions are provided as a study aid to you, the reader and prospective Security+ exam. We obviously can't guarantee that if you answer all of our questions correctly that you will absolutely pass the certification exam. Instead what we can guarantee is that the questions will provide you a feeling for how ready you are for the exam.

The CD-ROM

Security+ Certification All-in-One Exam Guide also provides you with a CD-ROM of even more test questions and their answers to help you prepare yourself for the certification exam. Read more about the companion CD-ROM in Appendix A.

Onward and Upward

At this point we hope that you are now excited about the topic of security, even if you weren't in the first place. We wish you luck in your endeavors and welcome you to the exciting field of computer and network security.

PART I

Authentication

General Security Concepts

In this chapter, you will

- Learn about the Security+ exam
- Learn basic terminology associated with computer and information security
- Discover the basic approaches to computer and information security
- Discover various methods to implement access controls
- Determine methods used to verify the identity and authenticity of an individual

So, why should you be concerned with taking the Security+ exam? The goal of the Computing Technology Industry Association (CompTIA) Security+ exam is to become the worldwide standard for foundation-level security practitioners. There is a growing need for trained security professionals, and the CompTIA Security+ exam is a perfect way to validate your knowledge and understanding of the computer security field. The exam is an appropriate mechanism for many different individuals, including network and system administrators, analysts, programmers, web designers, application developers, and database specialists to show proof of professional achievement in security. The exam's objectives were developed with input and assistance from industry and government agencies, including such notable examples as the Federal Bureau of Investigation (FBI), the National Institute of Standards and Technology (NIST), the U.S. Secret Service, the Information Systems Security Association (ISSA), Microsoft Corporation, RSA Security, Motorola, Novell, Sun Microsystems, Verisign, and Entrust.

The Security+ Exam

In terms of the exam itself, the Security+ exam is designed to cover a wide range of security topics—the type of subjects that a security practitioner would be expected to have knowledge of. The test includes information from five knowledge domains. The specific domains questions are taken from, and the relative weighting each is given on the exam according to CompTIA, are as follows:

Knowledge Domain	Percent of Exam
General Security Concepts	30%
Communication Security	20%
Infrastructure Security	20%
Basics of Cryptography	15%
Operational/Organizational Security	15%

The exam consists of a series of questions, each designed to have a single best answer or response. The other choices are designed to provide options that an individual might take if they had an incomplete knowledge or understanding of the security topic represented by the question. The questions can be in two different formats: multiple choice with a single correct answer or sample directions where the individual reads a statement or question and then must choose the correct option(s) from a list of possible options or responses. The exam questions will be chosen from the more detailed objectives listed in the outline shown in Figure 1-1, which was taken from the CompTIA web page, www.comptia.com/certification/Security/security_plus_objectives_10-23.pdf.

The Security+ exam is designed for individuals with at least two years of networking experience and who have a thorough understanding of TCP/IP. The exam is currently administered only in English and consists of 100 questions to be completed in 90 minutes. A minimum passing score is considered 764 out of a possible 900 points. The test results will be available immediately. An individual who fails to pass the test the first time will be required to pay the exam fee again to retake the test, but there is no mandatory waiting period before retaking it. For more information on retaking exams, consult CompTIA's retake policy, which can be found on their web site, www.comptia.org.

This All-in-One Exam Guide is designed to assist you in preparing for the Security+ exam. It is organized around the same objectives as the exam and attempts to cover the major areas the exam includes. Using this guide in no way guarantees that you will pass the exam, but it will greatly assist you in preparing to successfully meet the challenge posed by the Security+ exam.

Basic Security Terminology

The term hacking has been used frequently in the media. A *hacker* was once considered an individual who understood the technical aspects of computer operating systems and networks. Hackers were individuals you turned to when you had a problem and needed extreme technical expertise. Today, as a result of the media, the term is used more often to refer to individuals who attempt to gain unauthorized access to computer systems or networks. While some would prefer to use the terms *cracker* and *cracking* when referring to this nefarious type of activity, the terminology generally accepted by the public is that of hacker and hacking. A related term that may sometimes be seen is *phreaking*, which refers to the "hacking" of computers and systems used by the telephone company.

Security Basics

Computer security itself is a term that has many meanings and related terms. *Computer security* entails the methods used to ensure a system is secure. Subjects such as authentication and access controls must be addressed in broad terms of computer security. Seldom in today's world are computers not connected to other computers in networks.

DOMAIN 1.0: General Security Concepts

1.1. Access control
    1.1.1. MAC / DAC / RBAC
1.2. Authentication
    1.2.1. Kerberos
    1.2.2. CHAP
    1.2.3. Certificates
    1.2.4. Username / Password
    1.2.5. Tokens
    1.2.6. Multi-factor
    1.2.7. Mutual authentication
    1.2.8. Biometrics
1.3. Non-essential services and protocols
1.4. Attacks
    1.4.1. DOS / DDOS
    1.4.2. Back door
    1.4.3. Spoofing
    1.4.4. Man in the middle
    1.4.5. Replay
    1.4.6. TCP / IP hijacking
    1.4.7. Weak keys
    1.4.8. Mathematical
    1.4.9. Social engineering
    1.4.10. Birthday
    1.4.11. Password guessing
        1.4.11.1. Brute force
        1.4.11.2. Dictionary
    1.4.12. Software exploitation
1.5. Malicious code
    1.5.1. Viruses
    1.5.2. Trojan horses
    1.5.3. Logic bombs
    1.5.4. Worms
1.6. Social engineering
1.7. Auditing

DOMAIN 2.0: Communication Security

2.1. Remote access
    2.1.1. 802.1x
    2.1.2. VPN
    2.1.3. RADIUS
    2.1.4. TACACS / +
    2.1.5. L2TP / PPTP
    2.1.6. SSH
    2.1.7. IPSEC
    2.1.8. Vulnerabilities
2.2. E-Mail
    2.2.1. S / MIME
    2.2.2. PGP
    2.2.3. Vulnerabilities
        2.2.3.1. Spam
        2.2.3.2. Hoaxes
2.3. Web
    2.3.1. SSL / TLS
    2.3.2. HTTP / S
    2.3.3. Instant messaging
        2.3.3.1. Vulnerabilities
        2.3.3.2. 8.3. Naming conventions
        2.3.3.3. Packet sniffing
        2.3.3.4. Privacy
    2.3.4. Vulnerabilities
        2.3.4.1. Java script
        2.3.4.2. ActiveX
        2.3.4.3. Buffer overflows
        2.3.4.4. Cookies
        2.3.4.5. Signed applets
        2.3.4.6. CGI
        2.3.4.7. SMTP relay
2.4. Directory
    2.4.1. SSL / TLS
    2.4.2. LDAP
2.5. File transfer
    2.5.1. S / FTP
    2.5.2. Blind FTP / anonymous
    2.5.3. File sharing
    2.5.4. Vulnerabilities
        2.5.4.1. Packet sniffing
2.6. Wireless
    2.6.1. WTLS
    2.6.2. 802.11x
    2.6.3. WEP / WAP
    2.6.4. Vulnerabilities
        2.6.4.1. Site surveys

Figure 1-1   An outline taken from the CompTIA web page of objectives covering the Security+ certification exam

DOMAIN 3.0: Infrastructure Security

3.1. Devices
    3.1.1. Firewalls
    3.1.2. Routers
    3.1.3. Switches
    3.1.4. Wireless
    3.1.5. Modems
    3.1.6. RAS
    3.1.7. Telecom / PBX
    3.1.8. VPN
    3.1.9. IDS
    3.1.10. Network monitoring / Diagnostic
    3.1.11. Workstations
    3.1.12. Servers
    3.1.13. Mobile devices

3.2. Media
    3.2.1. Coax
    3.2.2. UTP / STP
    3.2.3. Fiber
    3.2.4. Removable media
        3.2.4.1. Tape
        3.2.4.2. CDR
        3.2.4.3. Hard drives
        3.2.4.4. Diskettes
        3.2.4.5. Flashcards
        3.2.4.6. Smartcards

3.3. Security topologies
    3.3.1. Security zones
        3.3.1.1. DMZ
        3.3.1.2. Intranet
        3.3.1.3. Extranet
    3.3.2. VLANs
    3.3.3. NAT
    3.3.4. Tunneling

3.4. Intrusion detection
    3.4.1. Network based
        3.4.1.1. Active detection
        3.4.1.2. Passive detection
    3.4.2. Host based
        3.4.2.1. Active detection
        3.4.2.2. Passive detection
    3.4.3. Honey pots
    3.4.4. Incident response

3.5. Security baselines
    3.5.1. OS / NOS Hardening
        3.5.1.1. File system
        3.5.1.2. Updates (hotfixes, service packs, patches)
    3.5.2. Network hardening
        3.5.2.1. Updates (firmware)
        3.5.2.2. Configuration
            3.5.2.2.1. Enabling and disabling services and protocols
            3.5.2.2.2. Access control lists

3.5.3. Application hardening
    3.5.3.1. Updates (hotfixes, service packs, patches)
    3.5.3.2. Web servers
    3.5.3.3. E-Mail servers
    3.5.3.4. FTP servers
    3.5.3.5. DNS servers
    3.5.3.6. NNTP servers
    3.5.3.7. File / Print servers
    3.5.3.8. DHCP servers
    3.5.3.9. Data Repositories
        3.5.3.9.1. Directory services
        3.5.3.9.2. Databases

DOMAIN 4.0: Basics of Cryptography

4.1. Algorithms
    4.1.1. Hashing
    4.1.2. Symmetric
    4.1.3. Asymmetric

4.2. Concepts of using cryptography
    4.2.1. Confidentiality
    4.2.2. Integrity
        4.2.2.1. Digital signatures
    4.2.3. Authentication
    4.2.4. Non-repudiation
        4.2.4.1. Digital signatures
    4.2.5. Access control

4.3. PKI
    4.3.1. Certificates
        4.3.1.1. Certificate policies
        4.3.1.2. Certificate practice statements
    4.3.2. Revocation
    4.3.3. Trust models

4.4. Standards and protocols

4.5. Key management / Certificate lifecycle
    4.5.1. Centralized vs. Decentralized
    4.5.2. Storage
        4.5.2.1. Hardware vs. Software
        4.5.2.2. Private key protection
    4.5.3. Escrow
    4.5.4. Expiration
    4.5.5. Revocation
        4.5.5.1. Status checking
    4.5.6. Suspension
        4.5.6.1. Status checking
    4.5.7. Recovery
        4.5.7.1. M of N control
    4.5.8. Renewal
    4.5.9. Destruction
    4.5.10. Key usage
        4.5.10.1. Multiple key pairs (single, dual)

Figure 1-1   An outline taken from the CompTIA web page of objectives covering the Security+ certification exam *(continued)*

DOMAIN 5.0: Operational/Organizational Security

5.1. Physical security
    5.1.1. Access control
        5.1.1.1. Physical barriers
        5.1.1.2. Biometrics
    5.1.2. Social engineering
    5.1.3. Environment
        5.1.3.1. Wireless cells
        5.1.3.2. Location
        5.1.3.3. Shielding
        5.1.3.4. Fire suppression
5.2. Disaster Recovery
    5.2.1. Backups
        5.2.1.1. Off-site storage
    5.2.2. Secure recovery
        5.2.2.1. Alternate sites
    5.2.3. Disaster recovery plan
5.3. Business continuity
    5.3.1. Utilities
    5.3.2. High availability / Fault tolerance
    5.3.3. Backups
5.4. Policy and procedures
    5.4.1. Security policy
        5.4.1.1. Acceptable use
        5.4.1.2. Due care
        5.4.1.3. Privacy
        5.4.1.4. Separation of duties
        5.4.1.5. Need to know
        5.4.1.6. Password management
        5.4.1.7. SLA
        5.4.1.8. Disposal / Destruction
        5.4.1.9. HR policy
            5.4.1.9.1. Termination
            5.4.1.9.2. Hiring
            5.4.1.9.3. Code of ethics
    5.4.2. Incident response policy

5.5. Privilege management
    5.5.1. User / Group / Role management
    5.5.2. Single sign-on
    5.5.3. Centralized vs. Decentralized
    5.5.4. Auditing (privilege, usage, escalation)
    5.5.5. MAC / DAC / RBAC
5.6. Forensics
    5.6.1. Chain of custody
    5.6.2. Preservation of evidence
    5.6.3. Collection of evidence
5.7. Risk identification
    5.7.1. Asset identification
    5.7.2. Risk assessment
    5.7.3. Threat identification
    5.7.4. Vulnerabilities
5.8. Education
    5.8.1. Communication
    5.8.2. User awareness
    5.8.3. Education
    5.8.4. Online resources
5.9. Documentation
    5.9.1. Standards and guidelines
    5.9.2. Systems architecture
    5.9.3. Change documentation
    5.9.4. Logs and inventories
    5.9.5. Classification
        5.9.5.1. Notification
    5.9.6. Retention / Storage
    5.9.7. Destruction

Figure 1-1   An outline taken from the CompTIA web page of objectives covering the Security+ certification exam *(continued)*

This then introduces the term *network security* to refer to the protection of the multiple computers and other devices that are connected together. Related to these two terms are two others: *information security* and *information assurance,* which place the focus of the security process not on the hardware and software being used but on the data that is processed by them. Assurance also introduces another concept, that of the availability of the systems and information when we want them.

Since the late 1990s, much has been seen in the media concerning computer and network security. Often the news is about a specific lapse in security, which has resulted in the penetration of a network or in the denial of service for a network. Over the last few years, the general public has become increasingly aware of its dependence on computers and networks and consequently has also become interested in the security of these same computers and networks.

As a result of this increased attention by the public, several new terms have become commonplace in conversations and print. Terms such as *hacking, virus, TCP/IP, encryption,* and *firewalls* are now frequently seen in mainstream news publications and have found their way into casual conversations. What was once the purview of scientists and engineers is now part of our everyday life.

With our increased daily dependence on computers and networks to conduct everything from making purchases at our local grocery store to driving our children to school (that new car you just bought is probably using a small computer to obtain peak engine performance), ensuring that computers and networks are secure has become of paramount importance. Medical information about each of us is probably stored in a computer somewhere. So is financial information and data relating to the types of purchases we make and store preferences (assuming you have and use a credit card to make purchases). Making sure that this information remains private is a growing concern to the general public, and it is one of the jobs of security to help with the protection of our privacy. Simply stated, computer and network security is now essential for us to function effectively and safely in today's highly automated environment.

The "CIA" of Security

Almost from its inception, the goal of computer security has been threefold: confidentiality, integrity, and availability—the "CIA" of security. The purpose of *confidentiality* is to ensure that only those individuals who have the authority to view a piece of information may do so. No unauthorized individual should ever be able to view data they are not entitled to. *Integrity* is a related concept but deals with the modification of data. Only authorized individuals should ever be able to change (or delete) information. The goal of *availability* is to ensure that the data, or the system itself, is available for use when the authorized user wants it.

As a result of the increased use of networks for commerce, two additional security goals have been added to the original three in the CIA of security. *Authentication* deals with the desire to ensure that an individual is who they claim to be. The need for this in an online transaction is obvious. Related to this is *nonrepudiation,* which deals with the ability to verify that a message has been sent and received. The requirement for this capability in online transactions should also be readily apparent.

The Operational Model of Security

For many years, the focus of security was on prevention. If we could prevent somebody from gaining access to our computer systems and networks, then we assumed that we had obtained security. Protection was thus equated with prevention. While the basic premise of this is true, it fails to acknowledge the realities of the networked environment our systems are part of. No matter how well we seem to do in prevention technology, somebody always seems to find a way around our safeguards. When this happens, our system is left unprotected. What is needed is multiple prevention techniques and also technology to alert us when prevention has failed and to provide ways to address the problem. This results in a modification to our original security equation with the addition of two new elements—detection and response. Our security equation thus becomes:

$$Protection = Prevention + (Detection + Response)$$

This is known as the *operational model of computer security*. Every security technique and technology falls into at least one of the three elements of the equation. Examples of the types of technology and techniques that represent each are depicted in Figure 1-2.

Security Principles

There are three ways an organization can choose to address the protection of its networks: ignore security issues, provide host security, and approach security at a network level. The last two, host and network security, have prevention as well as detection and response components.

If an organization decides to ignore security, it has chosen to utilize the minimal amount of security that is provided with its workstations, servers, and devices. No additional security measures will be implemented. Each "out of the box" system has certain security settings that can be configured, and they should be. To actually protect an entire network, however, requires work in addition to the few protection mechanisms that come with systems by default.

Host Security   Host security takes a granular view of security by focusing on protecting each computer and device individually instead of addressing protection of the network as a whole. When host security is used, each computer is relied upon to protect itself. If an organization decides to implement only host security and does not include network security, there is a high probability of introducing or overlooking vulnerabilities. Most environments are filled with different operating systems (Windows, UNIX, Linux, Macintosh), different versions of those operating systems, and different types of installed applications. Each operating system has security configurations that differ from other systems, and different versions of the same operating system may in fact have variations between them. Ensuring that every computer is "locked down" to the same degree as every other system in the environment can be overwhelming and often results in an unsuccessful and frustrating effort.

Host security is important and should always be addressed. Security, however, should not stop there, as host security is a complementary process to be combined with

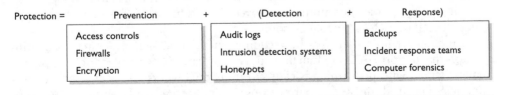

Protection =	Prevention	+	(Detection	+	Response)
	Access controls		Audit logs		Backups
	Firewalls		Intrusion detection systems		Incident response teams
	Encryption		Honeypots		Computer forensics

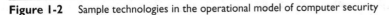

Figure 1-2   Sample technologies in the operational model of computer security

network security. If individual host computers have vulnerabilities embodied within them, then network security can provide another layer of protection that will hopefully stop any intruders getting that far into the environment. Topics covered in this book dealing with host security include: bastion hosts, host-based intrusion detection systems, antivirus software, and hardening of operating systems.

Network Security   In some smaller environments, host security by itself may be an option, but as systems become connected into networks, security should include the actual network itself. In network security, an emphasis is placed on controlling access to internal computers from external entities. This control can be through devices such as routers, firewalls, authentication hardware and software, encryption, and intrusion detection systems (IDSs).

Network environments have a tendency to be unique entities because usually no two networks will have exactly the same number of computers, the same applications installed, the same number of users, the exact same configurations, or the same available servers. They will not perform the same functions or have the same overall architecture. Since networks have so many differences, there are many different ways that they can be protected and configured. This chapter covers some foundational approaches to network and host security. Each approach may be implemented in a myriad of ways.

Least Privilege

One of the most fundamental approaches to security is *least privilege*. This concept is applicable to many physical environments as well as network and host security. Least privilege means that an object (which may be a user, application, or process) should have only the necessary rights and privileges to perform its task with no additional permissions. Limiting an object's privileges limits the amount of harm that can be caused, thus limiting an organization's exposure to damage. Users may have access to the files on their workstations and a select set of files on a file server, but no access to critical data that is held within the database. This rule helps an organization protect its most sensitive resources and helps ensure that whoever is interacting with these resources has a valid reason to do so.

Different operating systems and applications have different ways of implementing rights, permissions, and privileges. Before they are actually configured, an overall plan should be devised and standardized methods developed to ensure that a solid security baseline is actually implemented. For example, a company may want all of the Accounting employees, but no one else, to be able to access employee payroll and profit margin spreadsheets held on a server. The easiest way to implement this is to develop an Accounting group, put all Accounting employees in this group, and assign rights to the group instead of each individual person.

As another example, there may be a requirement to implement a hierarchy of administrators that perform different functions and require specific types of rights. Two people may be tasked with performing backups of individual workstations and servers; thus they do not need administrative permissions with full access to all resources. Three people may be in charge of setting up new user accounts and password management, which means they do not need full, or perhaps any, access to the company's routers and switches. Once these lines are delineated, indicating what subjects require which rights and permissions, then it is much easier to configure settings to provide the least privileges for different subjects.

The concept of least privilege applies to more network security issues than just providing users with specific rights and permissions. When trust relationships are created, they should not be implemented in such a way that everyone trusts each other simply because it is easier. One domain should trust another for very specific reasons, and the implementers should have a full understanding of what the trust relationship allows between two domains. If one domain trusts another, do all of the users automatically become trusted, and can they thus easily access any and all resources on the other domain? Is this a good idea? Is there a more secure way of providing the same functionality? If a trusted relationship is implemented such that users in one group can access a plotter or printer that is available on only one domain, it might make sense to simply purchase another plotter so that other, more valuable or sensitive, resources are not accessible by the entire group.

Another issue that falls under the least privilege concept is the security context in which an application runs. All applications, scripts, and batch files run in the security context of a specific user on an operating system. They will execute with specific permissions as if they were a user. The application may be Microsoft Word and run in the space of a regular user, or it may be a diagnostic program that needs access to more sensitive system files and so must run under an administrative user account, or it may be a program that performs backups and so should operate within the security context of a backup operator. The crux of this issue is that programs should execute only in the security context that is needed for that program to perform its duties successfully. In many environments, people do not really understand how to make programs run under different security contexts or it just seems easier to have them all run under the administrator account. If attackers can compromise a program or service running under the administrative account, they have effectively elevated their access level and have much more control over the system and many more possibilities to cause damage.

Layered Security

A bank does not just protect the money that it stores only by using a vault. It has one or more security guards as a first defense to watch for suspicious activities and to secure the facility when the bank is closed. It may have monitoring systems that watch various activities that take place in the bank, whether involving customers or employees. The vault is usually located in the center of the facility, and thus there are layers of rooms or walls before arriving at the vault. There is access control, which ensures that the people entering the vault have to be given the authorization beforehand. And the systems, including manual switches, are connected directly to the police station in case a determined bank robber successfully penetrates any one of these layers of protection.

Networks should utilize the same type of *layered security* architecture. There is no 100 percent secure system, and there is nothing that is foolproof, so a single specific protection mechanism should never be solely relied upon. Every piece of software and every device can be compromised in some way, and every encryption algorithm can be broken, given enough time and resources. The goal of security is to make the effort of actually accomplishing a compromise more costly in time and effort than it is worth to a potential attacker.

As an example, consider the steps an intruder might have to take to access critical data held within a company's back-end database. The intruder will first need to penetrate the firewall and use packets and methods that will not be identified and detected by the intrusion detection system (more on these devices can be found in Chapter 8). The attacker will then have to circumvent an internal router performing packet filtering and possibly penetrate another firewall that is used to separate one internal network from another. From here, the intruder must break the access controls that are on the database, which means having to do a dictionary or brute-force attack to be able to authenticate to the database software. Once the intruder has gotten this far, the data still needs to be located within the database. This may in turn be complicated by the use of access control lists outlining who can actually view or modify the data. That is a lot of work.

This example illustrates the different layers of security many environments employ. It is important to implement several different layers because if intruders succeed at one layer, you want to be able to stop them at the next. The redundancy of different protection layers assures that there is no one single point of failure pertaining to security. If a network used only a firewall to protect its assets, an attacker successfully able to penetrate this device would find the rest of the network open and vulnerable.

It is important that every environment have multiple layers of security. These layers may employ a variety of methods such as routers, firewalls, network segments, IDSs, encryption, authentication software, physical security, and traffic control. The layers need to work together in a coordinated manner so that one does not impede another's functionality and introduce a security hole. Security at each layer can be very complex, and putting different layers together can increase the complexity exponentially. Although having layers of protection in place is very important, it is also important to understand how these different layers interact either by working together or in some cases by working against each other.

One case of how different security methods can work against each other is exemplified when firewalls encounter encrypted network traffic. An organization may utilize encryption so that an outside customer communicating with a specific Web server is assured that sensitive data being exchanged is protected. If this encrypted data is encapsulated within Secure Sockets Layer (SSL) packets and then is sent through a firewall, the firewall will not be able to read the payload information in the individual packets. This may enable the customer, or an outside attacker, to send malicious code or instructions through the SSL connection undetected. There are other mechanisms that can be introduced in these situations, such as designing Web pages to accept information only in certain formats and having the Web server parse through the data for malicious activity. The important piece is to understand the level of protection that each layer provides and how each level of protection can be affected by things that take place in other layers.

The layers usually are depicted starting at the top, with more general types of protection, and progressing downward through each layer, with increasing granularity at each layer as you get closer to the actual resource, as you can see in Figure 1-3. This is because

Figure 1-3
Various layers
of security

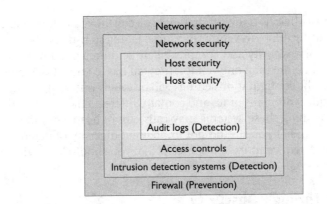

the top-layer protection mechanism is responsible for looking at an enormous amount of traffic, and it would be overwhelming and cause too much of a performance degradation if each aspect of the packet were inspected. Instead, each layer usually digs deeper into the packet and looks for specific items. Layers that are closer to the resource have to deal with only a fraction of the traffic that the top-layer security mechanism does, and thus it will not cause as much of a performance hit to look deeper and at more granular aspects of the traffic.

Diversity of Defense

Diversity of defense is a concept that complements the idea of various layers of security; it means to make the layers dissimilar so that even if attackers know how to get through a system making up one layer, they may not know how to get through a different type of layer that employs a different system for security.

If an environment has two firewalls that form a demilitarized zone (DMZ), for example, one firewall may be placed at the perimeter of the Internet and the DMZ. This firewall will analyze the traffic that is entering through that specific access point and will enforce certain types of restrictions. The other firewall may then be placed between the DMZ and the internal network. When applying the diversity of defense concept, you should set up these two firewalls to filter for different types of traffic and provide different types of restrictions. The first firewall, for example, may make sure that no FTP, SNMP, or Telnet traffic enters the network but allow SMTP, SSH, HTTP, and SSL traffic through. The second firewall may not allow SSL or SSH through and may interrogate SMTP and HTTP traffic to make sure that certain types of attacks are not part of that traffic.

Another type of diversity of defense is to use products from different vendors. Every product has its own security vulnerabilities that are usually known to experienced attackers in the community. A CheckPoint firewall has different security issues and settings than a Sidewinder firewall; thus different exploits can be used against them to crash them or compromise them in some fashion. Combining this type of diversity with the preceding example, you might utilize the CheckPoint firewall as the first line of defense. If attackers are able to penetrate it, they are less likely to get through the next firewall if it is one from another vendor, such as a Cisco PIX or Sidewinder firewall.

There is an obvious trade-off that must be considered before implementing diversity of security using different vendor products. Doing so usually also increases operational complexity, and security and complexity are seldom a good mix. When implementing products from more than one vendor, the staff has to know how to configure two different systems, the configuration settings will be totally different, the upgrades and patches will come out at different times and contain different changes, and the overall complexity of maintaining these systems may cause more headaches than security itself. This does not mean that you should not implement diversity of defense by installing products from different vendors; it just means that you should know the implications of this type of decision.

Security Through Obscurity

Another concept in security that should be discussed is the idea of *security through obscurity*. In this case, security is considered effective if the environment and protection mechanisms are confusing or supposedly not generally known. Security through obscurity uses the approach of protecting something by hiding it. Noncomputer examples of this concept include hiding your briefcase or purse if you leave it in the car so that it is not in plain view, hiding a house key under a ceramic frog, or pushing your favorite ice cream to the back of the freezer so that everyone else thinks it is all gone. The idea is that if something is out of sight, it is out of mind. This approach, however, does not provide actual protection of the object. Someone can still steal the purse by breaking into the car, lift the ceramic frog and find the key, or dig through the items in the freezer to find your favorite ice cream. Security through obscurity may make someone work a little harder to accomplish a task, but it does not prevent anyone from eventually succeeding.

Similar approaches are seen in computer and network security when attempting to hide certain objects. A network administrator may, for instance, move a service from its default port to a different port so that others will not know how to access it as easily, or a firewall may be configured to hide specific information about the internal network in the hope that potential attackers will not obtain the information for use in an attack on the network.

In most security circles, security through obscurity is considered a poor approach, especially if it is the only approach to security. An organization can use security through obscurity measures to try to hide critical assets, but other security measures should also be employed to provide a higher level of protection. For example, if an administrator moves a service from its default port to a more obscure port, an attacker can still actually find this service; thus a firewall should be used to restrict access to the service. Most people know that even if you do shove your ice cream to the back of the freezer, someone may eventually find it.

Keep It Simple

The terms security and complexity are often at odds with each other. This is because the more complex something is, the harder it is to understand, and you cannot truly secure something if you do not understand it. Another reason complexity is a problem within security is that it usually allows too many opportunities for something to go wrong. If an application has 4000 lines of code, there are a lot fewer places for buffer overflows, for example, than in an application of two million lines of code.

As with any other type of technology or problem in life, when something goes wrong with security mechanisms, a troubleshooting process is used to identify the actual issue. If the mechanism is overly complex, identifying the root of the problem can be overwhelming if not nearly impossible. Security is already a very complex issue because there are so many variables involved, so many types of attacks and vulnerabilities, so many different types of resources to secure, and so many different ways of securing them. You want your security processes and tools to be as simple and elegant as possible. They should be simple to troubleshoot, simple to use, and simple to administer.

Another application of the principle of keeping things simple concerns the number of services that you allow your system to run. Default installations of computer operating systems often leave many services running. The keep-it-simple principle tells us to eliminate those that we don't need. This is also a good idea from a security standpoint because it results in fewer applications that can be exploited and fewer services that the administrator is responsible for securing. The general rule of thumb should be to always eliminate all nonessential services and protocols. This of course leads to the question, how do you determine whether a service or protocol is essential or not? Ideally, you should know what your computer system or network is being used for, and thus you should be able to identify those elements that are essential and activate only them. For a variety of reasons, this is not as easy as it sounds. Alternatively, a stringent security approach that one can take is to assume that no service is necessary (which is obviously absurd) and activate services and ports only as they are requested. Whatever approach is taken, there is a never-ending struggle to try to strike a balance between providing functionality and maintaining security.

Access Control

The term *access control* has been used to describe a variety of protection schemes. It is sometimes used to refer to all security features used to prevent unauthorized access to a computer system or network. In this sense, it may be confused with authentication. More properly, *access* is the ability of a subject (such as an individual or a process running on a computer system) to interact with an object (such as a file or hardware device). Authentication, on the other hand, deals with verifying the identity of a subject. To help understand the difference, consider the example of an individual attempting to log in to a computer system or network. *Authentication* is the process used to verify to the computer system or network that the individual is who they claim to be. The most common method to do this is through the use of a userid and password. Once the individual has verified their identity, access controls regulate what the individual can actually do on the system. Just because a person is granted entry to the system, that does not mean that they should have access to all data the system contains.

To further illustrate, consider another example. When you go to your bank to make a withdrawal, the teller at the window will verify that you are indeed who you claim to be. This is usually done by asking you to provide some form of identification with your picture on it, such as your driver's license. You may also have to provide information such as your bank account number. Once the teller verifies your identity, you will have proved that you are a valid (authorized) customer of this bank. This does not, however, mean that you have the ability to view all information that the bank protects—such as your neighbor's balance. The teller will control what information, and funds, you may have access to and will grant you access only to that which you are authorized. In this example, your identification and bank account number serve as your method of authentication and the teller serves as the access control mechanism.

In computer systems and networks, there are several ways that access controls can be implemented. An *access control matrix* provides the simplest framework for illustrating the process. An example of an access control matrix is provided in Table 1-1. In this matrix, the system is keeping track of two processes, two files, and one hardware device. Process 1 can read both File 1 and File 2 but can write only to File 1. Process 1 cannot access Process 2, but Process 2 can execute Process 1. Both processes have the ability to write to the printer.

While simple to understand, the access control matrix is seldom used in computer systems because it is extremely costly in terms of storage space and processing. Imagine the size of an access control matrix for a large network with hundreds of users and thousands of files. The actual mechanics of how access controls are implemented in a system varies, though *access control lists (ACLs)* are common. An ACL is nothing more than a list that contains the subjects that have access rights to a particular object. The list will identify not only the subject but the specific access that that subject has for the object. Typical types of access include read, write, and execute as indicated in our example access control matrix.

No matter what specific mechanism is used to implement access controls in a computer system or network, the controls should be based on a specific model of access. Several different models are discussed in security literature, including discretionary access control (DAC), mandatory access control (MAC), and role-based access control (RBAC).

Discretionary Access Control

Both discretionary access control and mandatory access control are terms originally used by the military to describe two different approaches to controlling what access an individual had on a system. As defined by the "Orange Book," a Department of Defense document that at one time was the standard for describing what constituted a trusted computing system, discretionary access controls are "a means of restricting access to objects based on the identity of subjects and/or groups to which they belong. The controls are discretionary in the sense that a subject with a certain access permission is capable of

	Process 1	Process 2	File 1	File 2	Printer
Process 1	Read, write, execute		Read, write	Read	Write
Process 2	Execute	Read, write, execute	Read, write	Read, write	Write

Table 1-1   An Access Control Matrix

passing that permission (perhaps indirectly) on to any other subject." While this may appear to many to be typical "government-speak" and confusing, the principle is really rather simple. In systems that employ discretionary access controls, the owner of an object can decide which other subjects may have access to the object and what specific access they may have. One common method to accomplish this is the permission bits used in UNIX-based systems. The owner of a file can specify what permissions (read/write/execute) members in the same group may have and also what permissions all others may have. Access control lists are another common mechanism used to implement discretionary access control.

Mandatory Access Control

A less frequently employed system for restricting access is mandatory access control. This system, generally used only in environments where different levels of security classifications exist, is much more restrictive of what a user is allowed to do. Again referring to the Orange Book, we can find a definition for mandatory access controls, which is "a means of restricting access to objects based on the sensitivity (as represented by a label) of the information contained in the objects and the formal authorization (i.e., clearance) of subjects to access information of such sensitivity." In this case, the owner or subject can't determine whether access is to be granted to another subject; it is the job of the operating system to decide. In MAC, the security mechanism controls access to all objects and individual subjects cannot change that access. The key here is the label attached to every subject and object. The label will identify the level of classification for that object and the level that the subject is entitled to. Think of military security classifications such as Secret and Top Secret. A file that has been identified as Top Secret (has a label indicating that it is Top Secret) may be viewed only by individuals with a Top Secret clearance. It is up to the access control mechanism to ensure that an individual with only a Secret clearance never gains access to a file labeled as Top Secret. Similarly, a user cleared for Top Secret access will not be allowed by the access control mechanism to change the classification of a file labeled as Top Secret to Secret or to send that Top Secret file to a user cleared only for Secret information. The complexity of such a mechanism can be further understood when you consider today's windowing environment. The access control mechanism will not allow a user to cut a portion of a Top Secret document and paste it into a window containing a document with only a Secret label. It is this separation of differing levels of classified information that results in this sort of mechanism being referred to as multilevel security. A final comment should be made: just because a subject has the appropriate level of clearance to view a document, that does not mean that they will be allowed to do so. The concept of "need to know," which is a discretionary access control concept, also exists in mandatory access control mechanisms.

Role-Based Access Control

Access control lists can be cumbersome and can take time to administer properly. Another access control mechanism that has been attracting increased attention is the role-based access control (RBAC). In this scheme, instead of each user being assigned specific access permissions for the objects associated with the computer system or network, that user is assigned a set of roles that the user may perform. The roles are in turn assigned the access permissions necessary to perform the tasks associated with the role. Users will thus be granted permissions to objects in terms of the specific duties they must perform—not of a security classification associated with individual objects.

Authentication

Access controls define what actions a user can perform or what objects a user can have access to. These controls assume that the identity of the user has been verified. It is the job of authentication mechanisms to ensure that only valid users are admitted. Described another way, authentication is using some mechanism to prove that you are who you claim to be. There are three general methods used in authentication. In order to verify your identity, you can provide:

- Something you know
- Something you have
- Something about you (something that you are)

The most common authentication mechanism is to provide something that only you, the valid user, should know. The most frequently used example of this is the common userid (or username) and password. In theory, since you are not supposed to share your password with anybody else, only you should know your password, and thus by providing it you are proving to the system that you are who you claim to be. In theory, this should be a fairly decent method to provide authentication. Unfortunately, for a variety of reasons, such as the fact that people have a tendency to choose very poor and easily guessed passwords, this technique to provide authentication is not as reliable as it should be. Other authentication mechanisms are consequently always being developed and deployed.

Another method to provide authentication involves the use of something that only valid users should have in their possession. A physical-world example of this would be a simple lock and key. Only those individuals with the correct key will be able to open the lock and thus provide admittance to your house, car, office, or whatever the lock was protecting. A similar method can be used to authenticate users for a computer system or network (though the key may be electronic and may reside on a smart card or similar device). The problem with this technology is that people will lose their keys (or cards), which means they can't log in to the system and somebody else who finds the key may then be able to access the system, even though they are not authorized. To address this problem, a combination of the something-you-know/something-you-have methods is often used so that the individual with the key may also be required to provide a password or passcode. The key is useless unless you know this code. An example of this is the ATM card most of us carry. The card is associated with a personal identification number (PIN), which only you should know. Knowing the PIN without having the card is useless, just as having the card without knowing the PIN will also not provide you access to your account.

The third general method to provide authentication involves something that is unique about you. We are used to this concept in our physical world, where people's fingerprints, or a sample of their DNA, can be used to identify them. This same concept can be used to provide authentication in the computer world. The field of authentication that uses something about you or something that you are is known as *biometrics*. A number of different mechanisms can be used to accomplish this type of authentication, such as a voice print, a retinal scan, or hand geometry. All of these methods obviously require some additional hardware in order to operate.

While these three approaches to authentication appear to be easy to understand and in most cases easy to implement, authentication is not to be taken lightly, since it is such an important component of security. Potential attackers are constantly searching for ways to get past the system's authentication mechanism, and there have been some fairly ingenious methods employed to do so. Consequently, security professionals are constantly devising new methods, building on these three basic approaches, to provide authentication mechanisms for computer systems and networks.

Kerberos

Developed as part of MIT's project Athena, Kerberos is a network authentication protocol designed for a client/server environment. Taking its name from the three-headed dog of Greek mythology, Kerberos is designed to work across the Internet, an inherently insecure environment. Kerberos uses strong encryption so that a client can prove its identity to a server and the server can in turn authenticate itself to the client. The basis for authentication in a Kerberos environment is something known as a *ticket*. Tickets are granted by the *authentication server*, which is an entity trusted by both the client and the server the client wishes to access. The client can then present this ticket to the server to provide proof of identity. Since the entire session can be encrypted, this will eliminate the inherently insecure transmission of items such as a password that can be intercepted on the network. Since the tickets are time-stamped, attempting to reuse them will not be successful. To illustrate how the Kerberos authentication service works, think about the common driver's license. You have received a license that you can present to other entities to prove you are who you claim to be. Because these other entities trust the state the license was issued in, they will accept your license as proof of your identity. The state the license was issued in is analogous to the Kerberos authentication service. It is the trusted entity both sides rely on to provide valid identifications. This analogy is not perfect, because we all probably have heard of individuals who obtained a phony driver's license, but it serves to illustrate the basic idea behind Kerberos.

CHAP

CHAP, the Challenge Handshake Authentication Protocol, is used to provide authentication across a point-to-point link using the Point-to-Point Protocol (PPP). In this protocol, authentication after the link has been established is not mandatory. CHAP is designed to provide authentication periodically through the use of a challenge/response system sometimes described as a three-way handshake, as illustrated in Figure 1-4. The initial challenge (a randomly generated number) is sent to the client. The client uses a

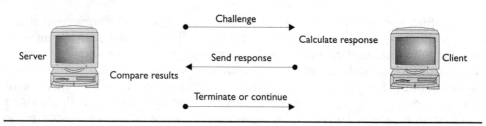

Figure 1-4   The CHAP challenge/response sequence

one-way hashing function to calculate what the response should be and then sends this back. The server compares the response with what it calculated the response should be. If it matches, communication continues. If the two values don't match, then the connection is terminated. This mechanism relies on a shared secret between the two entities so that the correct values can be calculated.

Certificates

Certificates are a method to establish authenticity of specific objects such as an individual's public key (more on this specific subject in Chapter 10) or downloaded software. A *digital certificate* is generally seen as an attachment to a message and is used to verify that the message did indeed come from the entity it claims to have come from. The digital certificate can also contain a key that can be used to encrypt further communication. For more information on this subject, refer to Chapter 10.

Tokens

A *token* is a hardware device that can be used in a challenge/response authentication process. In this way, it functions as both a something-you-have and something-you-know authentication mechanism. There have been several variations on this type of device, but they all work on the same basic principles. The device has an LCD screen and may or may not have a numeric keypad. Devices without a keypad will display a password (often just a sequence of numbers) that changes at a constant interval, usually about every 60 seconds. When an individual attempts to log in to a system, they enter their own user identification number and then the number that is showing on the LCD. The system knows which device they have and is synchronized with it so that it will know the number that should have been displayed. Since this number is constantly changing, a potential attacker who is able to see the sequence will not be able to use it later, since the code will have changed. Devices with a keypad work in a similar fashion (and may also be designed to function as a simple calculator). The individual who wants to log in to the system will first type their personal identification number into the calculator. They will then attempt to log in. The system will then provide a challenge; the user must enter that challenge into the calculator and press a special function key. The calculator will then determine the correct response and display it. The user provides the response to the system they are attempting to log in to, and the system verifies that this is the correct response. Since each user has a different PIN, two individuals receiving the same challenge will have different responses. The device can also use the date or time as a variable for the response calculation so that the same challenge at different times will yield different responses, even for the same individual.

Multifactor

Multifactor is a term used to describe the use of more than one authentication mechanism at the same time. An example of this is the hardware token, which requires both a personal identification number or password and the device itself to determine the correct response in order to authenticate to the system. This means that both the something-you-have and something-you-know mechanisms are used as factors in verifying authenticity of the user. Biometrics are also often used in conjunction with a personal identification number so that they too can be used as part of a multifactor authentication scheme, in this case something you are as well as something you know. The purpose of multifactor authentication is to increase the level of security, since more than one mechanism would have to be spoofed in order for an unauthorized individual to gain access to a computer system or network. The most common example of multifactor security is the common ATM card most of us have in our wallets.

Mutual Authentication

Mutual authentication is a term used to describe a process in which each side of an electronic communication verifies the authenticity of the other. We are used to the idea of having to authenticate ourselves to our Internet service provider (ISP) before we access the Internet, generally through the use of a user identification/password pair, but how do we actually know that we are really communicating with our ISP and not some other system that has somehow inserted itself into our communication (a man-in-the-middle attack). Mutual authentication would provide a mechanism for each side of a client/server relationship to verify the authenticity of the other to address this issue.

Chapter Review

In this chapter, you grew acquainted with the objectives that will be tested on the Security+ exam as well as the expected format for the exam. You met with a number of basic security concepts and terms. The operational model of computer security was described and examples provided for each of its components (prevention, detection, and response). The difference between authentication and access control was also discussed. Authentication is the process of providing some sort of verification for who you are to the computer system or network, and access controls are the mechanisms the system uses to decide what you can do once your authenticity has been verified. Authentication generally comes in one of three forms: something you know, something you have, or something you are/something about you. Examples include biometric devices and tokens. The most common authentication mechanism, however, is the simple username and password combination. Several approaches to access control were discussed, including discretionary access control, mandatory access control, and role-based access control.

Quick Tips

- Information assurance and information security place the security focus on the information and not the hardware or software used to process it.

- The original goal of computer and network security was to provide confidentiality, integrity, and availability—the "CIA" of security.

- As a result of the increased reliance on networks for commerce, authentication and nonrepudiation have been added to the original CIA of security.

- The operational model of computer security tells us that protection is provided by prevention, detection, and response.

- Host security focuses on protecting each computer and device individually instead of addressing protection of the network as a whole.

- Least privilege means that an object should have only the necessary rights and privileges to perform its task, with no additional permissions.

- Diversity of defense is a concept that complements the idea of various layers of security. It means to make the layers dissimilar so that if one layer is penetrated, the next layer can't also be penetrated using the same method.

- Access is the ability of a subject to interact with an object. Access controls are those devices and methods used to limit which subjects may interact with specific objects.

- Authentication mechanisms ensure that only valid users are provided access to the computer system or network.

- The three general methods used in authentication involve the users providing either something they know, something they have, or something unique about them (something they are).

- Multifactor is a term used to describe the use of more than one authentication mechanism at the same time.

- Mutual authentication is a term used to describe a process in which each side of an electronic communication verifies the authenticity of the other.

Questions

To further help you prepare for the Security+ exam, and to provide you a feel for your level of preparedness, answer the following questions and then check your answers against the list of correct answers found at the end of the chapter.

1. Which access control mechanism provides the owner of an object the opportunity to determine the access control permissions for other subjects?

    A. Mandatory

    B. Role-based

    C. Discretionary

    D. Token-based

2. What is the most common form of authentication used?

    A. Biometrics

    B. Tokens

    C. Access-card

    D. Username/password

3. A retinal scan device is an example of what type of authentication mechanism?

    A. Something you know

    B. Something you have

    C. Something about you/something you are

    D. Multifactor authentication

4. Which of the following is true about multifactor authentication?

    A. It employs more than one method to verify authenticity.

    B. It incorporates both access-control and authentication mechanisms into a single device.

    C. It allows for multiple levels of security classification in a single system.

    D. It bases access decisions on the role of the user, as opposed to using the more common access control list mechanism.

5. Tokens are

    A. An electronic signature used to verify authenticity

    B. A hardware device used in a challenge/response authentication process

    C. A software implementation of digital signature functionality

    D. Used in a challenge/response protocol to ensure the identity of both sides of a client/server relationship

6. What was described in the chapter as being essential in order to implement mandatory access controls?

    A. Tokens

    B. Certificates

    C. Labels

    D. Security classifications

7. The CIA of security includes

    A. Confidentiality, integrity, authentication

    B. Certificates, integrity, availability

    C. Confidentiality, inspection, authentication

    D. Confidentiality, integrity, availability

8. CHAP is the

    A. Certificate Handling Application Program

    B. Challenge Handshake Authentication Protocol

    C. Controlling Hierarchical Access Protocol

    D. Confidentiality Handling Application Protocol

9. The fundamental approach to security in which an object has only the necessary rights and privileges to perform its task with no additional permissions is a description of:

    A. Layered security

    B. Least privilege

    C. Role-based security

    D. Kerberos

10. What was the basis for authentication used in Kerberos?

    A. Token

    B. Certificate

    C. Ticket

    D. Biometrics

11. Mutual authentication describes:

    A. The three-way TCP handshake used for access control

    B. The process of asking for and receiving a digital certificate

    C. A process in which each side of an electronic communication verifies the authenticity of the other

    D. A process to verify both the integrity and confidentiality of a document

12. The ability of a subject to interact with an object describes:

    A. Authentication

    B. Access

    C. Confidentiality

    D. Mutual authentication

13. Information security places the focus of security efforts on:

    A. The system hardware

    B. The software

    C. The user

    D. The data

14. In role-based access control

    A. The user is responsible for providing both a password and a digital certificate in order to access the system or network.

    B. A set of roles that the user may perform will be assigned to each user, thus controlling what the user can do and what information they may access.

    C. The focus is on the confidentiality of the data the system protects and not its integrity.

    D. Authentication and nonrepudiation are the central focus.

15. Using different types of firewalls to protect various internal subnets is an example of:

    A. Layered security

    B. Security through obscurity

    C. Diversity of defense

    D. Implementing least privilege for access control

Answers

1. **C.** This is the definition of discretionary access control.

2. **D.** This is the single most common authentication mechanism in use today.

3. **C.** A retinal scan is an example of a biometric device, which falls into the category of something about you/something you are.

4. **A.** Multifactor authentication refers to the use of more than one type of authentication mechanism in order to provide improved security. An example of this would be a biometric device (something you know/something about you) and a personal identification number (something you know) in use at the same time.

5. **B.** This is the definition of a token.

6. **C.** Labels were discussed as being required for both objects and subjects in order to implement mandatory access controls. Here, D is not the correct answer, because mandatory access controls are often used to implement various levels of security classification but they are not needed in order to implement MAC.

7. **D.** Don't forget, even though authentication was described at great length in this chapter, the A in the CIA of security represents availability, which refers to both the hardware and data being accessible when the user wants it.

8. **B.** This is the definition for CHAP.

9. **B.** This was the description supplied for least privilege. Layered security referred to using multiple layers of security (such as at the host and network layers) so that if an intruder penetrates one layer, they still will have to face additional security mechanisms before gaining access to sensitive information.

10. **C.** A ticket was described as the basis for security in Kerberos. A ticket was granted by the authentication server in Kerberos. The analogy for a ticket in the physical world discussed in the chapter was the common driver's license.

11. **C.** This is the definition of the term mutual authentication.

12. **B.** This is the definition of access.

13. **D.** Information security places the focus of the security efforts on the data (information).

14. **B.** In role-based access controls, roles are assigned to the user. Each role will describe what the user can do and the data or information that can be accessed to accomplish that role.

15. **C.** This is an example of diversity of defense. The idea is to provide different types of security and not rely too heavily on any one type of product.

PART II

Malware and Attacks

Types of Attacks and Malicious Software

In this chapter, you will

- Learn about various types of computer and network attacks, including denial of service, spoofing, hijacking, and password guessing
- Understand the different types of malicious software that exists, including viruses, worms, Trojan horses, and logic bombs
- Explore how social engineering can be used as a means to gain access to computers and networks
- Discover the importance of auditing and what should be audited

There are two general reasons a particular computer system is attacked: it can be specifically targeted by the attacker, or it can be a target of opportunity.

Avenues of Attack

In the first case, the attacker has chosen the target not because of the hardware or software the organization is running but for another reason, such as a political reason. An example of this type of attack would be an individual in one country attacking a government system in another country. Alternatively, the attacker may be targeting the organization as part of a "hactivist" attack. An example, in this case, might be an attacker who defaces the web site of a company that sells fur coats because the attacker feels using animals in this way is unethical. Perpetrating some sort of electronic fraud is another reason a specific system might be targeted for attack. Whatever the reason, an attack of this nature is decided upon before the hardware and software of the organization is known.

The second type of attack, an attack against a target of opportunity, is conducted against a site that has hardware or software that is vulnerable to a specific exploit. The attackers, in this case, are not targeting the organization; they have instead learned of a vulnerability and are simply looking for an organization with this vulnerability that they can exploit. This is not to say that an attacker might not be targeting a given sector and looking for a target of opportunity in that sector. For example, an attacker may desire to obtain credit card or other personal information and may search for any exploitable company with credit card information in order to accomplish the attack.

Targeted attacks are more difficult and will take more time than attacks on a target of opportunity. The latter simply relies on the fact that with any piece of widely distributed software, there will almost always be somebody who has not patched the system as they should have.

The Steps in an Attack

The steps an attacker takes in attempting to penetrate a targeted network are similar to the ones that a security consultant performing a penetration test would take. The attacker will need to gather as much information about the organization as possible. There are numerous ways to do this, including studying the organization's own web site, looking for postings on newsgroups, or consulting resources such as the Securities and Exchange Commission's (SEC's) EDGAR web site (www.sec.gov/edgar.shtml). A number of different financial reports are available through the EDGAR web site that can provide information about an organization that is useful for an attack, especially for social engineering attacks. The type of information that the attacker wants includes IP addresses, phone numbers, names of individuals, and what networks the organization maintains.

The first step in the technical part of an attack is often to determine what target systems are available and active. This is often done with a ping sweep, which simply sends a "ping" (an ICMP echo request) to the target machine. If the machine responds, it is reachable. The next step is often to perform a port scan. This will help identify which ports are open, which gives an indication of which services may be running on the target machine. Determining the operating system that is running on the target machine, as well as specific application programs, follows along with determining the services that are available. Various techniques can be used to send specifically formatted packets to the ports on a target system to view the response. Often this response will provide clues as to which operating system and specific application is running on the target system. Once this is done, the attacker should have a list of possible target machines, the operating system running on them, and some specific applications or services to target.

Up until this point, the attacker has simply been gathering the information needed to take the next step, the actual attack on the target. Knowing the operating system and services on the target helps the attacker decide which tools to use in the attack.

There are numerous web sites that provide information on vulnerabilities in specific application programs and operating systems. This information is valuable to administrators, since they need to know what problems exist and how to patch them. In addition to information about specific vulnerabilities, some sites may also provide tools that can be used to exploit the vulnerabilities. An attacker can search for known vulnerabilities and tools that exploit them, download the information and tools, then use them against a site. If the administrator for the targeted system has not installed the correct patch, the attack may be successful; if the patch has been installed, the attacker will move on to the next possible vulnerability. If the administrator has installed all of the appropriate patches so that all known vulnerabilities have been addressed, the attacker may have to resort to a brute-force attack, which involves guessing a userid and password combination. Unfortunately, this type of attack, which could be easily prevented, sometimes proves successful.

This discussion of the steps in an attack is by no means complete. There are many different ways a system can be attacked. This, however, is the general process: gathering as much information about the target as possible (using both electronic and non-electronic means), gathering information about possible exploits based on the information about the system, and then systematically attempting to use each exploit. If the exploits don't work, other, less system-specific, attacks may be attempted.

Minimizing Possible Avenues of Attack

Understanding the steps an attacker will take enables you to limit the exposure of your system and to minimize the possible avenues an attacker can exploit.

The first step an administrator can take to minimize possible attacks is to ensure that all patches for the operating system and applications are installed. Many security problems that we read about, such as viruses and worms, exploit known vulnerabilities for which patches exist. The reason they have caused the damage they did is that administrators have not taken the appropriate actions to protect their systems.

The second step an administrator can take is to limit the services that are running on the system. As has been mentioned before, limiting the number of services to those that are absolutely needed does two things: it limits the possible avenues of attack (the possible services for which a vulnerability may exist that can be exploited), and it reduces the number of services the administrator has to worry about patching in the first place. This is one of the important first steps any administrator should take to secure a computer system.

Another step that can be taken to minimize possible avenues of attack is to provide as little information on your organization and its computing resources as possible. Since the attacker is after information, don't make it easy to obtain.

Attacking Computer Systems and Networks

While hackers and viruses receive the most attention in the news (due to the volume of these forms of attack), they are not the only methods for attacking computer systems and networks. This chapter will address the many different ways computers and networks come under attack on a daily basis. Each type of attack threatens at least one of the three security requirements mentioned in Chapter 1—confidentiality, integrity, and availability (the CIA of security). Attacks are thus attempts by unauthorized individuals to access or modify information, to deceive the system so that an unauthorized individual can take over an authorized session, or to disrupt service to authorized users.

From a high-level standpoint, attacks on computer systems and networks can be grouped into two broad categories: attacks on specific software (such as an application or the operating system itself) and attacks on a specific protocol or service. Attacks on a specific application or operating system are generally possible because of either an oversight in the code (and possibly in the testing of that code) or because of a flaw or bug in the code (again indicating a lack of thorough testing). Attacks on specific protocols or services are attempts to either take advantage of a specific feature of the protocol or service or to use the protocol or service in a manner for which it was not intended. The remainder of this section discusses the various forms of attacks that security professionals need to be aware of.

Denial of Service Attacks

Denial of service (DOS) attacks can exploit a known vulnerability in a specific application or operating system, or they may attack features (or weaknesses) in specific protocols or services. In this form of attack, the attacker is attempting to deny authorized users access either to specific information or to the computer system or network itself.

The purpose of such an attack can be to simply prevent access to the target system, or the attack can be used in conjunction with other actions in order to gain unauthorized access to a computer or network. For example, a SYN flooding attack may be used to temporarily prevent service to a system in order to take advantage of a trusted relationship that exists between that system and another.

SYN flooding is an example of a DOS attack that takes advantage of the way TCP/IP networks were designed to function, and it can be used to illustrate the basic principles of any DOS attack. SYN flooding utilizes the TCP three-way handshake that is used to establish a connection between two systems. Under normal circumstances, the first system sends a SYN packet to the system it wishes to communicate with. The second system will respond with a SYN/ACK if it is able to accept the request. When the initial system receives the SYN/ACK from the second system, it responds with an ACK packet, and communication can then proceed. This process is shown in Figure 2-1.

NOTE A SYN/ACK is really a combination of the SYN packet sent to the first system, combined with an ACK packet acknowledging the first's system's SYN packet.

In a SYN flooding attack, the attacker sends fake communication requests to the targeted system. Each of these requests will be answered by the target system, which then waits for the third part of the handshake. Since the requests are fake (a nonexistent IP address is used in the requests, so the target system is responding to a system that doesn't exist), the target will wait for responses that will never come, as shown in Figure 2-2. The target system will drop these connections after a specific time-out period, but if the attacker sends requests faster than the time-out period eliminates them, the system will quickly be filled with requests. The number of connections a system can support is finite, so when more requests come in than can be processed, the system will soon be reserving all its connections for fake requests. At this point, any further requests are simply dropped (ignored), and legitimate users who want to connect to the target system will not be able to. Use of the system has thus been denied to them.

Another simple DOS attack is the famous ping-of-death (POD), and it illustrates the other type of attack—one targeted at a specific application or operating system, as opposed

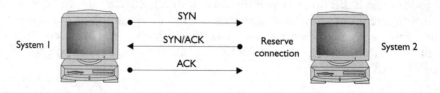

Figure 2-1   The TCP three-way handshake

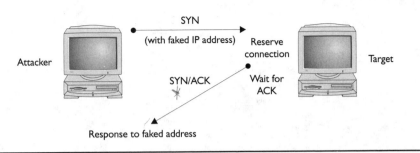

Figure 2-2   A SYN flooding DOS attack

to SYN flooding, which targets a protocol. In the POD attack, the attacker sends an Internet Control Message Protocol (ICMP) "ping" packet equal to, or exceeding 64KB (which is to say, greater than 64 * 1024 = 65,536 bytes). This type of packet should not occur naturally (there is no reason for a ping packet to be larger than 64KB). Certain systems were not able to handle this size of packet, and the system would hang or crash.

DOS attacks are conducted using a single attacking system. A denial of service attack employing multiple attacking systems is known as a distributed denial of service (DDOS) attack. The goal of a DDOS attack is the same: to deny the use of or access to a specific service or system. DDOS attacks were made famous in 2000 with the highly publicized attacks on eBay, CNN, Amazon, and Yahoo.

In a DDOS attack, the method used to deny service is simply to overwhelm the target with traffic from many different systems. A network of attack agents (sometimes called zombies) is created by the attacker, and upon receiving the attack command from the attacker, the attack agents commence sending a specific type of traffic against the target. If the attack network is large enough, even ordinary web traffic can quickly overwhelm the largest of sites, such as the ones targeted in 2000.

Creating a DDOS network is not a simple task. The attack agents are not willing agents—they are systems that have been compromised and on which the DDOS attack software has been installed. In order to compromise these agents, the attacker has to have gained unauthorized access to the system or tricked authorized users to run a program that installed the attack software. The creation of the attack network may in fact be a multistep process in which the attacker first compromises a few systems that are then used as handlers or masters, and which in turn compromise other systems. Once the network has been created, the agents wait for an attack message that will include data on the specific target before launching the attack. One important aspect of a DDOS attack that should be mentioned is that with just a few messages to the agents, the attacker can have a flood of messages sent against the targeted system. Figure 2-3 illustrates a DDOS network with agents and handlers.

How can you stop or mitigate the effects of a DOS or DDOS attack? One important precaution is to ensure that you have applied the latest patches and upgrades to your systems and the applications running on them. Once a vulnerability is discovered, it does not take long before multiple exploits are written to take advantage of it. Generally

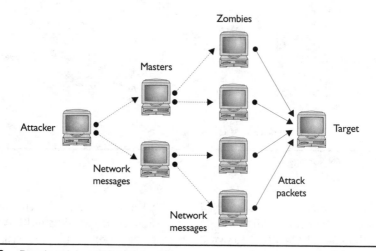

Figure 2-3   Distributed denial of service attacks

you will have a small window of opportunity in which to patch your system between the time a vulnerability is discovered and the time exploits become widely available.

Another approach involves changing the timeout option for TCP connections so that attacks such as the SYN flooding attack, described previously, are harder to perform because unused connections are dropped more quickly.

For DDOS attacks, much has been written about distributing your own workload across several systems so that any attack against your system would have to target several hosts in order to be completely successful. While this is true, if large enough DDOS networks are created (with tens of thousands of zombies, for example) any network, no matter how much the load is distributed, can be successfully attacked. This approach also involves an additional cost to your organization in order to establish this distributed environment. Addressing the problem in this manner is actually an attempt to mitigate the effect of the attack, as opposed to preventing or stopping an attack.

In order to prevent a DDOS attack, you have to either be able to intercept or block the attack messages or keep the DDOS network from being established in the first place. Tools have been developed that will scan your systems, searching for sleeping zombies waiting for an attack signal. The problem with this type of prevention approach, however, is that it is not something you can do to prevent an attack on your network—it is something you can do to keep your network from being used to attack other networks or systems. You have to rely on the rest of the community to test their own systems in order to prevent attacks on yours.

A final option you should consider that will address several forms of DOS and DDOS attacks is to block ICMP packets at your border, since many attacks rely on ICMP. Careful consideration should be given to this approach, because it will also prevent the use of some possibly useful troubleshooting tools.

Backdoors and Trapdoors

Backdoors were originally (and sometimes still are) nothing more than methods used by software developers to ensure that they could gain access to an application even if something were to happen in the future to prevent normal access methods. An example would be a hard-coded password that could be used to gain access to the program in the event that administrators forgot their own system password. The obvious problem with this sort of backdoor (also sometimes referred to as a *trapdoor*) is that, since it is hard-coded, it cannot be removed. Should an attacker learn of the backdoor, all systems running that software would be vulnerable to attack.

The term *backdoor* is also, and more commonly, used to refer to programs that attackers install after gaining unauthorized access to a system to ensure that they can continue to have unrestricted access to the system, even if their initial access method is discovered and blocked. Backdoors can also be installed by authorized individuals inadvertently, should they run software that contains a Trojan horse (more on these later in this chapter). Common backdoors include NetBus and Back Orifice. Both of these, if running on your system, will allow an attacker remote access to your system—access that allows them to perform any function on your system. A variation on the backdoor is the *rootkit*, and they are established not to gain root access but rather to ensure continued root access. Rootkits are generally installed at a lower level, closer to the actual kernel level of the operating system.

Sniffing

The group of protocols that make up the TCP/IP suite was designed to work in a friendly environment where everybody who connected to the network used the protocols as they were designed. The abuse of this friendly assumption is illustrated by network-traffic sniffing programs, sometimes referred to as *sniffers*.

A network sniffer is a software or hardware device that is used to observe traffic as it passes through a network on shared broadcast media. The device can be used to view all traffic, or it can target a specific protocol, service, or even string of characters (for example, looking for logins). Normally the network device that connects a computer to a network is designed to ignore all traffic that is not destined for that computer. Network sniffers ignore this friendly agreement and observe all traffic on the network, whether destined for that computer or others, as shown in Figure 2-4. A network card that is listening to all network traffic and not just its own is said to be in "promiscuous mode." Some network sniffers are designed not just to observe all traffic but to modify traffic as well.

Network sniffers can be used by network administrators for monitoring network performance. They can be used to perform traffic analysis, for example, in order to determine what type of traffic is most commonly carried on the network and to determine which segments are most active. They can also be used for network bandwidth analysis and to troubleshoot certain problems (such as duplicate MAC addresses).

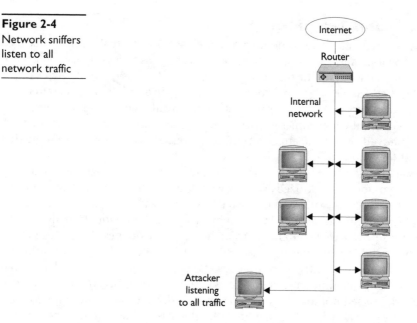

Figure 2-4
Network sniffers
listen to all
network traffic

Internet

Router

Internal
network

Attacker
listening
to all traffic

Network sniffers can also be used by attackers to gather information that can be used in penetration attempts. Information such as an authorized user's username and password can be viewed and recorded for later use. The contents of e-mail messages can also be viewed as the messages travel across the network. It should be obvious that administrators and security professionals will not want unauthorized network sniffers on their networks because of the security and privacy concerns they introduce. Fortunately, in order for network sniffers to be most effective, they need to be on the internal network, which generally means that the chances for outsiders to use them against you is extremely limited.

Spoofing

Spoofing is nothing more than making data look like it has come from a different source. This is possible in TCP/IP because of the friendly assumptions behind the protocols. When the protocols were developed, it was assumed that individuals who had access to the network layer would be privileged users who could be trusted.

When a packet is sent from one system to another, it includes not only the destination IP address and port but the source IP address as well. You are supposed to fill in the source with your own address, but there is nothing that stops you from filling in another system's address. This is one of the several forms of spoofing.

Spoofing E-Mail

E-mail spoofing is where you send a message with a From address different than your own. This can be easily accomplished, and there are several different ways to do it and programs that can assist you in doing so. A very simple method often used to demonstrate how simple it is to spoof an e-mail address is to telnet to port 25 (the port associated with e-mail) on a system. From there, you can fill in any address for the From and To sections of the message, whether or not the addresses are yours and whether they actually exist or not.

There are some simple ways to determine that an e-mail message was probably not sent by the source it claims to have been sent from, but most users do not question their e-mail and will accept where it appears to have come from. A variation on e-mail spoofing, though it is not technically spoofing, is for the attacker to acquire a URL close to the one they want to spoof so that e-mail sent from their system appears to have come from the official site unless you read the address carefully. For example, if attackers wanted to spoof XYZ Corporation, which owned XYZ.com, the attackers might gain access to the URL XYZ.Corp.com. An individual receiving a message from the spoofed corporation site would not normally suspect it to be a spoof but would take it to be official. This same method can be, and has been, used to spoof web sites. The most famous example of this is probably www.whitehouse.com. The www.whitehouse.gov site is the official site for the White House. The www.whitehouse.com URL takes you to a pornographic site. In this case, nobody is likely to take the pornographic site to be the official government site, and it was not intended to be taken that way. If, however, the attackers made their spoofed site appear similar to the official one, they could easily convince many viewers that they were at the official site.

IP Address Spoofing

The way the IP protocol is designed to work is to have the originators of any IP packet include their own IP address in the "From" portion of the packet. While this is the intent, there is nothing that prevents a system from inserting a different address in the "From" portion of the packet. This is known as IP Address Spoofing. An IP address may be spoofed for several reasons. In a specific DOS attack known as a *smurf* attack, the attacker sends a spoofed packet to the broadcast address for a network, which distributes the packet to all systems on that network. In the smurf attack, the packet sent by the attacker to the broadcast address is an echo request with the From address forged so that it appears that another system (the target system) has made the echo request. The normal response of a system to an echo request is an echo reply, and it is used in the ping utility to let a user know if a remote system is reachable and is responding. In the smurf attack, the request is sent to all systems on the network, so all will respond with an echo reply to the target system, as shown in Figure 2-5. The attacker has sent one packet and has been able to generate as many as 254 responses aimed at the target. Should the attacker send several of these spoofed requests, or send them to several different networks, the target can quickly become overwhelmed with the volume of echo replies it receives.

Spoofing and Trusted Relationships

Spoofing can also take advantage of a trusted relationship between two systems. If two systems are configured to accept the authentication accomplished by each other, an individual logged on to one system might not be forced to go through an authentication process again to access the other system. An attacker can take advantage of this arrangement

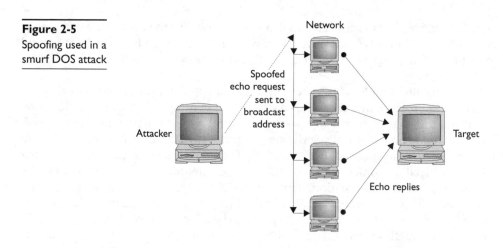

Figure 2-5
Spoofing used in a smurf DOS attack

by sending a packet to one system that appears to have come from a trusted system. Since the trusted relationship is in place, the targeted system may perform the requested task without authentication.

Since a reply will often be sent once a packet is received, the system that is being impersonated could interfere with the attack, since it would receive an acknowledgement for a request it never made. The attacker will often initially launch a DOS attack (such as a SYN flooding attack) to temporarily take out the spoofed system for the period of time that the attacker is exploiting the trusted relationship. Once the attack is completed, the DOS attack on the spoofed system would be terminated and possibly, apart from having a temporarily non-responsive system, the administrators for the systems may never notice that the attack occurred. Figure 2-6 illustrates a spoofing attack that includes a SYN flooding attack.

Because of this type of attack, administrators are encouraged to strictly limit any trusted relationships between hosts. Firewalls should also be configured to discard any packets from outside of the firewall that have From addresses indicating they originated from inside the network (a situation that should not occur normally and that indicates spoofing is being attempted).

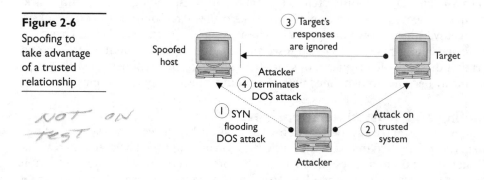

Figure 2-6
Spoofing to take advantage of a trusted relationship

NOT ON TEST

Spoofing and Sequence Numbers

How complicated the spoofing is depends heavily on several factors, including whether the traffic is encrypted and where the attacker is located in relationship to the target. Spoofing attacks from inside a network, for example, are much easier to perform than attacks from outside of the network because the inside attacker can observe the traffic to and from the target and can do a better job of formulating the necessary packets.

Formulating the packets is more complicated for external attackers because there is a sequence number associated with TCP packets. A sequence number is a 32-bit number established by the host that is incremented for each packet sent. Packets are not guaranteed to be received in order, and the sequence number can be used to help reorder packets as they are received and to refer to packets that may have been lost in transmission.

In the TCP three-way handshake discussed previously, two sets of sequence numbers are created, as shown in Figure 2-7. The first system chooses a sequence number to send with the original SYN packet that it sends. The system receiving this SYN packet acknowledges with a SYN/ACK. It sends back the first sequence number plus one (that is, it increments the sequence number sent to it by one). It then also creates its own sequence number and sends that along with it. The original system receives the SYN/ACK with the new sequence number. It increments the sequence number by one and uses it in an ACK package it responds with.

The difference in the difficulty of attempting a spoofing attack from inside a network and from outside involves determining the sequence number. If the attacker is inside of the network and can observe the traffic the target host responds with, the attacker can easily see the sequence number the system creates and can respond with the correct sequence number. If the attacker is external to the network, the sequence number the target system generates will not be observed, making it hard for the attacker to provide the final ACK with the correct sequence number. What the attacker has to do is guess what the sequence number might be.

Predicting sequence numbers is possible, because sequence numbers are somewhat predictable. Sequence numbers for each session are not started from the same number, so that different packets from different concurrent connections will not have the same sequence numbers. Instead, the sequence number for each new connection is incremented by some large number to keep them from being the same. The sequence number may also be incremented by some large number every second (or some other time period). What an external attacker has to do is determine what the values used for these

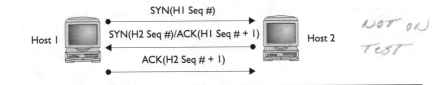

Figure 2-7   Three-way handshake with sequence numbers

increments are. The attacker can do this by attempting connections at various time intervals in order to observe how the sequence numbers are incremented. Once the pattern is determined, the attacker can attempt a legitimate connection to determine the current value, and then immediately attempt the spoofed connection. The spoofed connection sequence number should be the legitimate connection incremented by the determined value or values.

Sequence numbers are also important in session hijacking, which will be discussed in the "TCP/IP Hijacking" section of this chapter.

Man-in-the-Middle Attacks

A man-in-the-middle attack, as the name implies, generally occurs when attackers are able to place themselves in the middle of two other hosts that are communicating. Ideally, this is done by ensuring that all communication going to or from the target host is routed through the attacker's host (which may be accomplished if the attacker can compromise the router for the target host). The attacker can then observe all traffic before relaying it and can actually modify or block traffic. To the target host, it appears that communication is occurring normally, since all expected replies are received. Figure 2-8 illustrates this type of attack.

The amount of information that can be obtained in a man-in-the-middle attack will obviously be limited if the communication is encrypted. Even in this case, however, sensitive information may still be obtained, since knowing what communication is being conducted, and between which individuals, may in fact provide information that is valuable in certain circumstances.

Man-in-the-Middle Attacks on Encrypted Traffic

The term "man-in-the-middle attack" is sometimes used to refer to a more specific type of attack—one in which the encrypted traffic issue is addressed. Public and private key encryption will be discussed in much greater detail in Chapter 10, but for now it should be understood that public key encryption requires the use of two keys: your public key, which anybody can use to encrypt or "lock" your message, and your private key, which only you know and which is used to "unlock" or decrypt a message locked with your public key.

If you wanted to communicate securely with your friend Bob, you might ask him for his public key so you could encrypt your messages to him. You, in turn, would supply

Figure 2-8

A man-in-the-middle attack

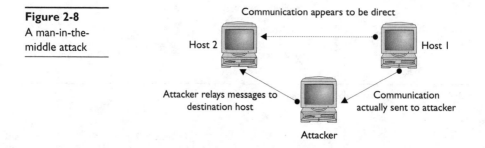

Communication appears to be direct

Host 2   Host 1

Attacker relays messages to destination host   Communication actually sent to attacker

Attacker

Bob with your public key. An attacker can conduct a man-in-the-middle attack by intercepting your request for Bob's public key and the sending of your public key to him. The attacker would replace your public key with the attacker's public key, and would send it on to Bob. The attacker's public key would also be sent to you by the attacker instead of Bob's public key. Now when either you or Bob encrypt a message, it will be encrypted using the attacker's public key. The attacker can now intercept it, decrypt it, and then send it on by re-encrypting it with the appropriate key for either you or Bob. Each of you thinks you are transmitting messages securely, but in reality your communication has been compromised. Well-designed cryptographic products use techniques such as mutual authentication to avoid this problem.

Replay Attacks

A replay attack is exactly what it sounds like: it is an attack where the attacker captures a portion of a communication between two parties and retransmits it at a later time. For example, an attacker might replay a series of commands and codes used in a financial transaction in order to cause the transaction to be conducted multiple times. Generally replay attacks are associated with attempts to circumvent authentication mechanisms, such as the capturing and reuse of a certificate or ticket.

The best way to prevent replay attacks is with encryption, cryptographic authentication, and time stamps. If a portion of the certificate or ticket includes a date/time stamp or an expiration date/time, and this portion is also encrypted as part of the ticket or certificate, replaying it at a later time will prove useless, since it will be rejected as having expired.

TCP/IP Hijacking

TCP/IP hijacking and *session hijacking* are terms used to refer to the process of taking control of an already existing session between a client and a server. The advantage to an attacker of hijacking over attempting to penetrate a computer system or network is that the attacker doesn't have to circumvent any authentication mechanisms, since the user has already authenticated and established the session. Once the user has completed the authentication sequence, the attacker can then usurp the session and carry on as if the attacker, and not the user, had authenticated with the system. In order to prevent the user from noticing anything unusual, the attacker may decide to attack the user's system and perform a denial of service attack on it, taking it down so that the user, and the system, will not notice the extra traffic that is taking place.

Hijack attacks generally are used against web and telnet sessions. The previous discussion on sequence numbers as they applied to spoofing also applies to session hijacking, since the hijacker will need to provide the correct sequence number to continue the appropriated sessions.

Attacks on Encryption

Cryptography is the art of "secret writing," and encryption is the process of transforming *plaintext* into an unreadable format known as *ciphertext* using a specific technique or algorithm. Most encryption techniques use some form of key in the encryption process. The key is used in a mathematical process to scramble the original message to arrive at the unreadable ciphertext. Another key (sometimes the same one and sometimes a different one) is used to decrypt or unscramble the ciphertext to re-create the original plaintext. The length of the key often directly relates to the strength of the encryption.

Cryptanalysis is the process of attempting to break a cryptographic system—it is an attack on the specific method used to encrypt the plaintext. There are various ways cryptographic systems can be compromised. Encryption will be discussed in greater detail in Chapter 10 of this book.

Weak Keys

Certain encryption algorithms may have specific keys that yield poor, or easily decrypted, ciphertext. Imagine an encryption algorithm that consisted solely of a single XOR function (an exclusive OR function where two bits are compared and a 1 is returned if either of the original bits, but not both, is a 1), where the key was repeatedly used to XOR with the plaintext. A key where all bits are 0's, for example, would result in ciphertext that is the same as the original plaintext. This would obviously be a weak key for this encryption algorithm. In fact, any key with long strings of 0's would yield portions of the ciphertext that were the same as the plaintext. In this simple example, there would be many keys that could be considered weak.

Encryption algorithms used in computer systems and networks are much more complicated than a simple, single XOR function, but some algorithms have still been found to have weak keys that make cryptanalysis easier.

Exhaustive Search of Key Space

Even if the specific algorithm used to encrypt a message is complicated and has not been shown to have weak keys, the key length will still play a significant role in how easy it is to attack the method of encryption. Generally speaking, the longer a key is, the harder it will be to attack. Thus, a 40-bit encryption scheme will be easier to attack using a brute-force technique (which tests all possible keys, one by one) than a 256-bit method will be. This is easily demonstrated by imagining a scheme that employed a 2-bit key. Even if the resulting ciphertext were completely unreadable, performing a brute-force attack until one key is found that can decrypt the ciphertext would not take long, since there are only four possible keys. Every bit that is added to the length of a key doubles the number of keys that have to be tested in a brute-force attack on the encryption. It is easy to understand why a scheme utilizing a 40-bit key would be much easier to attack than a scheme that utilized a 256-bit key.

Indirect Attacks

One of the most common ways of attacking an encryption system is to find weaknesses in mechanisms surrounding the cryptography. Examples include poor random number generators, unprotected key exchanges, keys stored on hard drives without sufficient protection, and other general programmatic errors, such as buffer overflows. In attacks that target these types of weaknesses, it is not the cryptographic algorithm itself that is being attacked, but rather the implementation of that algorithm in the real world.

Password Guessing

The most common form of authentication is the userid and password combination. While it is not inherently a poor mechanism for authentication, the userid and password combination can be attacked in several ways. All too often, these attacks will yield favorable results for the attacker not as a result of a weakness in the scheme but usually due to the user not following good password procedures.

Poor Password Choices

The least technical of the various password-attack techniques consists of the attacker simply attempting to guess the password of an authorized user of the system or network. It is surprising how often this simple method works, and the reason it does is because people are notorious for picking poor passwords. The problem the users face is that they need to select a password that they can remember. In order to do this, many select simple things, such as their birthday, their mother's maiden name, the name of their spouse or one of their children, or even simply their userid itself. All it takes is for the attacker to obtain a valid userid (often a simple matter, because organizations tend to use an individual's names in some combination—first letter of their first name combined with their last name, for example) and a little bit of information about the user before guessing can begin. Organizations sometimes make it even easier for attackers to obtain this sort of information by posting the names of their "management team" and other individuals, sometimes with short biographies, on their web sites.

Even if the person doesn't use some personal detail as their password, the attacker may still get lucky, since many people pick a common word for their password. Attackers can obtain lists of common passwords—there are a number of them on the Internet. Words such as "password" and "secret" have often been used as passwords. Names of favorite sports teams also often find their way onto lists of commonly used passwords.

Dictionary Attack

Another method of determining passwords is to use a password-cracking program. There are a number of both commercial and public-domain password cracking programs available. The programs use a variety of methods to crack passwords, including using variations on the userid. These programs often also use a dictionary of words—the words can be used by themselves, or two or more smaller ones may be combined to form a single possible password.

The programs often permit the attacker to create various rules that tell the program how to combine words to form new possible passwords. Users commonly substitute certain numbers for specific letters. If the user wanted to use the word *secret* for a password, for example, the letter *e* may be replaced with the number 3 yielding *s3cr3t*. This password will not be found in the dictionary, so a pure dictionary attack will not crack it.

At the same time, the password is still easy for the user to remember. If a rule were created that tried all words in the dictionary and then tried the same words substituting the number 3 for the letter *e*, the password would be cracked.

Rules can also be defined so that the cracking program will substitute special characters for other characters, or combine words together. The ability of the attacker to crack passwords is directly related to the method the user employed to create the password in the first place, as well as the dictionary and rules used.

Brute-Force Attack

If the user has selected a password that will not be found in a dictionary, even if various numbers or special characters are substituted for other letters, the only way the password can be cracked is to attempt a brute-force attack. This entails the password cracking program attempting all possible password combinations.

The length of the password and the size of the set of possible characters in the password will greatly affect the time a brute-force attack will take. A few years ago, this method of attack was very unreliable, since it took considerable time to generate all possible combinations. With the increase in computer speed, however, the time it takes to generate password combinations makes it much more feasible to launch brute-force attacks against certain computer systems and networks. A brute-force attack on a password can take place at two levels. It can be an attack on a system where the attacker is attempting to guess the password at a login prompt, or it can be an attack against the list of passwords contained in a password file. The first attack can be made more difficult by locking the account after a few failed login attempts. The second attack can be thwarted by securely maintaining your password file so that others may not obtain a copy of it.

Birthday Attack

The birthday attack is a special type of brute-force attack. It gets its name from something known as the *birthday paradox,* which states that in a group of at least 23 people, the chance that there will be two individuals with the same birthday is greater than 50 percent. Mathematically, we can use the equation $1.2k^{1/2}$ (with k equaling the size of the set of possible values), and in the birthday paradox, k would be equal to 365 (the number of possible birthdays). This same phenomenon applies to passwords, with k just being quite a bit larger.

Software Exploitation

An attack that takes advantage of bugs or weaknesses in software is referred to as *software exploitation.* These weaknesses can be the result of poor design, poor testing, or poor coding practices. They may also result from what are sometimes called "features." An example of this might be a debugging feature, which when used during debugging might allow unauthenticated individuals to execute programs on a system. If this feature is left in when the final version of the software is shipped, it creates a weakness that is just waiting to be exploited.

One common weakness that has been exploited on a number of occasions is buffer overflows. A buffer overflow occurs when a program is provided more data for input than it was designed to handle. For example, what would happen if a program that asks for a 7–10 character phone number instead receives a string of 150 characters? Many programs will provide some error checking to ensure that this will not cause a problem. Some programs, however, do not handle this error, and the extra characters continue to fill memory, overwriting other portions of the program. This can result in a number of problems, including causing the program to abort or the system to crash. Under certain circumstances the program may execute a command now supplied by the attacker.

Malicious Code

The term *malicious code* refers to software that has been designed for some nefarious purpose. Such software may be designed to cause damage to a system, such as by deleting all files, or it may be designed to create a backdoor in the system in order to grant access to unauthorized individuals. Generally the installation of malicious code is done so that it is not obvious to the authorized users. There are several different types of malicious software, such as viruses, Trojan horse, logic bombs, and worms, and they differ in the ways they are installed and their purposes.

Viruses

The best-known type of malicious code is the virus. Much has been written about viruses as a result of several high-profile security events that involved them. A virus is a piece of malicious code that replicates by attaching itself to another piece of executable code. When the other executable code is run, the virus also executes and has the opportunity to infect other files and perform any other nefarious actions it was designed to do. The specific way that a virus infects other files, and the type of files it infects, depends on the type of virus. The first viruses were of two types—boot sector or program viruses.

Boot Sector Virus A boot sector virus infects the boot sector portion of either a floppy disk or a hard drive (just a few years ago, not all computers had hard drives, and many booted from a floppy). When a computer is first turned on, a small portion of the operating system is initially loaded from hardware. This small operating system then attempts to load the rest of the operating system from a specific location (sector) on either the floppy or the hard drive. A boot sector virus infects this portion of the drive.

An example of this type of virus was the Stoned virus, which moved the true Master Boot Record (MBR) from the first to the seventh sector of the first cylinder, and replaced the original MBR with itself. When the system was then turned on, the virus was first executed, which had a one in seven chance of displaying a message stating the computer was "stoned"; otherwise it would not announce itself and would instead attempt to infect other boot sectors. This virus was rather tame in comparison to other viruses of its time, which often were designed to delete the entire hard drive after a period of time in which they would attempt to spread.

Program Virus   A second type of virus is the program virus, which attaches itself to executable files—typically files ending in .exe or .com on Windows-based systems. The virus is attached in such a way that it is executed before the program. Most program viruses also hide a nefarious purpose, such as deleting the hard drive, which is triggered by a specific event, such as a date or after a certain number of other files were infected. Like other types of viruses, program viruses are often not detected until after they execute their malicious payload. One method that has been used to detect this sort of virus before it has an opportunity to damage a system is to calculate checksums for commonly used programs or utilities. Should the checksum for an executable ever change, it is quite likely that this is due to a virus infection.

Macro Virus   In the late 90s, another type of virus appeared that now accounts for the majority of viruses. As systems became more powerful, as well as the operating systems that managed them, the boot sector virus, which once accounted for most reported infections, became less common. Systems no longer commonly booted from floppies, which were the main method for boot sector viruses to spread. Instead, the proliferation of software that included macro-programming languages resulted in a new breed of virus—the macro virus.

The Concept virus was the first known example of this new breed. It appeared to be created to demonstrate the possibility of attaching a virus to a document file, something that had been thought to be impossible before the introduction of software that included powerful macro language capabilities. By this time, however, Microsoft Word documents could include segments of code written in a derivative of Visual Basic. Further development of other applications that allowed macro capability, and enhanced versions of the original macro language, had the side effect of allowing the proliferation of viruses that took advantage of this capability.

This type of virus is so common today that it is considered a security best practice to advise users to never open a document attached to an e-mail if it seems at all suspicious. Many organizations now routinely have their mail servers eliminate any attachments containing Visual Basic macros.

Avoiding Virus Infection   Always being cautious about executing programs or opening documents given to you is a good security practice. "If you don't know where it came from or where it has been, don't open or run it" should be the basic guideline for all computer users.

Another security best practice for protecting against virus infection is to install and run an antivirus program. Since these programs are designed to protect against known viruses, it is also important to maintain an up-to-date listing of virus signatures for your antivirus software. Antivirus software vendors provide this, and administrators should stay on top of the latest updates to the list of known viruses.

Two advances in virus writing have made it more difficult for antivirus software to detect viruses. These advances are the introduction of *stealth virus* techniques and *polymorphic viruses*. A stealthy virus employs techniques to help evade being detected by antivirus software that uses checksums or other techniques. Polymorphic viruses also attempt to evade detection, but they do so by changing the virus itself (the virus "evolves"). Because the virus changes, signatures for that virus may no longer be valid, and the virus may escape detection by antivirus software.

Virus Hoaxes   Viruses have caused so much damage in the last few years that many Internet users have become extremely cautious anytime a rumor of a new virus is heard. Many users will not connect to the Internet when they hear about a virus outbreak, just to be sure they don't get infected themselves. This has given rise to virus hoaxes, in which word is spread about a new virus and the extreme danger it poses. It may warn users to not read certain files or connect to the Internet.

A good example of a virus hoax was the Good Times virus warning, which has been copied repeatedly and can still be seen in various forms today. It caused widespread panic as users read about this extremely dangerous virus, which could actually cause the processor to overheat (from being put into an "nth complexity infinite binary loop") and be destroyed. Many folks saw through this hoax, but many less experienced users did not, and they passed the warning along to all of their friends.

Hoaxes can actually be even more destructive than just wasting time and bandwidth. Some hoaxes warning of a dangerous virus have included instructions to delete certain files if found on the user's system. Unfortunately for those who follow the advice, the files may actually be part of the operating system, and deleting them could keep the system from booting properly. This suggests another good piece of security advice: make sure of the authenticity and accuracy of any virus report before following somebody's advice. Antivirus software vendors are a good source of factual data for this sort of threat as well (see http://www.symantec.com/avcenter/hoax.html or http://vil.mcafee.com/hoax.asp for examples of hoaxes).

Trojan Horses

A Trojan horse, or simply *Trojan*, is a piece of software that appears to do one thing (and may, in fact, actually do that thing) but that hides some other functionality. The analogy to the famous story of antiquity is very accurate. In the original case, the object appeared to be a large wooden horse, and in fact it was. At the same time, it hid something much more sinister and dangerous to the occupants of the city. As long as the horse was left outside the city walls, it could cause no damage to the inhabitants. It had to be taken in by the inhabitants, and it was inside the hidden purpose was activated. A computer Trojan works in much the same way. Unlike a virus, which reproduces by attaching itself to other files or programs, a Trojan is a standalone program that must be copied and installed by the user—it must be "brought inside" the system by an authorized user. The challenge for the attacker is enticing the user to copy and run the program. This generally means that the program must be disguised as something that the user would want to run—a special utility or game, for example. Once it has been copied and is "inside" the system, the Trojan will perform its hidden purpose with the user often still unaware of its true nature.

A good example of a Trojan is Back Orifice (BO), originally created in 1999 and now in several versions. BO can be attached to a number of types of programs. Once it is, and once an infected file is run, BO will create a way for unauthorized individuals to take over the system remotely, as if they were sitting at the console. BO is designed to work with Windows-based systems.

The single best method to prevent the introduction of a Trojan to your system is to never run software if you are unsure of its origin, security, and integrity. A virus-checking program may also be useful in detecting and preventing the installation of known Trojans.

Logic Bombs

Logic bombs, unlike viruses and Trojans, are a type of malicious software that is deliberately installed, generally by an authorized user. A logic bomb is a piece of code that sits dormant for a period of time until some event invokes its malicious payload. An example of a logic bomb might be a program that is set to automatically load and run, and that periodically checks an organization's payroll or personnel database for a specific employee. If the employee is not found, the malicious payload executes, deleting vital corporate files.

If the trigger is some event, such as not finding a specific name in the personnel file, the code is referred to as a *logic bomb*. If the event is a specific date or time, the program will often be referred to as a *time bomb*. In one famous example of a time bomb, a disgruntled employee left a time bomb in place just prior to being fired from his job. Two weeks later, thousands of client records were deleted. Police were able to eventually track the malicious code to the disgruntled ex-employee, who was prosecuted for his actions. He had hoped that the two weeks that had passed since his dismissal would have caused investigators to assume he could not have been the individual who had caused the deletion of the records.

Logic bombs are difficult to detect because they are often installed by authorized users and, in particular, have been installed by administrators who are also often responsible for security. This demonstrates the need for a separation of duties and a periodic review of all programs and services that are running. It also illustrates the need to maintain an active backup program so that if your organization loses critical files to this sort of malicious code, you only lose transactions since the most recent backup and don't permanently lose the data.

Worms

Originally it was easy to distinguish between a worm and a virus. Recently, with the introduction of new breeds of sophisticated malicious code, the distinction has blurred. Worms are pieces of code that attempt to penetrate networks and computer systems. Once a penetration occurs, the worm will create a new copy of itself on the penetrated system. Reproduction of a worm thus does not rely on the attachment of the virus to another piece of code or to a file, which is the definition of a virus.

The blurring of the distinction between viruses and worms has come about because of the attachment of malicious code to e-mail. Viruses were generally thought of as a system-based problem, and worms were network-based. If the malicious code is sent throughout a network, it may subsequently be called a worm. The important distinction, however, is whether the code has to attach itself to something else (a virus), or if it can "survive" on its own (a worm).

The Morris Worm   The most famous example of a worm was the Morris worm in 1988. Also sometimes referred to as the Internet worm, because of its effect on the early Internet, the worm was able to insert itself into so many systems connected to the Internet that it has been repeatedly credited with "bringing the Internet to its knees" for several days. It was this worm that provided the impetus for the creation of what was once the Computer Emergency Response Team Coordination Center though is now simply the CERT Coordination Center (CERT/CC) located at Carnegie Mellon University.

The Morris worm was created by a graduate student named Robert Morris. It utilized several known vulnerabilities to gain access to a new system, and it also relied on password guessing to obtain access to accounts. Once a system had been penetrated, a small bootstrap program was inserted into the new system and executed. This program then downloaded the rest of the worm to the new system. The worm had some stealth characteristics to make it harder to determine what it was doing, and it suffered from one major miscalculation. The worm would not be loaded if a copy of it was already found on the new system, but it was designed to periodically ignore this check, reportedly to ensure that the worm could not be easily eliminated. The problem with this plan was that interconnected systems were constantly being reinfected. Eventually the systems were running so many copies of the worm that the system response time ground to a stop. It took a concerted effort by many individuals before the worm was eliminated. While the Morris worm carried no malicious payload, it is entirely possible for worms to do so.

Protection Against Worms   How you protect a system against worms depends on the type of worm. Those attached and propagated through e-mail can be avoided by following the same guidelines about not opening files and not running attachments unless you are absolutely sure of their origin and integrity. Protecting against the Morris type of Internet worm involves securing systems and networks against penetration in the same way you would protect your systems against human attackers. Install patches, eliminate unused and unnecessary services, enforce good password security, and utilize firewalls and intrusion detection systems.

War-Dialing and War-Driving

War-dialing is the term used to describe an attacker's attempt to discover unprotected modem connections to computer systems and networks. The term's origin is the 1983 movie *War Games*, in which the star has his machine systematically call a sequence of phone numbers in an attempt to find a computer connected to a modem. In the case of the movie, the intent was to find a machine with games the attacker could play, though obviously an attacker could have other purposes once access is obtained.

War-dialing is surprisingly successful, mostly because of rogue modems. These are unauthorized modems attached to computers on a network by authorized users. Generally the reason for attaching the modem is not malicious—the individual may simply want to be able to go home and then connect to the organization's network in order to continue working. The problem is that if a user can connect, so can an attacker. If the authorized user has not implemented any security protection, this means of access could be totally open. This is often the case. Most organizations have a strict policy against connecting unauthorized modems, but it is hard to enforce this kind of policy. Recently, new technology has been developed to address this common backdoor into corporate networks. Telephone firewalls have been created, which block any unauthorized modem connections into an organization. These devices make it impossible for an unauthorized modem connection to be established and can also enforce strict access policies on any authorized modems.

Another avenue of attack on computer systems and networks has seen a tremendous increase over the last few years because of the increase in the use of wireless networks. Wireless networks have some obvious advantages—they free employees from the cable connection to a port on their wall, allowing them to wander throughout the building with their machine and still be connected. An employee could, for example, leave their desk with their laptop and move to a conference room where they could then make a presentation, all without ever having to disconnect their machine from the wall or find a connection in the conference room.

The problem with wireless networks is that it is hard to limit access to them. Since there is no physical connection, the distance that a user can go and still remain connected is a function of the wireless network itself and where the various components of the network are placed. In order to ensure access throughout a facility, stations are often placed at numerous locations, some of which may actually provide access to areas outside of the organization in order to ensure that the farthest offices in the organization can be reached. Frequently access extends into adjacent offices or into the parking lot or street. Attackers can locate these access areas that fall outside of the organization and attempt to gain unauthorized access.

The term *war-driving* has been used to refer to the activity where attackers wander throughout an area (often in a car) with a computer with wireless capability, searching for wireless networks they can access. There are security measures that can limit an attacker's ability to succeed at this activity, but, just as in war-dialing, the individuals who set up the wireless networks don't always activate these security mechanisms.

Social Engineering

Social engineering relies on lies and misrepresentation, which an attacker uses to trick an authorized user into providing information or access the attacker would not normally be entitled to. The attacker might, for example, contact a system administrator pretending to be an authorized user in order to have a password reset. Another common ploy is to pose as a representative from a vendor needing temporary access in order to perform some emergency maintenance. Social engineering also applies to physical access. Simple techniques include impersonating pizza or flower delivery personnel in order to gain physical access to a facility.

Attackers know that, due to poor security practices, if they can gain physical access to an office, the chances are good that, given a little unsupervised time, a userid and password pair might be found on a notepad or sticky note. Unsupervised access may not even be required, depending on how poor the security practices of the organization are. One of the authors of this book was once considering opening an account at a bank near his home. As he sat down at the desk across from the bank employee taking his information, the author noticed one of the infamous little yellow notes attached to the computer monitor the employee was using. The note read "password for July is julyjuly." It probably isn't too hard to guess what August's password might be. Unfortunately, this is all too often the state of security practices in most organizations. With that in mind, it is easy to see how social engineering might work and might provide all the information needed to gain unauthorized access to a system or network.

Auditing

Auditing, in the financial community, is done to verify the accuracy and integrity of financial records. There have been many standards established in the financial community about how to correctly record and report a company's financial status. In the computer security world, auditing serves a similar function. It is a process of assessing the security state of an organization compared against an established standard.

The important element here is the standards. Organizations from different communities may have widely different standards, and any audit will need to consider the appropriate elements for the specific community. Audits differ from security or vulnerability assessments in that assessments measure the security posture of the organization but may do so without any mandated standards to compare them against. In a security assessment, generally agreed-upon security "best practices" may be used, but they may lack the regulatory teeth that standards often provide. Penetration tests may also be encountered—these are tests conducted against an organization to see if any holes in the organization's security can be found. The goal of the penetration test is just that, to penetrate the security rather than measuring it against some standard. Penetration tests are often viewed as *white-hat hacking* in that the methods used often mirror those that an attacker might use.

It is important to conduct some form of security audit or assessment on a regular basis. Your organization may spend quite a bit on security, and it is important to measure how effective the efforts have been. In certain communities, audits may be regulated on a periodic basis with very specific standards that must be measured against. Even if your organization is not part of such a community, periodic assessments are important.

There are many things that may be evaluated during an assessment, but at a minimum, the security perimeter (with all of its components, including host-based security) should be examined, as well as the organization's policies, procedures, and guidelines governing security. Employee training is another aspect that should be examined, since employees are the targets of social engineering and password-guessing attacks.

Security audits, assessments, and penetration tests are a big business, and there are a number of organizations that can perform them. The cost of these varies widely depending on the extent of the test you desire, the background of the company you are contracting with, and the size of the organization to be tested.

Chapter Review

In attempting to attack a computer system or network, an attacker follows several general steps. These include gathering as much information about the target as possible, obtaining information about potential vulnerabilities that might exist in the operating system or applications running on the target system, and finally using tools to attempt to exploit those vulnerabilities. An administrator can make this process more difficult for the attacker by limiting the amount of information that can be obtained about the organization, by limiting the services offered, and by installing all appropriate patches for the remaining services.

There are a number of different ways to attack computer systems and networks. These vary from the non-technical social engineering attacks, where attackers attempt to lie and misrepresent themselves to authorized users in order to obtain key information, to DDOS attacks, which can incorporate thousands of penetrated systems in an attack on a targeted system or network.

In addition to human attackers, there are various forms of malicious software that must be guarded against. Security auditing and assessments are methods used to measure an organization's current security posture. It is important to have an understanding of the various types of attacks your organization could be subject to in order to better plan how you will address them, should they occur.

Questions

To further help you prepare for the Security+ exam, and to provide you a feel for your level of preparedness, answer the following questions then check your answers against the list of correct answers found at the end of the chapter.

1. A SYN flood is an example of what type of attack?

   A. Malicious code

   B. Denial of service

   C. Man-in-the-middle

   D. Spoofing

2. An attack in which the attacker simply listens for all traffic being transmitted across a network, in the hope of viewing something such as a userid and password combination, is known as

   A. A man-in-the-middle attack

   B. A denial of service attack

   C. A sniffing attack

   D. A backdoor attack

3. Which attack takes advantage of a trusted relationship that exists between two systems?

   A. Spoofing

   B. Password guessing

   C. Sniffing

   D. Brute force

4. In what type of attack does an attacker resend the series of commands and codes used in a financial transaction in order to cause the transaction to be conducted multiple times?

   A. Spoofing

   B. Man-in-the-middle

   C. Replay

   D. Backdoor

5. The trick in both spoofing and TCP/IP hijacking is in trying to

   A. Provide the correct authentication token.

   B. Finding two systems between which a trusted relationship exists.

   C. Guessing a password or brute forcing a password to gain initial access to the system or network.

   D. Maintaining the correct sequence numbers for the response packets.

6. 128-bit encryption schemes are generally considered better than schemes that employ keys of 40 bits because

   A. The larger number of possible keys in a 128-bit scheme makes it harder to attack.

   B. 128-bit encryption encrypts more bits at one time, and thus is faster.

   C. Keys should be a power of two to facilitate quicker encryption.

   D. It would not be considered better. A 40-bit key would be better because it would have fewer possible weak keys.

7. The ability of an attacker to crack passwords is directly related to the method the user employed to create the password in the first place, as well as

   A. The length of the password.

   B. The size of the character set used in generating the password.

   C. The speed of the machine cracking the password.

   D. The dictionary and rules used by the cracking program.

8. A piece of malicious code that must attach itself to another file in order to replicate is known as

   A. A worm

   B. A virus

   C. A logic bomb

   D. A Trojan

9. A piece of malicious code that appears to be designed to do one thing (and may in fact do that thing) but that hides some other payload (often malicious) is known as

   A. A worm

   B. A virus

   C. A logic bomb

   D. A Trojan

10. An attack in which the attackers attempt to lie and misrepresent themselves in order to gain access to information that can be useful in an attack is known as

    A. Social science

    B. White-hat hacking

    C. Social engineering

    D. Social manipulation

11. The first step in an attack on a computer system consists of

    A. Gathering as much information about the target system as possible.

    B. Obtaining as much information about the organization in which the target lies as possible.

    C. Searching for possible exploits that can be used against known vulnerabilities.

    D. Searching for specific vulnerabilities that may exist in the target's operating system or software applications.

12. The best way to minimize possible avenues of attack for your system is to

    A. Install a firewall and check the logs daily.

    B. Monitor your intrusion detection system for possible attacks.

    C. Limit the information that can be obtained on your organization and the services that are run by your Internet-visible systems.

    D. Ensure that all patches have been applied for the services that are offered by your system.

13. A war-driving attack is an attempt to exploit what technology?

    A. Fiber-optic networks whose cables often run along roads and bridges.

    B. Cellular telephones.

    C. The public switched telephone network (PSTN).

    D. Wireless networks.

14. How can you protect against worms of the type that Robert Morris unleashed on the Internet?

    A. Follow the same procedures as you would to secure your system from a human attacker.

    B. Install antivirus software.

    C. Ensure that no executable attachments to e-mails are executed unless their integrity has been verified.

    D. Monitor for changes to utilities and other system software.

15. Malicious code that is set to execute its payload on a specific date or at a specific time is known as

    A. A logic bomb

    B. A Trojan horse

    C. A virus

    D. A time bomb

Answers

1. **B.** A SYN flood attack involves launching a large number of SYN packets at a system. In TCP, the response to this is a SYN/ACK, and the system then waits for an ACK to complete the three-way handshake. If no ACK is received, the system will wait until a time-out occurs, and then it will release the connection. If enough SYN packets are received (requesting that communication be set up) the system can fill up and not process any more requests. This is one type of denial of service attack.

2. **C.** Sniffing consists of simply listening to all traffic on a network. It takes advantage of the friendly nature of the network, in which systems are only supposed to grab and examine packets that are destined to them. Sniffing looks at all packets traveling across the network.

3. **A.** One form of spoofing attack attempts to take advantage of the trusted relationship that may exist between two systems. This trusted relationship could mean that users on one system will not be required to authenticate themselves when accessing the other system—the second system trusts the first to have performed any necessary authentication. If packets are formed that claim to have come from one of the trusted systems, the target can be fooled into performing actions as if an authorized user had sent them.

4. **C.** This is the description of a replay attack.

5. **D.** Getting the correct sequence number is the tricky part of any attempt to spoof or take over a session. This is made easy if the attacker can observe (sniff) the network traffic. If, however, the attacker is external to the network, the task is much more complicated.

6. **A.** All other considerations being equal, the larger the key size, the harder it will be to attack the scheme because of the greater number of possible keys that must be checked in a brute-force attack. A 2-bit key would only yield 4 possible keys and would not take very long to guess. A 4-bit key, on the other hand, would have 16 possible keys and would thus take longer to guess.

7. **D.** This actually was a tricky question. All of the answers have a bearing on the ability of the attacker to crack the password, but, as discussed in the text, the dictionary and rule-set used will make or break the attempt (unless you *want* to try a brute-force attack, which is generally your last option). The size of the password will certainly have a bearing, but the difference between brute forcing a 13-character password and a 14-character password is not important—neither of them will be accomplished in the lifetime of the cracker. The same can be said of the size of the character set used to generate the password. The more characters that are available, the larger the number of passwords that must be tried in order to brute force it—but we want to try and stay away from using brute-force attacks. The speed of the machine will have some bearing, but speed will make little difference if we have to use a brute-force attack, since we still won't crack it in time to take advantage of it. If the attacker can pick a good dictionary and rule-set, there is a good chance that a password can be cracked (remember that users have this nasty tendency to select poor passwords).

8. **B.** This is how we defined a virus. This is the distinguishing aspect of a virus that separates it from other forms of malicious code, especially worms.

9. **D.** This is how we described a Trojan (or Trojan horse). A virus that is attached to another file and that appears to be that file, may also hide a malicious payload, but the description provided is the traditional description used to describe a Trojan.

10. **C.** This is a description of social engineering. The term *white-hat hacking* is often used to refer to authorized penetration tests on a network.

11. **B.** The first step is generally acknowledged to be to gather as much information about the organization as possible. This provides information that can be used in social engineering attacks that can result in even more information, or even access to the system. If access can be obtained without having to run any exploits, the chance of discovery is minimized. The second step is to gather information about the specific systems and networks—details on the actual hardware and software that is being used. It is not until both of these steps have been accomplished that possible vulnerabilities and tools to exploit them can be searched for. This sequence may differ if the attacker is not

targeting a specific system, but is instead looking for systems that are vulnerable to a specific exploit. In this case, the attacker would probably be searching for a vulnerability first, and then for a tool that exploits it, and may never even consider the organization that is being targeted.

12. **C.** In order to minimize the avenues of attack, you need to limit the information that can be obtained and the number of services you offer. The more services that are available, the greater the number of possible avenues that can be exploited. It is important to install patches, but this doesn't minimize the avenues; it protects specific avenues from attack. The use of firewalls and intrusion detection systems is important, but monitoring them doesn't aid in minimizing the avenues of attack (though a properly administered firewall can help to limit the exposure of your network).

13. **D.** War-driving is an attempt to locate wireless networks whose access area extends into publicly accessible space.

14. **A.** The Morris worm used the same type of techniques to penetrate the systems that human attackers use. Therefore, if you protect the system against one, you are protecting it against the other. Installing an antivirus package and not allowing executable attachments to e-mail to be executed are good ideas, but they address the other type of worm, not the Morris type of Internet worm. Monitoring the system for changes to utilities and other system software is also a good idea, but it is reactive in nature and discovering these changes means the individual or worm has already penetrated your system. Your goal should be to try to prevent this in the first place.

15. **D.** This is the definition of a time bomb. The more general term of *logic bomb* is sometimes used, but this term generally refers to a piece of software that is set to execute when some specified event occurs. When that event is a date or time, we often refer to the malicious code as a time bomb.

PART III

Security in Transmissions

Remote Access

In this chapter, you will

- Learn about the methods and protocols for remote access to networks
- Discover authentication, authorization, and accounting (AAA) protocols
- Be introduced to wireless protocols and the security implications in their use
- Cover virtual private networks (VPNs) and their security aspects
- Explore Internet Protocol Security (IPsec) and its use in securing communications

Remote access enables users outside a network to have network access and privileges as if they were inside the network. Being *outside* a network means that the user is using a machine that is not physically connected to the network in question and must therefore establish a connection through a remote means, such as dialing in, connecting via the Internet, or connecting through a wireless connection. A user accessing resources from the Internet through their ISP is also connecting remotely to the resources via the Internet.

To achieve these network connections, a variety of methods are used, varying depending upon network type, the hardware and software employed, and any security requirements. Microsoft Windows has a specific server component, the Remote Access Service, which is designed to facilitate the management of remote access connections through dial-up modems. Cisco has implemented a variety of remote access methods through its networking hardware and software. UNIX systems have built-in methods, as well.

The Remote Access Process

The process of connecting by remote access involves two elements: a temporary network connection and a series of protocols to negotiate privileges and commands. The temporary network connection can be via a dial-up service, the Internet, wireless access, or any other method of connecting to a network. Once the connection is made, the primary issue is identifying the user and establishing proper privileges for that user. This is done using a combination of protocols and the operating system on the host machine.

The three steps in the establishment of proper privileges are authentication, authorization, and accounting (AAA). *Authentication* is the matching of user-supplied credentials to previously stored credentials on a host machine, and it is usually done with an account name and password. Once the user is authenticated, the authorization step takes place. *Authorization* is the granting of specific permissions based on the privileges held by the account. Does the user have permission to use the network at this time, or is their use restricted? Does the user have access to specific applications, such as mail and FTP, or are some of these restricted? These checks are carried out as part of authorization, and in many cases, this is a function of the operating system in conjunction with its established security policies. A last function, *accounting*, is the collection of billing and other detail records. Network access is often a billable function, and a log of how much time, bandwidth, file transfer space, or other resources were used needs to be maintained. Other accounting functions include keeping detailed security logs to maintain an audit trail of tasks being performed. All of these standard functions are part of normal and necessary overhead in maintaining a computer system, and the protocols used in remote access provide the necessary input for these functions.

The primary role of the protocols is one of network connectivity, of which security plays an integral role. When defining security, the terms *confidentiality*, *integrity*, and *availability* are commonly used. All of these have a role in remote access, but availability is used specifically to mean authorized access. Confidentiality, integrity, and availability are major pieces of the foundation of security and they are well supported by properly implemented remote access protocols.

By using encryption, remote access protocols can establish a secure network connection, through which the operating system on the host machine can authenticate and authorize a user according to previously established privilege levels. The authorization phase can keep unauthorized users out, but after that, the encryption of the communications channel becomes very important in preventing others from breaking in on an authorized session and hijacking the authorized user's credentials. As more and more networks rely on the Internet for connecting remote users, the need for and importance of remote access protocols and security will continue to grow. When a user dials in to the Internet through their ISP, this is similarly a case of remote access—the user is establishing a connection to their ISP's network, and the same security issues apply. The issue of *authentication*, the matching of user-supplied credentials to previously stored credentials on a host machine, is usually done with an account name and password. Once the user is authenticated, then the authorization step takes place.

There are many different remote access protocols in use today, and more will be put into service in the future. Some are designed around specific methods of connection; others have specific functionality designed into them for special purposes. Some are private, some are based on common security mechanisms, and some have proprietary algorithms. This is important from a conceptual point of view, but in terms of functionality, these protocols are designed to do many of the same functions.

Identification

Identification is the process of ascribing a computer ID to a specific user, computer, or network device. User identification enables authentication and authorization, and these form the basis for accountability. This enables you to trace activities to individual users or computer processes so that they can be held responsible for their actions. Identification usually takes the form of logon ID or userid. A required characteristic of such IDs is that they must be unique. For accountability purposes they should not be shared, and for security purposes they should not be descriptive of job function.

Authentication

Authentication is the process of binding a specific ID to a specific computer connection. Historically, there have been three categories of things used to identify a user. Originally published by the U.S. Government in one of the Rainbow series of manuals on computer security, they are:

- What users know (such as a password)
- What users have (such as tokens)
- What users are (this can involve static biometrics such as fingerprints)

Today, because of technological advances, a new category has emerged, patterned after subconscious behavior:

- What users do (this can involve dynamic biometrics such as a voice print)

These methods can be used individually or in combination. The most common method is using a userid and password. For greater security, you can add an element from a separate group, such as a smart card token, something a user has in their possession. A common example is a bankcard and PIN. Although a 4-digit PIN (something you know) does not offer much security, when coupled with possession of the correct bankcard (something you have), together they form a reasonable level of security.

Authorization

Authorization is the process of permitting or denying access to a specific resource. Once identity is confirmed via authentication, specific actions can be authorized or denied. Many types of authorization schemes are used, but the purpose is the same: determine whether a given user who has been identified has permissions for a particular object or resource being requested. This functionality is frequently part of the operating system and is transparent to users.

The separation of tasks, from identification to authentication to authorization, has several advantages. There are many methods to perform each task, and on many systems several methods are concurrently present for each task. Separation of these tasks into individual elements allows combinations of implementations to all work together.

Authentication is a process of verifying properly presented credentials; the source of the credentials is not a relevant item. You can authenticate users and computer processes

(ID carried by script); the concept of authentication and implementation is identical. Different forms of authorization can be implemented, based on the resource being requested, such as database access or router admin access.

Any system or resource, be it hardware (router, workstation) or a software component (database system) that requires authorization can use its own authorization method once authentication for a connection has been resolved for it. This makes for efficient and consistent application of these principles.

Telnet

Telnet is the standard terminal-emulation protocol within the TCP/IP protocol series, and it is defined in RFC 854. Telnet allows users to log in remotely and access resources as if the user had a local terminal connection. Telnet is an old protocol and has little security. Information is passed in the clear over the TCP/IP connection, including account names and passwords.

Telnet makes its connection using TCP port 23. (A list of remote access networking port assignments is provided in Table 3-2 in the Chapter Review section.) As Telnet is implemented on most products using TCP/IP, it is important to control access to Telnet on machines and routers when setting them up. Failure to control access by using firewalls, access lists, and other security methods, or even by disabling the telnet daemon, is equivalent to leaving an open door for unauthorized users on a system.

SSH

Secure Shell (SSH) is a protocol series designed to facilitate secure network functions across an insecure network. SSH provides direct support for secure remote login, secure file transfer, and secure forwarding of TCP/IP and X Window System traffic.

SSH has its origins all the way back in the beginning of the UNIX operating system. An original component of UNIX was telnet, which allowed users to connect between systems. Telnet, although still in existence and in use today, had some drawbacks, such as passing information in the clear across the network, making it easy for anyone to obtain sensitive information, such as userids and passwords by sniffing. Some enterprising Berkeley students subsequently developed the **r-** commands, such as **rlogin**, to permit access based on the user and source system, as opposed to passing passwords. This was not perfect either, however, for when a login was required, it was still passed in the clear. This led to the development of Secure Shell (SSH), a protocol series designed to eliminate all of the insecurities associated with telnet, **r-** commands, and other means of remote access.

SSH opens a secure transport between machines by using an SSH daemon on each end. These daemons initiate contact over TCP port 22 and then communicate over higher ports in a secure mode. One of the strengths of SSH is its support for many different encryption protocols. SSH 1.0 started with RSA algorithms, but at the time they were still under patent, and this led to SSH 2.0 with extended support for 3DES and other encryption methods. Today, SSH can be used with a wide range of encryption protocols, including RSA, 3DES, Blowfish, IDEA, CAST128, AES256, and others.

The SSH protocol has facilities to automatically encrypt data, provide authentication, and compress data in transit. It can support strong encryption, cryptographic host authentication, and integrity protection. The authentication services are host-based and not user-based. If user authentication is desired in a system, it must be done separately at a higher level in the OSI model. The protocol is designed to be flexible and simple and it is specifically designed to minimize the number of round trips between systems. The key exchange, public key, symmetric key, message authentication, and hash algorithms are all negotiated at connection time. Individual data-packet integrity is assured through the use of a message authentication code that is computed from a shared secret, the contents of the packet, and the packet sequence number.

The SSH protocol consists of three major components:

- **Transport layer protocol**   Provides server authentication, confidentiality, integrity, and compression.
- **User authentication protocol**   Authenticates the client to the server.
- **Connection protocol**   Provides multiplexing of the encrypted tunnel into several logical channels.

SSH is very popular in the UNIX environment, and it is actively used as a method of establishing virtual private networks (VPNs) across public networks. As all communications between the two machines are encrypted at the OSI application layer by the two SSH daemons, this leads to the ability to build very secure solutions, and even solutions that defy the ability of outside services to monitor. As SSH is a standard protocol series with connection parameters established via TCP port 22, different vendors can build differing solutions that still can interoperate. As such, if SSH is enabled on a UNIX platform, it is a built-in method of establishing secure communications with that system.

Although Windows server implementations of SSH exist, this has not been a popular protocol in the Windows environment from a server perspective. The development of a wide array of commercial SSH clients for the Windows platform indicates the marketplace strength of interconnection from desktop PCs to UNIX-based servers utilizing this protocol.

L2TP and PPTP

Layer Two Tunneling Protocol (L2TP) and Point-to-Point Tunneling Protocol (PPTP) are both OSI layer two tunneling protocols, and PPTP is probably the most common implementation of tunneling today. Tunneling is the encapsulation of one packet within another, which allows you to hide the original packet from view, or to change the nature of the network transport. This can be done for both security and practical reasons.

From a practical perspective, assume that you are using the TCP/IP protocol to communicate between two machines. Your message may pass over an Asynchronous Transfer Mode (ATM) network as it moves from source to destination. As the ATM protocol can neither read nor understand TCP/IP packets, something must be done to make them passable. By taking a packet and encapsulating it as the payload in a separate protocol, so it can be carried across a section of a network, a tunnel is created. At each end of the tunnel, called the tunnel endpoints, the payload packet is read and understood. As it goes into the tunnel, you can envision your packet being placed in an envelope with the address of the appropriate tunnel endpoint on the envelope. When the envelope arrives at the tunnel endpoint, the original message (the tunnel packet's payload) is re-created, read, and sent to its appropriate next stop. The material being tunneled is only read and understood at the tunnel endpoints; it is not relevant to intermediate tunnel points because it is only a payload.

If you encrypt the original packet, intermediate points in the tunneled journey cannot read the original packet, thus ensuring message security. Additional use of cryptological tools can provide authenticity information and other protections; this will be described in the "IPsec" section of this chapter.

Point-to-Point Protocol (PPP) is a widely used protocol for establishing dial-in connections over serial lines or ISDN services. PPP has several authentication mechanisms, including Password Authentication Protocol (PAP), Challenge Handshake Authentication Protocol (CHAP), and the Extensible Authentication Protocol (EAP). These protocols are used to authenticate the peer device, not a user of the system. PPP is a standardized Internet encapsulation of IP traffic over point-to-point links, such as serial lines. The authentication process is performed only when the link is established.

PPTP

Microsoft led a consortium of networking companies to extend the PPP protocol to enable the creation of virtual private networks (VPNs). The result was the PPTP protocol. PPTP is a network protocol that enables the secure transfer of data from a remote PC to a server by creating a VPN across a TCP/IP network. This remote network connection can also span a public switched telephone network (PSTN) and is thus an economical way of connecting remote dial-in users to a corporate data network. The incorporation of the PPTP protocol into the Microsoft Windows product line provides a built-in secure method of remote connection using the operating system, and this has given PPTP a large marketplace footprint.

For most PPTP implementations, there are three computers involved: the PPTP client, the network access server (NAS), and a PPTP server, as shown in Figure 3-1. The connection between the remote client and the network is established in stages, as illustrated in Figure 3-2. First the client makes a PPP connection to a NAS, typically an ISP.

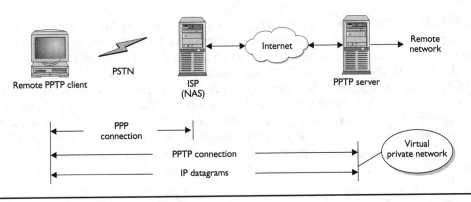

Figure 3-1   PPTP communication diagram

Once the PPP connection is established, a second connection is made over the PPP connection to the PPTP server. This second connection creates the VPN connection between the remote client and the PPTP server. This connection acts as a tunnel for future data transfers.

As mentioned earlier in this chapter, tunneling is the process of sending packets as data within other packets across a section of a network. This encapsulation enables a network to carry a packet type that it cannot ordinarily route, and it also provides the opportunity to secure the contents of the first packet through encryption. PPTP establishes

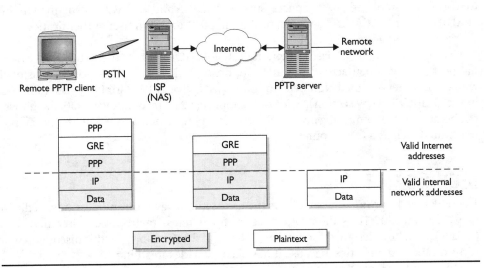

Figure 3-2   PPTP message encapsulation during transmission

a tunnel from the remote PPTP client to the PPTP server and enables encryption within this tunnel. This provides a secure method of transport. To do this and still enable routing, an intermediate addressing scheme, Generic Routing Encapsulation (GRE), is used.

To establish the connection, PPTP uses communications across TCP port 1723 (see Table 3-2 in the Chapter Review section), so this port must remain open across the network firewalls for PPTP to be initiated. Although PPTP allows the use of any PPP authentication scheme, CHAP is used when encryption is specified to provide an appropriate level of security. For the encryption methodology, Microsoft chose the RSA RC4 cipher, either with a 40-bit or 128-bit session key length, and this is operating-system driven.

L2TP uses, 1701 port

L2TP is also an Internet standard and came from the Layer Two Forwarding (L2F) protocol, a Cisco initiative designed to address issues with PPTP. Whereas PPTP is designed around PPP and IP networks, L2F, and hence L2TP, is designed for use across all kinds of networks including ATM and frame relay. Additionally, where PPTP is designed to be implemented in software at the client device, L2TP was conceived as a hardware implementation using a router or a special purpose appliance.

L2TP works in much the same way as PPTP, but it opens several items up for expansion. For instance, in L2TP, routers can be enabled to concentrate VPN traffic over higher bandwidth lines, creating hierarchical networks of VPN traffic that can be more efficiently managed across an enterprise. L2TP also has the ability to use IPsec and DES as encryption protocols, providing a higher level of data security. L2TP is also designed to work with established AAA services, such as RADIUS and TACACS+ (explained in the "RADIUS" and "TACACS+" sections of this chapter) to aid in user authentication, authorization, and accounting.

L2TP is established via User Datagram Protocol (UDP) port 1701, so this is an essential port to leave open across firewalls supporting L2TP traffic. This port is registered with the Internet Assigned Numbers Authority (IANA), as is 1723 for PPTP (see Table 3-2 in the Chapter Review section). Microsoft supports L2TP in Windows 2000 and above, but because of the computing power required, most implementations will use specialized hardware (such as a Cisco router).

IEEE 802.11

The IEEE 802.11 protocol series covers the use of microwave communications media in networks, and 802.16 is the protocol series for wireless metropolitan area networks (MANs). 802.11 is designed for wireless LANs, and the remainder of this discussion will focus on the 802.11 series, because it has become widespread in use.

This is not a single protocol, but an entire series of them, with 802.11b, 802.11a, and 802.11g being common wireless protocols that allow wireless connectivity to a

LAN and ad hoc peer-to-peer wireless networking. Products for these protocols have become very common, and they are available from a variety of vendors, often for under $100. These devices are beginning to find their use in corporate networks, metropolitan hot spots, and even home networks. The advantage of wireless communication is simple to understand—the requirement for a physical wire and various boxes is eliminated. This provides tremendous ease of setup for a network engineer from a cabling point of view, because there are no cables to connect. This pays off again if a corporation moves employees between desks, because again there are no wires to move when moving PCs. For laptop users, this means machines and devices can be mobile and remain connected to the network.

The lack of a physical cable does not change security requirements—the wireless solution has to face a tougher standard. Offering wireless connectivity is equivalent to giving an outsider a network drop, and it must be assumed that an intruder is connected at all times.

The actual communication method for 802.11 devices is via either direct-sequence spread spectrum (DSSS) or frequency-hopping spread spectrum (FHSS). These methods employ a range of frequencies to mitigate noise and propagation problems. These methods also prevent casual eavesdropping, as the frequency on which the data moves is always moving in time. This only affects casual eavesdropping, though, because a wireless access device is specifically designed to locate and track a signal from an access point. Frequency hopping has very little effect, from a security point of view.

For security purposes, the 802.11 standards contain an optional protocol called Wired Equivalent Privacy (WEP). This is an encryption method that is optional, so not all vendors support this option, nor do all network administrators enable this option. The default WEP method is a 40-bit form of the RC4 stream-cipher encryption algorithm, although many vendors offer a 128-bit version, as well. The WEP method uses a static shared secret key between devices, with a variable initialization vector.

The particular implementation of the initialization vector in WEP has been shown to have a fault that can allow an outsider to break the key in a 40-bit system after a few hours of studying traffic on a Pentium 4 class machine. The problem lies not with the RC4 algorithm, but with the initialization vector, which is repeated after a certain amount of time, and the way RC4 is used within WEP. Someone watching the pattern can find the repeated sequences and then break the shared secret key. This is one of the factors leading to the adoption of a new WEP method that does not cycle keys in the same manner as the current version. The weak initialization vector problem is not significantly improved upon by using a longer key. Even with a 128-bit key, the initialization vector stays the same length, and initialization vector collisions will therefore occur in the same relatively short period of time.

The current WEP method requires all clients that use the same access point to use the same key for session initiation. This introduces a key management issue and also adds concerns about eavesdropping between clients on the same access point. For this reason, many installations of wireless LANs also use other security protocols, such as layer three

Table 3-1	Protocol	Frequency	Maximum Network Speed
Comparison of 802.11 Protocol Parameters	802.11a	5 GHz	54 Mbps
	802.11b	2.4 GHz	11 Mbps
	802.11g	2.4 GHz	54 Mbps

tunneling, as in VPNs. Also, newer wireless access points have functionality built in to use access control lists against MAC addresses to filter LAN connections, but this adds significant management overhead in larger installations.

From a hardware point of view, a wireless network consists of two pieces: a wireless access point connected to a network, and a wireless network interface card on a client machine. The access point can be shared among multiple users, and users can move between access points. Each wireless access point has a usable range of up to about 200 feet, depending upon the antenna configuration, the building's configuration and interference sources. Transmission speed is dependent upon the range, with distant users running at slower speeds. The actual connection speed depends upon the protocol and signal strength, with Table 3-1 giving the standard values.

VPN

Virtual private networks (VPNs) are secure "virtual" networks built on top of physical networks. Their security lies in the encryption of packet contents between the endpoints that define the VPN network. The physical network upon which a VPN is built is typically a public network, such as the Internet. Because the packet contents between VPN endpoints are encrypted, to an outside observer on the public network, the communication is secure, and depending on how the VPN is set up, security may even extend to the two communicating parties machines.

Virtual private networking is not a protocol per se, but rather a method of using protocols to achieve a specific objective, secure communications, as shown in Figure 3-3. A user wishing to have a secure communication channel with a server across a public

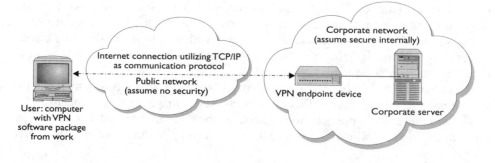

Figure 3-3   VPN service over an Internet connection

network can set up two intermediary devices, VPN endpoints, to accomplish this task. The user can communicate with his endpoint, and the server can communicate with its endpoint. The two endpoints then communicate across the public network. VPN endpoints can be software solutions, routers, or specific servers set up for specific functionality. This implies that VPN services are set up in advance and are not something negotiated on the fly.

A typical use of VPN services is a user accessing a corporate data network from a home PC across the Internet. The employee will install VPN software from work on their home PC. This software is already configured to communicate with the corporate network's VPN endpoint; it knows the location, the protocols that will be used, and so on. When the home user wishes to connect to the corporate network, they connect to the Internet and then start the VPN software. The user can then log in to the corporate network by using an appropriate authentication and authorization methodology. The sole purpose of the VPN connection is to provide a private connection between the machines. Identification, authorization, and all other standard functions are done with the standard mechanisms for the established system.

VPNs can use many different protocols to offer a secure method of communicating between endpoints. Common methods of encryption on VPNs include PPTP, IPsec, SSH, and L2TP, all of which are discussed in this chapter. The key is that both endpoints know the protocol and share a secret. All of this necessary information is established when the VPN is set up. At the time of use, the VPN only acts as a private tunnel between the two points, and does not constitute a complete security solution.

IPsec

IPsec, short for IP Security, is a set of protocols developed by the Internet Engineering Task Force (IETF) to securely exchange packets at the network layer of the OSI model (RFC 2401–2412). Although these protocols only work in conjunction with IP networks, once an IPsec connection is established, it is possible to tunnel across other networks at lower levels of the OSI model. The set of security services provided by IPsec occurs at the network layer of the OSI model, so higher layer protocols, such as TCP, UDP, ICMP, BGP, and the like, are unaffected by the implementation of IPsec services.

The IPsec protocol series has a sweeping array of services it is designed to provide, including, but not limited to, access control, connectionless integrity, traffic-flow confidentiality, rejection of replayed packets, data security (encryption), and data-origin authentication. IPsec has two defined methods—transport and tunneling—and these two methods provide different levels of security. IPsec also has three modes of connection: host to server, server to server, and host to host.

The transport method encrypts only the data portion of a packet, thus enabling an outsider to see source and destination IP addresses. This protects the data being transmitted, but allows knowledge of the transmission itself. Protection of the data portion of a packet is referred to as *content protection*.

Tunneling provides encryption of source and destination IP addresses, as well as of the data itself. This provides the greatest security, but it can only be done between IPsec servers (or routers) because the final destination needs to be known for delivery. Protection of the header information is known as *context protection*.

It is possible to use both methods at the same time, such as using transport within one's own network to reach an IPsec server, which then tunnels to the target server's network, connecting to an IPsec server there, and then using the transport method from the target network's IPsec server to the target host.

IPsec Configurations

There are four basic configurations for machine-to-machine connections using IPsec. The simplest is a host-to-host connection between two machines, as shown in Figure 3-4. In this case, the Internet is not a part of the security association between the machines. A security association is a formal manner of describing the necessary and sufficient portions of the IPsec protocol series to achieve a specific level of protection. As many options exist, both communicating parties must agree on the use of the protocols that are available, and this agreement is referred to as a security association.

The next level of implementation places two security devices in the stream, relieving the hosts of the calculation and encapsulation duties. These two gateways have a security association between them, but the network is assumed to be secure from each machine to its gateway, and no IPsec is performed in this hop. Figure 3-5 shows the two gateways with a tunnel across the Internet, although either tunnel or transport mode may be actually used.

A third case combines the first two. A separate security association exists between the gateway devices, but additionally, a security association exists between hosts. This could be considered a tunnel inside a tunnel, as shown in Figure 3-6.

A common situation is where a remote user connects through the Internet to an organization's network. The network has a security gateway through which it secures traffic to and from its servers and authorized users. In this case, illustrated in Figure 3-7, the user establishes a security association with the security gateway and then a separate association with the desired server, if required. This can be done using software on a remote laptop and hardware at the organization's network.

Windows has the ability to act as an IPsec server, as do routers and other servers. The primary issue is CPU usage, and where the computing power should be implanted. This consideration has led to the rise of IPsec appliances, hardware devices that perform the IPsec function specifically for a series of communications. Depending on the number of connections, network bandwidth, and so on, these devices can run as little as $150 (for small office or home office use) or as much as tens of thousands of dollars for large implementations.

IPsec Security

IPsec uses two protocols to provide traffic security:

- Authentication Header (AH)
- Encapsulating Security Payload (ESP)

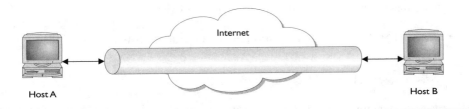

Figure 3-4   Host-to-host IPsec connection

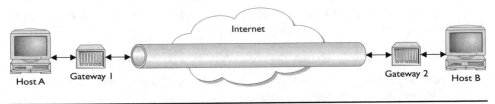

Figure 3-5   IPsec between machines using gateway security devices

Figure 3-6   Separate IPsec tunnels—gateway to gateway and host to host

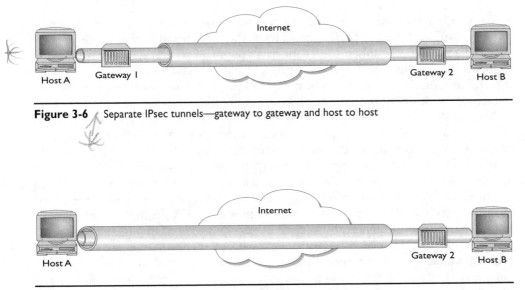

Figure 3-7   Remote connection across the Internet using IPsec

For key management and exchange, three protocols exist:

- Internet Security Association and Key Management Protocol (ISAKMP)
- Oakley
- Secure Key Exchange Mechanism for Internet (SKEMI)

These key management protocols can be collectively referred to as Internet Key Management Protocol (IKMP) or Internet Key Exchange (IKE).

IPsec does not define specific security algorithms, nor does it require specific methods of implementation. IPsec is an open framework that allows vendors to implement existing industry-standard algorithms suited for specific tasks. This flexibility is key in IPsec's ability to offer a wide range of security functions. IPsec allows several security technologies to be combined into a comprehensive solution for network-based confidentiality, integrity, and authentication. IPsec uses

- Diffie-Hellman key exchange between peers on a public network
- Public key signing of Diffie-Hellman key exchanges to guarantee identity and avoid man-in-the-middle attacks
- Bulk encryption algorithms, such as IDEA and 3DES, for encrypting data
- Keyed hash algorithms, such as HMAC, and traditional hash algorithms, such as MD5 and SHA-1, for packet-level authentication
- Digital certificates to act as digital ID cards between parties

To provide traffic security, two header extensions have been defined for IP datagrams. The Authentication Header (AH), when added to an IP datagram, ensures the integrity of the data and also the authenticity of the data's origin. By protecting the non-changing elements in the IP header, the AH protects the IP address, which enables data-origin authentication. The Encapsulating Security Payload (ESP) provides security services for the higher-level protocol portion of the packet only, not the IP header.

AH and ESP can be used separately or in combination, depending on the level and types of security desired. Both also work with the transport and tunnel modes of IPsec protocols. In transport mode, the two communication endpoints are providing security primarily for the upper layer protocols. The cryptographic endpoints, where encryption and decryption occurs, are located at the source and destination of the communication channel. For AH in transport mode, the original IP header is exposed, but its contents are protected via the AH block in the packet, as illustrated in Figure 3-8. For ESP in transport mode, the data contents are protected by encryption, as illustrated in Figure 3-9.

Tunneling, as described previously, is a means of encapsulating packets inside a protocol that is understood only at the entry and exit points of the tunnel. This provides security during transport in the tunnel, because outside observers cannot decipher packet contents, or even the identity of the communicating parties. IPsec has a tunnel mode that can be used from server to server across a public network. Although

Figure 3-8

IPsec use of AH in transport mode

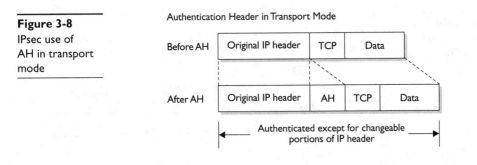

Authentication Header in Transport Mode

Before AH | Original IP header | TCP | Data

After AH | Original IP header | AH | TCP | Data

Authenticated except for changeable portions of IP header

the tunnel endpoints are referred to as servers, these devices can be routers, appliances, or servers. In tunnel mode, the tunnel endpoints merely encapsulate the entire packet with new IP headers to indicate the endpoints, and they encrypt the contents of this new packet. The true source and destination information is contained in the inner IP header, which is encrypted in the tunnel. The outer IP header contains the addresses of the endpoints of the tunnel.

As described earlier, AH and ESP can be employed in tunnel mode. When AH is employed in tunnel mode, portions of the outer IP header are given the same header protection that occurs in transport mode, with the entire inner packet receiving protection. This is illustrated in Figure 3-10. ESP affords the same encryption protection to the contents of the tunneled packet, which is the entire packet from the initial sender, as illustrated in Figure 3-11. Together, in tunnel mode, AH and ESP can provide complete protection across the packet, as shown in Figure 3-12. The specific combination of AH and ESP is referred to as a security association in IPsec.

In IP version 4 (IPv4), IPsec is an add-on, and its acceptance is vendor driven. It is not a part of the original IP protocol—one of the short-sighted design flaws of the original IP protocol. In the next version of the IP protocol suite, IPv6, IPsec is integrated into the IP protocol and is native on all packets. Its use is still optional, but its inclusion in the protocol suite will guarantee interoperability across vendor solutions when they are compliant with IPv6 standards. This is one of the major reasons firms will move to IPv6; the increased security will become a driving force behind the adoption of the new protocol series.

Figure 3-9

IPsec use of ESP in transport mode

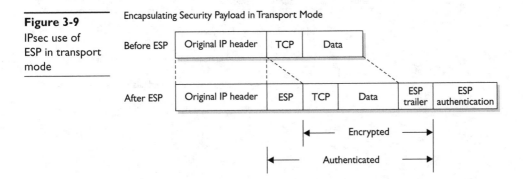

Encapsulating Security Payload in Transport Mode

Before ESP | Original IP header | TCP | Data

After ESP | Original IP header | ESP | TCP | Data | ESP trailer | ESP authentication

Encrypted

Authenticated

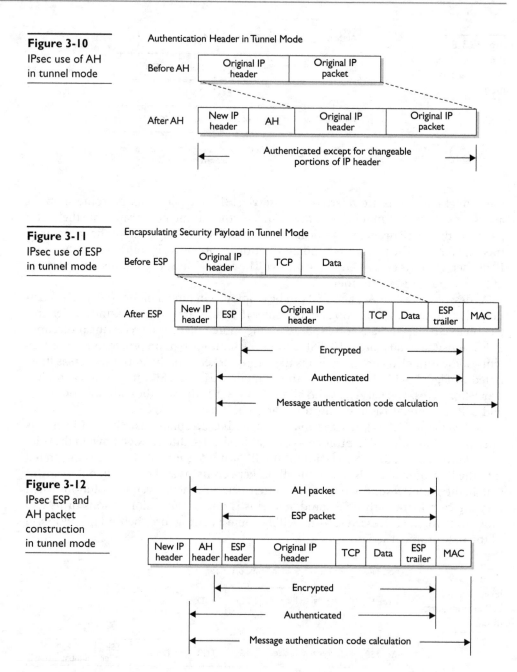

Figure 3-10
IPsec use of AH
in tunnel mode

Authentication Header in Tunnel Mode

Figure 3-11
IPsec use of ESP
in tunnel mode

Encapsulating Security Payload in Tunnel Mode

Figure 3-12
IPsec ESP and
AH packet
construction
in tunnel mode

IPsec uses cryptographic keys in its security process and has both manual and automatic distribution of keys as part of the protocol series. Manual key distribution is included, but is only practical in small static environments and does not scale to enterprise-level implementations. The default method of key management is automated and is typically referred to as IKE (Internet Key Exchange). IKE authenticates each peer involved in IPsec and negotiates the security policy, including the exchange of session keys. IKE creates a secure tunnel between peers and then negotiates the security association for IPsec across this channel. This is done in two phases: the first develops the channel, and the second the security association.

IEEE 802.1x

The IEEE 802.1x standard is for a protocol to support communications between a user and an authorization device, such as an edge router. This protocol describes methods to authenticate a user prior to granting access to an authentication server, such as a RADIUS server. 802.1x acts through an intermediate device, such as an edge switch, enabling ports to carry normal traffic if the connection is properly authenticated. This prevents unauthorized clients from accessing the publicly available ports on a switch, keeping unauthorized users out of a LAN. Until a client has successfully authenticated itself to the device, only Extensible Authentication Protocol over LAN (EAPOL) traffic is passed by the switch.

EAPOL is an encapsulated method of passing EAP messages over 802 frames. EAP is a general protocol that can support multiple methods of authentication, including one-time passwords, Kerberos, public keys, and security device methods such as smart cards. Once a client successfully authenticates itself to the 802.1x device, the switch opens ports for normal traffic. At this point, the client can communicate with the system's AAA method, such as a RADIUS server, and authenticate itself to the network.

RADIUS

Remote Authentication Dial-In User Service (RADIUS) is a protocol that was developed originally by Livingston Enterprises (acquired by Lucent) as an AAA protocol. It was submitted to the IETF as a series of RFCs: RFC 2058 (RADIUS specification), RFC 2059 (RADIUS accounting standard), and updated RFCs 2865–2869 are now standard protocols. The IETF AAA Working Group has proposed extensions to RADIUS (RFC 2882) and a replacement protocol DIAMETER (Internet Draft DIAMETER Base Protocol).

RADIUS is designed as a connectionless protocol utilizing UDP as its transport level protocol. Connection type issues, such as timeouts, are handled by the RADIUS application instead of the transport layer. RADIUS utilizes UDP ports 1812 for authentication and authorization and 1813 for accounting functions (see Table 3-2 in the Chapter Review section).

RADIUS is a client/server protocol. The RADIUS client is typically a NAS, and the RADIUS server is a process or daemon running on a UNIX or Windows NT machine. This is important to note, for if the user's machine (the PC) is not the RADIUS client (the NAS), then communications between the PC and the NAS are typically not encrypted and are passed in the clear. Communications between a RADIUS client and RADIUS server are encrypted using a shared secret that is manually configured into each entity and not shared over a connection. Hence, communications between a RADIUS client (typically a NAS) and a RADIUS server are secure, but the communications between a user (typically a PC) and the RADIUS client are subject to compromise.

RADIUS Authentication

The RADIUS protocol is designed to allow a RADIUS server to support a wide variety of methods to authenticate a user. When the server is given a username and password, it can support PPP, PAP, CHAP, UNIX login, and other mechanisms, depending on what was established when the server was set up. A user login authentication consists of a query (Access-Request) from the RADIUS client and a corresponding response (Access-Accept or Access-Reject) from the RADIUS server, as you will see in Figure 3-13.

The Access-Request message contains the username, encrypted password, NAS IP address, and port. The message also contains information concerning the type of session the user wishes to initiate. Once the RADIUS server receives this information, it searches its database for a match on the username. If a match is not found, either a default profile is loaded or an Access-Reject reply is sent. If the entry is found, or the default profile is used, the next phase involves authorization, for in RADIUS, these steps are performed in sequence.

RADIUS Authorization

In the RADIUS protocol, the authentication and authorization steps are performed together in response to a single Access-Request message, although they are sequential steps (see Figure 3-13). Once an identity has been established, either known or default, the authorization process determines what parameters are returned to the client. Typical authorization parameters include the service type allowed (shell or framed), the protocols allowed, the IP address to assign to the user (static or dynamic), the access list to apply or static route to place in the NAS routing table. These parameters are all defined in the configuration information on the RADIUS client and server during setup. Using this information, the RADIUS server returns an Access-Accept message with these parameters to the RADIUS client.

RADIUS Accounting

The RADIUS accounting function is performed independently of RADIUS authentication and authorization. The accounting function uses a separate UDP port, 1813 (see Table 3-2 in the Chapter Review section). The primary functionality of RADIUS accounting was established to support Internet service providers in their user accounting,

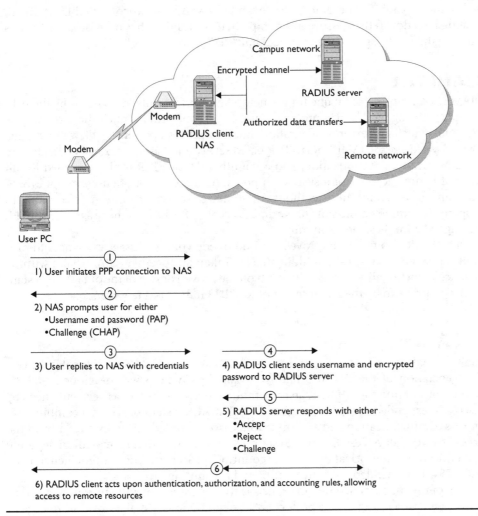

Figure 3-13 RADIUS communication sequence

and it supports typical accounting functions for time billing and security logging. The RADIUS accounting functions are designed to allow data to be transmitted at the beginning and end of a session, and it can indicate resource utilization, such as time, bandwidth, and so on.

When RADIUS was first designed in the mid 1990s, the role of ISP NASs was relatively simple. Allowing and denying access to a network and timing usage were the major concerns. Today, the Internet and its access methods have changed dramatically, and so have the AAA requirements. As individual firms extended RADIUS to meet these needs, interoperability became an issue, and a new AAA protocol called DIAMETER, designed to address these issues in a comprehensive fashion, has been proposed and is entering the final stages of the Internet Draft/RFC process.

DIAMETER

DIAMETER is a proposed name for the new AAA protocol suite, designated by the IETF to replace the aging RADIUS protocol. DIAMETER operates in much the same way as RADIUS, in a client/server configuration, but it improves upon RADIUS, resolving discovered weaknesses. DIAMETER is a TCP-based service and has more extensive capabilities in authentication, authorization, and accounting. DIAMETER is also designed for all types of remote access, not just modem pools. As more and more users adopt broadband and other connection methods, these newer services require more options to properly determine permissible usage and to account for and log the usage. DIAMETER is designed with these needs in mind.

DIAMETER also has an improved method of encrypting message exchanges to prohibit replay and man-in-the-middle attacks. Taken all together, DIAMETER, with its enhanced functionality and security, built on the proven design of the old RADIUS standard, will prove to be the replacement of RADIUS in the next few years.

TACACS+

The Terminal Access Controller Access Control System+ (TACACS+) protocol is the current generation of the TACACS family. Originally TACACS was developed by BBN Planet Corporation for MILNET, an early military network, but it has been enhanced by Cisco and expanded twice. The original BBN TACACS system provided a combination process of authentication and authorization. Cisco extended this to Extended Terminal Access Controller Access Control System (XTACACS), which provided for separate authentication, authorization, and accounting processes. The current generation, TACACS+, has extended attribute control and accounting processes.

One of the fundamental design aspects is the separation of authentication, authorization, and accounting in this protocol. Although there is a straightforward lineage of these protocols from the original TACACS, TACACS+ is a major revision and is not backward compatible with previous versions of the protocol series.

TACACS+ uses TCP as its transport protocol, typically operating over TCP port 49. This port is used for the login process and is reserved in the assigned numbers RFC, RFC 3232, manifested in a database from IANA. In the IANA specification, both UDP and TCP port 49 are reserved for TACACS login host protocol (see Table 3-2 in the Chapter Review section).

TACACS+ is a client/server protocol, with the client typically being a NAS and the server being a daemon process on a UNIX, Linux, or Windows NT server. This is important to note, for if the user's machine (usually a PC) is not the client (usually a NAS), then communications between PC and NAS are typically not encrypted and are passed in the clear. Communications between a TACACS+ client and TACACS+ server are encrypted using a shared secret that is manually configured into each entity and is not shared over a connection. Hence, communications between a TACACS+ client (typically a NAS) and a TACACS+ server are secure, but the communications between a user (typically a PC) and the TACACS+ client are subject to compromise.

TACACS+ Authentication

TACACS+ allows for arbitrary length and content in the authentication exchange sequence, enabling many different authentication mechanisms to be used with TACACS+ clients. Authentication is optional and is determined as a site-configurable option. When authentication is used, common forms include PPP PAP, PPP CHAP, PPP EAP, token cards, and Kerberos. The authentication process is performed using three different packet types: START, CONTINUE, and REPLY. START and CONTINUE packets originate from the client and are directed to the TACACS+ server. The REPLY packet is used to communicate from the TACACS+ server to the client.

The authentication process is illustrated in Figure 3-14, and it begins with a START message from the client to the server. This message may be in response to an initiation from a PC connected to the TACACS+ client. The START message describes the type of authentication being requested (simple plaintext password, PAP, CHAP, etc.). This START message may also contain additional authentication data, such as username and password. A START message is also sent as a response to a restart request from the server in a REPLY message. A START message always has its sequence number set to 1.

When a TACACS+ server receives a START message, it sends a REPLY message. This REPLY message will indicate whether the authentication is complete or needs to be continued. If the process needs to be continued, the REPLY message also specifies what additional information is needed. The response from a client to a REPLY message requesting additional data is a CONTINUE message. This process continues until the server has all the information needed, and the authentication process concludes with a success or failure.

TACACS+ Authorization

Authorization is defined as the action associated with determining permission associated with a user action. This generally occurs after authentication, as shown in Figure 3-14, but this is not a firm requirement. A default state of "unknown user" exists before a user is authenticated, and permissions can be determined for an unknown user. As with authentication, authorization is an optional process and may or may not be part of a site- specific operation. When it is used in conjunction with authentication, the authorization process follows the authentication process and uses the confirmed user identity as input in the decision process.

The authorization process is performed using two message types: REQUEST and RESPONSE. The authorization process is performed using an authorization session consisting of a single pair of REQUEST and RESPONSE messages. The client issues an authorization REQUEST message containing a fixed set of fields that enumerate the authenticity of the user or process requesting permission and a variable set of fields enumerating the services or options for which authorization is being requested.

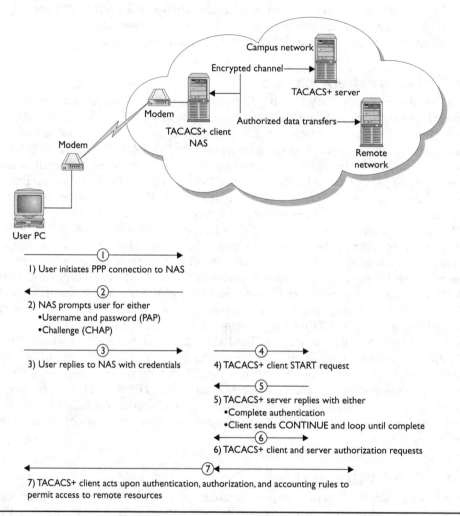

Figure 3-14 TACACS+ communication sequence

The RESPONSE message in TACACS+ is not a simple yes or no; it may also include qualifying information, such as a user time limit or IP restrictions. These limitations have important uses, such as enforcing time limits on shell access, or IP access list restrictions for specific user accounts.

TACACS+ Accounting

As with the two previous services, accounting is also an optional function of TACACS+. When utilized, it typically follows the other services. Accounting in TACACS+ is defined as the process of recording what a user or process has done. Accounting can serve two important purposes:

- It may be used to account for services being utilized, possibly for billing purposes.
- It may be used for generating security audit trails.

TACACS+ accounting records contain several pieces of information to support these tasks. The accounting process has the information revealed in the authorization and authentication processes, so it can record specific requests by user or process. To support this functionality, TACACS+ has three types of accounting records: START, STOP, and UPDATE. Note that these are record types, not message types as earlier discussed.

START records indicate the time and user or process that began an authorized process. STOP records enumerate the same information concerning the stop times for specific actions. UPDATE records act as intermediary notices that a particular task is still being performed. Together these three message types allow the creation of records that delineate the activity of a user or process on a system.

Vulnerabilities

The primary vulnerability associated with all of these methods of remote access is the passing of critical data in the clear. Plaintext passing of passwords provides no security if the password is sniffed, and sniffers are easy to use on a network. Even plaintext passing of usernames gives away data that can be correlated and possibly used. This is one of the fundamental flaws with telnet, and is why SSH was developed. This is also one of the flaws with RADIUS and TACACS+, as they have a segment unprotected. There are methods for overcoming these limitations, although they require discipline and understanding in setting up a system.

The strength of the encryption algorithm is also a concern. Should a specific algorithm or method prove to be vulnerable (such as WEP), services that rely solely on it are also vulnerable. To get around this dependency, many of the protocols allow numerous encryption methods, so that should one prove vulnerable, a shift to another restores security.

As with any software implementation, there always exists the possibility that a bug opens the system to attack. Bugs have been corrected in most software packages to close holes that left systems vulnerable, and remote access software is no exception. This is not a Microsoft-only phenomenon, as one might believe from the popular press. Critical flaws have been found in almost every product, from open system implementations such as OpenSSH to proprietary systems such as Cisco's IOS. The important issue is not the presence of software bugs, for as software continues to become more complex, this is an unavoidable issue. The true key is vendor responsiveness to fixing the bugs once they are discovered, and the major players, such as Cisco and Microsoft, have been very responsive in this area.

Chapter Review

There are many methods for achieving security under remote access conditions, and the number is growing as new protocols are developed to meet the ever-increasing use of remote access. From the beginnings of Telnet, to IPv6 with built-in IPsec, the options are many, but the task is basically the same. Perform the functions of authentication, authorization, and accounting while providing message and data security from outside intervention. (See Table 3-2.)

Some of the remote access solutions have a hardware component (such as L2F and RADIUS), some have software (SSH and PPTP) and some can have both (VPN and IPsec) depending upon the vendor's implementation and system requirements. The choice of a remote access solution will depend upon several factors, including security requirements, the type of network, the type of clients, required access methods, scalability, existing authentication mechanisms, and cost. Each system has its strengths and weaknesses, and when properly employed, each can be used effectively within its own limitations. There is no best solution at the present time, but as the Internet advances and IPv6 is adopted, IPsec will move up the list into a prime spot and provide a significant number of these required services as part of the TCP/IPv6 protocol suite.

TCP Port Number	UDP Port Number	Keyword	Protocol
20		FTP-Data	File Transfer (Default Data)
21		FTP	File Transfer Control
22		SSH	Secure Shell Login
23		TELNET	Telnet
25		SMTP	Simple Mail Transfer
37	37	TIME	Time
49	49	TACACS+	TACACS+ login
53	53	DNS	Domain Name Server
65	65	TACACS+	TACACS+ database service
88	88	Kerberos	Kerberos
500	500	ISAKMP	ISAKMP protocol
512		rexec	
513		rlogin	UNIX rlogin
	513	rwho	UNIX Broadcast Naming Svc
514		rsh	UNIX rsh and rep
	514	SYSLOG	UNIX system logs
614	614	SSHELL	SSL Shell
	1701	L2TP	L2TP
1723	1723	PPTP	PPTP
1812	1812	RADIUS	RADIUS authorization
1813	1813	RADIUS-actg	RADIUS accounting

Table 3-2 Common TCP/UDP Remote Access Networking Port Assignments

Questions

1. A firewall can be classified as an example of

    A. An ID-based access control

    B. A directory-based access control

    C. A rule-based access control

    D. A lattice-based access control

2. Authentication is typically based upon

    A. Something a user possesses

    B. Something a user knows

    C. Something measured on a user, such as a fingerprint

    D. None of the above

3. Passwords are an example of

    A. Something you have

    B. Something you know

    C. A shared secret

    D. None of the above

4. Which of these protocols is used for carrying authentication, authorization, and configuration information between a network access server and a shared authentication server?

    A. IPsec

    B. VPN

    C. SSH

    D. RADIUS

5. On a VPN, traffic is encrypted and decrypted at

    A. Endpoints of the tunnel only

    B. Users' machines

    C. Each device at each hop

    D. The data-link layer of access devices

6. What protocol is used for TACACS+?

    A. UDP

    B. NetBIOS

    C. TCP

    D. Proprietary

7. What protocol is used for RADIUS?

   A. UDP

   B. NetBIOS

   C. TCP

   D. Proprietary

8. Which protocols are supported by Microsoft Windows 2000 and XP for use in securing remote connections?

   A. SSH

   B. PPTP

   C. IPsec

   D. VPN

9. Which protocol is used to communicate over a serial interface channel between computers?

   A. CHAP

   B. IPsec

   C. SSH

   D. PPP

10. IPsec provides which options as security services?

   A. ESP and AH

   B. ESP and AP

   C. EA and AP

   D. EA and AH

11. Secure Shell uses which port to communicate?

   A. TCP port 80

   B. UDP port 22

   C. TCP port 22

   D. TCP port 110

12. PPTP connections occur at what level of the OSI model?

   A. Physical layer, level 1

   B. Data-link layer, level 2

   C. Network layer, level 3

   D. Transport layer, level 4

13. To establish a PPTP connection across a firewall, you must

    A. Do nothing; PPTP does not cross firewalls by design.

    B. Open TCP port 1723.

    C. Open a UDP port of choice and assign to PPTP.

    D. Do nothing; PPTP tunnels past firewalls.

14. To establish an L2TP connection across a firewall, you must

    A. Do nothing; L2TP does not cross firewalls by design.

    B. Do nothing; L2TP tunnels past firewalls.

    C. Open a UDP port of choice and assign to PPTP.

    D. Open UDP port 1701.

15. IPsec can provide which of the following types of protection?

    A. Context protection

    B. Content protection

    C. Both context and content protection

    D. Neither context nor content protection

Answers

1. **C.** A good example of rule-based access control is a firewall. Here, a set of rules defined by the network administrator is recorded in a file. Every time a connection is attempted (incoming or outgoing), the firewall software checks the rules to see if the connection is allowed. If it is not, the firewall closes the connection and does not permit the communication.

2. **A, B,** and **C.** Authentication is based on what you know, what you have, what you are, or what you can do.

3. **B.**

4. **D.** RADIUS is a protocol for performing authentication, authorization, and accounting. It involves an information exchange between a network access server, which desires authentication of specific connections, and a shared authentication server.

5. **A.** A virtual private network (VPN) is a secure communications protocol that encrypts traffic between two endpoints of a tunnel. At each endpoint of the secure VPN tunnel, the traffic is either encrypted or decrypted, depending upon whether the traffic is going into or out of the tunnel.

6. **C.**

PART III

7. **A.**

8. **B** and **C.** Both PPTP and IPsec are supported by Microsoft in Windows 2000 and XP. IPsec is more resource intensive, but also more versatile, and allows greater flexibility in connections.

9. **D.** PPP is a protocol for communication between computers using a serial interface, typically involving a PC connected via a phone line to a server.

10. **A.** IPsec utilizes Encapsulating Security Payload (ESP) and Authentication Headers (AH).

11. **C.** SSH initiates conversations over TCP port 22.

12. **B.** PPTP operates at the data-link layer of the OSI model and hence can carry TCP/IP traffic.

13. **B.** PPTP uses TCP port 1723 to establish communications, so this port must be open across a firewall for PPTP to function correctly.

14. **D.** L2TP uses UDP port 1701 to establish communications, so this port must be open across a firewall for L2TP to function correctly.

15. **C.** IPsec can provide both context protection and content protection by using both ESP and AH.

E-Mail

In this chapter, you will

- Learn about security issues associated with e-mail
- Understand some of the security practices for e-mail
- Learn about software to improve e-mail confidentiality

E-mail is the most popular application on the Internet. It is also by far the most popular application on intracompany networks. Roughly 12 million e-mails were sent each day in 2001, giving a rough total of 4.38 billion e-mails sent in that year. In 2000, there were 569 million e-mail boxes in the world.

Security of E-Mail Transmissions

Considering the old statistics, it is easy to see that e-mail needs to have security. E-mail started with mailbox programs on early time-sharing machines, allowing researchers to leave messages for others using the same machine. The first inter-machine e-mail was sent in 1972, and a new era in person-to-person communication was launched. E-mail proliferated, but it remained unsecured, only partly because most e-mail is sent in plaintext, providing no privacy in its default form.

Viruses started as simple self-replicating programs that spread via the transfer of floppy disks, but e-mail gave virus files a passport to travel. Sending themselves to every user that they possibly can, they have achieved record-breaking infection rates. Trojan horse programs are also often sent through the mail, with computer owners as accomplices, compromising hundreds of machines every day.

There is also the strange nature of e-mail hoaxes, those Internet-based urban legends that are spread through e-mail, with users forwarding them in seemingly endless loops around the globe. And, of course, there are the ubiquitous spam e-mails, which despite the remarkable advance of every other technology, people still haven't found a good way to block.

Securing e-mail is something that must be done by the users themselves, because they are the ones who will actually be sending and receiving the messages. However, security administrators can give users the tools they need to fight the problems. S/MIME and PGP are two very popular methods of encrypting e-mail. Server-based and desktop-based virus protection can help against malicious code, and spam filters attempt to block all unsolicited commercial e-mail. E-mail users need to be educated about security, though, because the popularity and functionality of e-mail is only going to increase.

Malicious Code

Viruses and worms are popular programs because they make themselves popular. When viruses were constrained to only one computer, they attempted to spread by attaching themselves to every executable program that they could find. This worked out very well for the viruses because they could piggyback onto a floppy disk with a program that was being transferred to another computer.

The advent of computer networks was a computer virus writer's dream, allowing viruses to attempt to infect every network share that the computer was attached to. This extended the virus's reach from a set of machines that might share a floppy disk to every machine on the network. Because the e-mail protocol permits users to attach files to e-mail messages, viruses can travel by e-mail from one local network to another, anywhere on the Internet. This changes the nature of virus programs, as they once were localized, but now can spread virtually everywhere. This changes the virus from having a local reach to a global one.

Viruses spread by e-mail further and faster than ever before, but viruses also evolved. This evolution started with viruses that were scripted to send themselves to other users, and this type of virus was known as a *worm*. A worm uses its code to automate the infection process. For example, when the worm program is executed, the code may seek out the user's e-mail address book and mail itself to as many people as the worm's programming dictates. This method of transmission depends on the user actually executing the worm file. Some worms use multiple methods of attack, not only sending multiple infected e-mails, but also scanning hosts on the Internet, looking for a specific vulnerability. Upon finding the vulnerability, the worm infects the remote host and starts the process all over again.

Viruses and worms are a danger not only to the individual user's machine, but also to network security because they can introduce malicious traffic to other machines. This can cause not only loss of data, but sometimes can send data out to other users. The Sircam worm attached random files from the infected user's hard drive to the e-mails the worm sent out.

Worms can also carry Trojan horse payloads, just as any e-mail message can. A Trojan horse is a program that seems to be one thing while actually having a more sinister hidden purpose. For example, an executable game program or an executable self-playing movie could be a Trojan. These programs will run and do what they claim, but they typically also install some other program, such as a remote control package like SubSeven or Back Orifice. These programs allow an attacker to remotely control an infected machine. Once control is achieved, the attacker can use the machine to perform a number of tasks, such as using it in distributed denial of service (DDOS) attacks, using it as a launching point to compromise other machines, or simply using it as a remote place to store some extra files.

While the distribution of malicious code in e-mail is tied to the files that are attached to the e-mail messages, in the past a user actually had to execute the attached file. The original system of e-mail used plain text to send messages, but the advent of the Web changed this. Hypertext Markup Language (better known as HTML) was created to allow plain text to represent complex page designs in a standardized way. HTML was soon adopted by e-mail programs so users could use different fonts and colors and embed pictures in their e-mails. E-mail programs then grew more advanced and, like web browsers, were designed to automatically open files attached to e-mails. When active content was designed for the Web, in the form of Java and ActiveX scripts, these scripts were interpreted and run by the e-mail programs, and that's when the trouble began. Some e-mail programs, most notably Microsoft Outlook, have what's known as a preview pane, which allows users to read e-mails without opening them in the full screen. Unfortunately, this preview still activates all the content in the e-mail message, and because Outlook supports VB scripting, it was vulnerable to e-mail worms. A user doesn't need to actually run the program or even open the e-mail to activate the worm—they just need to preview the e-mail in the preview pane. This form of automatic execution was the primary reason for the spread of the ILOVEYOU worm.

Viruses are a security threat, and one of the most common transfer methods is through e-mail. The solution to this problem comes in two parts: user education and virus scanning.

Although the great majority of users are now aware of viruses and the damage they can cause, further education may be needed to instruct them on the specific things that need to be addressed when the virus comes through the e-mail. These specific things can vary from organization to organization and from e-mail software to e-mail software; however, some useful examples of good practices are: examining all e-mails for a known source as well as a known destination, especially if the e-mails have attachments. Strange files or unexpected attachments should always be checked before execution. Users also need to know that some viruses can be executed simply by opening the e-mail or viewing it in the preview pane. Education and proper administration is also useful in configuring the e-mail software to be as virus resistant as possible; turning off scripting support and the preview pane are good examples.

The other protection is to have well thought out virus scanning procedures. If possible, perform virus scanning on every e-mail as it comes into the corporation's server. Some users will also attempt to retrieve e-mail off-site from their normal ISP account, which can bypass the server-based virus protection, so every machine should also be protected with a host-based virus protection program that scans all files on a regular basis and performs checks of files upon their execution. While these steps will not eliminate the security risks of malicious code in e-mail, it will limit infection and help to keep the problem to manageable levels.

✳ Hoax E-Mails

An interesting offshoot of e-mail viruses is the phenomenon of e-mail hoaxes. If you've had an Internet e-mail address for more than a couple of months, you've probably received at least one of these. The Neiman-Marcus cookie recipe that is sent to you because someone was charged $250, the "famous" commencement speech by Kurt Vonnegut, and the young dying boy whose last wish was to make it into the record books by receiving the most get well cards ever—these are the most famous of the e-mail hoaxes, though there are many others.

E-mail hoaxes are mostly a nuisance, but they do cost everyone, not only in the time wasted by receiving and reading the e-mail, but also in the Internet bandwidth and server processing time they take up. E-mail hoaxes are basically global urban legends, perpetually traveling from one e-mail account to the next, and most have a common theme of some story you must tell ten people about right away or some virus that everyone should beware of. Hoaxes are similar to chain letters, but instead of promising a reward, the story in the e-mail is typically what produces the action. Whether it's a call for sympathy from a dying boy, or an overly expensive recipe sent to the masses in the name of justice, all hoaxes prompt action of some sort, and this call for action is probably what keeps them going. Hoaxes have been circling the Internet for many, many years, and many web sites are dedicated to debunking them.

The power of the e-mail hoax is actually quite amazing. The Neiman-Marcus story, in which someone gets charged $250 for a chocolate chip cookie recipe, thinking that she is only being charged $2.50, used to have a fatal flaw: Neiman-Marcus did not sell chocolate chip cookies (but they do now simply because of the hoax). The Kurt Vonnegut hoax was convincing enough to fool his wife, and the dying boy, who is now 20, still receives cards in the mail. The power of these hoaxes probably means that they will never be stopped, though they might be slowed down. The most important thing to do in this case is educate e-mail users. Show them a hoax before you put them online, and teach them how to search the Internet for hoax information. Users need to apply the same common sense on the Internet that they would in real life: If it sounds too outlandish to be true, it probably isn't.

Unsolicited Commercial E-Mail (Spam)

Spam is something that every Internet user has received, usually on a daily basis. Spam is the common term for unsolicited commercial e-mail. These commercial e-mails got the name spam when the Internet was much smaller and commercial interests were rather rare. The term *spam* comes from a skit on Monty Python's Flying Circus where two people are in a restaurant that only serves spam. This concept of the repetition of unwanted things is the key to spam.

The first spam e-mail was sent in 1978 by a DEC employee. However, the first spam that really captured everyone's attention was in 1994 when two lawyers posted a commercial message to every Usenet newsgroup. This was the origin of using the Internet to send one message to as many recipients as possible via an automated program. Commercial e-mail programs have taken over, resulting in the variety of spam that most users receive in their mailboxes every day. In 2000, America Online estimated that nearly 30 percent of e-mail sent to its systems is spam, accounting for nearly 24 million messages a day.[*] The worst thing about spam is its apparent popularity—Jupiter Communications estimates that by 2005, every user will receive 1,600 spam e-mails a year.[*]

The appeal to the people generating the spam is the extremely low cost per advertising impression. The senders of spam e-mail can generally send the messages for less than a cent apiece. This is much less expensive than more traditional direct mail or print advertisements, and this low cost will ensure the continued growth of spam e-mail unless something is done about it. The amount of spam being transmitted has been large enough to trigger state and federal legislators to consider action, but no effective laws have been passed yet. This has forced most people to seek out technical solutions to the spam problem.

The first thing to be done is educate users about spam. A good way for users to fight spam is to be cautious about where on the Internet they post their e-mail address.

However, you can't keep e-mail addresses secret just to avoid spam, so one of the steps that the majority of system administrators running Internet e-mail servers have taken to reduce spam, and which is also a good e-mail security principle, is to shut down mail relaying. Port scanning occurs across all hosts all the time, typically with a single host scanning large subnets for a single port, and some of these people could be attempting to send spam e-mail. When they scan for TCP port 25, they are looking for open SMTP servers, and once they find a host that is an open relay, they can use that host to send as many commercial e-mails as possible. The reason that they look for an open relay is that spammers typically do not want the e-mails traced back to them.

Since it may not be possible to close all mail relays, and because some spammers will mail from their own mail servers, software must be used to combat spam at the recipient's end. There are two main places to filter spam: at the host itself, or at the server. Filtering spam at the host level is usually done with basic pattern matching, focusing on the sender, subject, or text of the e-mail. This is a fairly effective system, but it uses an inordinate amount of bandwidth and processing power on the host computer. These problems can be solved by filtering spam at the mail server level.

There is a benefit to the server-based approach, because there are other methods of filtering spam at the server: pattern matching is still used, but some mail software can also use the Realtime Blackhole List. This list is maintained in real time specifically for blocking spam mail. Started in 1997, this service is so popular that many programs include support for it by default, such as Sendmail, Postfix, and Eudora Internet Mail Server. This blacklist is effective because it is run by a not-for-profit organization devoted to reducing spam. As such, they have the most community participation and product support from multiple vendors, which helps them have a larger, more complete black-hole list. There are also commercial packages that block spam at the server level using both methods mentioned previously, maintaining their own blacklists and pattern-matching algorithms.

---

[*] Adam S. Marlin, "Spammers, Keep Out," *The Standard* (June 12, 2000): www.thestandard.com/article/0,1902,15586,00.html

These methods will take care of 90 percent of the junk mail clogging the networks, but they cannot stop it entirely. To truly combat spam, all network administrators will have to work together to eliminate it. One of the current better ideas is to block port TCP 25 from all hosts except for designated mail servers. This would stop spammers using remote open relays and prevent many users from running unauthorized e-mail servers of their own. This is a controversial measure and probably will not come to pass.

Because of the low cost of generating spam, until serious action is taken, or spam is somehow made unprofitable, spam will remain with us.

Mail Encryption

The e-mail concerns discussed so far in this chapter are all global issues involving security, but there is a more important security problem with e-mail—the lack of confidentiality or as it is sometimes referred to, privacy. E-mail has always been a plaintext protocol. When many people first got onto the Internet, there was a standard lecture about not sending anything through e-mail that you wouldn't want posted on a public bulletin board. Part of the reason for this was that e-mail is sent with the clear text of the message exposed to anyone who is sniffing the network. Any attacker at a choke point in the network could read all e-mail passing through that network segment. There are tools that solve this problem by encrypting the e-mail's content. The first method is called S/MIME and the second is called PGP.

S/MIME stands for Secure/Multipurpose Internet Mail Extensions, which means it is a secure implementation of the MIME (Multipurpose Internet Mail Extensions) protocol specification. MIME was created to allow Internet e-mail to support new and more creative features. The original e-mail RFC only specified text e-mail, so any non-text data had to be handled by a new specification—MIME. MIME handles audio files, images, applications, and multipart e-mails. This allows e-mail to handle multiple types of content in an e-mail, including file transfers. Every time you send a file as an e-mail attachment, you are using MIME. S/MIME takes this content and specifies a framework for encrypting the message as a MIME attachment.

S/MIME was developed by RSA Data Security and uses the X.509 format for certificates. The specification supports both 40-bit RC2 and 3DES for symmetric encryption. The protocol can affect the message in one of two ways: the host mail program can encode the message with S/MIME, or the server can act as the processing agent, encrypting all messages between hosts.

The host-based operation starts when the user clicks Send—the mail agent will then encode the message using the generated symmetric key. Then the symmetric key is encoded with the remote user's public key or the local user's private key. This enables the remote user to decode the symmetric key and then decrypt the actual content of the message. Of course, all of this is handled by the user's mail program, requiring the user simply to tell the program to decode the message. If the message is signed by the sender, it will be signed with the sender's public key, guaranteeing the source of the message. The reason that both symmetric and asymmetric encryption are used in the mail is to increase the speed of encryption and decryption. As encryption is based on difficult mathematical problems, it takes time to encrypt and decrypt. To speed this up, the more difficult process, asymmetric encryption, is used to only encrypt a relatively small amount of data, the symmetric key. The symmetric key is then used to encrypt the rest of the message.

The S/MIME process of encrypting e-mails provides integrity, privacy, and, if the message is signed, authentication. Several popular e-mail programs support S/MIME, including the popular Microsoft products, Outlook and Outlook Express. They both manage S/MIME keys and functions through the Security screen, as shown in Figure 4-1. This figure shows the different settings that can be used to encrypt messages and use X.509 digital certificates. This allows interoperability with web certificates, and trusted authorities are available to issue the certificates. Trusted authorities are needed to ensure the senders are who they claim to be, an important part of authentication. In Outlook Express the window is more simplistic (see Figure 4-2), but the same functions of key management and secure e-mail operation are available.

While S/MIME is a good and versatile protocol for securing e-mail, there are a few potential problems with its implementation. S/MIME allows the user to select low strength (40-bit) encryption, which means a user can send a message that is thought to be secure but that can be more easily decoded than messages sent with 3DES encryption. Also, as with any protocol, there can be bugs in the software itself. Just because an application is designed for security does not mean that it, itself, is secure. In October of 2002, a buffer overrun was found in Outlook Express's S/MIME error handling. Apart from potential flaws, S/MIME is a tremendous leap in security over regular e-mail.

Figure 4-1
S/MIME Options
in Outlook

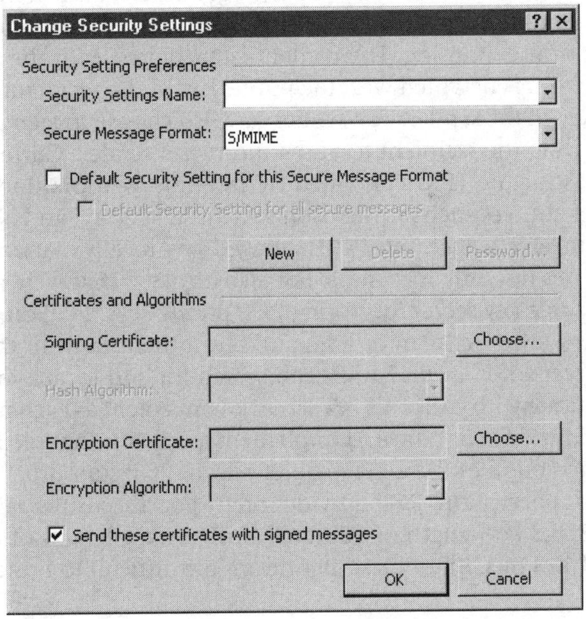

PART III

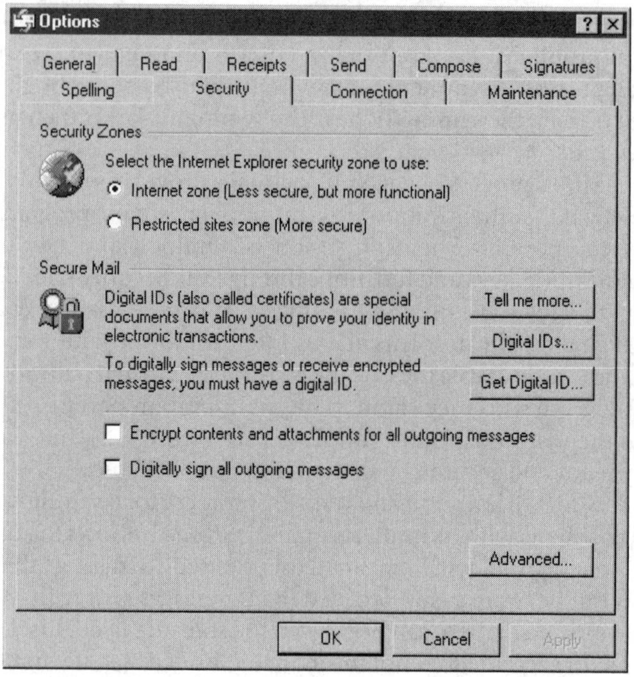

Figure 4-2
S/MIME Options
in Outlook
Express

Pretty Good Privacy (PGP) implements e-mail security in a similar fashion to S/MIME but using completely different protocols. The basic framework is the same. Again, the user sends the e-mail, and the mail agent applies encryption as specified in the mail program's programming. The content is encrypted with the generated symmetric key, and that key is encrypted with the public key of the recipient of the e-mail, or with the private key of the sender. The sender can also choose to sign the mail with their private key, allowing the recipient to authenticate the sender. Currently PGP supports Public Key Infrastructure (PKI) provided by multiple vendors, including X.509 certificates, LDAP key sources such as Microsoft's Active Directory, and Novell's NDS.

In Figure 4-3, we see how PGP managed keys locally in its own software. This is where a user stores not only local keys, but also any keys that were gotten from other people. There is a free key server for storing PGP public keys. PGP can generate its own keys using either Diffie-Hellman or RSA, and it can then transmit the public keys to the PGP LDAP server so other PGP users can search for and locate your public key in order to communicate with you. This key server is convenient as each person using PGP for communications does not have to implement a server to handle key management. For the actual encryption of the e-mail content itself, PGP supports IDEA, 3DES, and CAST for symmetric encryption. PGP provides pretty good security against brute-force attacks by using a 3DES key length of 168 bits, an IDEA key length of 128 bits, and a CAST key length of 128 bits. All of these algorithms are difficult to brute force with existing hard-

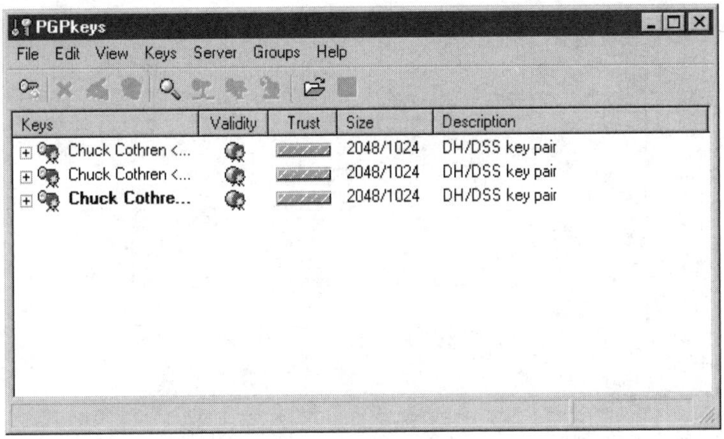

Figure 4-3
PGP key
management

ware, requiring well over a million years to break the code. While this is not a promise of future security against brute-force attacks, the security is reasonable today.

PGP has plug-ins for many popular e-mail programs, including Outlook, Outlook Express, and Qualcomm's Eudora. These plug-ins handle the encryption and decryption behind the scenes, and all that the user must do is enter the encryption key's passphrase to ensure that they are the owner of the key. In Figure 4-4 you can see the string of encrypted text that makes up the MIME attachment. This text includes the encrypted content of the message and the encrypted symmetric key. Also, you can see that the program does not decrypt the message upon receipt; it waits until instructed to decrypt it. PGP also stores encrypted messages in the encrypted format, as does S/MIME. This is important, as it provides end-to-end security for the message.

Like S/MIME, the PGP protocol is not problem free. Diligence must be applied to keep the software up to date and fully patched, because vulnerabilities are occasionally found. For example, a buffer overflow was found in the way PGP was handled in Outlook, causing the overwriting of heap memory and leading to possible malicious code execution. There is also a lot of discussion about the way PGP handles key recovery, or key escrow. PGP uses what's called Additional Decryption Key (ADK), which is basically an additional public key stacked upon the original public key. This, in theory, would give the proper organization a private key that would be used to retrieve the secret messages. In practice, the ADK is not always controlled by a properly authorized organization, and the danger exists for someone to add an ADK and then distribute it to the world. This creates a situation where other users will be sending messages that they believe can only be read by the first party, but that can be read by the third party who modified the key. These are just examples of the current vulnerabilities in the product, showing that PGP is just a tool, not the ultimate answer to security.

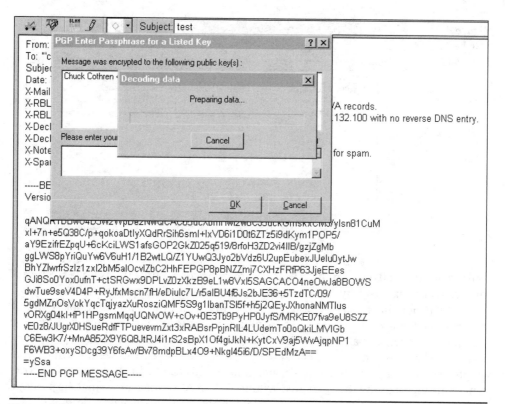

Figure 4-4   Decoding a PGP-encoded message in Eudora

Chapter Review

E-mail is one of the oldest and most popular applications on the Internet. Security was not a primary concern when it was created, and there have also been many extensions to the protocol that, while greatly increasing the functionality to users, increase security problems. The MIME extensions allowed file attachments and HTML mail, which allowed the e-mail transfer of viruses and Trojan programs. E-mail software that is capable of interpreting HTML also opened the door for self-installing e-mail worms. E-mail also offers simple annoyances, such as unwanted commercial spam and the hoax e-mails that never seem to die out. Worst of all is the complete lack of privacy and weak authentication inherent in e-mail. S/MIME and PGP attempt to reduce some of the limitations of e-mail, providing privacy, integrity, and authentication.

Questions

1. What symmetric encryption protocols does S/MIME support?

   A. AES and RC4

   B. IDEA and 3DES

   C. 3DES and RC2

   D. RC4 and IDEA

2. What is spam?

   A. Unsolicited commercial e-mail

   B. A Usenet archive

   C. A computer virus

   D. An encryption algorithm

3. How many bits are needed in a symmetric encryption algorithm to give decent protection from brute-force attacks?

   A. 24 bits

   B. 40 bits

   C. 56 bits

   D. 128 bits

4. What makes e-mail hoaxes popular enough to keep the same story floating around for years?

   A. They are written by award-winning authors.

   B. The story prompts action on the reader's part.

   C. The story will only give good luck if the user forwards it on.

   D. The hoax e-mail forwards itself.

5. What is end-to-end security?

   A. E-mail messages are stored in encrypted format before and after they have been decrypted.

   B. E-mail messages remain encrypted, no matter how many e-mail servers they pass through.

   C. E-mail messages are sent through special secure servers.

   D. E-mail is sent directly from the local host to the remote host, bypassing servers entirely.

6. Why do PGP and S/MIME need public key cryptography?

    A. Public keys are necessary to determine if the e-mail is encrypted.

    B. The public key is necessary to encrypt the symmetric key.

    C. The public key unlocks the password to the e-mail.

    D. The public key is useless and just gives a false sense of privacy.

7. Which standards support X.509 certificates?

    A. PGP

    B. S/MIME

    C. Both A and B

    D. Neither A nor B

8. What is one of the largest reasons spam is prevalent today?

    A. E-mail relays are left open.

    B. Regular mail is too slow.

    C. Spam is popular among recipients.

    D. Spam is sent from the government.

9. Why is HTML e-mail dangerous?

    A. It can't be read by some e-mail clients.

    B. It sends the content of your e-mails to web pages.

    C. It can allow launching of malicious code from the preview pane.

    D. It is the only way spam can be sent.

10. What is a Trojan horse program?

    A. A program that encrypts e-mail for security

    B. A program that appears legitimate but is actually malicious code

    C. A program that only runs on a single computer

    D. A program that self-compiles before it runs

11. Why is S/MIME sometimes considered unsecured?

    A. It doesn't actually encrypt the e-mail.

    B. It can send unsigned e-mails.

    C. It uses inferior Triple DES encryption.

    D. It can be used with only 40-bit ciphers.

12. What symmetric encryption protocols does PGP support?

    A. IDEA

    B. CAST

C. Triple DES

D. All of the above

13. What makes spam so popular as an advertising medium?

   A. Its low cost per impression

   B. Its high rate of return

   C. Its ability to canvass multiple countries

   D. Its quality of workmanship

14. What is one of the popular Trojan horse payloads?

   A. Word processor

   B. Web server

   C. Remote control programs

   D. Music sharing programs

15. How does the Realtime Blackhole List help fight spam?

   A. It is a universal Internet receptacle for spam.

   B. It maintains current signatures of all available spam for download.

   C. It takes all spam and returns it to the sender.

   D. It maintains a list of spam sources that e-mail servers can check messages against.

Answers

1. C.

2. A.

3. D. 128 bits is the current requirement to provide decent security from brute-force attacks against the key.

4. B. Hoax e-mails work by prompting action on the user's part. Typically the action is to forward the e-mail to everyone the reader knows, sometimes to right some moral injustice.

5. A. End-to-end security is when an e-mail is stored in its encrypted format both before and after it has been decrypted. PGP and S/MIME both provide this functionality.

6. B. The public key is used to encrypt the symmetric key, which is then used to encrypt the message contents, because encrypting the entire message would take too much processing power.

7. C. Both PGP and S/MIME support the use of X.509 certificates for the asymmetric key.

8. **A.** Spam is often sent through open e-mail relays to conceal the true identity of the senders.

9. **C.** HTML e-mail can carry embedded instructions to download or run scripts that can be launched from the preview pane in some e-mail programs, without requiring the user to actively launch the attached program.

10. **B.** A Trojan horse program looks like a legitimate game or video, but actually carries malicious code.

11. **D.** S/MIME currently supports a 40-bit cipher to perform the symmetric encryption, and this is considered unsecured by some, as 128 bits should be the minimum on symmetric keys.

12. **D.**

13. **A.** Spam is popular simply because of its low cost. Spam can be sent to thousands of people for less than a cent per reader.

14. **C.** Remote control programs, such as SubSeven and Back Orifice are popular Trojan horse programs because they give the attacker access to all the resources of the machine.

15. **D.** The Realtime Blackhole List is a list of sources known to send spam, and e-mail servers can use it to perform checks against the source of e-mail. If the source matches, often the e-mail is simply dropped from the server.

Web Components

In this chapter, you will

- Learn about the SSL/TLS protocol suite
- Study web applications, plug-ins, and associated security issues
- Understand secure file transfer options
- Discover directory usage for data retrieval
- Study scripting and other Internet functions that present security concerns
- Learn the use of cookies to maintain parameters between web pages

The World Wide Web was invented by Tim Berners-Lee to give physicists a convenient method of exchanging information. What began in 1990 as a physics tool in the European Laboratory for Particle Physics (CERN) has grown into a complex system that is used by millions of computer users for tasks from e-commerce, to e-mail, chatting, games, and even the original intended use—file and information sharing. Before the World Wide Web, there were plenty of methods to perform these tasks, and they were already widespread in use. File Transfer Protocol (FTP) was used to move files, and Telnet allowed access to other machines. What was missing was the common architecture brought by Berners-Lee. First, a common addressing scheme, built around the concept of a Uniform Resource Locator (URL). Second was the concept of linking documents to other documents by URLs through the Hypertext Markup Language (HTML).

Although these elements may seem minor, they formed a base that spread like wildfire. Berners-Lee developed two programs to demonstrate the usefulness of his vision: a web server to serve documents to users, and a web browser to retrieve documents for users. Both of these were key elements and contributed to the spread of this new technological innovation. The success of these components led to network after network being connected together in a "network of networks" known today as the Internet. Much of this interconnection was developed and funded through grants from the U.S. government to further technological and economic growth.

What enabled the Web's explosive growth into the PC market were the application programs, called browsers, that were developed to use these common elements and allow users ease of access to the new world of connected resources. Browsers became graphically based, and as more users began to use them, a market for more services via this new World Wide Web channel was born. Out of this market, standards emerged to provide the required levels of security necessary as the user base and functionality of the World Wide Web expanded.

The commercialization of browsers began with a program called Mosaic. Mosaic was developed at the National Center for Supercomputing Applications (NCSA) at the University of Illinois at Urbana-Champaign. A team headed by Marc Andreessen developed Mosaic for their own use, but a businessman, Jim Clark, from Silicon Valley realized the commercial potential and formed a company called Mosaic Communications to realize that potential. Andreessen and his team joined Clark, and the firm became Netscape Communications. Netscape was an early innovator and inventor of many of the protocols that drive the important elements of the Web today. Microsoft joined the browser world with its Internet Explorer and eventually became the leader in terms of market share.

Current Web Components and Concerns

The usefulness of the World Wide Web is due not just to browsers, but also to web components that enable services for end users through their browser interfaces. These web components use a wide range of protocols and services to deliver the desired content to end users. From a security perspective, these components offer end users an easy to use, secure method of conducting data transfers over the Internet. Many protocols have been developed to deliver this content, although for most users, the browser handles the details of these methods and protocols.

From a systems point of view, many security concerns have arisen, but they can be grouped in three main tasks:

- Securing a server that delivers content to users over the Web
- Securing the transport of information between users and servers over the Web
- Securing the user's computer from attack over a web connection

This chapter will present the components used on the Web to request and deliver information securely over the Internet.

Protocols

When two people communicate several things must happen for the communication to be effective. They must use a language that both parties understand, and they must correctly use the language, i.e. structure and syntax, to express their thoughts. The mode of communication is a separate entity entirely, for the previous statements are important in both spoken and written forms of communication. The same requirements are present with respect to computer communications and they are addressed through protocols. Protocols refer to agreed upon sets of rules that allow different vendors to produce hardware and software that can interoperate with pieces developed by other vendors. Because of the worldwide nature of the Internet, protocols are very important and form the basis by which all the separate parts can work together. The specific instantiation of protocols is done through hardware and software components. The majority of this chapter will concentrate on protocols related to the Internet as instantiated by software components.

Encryption (SSL and TLS)

Secure Sockets Layer (SSL) is a general-purpose protocol developed by Netscape for managing the encryption of information being transmitted over the Internet. It began as a competitive feature to drive sales of Netscape's web server product, which could then send information securely to end users. This early vision of securing the transmission channel between the web server and the browser became an Internet standard. Today, SSL is almost ubiquitous with respect to e-commerce—all browsers support it as do web servers, and virtually all sensitive financial traffic from e-commerce web sites uses this method to protect information in transit between web servers and browsers.

The Internet Engineering Task Force (IETF) embraced SSL in 1996 through a series of RFCs and named the group Transport Layer Security (TLS). Starting with SSL 3.0, in 1999 the IETF issued RFC 2246, "TLS Protocol Version 1.0," followed by RFC 2712, which added Kerberos authentication, and then RFCs 2817 and 2818, which extended TLS to HTTP version 1.1 (HTTP/1.1). Although SSL has been through several versions, TLS begins with an equivalency to SSL 3.0, so today SSL and TLS are essentially the same protocol although not interchangeable.

SSL/TLS is a series of functions that exist in the OSI model between the application layer and the TCP/IP implementation in the transport and network layers. The goal of TCP is to send an unauthenticated error-free stream of information between two computers. SSL/TLS adds message integrity and authentication functionality to TCP through the use of cryptographic methods. As cryptographic methods are an ever-evolving field, and for them to be used both parties must agree on an implementation method, SSL/TLS has embraced an open, extensible, and adaptable method to allow flexibility and strength. When two programs initiate an SSL/TLS connection, one of the first tasks is to compare available protocols and agree on an appropriate common cryptographic protocol for use in this particular communication. As SSL/TLS can use separate algorithms and methods for encryption, authentication, and data integrity, each of these is negotiated and determined depending upon need at the beginning of a communication. Currently the browsers from Netscape and Microsoft allow fairly extensive SSL/TLS setup options as illustrated in Figure 5-1, Figure 5-2, and Figure 5-3.

How SSL/TLS Works

SSL/TLS uses a wide range of cryptographic protocols. To effectively use these protocols between a client and a server, an agreement must be reached on which protocol to use. The SSL handshake process is used to accomplish this task. The handshake process begins with a client request for a secure connection, and a server's response. The questions that must be asked and answered are which protocol and which cryptographic algorithm will be used. For the client and server to communicate, both sides have to agree on a commonly held protocol (SSL v1, v2, v3, or TLS v1). Commonly available cryptographic

Figure 5-1
SSL and TLS options in Microsoft Internet Explorer

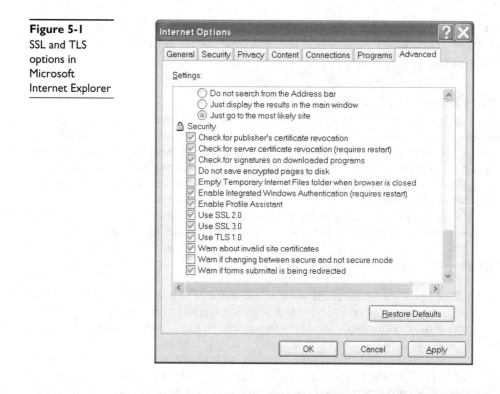

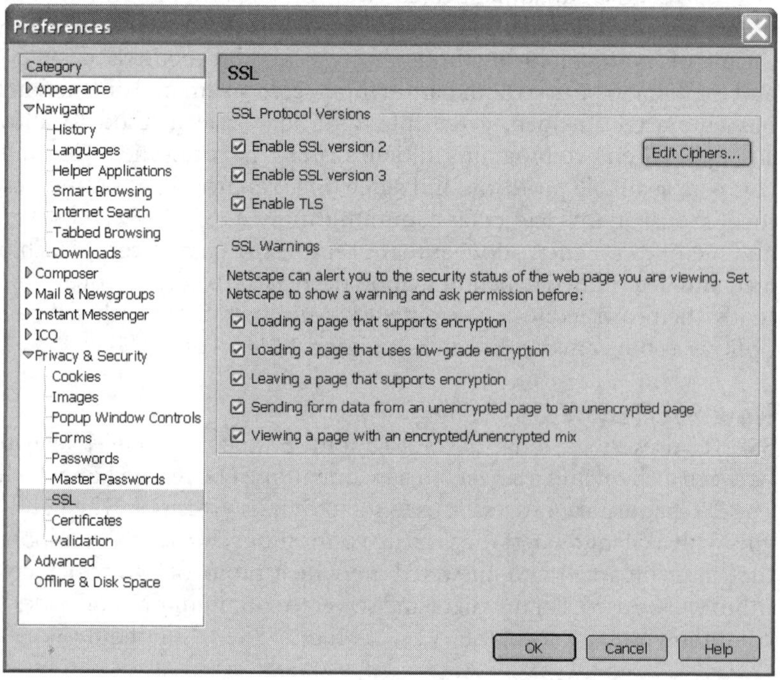

Figure 5-2
SSL and TLS options in Netscape Communicator

Figure 5-3

Cryptographic protocol options in Netscape Communicator

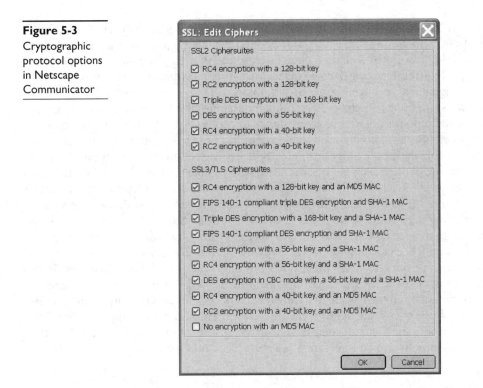

algorithms include Diffie-Hellman, and RSA. The handshake begins with the exchange to agree on parameters. The next step is to exchange certificates and keys as necessary to enable authentication. Authentication was a one-way process for SSL v1 and v2 with only the server providing authentication. In SSL v3/TLS, mutual authentication of both client and server is possible. The certificate exchange is via X.509 certificates, and public key cryptography is used to establish authentication. Once authentication is established, the channel is secured with symmetric key cryptographic methods and hashes, typically RC4 or 3DES for symmetric key and MD5 or SHA-1 for the hash functions.

At this point, the authenticity of the server and possibly the client has been established, and the channel is protected by encryption against eavesdropping. All of this work requires CPU time, hence SSL/TLS connections require significantly more overhead than unprotected connections. Establishing connections is particularly time consuming, so even stateless web connections are held in a stateful fashion when secured via SSL/TLS, to avoid repeating the handshake process for each request. This makes some web server functionality more difficult, such as implementing web farms, and it requires either an SSL/TLS appliance before the web server to maintain state, or the SSL/TLS state information must be maintained in a directory type service accessible by all of the web farm servers. Either method requires additional infrastructure and equipment. However, to enable secure e-commerce and other private data transactions over the Internet, this is a cost-effective method to establish a specific level of necessary security.

The use of certificates is a way to have a third party act as notary in the electronic world. A certificate is merely a standard set of formatted data that represents the authenticity of the public key associated with the signer. Microsoft is, in theory, the only firm that can offer a signed certificate saying they are in fact Microsoft. A certificate can be trusted as a notary to a signature. You would only trust a notary as far as you can verify their ability to vouch for something. A person using a notary assumes the notary is honest, and states have regulations and notaries have insurance to protect against fraud. The same idea is true with certificates, although the legal system has not caught up to the electronic age, nor has the business of liability insurance. Still, certificates provide a method of proving who someone is, provided you trust the issuer. If the issuer is a third party of stature, such as VeriSign or AT&T, then you may have something to rest your faith upon. If the issuer is a large firm such as Microsoft, then again you can probably trust them since you are downloading their code. If the issuer is Bob's Certificate Shack, well, unless you know Bob, then there may be cause for concern. Again, certificates do not vouch for code security, only that who is signing them is actually the person they say they are.

The use of certificates could present a lot of data and complication to a user. Fortunately, browsers have incorporated much of this desired functionality into a seamless operation. Once you have decided to always accept code from XYZ Corporation, subsequent certificate checks are handled by the browser. The ability to manipulate certificate settings is under the Options menus in both Microsoft Internet Explorer and Netscape Communicator, as shown in Figure 5-4, Figure 5-5, and Figure 5-6.

Figure 5-4
Certificate
options in
Microsoft
Internet Explorer

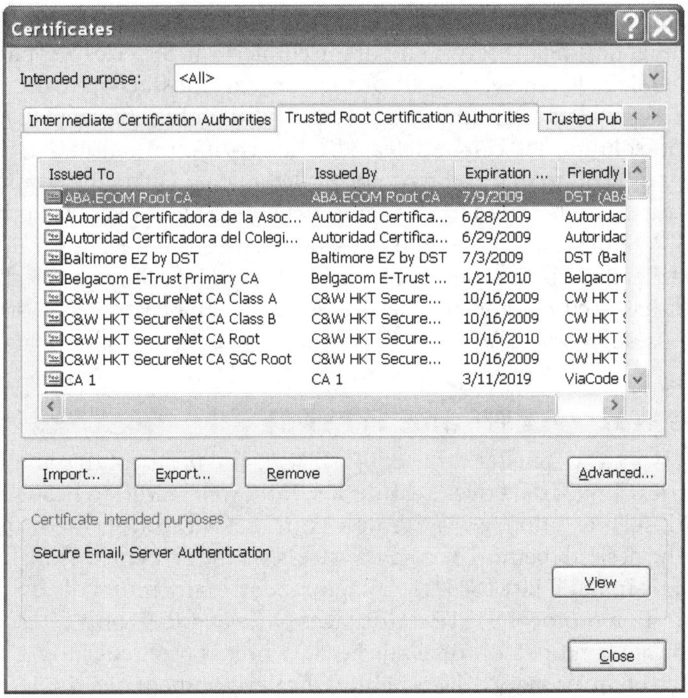

Figure 5-5
Certificate
management
options dialog
in Microsoft
Internet Explorer

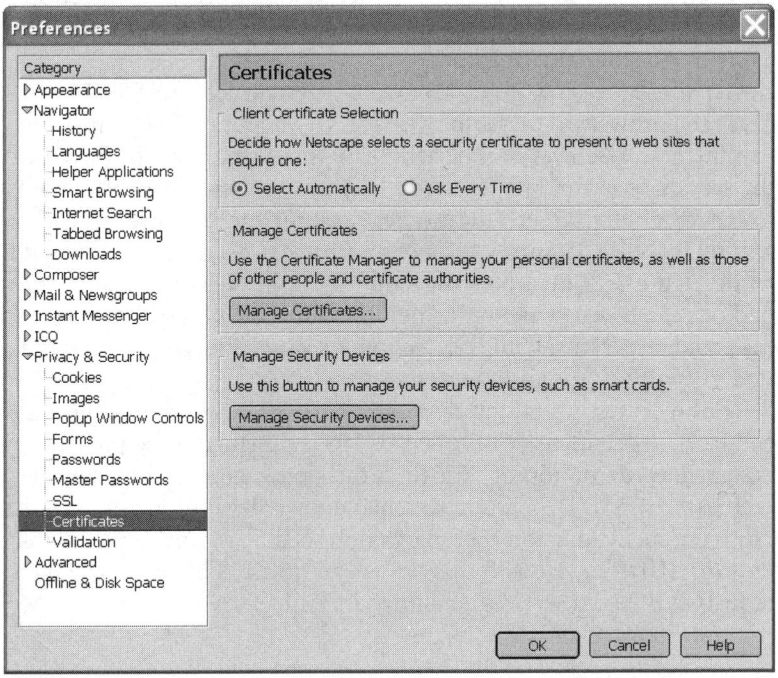

Figure 5-6
Certificate
management
options in
Netscape
Communicator

PART III

SSL/TLS is specifically designed to provide protection from man-in-the-middle attacks. By authenticating the server end of the connection, SSL/TLS prevents the initial hijacking of a session. By encrypting all of the conversations between the client and the server, SSL/TLS prevents eavesdropping. Even with all of this, though, SSL/TLS is not a complete security solution and can be defeated. Once a communication is in the SSL/TLS channel, it is very difficult to defeat the protocol. Before data enters the secured channel, however, defeat is possible. A Trojan program that copies keystrokes and echoes them to another TCP/IP address in parallel with the intended communication can defeat SSL/TLS, provided that the Trojan program copies the data prior to SSL/TLS encapsulation. This type of attack has occurred and has been used to steal passwords and other sensitive material from users, performing the theft as the user actually types in the data.

The Web (HTTP and HTTPS)

The Hypertext Transfer Protocol (HTTP) is the protocol designated for the transfer of hypertext-linked data over the Internet, from web servers to browsers. When a user types a URL such as http://www.example.com into a browser, the http:// portion indicates that the desired method of data transfer is via the Hypertext Transfer Protocol. Although this was initially just for HTML pages, today many protocols deliver content over this connection protocol. HTTP traffic takes place over TCP port 80 by default, and this port is typically left open on firewalls because of this protocol.

One of the primary drivers behind the development of SSL/TLS was the desire to hide the complexities of cryptography from end users. When using an SSL/TLS-enabled browser, this can be done simply by requesting a secure connection from a web server instead of nonsecure connection. With respect to HTTP connections, this is as simple as using https:// in place of http://.

When a browser is SSL/TLS-aware, the entry of an SSL/TLS-based protocol will cause the browser to perform the necessary negotiations with the web server to establish the required level of security. Once these negotiations have been completed and the session is secured by a session key, then a closed padlock icon is displayed in the lower right of the screen (in Internet Explorer and Communicator) to indicate that the session is secure. Figure 5-7 shows a secure connection in Microsoft Internet Explorer, while Figure 5-8 illustrates the same thing in Netscape Communicator. As the tiny padlock can be easily missed, when in doubt, the best solution is to look at the URL. If the protocol is https: your connection is secure, if it is http:, then the connection is carried by plaintext for anyone to see.

The objective of enabling cryptographic methods in this fashion is to make it easy for end users to use these protocols. SSL/TLS is designed to be protocol agnostic. Although designed to run on top of TCP/IP, it can operate on top of other lower-level protocols, such as X.25. SSL/TLS requires a reliable lower-level protocol, so it is not designed and cannot properly function on top of a non-reliable protocol such as the IP User Datagram Protocol (UDP). Even with this limitation, SSL/TLS has been used to secure many common TCP/IP-based services, as shown in Table 5-1.

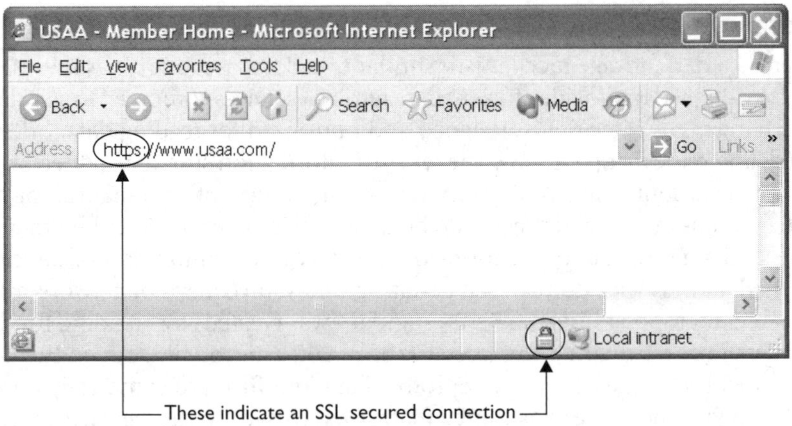

These indicate an SSL secured connection

Figure 5-7   HTTPS connection in Microsoft Internet Explorer

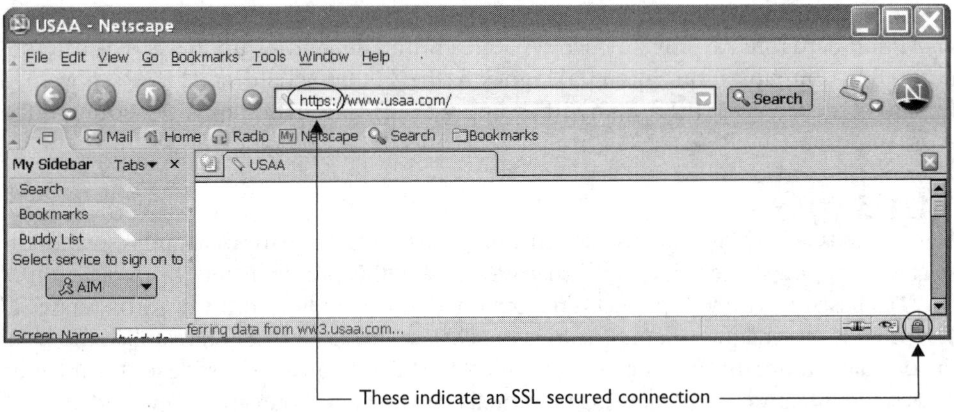

These indicate an SSL secured connection

Figure 5-8   HTTPS connection in Netscape Communicator

Protocol	TCP Port	Use
HTTPS	443	SSL/TLS secured HTTP traffic
SSMTP	465	SSL/TLS secured SMTP for mail sending
SPOP3	995	SSL/TLS secured POP3 for mail receiving
SNEWS	563	SSL/TLS secured Usenet news
SSL-LDAP	636	SSL/TLS secured LDAP services

Table 5-1   SSL/TLS Protected Services

Directory Services (DAP and LDAP)

A *directory* is a data storage mechanism similar to a database, but it has several distinct differences designed to provide efficient data retrieval services compared to standard database mechanisms. A directory is designed and optimized for reading data, offering very fast search and retrieval operations. The types of information stored in a directory tend to be descriptive attribute data. A directory offers a static view of data that can be changed without a complex update transaction. The data is hierarchically described in a tree-like structure, and a network interface for reading is typical. Common uses of directories include e-mail address lists, domain server data, and resource maps of network resources.

To enable interoperability, the X.500 standard was created as a standard for directory services. The primary method for accessing an X.500 directory is through the Directory Access Protocol (DAP), a heavyweight protocol that is difficult to completely implement, especially on PCs and more constrained platforms. This led to the Lightweight Directory Access Protocol (LDAP), which contains the most commonly used functionality. LDAP can interface with X.500 services, and, most importantly, LDAP can be used over TCP with significantly less computing resources than a full X.500 implementation. LDAP offers all of the functionality most directories will need and is easier and more economical to implement, hence LDAP has become the Internet standard for directory services. LDAP standards are governed by two separate entities depending upon use. The International Telecommunication Union (ITU) governs the X.500 standard, and LDAP is governed for Internet use by the IETF. Many RFCs apply to LDAP functionality, but some of the most important are RFCs 2251 through 2256 and RFCs 2829 and 2830.

SSL/TLS LDAP

LDAP over TCP is a plaintext protocol, meaning data is passed in the clear and is susceptible to eavesdropping. Encryption can be used to remedy this problem, and the application of SSL/TLS-based service will protect directory queries and replies from eavesdroppers. SSL/TLS provides several important functions to LDAP services. SSL/TLS can establish the identity of a data source through the use of certificates. SSL/TLS can also provide for the integrity and confidentiality of the data being presented from an LDAP source. As LDAP and SSL/TLS are two separate independent protocols, interoperability is more a function of correct setup than anything else. To achieve LDAP over SSL/TLS, the typical setup is to establish an SSL/TLS connection and then open an LDAP connection over the protected channel. To do this requires both the client and the server be enabled for SSL/TLS. In the case of the client, most browsers are already enabled. In the case of an LDAP server, this is a specific function that must be enabled by a system administrator. As setting this up initially is complicated, this is definitely a task for a competent system administrator.

Once an LDAP server is set up to function over an SSL/TLS connection, it essentially operates as it always has. The LDAP server responds to specific queries with the data returned from a node in the search. The SSL/TLS functionality operates to secure the channel of communication, and it is transparent to the data flow from the user's perspective. From the outside, SSL/TLS prevents observation of the data request and response, ensuring confidentiality.

File Transfer (FTP and SFTP)

One of the original intended uses of the Internet was for transferring files between machines. The ability to transfer files from one machine to another in a simple, secure, and reliable fashion was needed by scientific researchers. Today, file transfers represent the downloading of music content, reports, and other data sets from other computer systems to a PC-based client. Until 1995, the majority of Internet traffic was file transfers. With all of this need, a protocol was necessary so that two computers could agree on how to send and receive data. As such, the File Transfer Protocol (FTP) is one of the older protocols.

FTP

FTP is an application-level protocol, allowing it to operate over a wide range of lower-level protocols. FTP is embedded in most operating systems and provides a method of transferring files from a sender to a receiver. Most FTP implementations are designed to operate both ways, sending and receiving, and can enable remote file operations over a TCP/IP connection. FTP clients are used to initiate transactions and FTP servers are used to respond to transaction requests. The actual request can be either to upload (send data from client to server) or download (send data from server to client).

Clients for FTP on a PC can range from an application program to the command line ftp program in Windows/DOS to most browsers. To open an FTP data store in a browser, entering ftp://url in the browser's address field indicates that you wish to see the data associated with the URL via an FTP session—the browser handles the details. File transfers via FTP can be either binary or in text mode, but in either case, they are plaintext across the network.

Blind FTP (Anonymous FTP)

To access resources on a computer, an account must be used to allow the operating-system–level authorization function to work. In the case of an FTP server, you may not wish to control who gets the information, so a standard account called *anonymous* exists. This allows unlimited public access to the files and is commonly used when you wish to have unlimited distribution. On a server, access permissions can be established to allow only downloading or only uploading or both, depending upon the system's function. As FTP can be used to allow anyone access to upload files to a server, it is considered a security risk and is commonly implemented on specialized servers isolated from other critical functions. As FTP servers can present a security risk, they are typically not permitted on workstations and are disabled on servers without need for this functionality.

SFTP

FTP operates in a plaintext mode, so an eavesdropper can observe the data being passed. If confidential transfer is required, Secure FTP (SFTP) utilizes both Secure Shell (SSH) protocol and FTP to accomplish this task. SFTP is an application program that encodes both the commands and the data being passed and requires SFTP to be on both the client and the server. SFTP is not interoperable with standard FTP—the encrypted commands cannot be read by the standard FTP server program. To establish SFTP data transfers, the server must be enabled with the SFTP program, and then clients can access the server provided they have the correct credentials. One of the first SFTP operations is the same as with FTP: an identification function that uses a username, and an authorization function that uses a password. There is no anonymous SFTP account by definition, so access is established and controlled from the server using standard access control lists, IDs, and passwords.

Vulnerabilities

Modern encryption technology can provide significant levels of privacy, up to military-grade secrecy. The use of protocols such as SSL/TLS provide a convenient method for end users to use cryptography without having to understand the methods and steps. This can result in complacency—the impression that once SSL/TLS is enabled, the user is safe, and this is not necessarily the case. If a Trojan program is recording keystrokes and sending the information to another unauthorized user, SSL/TLS cannot prevent this security breach. If the user is connecting to an untrustworthy site, the mere fact that the connection is secure does not prevent the other site from running a scam. Using SSL/TLS and other encryption methods will not guard against your credit card information being "lost" by the company you do business with, as in the egghead.com credit card hack of 2000. In December 2000, egghead.com's credit card database was hacked into, and as many as 3.7 million credit card numbers were exposed. Other similar stories include 55,000 credit card records being compromised by creditcards.com in 2000 and over 300,000 records being compromised by the CD Universe hack in 1999.

The key to understanding what is protected and where it is protected requires an understanding of what these protocols can and cannot do. The SSL/TLS suite can protect data in transit, but not on either end in storage. It can authenticate users and servers, provided that the certificate mechanisms are established and used by both parties. Properly set up and used, SSL/TLS can provide a very secure method of authentication, followed by confidentiality in data transfers and data integrity checking. But again, all of this occurs during transit, and the protection ends once the data is stored.

Code-Based Vulnerabilities

The ability to connect many machines together to transfer data is what makes the Internet so functional for so many users. Browsers enable much of this functionality, and as the types of data have grown on the Internet, browser functionality has grown as well. But not all functions can be anticipated or included in each browser release, so the idea of extending browser functions through plug-ins became a standard. Browsers can perform many types of data transfer, and in some cases, additional helper programs, or plug-ins, can increase functionality for specific types of data transfers. In other cases, separate application programs may be called by a browser to handle the data being transferred. Common examples of these plug-ins and programs include Shockwave plug-ins, RealOne player (both plug-in and standalone application), Windows Media Player, and Adobe Acrobat (both plug-in and standalone). The richness that enables the desired functionality of the Internet has also spawned some additional types of interfaces in the form of ActiveX components and Java applets. In essence, all of these are pieces of code that can be written by third parties, distributed via the Internet, and run on your PC. If the code does what the user wants, the user is happy. But the opportunity exists for these applications or plug-ins to include malicious code that performs actions not desired by the end user.

Buffer Overflows

The most common exploit used to hack into software is the buffer overflow. The buffer overflow is a result of poor coding practices on the part of software programmers—when any program reads input into a buffer and does not validate the input for correct length, the potential for a buffer overflow exists. The concept is simple. A hacker writes an executable program that performs some action on the target machine and appends this code fragment to a legitimate response to a program on the target machine. When the target machine reads through the too-long response, a buffer overflow condition causes the original program to fail. The extra malicious code fragment is now in the machine's memory, awaiting execution. If the hacker executed it correctly, the program will skip into the hacker's code, running it before failing.

Buffer overflows have been shown to be exploitable in a wide range of programs, from UNIX to Windows to applications such as Internet Explorer, Netscape Communicator, and many more. It has been estimated that 50 percent of the security incidents by type are from buffer overflow exploits. This is one of the most common hacks used, and the primary defense a user has is to keep their machine up to date with patches from software manufacturers. This has not proven to be a very effective method of protection. Many people don't keep up to date with the patches, as demonstrated by the Slammer worm attack, which took place over three months after Microsoft had released a patch for the vulnerability. Even with the patch widely available, both in a hot-fix and a service pack, many SQL servers had not received the patch and were affected by this worm, which used a buffer overflow to propagate.

Java and JavaScript

Java is a computer language invented by Sun Microsystems as an alternative to Microsoft's development languages. Designed to be platform independent and based on C, Java offered a low learning curve and a way of implementing programs across an enterprise, independent of platform. Although platform independence never fully materialized, and the pace of Java language development was slowed by Sun, Java has found itself to be a leader in object-oriented programming languages.

Java, and its close cousin JavaScript, operates through an interpreter called a Java Virtual Machine (JVM) on each platform that interprets the Java code and this JVM enables the program's functionality for the specific platform. This reliance on an interpretive step has led to performance issues, and Java is still plagued by poor performance when compared to most other languages. Security was one of the touted advantages of Java, but in reality, security is not a built-in function but an afterthought and is implemented independent of the language core. This all being said, properly coded Java can operate at reasonable rates, and when properly designed can act in a secure fashion. These facts have led to the wide dependence on Java for much of the server-side coding for e-commerce and other Web-enabled functionality. Servers can add CPUs to address speed concerns, and the low learning curve has proven cost efficient for enterprises.

Java was initially designed to be used in trusted environments, and when it moved to the Internet for general use, safety became one of its much hyped benefits. Java has many safety features, such as type checking and garbage collection, that actually improve a program's ability to run safely on a machine and not cause operating-system–level failures. This isolates the user from many common forms of operating system faults that can end in the "blue screen of death" in a Windows environment, where the operating system crashes and forces a reboot of the system. Safety is not security, however, and although safe, a Java program can still cause significant damage to a system.

The primary mode of a computer program is to interact with the operating system and perform functional tasks for a user, such as getting and displaying data, manipulating data, storing data, and so on. Although these functions can seem to be benign, when enabled across the Web they can have some unintended consequences. The ability to read data from a hard drive and display it on the screen is essential for many programs, but when the program is downloaded and run from the Internet and the data is, without the knowledge of the user, sent across the Internet to an unauthorized user, this enables a program to spy on a user and steal data. Writing data to the hard drive can also cause deletions if the program doesn't write the data where the user expects. Sun recognized these dangers and envisioned three different security policies for Java that would be implemented via the browser and JVM, providing different levels of security. The first policy is to not run Java programs at all. The second restricts Java program functionality when the program is not run directly from the system's hard drive—programs being directly executed from the Internet have severe restrictions that block disk access and force other security-related functions to be performed. The last policy runs any and all Java programs as presented.

Most browsers adopted the second security policy, restricting Java functionality on a client unless the program was loaded directly from the client's hard drive. Although this solved many problems initially, this also severely limited functionality. Today, browsers allow much more specific granularity on security for Java, based on security zones and user settings.

JavaScript is a form of Java designed to be operated within a browser instance. The primary purpose of JavaScript was to enable features such as validation of forms before they are submitted to the server. Enterprising programmers found many other uses for JavaScript, such as manipulating the browser history files, now prohibited by design. JavaScript actually runs within the browser (see Figure 5-9), and the code is executed by the browser itself. This has led to compatibility problems, and not just between vendors, such as Microsoft and Netscape, but between browser versions.

Although JavaScript was designed not to be able to directly access files or network resources, except through the browser functions, this has not proven to be as secure as desired. This fault traces back to a similar fault in the Java language, where security was added on afterwards, without the benefit of a comprehensive security model. So, although designers

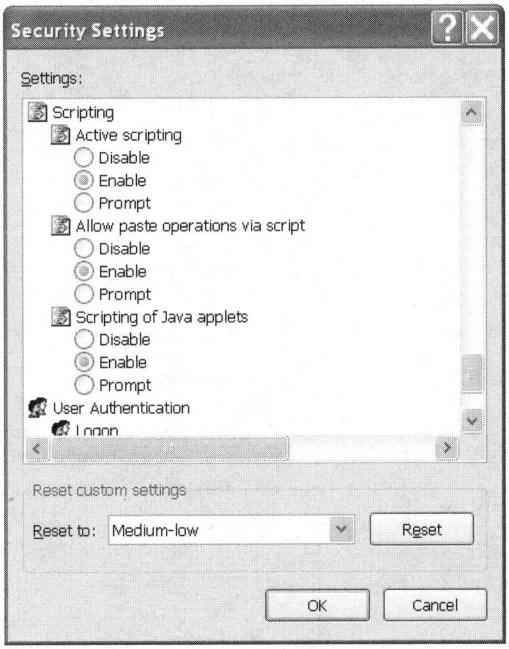

Figure 5-9
JavaScript settings in Microsoft Internet Explorer

put thought and common sense into the design, the lack of a comprehensive security model left some security holes. For instance, a form could submit itself via e-mail to an undisclosed recipient, either eavesdropping, or worse spamming or causing other problems—imagine your machine sending death threat e-mails to high-level government officials from a rogue JavaScript implementation.

Further, most browsers do not have a mechanism to halt a running script short of aborting the browser instance, and even this may not be possible if the browser has stopped responding to commands. Malicious JavaScripts can do many things, including opening two new windows every time you close one, each with the code to open two more. There is no way out of this one, short of killing the browser process from the operating system. JavaScripts can also spoof a user into thinking they are communicating with one entity, when in fact they are communicating with another. For example, a window may open asking whether you want to download and execute the new update from "http://www.microsoft.com..../update.exe", and what is covered by the ellipsis (three dots (...)) is actually "www.microsoft.com.attacker.org/"—the user just assumes this is a Microsoft address that is cut short by space restrictions on the display.

The number of ways a JavaScript can interact with a system is so high, with so many opportunities for malicious code, that the best advice is not to run JavaScripts or Java applets unless you trust the source. Again, browsers have the ability to limit Java functionality as shown in Figure 5-10 for Internet Explorer and Figure 5-11 for Netscape Communicator. A common recommendation for high-security clients is to disable JavaScript completely. Although this reduces the functionality, it also reduces the outside threat to a system.

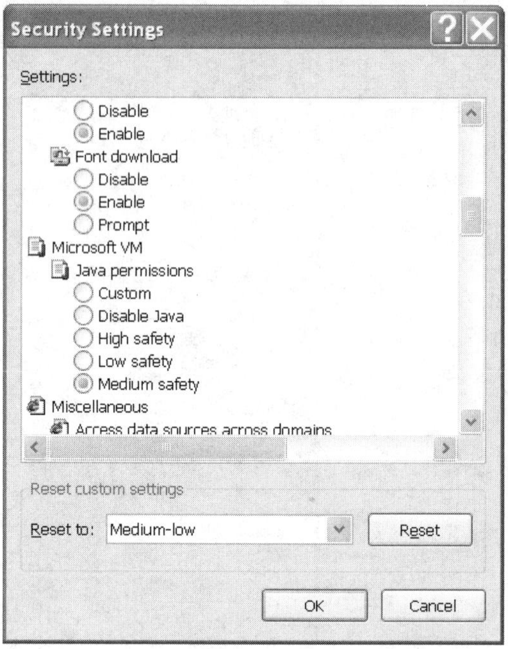

Figure 5-10
Java configuration options in Microsoft Internet Explorer

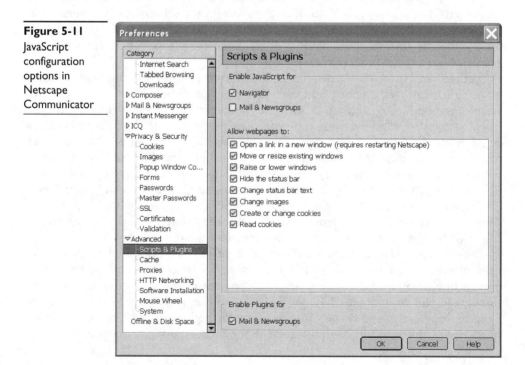

Figure 5-11
JavaScript configuration options in Netscape Communicator

As a browser scripting language, JavaScript is here to stay. Its widespread popularity for developing applets such as animated clocks, mortgage calculators, simple games, and the like will overcome its buggy nature and poor level of security. Similarly, Java as a development language is also here to stay, although it may never live up to its initial hype and will continue to have security issues. Both of these technologies boast many skilled developers, low learning curves (because of their heritage in the C language), and popularity in computer science courses. When viewed as a total package, the marketplace has decided that the benefits outweigh the drawbacks, and these two technologies will be a cornerstone for much Internet programming development.

ActiveX   *Browser plug-in*

ActiveX is the name given to a broad collection of APIs, protocols, and programs developed by Microsoft to automatically download and execute code over an Internet-based channel. The code is bundled together into an ActiveX control and given an .ocx extension. These controls are referenced in HTML using the **<object>** tag. ActiveX is a tool for the Windows environment and can be extremely powerful. ActiveX can do simple things, such as enable a browser to display a custom type of information in a particular way, and it can also perform complex tasks, such as update the operating system and application programs. This range of abilities gives ActiveX a lot of power, but this power can be abused as well as used for good purposes.

Microsoft Internet Explorer has several options to control the execution of ActiveX controls, as illustrated in Figure 5-12.

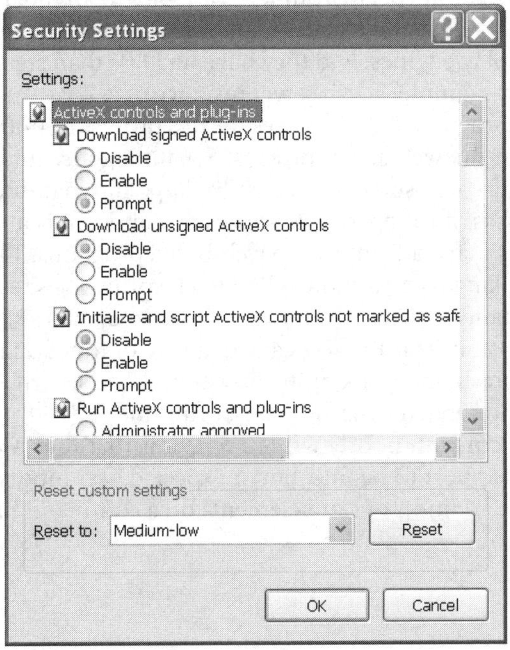

Figure 5-12

Some of the ActiveX control options in Microsoft Internet Explorer

To enable security and consumer confidence in downloaded programs such as ActiveX controls, Microsoft developed Authenticode, a system that uses digital signatures and allows Windows users to determine who produced a specific piece of code and whether or not the code has been altered. As in the case of Java, safety and security are different things, and Authenticode promotes neither in reality. Authenticode provides limited accountability at the time of download and guarantees that the code has not been changed since the time of signing. Authenticode does not identify whether a piece of code will cause damage to a system, nor does it regulate how code is used. A perfectly safe ActiveX control under one set of circumstances may be malicious if used improperly. As with a notary's signature, recourse is very limited—if code is signed by a terrorist organization and the code ruins your machine, all Authenticode did was make it seem legitimate. It is still incumbent upon the user to know from whom they are getting code and to determine whether or not they trust that organization.

Critics of Authenticode and other code-signing techniques are not against code signing, for this is a universally recognized good thing. What the critics argue is that code signing is not a panacea for security issues and that marketing it as doing more than it really does is irresponsible. Understanding the nuances of security is important in today's highly technical world, and leaving the explanations to marketing departments is not the ideal solution.

CGI

The Common Gateway Interface (CGI) was the original method of having a web server execute a program outside the web server process, yet on the same server. The intent was to pass information via environment variables to an independent program, execute the program, and return the results to the web server for display. Web servers are presentation and display engines, and they have had less than stellar results when used in other fashions. For example, a web server instance may have numerous independent connections, and a program failure that results in a process bounce can affect multiple users if it is run within the web server process. Separating any time consuming and more risky programming cores, such as database lookups and manipulation, complex calculations, and other tasks, into separate processes was and still is a prudent idea.

CGI offers many advantages to web-based programs. The programs can be written in a number of languages, although Perl is a favorite. These scripted programs embrace the full functionality of a server, allowing access to databases, UNIX commands, other programs, and so on. This provides a wide range of functionality to the web environment. With this unrestrained capability, however, come security issues. Poorly written scripts can cause unintended consequences at runtime.

The problem with poorly written scripts is that they are not always obvious. Sometimes scripts appear to be fine, but unexpected user inputs can have unintended consequences. The addition of extra elements on a command line, for example, can result in dramatically different outputs. The use of the Perl backquote function allows a user to programmatically encode user input to a UNIX shell, and this works properly given proper user input, but if the user appends **& /bin/ls -l** to a proper input, this could generate a directory listing of the cgi-bin directory, which in turn gives away script names for future exploitation attempts. Permitting users to execute other programs in such an uncontrolled fashion led many ISPs to prohibit the use of CGI scripts unless they were specifically approved by the ISP. This led to considerable overhead and code checking to ensure clean code and validated user inputs.

A variety of books have been written on how to code securely, and CGI has benefited. Properly coded, CGI offers no more and no less risk than any other properly coded solution. CGI's loss was that it was first and was abused first, and many developers learned by making mistakes early on CGI. On UNIX systems, CGI offers the ultimate in programmable diversity and capability, and now that security standard practices have been learned and put into use, the system is seeing new popularity.

Server-Side Scripts

CGI has been replaced in many web sites through newer server-side scripting technologies such as Java, Active Server Pages (ASP), and PHP. All of these technologies operate in much the same fashion as CGI: they allow programs to be run outside the web server and to return data to the web server to be served to end users via a web page. Each of these newer technologies has advantages and disadvantages, but all of them have stronger security models than CGI. With these security models comes reduced functionality and, as each is based on a different language, the learning curves are steeper. Still, the need for adherence to programming fundamentals exists in these newer technologies—code must be well designed and well written to avoid the same vulnerabilities that exist in all forms of code. Buffer overflows are still an issue, even with these newer technologies. Changing languages or technologies does not eliminate the basic security problems associated with incorporating open-ended user input into code. Understanding and qualifying user responses before blindly using them programmatically is essential to the security of a system.

Cookies

Cookies are small chunks of ASCII text passed within an HTML stream to temporarily store data in a web browser instance. Invented by Netscape, cookies pass back and forth between web server and browser and act as a mechanism to maintain state in a stateless world. *State* is a term that describes the dependence on previous actions. By definition, an HTTP session served by a web server is stateless—each request is completely independent of all previous requests, and the server has no memory of previous requests.

This dramatically simplifies the function of a web server, but it also significantly complicates the task of providing anything but the most basic functionality in a site. Cookies were developed to bridge this gap. Cookies are passed along with HTML data through a Set-Cookie message in the header portion of an HTML transaction, or via script in the HTML body.

A cookie is actually a series of name-value pairs that is stored in memory during a browser instance. The specification for cookies established several specific name-value pairs for defined purposes. Additional name-value pairs may be defined at will by a developer. The specified set of name-value pairs include the following:

- **Expires=** This specifies when the cookie expires. If no value exists, then the cookie is only good during the current browser session and will not be persisted to the user's hard drive. Should a value be given, the cookie will be written to the user's machine and persisted until this datetime value occurs.

- **Domain=** This name-value pair specifies the domain where the cookie is used. Cookies were designed as memory-resident objects, but as the user or data can cause a browser to move between domains, say from comedy.net to jokes.org, then some mechanism needs to tell the browser which cookies belong to which domains.

- **Path=** This name-value pair further resolves the applicability of the cookie into a specific path within a domain. If path=/directory, the cookie will only be sent for requests within /directory on the given domain. This allows a level of granular control over the information being passed between the browser and server, and it limits unnecessary data exchanges.

- **Secure** The presence of the keyword [secure] in a cookie indicates that it is only to be used when connected in an SSL/TLS session. This does not indicate any other form of security, as cookies are stored in plaintext on the client machine. In fact, one browser-based security issue was the ability to read another site's cookies from the browser cache and determine the values by using a script.

Cookie management on a browser is normally an invisible process, but both Internet Explorer and Communicator have methods for users to examine and manipulate cookies on the client side. Communicator stores the cookies in a long text file (see Figure 5-13). Note the file location in the browser address line. This will vary based on user account, but is generally representative of a default Netscape Communicator installation.

Netscape, the inventor of cookies, has maintained a strong cookie management option within its Communicator product line. Users have the ability to examine, delete, and block individual cookies through this interface, as shown in Figure 5-14.

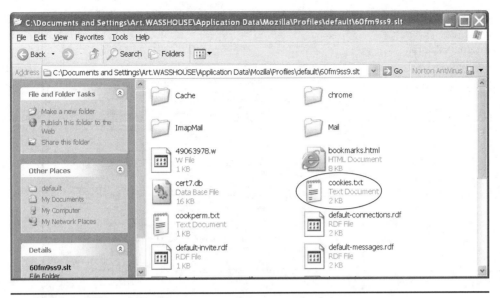

Figure 5-13   Netscape Communicator cookie file

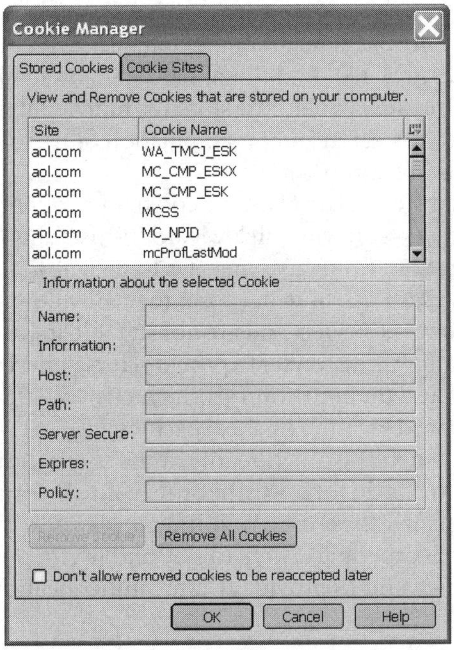

Figure 5-14

Netscape
Communicator
cookie
management
via browser

Figure 5-15
Microsoft
Internet Explorer
delete cookies
option

Internet Explorer has a much simpler interface, with just a Delete Cookies option in the browser (see Figure 5-15). Additional cookie manipulation is done through the file processing system, because cookies are stored as individual files as shown in Figure 5-16. This combination allows easier bulk manipulation, a useful option, as cookies can become quite numerous in short order.

So what good are cookies? Disable cookies in your browser and go to some common sites that you visit—you will quickly learn the usefulness of cookies. Cookies store a variety of information, from customer IDs to data about previous visits. Because cookies are stored on a user's machine in a form that will allow simple manipulation, they must always be considered suspect and are not suitable for use as a security mechanism. They can, however, allow the browser to provide crucial pieces of information to a web server. Advertisers can use them to control which ads you are shown, based on previous ads, and regardless of ad location by site. Specific sites can use them to pass state information between pages, enabling functionality at the user's desired levels. Cookies can also remember your ZIP code for a weather site, your ID for a stock tracker site, the items in your shopping cart—these are all typical cookie uses. In the end analysis, cookies are a part of daily web experience, here to stay and useful if not used improperly (such as to store security data and to provide ID and authentication).

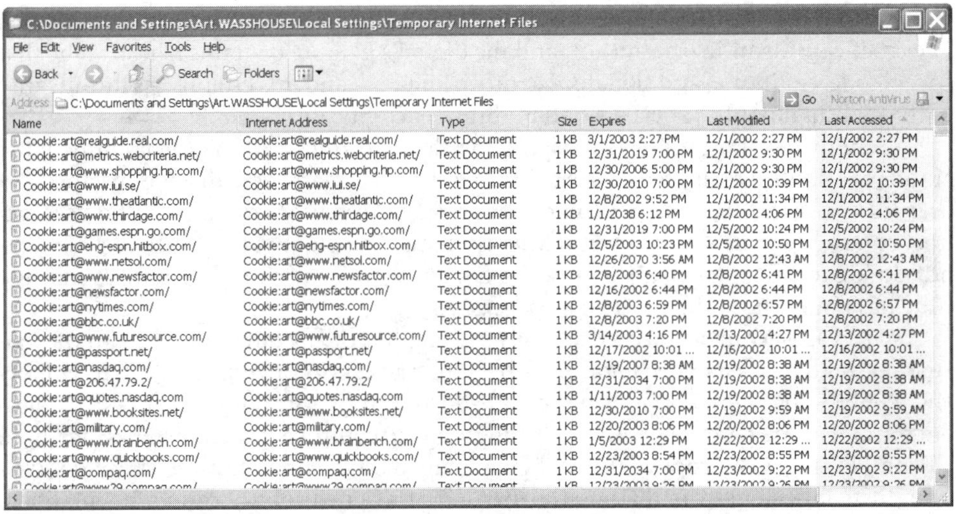

Figure 5-16   Cookie management in Microsoft Internet Explorer

Disabling Cookies

If the user disables cookies in a browser, this type of information will not be available for the web server to use. IETF RFC 2109 describes the HTTP state-management system (cookies) and specifies several specific cookie functions to be enabled in browsers, specifically

- The ability to turn on and off cookie usage
- An indicator as to whether cookies are in use
- A means of specifying cookie domain values and lifetimes

Several of these functions have already been discussed, but to surf cookie-free requires more than a simple step. Telling a browser to stop accepting cookies is a setup option available through an options menu, but this has no effect on cookies already received and stored on the system. To prevent the browser from sending cookies already received, the user must delete the cookies from the system. This bulk operation is easily performed, and then the browser can run cookie-free. There are also several third-party tools that enable even a finer granularity of cookie control.

Signed Applets

Code signing was an attempt to bring the security of shrink-wrapped software to software downloaded from the Internet. Code signing works by adding a digital signature and a digital certificate to a program file to demonstrate file integrity and authenticity. The certificate identifies the author, and the digital signature contains a hash value that covers code, certificate, and signature to prove integrity, and this establishes the integrity of the code and publisher via a standard browser certificate check.

The ability to use a certificate to sign an applet or a control allows the identity of the author of a control or applet to be established. This has many benefits. For instance, if a user trusts content from a particular vendor, such as Sun Microsystems, the user can trust controls that are signed by Sun Microsystems. This signing of a piece of code does not do anything other than identify the code's manufacturer and guarantee that the code has not been modified since it was signed.

A signed applet can be hijacked as easily as a graphic, or any other file. The two ways an attacker could hijack a signed control are by in-line access or copying the file in its entirety and republishing it. *In-lining* is using an embedded control from another site with or without the other site's permission. Republishing a signed control is done much like stealing a GIF or JPEG image—a copy of the file is maintained on the unauthorized site and served from there instead of from the original location. If a signed control cannot be modified, why be concerned with these thefts, apart from the issue of intellectual property? The primary security concern comes from how the control is used. A hacker may be able to use a control in an unintended fashion, resulting in file loss or buffer overflow—conditions that weaken a system and may allow exploitation of other vulnerabilities. A common programming activity is cleaning up installation files from a computer's hard drive after successfully installing a software package. If a signed control is used for this task, and permission has already been granted, then improperly using the control could result in the wrong set of files being deleted. The control will still function as designed, but the issue becomes who it is used by and how. These are concerns not addressed simply by signing a control or applet.

Browser Plug-Ins

The addition of browser scripting and ActiveX components allows a browser to change how it handles data, tremendously increasing its functionality as a user interface. But all data types and all desired functionality cannot be offered through these programming technologies. Plug-ins are used to fill these gaps.

Plug-ins are small application programs that increase a browser's ability to handle new data types and add new functionality. Sometimes these plug-ins are in the form of ActiveX components, which is the form Microsoft chose for its Office plug-in, which enables a browser to manipulate various Office files, such as pivot tables from Excel, over the Web. Adobe has developed Acrobat Reader, a plug-in that enables a browser to read and display Portable Document Format (PDF) files directly in a browser. PDF files offer platform independence for printed documents and are usable across a wide array of platforms—they are a compact way to provide printed information.

Dynamic data such as movies and music can be manipulated by a wide variety of plug-ins, and one of the most popular comes from Real Networks. RealOne player can operate both as a standalone program or run video and audio files in a web page. QuickTime from Apple Computer provides the same type of functionality, and not just for Apple computers, but for Windows PCs as well. Microsoft has responded with their own viewer technology, the Windows Media Player, which also acts as a standalone application in addition to enhancing browser capabilities.

Two strikingly different plug-ins that few computers are without are the Flash and Shockwave plug-ins. These plug-ins from Macromedia can provide developers with the ability to develop striking graphic and cartoon animations that greatly enhance the look and feel of a web experience. The combination of a development environment for developers and plug-in enabled browsers that can display the content has caused these technologies to see widespread use. The result is a tremendous increase in visual richness in web communications, and this, in turn, has made the Web more popular and has increased usage in various demographic segments.

To date, these plug-ins have had a remarkable safety record. Although a plug-in changes a browser and how it can manipulate data, security holes have not been the norm in this area. This does not mean that all plug-ins are safe—far from it. There are as many plug-ins as one could imagine, most from small single-programmer shops, designed for specific purposes that may or may not be needed by most users. Your trust in plug-ins should, as usual, be based on knowing whom you are trusting. Major vendors, such as Macromedia, Adobe, and the like, with their history of product safety, encourage trust. When it comes to Joe's programming house offering a plug-in to enhance 3-D images in porn files—you get what you pay for.

Chapter Review

This chapter covered a lot of web technologies that have been developed in response to challenges presented by the massive interconnectivity and data sharing across the Internet and the World Wide Web. The need for an easy way to handle the complexities of encryption and decryption led to the development of the SSL protocol series and then the TLS series. This session-layer protocol allows for the addition of authentication and data integrity checking for all activities that occur at lower levels, including TCP/IP functionality. SSL/TLS provides seamless integration through SSL/TLS-aware software, alleviating the user from tedious setups and data manipulation.

The World Wide Web has become a major forum for data exchange, and with this widespread application of computing came the need to rapidly retrieve attribute information from data stores for identifying users, resources, and other hierarchical data structures. Directory technologies were thus born from database technologies, providing methods to accomplish these narrowly defined data storage and retrieval tasks. FTP, a longtime protocol used on the Internet, continues to thrive and also has a secure form, the SSH-enabled SFTP.

One of the new possibilities enabled by the Internet's high degree of interconnectivity is downloadable application code that operates in a browser environment. Developers are using web browsers as user interfaces. Standard functionality and user familiarity make web browsers a good choice for many application interfaces. To enable this extensible use, browsers are now designed to be extended via plug-ins and scripting functions. These extensions offer much in the way of functionality and also introduce new levels of security concerns. Java applets, JavaScript, and ActiveX technologies are some of the examples of these new methods that enable developers to write browser-based applications. For more complex work, server-side implementations also exist, such as CGI and server-side scripts.

Cookies aren't just for snacking anymore; they have spread with the Internet and act as tiny data stores on computers everywhere. These small text files are essential little pieces of code that help to maintain state between web pages and web applications, and they can significantly enhance functionality for browser-based applications. As with any technology that offers to increase functionality, cookies also introduce security concerns that need to be understood and managed appropriately.

Questions

1. A cookie is

   A. A piece of data in a database that enhances web browser capability

   B. A small text file used in HTTP exchanges

   C. A segment of script to enhance a web page

   D. A favorite snack of web developers, so they named a program after it

2. The use of certificates in SSL is similar to

   A. A receipt proving purchase

   B. Having a notary notarize a signature

   C. A historical record of a program's lineage

   D. None of the above

3. SSL can be used to secure

   A. POP3 traffic

   B. HTTP traffic

   C. SMTP traffic

   D. All of the above

4. SFTP uses which method to secure its transmissions?

   A. IPsec

   B. VPN

   C. SSH

   D. SSL

5. Security for JavaScript is established by whom?

   A. The developer at the time of code development

   B. The user at the time of code usage

C. The user through browser preferences

D. Security for JavaScript is not necessary—the Java language is secure by design

6. ActiveX can be used for which of the following purposes?

A. Add functionality to a browser

B. Update the operating system

C. Both A and B

D. Neither A nor B

7. CGI has a weakness in its implementation because

A. It offers almost unlimited operating system access and functionality on a UNIX box

B. It is limited to Windows operating systems only

C. It is difficult to program in

D. It has a proprietary interface

8. The keyword [**secure**] in a cookie

A. Causes the system to encrypt its contents

B. Prevents it from passing over HTTP connections

C. Tells the browser that the cookie is a security upgrade

D. None of the above

9. Code signing is used to

A. Allow authors to take artistic credit for their hard work

B. Provide a method to demonstrate code integrity

C. Guarantee code functionality

D. Prevent copyright infringement by code copying

10. SSL provides which of the following functionality?

A. Data integrity services

B. Authentication services

C. Data confidentiality services

D. All of the above

11. SSL uses which port to carry HTTPS traffic?

A. TCP port 80

B. UDP port 443

C. TCP port 443

D. TCP port 8080

12. SSL protocol is performed at what level of the OSI model?

    A. Application layer, level 7

    B. Session layer, level 5

    C. Network layer, level 3

    D. Transport layer, level 4

13. To establish an SSL connection for e-mail and HTTP across a firewall, you must

    A. Open TCP ports 80, 25, 443 and 223

    B. Open TCP ports 443, 465, and 995

    C. Open a TCP port of choice and assign it to all SSL traffic

    D. Do nothing; SSL tunnels past firewalls

14. Directories are characterized by

    A. Read-only data

    B. Attribute type data

    C. More functionality than a simple database

    D. Better security model than a database

15. To prevent the use of cookies in a browser, a user must

    A. Tell the browser to disable cookies via a setup option

    B. Delete all existing cookies

    C. All of the above

    D. The user need do nothing—by design, cookies are necessary and cannot be totally disabled

Answers

1. **B.** Cookies are small pieces of ASCII text used in HTTP transfers to exchange data between client and server.

2. **B.** A certificate acts as a notary, providing a method of determining authenticity through a third party.

3. **D.** All of the above—SPOP3 is POP3 secured, HTTPS is secure HTTP, and SSMTP is secure SMTP.

4. **C.** SFTP uses SSH to enable secure file transfers.

5. **C.** JavaScript security is ultimately the responsibility of the end user, and the options exist in browsers to select various security levels or even disable it altogether.

6. **C.** ActiveX can be used to distribute all kinds of software and modifications to existing software.

7. **A.** Unlimited access to operating system functionality makes many CGI scripts security hazards to the system, and special care is required in their design and implementation.

8. **B.** Cookies with the **[secure]** tag are only passed by browsers over HTTPS connections.

9. **B.** Code signing includes data integrity checking through a hash value.

10. **D.**

11. **C.**

12. **B.** SSL operates at the session layer of the OSI model and hence can secure TCP/IP traffic.

13. **B.** HTTP uses 443, SSMTP uses 465, and POP3 uses 995.

14. **B.** Directories are used primarily for reading attribute type data to support fast lookups and searches.

15. **C.** The user must do both A and B. A will prevent future cookies from interacting, but B is necessary to stop cookies already downloaded from being passed back to the server on subsequent visits.

Wireless and Instant Messaging

In this chapter, you will
- Learn about the security implications of wireless networks
- Learn about the security implications of instant messaging

Wireless and instant messaging are two topics of great importance to computer and network security. Wireless network applications are very important to understand because the risks inherent in broadcasting a network signal across public airwaves are tantamount to posting all your company's passwords by the front door of your building. Instant messaging is another important application to people who control security, as currently, it can be hard to suppress these applications. When they are installed on any networked machine they can allow not only unencrypted chat traffic to and from the Internet-based messaging servers, but also file transfer capabilities.

Wireless

Wireless networking is the transmission of packetized data by means of a physical topology not using direct physical links. We will narrow this definition to apply to networks that use radio waves to carry the signals, over either public or private bands. While there are proprietary applications that use point-to-point technology with narrowband radios and highly directional antennas, this technology is not common enough to produce any significant research into its vulnerabilities, and anything that was developed would have little usefulness. So we will focus on point-to-multipoint systems, the two most common of which are the Wireless Application Protocol (WAP) and IEEE 802.11. The Wireless Application Protocol is a system developed to send data to small handheld devices such as cellular phones, wireless e-mail handhelds, and PDAs. The 802.11 protocol has been standardized by the IEEE for wireless local area networks. It has two versions currently in production, 802.11b and 802.11a. At the time of writing, a third standard, 802.11g, remains under development. While it is an IEEE draft specification, some manufacturers are already shipping products based upon it. This situation leads many people to think back to the 56K modem market, where manufacturers did something similar before V.90 was actually published. In the case of 802.11g, some equipment fails to interoperate with equipment from other manufacturers because of different implementation of the 802.11g draft.

The 802.11b standard was the first to market, 802.11a followed, and at the time of writing 802.11g products are just becoming available. The security world ignored wireless for a long time, and then within the space of a few months, it seemed like everyone was attempting to breach the security of wireless networks and transmissions. One reason that wireless suddenly found itself vulnerable is because wireless targets are so abundant and so unsecured, simply because they are not necessarily attached to crucial infrastructure. The dramatic proliferation of these inexpensive products has made the security ramifications of the protocol astonishing. No matter what the system, wireless security is a very important topic as more and more applications are designed to use wireless to send data. Wireless is particularly problematic from a security standpoint because there is no control over the physical layer of the traffic. In most wired local area networks, the administrators have physical control over the network and can control to some degree who can actually connect to the physical medium. This prevents large amounts of unauthorized traffic and makes snooping around and just listening to the traffic difficult. Wireless does away with the physical limitations. If an attacker can get close enough to the signal's source as it is being broadcast, he can at the very least listen to the radios talking and capture all the packets for examination. Attackers can also try to modify the traffic being sent, or to send their own traffic to disrupt the system. In this chapter, you will learn of the different types of attacks that wireless networks face.

 TIP Any wireless transmission is subject to interception and should be treated as such. Bluetooth, while not specifically covered in this chapter, can also be a security risk.

WAP and WTLS

Small and inexpensive products have made the wireless market grow by leaps and bounds, as traditional wireless devices such as cellular phones and pagers are replaced by wireless e-mail devices and PDAs. The newer generations of handheld cellular phones also have these features built in. All these new devices have generated a demand for additional services. The Wireless Application Protocol was designed to fulfill these needs. It uses a private-band, point-to-multipoint signal to deliver packet data to small wireless devices. To avoid broadcasting the data in the clear over the airwaves, the designers derived a lightweight encryption protocol called Wireless Transport Layer Security (WLTS) from the current Transport Layer Security protocol in use across the Internet. This new protocol was designed to meet the three fundamental requirements for security: confidentiality, integrity, and authentication. To have security in any network-based protocol, you must have these three things, and WAP is no different. So it's time to see how WTLS implements these three necessary attributes.

Confidentiality

Confidentiality is easy enough in theory: make sure that no one can read the packets that you are sending and receiving but you and the party you are intending to talk to. Confidentiality can be assured in several ways, but because wireless affords no control over the physical medium that the packets are traveling over, there is no way to stop another party from listening in. This is especially true with WAP, as the central aggregation point for the network is the cellular provider's tower. So given that anyone can listen in, the best way to ensure data confidentiality is through the use of data encryption. Encryption is explained in detail later in the book; the simplest explanation is that the data plaintext is encrypted and then sent over the airwaves as ciphertext. The originator and the recipient both have keys to decrypt the data and reproduce the plaintext. This method of ensuring confidentiality is very common, and if the encryption is well designed and implemented, then it is very hard for unauthorized users to take captured ciphertext and reproduce the plaintext that created it. WTLS uses a modified version of the TLS protocol, formerly known as SSL. The WTLS protocol supports several popular bulk encryption algorithms, including DES, Triple DES (more commonly referred to as 3DES), RC5, and IDEA. They can support 40- and 56-bit keys in the case of DES and 3DES, and 40-, 56-, and 128-bit keys in the case of RC5 and IDEA. These algorithms depend on the client and the server having a shared secret. To establish what this shared secret is, WTLS must carry out a key exchange, exactly as TLS does every time you log into a secure web site. WTLS supports several key exchange methods: Diffie-Hellman, Elliptic Curve Diffie-Hellman, and RSA. Both the algorithm used to encrypt the session and the method of key exchange in WTLS are decided during the WTLS handshake.

Integrity

Integrity means reliable information. When you are sending data to and receiving it from a specific place, you want assurances that what you sent is what was received. This is typically accomplished not by making the information completely invulnerable to replacement or substitution, but by giving indications if the information has been tampered with. Typically, this is done by generating a checksum of the message with a one-way hash function. When the receiver gets the data, it hashes it as well and compares the two sums; if they match, then the data was unaltered. WTLS implements integrity through the use of *message authentication codes (MACs)*. A MAC algorithm generates a one-way hash of the compressed WTLS data. WTLS supports the MD5 and SHA MAC algorithms. The MAC algorithm is also decided during the WTLS handshake.

Authentication

Authentication is the process by which each end of the data flow proves that they are who they say they are. This is necessary to prevent information flow to an unintended or unauthorized person. Authentication is typically accomplished by the sending party sending something that proves the sender is who they say they are. The sender will also want assurances that the party they are contacting is whom they mean to send data to.

Authentication can be performed in several ways, including digital certificates, tokens, or simple passwords. A popular way to perform authentication over the Internet is the use of digital certificates, cryptographic messages issued by a trusted third party. The key provided can then be used to encrypt a private shared key to enable ciphered communication. Authentication in WTLS is done with digital certificates; the types of certificates supported by WTLS include the native WTLS type, X509, and X9.68. Authentication is optional in the WTLS protocol; if the client and the server choose to use authentication, then the process begins immediately after the hello exchange. The server will send its certificate and the client will then provide its certificate, if possible, to the server. Once the certificates are processed, authentication is complete.

Security Issues with WTLS

As WTLS implements the three parts of security into the protocol, it also has to allow for the unique requirements of the devices that are using the protocol. The TLS protocol that WTLS is based on is designed around Internet-based computers, machines that have relatively high processing power, large amounts of memory, and sufficient bandwidth available for Internet applications. The PDAs and other devices that WTLS must accommodate are limited in all these respects. Thus WTLS has to be able to cope with small amounts of memory and limited processor capacity, as well as long round-trip times that TLS could not handle well. These requirements are the primary reasons that WTLS has security issues. As the protocol is designed around more capable servers than devices, the specification can allow connections with little to no security. Clients with low memory or CPU capabilities cannot support encryption, and choosing null or weak encryption greatly reduces confidentiality. Authentication is also optional in the protocol, and omitting authentication reduces security by leaving the connection vulnerable to a man-in-the-middle-type attack. In addition to the general flaws in the protocol's implementation, there are several known security vulnerabilities, including those to the chosen plaintext attack, the PKCS #1 attack, and the alert message truncation attack.

The chosen plaintext attack works on the principle of predictable initialization vectors (IVs). By the nature of the transport medium that it is using, WAP, WTLS needs to support unreliable transport. This forces the IV to be based upon data already known to the client, and WTLS uses a linear IV computation. Because the IV is based upon the sequence number of the packet and several packets are sent unencrypted, entropy is severely decreased. This lack of entropy in the encrypted data reduces confidentiality.

Now consider the PKCS #1 attack. PKCS, used in conjunction with RSA encryption, gives a standard for formatting the padding used to generate a correctly formatted block size. When the client receives the block, it will reply to the sender as to the validity of the block. An attacker takes advantage of this by attempting to send multiple guesses at the padding to force a padding error. In vulnerable implementations, WTLS will return error messages providing an oracle decrypting RSA with roughly 2^{20} chosen ciphertext queries.

Alert messages in WTLS are sometimes sent in plaintext and are not authenticated. This fact could allow an attacker to overwrite an encrypted packet from the actual sender with a plaintext alert message, leading to possible disruption of the connection through, for instance, a truncation attack.

TIP WAP is a point-to-multipoint protocol, but can face disruptions or attacks because it aggregates at well known points: the cellular antenna towers.

There has also been some concern over the so-called "WAP GAP." This concern involves confidentiality of information where the two different networks meet, the WAP gateway. WTLS acts as the security protocol for the WAP network, and TLS is the standard for the Internet, so the WAP gateway has to perform translation from one encryption standard to the other. This translation forces all messages to be seen by the WAP gateway in plaintext. This is a weak point in the network design, but from an attacker's perspective it is a much harder target than the WTLS protocol itself. Threats to the WAP gateway can be minimized through careful infrastructure design, such as secure physical location and allowing only outbound traffic from the gateway. There is still a risk of compromise, and an attacker would find a WAP gateway an especially appealing target, as plaintext messages are processed through it from all wireless devices, not just a single user. The solution for this is to have end-to-end security layered over anything underlying, in effect creating a VPN from the endpoint to the mobile device, or to standardize on a full implementation of TLS for end-to-end encryption and strong authentication. Neither of these solutions are currently possible with the majority of mobile devices, but one of them may be a viable solution in the future.

WAP in Sum

As with any wireless protocol, extra care should be taken to ensure that the security of the protocol is not compromised. WAP's biggest weakness is its lack of control over the physical medium of data transmission. The limited nature of the devices also hampers the ability of the security protocols to operate as intended, compromising any real security to be had on WAP networks. However, even wireless implementations intended for full-power computers don't always provide security, as you will see in the next section.

802.11

The 802.11b protocol was an IEEE standard that was ratified in late 1999, launching a range of products that would open the way to a whole new genre of attacks for the attackers and a new series of headaches for security administrators everywhere. This was a new standard for sending packetized data traffic over radio waves in the unlicensed 2.4 GHz band. As the products matured and became easy to use and affordable, security experts started to deconstruct the limited security that had been built into the standard. The 802.11a protocol is another standard for wireless networking, but it works only to improve the speed of the network and does not have security updates. At the time of writing, 802.11g has just started to appear on the market (when I say 802.11g, however, I mean the 802.11g draft specification, as the IEEE has not ratified the standard). This technology has been focused on making traffic in the 2.4 GHz band run at the data rates supported by the 802.11a's 5 GHz band. While the draft standard does support a longer WEP key, this does not solve the problems with WEP. What this means is that for security purposes, 802.11b and 802.11g are virtually identical. Now several new IEEE standards for wireless networks are also being worked on, but only one of them deals with increasing the security in 802.11. We will go over the 802.11b and 802.11a protocols and then discuss the security problems involved with them as well as some proposed solutions.

 TIP   The best place for current 802.11 standards and upcoming draft standard information is in the RFCs. You can find them at www.ietf.org/rfc.html.

The 802.11b protocol provides for multiple-rate Ethernet over 2.4 GHz spread-spectrum wireless. It provides transfer rates of 1 Mbps, 2 Mbps, 5.5 Mbps, and 11 Mbps and typically uses direct-sequence spread spectrum (DSSS). The most common layout is a point-to-multipoint environment with the available bandwidth being shared by all users. Typical range is roughly 100 yards indoors and 300 yards outdoors line of sight.

The 802.11a protocol is newer, with products only recently becoming available. It operates in the 5 GHz spectrum using orthogonal frequency division multiplexing (OFDM). Supporting rates of up to 54 Mbps, it is the faster brother of 802.11b. Although it is faster, the higher frequency used by 802.11a shortens the usable range of the devices. The 802.11g draft uses portions of both of the other standards: it uses the 2.4 GHz band for greater range but uses the OFDM transmission method to achieve the faster 54 Mbps data rates.

All these protocols operate in bands that are "unlicensed" by the FCC. This means that people operating this equipment do not have to be certified by the FCC, but it also means that the devices could possibly share the band with other devices, such as cordless phones, CCTV wireless transceivers, and other similar equipment. This other equipment can cause interference with the 802.11 equipment, possibly causing speed degradation. The 802.11 protocol designers knew that there were going to be some security concerns and attempted to build provisions into the 802.11 protocol that would ensure adequate security. The 802.11 standard includes attempts at rudimentary authentication and confidentiality controls. Authentication is handled in its most basic form by the 802.11 access point forcing the clients to perform a handshake when attempting to "associate" to the AP. Association is the process needed before the AP will allow the client to talk across the AP to the network. Association occurs only if the client has all the correct parameters needed in the handshake, among them the *service set identifier (SSID)*. This SSID setting should limit access to only the authorized users of the wireless network.

The designers of the standard also attempted to maintain confidentiality by introducing Wired Equivalent Privacy (WEP). WEP uses the RC4 stream cipher to encrypt the data as it is transmitted through the air. This encryption is synchronous and based upon a key shared by the AP and all the clients using the AP. WEP comes in both 40- and 104-bit key strengths, typically advertised as 60 and 128 bit. The 802.11a and 802.11g products typically have support for 152-bit WEP, but this greater key length does not affect the weaknesses. To understand what security problems 802.11 has, you must first look at some of the reasons it got to be as prominent a technology as it is.

Wireless networks came along in 2000 and became very popular. For the first time, it was possible to have almost full-speed network connections without having to be tied down to an Ethernet cable. The technology quickly took off, allowing prices to drop into the consumer range. Once the market shifted to focus on customers who were not necessarily technologists, the products also became very easy to install and operate. Default settings were designed to get the novice users up and running without having to alter anything substantial, and products were billed to be plug-in and work. These developments further enlarged the market for the low-cost, easy-to-use wireless access points. Then attackers realized that instead of attacking machines over the Internet, they could drive around and seek out these APs. Having physical control of an information asset is critical to its security. Physical access to a machine will enable an attacker to bypass *any* security measure that has been placed on that machine.

Typically, access to actual Ethernet segments is protected by physical security measures. This structure allows security administrators to plan for only internal threats to the network and gives them a clear idea of the types and number of machines connected to it. Wireless networking takes the keys to the kingdom and tosses them literally out the window and into the parking lot. A typical wireless installation broadcasts the network right through the physical controls that are in place. An attacker can now drive up and have the same access as by plugging into an Ethernet jack inside the building—in fact better access, because 802.11 is a shared medium, allowing sniffers to view all packets being sent to or from the AP and all clients. These access points were also typically behind any security measures the companies had in place, such as firewalls and IDSs. This kind of access into the internal network has caused a large stir among computer security professionals, and eventually, the media. War-driving, war-flying, war-walking, war-chalking—all of these terms have been splayed across security article after security article. However, wireless is a popular target for several reasons, as mentioned before: the access gained from wireless, the lack of default security, and the wide proliferation of devices.

There are also other reasons. The first of these is anonymity: an attacker can probe your building for wireless access from the street. Then he can log packets to and from the AP without giving any indication that an attempted intrusion is taking place. The attacker will announce his presence only if he attempts to associate to the access point. Even then, an attempted association is recorded only by the MAC address of the wireless card associating to it, and most APs do not have alerting functionality for when users associate to it. This fact gives administrators a very limited view of who is gaining access to their network, if they are even paying attention at all. It gives attackers the ability to seek out and compromise wireless networks with relative impunity.

The second reason is the low cost of the equipment needed. A single wireless access card costing less than a hundred dollars can give access to any unsecured access point within driving range. The final reason for the popularity of attacking wireless is the relative ease compared to other target hosts. Windows-based tools for locating and sniffing

PART III

wireless-based networks have turned anyone who can download files from the Internet and has a wireless card into a potential attacker.

The most common tools for an attacker to use are reception-based programs that will listen to the beacon frames put out by other wireless devices and programs that will promiscuously capture all traffic. The most widely used of these programs is called Netstumbler by Marius Milner, shown in Figure 6-1. This program listens for the beacon frames of access points that are within range of the card attached to the Netstumbler computer. When it receives them, it logs all available information about the access point for later analysis. If the computer has a GPS unit attached to it, the program also logs the access point's coordinates. This information can be used to return to the access point, or to plot maps of access points in a city. This is a Windows-based application, but there are programs that work on the same principle for Mac, BSD, Linux, and other operating systems.

Once an attacker has located a network, and assuming that they cannot directly connect and start active scanning and penetration of the network, they will use the best attack tool there is: a network sniffer. The network sniffer, when combined with a wireless network card it can support, is a powerful attack tool, as the shared medium of a wireless network exposes all packets to interception and logging. Popular wireless sniffers are Ethereal and WildPackets AiroPeek. Regular sniffers used on wireline Ethernet have also been updated to include support for wireless, with a popular example being Sniffer Pro 4.0, shown in Figure 6-2.

Specialized sniffer tools have come out recently, designed with a single objective, to crack WEP keys. Wired Equivalent Privacy is the encryption protocol that 802.11 uses to attempt to ensure confidentiality of wireless communications. Unfortunately, it has turned out to have several problems. These weaknesses are specifically targeted for attack by the specialized sniffer programs. They work by exploiting weak initialization vectors in the encryption algorithm. To exploit this weakness, you need a certain number of ciphertext packets; once you have captured enough packets, however, the program

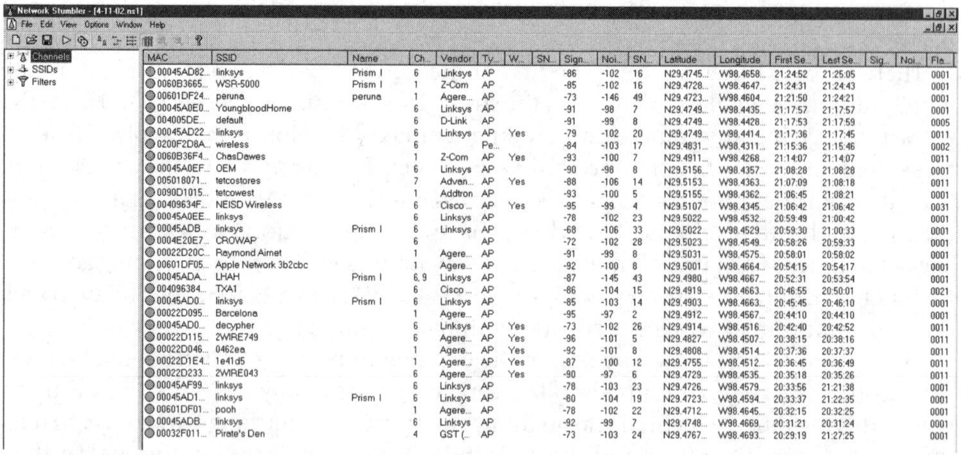

Figure 6-1 Netstumbler on a Windows PC

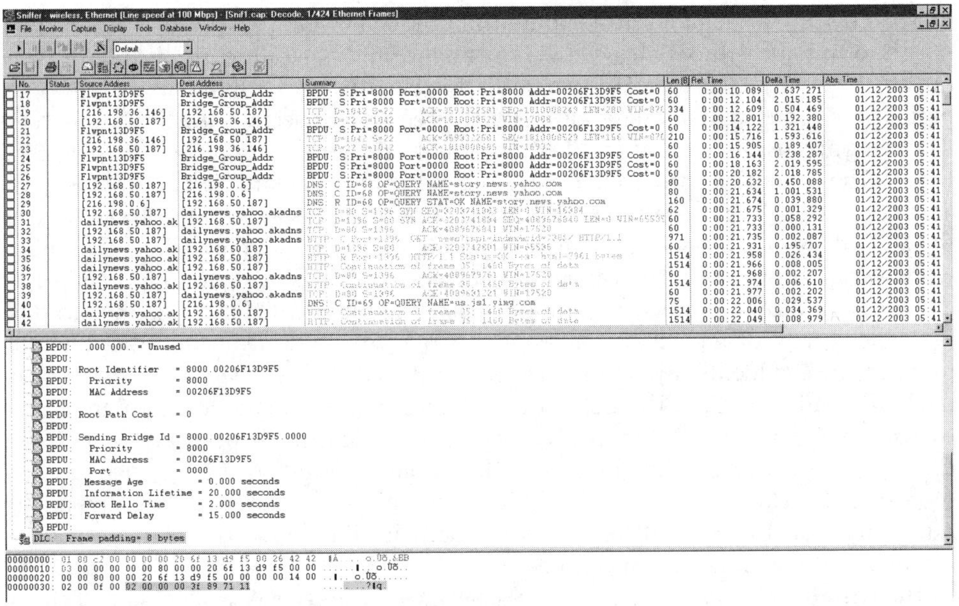

Figure 6-2   Sniffer Pro on a Windows PC

can very quickly decipher the encryption key being used. WEPCrack was the first available program to use this flaw to crack the WEP keys; however, WEPCrack depends on a dump of actual network packets from another sniffer program. AirSnort is a standalone program that captures its own packets; once it has captured enough ciphertext, it will provide the WEP key of the network.

All of these tools are used by the wireless attacker to compromise the network. They are also typically used by security professionals when doing a wireless site survey of an organization. The site survey has a simple purpose: to minimize the available wireless signal being sent beyond the physical controls of the organization. By using the sniffer and finding access point beacons, a security official can determine which access points are transmitting into uncontrolled areas. The access point can then be tuned, either by relocation or through the use of directional antennas, to minimize radiation beyond an organization's walls. A proper site survey is an important step in securing a wireless network because the other default tools for securing wireless are so ineffective.

802.11b has primarily two tools for security, one designed solely for authentication, and the other for authentication and confidentiality. The authentication function is known as the service set identifier (SSID). This is a unique 32-character identifier attached to the header of the packet. As this is, hopefully, a unique identifier, only people who know the identifier will be able to complete association to the access point. While this is a good idea in theory, the SSID is sent in plaintext in the packets, so in practice SSID has little security significance—any sniffer can determine the SSID, and some operating systems, Windows XP, for instance, will display a list of SSIDs active in the area and prompt the user to choose which one to connect to. This weakness is magnified by most access points' default setting, to transmit beacon frames. The beacon frame's purpose is to announce the wireless network's presence and capabilities so that WLAN cards can attempt to associate to it. This can be disabled in software for many access points, especially the more sophisticated ones. From a security perspective, the beacon frame is damaging because it contains the SSID, and this beacon frame is transmitted at a set interval. (The default interval is ten times a second.) Since a default access point without any other traffic is sending out its SSID in plaintext ten times a second, you can see why the SSID does not provide true authentication. Scanning programs like Netstumbler work by capturing the beacon frames and thereby the SSIDs of all access points.

WEP is the 802.11 protocol's method for ensuring confidentiality and authentication. WEP encrypts the data traveling across the network with an RC4 stream cipher, attempting to ensure confidentiality. This is a synchronous method of encryption, ensuring some method of authentication. The system depends on the client and the access point having a shared secret "key," ensuring that only authorized people with the proper key have access to the wireless network. WEP supports two key lengths, 40 and 104 bits, though these are more typically referred to as 64 and 128 bits. In 802.11a and 802.11g, manufacturers have extended this to 152-bit WEP keys. This is because in all cases, 24 bits of the overall key length are for the initialization vector.

The IV is the primary reason for the weaknesses in WEP. This IV is sent in the plaintext part of the message, and because the total keyspace is approximately 16 million keys, the same key will be reused. Once the key has been repeated, an attacker has two ciphertexts encrypted with the same key stream. This allows the attacker to examine the ciphertext and retrieve the key. This attack can be improved by examining only packets that have weak IVs, reducing the amount of packets needed to crack the key. Using only weak IV packets, the number of required captured packets is reduced to around four or five million, taking only a few hours on a fairly busy access point. For a point of reference, this means that equipment with an advertised WEP key of 128 bits can be cracked in under a day, whereas to crack a normal 128-bit key would take roughly 2,000,000,000,000,000,000 years on a computer able to attempt one trillion keys a second. As mentioned before, AirSnort is a modified sniffing program that takes advantage of this weakness to retrieve the WEP keys. The biggest weakness of the WEP protocol is that the IV problem exists regardless of key length, because the IV always remains at 24 bits. Most access points also have the capability to lock access in to only known MAC addresses, providing a limited authentication capability. Given sniffers' capacity to grab all active MAC addresses on the network, this capability is not very effective. An attacker simply configures their wireless cards to a known good MAC address.

After the limited security functions of a wireless network are broken, it behaves exactly like a regular Ethernet network and is subject to the exact same vulnerabilities. The host machines that are on or attached to the wireless network are vulnerable just as if they and the attacker were physically connected. Being on the network opens all machines up to vulnerability scanners, Trojan horse programs, virus and worm programs, and traffic interception via sniffer programs. Any unpatched vulnerability on any machine accessible from the wireless segment is now open to compromise.

Knowing all of these things, you can do several things to maximize the security of the wireless network. Even though WEP can be easily broken, employ it to defeat curious passers-by. Enable MAC address limiting on the access point, although this is also a security measure that will defeat only a casual attacker. If possible, disable beacon frames on the access point; this will help to keep your wireless off the majority of access point maps and defeat people that are not attempting a targeted attack against the organization. The most important tool that can be used to ensure that the 802.11 system does not get compromised is a good site survey. Making sure that wireless is not detectable casually will thwart the majority of attempts, as many attackers are seeking only the most simple of targets.

Note that 802.11 security is in the process of being improved. While future standards are attempting to replace WEP with an Advanced Encryption Standard–based protocol, most of the current work is being done on improving authentication. Since the current security and authentication methods are so weak, vendors have been turning to anything to improve the situation. One of the first things that they came up with was 802.1x, which is an authentication protocol designed for regular wired Ethernet networks. It is part of the IETF Extensible Authentication Protocol and uses its authentication framework. It is intended to provide strong authentication of both the client and the server, and then provide a key management structure for the underlying encryption mechanisms.

WEP was designed to provide some measure of confidentiality on an 802.11 network similar to what is found on a wired network, but that has not been the case. Accordingly, new standards are being developed to improve upon WEP. The 802.11i standard is to be the new IEEE standard for security in wireless networks. It will specify the use of 802.1x to provide authentication, and the use of AES as the encryption protocol. The 802.11i standard specifies the use of the Temporal Key Integrity Protocol (TKIP) and the Counter Mode with CBC-MAC Protocol (in full, the Counter Mode with Cipher Block Chaining–Message Authentication Codes Protocol, or simply CCMP). These two protocols have different functions, but they both serve to enhance security. TKIP works by using a shared secret combined with the card's MAC address to generate a new key, which is then mixed with the initialization vector to make per-packet keys that then encrypt a single packet using the same RC4 cipher that traditional WEP uses. This overcomes the WEP key weakness, as a key is used on only one packet. The other advantage to this method is that it can be retrofitted to current hardware with only a software change, unlike AES and 802.1X. CCMP is actually the mode that the AES cipher is used in to provide message integrity. Unlike TKIP, CCMP requires new hardware to perform the AES encryption. This should correct the weaknesses of the WEP protocol.

TIP   Cisco is currently shipping products that support LEAP, their implementation of the TKIP protocol. LEAP enabled products can be configured to be much more secure than other products that do not support dynamic WEP keys.

The 802.1X protocol can support a wide variety of authentication methods and also fits well into existing authentication systems such as RADIUS and LDAP. This allows 802.1X to interoperate well with other systems such as VPNs and dial-up RAS. Unlike other authentication methods such as the Point-to-Point Protocol over Ethernet (PPPoE), 802.1X does not use encapsulation, so the network overhead is much lower. Unfortunately, the protocol is just a framework for providing implementation, so there are no specifics guaranteeing strong authentication or key management. Implementations of the protocol vary from vendor to vendor in method of implementation and strength of security, especially when it comes to the difficult test of wireless security. There are four common ways of implementing 802.1X: EAP-TLS, EAP-TTLS, EAP-MD5, and EAP–Cisco Wireless, or LEAP.

EAP-TLS relies on Transport Layer Security, an attempt to standardize the SSL structure to pass credentials. The standard, developed by Microsoft, uses X.509 certificates and offers dynamic WEP key generation. This means that the organization must have the ability to support PKI in the form of X.509 digital certificates. Also, per-user per-session dynamically generated WEP keys help prevent anyone from cracking the WEP keys in use, as each user individually has their own WEP key. Even if a user were logged onto the access point and transmitted enough traffic to allow cracking of the WEP key, access would be gained to only that user's traffic. No other user's data would be compromised, and the attacker could not use the WEP key to connect to the access point. This standard authenticates the client to the access point, but it also authenticates the access point to the client, helping to avoid man-in-the-middle attacks. The main problem with the EAP-TLS protocol is that it is designed to work with only Microsoft's Active Directory and Certificate Services; it will not take certificates from other certificate issuers. Thus a mixed environment would have implementation problems.

EAP-TTLS (the acronym stands for EAP–Tunneled TLS Protocol) is a variant of the EAP-TLS protocol. EAP-TTLS works much the same way as EAP-TLS, with the server authenticating to the client with a certificate, but the protocol tunnels the client side of the authentication, allowing the use of legacy authentication protocols such as PAP, CHAP, MS-CHAP, or MS-CHAP-V2. This makes the protocol more versatile while still supporting the enhanced security features such as dynamic WEP key assignment.

EAP-MD5, while it does improve the authentication of the client to the access point, does little else to improve the security of your access point. The protocol works by using the MD5 encryption protocol to hash a user's username and password. The problems with this protocol are that it provides no way for the access point to authenticate with the client, and that it does not provide for dynamic WEP key assignment. In the wireless environment, without strong two-way authentication it is very easy for an attacker to perform a man-in-the-middle-type attack. Normally, these type of attacks are difficult to perform, requiring a traffic redirect of some kind, but wireless changes all those rules. By setting up a rogue access point, an attacker can attempt to get clients to connect to it as if it were authorized and then simply authenticate to the real access point, a simple way to have access to the network and the client's credentials. The problem of not dynamically generating WEP keys is that it simply opens up the network to the same lack of confidentiality that a normal access point is vulnerable to. An attacker only has to wait for enough traffic to crack the WEP key, and can then observe all traffic passing through the network.

LEAP is a protocol developed by Cisco to improve wireless security; it was then rolled into the EAP standard. LEAP works much like EAP-MD5 in that the access point accepts the username-password combination and forwards them to the RADIUS server. LEAP differs from EAP-MD5 in that it requires two-way authentication, causing the access point to authenticate to the client as well as the client to the access point. It also generates per-user per-session WEP keys, helping to defeat attackers sniffing the network. One of the drawbacks to using LEAP is that it operates only on Cisco equipment, though other vendors are sure to provide interoperability.

In summation, 802.1x is a very versatile protocol and can add a great deal of security to 802.11 networks.

Because the security of wireless LANs has been ineffective, many users have simply switched to a layered security approach. That is, they have moved their access points to untrustworthy portions of the network and have forced all clients to authenticate through the firewall to a third-party VPN system. The additional security comes at a price of putting more load on the firewall and VPN infrastructure and possibly adding cumbersome software to the users' devices. While wireless can be set up in a very secure manner in this fashion, it can also be set up poorly. Some systems lack strong authentication of both endpoints, leading to possibilities of a man-in-the-middle-type attack. Also, even though the data is tunneled through, IP addresses are still sent in the clear, giving an attacker information about what and where your VPN endpoint is. While VPNs may be the best stopgap measure currently, they need to be properly configured and carefully maintained if they are exposed on wireless LANs. True security will be much improved once the lower layers of encryption are fixed for wireless access points.

802.11 has enjoyed tremendous growth because of its ease of use and popularity, but that growth is threatened by many organizational rules prohibiting its use due to security measures. As you have seen here, the current state of wireless security is very poor, making attacking wireless a popular activity. With the addition of strong authentication and better encryption protocols, wireless should become both convenient and safe.

Instant Messaging

Instant messaging is another technology that has seen widespread acceptance in recent years. With the growth of the Internet threatening to pull customers away from America Online, one of the largest dial-up providers in the U.S., that company had to look at new ways of providing content. One of the things that it started was AIM, or AOL Instant Messenger. Conceived as a way to find people of like interests online, it was modeled after earlier chat programs. With GUI features and enhanced ease of use, it quickly became popular enough for AOL to release to regular users of the Internet as well. With several competing programs, AIM was now feeding the tremendous growth of the instant messaging segment. The programs had to appeal to a wide variety of users, so ease of use was paramount, and security was not a priority. Now that people are used to instant messaging applications, they see the benefit of using them not only for personal chatting on the Internet, but also for legitimate business use. When people install these applications, they unwittingly expose the corporate network to security breaches. Several of the security problems inhere in the nature of the programs themselves, while others are a function of the implementation.

Instant messaging programs are designed to attach to a server, or network of servers, and allow you to talk with other people on the same network of servers in near real time. The nature of this type of communication opens several holes in a system's security. First, the program has to attach to a server, typically announcing the IP address of the originating client. This is not a problem in most applications, but IM identifies a specific user associated with the IP address, making attacks more likely. Also associated with this fact is that for other users to be able to send you messages, the program is forced to announce your presence on the server. So now a user is displaying that their computer is on, and is possibly broadcasting the source IP address to anyone who is looking. This problem is compounded by the tendency for people to run these programs in the background so that they don't miss any messages.

The popular IM clients were not implemented with security in mind. All support sending files as attachments, few currently support encryption, and they do not have a virus scanner built into the file sharing utility. File sharing in any form must be a carefully handled application to prevent the spread of viruses and other malicious code. Chat programs produce security risks because the sharing is done ad hoc between end users, administrators have no control over the quality of the files being sent, and there is no monitoring of the original sources of those files. The only authentication for the files is the human interaction between the two users in question. This kind of vulnerability coupled with a social engineering attack can produce dramatic enough results for CERT to issue an incident note (CERT Incident Note IN-2002-03 Social Engineering Attacks via IRC and Instant Messaging). This personal type of authentication was abused, tricking people into downloading and executing backdoor or Trojan horse programs. A user can also be persuaded autonomously to download and run a file via IM. Several worms exist that attempt, via IM, to get users to download and run the payload. Goner, running via ICQ, asks users to download a screen saver. Choke, spreading via MSN, attempts to get users to download a game; if the game is downloaded, the worm will then attempt to spread to any user the infected user chats with. These worms and ones like it all depend on user interaction to run the payload. This file sharing mechanism bypasses all the server-side virus protection that is part of most organizations' e-mail infrastructure.

One of the largest problems with IM programs is the lack of support for encryption. AIM, ICQ, MSN Messenger, and Yahoo Messenger all currently do not support encryption of the text messages traveling between users. This flaw was not a significant concern while these programs were still primarily used for personal communication, but with businesses moving to adopt the systems, people are not aware of the infrastructure difference between IM and e-mail. Intracompany e-mail never leaves the company's network, but an intracompany instant message typically will do so unless the organization purchases a product and operates an internal IM server. This can and does expose large amounts of confidential business information to anyone who is physically in a spot to monitor and has the desire to capture the traffic.

TIP It is useful to remember that plaintext messages flow in both directions, if a company chooses to set up an internal IM server, then remote users should be using VPN technology to access the IM server.

If you think about how often client information is sent in e-mail between two people at a company, you start to see the danger that sending it via IM creates. IM is an application that is typically installed by the end user, without the knowledge of the administrator. These types of rogue applications have always been a danger to a network's security, but administrators have typically been able to control these types of applications by eliminating the applications' ports through the firewall.

Some instant messaging applications have even been programmed for use as rogue apps. In the event that they can't reach a server on the default ports, they begin to scan all ports looking for one that is allowed out of the firewall. As these applications can connect on any port, including common ones such as 23 Telnet and 80 HTTP, they are very hard to control. These types of security risks go above and beyond the routine security holes generated in IM software that arise as in any other piece of software, through coding errors.

IM applications work only in a networked environment and therefore are forced to accept traffic as well as send it, giving attackers a way to exploit flaws in the code of the program. AIM has had two buffer overflow problems, allowing a remote attacker to gain control of the user's computer. These flaws, which since have been patched, are just the beginning—with the proliferation of these applications, many more bugs are out there waiting to be exploited.

Several things can be done to improve the security of IM now, and new programs will have improved security features. The first thing businesses that use instant messaging should do is to use a local server. Keeping messages within the perimeter of the organization goes a long way to ensuring that confidential information does not get out. Microsoft Exchange can act as an internal IM server, routing employee-to-employee IMs within the organization. Trillian is a new chat client program that works with multiple chat networks; its most significant feature is that it can encrypt the chat messages, on AIM and ICQ networks, that the client sends to the server. While this does not help with file sharing problems, it will provide confidentiality in one direction. To have confidentiality across the entire chat session, both users must be using Trillian. Trillian and other tools exist to provide confidentiality, but to protect the method of file exchange the clients will have to be changed to integrate a virus scanner. These solutions and others should be applied widely to ensure that IM will be done securely.

Instant messaging is an application that can increase productivity by saving communication time, but it's not without risks. The protocol sends messages in plaintext and thus fails to preserve their confidentiality. It also allows for sharing of files between clients, allowing a backdoor access method for files. There are some methods to minimize security risks, but more development has to be done before IM is ready to be implemented in a secure fashion.

Chapter Review

Wireless and instant messaging are security risks anywhere they are installed. While they both have certain benefits, they are relatively new protocols and have not had enough development geared toward security. Wireless offers local network access to anyone within range. Instant messaging offers file sharing and plaintext messaging. When they both have better encryption and more security controls, they will be controllable by security administrators. Until these enhancements are made, both should be implemented with great care to ensure that security is maintained.

Questions

1. What encryption method does WEP use to try to ensure confidentiality of 802.11 networks?

   A. MD5

   B. AES

   C. RC4

   D. Diffie-Hellman

2. What is the one of the best tools for controlling access to the wireless network?

   A. Firewalls

   B. Samba

   C. Site surveys

   D. Routers

3. How does WTLS ensure integrity?

   A. Sender's address

   B. Message authentication codes

   C. Sequence number

   D. Public key encryption

4. What two key lengths does WEP support?

   A. 1024 and 2048

   B. 104 and 40

   C. 512 and 256

   D. 24 and 32

5. What instant messaging client currently supports encryption?

   A. Yahoo

   B. MSN

    C. Trillian

    D. AIM

6. Why does the SSID provide no real means of authentication?

    A. It cannot be changed.

    B. It is only 24 bits.

    C. It is broadcast in every beacon frame.

    D. SSID is not an authentication function.

7. The 802.1X protocol is a new protocol for Ethernet

    A. Authentication

    B. Speed

    C. Wireless

    D. Cabling

8. Why does WTLS have to support shorter key lengths?

    A. WAP doesn't need high security.

    B. The algorithm cannot handle longer key lengths.

    C. Key lengths are not important to security.

    D. WTLS has to support devices with low processor power and limited RAM.

9. Why is file sharing dangerous on instant messaging protocols?

    A. It bypasses server-based virus protections.

    B. Every file transfer sends corrupted data.

    C. It allows everyone you chat with to view all your files.

    D. File sharing is not dangerous.

10. Why is 802.11 wireless such a security problem?

    A. It has too powerful a signal.

    B. It provides access to the physical layer of Ethernet without needing physical access to the building.

    C. All the programs on wireless are full of bugs allowing buffer overflows.

    D. It draws too much power and the other servers reboot.

11. How are some instant messaging clients similar to attacker tools?

    A. They format your hard drive.

    B. They report your security weaknesses to the Internet.

    C. They run on regular Windows PCs.

    D. They can scan for open ports, trying to find a server.

12. What protocol is WTLS trying to secure?

    A. WAP

    B. WEP

    C. GSM

    D. SSL

13. Why should wireless have strong two-way authentication?

    A. Because you want to know when an attacker connects to the network.

    B. Because wireless is especially susceptible to a man-in-the-middle attack.

    C. Wireless needs authentication to prevent users from adding their home computers.

    D. Two-way authentication is needed so an administrator can ask the wireless user a set of questions.

14. Why is attacking wireless networks so popular?

    A. There are more wireless networks than wired.

    B. They all run Windows.

    C. It's easy.

    D. It's harder and more prestigious.

15. How are the security parameters of WTLS chosen between two endpoints?

    A. There is only one option for every parameter.

    B. The client dictates all parameters to the server.

    C. The user codes them through DTMF tones.

    D. The WTLS handshake determines what parameters to use.

Answers

1. **C.** WEP uses the RC4 stream cipher.

2. **C.** Site surveys are the only listed way to prevent wireless access from being transmitted into hostile areas.

3. **B.** WTLS uses a message authentication code generated with a one-way hash algorithm.

4. **B.** WEP currently supports 104 and 40, though it is sometimes packaged as 64-bit and 128-bit encryption. The initialization vector takes up 24 bits, leaving the 40- and 104-bit key strings.

5. **C.** Trillian, a third-party client, connects to all the major networks and currently supports encryption on the AIM and ICQ networks.

6. **C.** The SSID, or service set identifier, attempts to provide an authentication function, but because it is broadcast in every frame, it is trivial for an attacker to break.

7. **A.** Authentication; 802.1X is the new EAP framework for strong authentication over Ethernet networks.

8. **D.** WAP is designed to be used with small mobile devices, usually with low processor power and limited RAM, so it must support lower-grade encryption.

9. **A.** File sharing over instant messaging protocols is bad because it bypasses server-based virus protection, and most IM clients do not have integration with a virus scanner to check the incoming file.

10. **B.** The 802.11 protocol provides physical-layer access without having to have actual physical access to the building, thus promoting drive-by and parking lot attacks.

11. **D.** Some instant messaging clients are programmed in anticipation of being unauthorized, by scanning for an open outbound port when the default is not available.

12. **A.** WTLS is an attempt to secure the Wireless Application Protocol, or WAP.

13. **B.** Wireless is not connected to any physical medium, making it especially vulnerable to a man-in-the-middle attack.

14. **C.** Attacking wireless networks is extremely popular because it's easy—the majority of wireless networks have no security installed on them. This allows anyone to simply connect and have practically full access to the network.

15. **D.** The WTLS handshake lets both endpoints exchange capabilities, and then the parameters are agreed upon.

PART IV

Security for the Infrastructure

153

Infrastructure Security

In this chapter, you will

- Learn about the types of network devices used to construct networks
- Discover the types of media used to carry network signals
- Explore the types of storage media used to store information
- Consider the use of security zones and topologies to implement network-based security
- Grow acquainted with basic terminology for a series of network functions related to information security

Infrastructure security begins with the actual design of the infrastructure itself. The proper use of the right components not only improves performance but also improves security. Today a computing environment is not isolated from its network components. The network components are a part of the overall computing environment and have become an essential aspect of a total computing environment. From routers, switches, and cables that connect the devices, to the firewalls and gateways that manage communication, from the network design to the protocols employed—all of these items have essential roles, from both performance and security standpoints. In the CIA of security, the A for availability is often overlooked. Yet it is this concept, availability, that has moved computing into this networked framework, and again it is this concept that has a significant role in security. A failure in security can easily lead to a failure in availability, and hence a failure of the system to meet user needs. Security failures can occur in two ways. First, a failure can allow unauthorized users access to resources and data they are not authorized to use, compromising information security. Second, a failure can prevent an authorized user from access to resources and data they are authorized to use. This second failure is often overlooked, but it can be as serious as the first. The primary goal of network infrastructure security is to allow all authorized use and deny all unauthorized use of resources.

Devices

A complete network computer solution in today's business environment consists of more than just client computers and servers. Devices are needed to connect the clients and servers together and to regulate the traffic between them. Devices are also needed to expand this network beyond simple client computers and servers to include yet other devices such as wireless and handheld systems. Devices come in many forms and with many functions, from hubs and switches, to routers, wireless access points, and special-purpose devices such as VPN devices. Each of these devices has a specific network function, and each has a role in maintaining network infrastructure security.

Workstations

Workstations are the device that most users are familiar with. These are the client computers in the client/server model. The workstation is the machine that sits on a user's desktop and is used every day for tasks from e-mail, to spreadsheets, to application programs, even games. If a workstation is connected to a network, it is an important part of the security solution for the network. The list of threats to security from a workstation is large, but much can be done in a few simple steps to provide protection from many of these threats. Although safety is a relative term, the following basic steps should increase workstation security immensely:

- Remove unnecessary protocols such as Telnet, NetBIOS, IPX.
- Remove modems unless needed and authorized.
- Remove all shares that are not necessary.
- Rename the administrator account, securing it with a strong password.
- Remove unnecessary user accounts.
- Install an antivirus program and keep it up to date.
- If the floppy drive is not needed, remove or disconnect it.
- If there is no corporate firewall between machine and Internet, install a firewall.
- Keep the OS patched and up to date.

Antivirus Software for Workstations

Antivirus packages are available from a wide range of vendors. Running a network of computers without this basic level of protection will be an exercise in futility. Even if a virus attack is rare, the time and money spent cleaning it up will more than equal the cost of protection. Even more important, once connected by networks, computers can spread a virus between machines with even greater ease than simple floppy disk transfer. One unprotected machine can lead to problems throughout a network as other machines have to use their antivirus software to attempt to clean up a spreading infection. Even secure networks can fall prey to virus and worm contamination; there are even cases of infection from commercial packages. As important as antivirus software is, it is even more important to keep the virus definitions for the software up to date. Out-of-date definitions can lead to a false sense of security, and many of the most potent virus and worm attacks are the newest ones being developed. The risk associated with a new virus is actually higher than for many of the old ones, which have been eradicated to a great extent by antivirus software.

Workstations are the primary mode of entry for a virus into a network. A virus is a piece of software that must be introduced to the network and then executed on a machine. There are a lot of methods for introducing a virus to a network, but the two most common are transfer of an infected file from another machine and e-mail. A lot of work has gone into software to clean e-mail while in transit and at the mail server. But transferred files are a different matter altogether. People bring files from home, from friends, from places unknown and then execute them on a PC for a variety of purposes. It doesn't matter if it is a funny executable, a game, or even an authorized work application—the virus doesn't care what the original file is, it just uses it to gain access. Even sharing of legitimate work applications can introduce a virus.

The form of transfer is not an issue either; floppy, CD, or FTP, it really doesn't matter. When the transferred file is executed, the virus is propagated. Simple removal of floppy disks does not adequately protect against this threat; nor does training, for users will eventually justify a transfer. The only real defense is an antivirus program that monitors all file movements.

Personal firewalls are another necessity if a machine has an unprotected interface to the Internet. These are seen less often in commercial networks, as it is more cost effective to connect through a firewall server. With the advent of broadband connections for homes and small offices, this needed device is frequently missed. This can result in penetration of a PC from an outside hacker or a worm infection. Worst of all, the workstation may become part of a larger attack against another network, unknowingly joining forces with other compromised machines in a distributed denial of service attack.

The practice of disabling or removing unnecessary devices and software from workstations is also a sensible precaution. If there is no need for a particular service, device, or account, disabling or removing it will prevent unauthorized use by others. Having a standard image of a workstation and duplicating it across a bunch of identical workstations will reduce the workload for maintaining these requirements and reduce total cost of operations. Proper security at the workstation level can increase availability of network resources to users, enabling the business to operate as effectively as possible.

Servers

Servers are the computers in a network that host applications and data for everyone to share. Servers come in many sizes, from small single-CPU boxes that can be less powerful than a workstation to multiple-CPU monsters up to and including mainframes. The operating systems used by servers range from Windows Server to UNIX to MVS and other mainframe operating systems. The OS on a server tends to be more robust than a workstation system and is designed to service multiple users over a network at the same time. Servers can host a variety of applications, including web servers, databases, e-mail servers, file servers, print servers, and application servers for middleware applications.

TIP   The specific security needs for a server can vary depending on the server's specific use, but as a minimum:

- Remove unnecessary protocols such as Telnet, NetBIOS, IPX, FTP.
- Remove all shares that are not necessary.
- Rename the administrator account, securing it with a strong password.
- Remove unnecessary user accounts.
- Keep the OS patched and up to date.
- Control physical access to servers.

The key management issue behind running a secure server setup is to identify the specific needs of a server for its proper operation and enable only items necessary for those functions. Keeping all other services and users off the system improves system throughput and increases security. Once a server has been built and is ready to place into operation, the recording of MD5 checksums on all of its crucial files will provide valuable information later in case of a question concerning possible system integrity after a detected intrusion.

Antivirus Software for Servers

The need for antivirus protection on servers depends a great deal upon the use of the server. Some types of servers, such as e-mail servers, can require extensive antivirus protection because of the services they provide. Other servers (domain controllers and remote access servers, for example) may not require any antivirus software, as they do not allow users to place files on them. File servers will need protection, as will certain types of application servers. There is no general rule, so each server and its role in the network will need to be examined for applicability of antivirus software.

Network Interface Cards (NICs)

To connect a server or workstation to a network, a device known as a *network interface card (NIC)* is used. A NIC is a card with a connector port for a particular type of network connection, either Ethernet or Token Ring. The most common network type in use for local area networks is the Ethernet protocol, and the most common connector is the RJ-45 connector. Figure 7-1 shows a RJ-45 connector (lower) compared to a standard phone connector (upper). Additional types of connectors include coax cable connectors, frequently used with cable modems, from the wall to the cable modem.

The purpose of a NIC is to provide lower-level protocol functionality from the OSI model. As the NIC defines the type of physical layer connection, different NICs are used for different physical protocols. NICs come as single-port and multiport NICs. Most workstations use only a single-port NIC, for only a single network connection is needed. For servers, multiport NICs are used to increase the number of network connections, increasing the data throughput to and from the network.

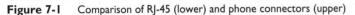

Figure 7-1   Comparison of RJ-45 (lower) and phone connectors (upper)

Hubs

Hubs are pieces of networking equipment that connect devices using the same protocol at the physical layer of the OSI model. The purpose for a hub is to allow multiple machines in an area to be connected together in a star configuration with the hub as the center of the star. This can save significant amounts of cable and is an efficient method of configuring an Ethernet backbone. Hubs are characterized as having all connections share a single collision domain. Hubs are basically simple signal conditioners that connect multiple devices to a common signal. This is equivalent to a party line, and as network traffic increases, it can become limited by collisions. What hubs lose in traffic management ability, they make up for in cost, with small, eight-port hubs being available for as little as $10. The collision issue has made hubs obsolete in newer, higher-performance networks, with low-cost switches and switched Ethernet keeping costs low and usable bandwidth high.

Bridges

Bridges are pieces of networking equipment that connect devices using the same protocol at the physical layer of the OSI model. Bridges can reduce collisions by separating pieces of a network into two separate collision domains, but this only cuts the collision problem in half. Although this is useful, a better solution is to use switches for network connections.

Switches

Switches form the basis for connections in most Ethernet-based local area networks. Although hubs and bridges still exist, in today's high-performance network environment switches have replaced hubs and bridges. A switch has separate collision domains for each port. This means for a particular port, there are two collision domains; one from the port to the client on the downstream side and one from the switch to the network upstream. When full duplex is employed, collisions are virtually eliminated from the two nodes, host and client. This also acts as a security factor in that a sniffer can see only limited traffic, as opposed to a hub-based system, where a single sniffer can see all of the traffic to and from connected devices.

As switches have replaced lower-level network equipment such as hubs and bridges, they are also moving into the network layer of the OSI model. Switches originally operated at the data-link layer, with routing occurring at the network layer. New breeds of switches can now switch at the network layer, bringing switching speed to network layer path optimization. For intranets, switches have become what routers are on the Internet—the device of choice for connecting machines.

Switches can also perform a variety of security functions. Switches work by moving packets from inbound connections to outbound connections. While moving the packets, it is possible to inspect the packet headers and enforce access control lists. Access control lists (ACLs) act as a series of rules governing whether a packet is allowed or blocked from a connection. This is the very function that a firewall uses for its determination, and this same functionality is what allows an 802.1x device to act as an edge device.

NOTE ACLs can be a significant effort to establish and maintain. Creating them is a straightforward task, but judicious use of this capability will yield security benefits with a limited amount of maintenance. This can be very important in security zones such as a DMZ and at edge devices, blocking undesired outside contact while allowing known inside traffic.

Virtual Local Area Networks

The other security feature that can be enabled in switches is the concept of virtual local area networks (VLANs). Cisco defines a VLAN as a "broadcast domain within a switched network," meaning that information is carried in broadcast mode only to devices within a VLAN. Switches that allow multiple VLANs to be defined enable broadcast messages to be segregated into the specific VLANs. If each floor of an office were to have a single switch and you had accounting functions on two floors, engineering functions on two floors, and sales functions on two floors, then separate VLANs for accounting, engineering, and sales would allow separate broadcast domains for each of these groups, even ones that spanned floors. This increases network segregation, increasing throughput and increasing security.

Unused switch ports can be preconfigured into empty VLANs that do not connect to the rest of the network. This significantly increases security against unauthorized network connections. If a building is wired with network connections in all rooms, including multiple connections for convenience and future expansion, then these unused ports become open to the network. One solution is to disconnect the connection at the switch, but this merely moves the network opening into the switch room. The better solution is to disconnect it and disable the port in the switch. One method for doing this is to connect all unused ports into a VLAN that isolates them from the rest of the network.

One of the security concerns with switches is that, like routers, they are intelligent network devices and are therefore subject to hijacking by hackers. Should a hijacker break into a switch and change its parameters, it would be possible to eavesdrop on specific or all communications, virtually undetected. Switches are commonly administered using the Simple Network Management Protocol (SNMP), which has a serious weakness in that it involves sending passwords across the network in the clear. A hacker armed with a sniffer that observes maintenance on a switch can capture the administrative password. This gives the hacker the ability to later come back to the switch and configure it as an administrator. An additional problem is that switches are shipped with default passwords, and if not changed when set up, they offer an unlocked door to a hacker.

CAUTION   To secure a switch, it is important to disable all access protocols other than a secure serial line, or a secure protocol such as Secure Shell (SSH). Using only secure methods to access a switch will limit the exposure to hackers and malicious users. Maintaining secure network switches is even more important than securing individual boxes, for the span of control to intercept data is much wider on a switch, especially if reprogrammed by a hacker.

Routers

Routers are network traffic management devices used to connect different network segments together. Routers operate at the network layer of the OSI model, routing traffic using the network address (typically an IP address) utilizing routing protocols to determine optimal routing paths across a network. Routers form the backbone of the Internet, moving traffic from network to network, inspecting packets from every communication as they move traffic in optimal paths.

Routers operate by examining each packet, looking at the destination address, and using algorithms and tables to determine where to send the packet next. This process of examining the header to determine the next hop can be done in quick fashion. It is also possible to examine the source address and determine whether or not to allow a packet to pass. This allows routers equipped with ACLs to drop packets according to rules. This can be a cumbersome process to set up and maintain, and as the list grows in size, routing efficiency can be decreased. It is also possible to configure some routers to act as quasi–application gateways, performing stateful packet inspection and using contents as well as IP addresses to determine whether or not to permit a packet to pass. This can tremendously increase the time for a router to pass traffic and can significantly decrease router throughput. Configuring ACLs and other aspects of setting up routers for this type of use are beyond the scope of this book.

One serious operational security concern of routers is over the access to a router and control of its internal functions. Like a switch, a router can be accessed using SNMP and programmed remotely. Because of the geographic separation of routers, this can become a necessity, for many routers in the world of the Internet can be hundreds of miles apart, in separate locked structures. Physical control over a router is absolutely necessary, for any device, be it server, switch, or router, if physically accessed by a hacker should be considered compromised, and thus such access must be prevented. As with switches, it is important to ensure that the administrative password is never passed in the clear, only secure mechanisms are used to access the router, and all of the default passwords are reset to strong passwords.

Routers come from numerous vendors and can come in sizes big and small. A typical small home office router for use with cable modem/DSL service is shown in Figure 7-2. Larger routers can handle traffic of up to tens of gigabytes per second per channel, using fiber optic inputs and moving tens of thousands of concurrent Internet connections across the network. These routers can cost hundreds of thousands of dollars and form an essential part of e-commerce infrastructure enabling large enterprises such as Amazon and eBay to serve multiple customers concurrently.

Firewalls

A *firewall* is a network device—hardware, software, or a combination—whose purpose is to enforce a security policy across its connections. It is much like a wall that has a window: the wall serves to keep things out, except those permitted through the window (see Figure 7-3). A security policy acts like the glass in the window; it permits some things to pass, light, while blocking others, air. The heart of a firewall is the security policy that it enforces.

Security policies are a series of rules that define what traffic is permissible and what traffic is to be blocked or denied. These are not universal rules, and there are many different sets of rules for a single company with multiple connections. A web server connected to the Internet may be configured only to allow traffic on port 80 for HTTP, and have all other ports blocked. An e-mail server may have only necessary ports for e-mail open, with others blocked. A key to security policies for firewalls is the same as has been seen for other security policies—the principle of least access. Only allow the necessary access for a function; block or deny all unneeded functionality. How a firm deploys its firewalls determines what is needed for security policies for each firewall.

As will be discussed later, the security topology will determine what network devices are employed at what points in a network. At a minimum, the corporate connection to the Internet should pass through a firewall. This firewall should block all network traffic except that specifically authorized by the security policy. This is actually easy to do: blocking communications on a port is simple, just tell the firewall to close the port. The issue comes in deciding what services are needed and by whom, and thus which ports should be open and which should be closed. This is what makes a security policy useful. The perfect security policy is one that the end user never sees and one that never allows

Figure 7-2 A small home office router for cable modem/DSL use

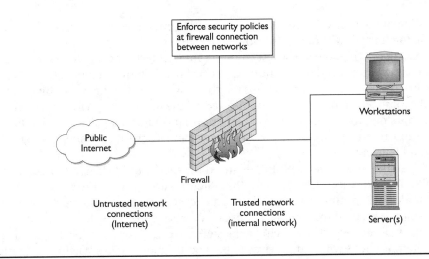

Figure 7-3   Firewall usage

even a single unauthorized packet to enter the network. As with any other perfect item, it will be rare to find the perfect security policy for a firewall.

In order to develop a complete and comprehensive security policy, it is first necessary to have a complete and comprehensive understanding of your network resources and their uses. Once you know what your network will be used for, you will have an idea of what to permit. Also, once you understand what you need to protect, you will have an idea of what to block. Firewalls are designed to block attacks before they get to a target machine. Common targets are web servers, e-mail servers, DNS servers, FTP services, and databases. Each of these has separate functionality, and each of these has separate vulnerabilities. Once you have decided who should receive what type of traffic and what types should be blocked, you can administer this through the firewall.

How Do Firewalls Work?

Firewalls are there to enforce the established security policies. They can do this through a variety of mechanisms, including

- Network Address Translation (NAT)
- Basic packet filtering
- Stateful packet filtering
- ACLs
- Application layer proxies

One of the most basic security functions provided by a firewall is Network Address Translation (NAT). This service allows you to mask significant amounts of information from outside of the network. This allows an outside entity to communicate with an entity inside the firewall without truly knowing its address.

Basic packet filtering, the next most common firewall technique, involves looking at packets, their protocols and destinations, and checking that information against the security policy. Telnet and FTP connections may be prohibited from being established to a mail or database server, but they may be allowed for the respective service servers. This is a fairly simple method of filtering based on information in each packet header, like IP addresses and TCP/UDP ports. This will not detect and catch all undesired packets, but it is fast and efficient.

To look at all packets, determining the need for each and its data, requires stateful packet filtering. Advanced firewalls employ stateful packet filtering to prevent several types of undesired communications. Should a packet come from outside the network, in an attempt to pretend that it is a response to a message from inside the network, the firewall will have no record of its being requested and can discard it, blocking access. As many communications will be transferred to high ports (above 1023), stateful monitoring will enable the system to determine which sets of high communications are permissible and which should be blocked. The disadvantage to stateful monitoring is that it takes significant resources and processing to do this type of monitoring and this reduces efficiency and requires more robust and expensive hardware. However, this type of monitoring is essential in today's comprehensive networks and given the variety of remotely accessible services.

As they are in routers, switches, servers, and other network devices, ACLs are a cornerstone of security in firewalls. Just as you must protect the device from physical access, ACLs do the same task for electronic access. Firewalls can extend the concept of ACLs by enforcing them as well at a packet level when packet-level stateful filtering is performed. This can add an extra layer of protection, making it more difficult for an outside hacker to breach a firewall.

Some high-security firewalls also employ application layer proxies. As the name implies, packets are not allowed to traverse the firewall, but data instead flows up to an application that in turn decides what to do with it. For example, an SMTP proxy may accept inbound mail from the Internet and forward it to the internal corporate mail server. While proxies provide a high level of security by making it very difficult for an attacker to manipulate the actual packets arriving at the destination, and while they provide the opportunity for an application to interpret the data prior to forwarding it to the destination, they generally are not capable of the same throughput as stateful packet inspection firewalls. The trade-off between performance and speed is a common one and must be evaluated with respect to security needs and performance requirements.

Wireless

Wireless devices bring additional security concerns. There is, by definition, no physical connection to a wireless device. Using radio waves or infrared to carry data allows anyone within range access to the data. This means that unless you take specific precautions, you have no control over who can see your data. Placing a wireless device behind a firewall does not do any good, for the firewall stops only physically connected traffic from getting to the device. Outside traffic can come literally from the parking lot directly to the wireless device.

The point of entry from a wireless device to a wired network is performed at a device called a *wireless access point*. Wireless access points can support multiple concurrent devices accessing network resources through the network node they provide. A typical wireless access point can be seen here.

A typical wireless access point

For notebooks and PCs, a PCMCIA adapter for wireless networks is available from several vendors. The following illustration shows one vendor's card—note the extended length used as an antenna. Not all cards have the same configuration, although they all perform the same function, to enable a wireless network connection. Wireless access points and cards must be matched by protocol for proper operation.

A typical PCMCIA wireless network card

PART IV

NOTE To prevent unauthorized wireless access to the network, configuration of remote access protocols to a wireless access point is common. Forcing authentication and verifying authorization is a seamless method of performing basic network security for connections in this fashion. These protocols are covered in Chapter 3.

Some wireless devices, such as those intended for operation on IEEE 802.11 wireless LANs, include security features such as the Wired Equivalent Privacy (WEP) protocol. This is designed to prevent wireless sniffing of network traffic over the wireless portion of the network. WEP is described in Chapter 3.

Modems

Modems were once a slow method of remote connection that was used to connect client workstations to remote services over standard telephone lines. Modem is a shortened form of modulator/demodulator, covering the functions actually performed by the device as it converts analog signals to digital and vice versa. To connect a digital computer signal to the analog telephone line required one of these devices. Today, the use of the term modem has expanded to cover devices connected to special digital telephone lines—DSL modems—and to cable television lines—cable modems. Although these devices are not actually modems in the true sense of the word, the term has stuck through marketing efforts directed to consumers. DSL and cable modems offer broadband high-speed connections and the opportunity for continuous connections to the Internet. Along with these new desirable characteristics come some undesirable ones as well. Although they both provide the same type of service, there are some differences between cable and DSL modems. A DSL modem provides a direct connection between a subscriber's computer and an Internet connection at the local telephone company's switching station. This private connection offers a degree of security, as it does not involve others sharing the circuit. Cable modems are set up in shared arrangements that theoretically would allow a neighbor to sniff a user's cable modem traffic.

Cable modems were designed to share a party line in the terminal signal area, and the cable modem standard, the Data Over Cable Service Interface Specification (DOCSIS), was designed to accommodate this concept. DOCSIS includes built-in support for security protocols, including authentication and packet filtering. Although this does not guarantee privacy, it prevents ordinary subscribers from seeing others' traffic without specialized hardware.

Both cable and DSL services are designed for a continuous connection, which brings up the question of IP address life for a client. Although some services originally used a static IP arrangement, virtually all have now adopted the Dynamic Host Configuration Protocol (DHCP) to manage their address space. A static IP has an advantage of being the same and enabling convenient DNS connections for outside users. As cable and DSL services are primarily designed for client services as opposed to host services, this is not a relevant issue. A security issue of a static IP is that it is a stationary target for hackers. The move to DHCP has not significantly lessened this threat, however, for the typical IP lease on a cable modem DHCP is for days. This is still relatively stationary, and some form of firewall protection needs to be employed by the user.

Cable/DSL Security

The modem equipment provided by the subscription service converts the cable or DSL signal into a standard Ethernet signal that can then be connected to a network interface card (NIC) on the client device. This is still just a direct network connection, without any security device separating the two devices. The most common security device used in cable/DSL connections is a firewall. The firewall needs to be installed between the cable/DSL modem and client computers. Two common methods exist for this in the marketplace. The first is software on each client device. Numerous software companies offer Internet firewall packages, which can cost under $50. Another solution is the use of a cable/DSL router with a built-in firewall. These are also relatively inexpensive, in the $100 range, and can be combined with software for an additional level of protection. Another advantage to the router solution is that most such routers allow multiple clients to easily share a common Internet connection; most can also be enabled with other networking protocols such as VPN. A typical small home office cable modem/DSL router is shown in earlier Figure 7-2. The bottom line is simple: Even if you connect only occasionally and you disconnect between uses, you need a firewall between the client and the Internet connection. Most commercial firewalls for cable/DSL systems come preconfigured for Internet use and require virtually no maintenance other than keeping the system up to date.

RAS

Remote Access Service (RAS) is a portion of the Windows OS that allows the connection between a client and a server via a dial-up telephone connection. Although slower than cable/DSL connections, this is still a common method for connecting to a remote network. When a user dials into the computer system, authentication and authorization are performed through a series of remote access protocols, described in Chapter 3. For even greater security, a callback system can be employed, where the server calls back to the client at a set telephone number for the data exchange.

RAS can also mean Remote Access Server, a term for a server designed to permit remote users access to a network and to regulate their access. A variety of protocols and methods exist to perform this function; they are described in detail in Chapter 3. Once connected to the RAS server, a client has all the benefits of a direct network connection. The RAS server treats its connected clients as extensions of the network. For security purposes, a RAS server should be placed in the DMZ and considered insecure. Additional security checks can be performed at the inner DMZ firewall before access to the internal network is granted.

Telecom/PBX

Private branch exchanges (PBXs) are an extension of the public telephone network into a business. Although typically considered a separate entity from data systems, they are frequently interconnected and have security requirements as part of this interconnection as well as of their own. PBXs are computer-based switching equipment designed to connect telephones into the local phone system. Basically digital switching systems, they can be compromised from the outside and used by phone hackers (phreakers) to make phone calls at the business' expense. Although this type of hacking has decreased with lower-cost long distance, it has not gone away, and as several firms learn every year, voice mail boxes and PBXs can be compromised and the long-distance bills can get very high, very fast.

Another problem with PBXs arises when they are interconnected to the data systems, either by corporate connection or by rogue modems in the hands of users. In either case, a path exists for connection to outside data networks and the Internet. Just as a firewall is needed for security on data connections, one is needed for these connections as well. Telecommunications firewalls are a distinct type of firewall designed to protect both the PBX and the data connections. The functionality of a telecommunications firewall is the same as that of a data firewall; it is there to enforce security policies. Telecommunication security policies can be enforced even to cover hours of phone use to prevent unauthorized long-distance usage through the implementation of access codes and/or restricted service hours.

VPN

A virtual private network (VPN) is a construct used to provide a secure communication channel between users across public networks such as the Internet. As described in Chapter 3, a variety of techniques can be employed to instantiate a VPN connection. The use of encryption technologies allows either the data in a packet to be encrypted or the entire packet to be encrypted. If the data is encrypted, the packets can still be sniffed and observed between source and destination, but the encryption protects the contents from inspection. If the entire packet is encrypted, it is then placed into another packet and sent via tunnel across the public network. Tunneling can protect even the identity of the communicating parties.

The most common implementation of VPN is via IPsec, a protocol for IP security devised for IPv6. This protocol series was back-fitted into the current IP protocol, IPv4, and can be implemented in hardware, software, or a combination of both.

IDS

Intrusion detection systems (IDSs) are systems designed to detect, log, and respond to unauthorized network or host use, both in real time and after the fact. IDSs are available from a wide selection of vendors and are an essential part of network security. These systems are implemented in software, but in large systems, dedicated hardware is required as well. IDSs can be broken into two categories, network-based systems and host-based systems, and there are two primary methods of detection, signature-based and anomaly-based.

Network-based IDS solutions are connected to a segment of the network where they examine all of the passing packets. Using signatures of known attacks, a network IDS can observe misuse as it is initiated and, if operating as a firewall, has the ability to stop it before it occurs. This approach represents an ideal solution but is hampered by two facts. First, seldom is all traffic passed over a single segment in a network. The same segmentation used to increase network bandwidth by separating signals across lines impairs an IDS by hiding a portion of the traffic from its view. The second issue is that not all attacks can be classified according to a signature that can be observed at a packet level. Although an IDS functioning this way can take care of many attacks, it will miss some.

To address the network connectivity and segmentation issue, it is common to place the IDS sensor just outside, or just inside the firewall at the port of entry into the network from the Internet, as shown by the leftmost dashed line in Figure 7-4. This seems like a solution to the segmentation problem except for two additional issues. Large networks can have multiple Internet connections for bandwidth and reliability, and many remote access protocols employ encryption technology that would hide the contents of packets from IDS inspection. To solve this problem, multiple network-based IDS sensors must be deployed at critical points inside a network and then the results combined.

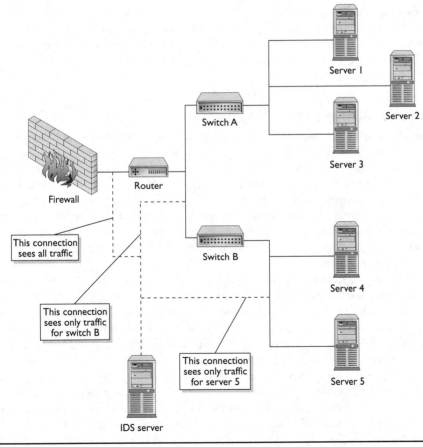

Figure 7-4   IDS location in a network

Host-based IDS solutions provide another method for looking at multiple points in a network. A host-based IDS works by collecting information from all of the servers on the network. Each server has an agent that collects specific performance and usage parameters, such as disk usage, network traffic, and CPU utilization and sends these to the IDS for analysis. The host-based IDS then looks at the collected information and can spot specific trends that have been shown to correlate with unauthorized use. Alerts to unusual activity can then be sent to a network monitoring center for investigation. The main drawback of this type of implementation is simple scaling. Host-based IDSs work very well in smaller networks, but in large commercial networks with hundreds of active servers, the ability to monitor all the traffic becomes an issue.

The other method of analyzing traffic or user behavior, the anomaly method, works by analyzing statistical patterns of usage of a network. Under normal conditions, a pattern of typical network usage is developed and then the system can alert operators to patterns that substantially deviate from this norm. Although this method is great in theory, the problem lies in execution. Anomaly detection works well in detecting large-scale changes and can do so rapidly, even for changes never seen before, the weakness of signatures. But as the level of difference is dialed down to provide finer-grain determination, normal statistical differences such as user behavior, employee movement between machines, and other normal random behavior forces false alarms. Too many false alarms render the system unusable, so research into solving this problem is underway at many locations.

Network Monitoring/Diagnostic

The computer network itself can be considered a large computer system, with performance and operating issues. Just as a computer needs management, monitoring, and fault resolution, so do networks. The Simple Network Management Protocol (SNMP) was developed to perform this function across networks. The idea is to enable a central monitoring and control center to maintain, configure, and repair network devices, such as switches and routers, as well as other network services such as firewalls, IDSs, and remote access servers. SNMP has some security limitations, and many vendors have developed software solutions that sit on top of SNMP, providing better security and better management tool suites.

The concept of a network operations center (NOC) comes from the old phone company network days, when central monitoring centers monitored the health of the telephone network and provided interfaces for maintenance and management. This same concept works well with computer networks, and companies with midsize and larger networks employ the same philosophy. The NOC allows operators to observe and interact with the network, using the self-reporting and in some cases self-healing nature of network devices to ensure efficient network operation. Although generally a boring operation under normal conditions, when things start to go wrong, as in the case of a virus or worm attack, the center can become a busy and stressful place as operators attempt to return the system to full efficiency while not interrupting existing traffic.

As networks can literally be spread out globally, it is not feasible to have a person go to each device for control functions. Software enables controllers at NOCs to measure the actual performance of network devices and make changes to the configuration and operation of devices. The ability to make remote connections with this level of functionality is both a blessing and a security issue. Although this allows efficient network operations management, it also is an opportunity for unauthorized entry into a network. For this reason, a variety of security controls are used, from secondary networks to VPNs and advanced authentication methods with respect to network control connections.

Network monitoring is an ongoing concern for any significant network. In addition to monitoring traffic flow and efficiency, monitoring of security is necessary. Intrusion detection systems act merely as alarms, indicating the possibility of a breach associated with a specific set of activities. These indications still need to be investigated and an appropriate response initiated by security personnel. Simple items such as port scans may be ignored by policy, but an actual unauthorized entry into a network router, for instance, would require NOC personnel to take specific actions to limit the potential damage to the system. The coordination of system changes, dynamic network traffic levels, potential security incidents, and maintenance activities is a daunting task requiring numerous personnel working together in any significant network. Software has been developed to help manage the information flow required to support these tasks. Such software can enable remote administration of devices in a standard fashion, so that the control systems can be devised in a hardware vendor–neutral configuration.

SNMP is the main standard embraced by vendors to permit interoperability. Although SNMP has received a lot of security-related attention of late due to various security holes in its implementation, it is still an important part of a security solution associated with network infrastructure. Many useful tools have security issues; the key is to understand the limitations and to use the tools within correct boundaries to limit the risk associated with the vulnerabilities. Blind use of any technology will result in increased risk, and SNMP is no exception. Proper planning, setup, and deployment can limit exposure to vulnerabilities. Continuous auditing and maintenance of systems with the latest patches is a necessary part of operations and is essential to maintaining a secure posture.

Mobile Devices

Mobile devices such as personal digital assistants (PDAs) and mobile phones are the latest devices to join the corporate network. These devices can perform significant business functions, and in the future, more of them will enter the corporate network and more work will be performed with them. These devices add several challenges for network administrators. When they synchronize their data with that on a workstation or server, the opportunity exists for viruses and malicious code to be introduced to the network. This can be a major security gap, as a user may access separate e-mail accounts, one personal, without antivirus protection, the other corporate. Whenever data is moved from one network to another via the PDA, the opportunity to put a virus onto the workstation exists. Although the virus may not affect the PDA or phone, these devices can act as a transmission vector. Currently, at least one vendor offers antivirus protection for PDAs, and similar protection for phones is not far away.

Media

The base of communications between devices is the physical layer of the OSI model. This is the domain of the actual connection between devices, whether by wire, fiber, or RF waves. The physical layer separates the definitions and protocols required to physically transmit the signal between boxes from higher-level protocols that deal with the details of the data itself. There are four common methods of connecting equipment at the physical layer:

- Coaxial cable
- Twisted-pair cable
- Fiber optics
- Wireless

Coax

Coaxial cable is very familiar to many households as a method of connecting televisions to VCRs or to satellite or cable services. It is used in these arenas because of its high bandwidth and shielding capabilities. Compared to standard twisted-pair lines such as telephone lines, coax is much less prone to outside interference. It is also much more expensive to run, both from a cost per foot measure and from a cable dimension measure. Coax costs much more per foot than standard twisted pair and carries only a single circuit for a large wire diameter.

A coax connector

An original design specification for Ethernet connections, coax was used from machine to machine in early Ethernet implementations. The connectors were easy to use and ensured good connections, and the limited distance of most office LANs did not carry a large cost penalty. The original ThickNet specification for Ethernet called for up to 100 connections over 500 meters at 10 Mbps.

Today, almost all of this older Ethernet specification has been replaced by faster, cheaper twisted-pair alternatives and the only place one is likely to see coax in a data network is from the cable box to the cable modem.

UTP/STP

Twisted-pair wires have all but completely replaced coaxial cables in Ethernet networks. Twisted-pair wires use the same technology used by the phone company for the movement of electrical signals. Single pairs of twisted wires reduce electrical crosstalk and electromagnetic interference. Multiple groups of twisted pairs can then be bundled together in common groups and easily wired between devices.

Twisted pairs come in two types, shielded and unshielded. Shielded twisted-pair (STP) has a foil shield around the pairs to provide extra shielding from electromagnetic interference. Unshielded twisted-pair (UTP) relies on the twist to eliminate interference. UTP has a cost advantage over STP and is usually sufficient for connections except in very noisy electrical areas.

A typical 8-wire UTP line

A typical 8-wire STP line

A bundle of UTP wires

Twisted-pair lines are categorized by the level of data transmission they can support. There are three current categories in use:

- Category 3 (Cat 3) minimum for voice and 10 Mbps Ethernet
- Category 5 (Cat 5) for 100 Mbps Fast Ethernet
- Category 6 (Cat 6) for Gigabit Ethernet

The standard method for connecting twisted-pair cables is via an 8-pin connector called an RJ-45 connector. This looks like a standard phone jack connector but is slightly larger. One nice aspect of twisted-pair cabling is its ease of splicing and changing of connectors. Many a network administrator has made Ethernet cables from stock Cat 5 wire, two connectors and a crimping tool. This ease of connection is also a security issue, as twisted-pair cables are very easy to splice into and rogue connections for sniffing could be made without detection in cable runs. Both coax and fiber are much more difficult to splice, with both of these needing a tap to connect, and taps are easier to detect.

Fiber

Fiber optic cable uses beams of laser light to connect devices over a thin glass wire. The biggest advantage to fiber is its bandwidth, with transmission capabilities into the terabits per second range. Fiber optic cable is what is used to make high-speed connections between servers and is the backbone medium of the Internet and large networks. For all of its speed characteristics, fiber has one major drawback—cost.

The cost of using fiber is a two-edged sword. It is cheaper when measured by bandwidth to use fiber than competing wired technologies. The length of runs of fiber can be much longer, and the data capacity of fiber is much higher. But connections to a fiber are difficult and expensive and fiber is impossible to splice. Making the precise connection on the end of a fiber optic line is a highly skilled job and is done by specially trained professionals who maintain a level of proficiency. Once the connector is fitted on the end, several forms of connectors and blocks are used, as shown in the images that follow.

A typical fiber optic fiber and terminator

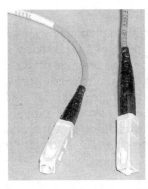

Another type of fiber terminator

A connector block for fiber optic lines

Splicing fiber optic is nearly impossible; the solution is to add connectors and connect through a repeater. This adds to the security of fiber in that unauthorized connections are all but impossible to make. The high cost of connections to fiber and the higher cost of fiber per foot also make fiber less attractive for the final mile in public networks where users are connected to the public switching systems. For this reason, cable companies use coax and DSL providers use twisted pairs to handle the last-mile scenario.

Unguided Media

Electromagnetic waves have been transmitted to convey signals literally since the inception of radio. Unguided media is a phrase used to cover all transmission media not guided by wire, fiber, or other constraints; it includes radio frequency (RF), infrared (IR), and microwave methods. Unguided media have one attribute in common, that they are unguided and as such can travel to many machines simultaneously. Transmission patterns may be modulated by antennas, but the target machine can be one of many in a reception zone. As such, security principles are even more critical, as they must assume that an unauthorized user has access to the signal.

Infrared

Infrared (IR) is a band of electromagnetic energy just beyond the red end of the visible spectrum. IR has been used in remote control devices for years and has the property that it cannot penetrate walls but instead bounces off them. IR made its debut in computer networking as a wireless method to connect to printers. Now there are wireless keyboards, wireless mice, PDAs exchanging data via IR—it seems to be everywhere. IR can also be used to connect devices in a network configuration, but a drawback is that it is slow compared to other wireless technologies. It also suffers from not being able to penetrate solid objects, so stack a few items in front of the transceiver and the signal is lost.

RF/Microwave

The use of radio frequency (RF) waves to carry communication signals goes back to the beginning of the twentieth century. Radio frequency (RF) waves are a common method of communicating in a wireless world. RF waves use a variety of frequency bands, each with special characteristics. The term microwave is used to describe a specific portion of the RF spectrum that is used for communication as well as other tasks such as cooking.

Point-to-point microwave links have been installed by many network providers to carry communications over long distances and rough terrain. Microwave communications of telephone conversations were the basis for forming the telecommunication company MCI. Many different frequencies are used in the microwave bands for many different purposes. Today, home users can use wireless networking throughout their house and enable laptops to surf the Web while walking between rooms. Corporate users are experiencing the same phenomenon, with wireless networking enabling corporate users to check e-mail on laptops while riding a shuttle bus on a business campus. These wireless solutions carry the information via microwaves; they are covered in detail in Chapter 3.

One key feature of microwave communications is that microwave RF energy can penetrate reasonable amounts of building structure. This allows one to connect network devices in separate rooms and can remove the constraints on equipment location imposed by fixed wiring. Another key feature is broadcast capability. By its nature, RF energy is unguided and can be received by multiple users simultaneously. Microwaves allow multiple users access in a limited area, and microwave systems are seeing application as the last mile of the Internet in dense metropolitan areas. Point-to-multipoint microwave devices can deliver data communication to all the business users in a downtown metropolitan area through rooftop antennas, reducing the need for expensive building-to-building cables. Just as microwaves carry cell phone and other data communications, the same technologies offer a method to bridge the last-mile solution. The "last mile" problem is the connection of individual consumers to a backbone, an expensive proposition because of the sheer number of connections and unshared line at this point in a network. Again, cost is an issue, as transceiving equipment is expensive, but in densely populated areas, such as apartments and office buildings in metropolitan areas, the user density can help defray individual costs. Speed on commercial microwave links can exceed 10 Gbps, so speed is not a problem for connecting multiple users, or for high-bandwidth applications.

Security Concerns for Transmission Media

The primary security concern for a system administrator has to be preventing physical access to a server by an unauthorized individual. Such access will almost always spell disaster, for with direct access and the correct tools, any system can be broken into. One of the next major concerns should be preventing unfettered access to a network connection. Access to switches and routers is almost as bad as direct access to a server, and access to network connections would rank third in terms of worst-case scenarios. To prevent such access is costly, yet the cost of replacing a server because of theft is also costly.

Physical Security

A balanced approach is the most sensible approach when addressing physical security, and this applies to transmission media as well. Keeping network switch rooms secure and cable runs secure seems obvious, but cases of using janitorial closets for this vital business purpose abound. One of the keys to mounting a successful attack on a network is information. Usernames, passwords, server locations—all of these can be obtained if someone has the ability to observe network traffic, in a process called sniffing. A sniffer can record all the network traffic, and this data can be mined for accounts, passwords, and traffic content, all of which may be useful to an unauthorized user. Many common scenarios exist when unauthorized entry to a network occurs, including:

- Insertion of a node and functionality that is not authorized on the network, such as a sniffer device or unauthorized wireless access point
- Modifying firewall security policies
- Modifying ACLs for firewalls, switches, or routers
- Modifying network devices to echo traffic to an external node

PART IV

One starting point for many intrusions is the first scenario, insertion of an unauthorized sniffer into the network, with the fruits of its labors driving the remaining unauthorized activities. The best first effort is to physically secure the actual network equipment to prevent this type of intrusion.

Network devices and transmission media become targets because they are dispersed through an organization and physical security of many dispersed items can be difficult to manage. This work is not glamorous and has been likened to guarding plumbing. The difference is that in the case of network infrastructure, unauthorized physical access strikes at one of the most vulnerable points and, in many cases, is next to impossible to detect. Locked doors and equipment racks are easy to implement, yet this step is frequently overlooked. Raised floors, cable runs, closets—there are many places to hide an unauthorized device. Add to this the fact that a large percentage of unauthorized users have a direct connection to the target of the unauthorized use—they are employees, students, or the like. Twisted pair and coax make it easy to tap into a network without signaling one's presence. A person with talent can make such a tap without interrupting network traffic.

Although limiting physical access is difficult, it is essential. The least level of skill is still more than sufficient to accomplish unauthorized entry into a network if physical access to the network signals is allowed. This is one factor driving many organizations to use fiber optics, for these are much more difficult to tap. Although many tricks can be employed with switches and VLANs to increase security, it is still essential to prevent unauthorized contact with the network equipment.

Wireless networks make the intruder's task even easier, as they take the network to the users, authorized or not. A new technique, called war-driving, involves using a laptop and software to find wireless networks from outside the premises. A typical use of war-driving is to locate a wireless network with poor (or no) security and obtain free Internet access, but the other uses can be more devastating. Methods for securing even the relatively weak WEP protocol are not difficult; they are just typically not followed. A simple solution is to place a firewall between the wireless access point and the rest of the network and authenticate users before allowing entry, even if the encryption setup matches the WEP setup. Home users can do the same thing to prevent neighbors from "sharing" their Internet connections. To ensure that unauthorized traffic does not enter your network through a wireless access point, you must either use a firewall with an authentication system or establish a VPN.

Removable Media

One task common to all computer users is storage of data. Sometimes this storage occurs on a file server; sometimes it is on movable media, allowing it to be transported between machines. Moving storage media represents a security risk from a couple of different angles, the first being the potential loss of control over the data on the moving media. Second is the risk of introducing unwanted items, such as a virus or a worm, when the media are attached back to a network. There are methods of combating both of these issues, through policies and software. The key is to ensure they are occurring. To describe media-specific issues, it is easiest to divide the media into three categories: magnetic, optical, and electronic.

Magnetic Media

Magnetic media store data through the rearrangement of magnetic particles on a nonmagnetic substrate. Common forms include hard drives, floppy disks, Zip disks, and magnetic tape. Although the specific format may differ, the basic concept is the same. All of these devices share some common characteristics. Each has sensitivity to external magnetic fields. Attach a floppy disk to the refrigerator door with a magnet if you wish to test the sensitivity. They are also affected by high temperatures as in fires, and by exposure to water.

Hard Drives

Hard drives used to be large machines in mainframes. Now they can be found small enough to attach to PDAs and small handheld devices. The concepts remain the same among all of them: a spinning patter rotates the magnetic media beneath heads that read the patterns in the oxide coating. As drives have gotten smaller and rotation speeds increased, the capacities have also grown. Today gigabytes can be stored in a device slightly larger than a bottle cap. Portable hard drives in the 20–120GB range are now available and affordable, some for less than $300.

External Portable 80GB hard drive with USB connection

Diskettes

Floppy disks were the industry's first attempt at portable magnetic media. The movable medium was placed in a protective sleeve, and the drive remained in the machine. Capacities up to 1.4MB were achieved, but the fragility of the device as the size increased, as well as competing media, has rendered floppies almost obsolete. A better floppy, the Zip disk from Iomega Corporation, improved on the floppy with a stronger case and higher capacity (100MB and 250MB); it has become a common backup and file transfer medium. But even the increased size of 250MB is not large enough for some multimedia files, and recordable optical (CD-R) drives have arrived to fill the gap; they will be discussed shortly in this chapter.

Comparison of 3.5-inch floppy (left) and Zip disk (right)

Tape

Magnetic tape has had a place in computer centers since the beginning of computing. The primary use has been bulk offline storage and backup. Tape functions well in this role because of its low cost. The disadvantage of tape is its nature as a serial access medium, making it a slow medium to work with for large quantities of data. Several types of magnetic tape are in use today, ranging from quarter inch to digital linear tape (DLT) and digital audio tape (DAT). These cartridges can hold upward of 60GB of compressed data. Tapes are still a major concern from a security perspective, as they are still used to back up many types of computer systems. The security concern is over the physical protection afforded the tapes, for if they were stolen, then an unauthorized user could establish a network and recover your data on his system, where he has access to it all. Offsite storage is needed for proper disaster recovery protection, but secure offsite storage and transport is what is really needed. This important issue is frequently overlooked in many facilities.

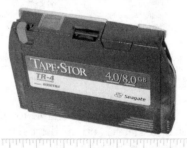

A magnetic tape used for backups

Optical Media

Optical media are characterized by the use of a laser to read data stored on a physical device. Rather than a magnetic head picking up magnetic marks on a disk, a laser picks up deformities embedded in the media that contain the information. As with magnetic media, optical media can be read/write, although the read-only version is still more common.

CD-R/DVD

The compact disc (CD) took the music industry by storm, and then it took the computer industry by storm as well. A digital record, a standard CD holds over 640MB of data. A newer form, the digital video disc (DVD), can hold almost 4GB of data. These new devices operate as optical storage, with little marks burned in them to represent 1's and 0's on a microscopic scale. The most common type of CD is the read-only version, where the data is written to the disc once and only to read afterward. This has become a popular method for distributing computer software, although recently higher-capacity DVDs have begun to replace CDs for program distribution.

A DVD (left) and a CD-R (right)

A second-generation device, the recordable compact disc (CD-R), allows users to create their own CDs using a burner device in their PC and special software. This has enabled users to back up data, make their own audio CDs, and use CDs as high-capacity diskettes. Their relatively low cost (less than 50 cents each in bulk) has made it economical to use them only once. CDs have a thin layer of aluminum inside the plastic, upon which bumps are burned by the laser when recorded. CD-Rs use a reflective layer, such as gold, upon which a dye is placed that changes upon impact by the recording laser. A newer type, CD-RW, has a different dye that allows discs to be erased and reused. The cost of the media increases from CD to CD-R to CD-RW.

DVDs may in the future occupy the same role that CDs have in the recent past, except that they hold over seven times the data of a CD. This makes full-length movie recording possible on a single disc. The increased capacity comes from finer tolerances and the fact that DVDs can hold data on both sides. Formats for burners to allow home burning of DVDs are still in their infancy, with a couple of competing formats available. They have raised digital rights management issues as well, to prevent the copying of digital media such as movies.

PART IV

Electronic Media

The latest form of removable media is electronic memory. Electronic circuits of static memory, which can retain data even without power, fill a niche where high density and small size are needed. Primarily used in audio devices and digital cameras, these electronic media come in a variety of vendor-specific types, such as Smart Cards, Smart Media, Flash Cards, Memory Sticks, and CompactFlash devices. Several recent photo-quality color printers have been released with ports to accept the cards directly, so that a computer is not required for printing. Computer readers are also available to permit storing data from the card onto hard drives and other media in a computer. The size of storage on these devices ranges from 16MB to 256MB, with 512MB on the horizon.

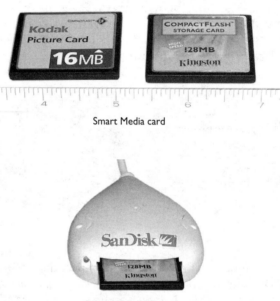

Smart Media card

Smart Media USB reader

Although they are primarily used for photos and music, there is nothing to prevent these devices from moving any digital data from one machine to another. To a machine, equipped with a connector port, these look like any other file storage location. Being able to hold 256MB on a chip the size of a postage stamp and 1/8-inch thick brings a lot of uses to mind. Cost is still fairly high, with a 256MB card costing $75, but it wasn't so many years ago we would have gladly paid that for a hard drive with the same capacity but a significantly larger footprint.

These devices can be connected to a system through a special reader or directly via a USB port. In newer PC systems, a USB boot device is being used to replace the older floppy drive. These devices are small, can hold a significant amount of data, up to 2GB at time of writing, and are easy to move from machine to machine. Another novel interface is a mouse that has a slot for a memory stick. This dual-purpose device conserves space, conserves USB ports, and is intuitively easy to use. You put the memory stick in the mouse and use the mouse normally. When you are finished, you take the stick with you. The mouse works with or without the memory stick; it is just a convenient device to use for a portal.

Security Topologies

Networks are different than single servers; networks exist as connections of multiple devices. A key characteristic of a network is its layout, or topology. A proper network topology takes security into consideration and assists in "building security" into the network. Security-related topologies include separating portions of the network by use and function, strategically designing in points to monitor for IDS systems, building in redundancy, and adding fault-tolerant aspects.

Security Zones

The first aspect of security is a layered defense. Just as a castle has a moat, an outside wall, an inside wall, and even a keep, so too does a modern secure network have its different layers. Different zones are designed to provide layers of defense, with the outermost layers providing basic protection and the innermost layers providing the highest level of protection. A constant issue is that accessibility tends to be inversely related to level of protection, so it is harder to provide complete protection and unfettered access at the same time. Trade-offs between access and security are handled through zones, with successive zones guarded by firewalls enforcing ever increasingly strict security policies. The outermost zone is the Internet, a free area, beyond any specific controls. Between the inner secure corporate network and the Internet is an area where machines are considered at risk. This zone has come to be called the DMZ, after its military counterpart, the demilitarized zone, where neither side has any specific controls. Once inside the inner secure network, separate branches are frequently carved out to provide specific functionality; under this heading, we will discuss intranets, extranets, and virtual LANs.

DMZ

The demilitarized zone, or DMZ, is a military term for ground separating two opposing forces, by agreement and for the purpose of acting as a buffer between the two sides. A DMZ in a computer network is used in exactly the same way; it acts as a buffer zone between the Internet, where no controls exist, and the inner secure network, where an organization has security policies in place (see Figure 7-5). To demarcate the zones and enforce separation, a firewall is used on each side of the DMZ. The area between these firewalls is accessible from either the inner, secure, network or the Internet. Figure 7-5 illustrates these zones as caused by firewall placement. The firewalls are specifically designed to prevent access across the DMZ directly, from the Internet to the inner, secure, network.

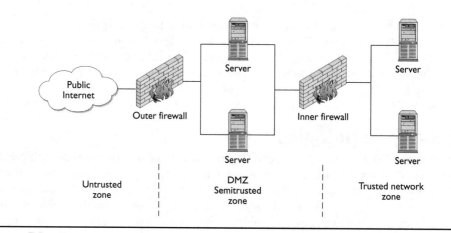

Figure 7-5   The DMZ and zones of trust

Special attention should be paid to the security settings of network devices placed in the DMZ, and they should be considered at all times to be compromised to unauthorized use. A common industry term, *hardened operating system*, applies to machines where special attention is paid to locking down the functionality to preserve security. This approach needs to be applied to the machines in the DMZ, and although it limits functionality, it enables them to work properly in this less-secure environment.

Many types of servers belong in this area, including web servers that are serving content to Internet users, as well as remote access servers and external e-mail servers. In general, any server directly accessed from the outside, untrusted Internet zone needs to be in the DMZ. Other servers should not be placed in the DMZ. Domain name servers for your inner, trusted, network should not be accessible from the outside, nor should the database servers that house corporate databases. Application servers, file servers, print servers—all of the standard servers used in the trusted network should be behind both firewalls. And not just the servers, but the routers and switches that connect these machines together.

The idea behind the use of the DMZ topology is to force a user to make at least one hop in the DMZ before accessing information inside the trusted network. If the outside user makes a request for a resource from the trusted network, say a data element from a database via a web page, then this request needs to follow the following scenario:

1. A user from the untrusted network (the Internet) requests data via a web page from a web server in the DMZ.

2. The web server in the DMZ requests the data from the application server, which can be in the DMZ or in the inner, trusted network.

3. The application server requests the data from the database server in the trusted network.

4. The database server returns the data to the requesting application server.

5. The application server returns the data to the requesting web server.

6. The web server returns the data to the requesting user from the untrusted network.

This separation accomplishes two specific, independent tasks. First, the user is separated from the request for data on a secure network. By having intermediaries do the requesting, this layered approach allows significant security levels to be enforced. Users do not have direct access or control over their requests, and this filtering process can put controls in place. Second, scalability is more easily realized. The multiple-server solution can be made to be very scalable to literally millions of users, without slowing down any particular layer.

Internet

The Internet is the name given to the worldwide connection of networks. This network can be used to transport e-mail, files, financial records, remote access—you name it, and the Internet carries it today from one network to another. A formal way of looking at the Internet is not as a single network, but as a series of interconnected networks that allow protocols to operate to enable data to flow across it. This means that even if your network doesn't have direct contact with a resource, as long as a neighbor, or a neighbor's neighbor, etc., can get there, so can you. This large mesh allows users almost infinite ability to communicate between systems.

Because everything and everyone can access this interconnected mesh and it is outside of your control and ability to enforce security policies, the Internet should be considered to be untrusted. A firewall should exist at any connection between your trusted network and the Internet. This is not to imply that the Internet is a bad thing—it is a great resource for all networks and adds significant functionality to our computing environments. It is just not an area where you can use your own security policies and trust content or identities.

The term World Wide Web (WWW) is frequently used synonymously with the term Internet, but it actually is just one set of services available via the Internet. WWW is more specifically the Hypertext Transfer Protocol (HTTP)–based services that are made available over the Internet. This can include a variety of actual services and content, including text files, pictures, streaming audio and video, even viruses and worms.

Intranet

The intranet is a term used to describe a network that has the same functionality as the Internet for users but lies completely inside the trusted area of a network and is under the security control of the system and network administrators. Typically referred to as *campus* or *corporate* networks, intranets are used everyday in companies around the world. An intranet allows a developer and a user the full set of protocols, HTTP, FTP, instant messaging, etc., that is offered on the Internet, but with the added advantage of trust from the network. Content on web servers on intranets by definition is not available over the Internet to untrusted users. This layer of security offers a significant amount of control and regulation, allowing users to fulfill business functionality while ensuring security.

Should information need to be made available to outside users, two methods exist. Duplication onto machines in the DMZ can place the material in a position to be made available for other users. Proper security checks and controls can be made prior to duplicating the material to ensure security policies concerning specific data availability are being followed. The other method to extend distribution is through the use of extranets, which are the publishing of material to trusted partners.

Should users inside the intranet require access to information from the Internet, then a proxy server can be used to mask the requestor's location. This helps secure the intranet from outside mapping of its actual topology. All Internet requests go to the proxy server. If a request passes filtering requirements, the proxy server, assuming it is also a cache server, looks in its local cache of previously downloaded web pages. If it finds the page in its cache, it returns the page to the requestor without needing to send the request to the Internet. If the page is not in the cache, the proxy server, acting as a client on behalf of the user, uses one of its own IP addresses to request the page from the Internet. When the page is returned, the proxy server relates it to the original request and forwards it on to the user. This masks the user's IP address from the Internet. Proxy servers can perform several functions for a firm; for example, they can monitor traffic requests, eliminating improper requests, i.e., inappropriate content for work. They can also act as a cache server, cutting down on outside network requests for the same object. Finally, proxy servers protect the identity of internal IP addresses, although this function can also be done through a router or firewall using NAT.

Extranet

An *extranet* is an extension of a selected portion of a company's intranet to external partners. This allows a business to share information with customers, suppliers, partners, and other trusted groups while using a common set of Internet protocols to facilitate operations. Extranets can use public networks to extend their reach beyond a company's own internal network, and some form of security, typically VPN, is used to secure this channel. The use of the term extranet implies both privacy and security. Privacy is required for many communications, and security is needed to prevent unauthorized use and events from occurring. Both of these functions can be achieved through the use of technologies described in this chapter and other chapters in this book. Proper firewall management, remote access, encryption, authentication, secure tunnels across public networks—these are all methods used to ensure privacy and security for extranets.

VLANs

A local area network (LAN) is a set of devices with similar functionality and similar communication needs, typically collocated and operated off a single switch. This is the lowest level of a network hierarchy and defines the domain for certain protocols at the data-link layer for communication. Virtual local area networks (VLANs) are a method of using a single switch and dividing it into multiple broadcast domains and/or multiple network segments. This is a very powerful technique that allows significant network flexibility, scalability, and performance. VLANs are implemented at a switch level and are often combined with a technique known as trunking.

Trunking

Trunking is the process of spanning a single VLAN across multiple switches. A trunk-based connection between switches allows packets from a single VLAN to travel between switches, as shown in Figure 7-6. Two trunks exist in Figure 7-6, VLAN 10 is implemented with one trunk and VLAN 20 is implemented by the other. Hosts on different VLANs cannot communicate using trunks and are switched across the switch network. Trunks enable network administrators to set up VLANs across multiple switches with minimal effort. With a combination of trunks and VLANs, network administrators can subnet a network by user functionality without respect to host location on the network or recabling machines.

Security Implications

VLANs have several security implications. First and foremost is the ability to divide a single network into multiple subnets based on functionality. This would permit engineering and accounting to share a switch because of proximity and yet have separate

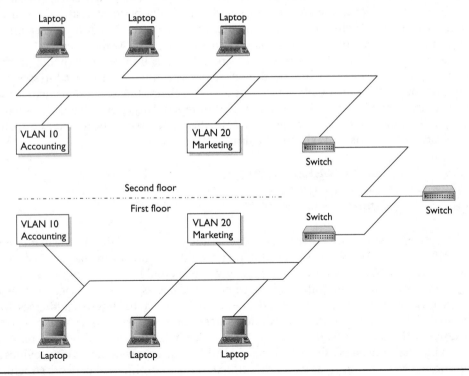

Figure 7-6   VLANs and trunks

traffic domains. The physical placement of equipment and cables is logically and programmatically separated so adjacent ports on a switch can reference separate subnets. This prevents unauthorized use of physically close devices through separate subnets, but the same equipment. VLANs also allow a network administrator to define a VLAN that has no users and map all of the unused ports to this VLAN. Then if an unauthorized user should gain access to the equipment, they will be unable to use unused ports, as those ports will be securely defined to nothing.

 CAUTION Trunks and VLANs also have security implications that need to be heeded so that firewalls and other segmentation devices are not breached through their use. They also require understanding of their use to prevent an unauthorized user from reconfiguring them to gain undetected access to secure portions of a network.

NAT

Network Address Translation (NAT) is a method for using two sets of IP addresses for resources, one for internal use and a different one for external (Internet) use. NAT was developed as a solution to the rapid depletion of IP addresses in the IPv4 address space; it has since became an Internet standard (see RFC 1631 for details). NAT is used to translate between the two addressing schemes and is typically performed at a firewall or router. This permits enterprises to use the nonroutable private IP address space internally and reduce the number of external IP addresses used across the Internet.

There are three sets of IP addresses that are defined as nonroutable. By definition, nonroutable addresses will not be routed across the Internet. These addresses are routable internally and routers can be set to route them, but the routers across the Internet are set to discard packets sent to these addresses. This approach enables a separation of internal and external traffic and allows these addresses to be reused by anyone and everyone who wishes to do so. The three address spaces are:

Class A	10.0.0.0 – 10.255.255.255
Class B	172.16.0.0 – 172.31.255.255
Class C	192.168.0.0 – 192.168.255.255

The use of these addresses inside a network is unrestricted, and they function like any other IP addresses. When outside, i.e., Internet-provided resources are needed for one of these addresses, NAT is required to produce a valid external IP address for the resource. NAT operates by translating the address when traffic passes the NAT device, such as a firewall. The external addresses used are not mappable 1:1 to the internal addresses, for this would defeat the purpose of reuse and address space conservation. Typically, a pool of external IP addresses is used by the NAT device, with the device keeping track of which internal address is using which external address at any given time. This provides a significant layer of security, as it makes it difficult to map the internal network structure behind a firewall and directly address it from the outside. NAT is one of the methods for enforcing perimeter security by forcing users to access resources through defined pathways such as firewalls and gateway servers.

To accomplish NAT, several different techniques are used. *Static* NAT is where there is a 1:1 binding of external address to internal address; it is needed for services where external sources reference internal sources, such as web servers or e-mail servers. For DMZ resources that reference outside resources, addresses can be shared, through dynamic NAT. In *dynamic* NAT, a table is constructed and used by the edge device to manage the translation. As the address translation can change over time, the table changes as well. Even finer-grained control can be obtained through port address translation (PAT), where actual TCP/UDP ports are translated as well. This will enable a single external IP address to serve two internal IP addresses through the use of ports. Resources that need long-running NAT, but only specific ports, for instance, a web server on port 80 or e-mail on port 25, can share a single external IP, conserving resources.

Tunneling

Tunneling is a method of packaging packets so that they can traverse a network in a secure, confidential manner. Tunneling involves encapsulating packets within packets, enabling dissimilar protocols to coexist in a single communication stream, as in IP traffic routed over an ATM network. Tunneling also can provide significant measures of security and confidentiality through encryption and encapsulation methods. The best example of this is the VPN method, where a virtual private network is established over a public network through the use of a tunnel, as shown in Figure 7-7, connecting a firm's Boston office to its NYC office.

Assume a company has multiple locations and decides to use the public Internet to connect the networks at these locations. To make these connections secure from outside unauthorized use, the company can employ a VPN connection between the different networks. On each network, an edge device, usually a router, connects to another edge device on the other network. Then using IPsec protocols, these routers establish a secure, encrypted path between them. This securely encrypted set of packets cannot be read by outside routers; only the addresses of the edge routers are visible. This arrangement thus acts as a tunnel across the public Internet and establishes a private connection, secure from outside snooping or use.

Because of ease of use, low-cost hardware, and strong security, tunnels and the Internet are a combination that will see more use in the future. IPsec, VPN, and tunnels will become a major set of tools for users requiring secure network connections across public segments of networks.

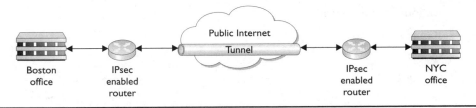

Figure 7-7   Tunneling across a public network

Chapter Review

This chapter covered a wide range of topics—from devices, to media, to topologies—and showed you how to use these items together to create secure networks. These are all complementary items, and each can support the other in an effort to build a secure network structure. Designing a secure network begins with defining a topology and then laying out the necessary components. Separate the pieces using firewalls with clearly defined security policies. Use devices and media to the advantage of the overall network design and implement usable subnets with VLANs. Use encryption and encapsulation to secure communications of public segments to enable extranets and cross-Internet company traffic. Use items such as intrusion detection systems and firewalls to keep unauthorized users out and monitor activity. Taken together, these pieces can make a secure network that is efficient, manageable, and effective.

Questions

1. An extranet could be considered an extension of a company's network to include which of the following?

   A. Internet-based customers

   B. Suppliers

   C. Salespersons for the company

   D. System administrators

2. UTP cables are terminated for Ethernet using what type of connector?

   A. A BNC plug

   B. An Ethernet connector

   C. A standard phone jack connector

   D. An RJ-45 connector

3. Coaxial cable carries how many physical channels?

   A. Two

   B. Four

   C. One

   D. None of the above

4. NAT is found on which types of devices in a network?

   A. Routers and firewalls

   B. NICs

   C. Switches

   D. Hubs

PART IV

5. Trunking is associated with which of the following?

A. VLANs

B. IPsec

C. Routers

D. NAT

6. The purpose of twisting the wires in twisted-pair circuits is to

A. Increase speed

B. Increase bandwidth

C. Reduce crosstalk

D. Allow easier tracing

7. The shielding in STP acts as

A. A physical barrier strengthening the cable

B. A ground to reduce interference

C. An amplifier allowing longer connections

D. None of the above

8. The purpose of a DMZ in a network is to

A. Provide easy connections to the Internet without an interfering firewall

B. Allow server farms to be divided into similar functioning entities

C. Provide a place to lure and capture hackers

D. Act as a buffer between untrusted and trusted networks

9. One of the greatest concerns addressed by physical security is to prevent unauthorized connections having what intent?

A. Sniffing

B. Spoofing

C. Data diddling

D. Free network access

10. SNMP is a protocol used for which of the following functions?

A. Secure e-mail

B. Secure encryption of network packets

C. Remote access to user workstations

D. Remote access to network infrastructure

11. Firewalls can use which of the following in their operation?

A. Stateful packet inspection

B. Port blocking to deny specific services

      C. NAT to hide internal IP addresses

      D. All of the above

12. SMTP is a protocol used for which of the following functions?

      A. E-mail

      B. Secure encryption of network packets

      C. Remote access to user workstations

      D. None of the above

13. Microwave communications are limited by

      A. Speed—the maximum for microwave circuits is 1 Gbps

      B. Cost—microwaves take a lot of energy to generate

      C. Line of sight—microwaves don't propagate over the horizon

      D. Lack of standard operation protocols for widespread use

14. NAT is used for which of the following functions:

      A. To bind multiple machines to a single IP address

      B. To eliminate the need for a firewall on a network

      C. To mask IP addresses within a network

      D. To resolve IP addressing errors upon arrival at the firewall

15. VLANs use which of the following methods to achieve their objective purpose in a network?

      A. Security associations

      B. Encryption of network packets

      C. Tunneling across network boundaries

      D. Trunking to combine circuits

Answers

1. **B.** An extranet is an extension of a company's network to include selected firms such as suppliers.

2. **D.** The standard connector for UTP in an Ethernet network is the RJ-45 connector. An RJ-45 is much larger than a standard phone connector.

3. **C.** A coaxial connector carries one wire, one physical circuit.

4. **A.** Routers and firewalls can both perform network address translation functions.

5. **A.** Trunking is the process of spanning a single VLAN across multiple switches.

6. **C.** The twist in twisted-pair wires is to reduce crosstalk between wires.

7. **B.** The shielding on STP is for grounding and reducing interference.

8. **D.** The purpose of the DMZ is to act as a buffer zone. Honeypots are used to lure and catch hackers. DMZs typically have firewalls on both sides, and the mix of servers is just that: a mix of functions inside the DMZ.

9. **A.** Sniffing is the greatest threat, for passwords and accounts can be captured and used later.

10. **D.** The Simple Network Management Protocol is used to control network devices from a central control location.

11. **D.** Firewalls can do all of these things.

12. **A.** SMTP, the Simple Mail Transfer Protocol, is used to move e-mail across a network.

13. **C.** Microwave energy is a line-of-sight transmission medium; hence, towers must not be spaced too far apart or the horizon will block transmissions.

14. **C.** NAT performs IP address translation, masking internal IP addresses from outside users.

15. **D.** VLANs use trunking to span several switches.

Intrusion Detection Systems

In this chapter, you will

- Understand host-based intrusion detection systems
- Explore network-based intrusion detection systems
- Learn what honeypots are used for
- Learn how to conduct incident response operations

Network security can be fairly easily compared to physical security—the more you wish to protect something and restrict access to it, the more security you need. In the world of physical security, you have locks, walls, gates, guards, motion sensors, pressure plates, etc. As you add more protective devices, you are adding "layers" of security that an intruder would have to overcome or breach to obtain access to whatever you are protecting. Correspondingly, in the network and data security arenas you have protective layers in the form of passwords, firewalls, access lists, file permissions, and intrusion detection systems. Most organizations have their own approach to network security, choosing the "layers" that make sense for them after they weigh risks, potential for loss, cost, and manpower requirements.

The foundation for a layered network security approach usually starts with a well-secured system regardless of the system's function (whether it's a user PC or a corporate e-mail server). A well-secured system is one with up-to-date application and operating system patches, well-chosen passwords, the minimum number of services running, and restricted access to available services. On top of that foundation, you can add layers of protective measures such as antivirus products, firewalls, sniffers, and intrusion detection systems.

Some of the more complicated and interesting types of network/data security devices are intrusion detection systems. Intrusion detection systems (IDSs) are to the network world what burglar alarms are to the physical world. The main purpose of an intrusion detection system is to identify suspicious or malicious activity, note activity that deviates from normal behavior, catalog and classify the activity, and if possible, respond to the activity. In this chapter, you will look at the history of IDS, various types of intrusion detection systems, how they work, benefits and weaknesses of specific types, and what the future may hold for these systems. You'll also look at some complementary topics to intrusion detection systems: honeypots and incident response.

History of Intrusion Detection Systems

Like much of the network technology we see today, intrusion detection systems grew from a need to solve specific problems. Like the Internet itself, the IDS concept came from Department of Defense–sponsored research. In the early 1970s, the U.S. government and military became increasingly aware of the need to protect the electronic networks that were becoming critical to daily operations. In 1972, James Anderson published a paper for the United States Air Force outlining the growing number of computer security problems and the immediate need to secure Air Force systems (James P. Anderson, "Computer Security Technology Planning Study Volume 2," October 1972, http:// seclab.cs.ucdavis.edu/projects/history/papers/ande72.pdf). Anderson continued his research and in 1980 published a follow-up paper outlining methods to improve security auditing and surveillance methods (James P. Anderson, "Computer Security Threat Monitoring and Surveillance," 15 April 1980, http://seclab .cs.ucdavis.edu/projects/history/ papers/ande80.pdf). In this paper, Anderson pioneered the concept of using system audit files to detect unauthorized access and misuse. He also suggested the use of automated detection systems, which paved the way for misuse detection on mainframe systems in use at the time.

While Anderson's work got the efforts started, the concept of a real-time, rule-based IDS didn't really exist until Dorothy Denning and Peter Neumann developed the first real-time IDS model, called "The Intrusion Detection Expert System (IDES)," from their research between 1984 and 1986. In 1987, Denning published "An Intrusion-Detection Model," a paper that laid out the model on which most modern intrusion detection systems are based, which appears in *IEEE Transactions on Software Engineering*, Vol. SE-13, No. 2 (February 1987): 222–232.

With a model and definitions in place, the U.S. government continued to fund research that led to projects such as Discovery, Haystack, Multics Intrusion Detection and Alerting System (MIDAS), and Network Audit Director and Intrusion Reporter (NADIR). Finally, in 1989, Haystack Labs released "Stalker," the first commercial intrusion detection system. Stalker was host-based and worked by comparing audit data to known patterns of suspicious activity. While the military and government embraced the concept, the commercial world was very slow to adopt IDS products and it was several years before other commercial products began to emerge.

In the early to mid-1990s, computer systems continued to grow and companies were starting to realize the importance of intrusion detection systems; however, the solutions available were host-based and required a great deal of time and money to manage and operate effectively. Focus began to shift away from host-based systems, and network-based intrusion detection systems began to emerge. In 1995, WheelGroup was formed in San Antonio, Texas, to develop the first commercial, network-based intrusion detection product, called NetRanger. NetRanger was designed to monitor network links and the traffic moving across the links to identify misuse as well as suspicious and malicious activity. NetRanger's release was quickly followed by Internet Security Systems'

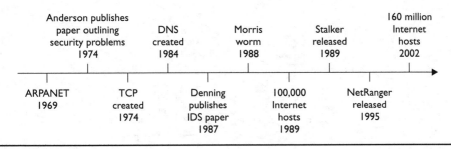

Figure 8-1   History of the Internet and IDS

RealSecure in 1996. Several other players followed suit and released their own IDS products, but it wasn't until the networking giant Cisco Systems acquired WheelGroup in February 1998 that intrusion detection systems were recognized as a vital part of any network security infrastructure. Figure 8-1 offers a timeline for these developments.

IDS Overview

As we mentioned before, an IDS is somewhat like a burglar alarm. An IDS watches the activity going on around it and tries to identify undesirable activity. Intrusion detection systems are typically divided into two main categories, depending on how they monitor activity: host-based and network-based.

- A *host-based* IDS examines activity on an individual system, such as a mail server, web server, or individual PC. It is concerned only with an individual system and usually has no visibility into the activity on the network or systems around it.

- A *network-based* IDS examines activity on the network itself. It has visibility only into the traffic crossing the network link it is monitoring and typically has no idea of what is happening on individual systems.

Whether or not it is network- or host-based, an intrusion detection system will typically consist of several specialized components working together as illustrated in Figure 8-2. These components are often logical and software-based rather than physical and will vary slightly from vendor to vendor and product to product. Typically, an IDS will have the following logical components:

- **Traffic collector**   This component collects activity/events for the IDS to examine. On a host-based IDS, this could be log files, audit logs, or traffic coming to or leaving a specific system. On a network-based IDS, this is typically a mechanism for copying traffic off the network link—basically functioning as a sniffer.

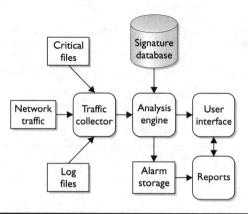

Figure 8-2   Logical depiction of IDS components

- **Analysis engine**   This component examines the collected network traffic and compares it to known patterns of suspicious or malicious activity stored in the signature database. The analysis engine is the "brains" of the IDS.

- **Signature database**   The signature database is a collection of patterns and definitions of known suspicious or malicious activity.

- **User interface and reporting**   This is the component that interfaces with the human element, providing alerts when appropriate and giving the user a means to interact with and operate the IDS.

Most IDSs can be "tuned" to fit a particular environment. Certain signatures can be turned off, telling the IDS not to look for certain types of traffic. For example, if you are operating in a pure UNIX environment, you may not wish to see Windows-based alarms, as they will not affect your systems. Additionally, the severity of the alarm levels can be adjusted depending on how concerned you are over certain types of traffic. Some IDSs will also allow the user to "exclude" certain patterns of activity from specific hosts. In other words, you can tell the IDS to ignore the fact that some systems generate traffic that looks like malicious activity, because it really isn't.

Host-Based Intrusion Detection Systems

As we mentioned in our history of intrusion detection systems, the first IDSs were host-based and designed to only examine activity on a specific host. A host-based IDS (HIDS) is a system that examines log files, audit trails, and network traffic coming in to or leaving a specific host. Host-based IDSs can operate in real time, looking for activity as it occurs, or batch mode, looking for activity on a periodic basis. Host-based systems are typically self-contained, but many of the newer commercial products have been designed to report to and be managed by a central system. Host-based systems also take local system resources to operate. In other words, a host-based IDS will use up some of

the memory and CPU cycles of the system it is protecting. Early versions of host-based IDSs ran in batch mode, looking for suspicious activity on an hourly or daily basis, and typically only looked for specific events in the system's log files. As processor speeds increased, later versions of host-based IDSs began to look through the log files in real time and even added the ability to examine the data traffic the host was generating and receiving.

Most host-based intrusion detection systems focus on the log files or audit trails generated by the local operating system. On UNIX systems, the examined logs usually include those created by syslog such as messages, kernel logs, and error logs. On Windows systems, the examined logs are typically the three event logs: Application, System, and Security. Some host-based IDSs have the ability to cover specific applications, such as FTP or web services, by examining the logs produced by those specific applications or examining the traffic from the services themselves. Within the log files, the IDS is looking for certain activities that typify hostile actions or misuse such as:

- Logins at odd hours
- Login authentication failures
- Adding new user accounts
- Modification or access of critical system files
- Modification or removal of binary files (executables)
- Starting or stopping processes
- Privilege escalation
- Use of certain programs

In general, most host-based intrusion detection systems will operate in a very similar fashion. (Figure 8-3 shows the logical layout of a host-based IDS.) By considering the function and activity of each component, you can gain some insight into how they operate.

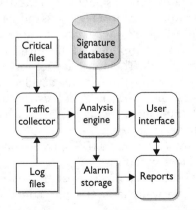

Figure 8-3   Host-based IDS components

As on any IDS, the *traffic collector* on a host-based IDS pulls in the information the other components, such as the analysis engine, need to examine. For most host-based systems, the traffic collector pulls data from information the local system has already generated, such as error messages, log files, and system files. The traffic collector is responsible for reading those files, selecting which items are of interest, and forwarding them to the analysis engine. On some host-based systems, the traffic collector will also examine specific attributes of critical files such as file size, date modified, or checksum.

> **NOTE** Critical files are those that are vital to the system's operation or overall functionality. They may be program (or binary) files, files containing user accounts and passwords, or even scripts to start or stop system processes. Any unexpected modifications to these files could mean the system has been compromised or modified by an attacker. By monitoring these files, the IDS can warn users of potentially malicious activity.

The *analysis engine* is perhaps the most important component of the IDS, as it must decide what activity is "okay" and what activity is "bad." The analysis engine is a sophisticated decision and pattern matching mechanism—it looks at the information given to it by the traffic collector and tries to match it against known patterns of activity stored in the signature database. If the activity matches a known pattern, the analysis engine can react, usually by issuing an alert or alarm. An analysis engine may also be capable of remembering how the activity it is looking at right now compares to traffic it has already seen or may see in the near future so that it can match more complicated, multistep malicious activity patterns. An analysis engine must also be capable of examining traffic patterns as quickly as possible, as the longer it takes to match a malicious pattern, the less time the IDS or human operator has to react to malicious traffic. Most IDS vendors will build a "decision tree" into their analysis engines to expedite pattern matching.

The *signature database* is a collection of predefined activity patterns that have already been identified and categorized—activity patterns that typically indicate suspicious or malicious activity. When the analysis engine has a traffic pattern to examine, it will compare that pattern to the appropriate signatures in the database. The signature database can contain anywhere from a few to a few thousand signatures, depending on the vendor, type of IDS, space available on the system to store signatures, etc.

The *user interface* is the visible component of the intrusion detection system—this is the part that humans interact with. The user interface varies widely depending on the product and vendor and could be anything from a detailed graphical interface to a simple command line. Regardless of the type and complexity, the interface is provided to allow the user to interact with the system: changing parameters, receiving alarms, tuning signatures and response patterns, etc.

To better understand how a host-based IDS operates, take a look at examples from a UNIX system and a Windows system.

On a UNIX system, the host-based IDS is most likely going to be examining any of a number of system logs—basically large text files containing entries about what is

Decision Tree

In computer systems, a "tree" is a data structure where each element in the structure is attached to one or more structures directly beneath it (the connections are called "branches"). Structures on the end of a branch without any elements below them are called "leaves." Trees are most often drawn inverted, with the "root" at the top and all subsequent elements branching down from the root. Trees where each element has no more than two elements below it are called "binary" trees.

In intrusion detection systems, a decision tree is used to help the analysis engine quickly examine traffic patterns. The decision tree helps the analysis engine eliminate signatures that don't apply to the particular traffic being examined so that the fewest number of comparisons can be made. For example, in the following illustration, the sample IDS decision tree shown may contain a section dividing the traffic into three sections based upon origin of the traffic (a log entry for events taken from the system logs, file changes for modifications to critical files, or user actions for something a user has done). When the analysis engine looks at the traffic pattern and starts down the decision tree, it must decide which path to follow. If it is a log entry, the analysis engine can then concentrate on only the signatures that apply to log entries; it does not need to worry about signatures that apply to file changes or user actions. This type of decision tree allows the analysis engine to function much faster, as it does not have to compare traffic to every signature in the database, just the signatures that apply to that particular type of traffic.

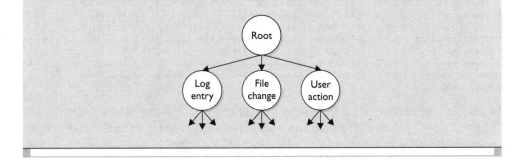

happening on the system. For our example, we'll use the following lines from the "messages" log on a Red Hat 8.0 system:

```
Jan 5 18:20:39 jeep su(pam_unix)[32478]: session opened for user bob by (uid=0)
Jan 5 18:20:47 jeep su(pam_unix)[32516]: authentication failure;
   logname= uid=502 euid=0 tty= ruser=bob rhost= user=root
Jan 5 18:20:53 jeep su(pam_unix)[32517]: authentication failure; logname= id=5
```

Bob tRying To be come su (Super usek)

```
02 euid=0 tty= ruser=bob rhost= user=root
Jan 5 18:21:06 jeep su(pam_unix)[32519]: authentication failure; logname= uid=5
02 euid=0 tty= ruser=bob rhost= user=root
```

In the first line, you see a session being opened by a user named "bob." This usually indicates that whoever owns the account "bob" has logged into the system. On the next three lines, you see authentication failures as Bob tries to become "root"—the superuser account that can do anything on the system. In this case, "bob" tries three times to become root and fails on each try. This pattern of activity could mean a number of different things—"bob" could be an admin and have forgotten the password for the root account, "bob" could be an admin and someone changed the root password without telling him, "bob" could be a user attempting to guess the root password, or an attacker could have compromised Bob's account and is now trying to compromise the root account on the system. In any case, our host-based IDS will work through its decision tree to see if an "authentication failure" in the message log is something it needs to examine. In this instance, when the IDS examines these lines in the log, it will note the fact that three of the lines in the log match one of the patterns it has been told to look for (as determined by information from the decision tree and the signature database) and it will react accordingly, usually by generating an alarm or alert of some type that appears on the user interface or in an e-mail, page, or other form of message.

On a Windows system, the host-based IDS is most likely going to be examining the application logs generated by the operating system. These three logs (application, system, and security) are similar to the logs on a UNIX system, though the Windows logs are not stored as text files and typically require a utility or application to read them. For our example, we will be using the security log from a Windows 2000 Professional system.

```
Failure Audit   1/5/2003   6:47:29 PM   Security   Logon/Logoff          529   SYSTEM
Failure Audit   1/5/2003   6:47:27 PM   Security   Logon/Logoff          529   SYSTEM
Failure Audit   1/5/2003   6:47:26 PM   Security   Logon/Logoff          529   SYSTEM
Success Audit   1/5/2003   6:47:13 PM   Security   Privilege Use         578   Administrator
Success Audit   1/5/2003   6:47:12 PM   Security   Privilege Use         577   Administrator
Success Audit   1/5/2003   6:47:12 PM   Security   Privilege Use         577   Administrator
Success Audit   1/5/2003   6:47:06 PM   Security   Account Management    643   SYSTEM
Success Audit   1/5/2003   6:46:59 PM   Security   Account Management    643   SYSTEM
```

In the first three lines of our security log, you see a "Failure" audit entry for the "Logon/Logoff" process. This indicates someone has tried to log in to the system three times and has failed each time (much like our UNIX example). You don't see the name of the account until you expand the log entry within the Windows event viewer tool, but for this example, let's assume it was the "Administrator" account—the Windows equivalent of the root account. Here again, you see three login failures—if our host-based IDS has been programmed to look for failed login attempts, then it will generate alerts when it examines these log entries.

Advantages of Host-Based IDSs

Host-based IDSs have certain advantages that make them a good choice for certain situations:

- **They can be very operating system–specific and have more detailed signatures**   A host-based IDS can be very specifically designed to run on a certain operating system or to protect certain applications. This narrow focus lets developers concentrate on only the things that affect the specific environment they are trying to protect. With this type of focus, the developers can avoid generic alarms and develop much more specific, detailed signatures to more accurately identify malicious traffic.

- **They can reduce false positive rates**   When running on a specific system, the IDS process is much more likely to be able to determine whether or not the activity being examined is malicious or not. By more accurately identifying which activity is "bad," the IDS will generate fewer "false positives" (alarms generated when the traffic matches a pattern but is not actually malicious).

- **They can examine data after it has been decrypted**   With security concerns constantly on the rise, many developers are starting to encrypt their network communications. When designed and implemented in the right manner, a host-based IDS will be able to examine traffic that is unreadable to a network-based IDS. This particular ability is becoming more important each day as more and more web sites start to encrypt all of their traffic.

- **They can be very application specific**   On a host level, the IDS can be designed, modified, or tuned to work very well on specific applications without having to analyze or even hold signatures for other applications that are not running on that particular system. Signatures can be built for specific versions of web server software, FTP servers, mail servers, or any other application housed on that host.

- **They can determine whether or not an alarm may impact that specific system**   The ability to determine whether or not a particular activity or pattern will really affect the system being protected assists greatly in reducing the number of generated alarms. As the IDS resides on the system, it can verify things such as patch levels, presence of certain files, and system state when it analyzes traffic. By knowing what state the system is in, the IDS can more accurately determine if an activity is potentially harmful to the system.

Disadvantages of Host-Based IDSs

Host-based IDSs also have certain disadvantages that must be weighed into the decision to deploy this type of technology:

- **The IDS must have a process on every system you want to watch**   In order to watch a host, you must have an IDS process or application on every host you want to watch. To cover 100 systems, you will need to deploy 100 host-based IDSs to watch those systems.

- **The IDS can have a high cost of ownership and maintenance** Depending on the specific vendor and application, a host-based IDS can be fairly costly in terms of time and manpower to maintain. Unless there is some type of central console that allows you to maintain remote processes, administrators must maintain each IDS process individually. Even with a central console, with a host-based IDS there will be a high number of processes to maintain, software to update, and parameters to tune.

- **The IDS uses local system resources** In order to function, the host-based IDS must use CPU cycles and memory from the system it is trying to protect. Whatever resources the IDS uses are no longer available for the system to perform its other functions. This becomes extremely important on applications such as high-volume web servers where fewer resources usually means fewer visitors served and the need for more systems to handle expected traffic.

- **The IDS has a very focused view and cannot relate to activity around it** The host-based IDS has a very limited view of the world, as it can only see activity on the host it is protecting. It has little to no visibility into traffic around it on the network or events taking place on other hosts. Consequently, a host-based IDS can tell you only if the system it is running on is under attack.

- **The IDS, if logged locally, could be compromised or disabled** When an IDS generates alarms, it will typically store the alarm information in a file or database of some sort. If the host-based IDS stores its generated alarm traffic on the local system, an attacker that is successful in breaking into the system may have the capability to modify or delete those alarms. This makes it difficult for security personnel to discover the intruder and conduct any type of postincident investigation. A capable intruder may even be able to turn off the IDS process completely.

Active vs. Passive Host-Based IDSs

Most intrusion detection systems can be distinguished by how they examine the activity around them and whether or not they interact with that activity. This is certainly true for host-based IDSs. On a passive system, the IDS is exactly that—"passive." It simply watches the activity, analyzes it, and generates alarms. It does not interact with the activity itself in any way, and it does not modify the defensive posture of the system to react to the traffic. A passive IDS is very similar to a simple motion sensor—it generates an alarm when it matches a pattern much as the motion sensor generates an alarm when it sees movement. An *active* IDS will contain all the same components and capabilities of the passive IDS with one critical exception—the active IDS can *react* to the activity it is analyzing. These reactions can range from something simple, such as running a script to turn a process on or off, to something as complex as modifying file permissions, terminating the offending processes, logging off specific users, and reconfiguring local capabilities to prevent specific users from logging in for the next 12 hours.

Network-Based Intrusion Detection Systems

Network-based intrusion detection systems came along a few years after host-based systems. After running host-based systems for a while, many organizations grew tired of the time, energy, and expense involved with managing the first generation of these systems. The desire for a "better way" grew along with the amount of interconnectivity between systems and consequently the amount of malicious activity seen coming across the networks themselves. This fueled development of a new breed of IDS designed to focus on the source for a great deal of the malicious traffic—the network itself. The network IDS integrated very well into the concept of "perimeter security." More and more companies began to operate their computer security like a castle or military base with attention and effort focused on securing and controlling the means in and out—the idea being that if you could restrict and control access at the perimeter, you didn't have to worry as much about activity inside the organization. Even though the idea of a security perimeter is somewhat flawed (many security incidents originate inside the perimeter), it caught on very quickly, as it was easy to understand and devices such as firewalls, bastion hosts, and routers were available to define and secure that perimeter. The best way to secure the perimeter from outside attack is to reject all traffic from external entities, but as it is impossible and impractical to do so, security personnel needed a way to let traffic in but still be able to determine whether or not the traffic was malicious. This is the problem that network-based intrusion detection system developers were trying to solve.

A network-based IDS, as the name suggests, focuses on network traffic—the bits and bytes traveling along the cables and wires that interconnect the systems. A network IDS (NIDS) must examine the network traffic as it passes by and be able to analyze traffic according to protocol, type, amount, source, destination, content, traffic already seen, etc. This analysis must happen quickly, and the IDS must be able to handle traffic at whatever speed the network operates on to be effective. Network-based IDSs are typically deployed so that they can monitor traffic in and out of an organization's major links: connections to the Internet, remote offices, partners, etc. Like host-based systems, network-based IDSs look for certain activities that typify hostile actions or misuse such as:

- Denial of service attacks
- Port scans or sweeps
- Malicious content in the data payload of a packet or packets
- Vulnerability scanning
- Trojans, viruses, or worms
- Tunneling
- Brute-force attacks

In general, most network-based intrusion detection systems will operate in a fairly similar fashion. Figure 8-4 shows the logical layout of a network-based IDS and by

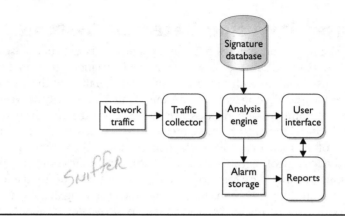

Figure 8-4   Network IDS components

considering the function and activity of each component you can gain some insight into how they operate.

As you can see, the logical components of a network-based intrusion detection system are very similar to those of the host-based system. In the simplest form, a network-based IDS has the same major components: traffic collector, analysis engine, reports, and a user interface.

In a network-based IDS, the *traffic collector* is specifically designed to pull traffic from the network. This component usually behaves in much the same way as a network traffic sniffer—it simply pulls every packet it can see off the network it is connected to. In a network-based IDS, the traffic collector will logically attach itself to a network interface card (NIC) and instruct the NIC to accept every packet it can. A NIC that accepts and processes every packet regardless of the packet's origin and destination is said to be in "promiscuous" mode.

The *analysis engine* in a network-based IDS has the same function as its host-based counterpart, with some substantial differences. The network analysis engine must be capable of collecting packets and examining them individually or, if necessary, reassembling them into an entire traffic session. The patterns and signatures being matched are far more complicated than host-based signatures, so the analysis engine must be capable of remembering what traffic preceded the traffic currently being analyzed so that it can determine whether or not that traffic fits into a larger pattern of malicious activity. Additionally, the network-based analysis engine must be able to keep up with the flow of traffic on the network, rebuilding network sessions and matching patterns in real time.

The network-based IDS *signature database* is usually much larger as well. When examining network patterns, the IDS must be able to recognize traffic targeted at many different applications and operating systems as well as traffic from a wide variety of threats (worms, assessment tools, attack tools, etc.). Some of the signatures themselves can be quite large, as the IDS must look at network traffic occurring in a specific order over a period of time in order to match a particular malicious pattern.

With the lessons learned from the early host-based systems, the network-based IDS developers modified the logical component design somewhat to distribute the user interface and reporting functions. As many companies had more than one network link, they would need an IDS capable of handling multiple links in many different locations. The early IDS vendors solved this dilemma by dividing the components and assigning them to separate entities. The traffic collection, analysis engine, and signature database were bundled into a single entity usually called a "sensor" or "appliance." The sensors would report to and be controlled by a central system or master console. This central system, shown in Figure 8-5, consolidated alarms and provided the user interface and reporting functions that allowed users in one location to manage, maintain, and monitor sensors deployed in a variety of remote locations.

By creating separate entities designed to work together, the network IDS developers were able to build a more capable and flexible system. With encrypted communications, network sensors could be placed around both local and remote perimeters and still be monitored and managed securely from a central location. Placement of the sensors very quickly became an issue for most security personnel, as the sensors obviously had to have visibility of the network traffic in order to analyze it. Because most organizations with network-based IDSs also had firewalls, location of the IDS relative to the firewall had to be considered as well. Placed before the firewall, as shown in Figure 8-6, the IDS will see all traffic coming in from the Internet, including attacks against the firewall itself. This includes traffic that the firewall stops and does not permit into the corporate network. With this type of deployment, the network IDS sensor will generate a large number of alarms (including alarms for traffic that the firewall would stop) that tends to overwhelm the human operators managing the system.

Placed after the firewall, as shown in Figure 8-7, the network IDS sensor sees and analyzes the traffic that is being passed through the firewall and into the corporate network. While this does not allow the IDS to see attacks against the firewall, it generally results in far fewer alarms and is the most popular placement for network IDS sensors.

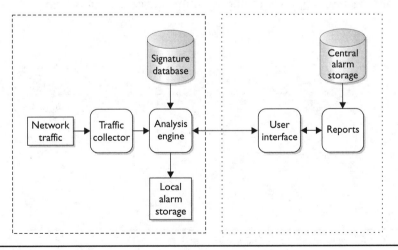

Figure 8-5   Distributed network IDS components

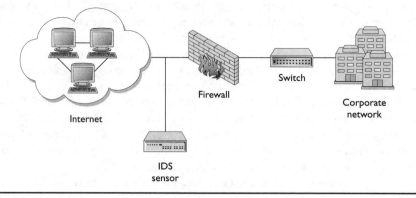

Figure 8-6   IDS sensor placed in front of firewall

As you already know, network-based intrusion detection systems examine the network traffic for suspicious or malicious activity. Here are two examples to illustrate the operation of a network IDS:

- **Port scan**   A port scan is a reconnaissance activity a potential attacker will use to find out information about the systems they wish to attack. Using any of a number of tools, the attacker will attempt to connect to various services (Web, FTP, SMTP, etc.) to see if they exist on the intended target. In normal network traffic, a single user might connect to the FTP service provided on a single system. During a port scan, an attacker may attempt to connect to the FTP service on every system. As the attacker's traffic passes by the IDS, this pattern of attempting to connect to different services on different systems will be noticed. When the IDS compares the activity to its signature database, it will very likely match this traffic against the port scanning signature and generate an alarm.

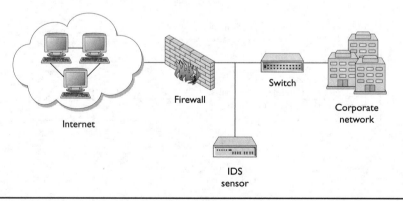

Figure 8-7   IDS sensor placed behind firewall

- **Ping of death**   Toward the end of 1996, it was discovered that certain operating systems, such as Windows, could be crashed by sending a very large ICMP echo request packet to that system. The vulnerable operating systems did not handle the packet correctly and would subsequently reboot or lock up after receiving the packets. This is a fairly simple traffic pattern for a network IDS to identify, as it simply has to look for ICMP packets over a certain size.

Advantages of a Network-Based IDS

A network-based IDS has certain advantages that make it a good choice for certain situations:

- **It takes fewer systems to provide IDS coverage**   With a few well-placed network IDS sensors, you can monitor all the network traffic going in and out of your organization. Fewer sensors usually equates to less overhead and maintenance, meaning you can protect the same number of systems at a lower cost.

- **Deployment, maintenance, and upgrade costs are usually lower**   The fewer systems that have to be managed and maintained to provide IDS coverage, the lower the cost to operate the IDS will be. Upgrading and maintaining a few sensors is usually much cheaper than upgrading and maintaining hundreds of host-based processes.

- **A network-based IDS has visibility into all network traffic and can correlate attacks among multiple systems**   Well-placed network IDS sensors can see the "big picture" when it comes to network-based attacks. The network sensors can tell you if attacks are widespread and unorganized or focused and concentrated on specific systems.

Disadvantages of a Network-Based IDS

A network-based IDS has certain disadvantages:

- **It is ineffective when traffic is encrypted**   When network traffic is encrypted from application to application or system to system, a network-based IDS sensor will not be able to examine that traffic. With the increasing popularity of encrypted traffic, this is becoming a bigger problem for effective IDS operations.

- **It can't see traffic that does not cross it**   The IDS sensor can examine only traffic crossing the network link it is monitoring. With most IDS sensors being placed on perimeter links, traffic traversing the internal network is never seen.

- **It must be able to handle high volumes of traffic**   As network speeds continue to increase, the network sensors must be able to keep pace and examine the traffic as quickly as it can pass the network. When network-based intrusion detection systems were introduced, 10 Mbps networks were the norm. Now 100 Mbps and even 1 Gbps networks are commonplace. This increase in traffic speeds means IDS sensors must be faster and more powerful than ever before.

- **It doesn't know about activity on the hosts themselves**   As the name suggests, network-based intrusion detection systems focus on network traffic. Activity that occurs on the hosts themselves will not be seen by a network IDS.

Active vs. Passive Network-Based IDSs

Most network-based intrusion detection systems can be distinguished by how they examine the traffic and whether or not they interact with that traffic. On a *passive* system, the IDS is exactly that—"passive." It simply watches the traffic, analyzes it, and generates alarms. It does not interact with the traffic itself in any way, and it does not modify the defensive posture of the system to react to the traffic. A passive IDS is very similar to a simple motion sensor—it generates an alarm when it matches a pattern much as the motion sensor generates an alarm when it sees movement. An *active* IDS will contain all the same components and capabilities of the passive IDS with one critical addition— the active IDS can *react* to the traffic it is analyzing. These reactions can range from something simple, such as sending a TCP reset message to interrupt a potential attack and disconnect a session, to something complex such as dynamically modifying firewall rules to reject all traffic from specific source IP addresses for the next 24 hours.

The most common defensive capability for an active IDS is to send a TCP reset message. Within the TCP protocol, the reset message (RST) essentially tells both sides of the connection to drop the session and stop communicating immediately. While this mechanism was originally developed to cover situations like systems accidentally receiving communications intended for other systems, the reset message works fairly well for intrusion detection systems. There is one serious drawback—a reset message affects only the current session. There is nothing to prevent the attacker from coming back and trying again and again. Despite the "temporariness" of this solution, sending a reset message is usually the only defensive measure implemented on IDS deployments, as the fear of blocking legitimate traffic and disrupting business processes, even for a few moments, often outweighs the perceived benefit of discouraging potential intruders.

Signatures

As you have probably deduced from our discussion so far, one of the critical elements of any good intrusion detection system is the signature set—that set of patterns the IDS uses to determine whether or not activity is potentially hostile. Signatures can be very simple or remarkably complicated, depending on the activity they are trying to highlight. In general, signatures can be divided into two main groups, depending on what the signature is looking for.

Content-based signatures are generally the simplest. They are designed to look at the content of such things as network packets or log entries. Content-based signatures are typically easy to build and look for something simple such as a certain string of characters or a certain flag set in a TCP packet. Here are some example content-based signatures:

- *Matching the characters "/etc/passwd" in a telnet session.* On a UNIX system, the names of valid user accounts (and sometimes the passwords for those user accounts) are stored in a file called "passwd" located in the "etc" directory.

- *Matching a TCP packet with the synchronize, reset, and urgent flags all set.* This combination of flags is impossible to generate under normal conditions, and the presence of all of these flags in the same packet would indicate this packet was likely "created" by a potential attacker for a specific purpose.

- *Matching the characters "to: decode" in the header of an e-mail message.* On certain older versions of sendmail, sending an e-mail message to "decode" would cause the system to execute the contents of the e-mail.

Context-based signatures are generally more complicated, as they are designed to match large patterns of activity and examine how certain types of activity fit into the other activities going on around them. Context signatures generally address the question "how does this event compare to other events that have already happened or might happen in the near future?" Context signatures are more difficult to analyze and take more resources to match, as the IDS must be able to "remember" past events to match certain context signatures. Some example context-based signatures:

- *Match a potential intruder scanning for open web servers on a specific network.* A potential intruder may use a port scanner to look for any systems accepting connections on port 80. To match this signature, the IDS must analyze all attempted connections to port 80 and then be able to determine which connection attempts are coming from the same source but are going to multiple, different destinations.

- *Identify a Nessus scan.* Nessus is an open-source vulnerability scanner that allows security administrators (and potential attackers) to quickly examine systems for vulnerabilities. Depending on the tests chosen, Nessus will typically perform the tests in a certain order, one after the other. To be able to determine the presence of a Nessus scan, the IDS must know which tests Nessus runs as well as the typical order the tests are run in.

- *Identify a ping flood attack.* A single ICMP packet on its own is generally regarded as harmless, certainly not worthy of an IDS signature. Yet, thousands of ICMP packets coming to a single system in a short period of time can have a devastating effect on the receiving system. By flooding a system with thousands of valid ICMP packets, an attacker can keep a target system so busy it doesn't have time to do anything else—a very effective denial of service attack. To identify a ping flood, the IDS must recognize each ICMP packet and keep track of how many ICMP packets different systems have received in the recent past.

To function, the IDS must have a decent signature base with examples of known, undesirable activity that it can use when analyzing traffic or events. Any time an IDS matches current events against a signature, the IDS could be considered successful, as it has correctly matched the current event against a known signature and reacted accordingly (usually with an alarm or alert of some type).

False Positives and Negatives

Viewed in its simplest form, an IDS is really just taking activity (be it host-based or network-based) and matching it against a predefined set of patterns. When it matches activity to a specific pattern, there is no way for the IDS to know the true intent behind that activity—whether or not it is benign or hostile—and therefore the IDS can react only as it has been programmed to do. In most cases, this means generating an alert that must then be analyzed by a human who tries to determine the intent of the traffic from whatever information they have available. When an IDS matches a pattern and generates an alarm for benign traffic, meaning the traffic was not hostile and not a threat, this is called a *false positive.* In other words, the IDS matched a pattern and raised an alarm when it didn't really need to. Again, keep in mind that the IDS can only match patterns and has no capability to determine intent behind the activity, so in some ways this is an unfair label. Technically, the IDS is functioning correctly by matching the pattern, but from a human standpoint this is not information the analyst needed to see, as it does not constitute a threat and does not require intervention.

An IDS is also limited by its signature set—it can match only activity for which it has stored patterns. Hostile activity that does not match an IDS signature and therefore goes undetected is called a *false negative.* In this case, the IDS is not generating any alarms, even though it should be, giving a false sense of security.

IDS Models

In addition to being divided along the host and network lines, intrusion detection systems are often classified according to the detection model they use: anomaly or misuse. For an IDS, a model is a method for examining behavior so that the IDS can determine if that behavior is "not normal" or in violation of established policies.

An *anomaly* detection model is the more complicated of the two. In this model, the intrusion detection system must know what "normal" behavior on the host or network being protected really is. Once the "normal" behavior baseline is established, the IDS can then go to work identifying deviations from the norm, which are further scrutinized to determine if that activity is malicious. Building the profile of normal activity is usually done by the IDS, with some input from security administrators, and can take anywhere from days to months. The IDS must be flexible and capable enough to account for things such as new systems, new users, movement of information resources, etc., but be sensitive enough to detect a single user illegally switching from one account to another at 3 A.M. on a Saturday. Anomaly detection was developed to make the system capable of dealing with variations in traffic and better able to determine which activity patterns were malicious. A perfectly functioning anomaly-based system would be able to ignore patterns from legitimate hosts and users but still identify those patterns as suspicious should they come from a potential attacker. Unfortunately, most anomaly-based systems suffer from extremely high false positives, especially during the "break-in" period while the IDS is learning the network. On the other hand, an anomaly-based system is not restricted to a specific signature set and is far more likely to identify a new exploit or attack tool that would go unnoticed by a traditional intrusion detection system.

A *misuse* detection model is a little simpler to implement, and therefore the more popular of the two models. In a misuse model, the IDS looks for suspicious activity or activity that violates specific policies and then reacts as it has been programmed. This reaction may be an alarm, e-mail, router reconfiguration, or TCP reset message. Technically, this is the more efficient model, as it takes fewer resources to operate, does not need to learn what "normal" behavior is, and will generate an alarm whenever a pattern is successfully matched. However, the misuse model's greatest weakness is its reliance on a predefined signature base—any activity, malicious or otherwise, that the misuse-based IDS does not have a signature for will go undetected. Despite that drawback and because it is easier and cheaper to implement, most commercial IDS products are based on the misuse detection model.

Preventative Intrusion Detection Systems

While current intrusion detection systems do a fairly decent job of alerting the user to suspicious or malicious activity, they don't really provide too many capabilities to prevent the attacker from damaging your information systems. As many security personnel and system administrators have found out, there's less value in knowing what happened after the fact than there is in preventing the damage from occurring in the first place. This is the philosophy behind a new movement in intrusion detection systems—systems designed to both identify malicious activity and prevent it from having any impact on your network and information systems. This new breed of IDS, called a *preventative IDS*, is rapidly gaining in popularity, and several commercial vendors are already offering products with this type of capability.

The concept behind a preventative IDS is simple: identify bad traffic and make sure it doesn't do any harm. In many ways, a preventative IDS is similar to an antivirus product. An antivirus product may spot an infected e-mail attachment coming into the mail server and will quarantine the incoming message, preventing the message from being opened and the virus from being executed. In the same fashion, a preventative IDS may see an attacker attempting to execute a buffer overflow on a local system and will intercept the attacker's system call to prevent it from executing. To be effective, a preventative IDS will typically be some type of hybrid system, having both network-based and host-based portions. The host-based portion serves as a security wrapper for the protected system, filtering such things as system calls, user input, and program executions. Activity that matches a known, malicious pattern, such as a buffer overflow, is caught by the host wrapper and stopped before the attack is allowed to execute and affect the local system. The network-based portion operates in a similar manner, filtering network traffic for things like scans, network-based attacks, and denial of service attacks. Like its host counterpart, the preventative network IDS catches the malicious activity and prevents it from reaching the intended target.

In many ways, preventative intrusion detection systems are the wave of the future. Traditional misuse model–based IDSs are continually playing catch-up to increasingly sophisticated attackers. Additionally, most IDSs are limited to a detection role much like a burglar alarm—they can tell you when certain things have happened, but they have a limited ability to prevent things from happening. Even when the ability to prevent malicious activity is available, as by sending a TCP reset or reconfiguring firewall rulesets, it is often not used, as the potential for accidentally blocking legitimate traffic is extremely high. By contrast, a preventative IDS will still have the ability to detect and identify malicious activity, but it will also have the capability to prevent that activity from damaging or disabling critical information assets. This promise of a "better way" to perform security operations is attracting a large audience whose interest ensures preventative intrusion detection systems will receive some serious attention from commercial security companies in the very near future.

IDS Products and Vendors

There are quite a few intrusion detection products available on the market today, with prices ranging from free to very expensive. Table 8-1 provides a list of some of the IDS products and vendors currently available.

Honeypots

As is often the case, one of the best tools available to information security personnel has always been knowledge. To properly secure and defend a network and the information systems on that network, security personnel need to know what they are up against. What types of attacks are being used? What are the tools and techniques that are popular right now? How effective is a certain technique? What sort of impact does this specific tool have on my network? Often this sort of information is passed through white papers, conferences, mailing lists, or even word of mouth. In some cases, the tool developers themselves provide much of the information in the interest of promoting better security for everyone. Information is also gathered through examination and forensic analysis, often after a major incident has already occurred and information systems are

Name	Product	Where to Find More Information
Cisco Systems, Inc.	Cisco IDS	www.cisco.com
Computer Associates	eTrust	www.ca.com
Enterasys Network	Dragon	www.enterasys.com
Internet Security Systems, Inc.	RealSecure	www.iss.net
Intrusion, Inc.	SecureNet, SecureHost	www.intrusion.com
Intruvert Networks	IntruShield	www.intruvert.com
iPolicy Networks	ipEnforcer	www.ipolicynetworks.com
NetScreen	NetScreen IDP	www.netscreen.com
NFR Security, Inc.	NFR	www.nfr.com
Snort	Snort (free, open source)	www.snort.org
Symantec Corporation	Intruder Alert	www.symantec.com
TippingPoint Technologies	UnityOne	www.tippingpoint.com
Tripwire, Inc.	Tripwire	www.tripwiresecurity.com

Table 8-1   List of IDS Vendors and Products

BackOfficer (free)

already damaged. One of the most effective techniques for collecting this type of information is to observe activity first-hand—watching an attacker as they probe, navigate, and exploit their way through a network. To accomplish this without exposing critical information systems, security researchers often use something called a "honeypot."

A *honeypot* or *honeynet* is sometimes called a digital sandbox. In essence, a honeypot is an artificial environment where attackers can be contained and observed without putting real systems at risk. A good honeypot gives the appearance of a real network, application servers, users systems, network traffic, etc., but in most cases is made up of one or a few systems running specialized software to simulate the user and network traffic common to most targeted networks. Figure 8-8 illustrates a simple honeypot layout where a single system is placed on the network to deliberately attract attention from potential attackers.

Figure 8-8 shows the security researcher's view of the honeypot, while Figure 8-9 shows the attacker's view. The security administrator knows that the honeypot, in this case, really only consists of a single system running software designed to react to probes, reconnaissance attempts, and exploits as if it were an entire network of systems. When the attacker connects to the honeypot, they are presented with an entire "virtual" network of servers and PCs running a variety of applications. In most cases, the honeypot will appear to be running versions of applications that are known to be vulnerable to specific exploits. All this is designed to provide the attacker with an enticing, hopefully irresistible target.

Anytime an attacker has been lured into probing or attacking the virtual network, the honeypot records the activity for later analysis: what the attacker does, which systems and applications they concentrate on, what tools are run, how long they stay, etc. All this information is collected and analyzed in the hopes that it will allow security personnel to better understand and protect against the threats to their systems.

There are many honeypots in use, specializing in everything from wireless to denial of service attacks; most are being run by research, government, or law enforcement organizations. Why aren't more businesses running honeypots? Quite simply, the time and cost are prohibitive. Honeypots take quite a bit of time and effort to manage and maintain and even more effort to sort, analyze, and classify the traffic the honeypot collects.

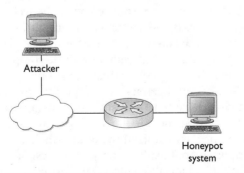

Figure 8-8   Logical depiction of a honeypot

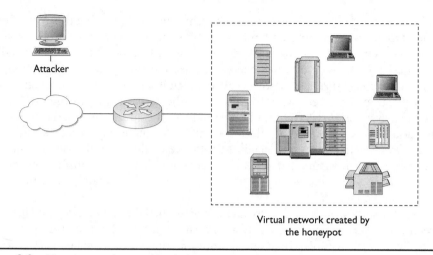

Virtual network created by
the honeypot

Figure 8-9   Virtual network created by the honeypot

Unless they are developing security tools, most companies focus their limited security efforts on preventing attacks, and in many cases, companies aren't even that concerned with detecting attacks as long as the attacks are blocked, are unsuccessful, and don't affect business operations. So for now, honeypots will probably continue to be specialized research tools that you aren't likely to find in most companies' security deployments.

Incident Response

If you spend any time at all in the fields of network security or system administration, you will likely be involved in some sort of incident response or recovery effort. An "incident" can be anything from a hardware failure to a full-scale security breach, and while each one is handled in a slightly different manner, there are some similarities we will discuss in this section. Essentially, incident response is how an organization reacts to an unusual negative situation. Incident response covers the technical and administrative aspects of dealing with incidents and can range in formality from a simple "call Superman" approach to a formal, detailed step-by-step response plan including procedures and tools that covers every situation imaginable. Some companies have a full-scale response team, while others have that proverbial "go to" person that handles everything on their own. Entire books have been written about this topic, and while we won't attempt to cover it in anywhere close to that amount of detail, we will cover a few fundamental concepts that should be included in any incident response approach.

Regardless of your particular organization's approach, it is always a good idea to start with an incident response plan. Ideally, your incident response plan is a well-thought-out set of documents that include all the necessary processes and pieces of information to deal with specific incidents. The idea is to sit down ahead of time and plan out how you need to react to and deal with different kinds of incidents. Make your response procedures as specific as you can—the less you leave to chance, the less likely you are to make a mistake when handling an incident. When building your response procedures, think about topics such as:

- What immediate steps need to be taken?
- Does the security posture need to be modified? When? How?
- Who needs to be notified of this event? When? How?
- What impact does this have on business operations?
- What tools will be used to investigate this incident? Who will use them and how?
- Which is more important, system recovery or evidence collection?
- Will forensic activity occur? What evidence will be collected, and how will it be preserved?
- At what point do you contact law enforcement? Who makes that call, and whom do you call?
- What other resources are available?
- Where are things like replacement hardware and software located?
- Do system images or backups exist to aid in recovery?
- How do you contact hardware, software, or security vendors if you need to?
- Will this incident become public knowledge? Is a press release needed?

These questions are just examples—not every incident is the same, and while you can't plan for everything, you do need to plan for everything you can. The biggest advantage to prebuilt incident response plans is that they provide a framework and offer guidance during what is usually a frantic and tense situation. By following a plan, organizations can usually recover faster and with less impact than by "winging it" when something happens.

Another key factor you have to consider when responding to an incident, particularly an intrusion or security breach, is the involvement of law enforcement. If you have any notion of attempting to track down and prosecute the intruder, you will need to involve law enforcement as quickly as possible. Start with your local police department and the FBI; you may also want to engage one of the many consulting firms that specialize in incident response and computer forensics. Keep in mind that there are specific guidelines for handling and preserving digital evidence and in many cases, the steps necessary to preserve evidence are contrary to business recovery efforts. For example, if your main e-commerce web server is attacked, business recovery would want the system up and on-line as soon as possible. To properly examine and preserve evidence, though, you may not be able to return that system to operation for days or months. These conflicting priorities make it difficult for many companies, particularly smaller ones, to properly investigate and respond to incidents.

Computer incidents are increasing at such high rate that some insurance firms are now offering "incident insurance" to protect your organization in the event of a serious computer-related incident. As with most insurance policies, premium reductions are granted for proactive measures like installing firewalls and intrusion detection systems. While insurance may protect you from immediate monetary losses, your organization may sustain more permanent long-term damage such as a loss of public confidence as a result of the incident—particularly damaging if you are a financial or retail organization.

Chapter Review

Intrusion detection is a mechanism for detecting unexpected or unauthorized activity on computer systems. Intrusion detection systems can be host-based, examining only the activity applicable to a specific system; or network-based, examining network traffic for a large number of systems. Intrusion detection systems match patterns known as "signatures" that can be content or context based. Some intrusion detection systems are model based and alert when activity does not match normal patterns (anomaly based) or when it matches known suspicious or malicious patterns (misuse detection). Newer versions of IDS include prevention capabilities that will automatically block suspicious or malicious traffic before it reaches its intended destination.

Honeypots are specialized forms of intrusion detection that involve setting up simulated hosts and services for attackers to target. Honeypots are based on the concept of luring attackers away from legitimate systems by presenting more tempting or interesting systems that, in most cases, appear to be easy targets. By monitoring activity within the honeypot, security personnel are better able to identify potential attackers along with their tools and capabilities.

Incident response is the formalized response of reacting to a situation such as a security breach or system outage. Incident response requires procedures that outline steps to take for notification, analysis, and remediation. While many incident response systems are based on threats from potential attackers, incident response can be used to deal with other situations such as virus outbreaks, hardware outages, and loss of network connectivity.

Questions

1. What are the three types of event logs generated by Windows NT or 2000 systems?

    A. Event, Process, and Security

    B. Application, User, and Security

    C. User, Event, and Security

    D. Application, System, and Security

2. What are the two main types of intrusion detection systems?

    A. Network-based and host-based

    B. Signature-based and event-based

    C. Active and reactive

    D. Intelligent and passive

3. The first commercial IDS product was

    A. Stalker

    B. NetRanger

    C. IDES

    D. RealSecure

4. What are the two main types of IDS signatures?

    A. Network-based and file-based

    B. Context-based and content-based

    C. Active and reactive

    D. None of the above

5. A passive, host-based IDS

    A. Runs on the local system

    B. Does not interact with the traffic around it

    C. Can look at system event and error logs

    D. All of the above

6. Which of the following is *not* a capability of a network-based IDS?

    A. Can detect denial of service attacks

    B. Can decrypt and read encrypted traffic

    C. Can decode UDP and TCP packets

    D. Can be tuned to a particular network environment

7. An active IDS can

    A. Respond to attacks with TCP resets

    B. Monitor for malicious activity

    C. A and B

    D. None of the above

8. Honeypots are used to

    A. Research behavior of attackers

    B. Collect evidence for prosecution

    C. Process alarms from other IDSs

    D. Attract customers to e-commerce sites

PART IV

9. Incident response

   A. Usually involves a response plan

   B. Is a reaction to a security incident

   C. May involve law enforcement

   D. All of the above

10. Preventative intrusion detection systems

    A. Are cheaper

    B. Are designed to stop malicious activity from occurring

    C. Can only monitor activity

    D. Were the first types of IDS

Answers

1. **D.** The three main types of event logs generated by Windows NT or 2000 systems are: Application, System, and Security.

2. **A.** The two main types of intrusion detection systems are network-based and host-based. Network-based systems monitor network connections for suspicious traffic. Host-based systems reside on an individual system and monitor that system for suspicious or malicious activity.

3. **A.** The first commercial IDS product was Stalker, released by Haystack Labs in 1989.

4. **B.** The two main types of IDS signatures are context-based and content-based. Context-based signatures examine traffic and how that traffic fits into the other traffic around it. A port scan is a good example of a context-based signature. A content-based signature looks at what is inside the traffic, such as the contents of a specific packet.

5. **D.** A passive, host-based IDS runs on the local system, cannot interfere with traffic or activity on that system, and would have access to local system logs.

6. **B.** A network-based IDS typically cannot decrypt and read encrypted traffic. This is one of the principle weaknesses of network-based intrusion detection systems.

7. **C.** An active IDS can perform all the functions of a passive IDS (monitoring, alerting, reporting, etc.) with the added ability of responding to suspected attacks with capabilities such as sending TCP reset messages to the source and destination IP addresses.

8. **A.** Honeypots are designed to attract attackers by providing what appear to be easy, inviting targets. The honeypot collects and records the activity of attackers and their tools so that security researchers can better understand how attackers operate.

9. **D.** Incident response is the act of responding to a negative situation, usually a security breach or attack in the area of network security. Most organizations have response plans to guide their actions during an incident; more serious incidents, such as a security breach where sensitive information such as credit card numbers are stolen, will likely involve law enforcement participation.

10. **B.** Preventative intrusion detection systems are designed to "prevent" malicious actions from having any impact on the targeted system or network. For example, a host-based preventative IDS may intercept an attacker's buffer overflow attempt and prevent it from executing. By stopping the attack, the IDS prevents the attacker from affecting the system.

Security Baselines

In this chapter, you will
- Learn about hardening operating systems
- Understand hardening network devices
- Explore hardening applications

Computers are such an integral part of everything we do now that it is difficult imagining life without them. Operating systems, network devices, and applications all work together on millions of computers to process, transmit, and store the billions of pieces of information exchanged every day. Everything from cars to credit cards require computers to operate.

The many uses for systems and operating systems require flexible components, allowing users to design, configure, and implement the systems they need. Yet, it is this very flexibility that causes some of the biggest weaknesses in computer systems. Computer and operating system developers often build and deliver systems in "default" modes that do little to secure the system from external attacks. From the view of the developer, this is the most efficient mode of delivery, as there is no way they could anticipate what every user in every situation will need. From the user's view, however, this means a good deal of effort must be put into protecting and securing the system before it is ever put into service. The process of securing and preparing a system for the production environment is called *hardening*. Unfortunately, many users don't understand the steps necessary to effectively secure their systems, resulting in hundreds of compromised systems every day.

Overview Baselines

To effectively and consistently secure systems, one must take a structured and logical approach. This starts with an examination of the system's intended functions and capabilities to determine what processes and applications will be housed on the system. As a best practice, anything that is not required for operations should be removed or disabled on the system. Then all the appropriate patches, hotfixes, and settings are applied to protect and secure the systems.

This process of establishing a system's security state is called *baselining,* and the resulting product is a security *baseline* that allows the system to run safely and securely. Once the process has been completed for a particular hardware and software combination, any like systems can be configured with the same baseline and achieve the same level and depth of security and protection. Uniform baselines are critical in large-scale operations, as it is far too costly to maintain separate configurations and security levels for hundreds or thousands of systems.

Password Selection

Password selection is one of those critical activities that is often neglected as part of a good security baseline. The heart of the problem is this—most systems today are only protected by a simple userid and password. If an attacker guesses the right userid and password combination, then they are in, and have completely bypassed all the other steps taken to secure the system. Worse still, on a system supporting multiple users, the attacker only has to guess one correct userid and password combination to gain access.

This basic security challenge exists for every other topic we will examine in this chapter, from operating systems to applications. Selecting a good password for all user accounts is critical to protecting information systems. So how does one select a good password? One that is still relatively easy to remember but still difficult to "guess?" Unfortunately, there is no magic answer to cover all situations, but there are some basic guidelines and principles to help ensure good password selection.

Password Policy Guidelines

The username and password challenge is arguably the most popular security mechanism in use today. Unfortunately, it's also the most poorly configured, neglected, and easily circumvented. The first step in addressing the password issue is to create an effective and manageable *password policy* that both system administrators and users can work with. In creating a policy, you should examine your business and security needs carefully. What level of risk is acceptable? How secure does the system need to be? How often should users change their passwords? Should you ever lock accounts? What guidelines should users use when selecting passwords? Your list of questions will vary greatly, but the key is to spend time identifying your concerns and addressing them specifically in your password policy.

Once you have created your password policy, spread the word. Make sure every user gets a copy. Post it on your company intranet. Have new users read a copy of the policy before creating an account for them. Periodically send out e-mail reminders highlighting items in the password policy. Make announcements at company gatherings. The method is not important—the goal is simply to ensure that every single user understands what the policy is.

Once you have taught everyone what the policy is, you have to enforce it to make it effective. Set a minimum number of characters for passwords, and never accept a shorter password. Implement password aging and prompt users to change passwords on a regular basis. Do not accept passwords based on dictionary words. Do not allow users to use the same password over and over. Many operating systems have built-in utilities or add-ons that allow administrators to enforce good password selection, force password aging, and prevent password reuse. Here are some useful references for different operating systems:

- **Microsoft Windows NT 4.0, Service Pack 2**   Introduced PASSFILT.DLL, which forces users to follow specific conventions when creating new passwords: http://support.microsoft.com/support/kb/articles/q161/9/90.asp

- **Linux**
  - **Npasswd**   A replacement for passwd that provides intelligent password screening to help users select a more secure password: www.utexas.edu/cc/unix/software/npasswd/
  - **PAM (Pluggable Authentication Modules)**   Provides a common authentication scheme that can be used for a variety of applications. Go to www.redhat.com and search for "PAM."

- **Solaris**
  - **PAM (Pluggable Authentication Modules:**   Is the Solaris implementation of a common authentication scheme: www.sun.com/solaris/pam/

Take the time to audit your own password files by running some of the more popular password cracking utilities against them. In a large organization with many user accounts (over a thousand), this will take some time and computing power, but it is well worth the effort. Perform these audits as often as you can—monthly, every other month, or every quarter. If you find accounts with easily cracked passwords, have the users review your password policy and change the passwords immediately. Remember, there are many publicly available password cracking tools, and any account you crack easily can be cracked by someone else. Here are some of the more popular password cracking utilities:

- **LC4 (formerly L0phtCrack) for Windows 2000 and NT** www.atstake.com/research/lc/
- **John the Ripper (UNIX and DOS)**   www.openwall.com/
- **Crack (UNIX)**   packetstormsecurity.nl/Crackers/crack/

Selecting a Password

There are many different methods of selecting a password, ranging from random generation to one-time use. Each method has its own advantages and weaknesses, but typically when security increases, usability tends to decrease. For example, random generation tends to produce secure passwords composed of random letters (no dictionary words, and a mix of upper- and lowercase letters with usually one or two numbers) that are very difficult to guess and will defeat most password cracking utilities. Unfortunately, randomly generated passwords tend to be difficult to remember, and users often write such passwords down, usually in a location close to the machine, thus defeating the purpose of the password. The best compromise between security and usability lies in teaching users how to select their own secure password based on an easy to remember *passphrase*.

A password based on a passphrase can be formed in many ways: taking the first letter of each word in a sentence; taking the first letter from the first word, second letter from the second word, and so on; combining words; or replacing letters with other characters. Here are some passphrase examples and the resulting passwords:

- Use the first letter of each word in the following sentence:
  Sentence   I love to drive my 1969 Mustang!
  Password   Iltdm69M!

- Combining words and replacing letters with characters:
  Sentence   Bad to the Bone
  Password   Bad2theB1

Passphrases can be almost anything—lines from your favorite movie, lyrics from your favorite song, or something you make up on the spot. Use any method you choose, but the end result should be a difficult-to-guess, easy-to-remember password.

Components of a Good Password

By using the passphrase method, users should be able to create their own easy-to-remember passwords. However, since a password is meant to protect access and resources from intruders, it should not be easy for someone else to guess or obtain using password cracking utilities, such as John the Ripper, L0phtCrack, or Crack. To make a password more difficult to guess or obtain, make sure your new password meets the following guidelines:

- Should be at least eight characters long (some operating systems require longer passwords by default)
- Should have at least three of the following four elements:
  - One or more uppercase letters (A – Z)
  - One or more lowercase letters (a – z)
  - One or more numerals (0 – 9)
  - One or more special characters or punctuation marks (!@#$%^&*,.:;?)
- Should not consist of dictionary words
- Should never be the same as the user's login name or contain the login name
- Should not consist of the user's first or last name, family member's names, birth dates, pet names, or any other item that is easily identified with the user

Password Aging

Given enough time and computing power, virtually any password can be cracked by simply testing all possible passwords. It is therefore necessary to have users change their passwords on a regular basis. Additionally, since any password can be cracked eventually, it is necessary to prevent users from "recycling" passwords (using the same password over and over). Many operating systems have options allowing system administrators to enforce password aging and prevent password reuse. Consider using the following guidelines:

- Have users change their passwords every 60 to 90 days (very secure facilities may want to change passwords every 30 to 45 days)

- Have the system "remember" the user's last five to ten passwords, and do not allow the user to use those passwords again

Operating System and Network Operating System Hardening

The *operating system (OS)* of a computer is the basic software that handles things such as input, output, display, memory management, and all the other highly detailed tasks required to support the user environment and associated applications. Most users are familiar with the Microsoft family of operating systems: Windows 95, Windows 98, Windows NT, Windows 2000, Windows ME, and Windows XP. Indeed, the vast majority of home and business PCs run some version of a Microsoft operating system. Other users may be familiar with Mac OS, Solaris, or one of the many varieties of the UNIX operating system.

A *network operating system (NOS)* is an operating system that includes additional functions and capabilities to assist in connecting computers and devices, such as printers, to a local area network. Some of the more common network operating systems include Novell's Netware and SpartaCom's LANtastic. For most modern operating systems, including Windows 2000, Solaris, and Linux, the terms *operating system* and *network operating system* are used interchangeably as they perform all the basic function and provide enhanced capabilities for connecting to LANs.

Operating system developers and manufacturers all share a common problem. There is no possible way they can anticipate the many different configurations and variations that the user community will require from their products. So, rather than spending countless hours and funds attempting to meet every need, manufacturers provide a "default" installation for their products that usually contains the base operating system and some more commonly desirable options, such as drivers, utilities, and enhancements. As the operating system could be used for any of a variety of purposes, and could be placed in any number of logical locations (local LAN, DMZ, WAN, and so on) the manufacturer typically does little to nothing with security. The manufacturer may provide some recommendations or simplified tools and settings to facilitate securing the system, but in general, the end users are responsible for securing their own systems. Generally this involves removing unnecessary applications and utilities, disabling unneeded services, setting appropriate permissions on files, and updating the operating system and application code to the latest version.

This process of securing an operating system is called *hardening*, and it is intended to make the system more resistant to attack, much like armor or steel is hardened to make it less susceptible to breakage or damage. Each operating system has its own approach to security, and while the process of hardening is generally the same, different steps must be taken to secure each operating system.

Hardening Microsoft Operating Systems

When we talk about securing or hardening Windows operating systems, we generally only discuss the Windows NT, Windows 2000, or Windows XP family of operating systems. Older Microsoft operating systems, such as Windows 3.11, Windows 95, Windows 98, and Windows ME were designed with very little in the way of security capabilities, and not much can be done to harden those particular operating systems. For the purposes of this discussion, we will focus on hardening the Windows 2000 and Windows XP operating systems, as they are the most popular choices for business servers and desktops.

General Steps for Securing Windows Operating Systems

The following is a general guide for securing Windows operating systems such as Windows 2000 or XP Professional. It is by no means an exhaustive list, but can help you address some of the more critical areas of Windows security.

1. *Disable all unnecessary services.* In general, Windows systems will serve one main purpose (web server, mail server, DNS server, domain/login server, and so on). Once you have determined what the main purpose of the system will be, disable any service not absolutely necessary to support that purpose.

2. *Restrict permissions on files and access to the Registry.* While this step may take some time, restricting who can read, write, and execute certain files can provide some much-needed security. Additionally, the Windows Registry must be protected to ensure that entries are not modified or deleted.

3. *Remove unnecessary programs.* Any application or utility not needed should be removed. This reduces the chances of an attacker exploiting a weakness or enabling unneeded services.

4. *Apply the latest patches and fixes.* Ensure the operating system and all applications have the latest vendor-supplied patches applied.

5. *Remove unnecessary user accounts and ensure password guidelines are in place.* Default accounts such as "guest" should be disabled or removed. Password guidelines should be enabled and enforced to ensure that users choose appropriate passwords.

Hardening Windows 2000

When Microsoft introduced Windows 2000 in February of 2000, many users were thrilled at the additional stability and security promised by this new operating system. While Windows 2000 did deliver on some fronts, like many previous Microsoft products there were some significant vulnerabilities discovered, and these vulnerabilities were used by attackers to disable, disrupt, or modify hundreds of thousands of systems over the last two years. A large number of these vulnerabilities came from default settings or applications that were never addressed by the end users when they installed the operating system and attached their computer to the Internet. Windows 2000 security can be significantly improved, and there are a number of guides out there to assist you in securing your Windows system. In this chapter, we will examine the steps recommended by Microsoft's own security team.

 NOTE Microsoft updates their on-line content on a fairly frequent basis. Should the Microsoft checklist be updated from the material available in this text, please use the suggested checklist from Microsoft.

The first step, though it is not covered in Microsoft's own checklist, is rather obvious but extremely important. You must determine which version of the operating system you are securing (Professional, Server, or Advanced Server) and what purpose the system will serve (user desktop, web server, file server, and so on). We will assume we are working on a Windows 2000 Server system destined to be a file server (web servers are a special case, and we will discuss them in the "Web Servers" section later in this chapter). There are six recommended steps in the Windows security checklist on Microsoft's TechNet (http://www.microsoft.com/technet/treeview/default.asp?url=/technet/security/tools/ChkList/wsrvSec.asp

NOTE Step 7 applies to web servers only so we will not include that step in this particular discussion):

1. Install the latest Windows 2000 service pack, following the recommended steps in the "Microsoft Windows 2000 Service Pack Installation and Deployment Guide." Visit the Windows Update site to receive any additional updates released after the latest service pack.

2. Configure Window's "Automatic Updates" service to check the Microsoft site and inform you when new security fixes become available. As an option, the automatic update service can be configured to download and install updates without manual intervention.

3. Keep up with the latest security patches using Microsoft's Security Bulletins Search.

4. Follow the guidelines in the "Microsoft Windows 2000 Server Baseline Security Checklist" and update your antivirus tools and signature files against viruses. Check Microsoft's virus alerts regularly.

5. Read "Securing Windows 2000 Server," "Security Operations Guide for Windows 2000 Server" and the "Security Administration Operations Guide"—all available from Microsoft.com.

6. Use the "Baseline Security Analyzer" tool to scan and evaluate the security of your system. mBSA

Step 1 recommends installing the latest Windows 2000 service pack and critical updates using the Windows Update site. *Service packs* are Microsoft's way of bundling updates, fixes, and new functions into a large, self-installing package. Service packs can be found on Microsoft's main download page and vary in size from less than 1MB to over 100MB. Installing a service pack is usually quite simple and consists of downloading an executable file from Microsoft and running it. While this may seem to be an easy and agreeable process, service packs themselves have introduced new functions and vulnerabilities, disabled old functions, and caused third-party applications to fail. Even so, to secure your Windows systems, you must make sure you update them with the latest service pack—in this case, the good outweighs the bad. Critical updates are small, but important updates, that are provided on an individual basis as they become available. Eventually, critical updates get rolled up into the next service pack.

Step 2 recommends configuring the "Automatic Updates" service that is installed automatically with Service Pack 3. Once configured, the service automatically checks the Windows Update site for any new security fixes. This utility can be configured to download and install security updates without manual intervention.

Step 3 urges you to keep up with the latest security patches using the Security Bulletins Search. Microsoft provides security bulletins to alert its user community to problems, issues, or vulnerabilities with Microsoft's products. The security bulletins usually identify the problem, the affected software and versions, and how the problem can be addressed.

Step 4 recommends following the "Microsoft Windows 2000 Server Baseline Security Checklist." This is a 17-step checklist that we will examine in more detail in the next section. Step 4 also recommends keeping your antivirus software and associated signature files updated.

Step 5 instructs us to read three documents available from Microsoft that detail best practices for securing, running, and maintaining Windows 2000 servers.

Step 6 recommends use of the "Baseline Security Analyzer." This free tool from Microsoft can scan and evaluate the security state of your Windows system to ensure the latest patches and fixes are in place, user accounts are secured, and appropriate permissions have been applied to files and directories.

Microsoft Windows 2000 Server Baseline Security Checklist   To assist its end-user community, Microsoft has provided a baseline security checklist specifically for Windows 2000 servers. This checklist applies to both the Windows 2000 Server and Advanced Server operating systems and outlines the steps to achieve a minimum baseline of security. The following list reviews each step to better understand what each step requires and the benefit it provides.

- *Verify that all disk partitions are formatted with NTFS.* NTFS is the NT file system, a Microsoft-developed file system that provides features, such as enhanced security and reliability, that its previous file systems lacked. NTFS allows you to set access permissions using an *access control list* on files and directories, so you can control what users or groups of users can read the contents of a particular file, or modify it. Microsoft's permissions consist of *none, read, write, execute, delete, change permissions,* and *take ownership,* and they can be applied to both files and directories in various combinations.

  In most cases, the choice to format a particular disk partition as NTFS occurs during installation, but you can convert a partition from FAT or FAT32 to NTFS by using the Disk Management tools provided with Windows 2000, as shown in Figure 9-1. In this example, you can see that the first partition (C:) is NTFS but the second (OTHER HALF) is FAT32. You could apply ACLs to the files and directories in the first partition, but not the second. Anyone with access to this system would be able to read, write, modify, and delete files on the FAT32 partition.

- *Verify that the Administrator account has a strong password.* The Administrator account is a special account under the Windows 2000 operating system. This is the "superuser" account that has the ability to control virtually everything on that

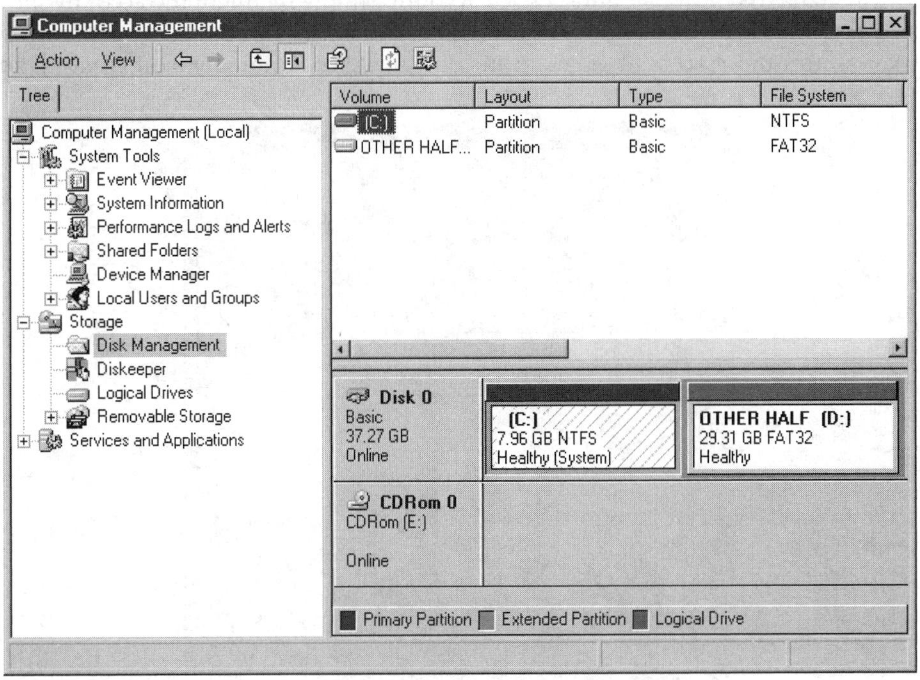

Figure 9-1   Viewing disk partitions with the Windows 2000 Disk Management utility

system, much like the "root" account on UNIX systems. As such, the Administrator account is a frequent target, as attackers attempt to guess or otherwise obtain the password for this account. In general, a password should be selected with care, and this is even more important for an account with this level of privilege. Good passwords typically consist of eight or more characters, at least one change in case, one number, and one special character.

- *Disable unnecessary services.* Any service not absolutely required to support the intended function of the server should be disabled or removed from the system completely. For example, a dedicated web server should not have SMTP or FTP services running on it, and there's usually no legitimate reason for file and print sharing to be enabled on a publicly viewable system. Additionally, there are often components of services that should be removed. For example, within IIS there are often data-access components and sample files that are placed on the system during installation. Like any component not vital to the operation of the system, sample files and unnecessary functions, plug-ins, and expansion packs should be removed.

- *Disable or delete unnecessary accounts.* Removing or disabling unnecessary accounts is a standard best practice for any system, but is particularly applicable for servers. User accounts on public systems should be limited to only those absolutely necessary. On a Windows 2000 system, use the Users and Passwords tool (see the following illustration) to view and remove accounts from the system. To remove an unnecessary account, simply highlight the account and click Remove. For additional security, some organizations will also rename the Administrator account or create an equivalent account under a different name.

- *Protect files and directories.* Certain Windows operating systems (such as 2000 and XP) have the ability to restrict access to files and directories through the use of access control lists (ACLs). An ACL is a list of permissions that controls who may write, modify, delete, or access a specific file or directory. A default, "clean" installation of Windows 2000 places restrictive permissions on certain system files and directories that prevent the average user from tampering with or removing those system files. An upgraded version of Windows 2000 (from Windows 98 or NT) will not have the same default permissions in place, so to secure the system, an administrator must enable those permissions and protect the system files. It is important to note that file and directory permissions can only be implemented on NTFS disk partitions—FAT and FAT32 partitions do not support ACLs for files and directories. The next illustration shows the ACLs placed on the WINNT directory in a default Windows 2000 install. By right-clicking any file or directory on an NTFS partition, selecting Properties, and clicking the Security tab, you can see the permissions associated with each group or user account for that particular file or directory. For more specific information on what each permission setting means, see Table 9-1.

- *Make sure the Guest account is disabled.* In a default installation of Windows 2000, the Guest account is disabled, meaning that it is no longer accessible for use on that system. Older versions of Windows NT and older systems that have been upgraded to Windows 2000 may not have the Guest account disabled. To ensure that the Guest account (or any other account) is disabled, use the Users and Passwords tool found in the Control Panel.

Permissions	Full Control	Modify	Read & Execute	List Folder Contents (folders only)	Read	Write
Traverse Folder/Execute File	x	x	x	x		
List Folder/Read Data	x	x	x	x	x	
Read Attributes	x	x	x	x	x	
Read Extended Attributes	x	x	x	x	x	
Create Files/Write Data	x	x				x
Create Folders/ Append Data	x	x				x
Write Attributes	x	x				x
Write Extended Attributes	x	x				x
Delete Subfolders and Files	x					
Delete	x	x				
Read Permissions	x	x	x	x	x	x
Change Permissions	x					
Take Ownership	x					
Synchronize	x	x	x	x	x	x

Table 9-1 Permissions on Windows 2000

- *Protect the Registry from anonymous access.* By default, Windows does not restrict remote access to the Registry, a fact that many attackers take advantage of when collecting information (such as user accounts, shared drives, resources, and so on) from potential Windows targets. To restrict network access to the Registry, Microsoft recommends following these steps:

NOTE Editing the registry incorrectly can lead to an unstable Windows system. If you are not familiar with the tools and techniques required to complete these steps contact your local system administrator or a qualified professional.

1. Add the following key to the Registry using regedit:
   Hive   HKEY_LOCAL_MACHINE \SYSTEM
   Key   \CurrentControlSet\Control\SecurePipeServers
   Value Name   \winreg

2. Select winreg (the key you just created), click the Security menu, and then click Permissions.

3. Set the Administrators permission to Full Control, make sure no other users or groups are listed, and then click OK.

- *Apply appropriate Registry ACLs.* In a default installation of Windows 2000, the Registry has secure ACLs enabled by default. Unfortunately, this is not the case for systems upgraded to Windows 2000. To enable the appropriate Registry ACLs, refer to Microsoft's TechNet web site (www.microsoft.com/technet) for more information, and search for a white paper entitled "Default Access Control Settings in Windows 2000."

- *Restrict access to public local security authority (LSA) information.* The LSA within Windows handles specific aspects of security administration on the local computer, including access to the system itself, and permissions checking for files and folders. To prevent potential attackers from extracting information from your system anonymously, create the following Registry key using regedit:

Hive   HKEY_LOCAL_MACHINE\SYSTEM
Key   CurrentControlSet\Control\LSA
Value Name   RestrictAnonymous
Type   REG_DWORD
Value   1

For additional security, you can also use the Local Security Policy Setting tool to restrict anonymous connections, as shown in the following illustration. Select Administrative Tools from the Control Panel, then select Local Security Policy, Local Policies, Security Options, and Additional Restrictions for Anonymous Connections. In the drop-down box, select None, Do Not Allow Enumeration Of SAM Accounts And Shares, or No Access Without Explicit Anonymous Permissions. The most secure setting is the latter, which will help prevent potential attackers from anonymously gathering information from your Windows systems.

- *Set stronger password policies.* Password policies are extremely important to the security of any system. More often than not, the only thing that stands between an attacker and access to the system is a simple userid and password pair. You can always educate a user on how to select a good password, but it often helps to have the system itself enforce good password selection. Within Windows 2000, you can enable certain features regarding password selection by using the Password Policy Tool found by selecting Administrative Tools from the Control Panel. Then select Local Security Policy, Account Policies, and Password Policies. This will open the Local Security Settings window shown here.

In the preceding illustration, there are six options for local password policies. Enforce Password History allows you to specify the number of previous passwords that the system should remember and prevent users from reusing. Maximum Password Age specifies how long a user may maintain the same password before being forced to select a new one. Minimum Password Age specifies the minimum number of days that must pass after a successful password change before a user is allowed to change their password again. Minimum Password Length specifies the minimum number of characters the user must include in an acceptable password. For example, if the minimum password length were set at 4, then the user's password must be at least four characters long. Passwords Must Meet Complexity Requirements specifies additional restrictions on password selection. When this option is enabled, all passwords must be at least six characters long (regardless of the minimum password length setting), the password cannot contain the username or any part of the user's full name, and the password must contain at least one character from three of the four classes of characters identified in the following table:

Character Class	Examples
Uppercase letters	A, B, C, ... Z
Lowercase letters	a, b, c, ... z
Numerals	0, 1, 2, ... 9
Non-alphanumeric ("special characters")	Punctuation marks and other symbols

Storing passwords using reversible encryption is essentially the same as storing a cleartext version of the password as it makes the password easy to access for third-party applications. In most environments this option should never be enabled.

- *Set the account lockout policy.* To protect against brute-force password-guessing attacks, Windows 2000 includes an account lockout feature that will disable an account after a specified number of login failures. For example, the administrator may choose to enable account lockout after three unsuccessful login attempts. The account lockout policies shown in the following illustration give the administrator three distinct capabilities. Account Lockout Duration tells the system how long to leave an account locked once the account lockout threshold has been reached (this can be anywhere from minutes to hours to until the administrator manually unlocks the account). Account Lockout Threshold tells the system how many unsuccessful login attempts to allow before locking a user account. Reset Account Lockout Counter After tells the system how long to wait after the last unsuccessful login attempt before clearing out the unsuccessful-login-attempt counter.

NOTE It is highly recommended that you enable reset options and account lockout durations if you choose to enable an account lockout threshold. If each account must be manually unlocked by an administrator once it is locked, then a large-scale brute-force attack will cause a great deal of additional effort for your system administrators.

- *Configure the Administrator account.* While in actual practice this is rarely done, for additional security, the built-in Administrator account can be modified and hidden to make it less obvious to potential attackers. For added security, the Administrator account can be renamed to something obscure that does not indicate that this is the administrator level account (do not use names such as "admin" or "root"). Once the Administrator account has been renamed, you can create a dummy account called "Administrator" but ensure that it has no privileges of any kind. This gives you the ability to still look for password-guessing attacks against the dummy Administrator account in the event logs, but it does not risk the actual administration account. By disabling the Administrator account, attackers won't be able to use the account in any way, even if they are able to guess the password assigned to the account. If you are really concerned about security, you can enable account lockout features on the admin account you created, but be warned that this could cause problems if the entire system comes under a brute-force attack and every account on the system becomes locked.

- *Revoke the Debug programs user right.* By default, Windows 2000 grants administrators the "Debug programs" user right. If abused, this capability allows administrators (or a virus, Trojan, or malicious piece of code accidentally run by the administrator) to obtain sensitive information from system memory, such as hashed passwords. Unless absolutely required, this right should be removed from all administrator accounts.

- *Remove all unnecessary file shares.* In any operating system, information that does not absolutely have to be shared should not be. In Windows this means removing sharing on every file and folder unless it is absolutely necessary. Be aware that Windows creates hidden administrative shares for certain resources by default (a hidden share is created for each drive on the system as well as the WINNT directory). Hidden shares are marked with a dollar sign ($) in front of the name. For example $C is the admin share for the C drive on a Windows 2000 system. The admin shares function much like other shared files and folders—anyone accessing the $C share would be accessing the C drive as if it were one large, shared folder. You can disable these admin shares after installation, but doing so may cause many Microsoft or third-party administration tools to fail. If you do wish to disable the admin shares, you can do so by following these steps:

1. Start the Registry Editor (Regedt32.exe).

2. Locate and then click the following key in the Registry: HKEY_LOCAL_MACHINE\SYSTEM\CurrentControlSet\Services\ LanmanServer\Parameters\AutoShareServer

3. Change the value of the AutoShareServer key to 0 (zero).

NOTE A setting of 0 prevents the administrative shares, such as C$, D$, and Admin$ from being created automatically.

4. Quit the Registry Editor.

CAUTION Editing of the Registry should only be performed by qualified individuals. Alterations to the system Registry can cause the system to become unstable or even nonfunctional.

- *Set appropriate ACLs on all necessary file shares.* By default, any newly created file shares on an NTFS file system will give Full Control access to all users. To prevent unauthorized access and manipulation of these files, administrators must modify permissions by right-clicking on the shared folder or file and selecting Properties then clicking the Security tab. In the Security tab, the administrator can manually assign or remove permissions for the appropriate users or groups.

- *Enable security event auditing.* By default, Windows 2000 does not perform logging of security events such as successful or failed logons. The Audit Policy section found under the Local Policies section of the Local Security Settings tool allows administrators to record the success or failure of certain actions. Microsoft recommends carefully selecting which events to log as logging too many events creates extremely large log files. Microsoft recommends enabling only Success and Failure auditing for the Audit account logon events policy.

- *Set log on warning message.* Windows 2000 provides administrators with the ability to display a message to any users attempting to log in to the system. By displaying a message indicating that system use is restricted to authorized users as well as information regarding monitoring and the prosecution of unauthorized access attempts, organizations can enhance their ability to perform forensic and legal actions.

- *Install antivirus software and updates.* With damage estimates for recent virus outbreaks and their associated clean-up efforts in the billions of dollars, installing antivirus software is a critical best practice for maintaining a functional and secure system. Installing antivirus software is merely the first step though. The antivirus signatures must be kept up to date as new viruses, worms, and Trojans are discovered every day. Most antivirus software programs contain utilities that will automatically update antivirus signatures for you at preset intervals. In general, antivirus signatures should be updated at least once a week.

- *Automate patch deployment.* With the release of Service Pack 3, Microsoft added a capability called "Automatic Updates." By enabling this utility, administrators can have systems automatically check Microsoft for new security updates and, if desired, download and install those updates automatically.

- *Scan system with the Baseline Security Analyzer.* To help address the complexity of keeping Windows systems up to date, Microsoft introduced a free utility that can be used to scan the local system, identify potential vulnerabilities and missing updates, and assist the user in addressing any discovered issues. At a minimum this utility should be run on any newly installed Windows system.

- *Install the latest service pack.* Keeping operating system and application software up to date is also critical for maintaining the security and functionality of your systems. Microsoft releases major revisions to its operating systems called *service packs*, which contain a large collection of modifications and corrections to eliminate bugs, vulnerabilities, or misconfigurations in previous versions of the code. Service packs are usually numbered, inclusive of previous updates (service pack 3 contains the fixes from service packs 1 and 2), and they can be found on the Microsoft web site in the download section. In general, service packs are quite large and can be ordered in CD format if your Internet connection does not support downloading 20MB to 100MB files.

- *Install the appropriate post-service-pack security hotfixes.* New service packs are not released for each discovered vulnerability—this would simply be too much effort for an organization like Microsoft. Instead, Microsoft will release *hotfixes* designed to correct specific vulnerabilities. These hotfixes are

PART IV

eventually collected into a service pack over time, but in order to maintain security on your system, you must install the latest service pack and then any appropriate hotfixes. Fortunately, Microsoft has made this task a little easier through the Windows Update function found in Internet Explorer. From an Internet Explorer window, select Tools and then Windows Update. This will launch the Windows Update utility, shown in Figure 9-2, which will scan your system and provide a list of appropriate updates and hotfixes for your system. Running this Windows Update tool each week will help ensure that your system is kept up to date.

- *Remove File And Printer Sharing protocol.* On certain systems, such as web servers or any other system maintained in your DMZ, you should consider removing or disabling the File And Printer Sharing For Microsoft Networks protocol from all network interfaces. This prevents administrators from accidentally sharing out directories and files on publicly visible systems and will help prevent certain types of reconnaissance and network-based attacks.

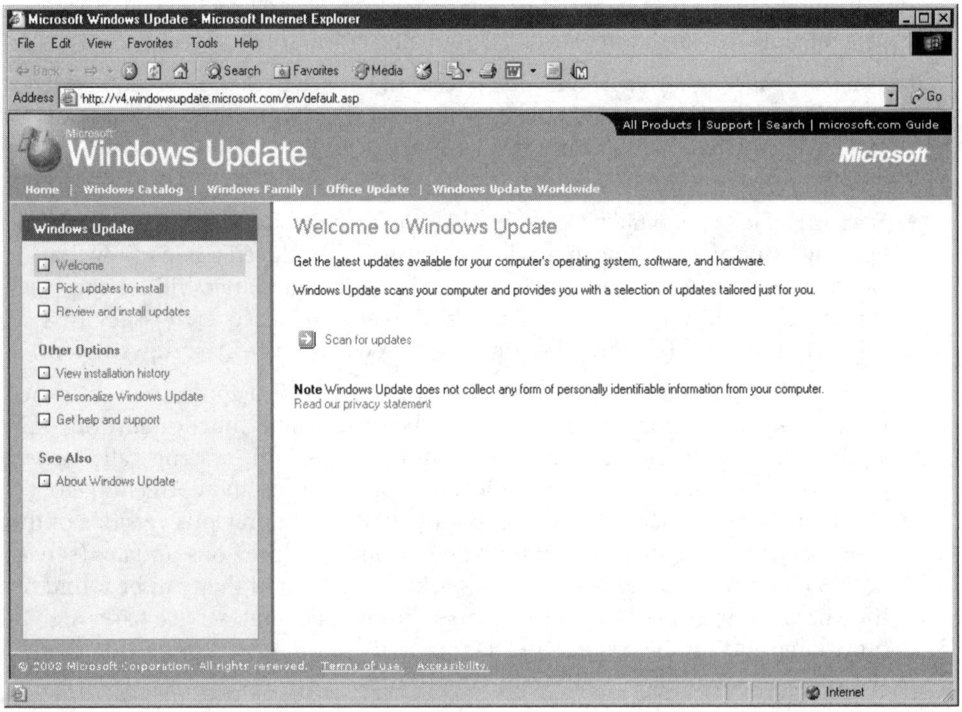

Figure 9-2   Microsoft's Windows Update site

In addition to the Windows 2000 hardening checklist, Microsoft has provided some additional tools to help you keep your Windows systems up to date. The Microsoft Security Baseline Analyzer (MSBA) is an automated tool that scans your Windows systems and does the following:

- Checks to ensure the latest security patches and service packs have been installed
- Checks to ensure the strong passwords requirements are enabled
- Scans Internet Information Server and SQL Server for common security-related misconfigurations
- Checks for misconfigured security zone settings in Microsoft Office, Outlook, and Internet Explorer

The MSBA is available from Microsoft's TechNet (www.microsoft.com/technet/default .asp) by selecting Security, Tools and Checklists, and MBSA (www.microsoft.com/technet/treeview/default.asp?url=/technet/security/tools/Tools/mbsaqa.asp).

In addition to the MSBA, the Internet Information Server (IIS) Lockdown Tool is available to help secure IIS servers from attack (we will discuss this tool in the "Microsoft's Internet Information Server" section later in this chapter). If you don't wish to run the fully implemented version of the MSBA, you can run HFNetChk—a command-line tool that will scan your system to ensure it is up to date with the latest security fixes and service packs.

As you can see, the Microsoft checklist for securing Windows 2000 systems contains many different steps, all designed to help secure the system by examining a specific area. This checklist is designed to help you create a secure baseline for your Windows 2000 systems by following the same basic tenets as any other operating system baselining process: remove unnecessary components and services, restrict and limit access to files and directories, and apply the latest patches. After following the checklist and making the appropriate choices for your specific environment, you should end up with your own secure Windows baseline.

One item the Microsoft checklist does not adequately cover is logging. Logging, or auditing, is the process of recording events or actions that take place. More specifically in this case, the recording of events or actions that take place on the system itself—events such as logins, program executions, file or directory modifications, and so on. Recording these events makes it possible for security personnel and administrators to determine what has happened on the system and whether or not the security of the system has been compromised in any way. The logging facilities within Windows are fairly simple and essentially consist of turning logging on or off for certain events. Logged events within Windows are placed into one of three event logs: Application Log, Security Log, or System Log. The event logs can be accessed through the Event Viewer provided with Windows, as shown in the following illustration, or through any of a number of third-party tools.

Determining your logging and auditing requirements is an important part of the overall baselining process. You must decide which events to record, what the records will be used for, when and how to examine the records, and how long to maintain these records. Setting up logging should be a part of every security baseline checklist or process, and it is typically done just after the system is installed and configured, but before the system has been placed on the network or into production.

Removing or disabling programs or services in Windows is usually relatively simple. Many applications contain their own uninstaller, which is designed to remove the application from the system. Others rely on the built-in Windows Add/Remove Programs utility found in the Control Panel and shown in the following illustration. Removing an application is a simple process: select the application you want to remove by clicking it, and then click the Remove button. In most cases this works quite well, but there are many cases where files and directories get left behind and require manual intervention to completely remove them from the system.

Removing or disabling services is fairly simple, as Microsoft has provided a Services utility under the Administrative Tools section of the Control Panel. By using this utility, shown in Figure 9-3, administrators can examine those services that are running on their system, how the services are started, and when they are started. Administrators can also use this utility to stop or start specific services, as well as disable services that should not be running on the system.

Hardening UNIX- or Linux-Based Operating Systems

As a general rule, any operating system can be made relatively secure, but by default UNIX operating systems tend to be more secure than default installations of Windows operating systems. However, that does not mean that UNIX systems are *completely* secure by default and don't need any additional security configuration. UNIX systems, like Windows systems, need to be carefully examined, modified, and baselined to provide secure operations.

Depending on the skill and knowledge of the system administrator, securing UNIX systems can be more challenging than securing Windows systems because the operating system is so powerful and flexible and so much control is placed in the hands of the administrator. Unlike Windows, there is no single manufacturer to provide specific guidelines and step-by-step checklists for securing UNIX systems. Instead, there are many general and version-specific guidelines that must be adapted and applied to your specific version of UNIX to complete the baselining process. This section examines some of the common guidelines for a sampling of the more popular versions of UNIX.

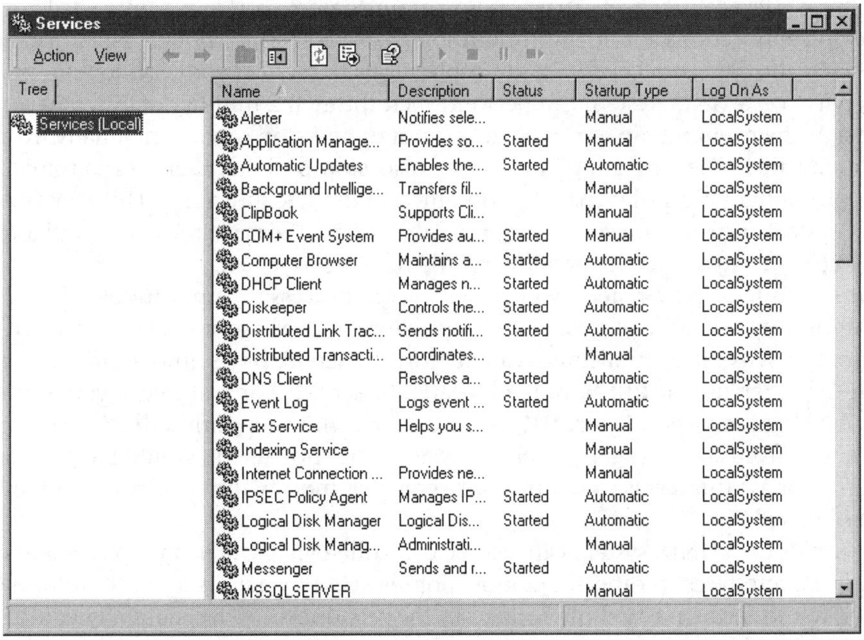

PART IV

Figure 9-3   Starting or stopping services with the Windows Services utility

General UNIX Baselines

General UNIX baselining is the same as for Windows operating systems: disable unnecessary services, restrict permissions on files and directories, remove unnecessary software, apply patches, remove unnecessary users, and apply password guidelines. Some versions of UNIX provide GUI-based tools for these tasks, while others require administrators to manually edit configuration files. In most cases, anything that can be accomplished through a GUI interface can be accomplished from the command line or by manually editing configuration files.

Like Windows systems, UNIX systems are easiest to secure and baseline if they are providing a single service or performing a single function, such as acting as an SMTP or web server. Prior to performing any installing or baselining, the purpose of the system should be defined and all required capabilities and functions should be identified. One nice advantage of UNIX systems is that you typically have complete control over what does or does not get installed on the system. During the installation process, you can select which services and applications are placed on your system, giving administrators a good opportunity to simply not install services and applications that will not be required. However, this assumes that the administrator knows and understands the purpose of this system, which is not always the case. In other cases, the function of the system, itself, may have changed.

Regardless of the installation decisions, the administrator may sometimes need to remove applications or components that are no longer needed. With UNIX systems, there is typically no "add/remove program" wizard as there is with Windows, but you will often encounter package managers that enable administrators to remove unneeded components and applications automatically. On some UNIX versions, though, you must manually delete the files associated with the applications or services you wish to remove.

Services on a UNIX system can be controlled through a number of different mechanisms. As the root user, an administrator can start and stop services manually from the command line. The operating system can also stop and start services automatically through configuration files (usually contained in the /etc directory). Unlike Windows, UNIX systems can also have different *run levels*, where the system can be configured to bring up different services depending on the run level selected.

On a running UNIX system, you can see which processes, applications, and services are running by using the process status or **ps** command, as shown in Figure 9-4. To stop a running service, an administrator can identify the service by its unique *process identifier* or *PID* and then use the **kill** command to stop the service. For example, if you wanted to stop the klogd service in Figure 9-4, you would use the command **kill 743**. To prevent this service from starting again when the system is rebooted, you would have to modify the appropriate run levels to remove this service or modify the configuration files that control this service.

Accounts on a UNIX system can also be controlled via GUIs in some cases and command-line interfaces in others. On most popular UNIX versions, the user information can be found in the passwd file located in the /etc directory. By manually editing this file, you can add, delete, or modify user accounts on the system. By examining this file, an administrator can see which user accounts exist on the system and then determine

```
C:\WINNT\System32\telnet.exe                                     _ □ ×
UID          PID   PPID  C STIME TTY          TIME CMD
root           1     0   0 May13 ?        00:00:04 init
root           2     1   0 May13 ?        00:00:00 [keventd]
root           3     1   0 May13 ?        00:00:00 [kapmd]
root           4     1   0 May13 ?        00:00:00 [ksoftirqd_CPU0]
root           5     1   0 May13 ?        00:00:24 [kswapd]
root           6     1   0 May13 ?        00:00:05 [bdflush]
root           7     1   0 May13 ?        00:00:00 [kupdated]
root           8     1   0 May13 ?        00:00:00 [mdrecoveryd]
root          16     1   0 May13 ?        00:00:04 [kjournald]
root          95     1   0 May13 ?        00:00:00 [khubd]
root         223     1   0 May13 ?        00:00:00 [kjournald]
root         224     1   0 May13 ?        00:00:13 [kjournald]
root         225     1   0 May13 ?        00:00:00 [kjournald]
root         739     1   0 May13 ?        00:00:01 syslogd -m 0
root         744     1   0 May13 ?        00:00:00 klogd -x
rpc          764     1   0 May13 ?        00:00:00 portmap
rpcuser      792     1   0 May13 ?        00:00:00 rpc.statd
root         904     1   0 May13 ?        00:00:00 /usr/sbin/apmd -p 10 -w 5 -W -P
root         959     1   0 May13 ?        00:00:00 /usr/sbin/sshd
root         992     1   0 May13 ?        00:00:00 xinetd -stayalive -reuse -pidfil
root        1020     1   0 May13 ?        00:00:00 sendmail: accepting connections
root        1039     1   0 May13 ?        00:00:00 gpm -t ps/2 -m /dev/mouse
--More--
```

Figure 9-4   Running the **ps** command on a UNIX system

which accounts to remove or disable. On most UNIX systems, if you remove the user account from the passwd file, you must manually remove any files that belong to that user, including their home directories.

How you patch a UNIX system depends a great deal on the UNIX version in use and the patch being applied. In some cases, a patch will consist of a series of manual steps requiring the administrator to replace files, change permissions, and alter directories. In other cases, the patches are executable scripts or utilities that perform the patch actions automatically. Some UNIX versions, such as Red Hat and Solaris, have built-in utilities that handle the patching process. In those cases, the administrator downloads a specifically formatted file that the patching utility then processes to perform any modifications or updates that need to be made.

To better illustrate UNIX baselines, we will examine two popular UNIX-based operating systems: Solaris and Red Hat Linux.

Solaris   The Solaris operating system is developed and distributed by Sun Microsystems and has been an extremely popular choice in high-performance and high-availability environments. As a commercial operating system, Solaris is typically bundled with a hardware platform from Sun, but it can be purchased separately and is even available for Intel-based processor platforms (Solaris x86). For more secure environments, a specially hardened version called Trusted Solaris is available, though this is typically only used by the government, military, and banking communities.

Baselining a Solaris system is fairly simple. Once the system's purpose is defined, installation is typically done through a graphical interface that allows the administrator to select which applications and services should be loaded on the system. On a running Solaris system, patches and services can be added or removed using the **pkgadd** command, which adds binary packages, and the **pkgrm** command, which removes binary packages.

The binary packages themselves are unusable in the format in which they are downloaded or delivered on removable media. The pkg utilities take care of interpreting the package's software control files to determine where to either install or remove files or directories. Any package handled by the Solaris system is stored in a package information database, so administrators can easily obtain a list of currently installed software. Software can also be installed or removed using the Admintool shown in Figure 9-5.

Obtaining a list of running services on a Solaris system is much the same as on all UNIX systems. You can use the **ps** command to view running processes, and you can examine the Internet servers configuration file, called inetd.conf in Solaris. The inetd.conf file, located in the /etc directory, contains a list of services controlled by the Internet services daemon, simply called *inetd*. On Solaris, and many other UNIX variants, inetd listens for incoming connections on the TCP and UDP ports associated with each of the services listed in its configuration file, inetd.conf. When a connection request is received, inetd will launch the program or process associated with that service, if necessary, and pass the connection request to the appropriate service. To prevent unwanted services from running and processing requests, administrators can edit inetd.conf and either comment out or remove the lines for the services they wish to disable.

In addition to disabling or removing unnecessary network services, Solaris allows administrators to use local security mechanisms called *tcp wrappers* that provide additional layers of security for network services. TCP wrappers are essentially filters that compare incoming connection requests to lists of authorized and unauthorized connections. If a connection is authorized, then it is permitted to reach the network service it is attempting to contact. If a connection is unauthorized, it is dropped by the TCP wrappers. These functions are controlled by two files: hosts.allow and hosts.deny. The hosts.allow file contains a list of IP addresses or subnets that are allowed to connect to a specific service, such as "10.0.0.0: FTP," which would allow any address in the 10.X.X.X network to connect to the FTP service on the local machine. In more secure installations, the hosts.allow file is populated, and the entry "ALL: ALL" is placed in the hosts.deny file. This type

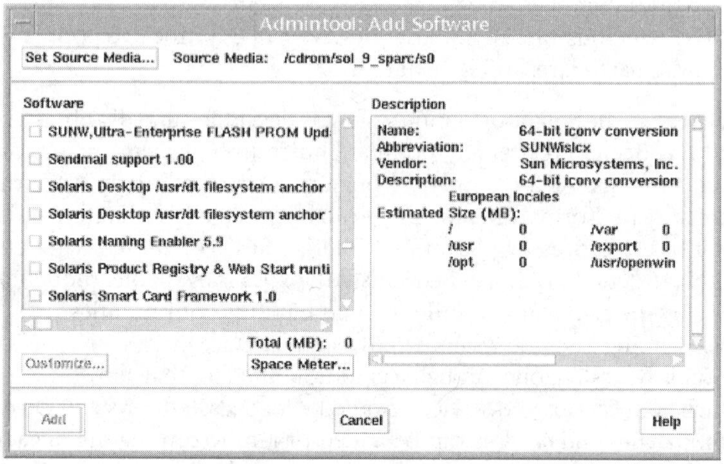

Figure 9-5 The Solaris Admintool is used to add or remove software

of configuration will reject any inbound connections to the local system unless they are specifically authorized by the hosts.allow file.

Securing access to files and directories in Solaris is done in the same manner as in most UNIX variants. Each file and directory has a list of associated permissions for the owner of the file or directory, the group owner of the file or directory, and anyone else (often called the "world"). The permissions are listed in owner-group-world order and consist of three values for each grouping: read, write, and execute. The logical representation looks like this: rwx rwx rwx. Read (r) allows for viewing of the file or listing of the directory. Write (w) allows for modification of the file or directory. Execute (x) allows the file, usually an executable or script, to be run. If you want a file to have read, write, and execute permissions for the owner, read and write permissions for the group, and no permissions for the world, the permissions could be logically represented as shown here.

Owner	Group	World
rwx	rw-	---

In Solaris, you can use the **chmod** command to modify the permissions associated with a file or directory. Similarly the **chown** command allows you to modify the ownership of a file or directory, and **chgrp** allows you to change the group ownership of a file or directory. To adequately secure a Solaris system, you should ensure that all configuration and system files have appropriately restrictive permissions—you don't want any user on the system to be able to modify inted.conf without appropriate access. To assist you in securing files and directories, there are many different resources available on Sun's web site, as well as on security-related web sites.

A crucial step in baselining a Solaris system is to ensure that all the latest patches and fixes are in place. Patches for Solaris systems are typically distributed from Sun and are available from Sun's web site but can also be obtained on CD, floppy, or tape in some cases. Once obtained, patches must be processed, and Solaris provides several tools to assist administrators in managing and maintaining patches: **patchadd**, **patchrm**, **smpatch**, and **pkgparam**. The **patchadd** command can be used to add patches to the system as well as obtain information about what patches are currently installed on the system. The **patchrm** command can be used to remove installed patches from the system. The **smpatch** command is used to process signed patches. The **pkgparam** command shows patches installed for a specific software package. In addition to the command-line tools, Solaris provides a GUI-based management console, called the Solaris Management Console, that provides the same level of functionality. The Solaris Management Console is shown in Figure 9-6.

In spite of the security efforts identified so far, a Solaris system can still be easily compromised if the user base is not effectively managed and maintained. The keys to protecting accounts and system access are to remove or disable unused accounts and to ensure that all accounts are secured with a good, strong password. In Solaris, user accounts are maintained in the passwd file, and groups are maintained in the groups file, both of which are located in the /etc directory. There are three main methods for maintaining users and groups on a Solaris system: manually editing the required configuration files,

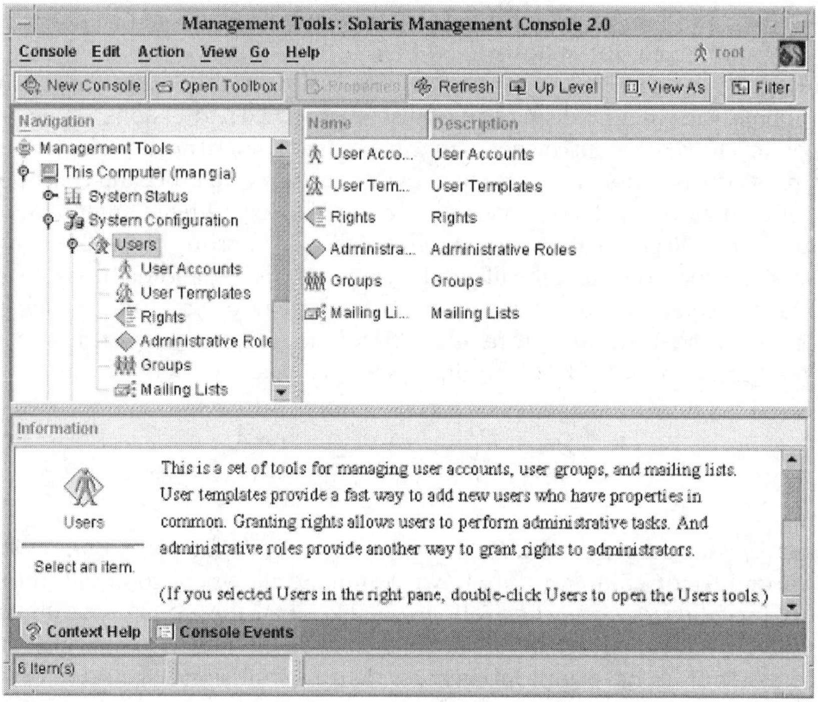

Figure 9-6   Solaris Management Console

using command line interface tools such as **useradd**, and using the management console. Each method can be used interchangeably, offering a level of flexibility not found on Windows systems. Removing unused user accounts can be accomplished through any of these methods—the end result is the same.

The second step to effectively managing your user base is to ensure that users select good passwords. On Solaris systems, passwords are generally stored in a separate file called shadow. This file contains the encrypted password for each account on the system, and it must therefore be guarded and protected appropriately. An administrator can use any of a number of popular password cracking programs to check the user passwords to ensure that they are not easily guessed or based on a simple dictionary word. Additionally, Solaris already imposes some restrictions on what is considered a "suitable" password for users. In most implementations, a password must be at least six characters long, must contain at least two letters and one number or symbol, must not be the same as the login ID, and must be different than the previous password. If these are not strict enough guidelines, the administrator can alter these parameters by using the **passwd** command and the appropriate option flag or by modifying the parameters in /etc/default/passwd. Solaris also supports PAM (Pluggable Authentication Modules), a mechanism for providing interoperation and secure access to a variety of services on different platforms.

Linux   Linux is a rather unique operating system. It is UNIX-based, very powerful, open source, can be obtained for free, and is available in many different "distributions" from several vendors. Linux was initially conceived and written by Linus Torvalds in 1991. His concept of creating a lightweight, flexible, and free operating system gave rise to an entirely new operating system that is very popular and is installed on millions of computers around the world. Due to its open nature, the entire source-code base for the operating system is available to anyone who wants to examine it, modify it, or recompile it for their own specific uses. Linux is a favored operating system among security professionals, system administrators, and other highly technical users who enjoy the flexibility and power that Linux provides.

While most versions of Linux can be obtained for free simply by downloading them from the Internet (including major commercial distributions), you can also purchase commercial versions of the Linux operating system from vendors, such as Red Hat, Slackware, SuSE, and Debian, who have built a business out of providing custom versions of Linux along with support and training. Red Hat is arguably the most popular of these commercial Linux distributions, and we will use it as the example for the rest of this section. Regardless of which Linux version you prefer, baselining a Linux system follows the same guidelines as any other UNIX system: disable unnecessary services, restrict permissions on files and directories, remove unnecessary software, apply patches, remove unnecessary users, and apply password guidelines.

Services under Linux are normally controlled by their own configuration files or by xinetd, the extended Internet services daemon. Instead of starting all Internet services, such as FTP servers, at system startup, Linux uses xinetd to listen for incoming connections. Xinetd listens to all the appropriate ports (those that match the services in its configuration files) and when a connection request comes in, xinetd starts the appropriate server and hands over the connection request. This "master process" approach makes it fairly simple to disable unwanted services—all the configuration information for each server is located in /etc/xinetd.d with a configuration file for each process, as shown in Figure 9-7.

```
[root@Jeep xinetd.d]# ls -la
total 64
drwxr-xr-x    2 root     root       4096 Feb 16 17:54
drwxr-xr-x   62 root     root       4096 Apr  5 15:18
-rw-r--r--    1 root     root        563 Nov 19 11:00 chargen
-rw-r--r--    1 root     root        580 Nov 19 11:00 chargen-udp
-rw-r--r--    1 root     root        419 Nov 19 11:00 daytime
-rw-r--r--    1 root     root        438 Nov 19 11:00 daytime-udp
-rw-r--r--    1 root     root        341 Nov 19 11:00 echo
-rw-r--r--    1 root     root        360 Nov 19 11:00 echo-udp
-rw-r--r--    1 root     root        312 Nov 19 11:00 servers
-rw-r--r--    1 root     root        314 Nov 19 11:00 services
-rw-r--r--    1 root     root        392 Apr  7  2002 sgi_fam
-rw-r--r--    1 root     root        363 Nov 20 11:24 swat
-rw-r--r--    1 root     root        304 Feb 16 16:54 telnet
-rw-r--r--    1 root     root        497 Nov 19 11:00 time
-rw-r--r--    1 root     root        518 Nov 19 11:00 time-udp
-rw-r--r--    1 root     root        329 Feb 16 16:55 wu-ftpd
[root@Jeep xinetd.d]# _
```

Figure 9-7   Listing of server configuration files for xinetd

```
[root@Jeep xinetd.d]# more telnet
# default: on
# description: The telnet server serves telnet sessions; it uses \
#       unencrypted username/password pairs for authentication.
service telnet
{
        flags           = REUSE
        socket_type     = stream
        wait            = no
        user            = root
        server          = /usr/sbin/in.telnetd
        log_on_failure  += USERID
        disable         = no
}

[root@Jeep xinetd.d]#
```

Figure 9-8   Telnet service configuration file under Red Hat Linux

Inside each configuration file are the options to be used when starting the service, the location where the server binary is located, and the disable flag. By changing the value of the disable flag to "yes," you can disable any process controlled by xinetd. Figure 9-8 shows the configuration file for the telnet service on a Red Hat Linux system. Services in Red Hat Linux can also be configured via a GUI-based utility, as shown in Figure 9-9. Regardless of the method chosen, the end result should the same—all unnecessary services should be removed or disabled.

Permissions under Linux are the same as for other UNIX-based operating systems. There are permissions for owner, group, and others (or world). Permissions are based on the same read-write-execute principle and can be adjusted using the **chmod** command.

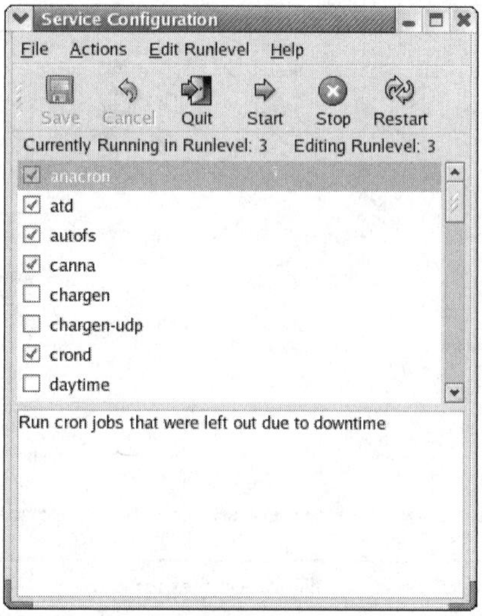

Figure 9-9

Red Hat Linux's GUI-based service configuration

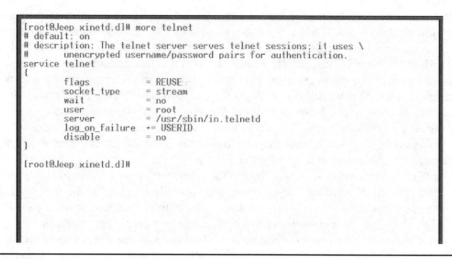

Individual and group ownership information can be changed using **chown** and **chgrp** respectively. As with other baselining exercises, permissions should be as restrictive as functionally possible, giving read-only access when possible and write or execute access when necessary.

Adding and removing software under Linux is typically done through a package manager. In Red Hat Linux, the package manager is called Red Hat Package Manager, or rpm for short. Using rpm, you can add, modify, update, or remove software packages from your system. Using the **rpm -qa** command will give you a list of all the software packages installed on your Red Hat system. You can remove any packages you do not wish to leave installed using the **rpm -e** command. As with most things under Linux, there is a GUI-based utility to accomplish this same task. The GUI-based Package Management utility is shown in Figure 9-10.

Patching and keeping a Red Hat Linux system up to date is a fairly simple exercise, as well. Red Hat has provided an Update Agent that, once configured, will examine your system, obtain the list of available updates from Red Hat, and, if desired, install those updates on your system. Like any other operating system, it is important to maintain the patch level of your Red Hat system. For more information on the Red Hat Update Agent, see the "Updates (aka Hotfixes, Service Packs, and Patches)" section later in this chapter.

Managing and maintaining user accounts under Linux can be accomplished with either the command line or a GUI interface. Unlike certain other operating systems, there's really only one default account for Linux systems—the root or superuser account. The root account has complete and total control over the system and should therefore be protected with an exceptionally strong password. Many administrators will configure their systems to prevent anyone from logging in directly as root; instead they

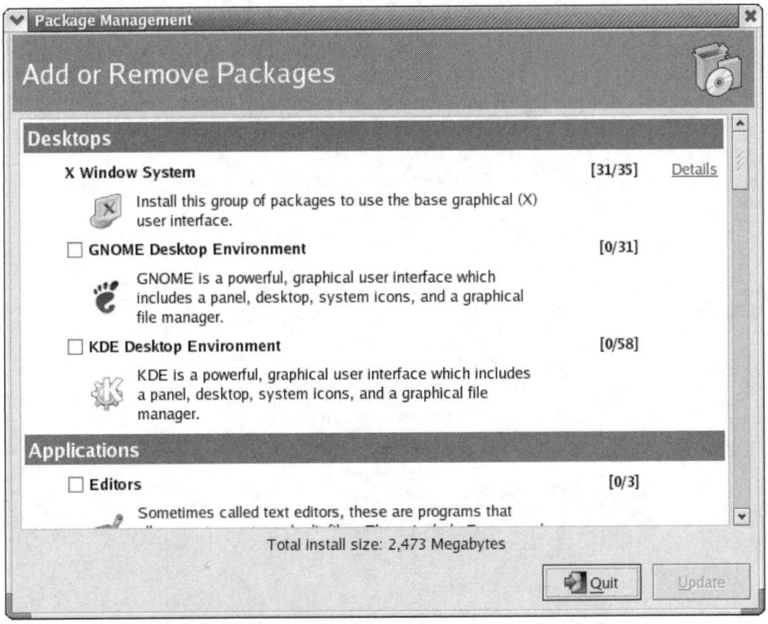

Figure 9-10   Red Hat Package Management utility

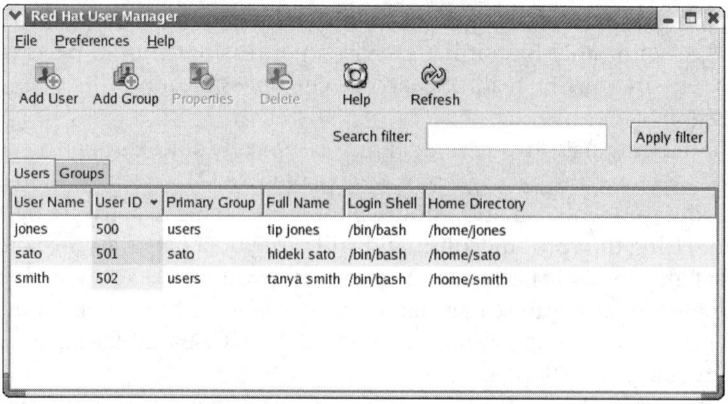

Figure 9-11   Managing user accounts with the Red Hat User Manager

must log in with their own personal accounts and switch to the root account using the **su** command. Adding user accounts can be done with the **useradd** command, and unwanted user accounts can be removed using the **userdel** command. Additionally you can manually edit /etc/passwd to add or remove user accounts. User accounts can also be managed via a GUI interface, as shown in Figure 9-11.

For increased local security, Red Hat also provides a built-in firewall function that can be managed either via the command line or through a GUI interface, as shown in the following illustration. To protect network access to the local system, administrators can control which ports external users may connect to, such as mail, FTP, or web. Administrators may choose a security level, from high, medium, off, and a customized option, where they can individually select which ports on which interfaces external users may connect to.

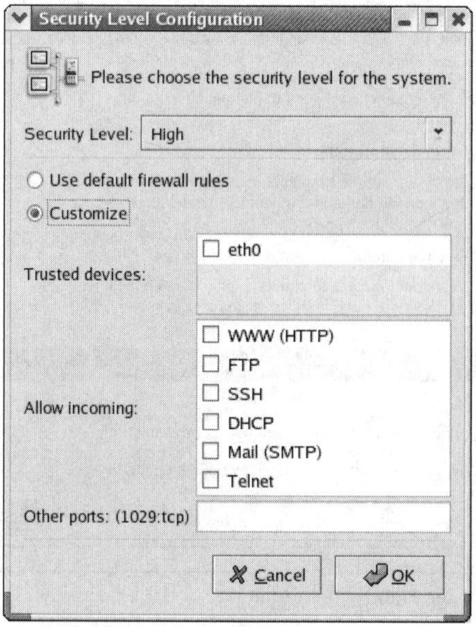

In addition to the built-in firewall functions, administrators may also use TCP wrappers like those discussed earlier in the Solaris section of this chapter. By specifying host and port combinations in /etc/hosts.allow, administrators can allow certain hosts to connect on certain ports. The firewall function and hosts.allow must work together if both functions are used on the same system. The connection must be allowed by both utilities or it will be dropped.

Mac OS X

Apple's latest version of its operating system is essentially a new variant of the UNIX operating system. While this brings a new level of power, flexibility, and stability to Mac users everywhere, it also brings a new level of security concerns. Traditionally, the Mac OS was largely ignored by the hacker community—the deployment was relatively small, largely being restricted to individual users or departments, and harder to obtain information on. With the migration to a UNIX-based OS, Mac users should anticipate a sharp increase in unwanted attention and scrutiny from potential attackers.

Because it is a UNIX-based operating system, the same rough guidelines for all UNIX systems apply to Mac OS X. As with Solaris, Linux, and all the other UNIX variants, each workstation can become an instant server by installing the right application or enabling a specific service. As with other UNIX variants, it is important with Mac OS X to disable unnecessary services, such as web, mail, FTP, and so on, unless they are going to be properly configured and secured. Mac OS X services can be manually controlled by editing the appropriate files, as with other UNIX variants, but one of Apple's strengths (or weaknesses, depending on how you look at it) is providing user interfaces that greatly simplify tasks for their user base. For example, within Mac OS X, Apple has provided Services, Firewall, and Internet tabs under the Sharing window. As Figure 9-12 shows, certain services can be turned on or off simply by clicking the box next to the appropriate service.

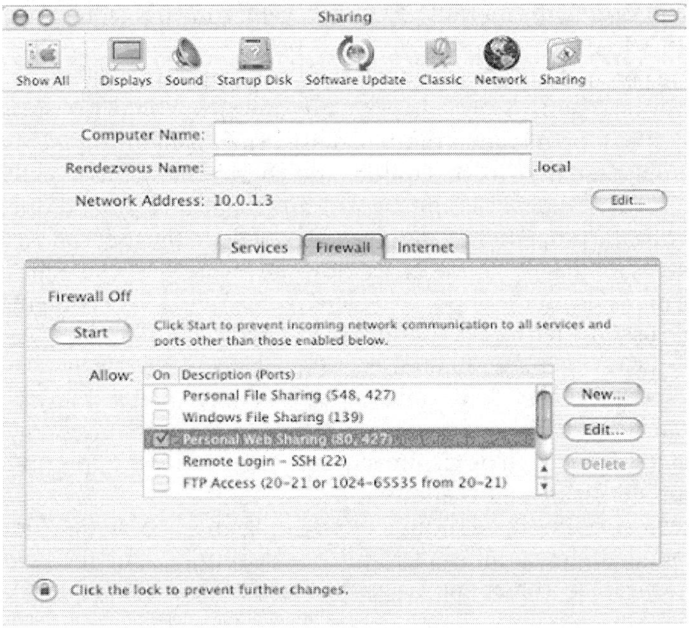

Figure 9-12
Turning services on and off in the Services tab in Mac OS X

Figure 9-13

Turning the firewall settings on and off in the Firewall tab in Mac OS X

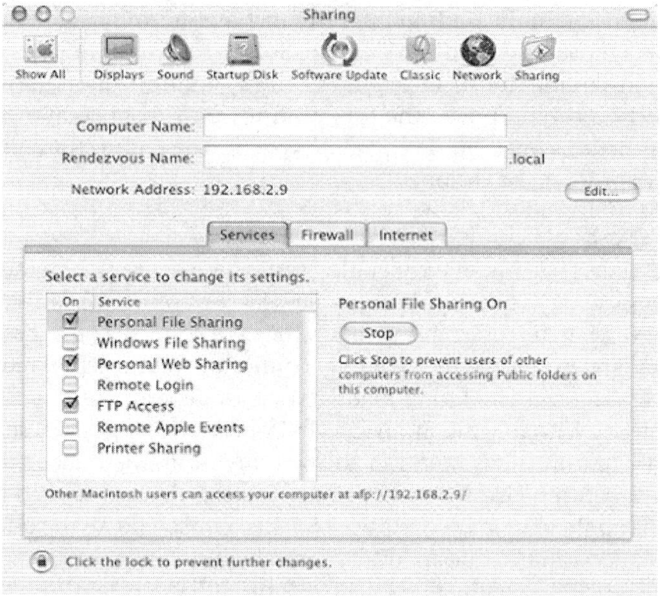

The Firewall tab similarly provides users with the ability to restrict incoming connections to the system, again by simply clicking on the box next to the service you wish to allow to reach your computer, as shown in Figure 9-13.

For Mac OS X users, the task of identifying and disabling unwanted services is relatively simple compared to some other operating systems. Apple has conveniently located the services and the firewall functions together and has reduced the administration tasks to just selecting the appropriate check boxes.

File permissions in Mac OS X are nearly identical to any other UNIX variant and are based on separate read, write, and execute permissions for owner, group, and world. While these permissions can be adjusted manually using a command line interface, with the standard **chown**, **chmod**, and **chgrp** commands, Apple again provides some nice interface capabilities for viewing and managing file and directory permissions. By selecting the properties of any given file or folder, the user can view and modify the permissions for that file or folder, as shown in Figure 9-14. Note that the GUI interface follows the same user-group-world pattern of permissions as other UNIX variants, though Apple uses the term *others* as opposed to *world*.

This GUI interface allows users to quickly and effectively restrict access to sensitive files and directories. By default, Mac OS X limits a user's ability to access or modify certain areas of the file system, including those areas containing system binaries. However, these restrictions can be circumvented by a user with the appropriate permissions or by certain third-party applications.

Removing unwanted or unnecessary programs in Mac OS X is usually done through the program's own uninstaller utility or by simply using the Finder to locate and then delete the folder containing the program and associated utilities. Like Windows, Mac OS X

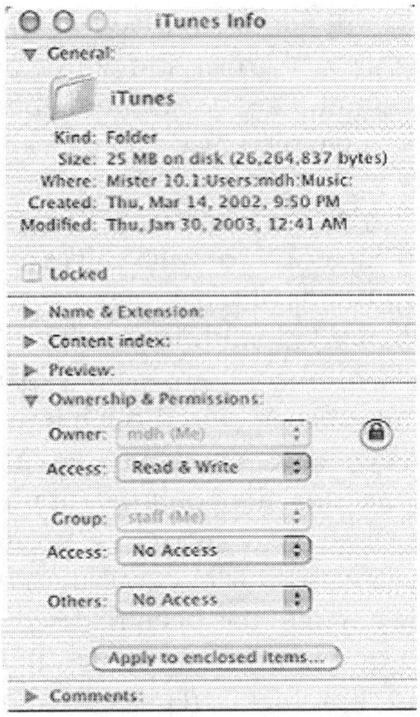

Figure 9-14

Setting file
permissions in
Mac OS X

maps certain file extensions to specific programs, so deleting a program that handles specific extension types may require administrators to clear up associated extensions.

Like most UNIX-based operating systems, Mac OS X is a multiuser platform. As part of the baselining effort, the active user accounts should be examined to ensure they have the right level of access, permissions, group memberships, and so on. In addition, any accounts that are not used should be removed from the system completely. To access the user accounts under Mac OS X, select the Users icons under System Preferences—this should display the Users window, as shown here.

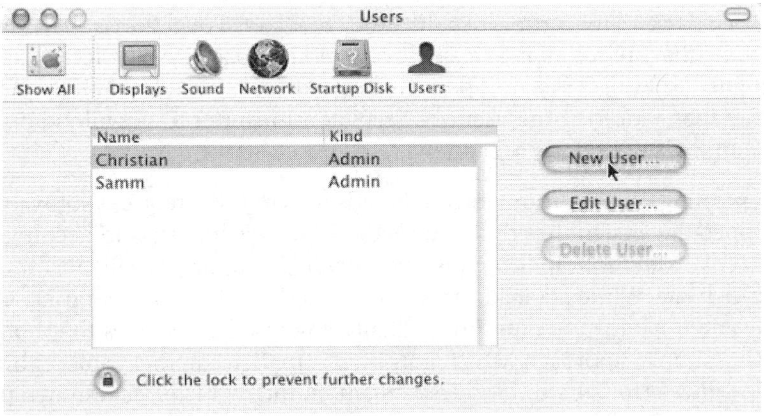

As can be seen in the preceding illustration, adding, editing, and deleting users is simply a matter of selecting the user account and clicking the correct button on the right side of the window. Mac OS X also permits administrators to lock accounts so they can only be modified by users with administrative-level privileges. Those who are familiar with UNIX operating systems may notice something odd about Mac OS X—there is no root account enabled by default. The root account does exist and can be enabled, but for "security reasons," it is not enabled by default.

Updates (a.k.a. Hotfixes, Service Packs, and Patches)

Operating systems are large and complex mixes of interrelated software modules written by dozens or even thousands of separate individuals. With the push toward GUI-based functionality and enhanced capabilities that has occurred over the past several years, operating systems have continued to grow and expand. Windows 2000 contains approximately 29 million lines of code, and though it may be the largest in that respect, other modern operating systems are not far behind. As operating systems continue to grow and introduce new functions, the potential for problems with the code grows as well. It is almost impossible for an operating system vendor to test their product on every possible platform under every possible circumstance, so functionality and security issues do arise after an operating system has been released.

To the average user or system administrator, this means a fairly constant stream of updates designed to correct problems, replace sections of code, or even add new features to an installed operating system. Vendors typically follow a hierarchy for software updates:

- **Hotfix**   This is a term given to a (usually) small software update designed to address a specific problem, such as a buffer overflow in an application that exposes the system to attacks. Hotfixes are typically developed in reaction to a discovered problem and are produced and then released rather quickly.

- **Patch**   This term is usually applied to a more formal, larger software update that may address several or many software problems. Patches often contain enhancements or additional capabilities as well as fixes for known bugs. Patches are usually developed over a longer period of time.

- **Service pack**   This term is usually given to a large collection of patches and hotfixes that are rolled into a single, rather large package. Service packs are designed to bring a system up to the latest known, good level all at once, rather than requiring the user or system administrator to download dozens or hundreds of updates separately.

Every operating system, from Linux to Solaris to Windows, requires software updates, and each operating system has different methods of assisting users in keeping their systems up to date. Microsoft, for example, typically makes updates available for download from their web site. While most administrators or technically proficient users may prefer to identify and download updates individually, Microsoft recognizes that nontechnical users prefer a simpler approach, which they built into their Internet Explorer browser. By selecting Windows Update from the Tools menu in Internet Explorer (shown previously in Figure 9-2), users will be taken to the Microsoft web site. By selecting Scan For Updates, users can allow their systems to be examined for needed or required updates. The web site will identify which updates the user's system needs and will provide the user with the option to download and install the required updates. While this typically requires admin or power-user level access, it does simplify the update process for most users.

In addition to a web-based update utility, Microsoft also provides an automated update functionality that will, once configured, locate any required updates, download them to your system, and even install the updates if that is your preference. Figure 9-15 shows the Automatic Updates window, which can be found in the Control Panel. Note that both the web-based updates and automatic updates require active Internet connections to retrieve information and updates from Microsoft.

Microsoft is not alone in providing utilities to assist users in keeping their systems up to date and secure. The latest versions of Red Hat Linux contain a utility called the Red Hat Update Agent, which does essentially the same thing. By registering your system and user profile with Red Hat, you can obtain a customized list of updates for your specific system. By customizing your system profile, as shown in Figure 9-16, you can even tell the Red Hat Update Agent to look for updates on specific packages only.

Once the profile has been built, the Update Agent contacts the Red Hat update server to obtain information on available updates for the packages selected in the profile. Once a list of updates is obtained, the Update Agent allows the user to select which updates to download and install, as shown in Figure 9-17. This gives the user the ability to selectively download and install updates at their convenience. Again, an active Internet connection is required to use the Red Hat Update Agent.

Regardless of the method used to update the operating system, it is critically important to keep systems up to date. New security advisories come out every day, and while a buffer overflow may be a "potential" problem today, it will almost certainly become a "definite" problem in the near future. Much like the steps taken to baseline and initially secure an operating system, keeping every system patched and up to date is critical to protecting the system and the information it contains.

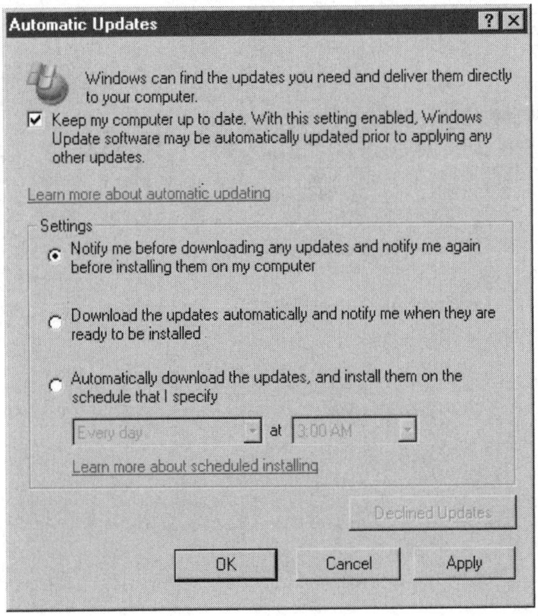

PART IV

Figure 9-15

Setting up Microsoft's Automatic Updates utility in Windows 2000

Figure 9-16
Registering a
system with the
Red Hat Update
Agent

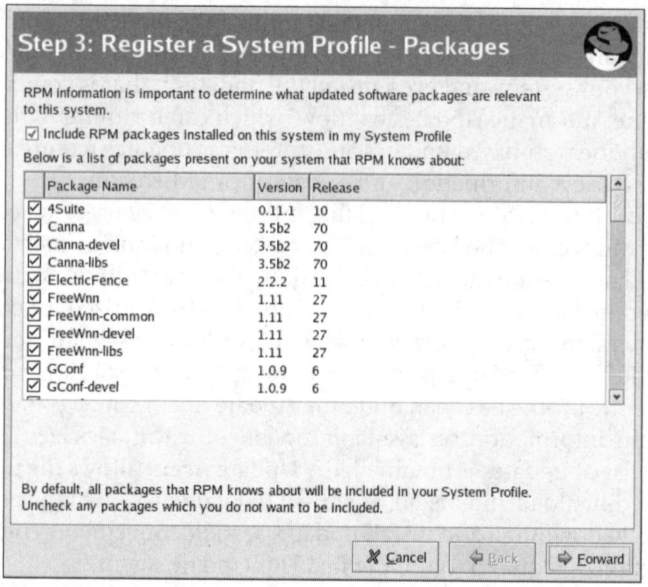

Network Hardening

While considering the baseline security of systems, attention must be given to the role the network connection plays in the overall security profile. The tremendous growth of the Internet and the affordability of multiple personal computers and Ethernet networking have caused almost every computer to be attached to some kind of network, and once computers are attached to a network, they are open to access from any other user on that

Figure 9-17
Selecting from
available updates
in the Red Hat
Update Agent

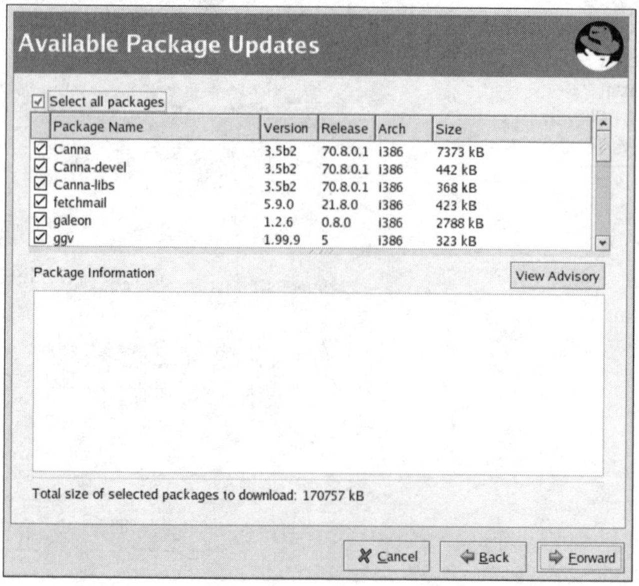

network. Proper controls over network access must be established. On computers, this is done by controlling the services that are running and the ports that are opened for network access. In addition to servers and workstations, however, network devices must also be examined: routers, switches, and modems, as well as other various components.

Today's network infrastructure components are similar to other computing devices on the network—they have dedicated hardware that runs an operating system, typically with one or more open ports for direct connection to the operating system, as well as ports supporting various network services. Any flaws in the coding of the operating system can be exploited to gain access as with any "regular" computer. These network devices should be configured with very strict parameters to maintain network security. Like normal computer operating systems that need to be patched and updated, the software that runs network infrastructure components needs to be updated regularly, as well. Finally, an outer layer of security should be added by implementing appropriate firewall rules and router access control lists.

Software Updates

Maintaining current vendor patch levels for your software is one of the most important things you can do to maintain security. This is also true for the infrastructure that runs the network. While some equipment is unmanaged and typically has no network presence and few security risks, any managed equipment that is responding on network ports will have some software or firmware controlling it. This software or firmware needs to be updated on a regular basis.

The most common device that connects people to the Internet is the network router. There are dozens of brands of routers, but the market is dominated by Cisco Systems. Their popular Internetwork Operating System (IOS), runs on over 70 of Cisco's devices and is installed countless times at countless locations. This popularity has fueled research into vulnerabilities in the code, and over the past few years quite a few vulnerabilities have been reported. These vulnerabilities can take many forms as routers send and receive several different kinds of traffic, from the standard Telnet remote terminal, to routing information in the form of Routing Information Protocol (RIP) or Open Shortest Path First (OSPF) packets, to Simple Network Management Protocol (SNMP) packets. This highlights the need to update the IOS software on a regular basis.

Cisco's IOS also runs on many of their Ethernet switching products. Like routers, these too have capabilities for receiving and processing protocols like Telnet and SNMP. Smaller network components do not usually run large software suites and typically have smaller software loaded on internal Non-Volatile RAM (NVRAM). While the update process for this kind of software is typically called a *firmware update*, this does not change the security implications of keeping it up to date. In the case of a corporate network with several devices, someone must take ownership of updating the devices, and updates must be performed regularly according to security and administration policies.

Device Configuration

As important as it is to keep software up to date, properly configuring network devices is equally, if not more, important. Many network devices, such as routers and switches, now have advanced remote management capabilities and can have multiple open ports accepting network connections. Proper configuration is necessary to keep these devices secure. Choosing a good password is very important in maintaining external and internal security, and closing or limiting access to any open ports is also a good step for securing the devices. On the more advanced devices, care must also be taken about what services the device is running, just like with a computer.

In many cases, a network device's primary protection method is a password. Good passwords are one of the most effective security tools, because a good password can be resistant to several forms of attack. This resistance makes an attacker use simple brute forcing methods, taking tremendous amounts of time and generating a large amount of network traffic, both increasing the likelihood of the attacker's efforts being detected. Unfortunately, good passwords are often hard to remember, so weaker passwords are usually used.

To recognize the impact on security a bad password can have, consider the fact that a typical brute forcing program can try every word in the unabridged English dictionary in under a day, but it would take several thousand years to attempt to brute force an eight-character password. This is based upon using not only the standard 26 character alphabet, but also adding capitalization for 26 more characters, numeric digits for 10 more, and special characters, adding another 32 different characters. This totals 95 different characters that can be used, giving 6,704,780,954,517,120 or six quadrillion different possibilities for a one to eight character password. This is in stark contrast to the estimated two million words in the English language, or the 217 billion possibilities provided by simple lowercase alphabetic characters.

The best kinds of passwords are ones that bear no resemblance to actual words, such as "AvhB42^&nFh". However, although such passwords provide greater security, they are difficult to remember, leading users to use passwords that are based upon regular dictionary words. While this is a concern for any password on any system, it is of greater concern on network infrastructure equipment because many pieces of network equipment require only password authentication for access—there is typically no username.

One of the password-related issues that many administrators overlook is SNMP. SNMP was developed in 1988 and has been implemented on a huge variety of network devices. Its wide implementation is directly related to its simplicity and extensibility. Since every manufacturer can add objects to the Management Information Base (MIB), they can add functionality without interfering with any other manufacturer's portion of the MIB tree. This feature of the protocol lets manufacturers make SNMP very powerful for configuration and monitoring purposes. The downside is that many devices have SNMP turned on by default. Network administrators not using SNMP will often forget to disable SNMP or will forget to change the well-known default passwords—typically "public" for read-only access and "private" for read/write access. With the SNMP service active and using a default password, an attacker can retrieve a great deal of interesting information from a network device, as well as altering any SNMP-capable settings. If SNMP is employed, well thought out passwords should be used, as well as a schedule for password updates.

Keep in mind that SNMP passwords are often passed in the clear, so it should never be treated as a trusted protocol. The SNMP service should also be limited to only connections from the management station's IP address. If SNMP is not used, the service should be disabled, if possible. Otherwise the ports for SNMP should not be accessible from anywhere on the external or internal network.

As with any system, security is largely dependant on proper configuration of the system itself. A router can be secured with proper configuration just as easily as it can be left unsecured through poor configuration. Good passwords and knowledge of what services the devices are running is important to maintaining the security of those devices.

Ports and Services

A part of configuration that deserves its own section is the configuration of ports and services. For any networked machine, you need to take care to establish which ports and services are running and then conduct regular audits to ensure that only the authorized ports and services are open.

The advent and growth of networks permit almost any machine to be electronically connected to any other machine. This is a danger, as many machines are designed around a principle of trusting any other system on their local network. This causes problems because many machines have default configurations that offer a wide variety of services to the network, resulting in a large number of open ports. The overarching rule of security, here, is to give an attacker as little information or opportunity as possible, whether the attacker is inside or outside your network. While not all ports can be dangerous, they might provide information, so it is best to only have ports open that are necessary to run the services that the machine provides. By limiting the number of open ports, you reduce not only the possible avenues an attacker can use to compromise a machine, but also the amount of information that they can retrieve about the system. Table 9-2 shows an example output from a very popular port scanning program called "nmap." This tool checks remote systems for open services and reports back which services are "open" and accepting connections and which ports are "closed" and not accepting connections. In this example, nmap has scanned for open services on 1,013 different ports—any port not listed in Table 9-2 is "closed."

Table 9-2 shows interesting ports on localhost (127.0.0.1). The 1013 ports scanned but not shown are in state: Closed.

> **NOTE** Nmap typically lists open services as "number/protocol" as shown in Table 9-2. The service name is a "best guess" by nmap based on the service typically running on that specific port.

There are also many ports left open by default on Windows systems, such as 135 epmap, 139 netbios-ssn, and 445 microsoft-ds.

Typically most servers are only used to provide one or two services, the most prevalent service on Internet servers being web and secure web, or 80/tcp and 443/tcp, respectively. Having web servers that also run telnet, SMTP, or POP3 provides multiple paths for an attacker who is attempting to compromise the system. It also requires more administration, as every service that is running needs to have its patch level kept up to date to ensure security. Figure 9-18 shows the output of a **netstat –a** command on a workstation running Windows 2000 Professional.

Table 9-2	Port	State	Service
Open Ports and Services on a Typical UNIX Machine	21/tcp	open	ftp
	22/tcp	open	ssh
	23/tcp	open	telnet
	25/tcp	open	smtp
	80/tcp	open	http
	110/tcp	open	pop
	111/tcp	open	pop
	113/tcp	open	ident
	143/tcp	open	imap2
	512/tcp	open	exec
	513/tcp	open	login
	514/tcp	open	shell
	587/tcp	open	unknown
	783/tcp	open	unknown
	940/tcp	open	unknown
	946/tcp	open	unknown
	7256/tcp	open	smtp-stats

TIP To list open, or listening, ports on most machines, use the command **netstat -l** or **netstat -a** (shown in Figure 9-18).

```
C:\WINNT\System32\cmd.exe                                        _ □ ×

Active Connections

  Proto  Local Address          Foreign Address        State
  TCP    piii:epmap             piii:0                 LISTENING
  TCP    piii:microsoft-ds      piii:0                 LISTENING
  TCP    piii:1025              piii:0                 LISTENING
  TCP    piii:1030              piii:0                 LISTENING
  TCP    piii:1114              piii:0                 LISTENING
  TCP    piii:2446              piii:0                 LISTENING
  TCP    piii:2711              piii:0                 LISTENING
  TCP    piii:netbios-ssn       piii:0                 LISTENING
  TCP    piii:1103              piii:0                 LISTENING
  TCP    piii:1103              TANK:netbios-ssn       ESTABLISHED
  TCP    piii:1114              192.168.1.33:telnet    ESTABLISHED
  TCP    piii:2608              piii:0                 LISTENING
  TCP    piii:4659              piii:0                 LISTENING
  UDP    piii:epmap             *:*
  UDP    piii:microsoft-ds      *:*
  UDP    piii:1026              *:*
  UDP    piii:netbios-ns        *:*
  UDP    piii:netbios-dgm       *:*
  UDP    piii:isakmp            *:*

C:\>
```

Figure 9-18 Output from netstat—a command on Windows 2000

Once the running services are known, the best thing to do is to shut off the unused ones. This is done by editing the inetd.conf file found in /etc on most UNIX systems, or by erasing the software that is providing the service (such as by completely removing Sendmail from the system). In Windows NT or 2000, the service must be stopped and set to "disable" in the Services Control Panel. Netstat can be rerun multiple times while editing the configuration files to ensure that all unnecessary services are shut down.

Any networked computer is typically going to have open ports and services, but many networked devices are being delivered with advanced remote management capabilities and have their own open ports and services. The most common are remote terminal services, such as telnet 23/tcp, SSH 22/tcp, embedded web services on HTTP 80/tcp or HTTPS 443/tcp, and SNMP services on 161/udp. These types of services are harder to disable on network equipment, but is sometimes possible. In Cisco's IOS, the command **no snmp-server** in config mode will disable the server service and close the port. Contact the vendor of your network equipment for information on disabling unnecessary services or limiting access to network services.

Some equipment will simply not allow you to disable the running service, but there is almost always another way to restrict access. Quite often, the most effective method is to perform filtering on the equipment itself, in the form of access control lists.

Traffic Filtering

Filtering is one of the most common tools used in security. If something is trying to get in that you don't want to get in, you filter it. This is accomplished in a variety of ways, but they all consist of the same basic elements—rules that accept traffic and rules that deny traffic. These rules are typically arranged into sequential lists that the device steps through, one by one, as it receives traffic and attempts to find a match between rule and traffic. If this methodology looks familiar, that's because it is also how many brands of firewalls handle network traffic. While routers and other network devices typically make poor firewalls, they do have filtering capabilities that can be used to help secure the network as well as the routers and network devices themselves.

Filtering, while always following the same basic principle, is accomplished in many ways on different types of equipment. One of the most common places to do at least rudimentary filtering for your network is at the border routers. In Cisco's IOS, these filters are referred to as *access control lists (ACLs)*. Routers were originally built for the forwarding of traffic between networks, and current ones are optimized for that task. Traffic filtering was later added as a convenience, so ACLs can assist in the control of traffic across the network, but they will not make a router into a true firewall.

Access lists, like the majority of filtering rules, work on the principle of pattern matching. Every packet that the router accepts is examined for a match between the packet and the rules in the ACL. The ACL rules are processed in sequential order, meaning that the packet is compared against the first rule, then the second, then the third, and so on, until a match is found or the packet has been compared to every rule. At very high data rates, or for very long lists of rules, this can become computationally intensive. This large drain on resources is the primary reason to avoid using a router as a firewall, but using ACLs to drop known rogue traffic at the borders to the network makes good sense.

A typical access-list entry would be something like this:

```
Access-List 201 deny icmp any 192.168.1.0 255.255.255.0
```

This will drop Internet Control Message Protocol (ICMP) traffic from anywhere to the 192.168.1.0 network. These ACL entries must follow a specific syntax. The first component is an access-list name, in this case 201. The next part of the rule is the action that the rule will take—"permit" or "deny" if the traffic matches this particular rule. The type of traffic that the rule applies to is next, and while it is ICMP in this case, it can be set to any particular type of traffic you wish to allow or deny. The next required component is the source address and mask. This can be as specific as a single address, a list of addresses, or it can be set to all 0's or a wildcard to signify all addresses. In this case "any" is used as an abbreviation of the all 0's address. The last component is the destination address and mask. This follows the same format as the source address and mask, and it can also be a single address, a list of addresses, or all addresses.

While Cisco dominates the router market, other manufacturers do produce similar products. These products generally follow a similar format for their filtering rules, possibly with different syntax; however, they generally have statements involving traffic type, source, destination, and the action to be performed on the traffic. The versatility of ACLs allows a lot of filtering power, but filtering on a router should primarily be used to drop large blocks of the Internet that are known to not have contact with your organization, or to drop entire types of traffic from the entire Internet. This allows the firewall to handle the more complex rules for traffic filtering.

The next piece of equipment that should handle traffic after it passes through the router is the firewall. This is where the most complex filtering is performed, but it is typically still done with ACL-like statements. However, while the configuration is similar, extra care must be taken with firewalls, as they typically bridge public networks and private ones—if an attacker breaches the firewall, they will have a great deal of access to all the networks that the firewall is in contact with.

Firewalls should have all their open ports and services restricted to a very limited number of source addresses, typically the authorized control stations. Once traffic has been allowed inside the firewall, it can also be filtered on the host itself, as both Windows 2000 and most variants of UNIX support traffic filtering natively. Almost any other operating system can have traffic filtering added as an application. Windows 2000 provides traffic filtering on a per-port basis, and many versions of UNIX support traffic filtering to the point that they are well suited to be firewalls. IPFW, ipchains, and iptables are all programs that implement the same filtering concept, which is once again based upon access control statements formed into lists. Ipchains and iptables both have multiple lists allowing further specialization of inbound and outbound traffic on each interface. The statements that make up the lists follow the same format of list, action, type of traffic, source, and destination.

There is also the capability in many UNIX flavors to do filtering within certain applications. Tcpwrapper is a program that sits between inetd (the UNIX Internet superserver described in the Solaris and Linux sections of this chapter) and the individual services.

When a request comes in, inetd starts tcpwrapper, and it will allow authorized connections to the associated daemon when that specific service, such as FTP or Telnet, is needed by an authorized connection. Some newer versions of inetd now contain tcpwrapper-like functionality.

Filtering rules for tcpwrapper are typically contained in two separate files: /etc/hosts.allow and /etc/hosts.deny. These files enumerate the hosts allowed to connect to certain services, as well as those that are denied access to certain services. These files are processed from top to bottom until a matching rule is found, but they work on only source address and service. The rules in the files are formatted as "SERVICE:SOURCE", so an example hosts.allow might read as follows:

```
telnetd: ALL
ftpd: 192.168.1
sendmail: localhost
```

Any traffic that matches a rule in the hosts.allow file is allowed to connect to the system. The hosts.deny file has the same format, but it denies traffic that matches its rules. This functionality can be very useful for protecting not only against external threats, but also against internal threats, because you are locking down services to only the machines authorized to make use of them. TCP wrappers checks hosts.allow first and then hosts.deny—any traffic permitted by hosts.allow will be allowed in regardless of any rules contained in hosts.deny. This allows administrators to specify connections in hosts.allow and then place a generic "deny all" statement in hosts.deny to reject anything not specifically allowed in the hosts.allow file.

Network hardening is, on first glance, a fairly simple task. Disallow any traffic that is unauthorized by filtering it at all possible junctures in the network, and keep all software up to date on any devices that have contact with the network. Actually accomplishing that task is much more complex and maintenance oriented. The tools for controlling traffic are ACLs, traffic filters like tcpwrapper, and closing all unnecessary ports by properly configuring them. Vendor patches and firmware updates should be installed regularly. As always, any open services should be configured with maximum authentication and good passwords. Taking these steps will not completely solve the problem of security, but will ensure that an attack is as difficult as it can be.

Application Hardening

Perhaps as important as operating system and network hardening is application hardening—securing an application against local and Internet-based attacks. Hardening applications is fairly similar to hardening operating systems—you remove the functions or components you don't need, restrict access where you can, and make sure the application is kept up to date with patches. In most cases, the last step in that list is the most important for maintaining application security. After all, you need to make applications accessible to users or they serve no purpose. As most problems with applications tend to be buffer overflows in legitimate user input fields, patching the application is often the only way to secure it from attack.

Application Patches

As obvious as this seems, application patches are most likely going to come from the vendor that sells the application. After all, who else has access to the source code? In some cases, such as with Microsoft's Internet Information Server, this is the same company that sold the operating system that the application runs on. In other cases, such as Apache, the vendor is operating-system independent and provides an application with versions for many different operating systems.

Application patches are likely to come in three varieties: hotfixes, patches, and upgrades. As for operating systems, *hotfixes* are usually small sections of code designed to fix a specific problem. For example, a hotfix may be released to address a buffer overflow in the login routine for an application. *Patches* are usually collections of fixes, they tend to be much larger, and they are usually released on a periodic basis or whenever enough problems have been addressed to warrant a patch release. *Upgrades* are another popular method of patching applications, and they tend to be received with a more positive spin than patches. Even the term *upgrade* has a positive connotation—you are moving up to a better, more functional, and more secure application. For this reason, many vendors will release "upgrades" that consist mainly of fixes rather than new or enhanced functionality.

Application patches can come in a variety of forms. They can be downloaded from the vendor's web site or FTP site, or they can be received on a CD. In many cases, a patch is a small binary application that, when run, automatically replaces defective application binaries with updated ones. The patch may also change settings or modify configuration files. In other cases, the patch will be a zipped archive of files with a set of instructions that require the user or administrator to manually replace defective applications with the updated ones. Some advanced applications will have automatic update routines that update the application automatically in much the same fashion as an operating system.

Web Servers *IIS*

Without a doubt, the most common Internet server-side application in use is the web server. Web servers are designed to provide content and functionality to remote users through a standard web browser. Web servers are used to deliver news, sell just about every product ever created, conduct auctions, and show pictures of someone's wedding. Due to their popularity and prolific use, web servers have become extremely popular targets for attackers. Web sites are defaced, and the original content is replaced with something the owner did not intend to display. E-commerce sites are attacked, and credit card numbers and user information is stolen.

Vendors have made setting up a web server remarkably easy, and this is one of the reasons for their enormous popularity. Unfortunately, vendors don't always provide good security configurations as part of the default installation. Fortunately, hardening a web server is not that difficult, as will be illustrated with examples of the two most popular web servers: IIS and Apache.

Microsoft's Internet Information Server

Microsoft's Internet Information Server (IIS) is one of the most popular web server applications in use today. IIS comes as a standard package with the Windows 2000 Server and Advanced Server operating systems and can be loaded at install time or added to the configuration of a running system. Due to its widespread use, IIS is a very popular target, and new vulnerabilities and exploits are released on an almost weekly or even daily basis.

The first step in securing an IIS server is to remove all sample files. To assist users in setting up their new web servers, Microsoft provides a number of sample files that users can examine and use as references when constructing their web sites. Unfortunately, these sample applications tend to be full of vulnerabilities and holes and should therefore never be present on a production web server. To remove IIS sample applications, remove the virtual and physical directories where the samples exist. For more information on the location of the sample files, refer to the following table:

Sample Name	Virtual Directory	Location
IIS Samples	\IISSamples	C:\Inetpub\IISsamples
IIS Documentation	IISHelp	C:\Winnt\Help\IIShelp
Data Access	\MSADC	C:\Program files\Common files\System\MSadc

Next, you should set up the appropriate permissions for the web server's files and directories. In IIS you can do this using access control lists (ACLs), which are essentially the same file permissions that were discussed in the context of operating system hardening. As web servers are usually designed to give the public at large access, the key is to limit the user's ability to browse or navigate outside the intended path. This will typically involve removing permissions for the "everyone" group from certain files and directories. In most cases, you should never allow the "everyone" group to have write and execute privileges to the same directory. For that matter, in most cases you will not want to allow users to have write permissions for any of the web server's directories. Microsoft has provided some suggested ACL settings that are outlined in the following table:

File Type	ACL
CGI (exe, dll, cmd, pl)	Everyone (execute) Administrators (full control) System (full control)
Script files (asp)	Everyone (execute) Administrators (full control) System (full control)
Include files (inc, shtm, shtml)	Everyone (execute) Administrators (full control) System (full control)
Static content (txt, gif, jpg, html)	Everyone (read-only) Administrators (full control) System (full control)

Patching is also an extremely important part of the process of securing an IIS server. Since IIS is almost an integral part of the Windows Server operating system, the service packs for the operating system often contain patches and fixes for IIS. Microsoft also releases security bulletins to address each specific vulnerability that is discovered. Within each security bulletin there are links to the patch or hotfix that will mitigate or remove

PART IV

the reported vulnerability or manual steps an administrator can perform until a formal patch is released.

IIS is such a popular target that it is often very difficult for an administrator to keep pace with all the discovered vulnerabilities and patches required to keep it up to date and secure from attack. To ease the burden somewhat, Microsoft has developed two tools specifically designed to help secure IIS servers: the URLScan and IIS LockDown tools. URLScan is a monitoring utility and preprocessor that examines all incoming URLs and rejects any requests for files, directories, or services outside the intended scope of the web site. The IIS LockDown tool asks the administrator a series of questions to determine which features are needed. Based on the answers, IIS LockDown can deny write permissions for anonymous accounts, disable WebDAV, remove dynamic script type associations, restore default security settings, and back up the IIS Metabase and ACLs.

Apache

The Apache HTTP server from the Apache Software Foundation is the most popular web server in use today. Its Internet presence is greater than all the other web server versions combined. In 1995, a group of individuals known as the Apache Group joined to develop the Apache HTTP server. By 1999, the web server software and associated projects had become so popular that the organization grew into the Apache Software Foundation, a non-profit corporation. According to the Apache.org web site "The Apache HTTP Server Project is an effort to develop and maintain an open-source HTTP server for modern operating systems including UNIX and Windows NT. The goal of this project is to provide a secure, efficient and extensible server that provides HTTP services in sync with the current HTTP standards." This statement highlights two of the keys to Apache's popularity—the software is open source, and it is available for virtually every popular operating system.

The first step in securing an Apache web server is to secure the host operating system. Due to the fact that Apache is available for most popular operating systems, outlining the possible security issues here could be a large task and would depend heavily on the operating system chosen. For the sake of brevity, we'll just say that a secure host operating system is one that is patched, has strong passwords for all user accounts, has no unnecessary services or software, has strong file and directory permissions, and has auditing enabled.

Once the host operating system has been taken care of, you will need to create an unprivileged account that will run the Apache server. This account, typically called "httpd" or "apache" is given the minimum permissions necessary to run the server software. Additional security measures include locking the account so it can never be used to log in to the system and assigning it to a special group where it is the only member. What you essentially end up creating is a user account that is only able to run the web server software and nothing more—this is fairly close to the ideal for Internet-visible services. By running the Apache software under an unprivileged account, you reduce the risk of potential compromise.

How you install the Apache software depends on whether you choose a precompiled binary or choose to compile it from the source code yourself. Regardless of the method you choose for installation, it is essential that you delete unneeded files and directories immediately after installation. Any source code files, samples, cgi-bin scripts, HTML pages, or documentation files that you don't absolutely need should be removed from the system. Like IIS, some of Apache's vulnerabilities have been in sample files and scripts that should not be placed on a production web server.

Locking down file and directory permissions is also important when securing an Apache server. In most cases, you are going to restrict access to web server configuration files to highly privileged users only, such as the root user. Files used for development or for maintaining the site itself are usually restricted to the web server development or maintenance team. The unprivileged user that was created to run the server is typically given read access to the web site content, and in some cases read and execute permission on any scripts required to support web site functionality. By restricting permissions and access to files and directories in this manner, you can help prevent web site visitors from wandering off the intended path or gaining access to files they should not see.

Patching an Apache server is just as critical as patching or maintaining any other application. New vulnerabilities are discovered on a frequent basis, and in some cases the only defense is to either disable functionality or implement the patch to correct the issue. There are no specific tools available to ensure that your version of Apache is up to date, so the best defense is to regularly visit the main Apache web site at www.apache.org for more information.

Mail Servers

Electronic mail is such an integral part of business and, for many of us, our daily lives that it is hard to imagine getting by without it. It has literally changed the way the world communicates and is so popular that there are millions of mail servers spread across the Internet sending billions of messages each day. As with so many things, increased popularity, use, and presence on the Internet also bring an increase in attention from potential attackers. Mail servers have become very popular targets, which makes securing them a constant challenge for administrators.

Securing a mail server typically means removing or disabling unwanted functionality and ensuring the software is patched. Earlier versions of mail server packages often contained bugs or even backdoors, such as the **wiz** command that gave potential attackers complete access to the host system. As mail server software matured, attacks started to focus on three areas: reconnaissance, relaying, and buffer overflows.

Reconnaissance or *information discovery* on a mail server is rather simple. The attacker's goal is to pull information from the system without having to authenticate or provide any information in return. Reconnaissance usually involves an attacker attempting to discover the names and addresses of valid user accounts, which are used for other purposes later. The two most common techniques use the **vrfy** and **expn** commands. When an attacker connects to a mail server, usually by telnetting to port 25 on the target system, the attacker can then enter commands and interact with the mail server itself. The **vrfy** command was initially designed to allow servers to verify e-mail addresses. For example, **vrfy jones** may yield a result of "jones@sample.com". This tells the attacker that the account "jones" does exist and gives the correct e-mail address for that account. The **expn** command expands an alias list into the full list of e-mail addresses belonging to that list. For example **expn all-users** would provide a list of every e-mail address belonging to the mailing list called "all-users", if that mailing list existed. As you can see, while neither of these commands causes any direct harm, they do provide some useful information. For that reason, most administrators disable the **vrfy** and **expn** functions on their mail servers.

Relaying occurs when a mail server handles a message and neither the sender nor the recipient is a local user. Essentially, an attacker can take advantage of the mail server to send out e-mail on their behalf, even though they are not a legitimate user of that system. Spammers—those parties responsible for filling your e-mail inbox with unwanted junk messages promising to make you rich beyond your wildest dreams—actively seek out open mail relays so they can take advantage of someone else's resources to do their dirty work. Attackers also seek out open relays and leverage them to launch e-mail attacks, flooding a recipient with so many messages that their mailbox fills up or their mail server crashes. Preventing your mail server from becoming an open relay usually involves ensuring only authenticated users are allowed to send outgoing mail. Many mail server software packages, such as Sendmail, now provide relay-prevention capabilities as part of the default install. In most cases, you can also specify which systems, by system and domain name or IP address, are allowed to send mail through the server.

Buffer overflows continue to be the greatest danger to mail server security. A buffer overflow is a rather simple attack—you find a place where the server is accepting input, and you provide more input than the server is expecting to receive. Depending on the "extra" input provided and the software being attacked, a buffer overflow can do anything from crashing the server to giving the attacker remote access to the system. These continue to be extremely popular attacks, and the most effective way to prevent them is to ensure your mail server software is kept patched and up to date.

Microsoft's Exchange

Microsoft's mail server implementation is called Exchange, and, like other Microsoft products, it has had its share of vulnerabilities. By default, **vrfy** and **expn** are disabled in later versions of Exchange, but they can be enabled if required by modifying certain Registry settings. Service packs and patches for later versions of Exchange also provide anti-relay capabilities that can be configured through the Routing tab of the Internet Mail Service Properties.

Microsoft also provides a tool called the Baseline Security Analyzer, designed to scan Exchange, along with other applications and the operating system itself, to ensure that the software is up to date and patched appropriately. Running this tool on a regular basis will help ensure your Exchange system is patched against the latest vulnerabilities.

Microsoft also offers several useful guides, such as "Security Operations Guide for Exchange 2000 Server," to assist administrators in securing Exchange servers.

Sendmail

Sendmail was the initial mail server software, and it is still extremely popular. It is available as a completely free, open source product or as a fully licensed commercial product.

By default, recent versions of Sendmail disable the **expn** and **vrfy** functions, but they can be disabled in earlier versions by adding **PrivacyOptions=noexpn novrfy** to the sendmail.cf configuration file. Relaying is also restricted by default in recent versions, though an administrator can allow relaying for specific IPs or domains by modifying the relay-domains configuration file. Buffer overflows have been a frequent problem for

Sendmail—as usual, the best defense is to ensure your Sendmail software is patched and up to date. For more information on Sendmail, refer to www.sendmail.org.

FTP Servers

The File Transfer Protocol (FTP) allows users to access remotely stored files, and the applications that provide FTP services are very popular. Users can typically download files from FTP sites and, in certain cases, may even be allowed to upload files to the server. FTP is most commonly used as a distribution method for application updates, device drivers, free software—anything that needs to be made available to a large group of people.

FTP servers are typically configured as read-only services, meaning that you can download files from the server but cannot upload files or modify anything on the server itself. The most interesting dilemma concerning FTP servers is the use of anonymous access. In many cases, this is exactly what the system has been designed to do—permit thousands of remote users to anonymously download files and information. So in some cases, anonymous is the expected condition, assuming all related security precautions have been taken. Anonymous access to FTP servers only becomes a problem when the administrator does not mean to provide anonymous access or does not properly secure the FTP service. This typically involves setting the appropriate permissions, having the FTP process run by a nonprivileged user, and not allowing users to upload or modify files. Some FTP servers are meant as an upload and download service for authorized users only—in those cases, anonymous access should be completely removed.

Like many other Internet services, buffer overflows have been a consistent problem for FTP servers. Ensuring your FTP server software is up to date and patched is the best defense against buffer overflows. If you are not providing anonymous FTP services, you may also wish to restrict which external IP addresses are allowed to connect to the FTP service.

DNS Servers

Domain Name Service (DNS) is an integral part of making the Internet work. Human beings are not good at remembering long strings or numbers like IP addresses, but we are pretty good at remembering names like cnn.com, yahoo.com, or amazon.com. To navigate the Internet, your computer will need to know the IP address of your destination system, and DNS provides the translation from name to IP address that makes it all possible. DNS services are built as a hierarchical structure with many systems, called nameservers, working together to resolve names into IP addresses. When you request a name resolution, your system queries a local nameserver. If the nameserver does not know how to perform the translation (doesn't know the name-to-IP address translation), it asks the next nameserver up in that chain. This continues until the answer is found and is passed back down to your system. At the top of the DNS tree are 13 root nameservers that provide the definitive answers for all DNS queries.

The most popular DNS server implementation is Berkeley Internet Name Domain (BIND). BIND is an open-source, free server package that can be downloaded and run on a variety of operating systems. The two most common types of attacks against DNS servers are reconnaissance attacks and buffer overflows.

PART IV

Reconnaissance attacks against DNS servers usually consist of an attacker attempting a zone transfer. A *zone transfer* occurs whenever a DNS server provides all the information it knows about an entire zone, which usually corresponds to an entire domain name. This information typically consists of all the names and IP addresses of systems in that zone—a very useful set of information for a potential attacker. Zone transfers also have a legitimate use, as they can be used to update zone information between nameservers. To protect against zone transfers, some organizations employ a split DNS architecture by using one nameserver to handle internal name queries and another server to handle external name queries. The two nameservers are never connected and never share information—the internal server is only visible from inside the network, and the external server knows nothing about the internal organization. Other organizations block all inbound connections on TCP port 53—the port used for zone transfers. You can also specify on your nameserver which external systems are allowed to execute zone transfers.

Buffer overflows are best defeated by ensuring the DNS software is patched and up to date. BIND, due to its popularity and widespread use, has been an extremely popular target in the last few years, and new vulnerabilities are introduced on a fairly regular basis. For the latest version and patches, see the main BIND web site at www.isc.org/products/BIND.

File and Print Services

Securing file and print services really boils down to a matter of permissions and ensuring legitimate users have access while unauthorized users do not. Network print services should be configured so that they receive print jobs from authorized, authenticated users. Users should, in most cases, be allowed to stop, pause, or delete their own print jobs. Only administrators should be able to control or modify the entire print queue or the printer itself.

In a similar manner, securing file services is usually a matter of permissions. Users should be given full control over their own files, read access to public resources that should not be modified, and possibly read and write access to group folders. In most cases, file services are extensions of the operating system itself, but there are some specialized file-service applications, such as Network File System (NFS), that are specifically designed to provide network access to stored data and files. NFS, a service that has a long history of security problems, has made advancements in recent versions, including better authentication methods, encryption, and PKI support.

Active Directory

The old adage "the network is the system" comes much closer to reality with systems like Microsoft's Active Directory services. Active Directory allows single login access to multiple applications, data sources, and systems, and includes advanced encryption capabilities, such as Kerberos and PKI.

Active Directory is built around a database, called a *schema*, containing information about network objects, such as domains, servers, workstations, printers, groups, and users. Each object is placed into a domain, which can then be used to control which users may access which objects. Each domain has its own security policies, administrative control, privileges, and relationships to other domains.

Domains are organized into a hierarchical structure called a forest, with the forest root domain being at the top of the tree. Branching off the main domain are trees containing parent and child domains. Every child domain has a two-way trust with its parent, which, by virtue of design, extends to every other child domain under that parent. Under this concept, when a user authenticates successfully into one child domain, all the other child domains under the same parent will accept the authentication as well, due to the two-way trust system. While the other child domains may accept the authentication information, access to resources is still controlled by the access controls for each specific child domain. So while a child domain may recognize you as an authenticated user from another child domain, it may not grant you access to its resources, due to local access controls.

Another key feature of Active Directory is delegation—the ability to selectively push administrative control to users in each domain. While enterprise-level administrative accounts only exist in the root domain, local admin accounts can exist in child domains. This means that you can have a high level admin in the central office grant local authority to add users, configure printers, and so on, to local admins in remote offices. This type of selective, localized administrative control can be very useful in large, distributed organizations.

Each object in Active Directory also has an access control list to determine who can view the object, what attributes they can read, and what actions each user can perform on the object. Access controls can be inherited or passed down from a parent to a child. For example, administrators can set permissions on a specific folder and specify that every subfolder or file in that folder receive the same permissions.

Active Directory also maintains a global catalog that contains a subset of information on all the objects in the Active Directory database. The global catalog is used for many functions within Active Directory, including user identification and e-mail addresses. The global catalog must be available and queryable for Active Directory to function properly. To update and query Active Directory, Microsoft uses the Lightweight Directory Access Protocol (LDAP). Every object in Active Directory has a unique name for use in LDAP queries and updates. Unfortunately, LDAP is not, by default, an encrypted protocol, meaning that anyone on the network could intercept and examine LDAP queries and updates.

The key to securing Active Directory is carefully planning and using appropriate permissions. While the granular control and enhanced capabilities of Active Directory could lead to more secure systems, its complexity can also lead to administrators overwriting each other's changes or accidentally granting access to unauthorized individuals. Microsoft provides some very good Active Directory resources on its web site.

Chapter Review

Security baselines are critical to protecting information systems, particularly those allowing connections from external users. Hardening is the process by which operating systems, network resources, and applications are secured against possible attacks. Securing operating systems consists of removing or disabling unnecessary services, restricting permissions on files and directories, removing unnecessary software (or not installing it in the first place), applying the latest patches, removing unnecessary user accounts, and ensuring strong password guidelines are in place. Securing network resources consists of disabling unnecessary functions, restricting access to ports and services, ensuring strong passwords are used, and ensuring the code on the network devices is patched and up to date. Securing applications depends heavily on the application involved, but typically consists of removing samples and default materials, preventing reconnaissance attempts, and ensuring the software is patched and up to date.

Questions

1. Which of the following steps is part of the hardening process for operating systems?

   A. Removing unnecessary applications and utilities

   B. Disabling unneeded services

   C. Setting appropriate permissions on files

   D. All of the above

2. Buffer overflow attacks are best defeated by

   A. Removing sample files

   B. Selecting strong passwords

   C. Setting appropriate permissions on files

   D. Installing the latest patches

3. Traffic filtering is used to

   A. Scan incoming web requests for malformed code

   B. Restrict access to ports and services

   C. Prevent buffer overflows

   D. Optimize the flow of time-sensitive traffic

4. File permissions under UNIX consist of what three types?

   A. Modify, read, and execute

   B. Full control, read-only, and run

   C. Write, read, and open

   D. Read, write, and execute

5. The **netstat** command

   A. Lists active network connections

   B. Provides the status of all hardware interfaces

   C. Shows open files and directories

   D. All of the above

6. The inetd daemon

    A. Listens for incoming connections

    B. Starts the appropriate service when required

    C. Runs at system startup

    D. All of the above

7. To provide an immediate solution addressing a specific vulnerability, a vendor may release

    A. A hotfix

    B. A service pack

    C. A patch

    D. None of the above

8. Password security consists of

    A. Selecting a password with at least eight characters, at least one change in case, and at least one number or nonalphanumeric character

    B. Storing the password in your wallet or purse

    C. Using the same password on every system

    D. Changing passwords at least once a year

9. TCP wrappers

    A. Verify checksums on every packet entering or leaving the system

    B. Help prioritize network traffic for optimal throughput

    C. Help restrict access to the local system

    D. None of the above

10. Ensuring software is patched and up to date is important for

    A. Operating systems

    B. Network devices

    C. Applications

    D. All of the above

Answers

1. D.

2. D. The best defense against buffer overflows is to apply the appropriate patches or fixes that eliminate the buffer overflow condition.

3. B.

4. **D.**

5. **A.**

6. **D.** The Internet superserver daemon, inetd, performs all of the functions listed. This helps prevent other services from using system resources until they need to do so.

7. **A.** Immediate solutions designed to address a specific vulnerability are usually called hotfixes. Patches and service packs tend to be larger, they are released on a slower timetable, and they often contain fixes for many different problems.

8. **A.**

9. **C.** TCP wrappers help restrict access to the local system by controlling what systems are allowed to connect to what services. This functionality is typically implemented in the hosts.allow and hosts.deny files on a specific system.

10. **D.**

PART V

Cryptography and Applications

CHAPTER 10

Cryptography

In this chapter, you will

- Learn about the three types of cryptography
- Learn about the current cryptographic algorithms
- Understand how cryptography is applied for security

Cryptography is the science of encrypting information. People's desire to hide information from each other extends well back into ancient times. Once people had determined that they could apply language to writing, they knew how to share information with others. The next step was to keep information from others. The easiest way for people to do this was to not teach others how to read and write the language. As that became ineffective, methods of shifting the letters around to make the text unreadable were attempted.

Spartans used a ribbon wrapped around a specific gauge cylinder and then wrote on the ribbon. When unwrapped, the ribbon appeared to hold a strange string of letters. The message could only be read when someone wrapped the ribbon back around the same gauge cylinder. This is an example of a *transposition cipher*, where the same letters are used but the order is changed.

The Romans typically used a different method known as a *shift cipher*. In this case, one letter of the alphabet is shifted a set number of places in the alphabet for another letter. A common modern-day example of this is the ROT13 cipher, where every letter is rotated 13 positions in the alphabet; *n* is written instead of *a*, *o* instead of *b*, etc.

These ciphers were simple to use and unfortunately also simple to break. This led to the need for more advanced transposition and substitution ciphers. As the systems became more complex, they were frequently automated by some mechanical or electro-mechanical device. A famous example of a modern encryption machine is the German Enigma machine from World War II. This machine used a complex series of substitutions to perform encryption, and interestingly enough gave rise to great amounts of research in computers.

Cryptanalysis, which is the process of analyzing available information to attempt to return the encrypted message to its original form, required advances in computer technology for the more complex encryption methods. The birth of the computer made it possible to easily execute more complex encryption algorithms, which is how encryption is performed today. Computer technology has also aided cryptanalysis, allowing new methods to be tried, such as linear and differential cryptanalysis. *Differential cryptanalysis is* done by comparing the input plaintext to the output ciphertext to try and determine the key. *Linear cryptanalysis* is similar in that it uses both plaintext and ciphertext, but it puts the plaintext through a simplified cipher to try and deduce what the key is likely to be in the full version of the cipher.

In this chapter, we will take a look at the most common algorithms in use today, both symmetric and asymmetric, as well as some of the things encryption is used to achieve on computer networks.

Algorithms

All current encryption schemes are based upon an *algorithm*, which is a step-by-step problem-solving procedure—a recursive computational procedure for solving a problem in a finite number of steps. The cryptographic algorithm, or what we commonly call the encryption algorithm or cipher, is made up of mathematical steps for encrypting and decrypting information. Figure 10-1 shows the process and will hopefully give better sense to the terms used in this chapter.

The best algorithms are always public algorithms that have been published for peer review by other cryptographic and mathematical experts. The actual steps for encrypting data can be published because of the design of the systems. They are designed to use a *key*, which is a special piece of data used in both the encryption and decryption processes. The algorithms that are used stay the same, but every implementation uses a different key, which ensures that even if someone knows the algorithm you are using, they cannot break your security. The classic example of this is the early shift cipher, known as Caesar's cipher.

Caesar's cipher uses an algorithm and a key, the algorithm specifying that you offset the alphabet either to the right (forwards) or to the left (backwards), and the key specifying how many letters the offset should be. For example, if the algorithm specified offsetting the alphabet to the right, and the key was three, the cipher would substitute for the real letter the letter three to the right in the alphabet. In this example, both the algorithm and key are simple, allowing for easy cryptanalysis of the cipher and easy recovery of the plaintext message.

The ease with which shift ciphers were broken led to the development of substitution ciphers. Substitution ciphers were very popular in Elizabethan England and are more complex than shift ciphers. They work on the principle of substituting a different letter for every letter: A becomes G, B becomes D, and so on. This system permits 26 possible values for every letter in the message, making the cipher many times more complex than a standard shift cipher. Simple analysis of the cipher could be performed to retrieve the

Figure 10-1

Diagram of the encryption and decryption process

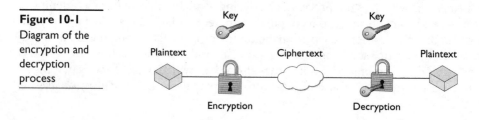

key, however. By looking for common letters and patterns that would become words, you can determine which cipher letter corresponds to which plaintext letter and therefore you can determine this system's key value.

To correct this problem, more complexity had to be added to the system. The Vigenère cipher works as a polyalphabetic substitution cipher that depends on a password. This is done by setting up a substitution table like this one:

```
A B C D E F G H I J K L M N O P Q R S T U V W X Y Z
B C D E F G H I J K L M N O P Q R S T U V W X Y Z A
C D E F G H I J K L M N O P Q R S T U V W X Y Z A B
D E F G H I J K L M N O P Q R S T U V W X Y Z A B C
E F G H I J K L M N O P Q R S T U V W X Y Z A B C D
F G H I J K L M N O P Q R S T U V W X Y Z A B C D E
G H I J K L M N O P Q R S T U V W X Y Z A B C D E F
H I J K L M N O P Q R S T U V W X Y Z A B C D E F G
I J K L M N O P Q R S T U V W X Y Z A B C D E F G H
J K L M N O P Q R S T U V W X Y Z A B C D E F G H I
K L M N O P Q R S T U V W X Y Z A B C D E F G H I J
L M N O P Q R S T U V W X Y Z A B C D E F G H I J K
M N O P Q R S T U V W X Y Z A B C D E F G H I J K L
N O P Q R S T U V W X Y Z A B C D E F G H I J K L M
O P Q R S T U V W X Y Z A B C D E F G H I J K L M N
P Q R S T U V W X Y Z A B C D E F G H I J K L M N O
Q R S T U V W X Y Z A B C D E F G H I J K L M N O P
R S T U V W X Y Z A B C D E F G H I J K L M N O P Q
S T U V W X Y Z A B C D E F G H I J K L M N O P Q R
T U V W X Y Z A B C D E F G H I J K L M N O P Q R S
U V W X Y Z A B C D E F G H I J K L M N O P Q R S T
V W X Y Z A B C D E F G H I J K L M N O P Q R S T U
W X Y Z A B C D E F G H I J K L M N O P Q R S T U V
X Y Z A B C D E F G H I J K L M N O P Q R S T U V W
Y Z A B C D E F G H I J K L M N O P Q R S T U V W X
Z A B C D E F G H I J K L M N O P Q R S T U V W X Y
```

Then the password is matched up to the text it is meant to encipher. If the password is not long enough, the password is repeated until one character of the password is matched up with each character of the plaintext. For example, if the plaintext is "Sample Message" and the password is "password" the resulting match is

passwordpassw

samplemessage

The cipher letter is determined by use of the previous grid, matching the plaintext character's row with the password character's column, resulting in a single ciphertext character from where the two meet. Taking the preceding example, the first two letters are "p" and "s"; when plugged into the grid they output a ciphertext character of "h". This process is repeated for every letter of the message.

In this example, the key in the encryption system is the password. It also illustrates that an algorithm can be simple and still have security. If someone knows what the table is, they can determine how the encryption was performed, but they still will not know the key to decrypting the message.

The more complex the key, the greater the security of the system. The Vigenère cipher system and systems like it make the algorithms rather simple but the key rather complex, with the best keys being very long and very random data. Key complexity is achieved by giving the key a large number of possible values. The *keyspace* is the size of every possible key value. When an algorithm lists a certain number of bits as a key, it is defining the keyspace. It is important to note that because keyspace is a numerical value, it is very important to ensure that comparisons are done using similar key types. Comparing a key made of 1 bit (2 possible values) and a key made of 1 letter (26 possible values) would not yield accurate results. Fortunately, the widespread use of computers have made almost all algorithms state their keyspace values in terms of bits.

It is easy to see how key complexity affects an algorithm when you look at some of the encryption algorithms that have been broken. DES (Data Encryption Standard) used a 56-bit key, allowing 72,000,000,000,000,000 possible values, but it has been broken by modern computers. The modern implementation of DES, Triple DES (commonly known as 3DES) uses a 128-bit key, or 340,000,000,000,000,000,000,000,000,000,000,000,000 possible values. You can see the difference in the possible values, and why 128 bits is generally accepted as the minimum to protect sensitive information.

When an algorithm is listed as being broken, it may be a result of the algorithm being faulty or having been based on poor math, but more likely the algorithm has been rendered obsolete by advancing technology. All encryption ciphers besides a "one-time pad" cipher are susceptible to a brute-force attack—attempting every possible key. With a very small key, such as a 2-bit key, trying every possible value is simple, as you only have 4 possibilities: 00, 01, 10, or 11. The 56-bit DES hs 72 quadrillion values, and while that seems like a lot, computers have advanced to the extent that they can attempt billions of keys every second. This makes brute forcing a key only a matter of time, so large keys are required to make brute-force attacks against the cipher take longer than the effective value of the information that is enciphered by them. One-time Pad ciphers are interesting because they have a key that is equal to the length of the message, and must use **completely** random data for the key. This allows the keyspace to be unlimited, therefore making a brute-force attack impossible.

Computers in cryptography and cryptanalysis have to handle all this data in a bit format. They would have difficulty in using the table shown earlier, so many encryption functions use a logical function to perform the encipherment. This function is typically XOR which is the bitwise exclusive OR. XOR is used because

$$\text{If} \quad (P\,XOR\,K) = C \quad \text{then} \quad (C\,XOR\,K) = P$$

If P is the plaintext and K is the key, then C is the ciphertext, making a simple symmetric key cipher in the case where the sender and the receiver both have a shared secret (key) to encrypt and decrypt data. While symmetric encryption is the most common type of encryption, there are other types of encryption, such as public key or asymmetric encryption, and hashing or one-way functions. They all have situations that they are naturally suited for, and we will go over the way each type works and look at what they are commonly used for.

Hashing

Hashing functions are one of the most commonly used encryption methods. A *hash* is a special mathematical function that performs one-way encryption, meaning that once the algorithm is processed, there is no feasible way to take the ciphertext and retrieve the plaintext that was used to generate it. Also, ideally, there is no feasible way to generate two different plaintexts that compute to the same hash value. Figure 10-2 shows a generic hashing process.

Common uses of hashing functions are storing computer passwords and ensuring message integrity. The idea is that hashing can produce a unique value corresponding to the data entered, but the hash value is also reproducible by anyone else running the same algorithm against the data. So, you could hash a message to get a message authentication code (MAC), and the computational number of the message would show that no intermediary has modified the message. This process works because hashing methods are typically public, and anyone can hash data using the specified method. It is computationally simple to generate the hash, so it is simple to check the validity or integrity of something by matching the given hash to one that is locally generated.

A hash algorithm can be attacked with what is called a *collision attack*, where an attacker finds two different messages that hash to the same value. Two of the popular hash algorithms are Secure Hash Algorithm (SHA) and Message Digest of varying versions (MD2, MD4, MD5). ✕

SHA ✕ = / 60 bit

SHA was developed in 1993 by the National Institute of Standards and Technology (NIST) and the National Security Agency (NSA). It was designed as the algorithm to be used for secure hashing in the U.S. Digital Signature Standard (DSS). It is modeled on the MD4 algorithm and implements fixes in that algorithm discovered by the NSA. It creates message digests 160 bits long that then can be used by the Digital Signature Algorithm (DSA), which can then compute the signature of the message. This is computationally simpler, as the message digest is typically much smaller than the actual message. Smaller message = less work.

SHA works, as all hashing functions work, by applying a compression function to the data input. It accepts an input of up to 2^{64} bits or less and then compresses down to a hash of 160 bits. SHA works in block mode, separating the data into words first, and then grouping the words into blocks. The words are 32-bit strings converted to hex; grouped together as 16 words they make up a 512-bit block. If the data that is input to SHA is not a multiple of 512, the message is padded with zeros and an integer describing the original length of the message.

Figure 10-2
How hashes work

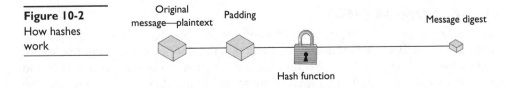

Original message—plaintext   Padding   Message digest

Hash function

PART V

Once the message has been formatted for processing, the actual hash can be generated. The 512-bit blocks are taken in order $B_1, B_2, B_3, \ldots, B_n$ until the entire message has been processed. The computation uses 80 32-bit words labeled $W_0, W_1, W_2, \ldots, W_{79}$ being sent to two 5-word buffers. The first 5-word buffer's words are labeled A, B, C, D, E, and the second 5-word buffer has them labeled H_0, H_1, H_2, H_3, H_4. There is also a single-word buffer, TEMP. Before processing any blocks, the H_i are initialized as follows:

$$H_0 = 67452301$$

$$H_1 = \text{EFCDAB89}$$

$$H_2 = \text{98BADCFE}$$

$$H_3 = 10325476$$

$$H_4 = \text{C3D2E1F0}$$

The first block now gets processed by dividing the first block into 16 words:

W_0 through W_{15}

For $t = 16$ through 79

$$W_t = S1(W_{t-3} \text{ XOR } W_{t-8} \text{ XOR } W_{t-14} \text{ XOR } W_{t-16})$$

Let $A = H_0\ B = H_1\ C = H_2\ D = H_3\ E = H_4$

For $t = 0$ through 79

Let $\text{TEMP} = S^5(A) + f_t(B,C,D) + E + W_t + K_t;$

$$E = D;\ D = C;\ C = S^{30}(B);\ B = A;\ A = \text{TEMP}$$

Let $H_0 = H_0 + A;\ H_1 = H_1 + B;\ H_2 = H_2 + C;\ H_3 = H_3 + D;\ H_4 = H_4 + E$

After this has been completed for all blocks, the entire message is now represented by the 160-bit string $H_0\ H_1\ H_2\ H_3\ H_4$.

SHA is one of the more secure hash functions, with no known successful attacks against it. Also, its output is 160 bits long versus the more common 128-bit result from MD5. This added security and resistance to attack in SHA requires more processing power.

Message Digest (MD)

Message Digest (MD) is the generic version of one of three algorithms, all designed to create a message digest or hash from data input into the algorithm. MD algorithms work in the same manner as SHA in that they use a secure method to compress the file and generate a computed output of a specified number of bits. They were all developed by Ronald L. Rivest of MIT.

MD2

Message Digest 2 was developed in 1989 and is in some ways an early version of the later MD5 algorithm. It takes a data input of any length and produces a hash output of 128 bits. It is different from MD4 and MD5 in that MD2 is optimized for 8-bit machines, whereas the other two are optimized for 32-bit machines. As with SHA, the input data is padded to become a multiple—in this case a multiple of 16 bytes. After padding, a 16-byte checksum is appended to the message. The message is then processed in 16-byte blocks. After initialization, the algorithm invokes a compression function.

The compression function operates as shown here:

$$T = 0$$

For $J = 0$ through 17

For $k = 0$ through 47

$$T = Xk \text{ XOR } St$$

$$Xk = T$$

$$T = (T + J)\text{mod } 256$$

After the function has been run for every 16 bytes of the message, the output result is a 128-bit digest. The only known attack that is successful against MD2 is dependant on the checksum not being appended to the message before the hash function is run. Without a checksum, the algorithm can be vulnerable to a collision attack.

MD4

Message Digest 4 was developed in 1990 and is optimized for 32-bit computers. It is a fast algorithm, but it is not as secure. Like MD2 it takes a data input of some length and outputs a digest of 128 bits. The message is padded to become a multiple of 512, which is then concatenated with the representation of the message's original length.

As with SHA, it is then divided into blocks and also into 16 words of 32 bits. All blocks of the message are processed in three distinct rounds. The digest is then computed using a four-word buffer. The final four words left after compression are the 128-bit hash.

There is also an extended version of MD4 that computes the message in parallel and produces two 128-bit outputs—effectively a 256-bit hash. Even though a longer hash is produced, security has not been improved because of basic flaws in the algorithm. Dobbertin has shown how collisions in MD4 can be found in under a minute using just a PC. This vulnerability to collisions applies to 128-bit MD4 as well as 256-bit MD4. Most people are moving away from MD4 to MD5 or SHA.

MD5

Message Digest 5 was developed in 1991 and is structured after MD4 but with additional security to overcome the problems in MD4. Therefore, it is very similar to the MD4 algorithm, only slightly slower and more secure.

PART V

MD5 creates a 128-bit hash of a message of any length. Like MD4, it segments the message into 512-bit blocks and then into 16 32-bit words. First the original message is padded to be 64 bits short of a multiple of 512 bits. Then a 64-bit representation of the original length of the message is added to the padded value to bring the entire message up to a 512-bit multiple.

After padding is complete, four 32-bit variables, A, B, C, D, are initialized. A, B, C, D are copied into a, b, c, d, and then the main function begins. This has four rounds, each using a different nonlinear function 16 times. These functions operate on three of a, b, c, d, adding the result to the fourth variable, the fourth variable being a sub-block of the text and a constant, then rotating the result of that addition to the right a variable number of bits, specified by the round of the algorithm. After adding the result of this operation to one of a, b, c, d, that sum replaces one of a, b, c, d. After the four rounds are completed, a, b, c, d are added to A, B, C, D, and the algorithm moves on to the next block. After all blocks are completed, A, B, C, D are concatenated to form the final output of 128 bits.

Currently there are no true known attacks against MD5, but there has been cryptanalysis that displays weaknesses in the compression function. However, this weakness does not lend itself to an attack on MD5, itself. There are also methods to brute force hash functions for collisions, but the cost of hardware to perform the attack and the length of time required to produce the collision make the technique impractical. A custom machine to search for collisions was estimated to cost $10 million and require 24 days of run time by Paul C. van Oorschot and Michael J. Wiener in "Parallel Collision Search with Application to Hash Functions and Discrete Logarithms." The combination of these problems with MD5 has pushed people to adopt SHA for security reasons.

Hashing Summary

Hashing functions are very common, and they play an important role in the way information, such as passwords, is stored securely, and the way in which messages can be signed. By computing a digest of the message, less data needs to be signed by the more complex asymmetric encryption, and this still maintains assurances about message integrity. This is the primary purpose for which the protocols were designed, and their success will allow greater trust in electronic protocols and digital signatures.

Symmetric Encryption

Symmetric encryption is the older and more simple method of encrypting information. The basis of symmetric encryption is that both the sender and the receiver of the message have previously obtained the same key. This is, in fact, the basis for even the oldest ciphers—the Spartans needed the exact same size cylinder, making the cylinder the "key" to the message, and in shift ciphers both parties need to know the direction and amount of shift being performed. All symmetric algorithms are based upon this *shared secret* principle, including even the unbreakable one-time pad method. Figure 10-3 is a simple diagram showing the process that a symmetric algorithm goes through to provide encryption from plaintext to ciphertext. This ciphertext message is, presumably, transmitted to the message recipient who goes through the process to decrypt the message. Figure 10-3 shows the keys to the algorithm, which are the same value in the case of symmetric encryption.

Unlike hash functions, there is a cryptographic key involved in symmetric encryption, so there must be a mechanism for key management. Managing the cryptographic keys is very important in symmetric algorithms because the key unlocks the data you are trying to protect. However, the key also needs to be known or transmitted in a secret way to the other party that you wish to communicate with. This key management applies to all things that could happen to a key, securing it on the local computer, securing it on the remote one, protecting it from data corruption, protecting it from loss, as well as probably the most important step, protecting the key while it is transmitted between the two parties.

Later in the chapter we will look at public key cryptography, which greatly eases the key management issue, but for symmetric algorithms the most important lesson is to store and send the key only by known secure means. We will also look at some of the more popular symmetric encryption algorithms in use today, such as DES, 3DES, AES, IDEA, and others, as well as their key lengths.

DES

DES stands for Data Encryption Standard. It was first developed over twenty years ago. In 1973 the National Bureau of Standards (NBS), now known as the National Institute of Standards and Technology (NIST), issued a request for proposals for a standard cryptographic algorithm. They received a promising response in an algorithm called Lucifer, originally developed by IBM. The NBS and the NSA worked together to analyze the algorithm's security, and eventually DES was adopted as a federal standard in 1976.

NBS specified that the DES standard had to be recertified every five years. While DES passed without a hitch in 1983, the NSA said it would not recertify it in 1987. However, since there was no alternative for many businesses, there were many complaints, and the NSA and NBS were forced to recertify it again. The algorithm was then recertified in 1993, but NIST is now looking at the Advanced Encryption Standard (AES) to replace DES.

DES is what is known as a *block cipher*, segmenting the input data into blocks of a specified size, typically padding the last block to make it a multiple of the block size required. In the case of DES, the block size is 64 bits, which means DES takes a 64-bit input and outputs 64 bits of ciphertext. This process is repeated for all 64-bit blocks in the message. DES uses a key length of 56 bits, and all security rests within the key. The same algorithm and key are used for both encryption and decryption.

Figure 10-3

Layout of a symmetric algorithm

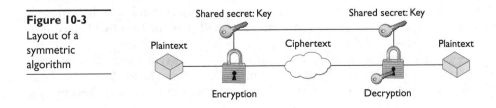

Shared secret: Key   Shared secret: Key

Plaintext   Ciphertext   Plaintext

Encryption   Decryption

At the most basic level, DES performs a substitution and then a permutation (a form of transposition) on the input, based upon the key. This action is called a *round*, and DES performs this 16 times on every 64-bit block. It works in three stages:

1. The algorithm accepts plaintext, P, and performs an initial permutation, IP, on P producing P_0. The block is then broken into left and right halves, the left (L_0) being the first 32 bits of P_0 and the right (R_0) being the last 32 bits of P_0.

2. With L_0 and R_0, 16 rounds are performed until L_{16} and R_{16} are generated.

3. The inverse permutation, IP^{-1}, is applied to $L_{16}R_{16}$ to produce ciphertext C.

The second stage mentions executing 16 times, and these rounds are where the bulk of the encryption is performed. The individual rounds work with the following computation:

Where i represents the current round,

$$L_i = R_{i-1}$$

$$R_i = L_{i-1} \text{ XOR } f(R_{i-1}, K_i)$$

K_i represents the current round's 48-bit string derived from the 56-bit key, and f represents the diffusion function. This function operates as follows:

1. 48 bits are selected from the 56-bit key.

2. The right half is expanded from 32 bits to 48 bits via an expansion permutation.

3. Those 48 bits are combined via XOR with the 48-key bits.

4. This result is then sent through 8 S-boxes, producing 32 new bits, and then it is permuted again.

After all 16 rounds have been completed and the inverse permutation has been completed, the ciphertext is output as 64 bits. Then the algorithm picks up the next 64 bits and starts all over again. This is carried on until the entire message has been encrypted with DES. As mentioned before, the same algorithm and key are used to decrypt DES as to encrypt. The only difference is that the sequence of key permutations are used in reverse order.

Over the years that DES has been a cryptographic standard, there has been a lot of cryptanalysis, and while the algorithm has held up very well, there have been some concerns. Weak keys are keys that are less secure than the majority of keys allowed in the keyspace of the algorithm. In the case of DES, because of the way the initial key is modified to get the subkey, certain keys are weak keys. The weak keys are ones that equate in binary to having all ones or all zeros, or where half is all ones and the other half is all zeros, like these shown in Figure 10-4.

There are also semi-weak keys, where two keys will encrypt plaintext to identical ciphertext, meaning that either key will decrypt the ciphertext. The total number of possibly weak keys is 64, which is very small compared with the 2^{56} possible keys in DES.

Figure 10-4
Weak DES keys

Binary Key

```
0000000 0000000
0000000 FFFFFFF
FFFFFFF 0000000
FFFFFFF FFFFFFF
```

There is also the question of 16 rounds. There have been multiple successful attacks against DES algorithms that use fewer rounds. Any DES with fewer than 16 rounds could be analyzed more efficiently with chosen plaintext than via a brute-force attack using differential cryptanalysis. With 16 rounds and not using a weak key, DES is reasonably secure, and amazingly has been for over 20 years. In 1999 there was a distributed effort consisting of a supercomputer and 100,000 PCs over the Internet to break a 56-bit DES key. By attempting over 240 billion keys per second, they were able to retrieve the key in less than a day. This demonstrates an incredible resistance to cracking a 20-year-old algorithm, but it also demonstrates that more stringent algorithms are needed to protect data today.

3DES

3DES (Triple DES) is a variant of DES. Depending on the specific variant, it uses either two or three keys instead of the single key that DES uses. It also spins through the DES algorithm three times via what's called *multiple encryption*.

Multiple encryption can be performed several different ways. The simplest method of multiple encryption is just to stack algorithms on top of each other—taking plaintext, encrypting it with DES, then encrypting the first ciphertext with a different key, then encrypting the second ciphertext with a third key. In reality, this technique is less effective than the technique that 3DES uses, which is to encrypt with one key, then decrypt with a second, and then encrypt with a third, as shown in Figure 10-5.

Figure 10-5
Diagram of 3DES

Triple DES (3DES)

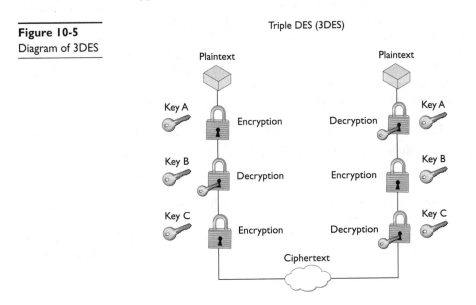

This greatly increases the number of attempts needed to retrieve the key, and this is a significant enhancement of security. The additional security comes with a price, though. It can take up to three times as long to compute 3DES as it does to compute DES. However, the advances in memory and processing power in today's electronics should make this problem irrelevant in all devices except for very small low power handhelds.

The only weaknesses of 3DES are the ones that already exist in DES, and due to the use of different keys in the same algorithm, affecting a longer key length by adding the first keyspace to the second keyspace, and the greater resistance to brute forcing, 3DES has less actual weakness. 3DES is a good interim step before the new encryption standard, AES, is fully implemented to replace DES.

AES   *256 bits*

Because of the advancement of technology and the progress being made in quickly retrieving DES keys, NIST put out a request for proposals for a new Advanced Encryption Standard (AES). It called for a block cipher using symmetric key cryptography and supporting key sizes of 128, 192, and 256 bits. After evaluation, the NIST had five finalists:

- **MARS**   IBM
- **RC6**   RSA
- **Rijndael**   John Daemen and Vincent Rijmen
- **Serpent**   Ross Anderson, Eli Biham, and Lars Knudsen
- **Twofish**   Bruce Schneier, John Kelsey, Doug Whiting, David Wagner, Chris Hall, and Niels Ferguson

In the fall of 2000, NIST picked Rijndael to be the new AES. It was chosen for its overall security as well as its good performance on limited capacity devices. Rijndael's design was influenced by Square, also written by John Daemen and Vincent Rijmen. Like Square, Rijndael is a block cipher separating data input in 128-bit blocks. Rijndael can also be configured to use blocks of 192 or 256 bits, but AES will standardize on 128-bit blocks. AES can have key sizes of 128, 192, and 256 bits, with the size of the key affecting the number of rounds used in the algorithm.

Like DES, AES works in three steps on every block of input data:

1. Add round key, performing an XOR of the block with a subkey.
2. Perform the number of normal rounds required by the key length.
3. Perform a regular round without the mix-column step found in the normal round.

After these steps have been performed, a 128-bit block of plaintext produces a 128-bit block of ciphertext. As mentioned in Step 2, AES performs multiple rounds. This is determined by the key size. A key size of 128 bits requires 9 rounds, 192-bit keys will require 11 rounds, and 256-bit keys use 13 rounds. There are four steps performed in every round:

- **Byte sub**   Each byte is replaced by its S-box substitute.
- **Shift row**   Bytes are arranged in a rectangle and shifted.
- **Mix column**   Matrix multiplication is performed based upon the arranged rectangle.
- **Add round key**   This round's subkey is cored in.

These steps are performed until the final round has been completed, and when the final step has been performed, the ciphertext is output.

This new algorithm is well thought out and has suitable key length to provide security for many years to come. While there are currently no efficient attacks against AES, more time and analysis will tell if this standard can last as long as DES has.

CAST

CAST is an encryption algorithm similar to DES in its structure. It was designed by Carlisle Adams and Stafford Tavares. CAST uses a 64-bit block size for 64- and 128-bit key versions, and a 128-bit block size for the 256-bit key version. Like DES, it divides the plaintext block into a left half and a right half. The right half is then put through function f and then is XORed with the left half. This becomes the new right half, and the original right half becomes the new left half. This is repeated for eight rounds for a 64-bit key, and the left and right output is concatenated to form the ciphertext block.

As mentioned before, CAST supports longer key lengths than the original 64-bit one. Changes to the key length affect the number of rounds: CAST-128 specifies 16 rounds, and CAST-256 has 48 rounds. This algorithm in CAST-256 form was submitted for the AES standard but was not chosen. CAST has been through thorough analysis with only minor weaknesses discovered that are dependent on low numbers of rounds. There is currently no better way known to break high-round CAST than by brute forcing the key, meaning that with sufficient key length, CAST should be placed with other trusted algorithms.

RC

RC is a general term for several ciphers all designed by Ron Rivest—RC officially stands for Rivest Cipher. RC1, RC2, RC3, RC4, RC5, and RC6 are all ciphers in the series. RC1 and RC3 never made it to release, but RC2, RC4, RC5, and RC6 are all working algorithms.

RC2

RC2 was designed to be a DES replacement, and it is a variable-key-size block-mode cipher. The key size can be from 8 bits to 1,024 bits with the block size being fixed at 64 bits. RC2 breaks up the input blocks into four 16-bit words, and then puts them through 18 rounds of one of two operations. The two operations are mix and mash. The sequence in which the algorithms works is as follows:

1. Initialize the input block to words R_0 through R_3
2. Expand the key into K_0 through K_{63}

3. Initialize $j = 0$

4. Five mix rounds

5. One mash round

6. Six mix rounds

7. One mash round

8. Five mix rounds

This outputs 64 bits of ciphertext for 64 bits of plaintext. The individual operations are performed as follows, with "rol" in this description meaning to rotate the word left.

This is the mix operation:

$$Ri = R_i + K_j + (R_{i-1} \ \& \ R_{i-2}) + ((\sim R_{i-1}) \ \& \ R_{i-1})$$

$$j = j + 1$$

$$R_i = R_i \text{ rol } s_i$$

This is the Mash operation:

$$R_i = R_i + K[R_{i-1} \ \& \ 63]$$

According to RSA, RC2 is up to three times faster than DES. RSA maintained RC2 as a trade secret for a long time, with the source code eventually being illegally posted on the Internet. The ability of RC2 to accept different key lengths is one of the larger vulnerabilities in the algorithm. Any key length below 64 bits can be easily retrieved by modern computational power.

RC5

RC5 is a block cipher, written in 1994. It has multiple variable elements, numbers of rounds, key sizes, and block sizes. The algorithm starts by separating the input block into two words, A and B.

$$A = A + S_0$$

$$B = B + S_1$$

$$\text{For} \quad i = 1 \quad \text{to} \quad r$$

$$A = ((A \text{ XOR } B) <<< B) + S_{2i}$$

$$B = ((B \text{ XOR } A) <<< A) + S_{2i+1}$$

A and B represent the ciphertext output. This algorithm is relatively new, but if configured to run enough rounds, RC5 seems to provide adequate security for current brute forcing technology. Rivest recommends using at least 12 rounds. With 12 rounds in the algorithm cryptanalysis in a linear fashion proves less effective than brute force against RC5, and differential analysis fails for 15 or more rounds. There is also a newer algorithm, RC6.

RC6

RC6 is based on the design of RC5. It uses a 128-bit block size, separated into four words of 32 bits each. It uses a round count of 20 to provide security, and it has three possible key sizes: 128, 192, and 256 bits. The four words are named A, B, C, D, and the algorithm works like this:

$$B = B + S_0$$

$$D = D + S_1$$

$$\text{For} \quad i = 1 - 20$$

$$[t = (B * (2B + 1)) <<< 5$$

$$u = (D * (2D + 1)) <<< 5$$

$$A = ((A \text{ XOR } t) <<< u) + S_{2i}$$

$$C = ((C \text{ XOR } u) <<< t) + S_{2i+1}$$

$$(A, B, C, D) = (B, C, D, A)]$$

$$A = A + S_{42}$$

$$C = C + S_{43}$$

The output of A, B, C, D after 20 rounds is the ciphertext.

RC6 is a modern algorithm that runs well on 32-bit computers. With a sufficient number of rounds, the algorithm makes both linear and differential cryptanalysis infeasible. The available key lengths make brute-force attacks extremely time consuming. RC6 should provide adequate security for some time to come.

RC4   web

RC4 was created before RC5 and RC6, but it differs in operation. RC4 is a *stream cipher*, whereas all the symmetric ciphers we have looked at so far have been block-mode ciphers. A stream-mode cipher works by enciphering the plaintext in a stream, usually bit by bit. This makes stream ciphers faster than block-mode ciphers. Stream ciphers accomplish this by performing a bitwise XOR with the plaintext stream and a generated keystream.

RC4 operates in this manner. It was developed in 1987 and remained a trade secret of RSA until it was posted to the Internet in 1994. RC4 can use a key length of 8 to 2,048 bits, though the most common versions use 128-bit keys, or if subject to the old export restrictions, 40-bit keys. The key is used to initialize a 256-byte state table. This table is used to generate the pseudo-random stream that is XORed with the plaintext to generate the ciphertext.

The operation is performed as follows:

$$I = 0$$

$$j = 0$$

$$I = (I + 1) \bmod 256$$

$$j = (j + S_i) \bmod 256$$

Swap S_i and S_j

$$t = (S_i + S_j) \bmod 256$$

$$K = S_t$$

K is then XORed with the plaintext. Alternatively, K is XORed with the ciphertext to produce the plaintext.

The algorithm is fast, sometimes 10 times faster than DES. The most vulnerable point of the encryption is the possibility of weak keys. One key in 256 can generate bytes closely correlated with key bytes.

Blowfish

Blowfish was designed in 1994 by Bruce Schneier. It is a block-mode cipher using 64-bit blocks and a variable key length from 32 to 448 bits. It was designed to run quickly on 32-bit microprocessors and is optimized for situations where there are few key changes. Encryption is done by separating the 64-bit input block into two 32-bit words, and then a function is executed every round. Blowfish has 16 rounds. Once the input has been split into left and right words, the following function is performed:

For $I = 1 - 16$

$$X_L = X_L \text{ XOR } P_i$$

$$X_R = F(X_L) \text{ XOR } X_R$$

Swap X_L and X_R

Then, swap X_L and X_R

$$X_R = X_R \text{ XOR } P_{17}$$

$$X_L = X_L \text{ XOR } P_{18}$$

The two words are then recombined to form the 64-bit output ciphertext.

The only successful cryptanalysis to date against Blowfish has been against variants that used reduced rounds. There does not seem to be a weakness in the full 16-round version.

IDEA

IDEA started out as PES, or Proposed Encryption Cipher, in 1990. It was modified to improve its resistance to differential cryptanalysis and its name was changed to IDEA (International Data Encryption Algorithm) in 1992. It is a block-mode cipher using a 64-bit block size and a 128-bit key. The input plaintext is split into four 16-bit segments, A, B, C, D. The process uses eight rounds with each round performing the following function:

$$A * S_1 = X_1$$

$$B + S_2 = X_2$$

$$C + S_3 = X_3$$

$$D * S_4 = X_4$$

$$X_1 \text{ XOR } X_3 = X_5$$

$$X_2 \text{ XOR } X_4 = X_6$$

$$X_5 * S_5 = X_7$$

$$X_6 + X_7 = X_8$$

$$X_8 * S_6 = X_9$$

$$X_7 + X_9 = X_{10}$$

$$X_1 \text{ XOR } X_9 = X_{11}$$

$$X_3 \text{ XOR } X_9 = X_{12}$$

$$X_2 \text{ XOR } X_{10} = X_{13}$$

$$X_4 \text{ XOR } X_{10} = X_{14}$$

$$X_{11} = A$$

$$X_{13} = B$$

$$X_{12} = C$$

$$X_{14} = D$$

PART V

Then the next round starts. After eight rounds are completed, four more steps are done:

$$X_{11} * S_{49} = C_1$$

$$X_{12} + S_{50} = C_2$$

$$X_{13} + S_{51} = C_3$$

$$X_{14} + S_{52} = C_4$$

The output of the last four steps is then concatenated to form the ciphertext.

This algorithm is new, but all current cryptanalysis on full, eight-round IDEA shows that the most efficient attack would be to brute force the key. The 128-bit key would prevent this attack being accomplished, given current computer technology. The only known issue is that IDEA is susceptible to a weak key—a key that is made of all zeros. This weak key is easy to check for, and the weakness is simple to mitigate.

Symmetric Encryption Summary

Symmetric algorithms are important because they are comparatively fast and have fewer computational requirements. Their main weakness is that two geographically distant parties need to have a key that matches exactly. In the past, keys could be much simpler and still be secure, but with today's computational power, simple keys can be brute forced very quickly. This means that larger and more complex keys must be used and exchanged. This exchange of keys is greatly facilitated by our next subject, asymmetric or public key cryptography.

Asymmetric Encryption

Asymmetric cryptography is in many ways completely different than symmetric cryptography. While both are used to keep data from being seen by unauthorized users, asymmetric cryptography uses two keys instead of one. It was invented by Whitfield Diffie and Martin Hellman in 1975. Asymmetric cryptography is more commonly known as public key cryptography. The system uses a pair of keys: a private one that is kept secret, and a public key that can be sent to anyone. The system's security relies upon resistance to deducing one key, given the other, and thus retrieving the plaintext from the ciphertext.

Public key systems typically work by using hard math problems. One of the more common methods is through the difficulty of factoring large numbers. These functions are often called *trapdoor functions*, as they are difficult to process without the key, but easy when you have the key—the trapdoor through the function. For example, given a prime number, say 293, and another prime, such as 307, it is an easy function to multiply them together to get 89,951. Given 89,951, it is not simple to find the factors 293 and 307 unless you know one of them already. Computers can easily multiply very large primes with hundreds or thousands of digits but cannot easily factor the product.

The strength of these functions is very important: because an attacker is likely to have access to the public key, they can run tests of known plaintext and produce ciphertext. This allows instant checking of guesses that are made about the keys of the algorithm. RSA, Diffie-Hellman, ECC, and ElGamal are all popular asymmetric protocols. We will look at all of them and their suitability for different functions.

RSA

RSA is one of the first public key cryptosystems ever invented. It can be used for both encryption and digital signatures. RSA is named after its inventors, Ron Rivest, Adi Shamir, and Leonard Adleman, and was first published in 1977.

This algorithm uses the product of two very large prime numbers and works on the principle of difficulty in factoring such large numbers. It's best to choose large prime numbers from 100 to 200 digits in length and that are equal in length. These two primes will be P and Q. Randomly choose an encryption key, E, so that E is greater than 1, E is less than $P * Q$, and E must be odd. E must also be relatively prime to $(P - 1)$ and $(Q - 1)$. Then compute the decryption key D:

$$D = E^{-1} \bmod ((P - 1)(Q - 1))$$

Now that the encryption key and decryption key have been generated, the two prime numbers can be discarded, but they should not be revealed. To encrypt a message, it should be divided into blocks less than the product of P and Q. Then,

$$C_i = M_i^E \bmod (P * Q)$$

C is the output block of ciphertext matching the block length of the input message, M. To decrypt a message take ciphertext, C, and use this function:

$$M_i = C_i^D \bmod (P * Q)$$

This use of the second key retrieves the plaintext of the message.

This is a simple function, but its security has withstood the test of over 20 years of analysis. Considering the effectiveness of RSA's security and the ability to have two keys, why are there symmetric encryption algorithms at all? The answer is speed. RSA in software can be 100 times slower than DES, and in hardware it can be even slower.

RSA can be used to do both regular encryption and digital signatures. Typically RSA and the other public key systems are used in conjunction with symmetric key cryptography. Public key, the slower protocol, is used to exchange the private key, and then the communication uses the faster symmetric key protocol. This process is known as *electronic key exchange*.

Since the security of RSA is based upon the supposed difficulty of factoring large numbers, the main weaknesses are in the implementations of the protocol. Until recently, RSA was a patented algorithm, but it was a de facto standard for many years.

PART V

Diffie-Hellman

Diffie-Hellman was created in 1976 by Whitfield Diffie and Martin Hellman. This protocol is one of the most common encryption protocols in use today. It plays a role in the electronic key exchange method of the Secure Sockets Layer (SSL) protocol. It is also used by the SSH and IPsec protocols. This protocol is important because it enables the sharing of a secret key between two people who have not contacted each other before.

The protocol, like RSA, uses large prime numbers to work. Two users agree to two numbers, P and G, with P being a sufficiently large prime number, and G being the generator. Both users pick a secret number, a and b. Then both users compute their public number:

User 1 $X = Ga \bmod P$, with X being the public number

User 2 $Y = Gb \bmod P$, with Y being the public number

The users then exchange public numbers. User 1 knows P, G, a, X, Y.

User 1   Computes $Ka = Y^a \bmod P$

User 2   Computes $Kb = X^b \bmod P$

With $Ka = Kb = K$, now both users know the new shared secret K.

This is the basic algorithm, and though there have been methods to strengthen it, Diffie-Hellman is still in wide use. It remains very effective because of the nature of what it is protecting, which is just a temporary automatically generated secret key that is only good for a single communication session.

ElGamal

ElGamal can be used for both encryption and digital signatures. Taher ElGamal designed the system in the early 1980s. This system was never patented and is free for use. It is used as the U.S. government standard for digital signatures.

The system is based upon the difficulty of calculating discrete logarithms in a finite field. Three numbers are needed to generate a key pair. User 1 chooses a prime, P, and two random numbers, F and D. F and D should both be less than P. Then you can calculate the public key A:

$$A = D^F \bmod P$$

Then A, D, and P are shared with the second user, with F being the private key. To encrypt a message, M, a random key, k, is chosen that is relatively prime to $P - 1$. Then,

$$C_1 = D^k \bmod P$$

$$C_2 = A^k M \bmod P$$

C_1 and C_2 makes up the ciphertext. Decryption is done by

$$M = C_2/C_1^F \bmod P$$

ElGamal uses a different function for digital signatures. To sign a message, M, once again choose a random value k that is relatively prime to $P - 1$. Then,

$$C_1 = Dk \bmod P$$

$$C_2 = (M - C_1*F)/k \;(\bmod\; P - 1)$$

C_1 concatenated to C_2 is the digital signature.

ElGamal is an effective algorithm and has been in use for some time. It is used primarily for digital signatures. Like all asymmetric cryptography, it is slower than symmetric cryptography.

ECC

Elliptic curve cryptography (ECC) works on the basis of elliptic curves. An elliptic curve is a simple function that is drawn as a gently looping curve on the X, Y plane. They are defined by this equation:

$$y^2 = x^3 + ax^2 + b$$

Elliptic curves work because they have a special property—that you can add two points on the curve together and get a third point on the curve.

For cryptography, the elliptic curve works as a public key algorithm. Users agree on an elliptic curve and a fixed curve point. This information is not a shared secret, these points can be made public without compromising the security of the system. User 1 then chooses a secret random number, K_1, and then computes a public key based upon a point on the curve:

$$P_1 = K_1 * F$$

User 2 performs the same function and generates $P2$. Now user 1 can send user 2 a message by generating a shared secret:

$$S = K_1 * P_2$$

User 2 can generate the same shared secret independently:

$$S = K_2 * P_1$$

This is true because

$$K_1 * P_2 = K_1 * (K_2 * F) = (K_1 * K_2) * F = K_2 * (K_1 * F) = K_2 * P_1$$

The security of elliptic curve systems has been questioned, mostly because of lack of analysis. However, all public key systems rely on the difficulty of certain math problems. It would take a breakthrough in math for any of the mentioned systems to be weakened dramatically, but research has been done about the problems and has shown that the elliptic curve problem has been more resistant to incremental advances. Again, as with all cryptography algorithms, only time will tell how secure they really are.

Asymmetric Encryption Summary

Asymmetric encryption creates the possibility of digital signatures and also corrects the main weakness of symmetric cryptography. The ability to send messages securely without having to have had prior contact is growing to be one of the basic blocks of secure communication. Digital signatures will enable faster and more efficient exchange of all kinds of documents, including legal documents. With strong algorithms and good key lengths, security can be assured.

Usage

The use of cryptographic algorithms grows every day as more and more information becomes digitally encoded or put online. All of this data needs to be secured, and the best current way to do that has been encryption. We have looked at the algorithms; we will now consider some of the tasks they accomplish and things that they are best suited for. Security is typically defined as a product of five components: confidentiality, integrity, availability, authentication, and nonrepudiation. Encryption can address four of these five components with confidentiality, integrity, nonrepudiation, and authentication.

Confidentiality

Confidentiality is what is typically thought about when the term *security* comes up. Confidentiality is the ability to keep some piece of data a secret. In the digital world, confidentiality is something that encryption excels at providing.

There are two uses of confidentiality: on stored data and on transmitted data. In both cases, symmetric encryption is favored because of its speed and because some asymmetric algorithms can significantly increase the size of the object being encrypted. In the case of a stored item, there is typically no need to have a public key, as the item is being encrypted to protect it from others. In the case of transmitted data, the typical case is to use public key cryptography to exchange the secret key, and then to use symmetric cryptography to ensure the confidentiality of the data being sent.

Asymmetric cryptography does protect confidentiality, but its size and speed make it more efficient at protecting the confidentiality of small units, such as for electronic key exchange. In all cases, it is the strength of the algorithms and the length of the keys that ensure the secrecy of the data in question.

Integrity

Integrity is better known as *message integrity*, and it is a crucial component of message security. When a message is sent, both the sender and recipient need to know that the message was not altered in transmission. This is especially important when it comes to legal contracts—recipients need to know that the contracts have not been altered. The signers also have to have a way to validate that the contract they signed is not altered in the future.

This integrity is provided with one-way hash functions and digital signatures. The hash functions compute the message digests, and this guarantees the integrity of the message by allowing easy testing to determine whether any part of the message has been changed. The message now has a computed function (the hash value) to tell the users to resend the message if it was intercepted and interfered with.

This hash value is combined with asymmetric cryptography by taking the message's hash value and encrypting it with the user's private key. This lets anyone with the user's public key decrypt the hash and compare it to the locally computed hash, ensuring not only the integrity of the message but positively identifying the sender.

Nonrepudiation

An item of some confusion, nonrepudiation is actually fairly simple. It means that the sender cannot later deny that they sent the message. This is important in electronic exchanges of data because of the lack of face-to-face meetings. Nonrepudiation is based upon public key cryptography and the principle of only you knowing your private key. The presence of a message signed by you, using your private key, which nobody else should know, is an example of nonrepudiation. When a third party can check your signature using your public key, that disproves any claim that you were not the one who actually sent the message. Nonrepudiation is tied to asymmetric cryptography and cannot be implemented with symmetric algorithms.

Authentication

Authentication is simply being able to prove you are who you say you are. Authentication is similar to nonrepudiation, except that it is often used before communication begins, not after. Authentication is also typically used in both directions as part of a protocol.

Authentication can be done in a multitude of ways, the most basic being the use of a simple password. Every time you check your e-mail, you authenticate yourself to the server. This process can grow to need two or three identifying factors, like a password, a token, and a biometric.

Digital certificates are one form of such tokens. When you log in to a secure web site, one-way authentication occurs. You want to know that you are logging into the server that you mean to, so your browser checks the server's digital certificate. This is a token that is digitally signed by a trusted third party, assuring you that the sender is genuine.

This authentication is one way because the server does not need to know that you are who you say you are—it will authenticate your credit card later on. However, two-way authentication can work the same way, where you send your digital certificate signed by a third party, and the other entity you are communicating with sends theirs.

While symmetric encryption can be used as a simple manner of authentication (only the authorized should know the secret, after all) asymmetric encryption is better suited to show, via digital signatures and certificates, that you are who you say you are.

Digital Signatures

Digital signatures have been touted as being the key to truly paperless document flow, and they do have promise for improving the system. Digital signatures are based upon both hashing functions and asymmetric cryptography. Both encryption methods play an important role when signing digital documents.

Unprotected digital documents are very easy for anyone to change. If a document is edited after an individual signs it, it is important that this modification can be detected. To protect against document editing, hashing functions are used to create a digest of the message that is unique and easily reproducible by both parties. This ensures that the message integrity is complete.

Protection must also be provided that the intended party actually did sign the message, and that someone did not edit the message and the hash of the message. This is done by asymmetric encryption. The properties of asymmetric encryption allow anyone to use a person's public key to generate a message that can only be read by that person, as they are theoretically the only one with access to the private key. In the case of digital signatures, this process works exactly in reverse. When a user can decrypt the hash with the public key of the originator, that user knows that the hash was encrypted by the corresponding private key. This use of asymmetric encryption is a very good example of nonrepudiation, because only the signer would have access to the private key. This is how digital signatures work, by using integrity and nonrepudiation to prove not only that the people signed, but also what they signed.

Key Escrow

The impressive growth of the use of encryption technology has led to new issues in the handling of keys. Key escrow and key recovery are two issues in the use of asymmetric encryption that are often discussed.

Encryption became very good at hiding secrets, and with computer technology being affordable to everyone, criminals and other ill-willed people began using it to conceal communications and business dealings from law enforcement agencies. Government agencies, because they could not break the encryption, began asking for key escrow. *Key escrow*, in a simple form, is a system by which your private key is kept both by you and by the government. This allows people with a court order to retrieve your private key and have access to anything encrypted with your public key. Technically, this is typically done by encrypting the data with two keys, thereby giving the government access to your plaintext data. This has a tendency to negate the security provided by encryption, because the government will now have a huge complex infrastructure of systems to hold every escrowed key, and the security of those systems is less efficient than the security of your memorizing the key. These issues will affect the design and security of encryption technologies for the foreseeable future.

Chapter Review

Cryptography is in many ways the key to security in other systems. The progression of technology has allowed systems to be built to retrieve the secrets of others. More and more information is being digitized, then stored and sent via computers. Storing and transmitting valuable data and keeping it secure can be best accomplished with encryption.

We have seen the message digest one-way functions for passwords and message integrity checks. We have also seen the symmetric encryption algorithms used for encrypting data at high speeds. Finally we have seen the operation of asymmetric cryptography that is used for key management and digital signatures. These are three distinct types of encryption with different purposes. The material that makes up this chapter is based upon current algorithms and techniques. When implemented properly, they will improve security; however, they will need to be updated as encryption strength decays. Encryption, being based on traditionally difficult mathematical problems, can only keep data secure for a limited amount of time, as technology for solving those problems improves. The encryption that was incredibly effective 50 years ago is now easily broken. However, if one stays current with technology, encryption can provide a reasonable assurance of security.

Questions

1. Why is integrity important to cryptographic messages?

   A. To ensure that the message is properly formatted for decryption

   B. To protect the keys from exposure

   C. To show that a message has not been edited in transit

   D. To show that no one has read the message

2. What is Diffie-Hellman most commonly used for?

   A. Symmetric encryption key exchange

   B. Signing digital contracts

   C. Secure e-mail

   D. Storing encrypted passwords

3. What is AES meant to replace?

   A. IDEA

   B. DES

   C. Diffie-Hellman

   D. MD5

4. What does a hash function do?

   A. Creates a secure tunnel

   B. Breaks encryption by trying every possible key

   C. Multiplies two very large primes

   D. Creates a unique digest of a message

5. What is public key cryptography a more common name for?

   A. Asymmetric encryption

   B. SHA

   C. An algorithm that is no longer secure against cryptanalysis

   D. Authentication

6. How many bits are in a block of the SHA algorithm?

   A. 128

   B. 64

   C. 512

   D. 1,024

7. What is the advantage of using symmetric encryption on large quantities of data?

   A. Uniqueness of message digests

   B. Speed

   C. Anyone with the public key could decrypt the data

   D. Nonrepudiation

8. How do hash functions provide integrity?

   A. If the message is edited, the hash will no longer match.

   B. The hash makes the message uneditable.

   C. Hashing encrypts the message so that only the private key holder can read it.

   D. Hashing destroys the message so it cannot be read by anyone.

9. How is 3DES an improvement over normal DES?

   A. It uses public and private keys.

   B. It hashes the message before encryption.

   C. It uses three keys and multiple encryption and/or decryption sets.

   D. It is faster than DES.

10. What is the best kind of key to have?

   A. One that is easy to remember

   B. Long and random

C. Long and predictable

D. Short

11. What is a shift cipher?

    A. A cipher with public and private keys

    B. A cipher that cannot be broken except by hand calculations

    C. One that uses the geometry of elliptical curves

    D. A cipher that shifts the letters in the alphabet by a numeric amount

12. What kinds of encryption does a digital signature use?

    A. Hashing and asymmetric

    B. Asymmetric and symmetric

    C. Hashing and symmetric

13. What does differential cryptanalysis require?

    A. The key

    B. Large amounts of plaintext and ciphertext

    C. Just large amounts of ciphertext

    D. Computers able to guess at key values faster than a billion times per second

14. What is a brute-force attack?

    A. Feeding certain plaintext into the algorithm to deduce the key

    B. Capturing ciphertext with known plaintext values to deduce the key

    C. Sending every key value at the algorithm to find the key

    D. Sending two large men to the key owner's house to retrieve the key

15. What cipher was chosen to be the new AES standard?

    A. IDEA

    B. 3DES

    C. Blowfish

    D. Rijndael

Answers

1. C. Integrity is important for encryption to show that a message has not been edited or altered since it was created.

2. A. Diffie-Hellman is most commonly used to protect the exchange of keys used to create a connection using symmetric encryption. It is often used in Transport Layer Security (TLS) implementations for protecting secure web pages.

3. **B.** AES or Advanced Encryption Standard is designed to replace the old U.S. government standard of DES.

4. **D.** A hash function creates a message digest that should be unique to the message. This ensures that a different message would create a different digest, guaranteeing the integrity of the message.

5. **A.** Asymmetric encryption

6. **C.** 512 bits make up the blocks in SHA.

7. **B.** Symmetric encryption is several times faster computationally than asymmetric encryption.

8. **A.** Hashing makes a digest unique to the message, so if the message is altered, the hash will no longer match.

9. **C.** 3DES uses multiple keys and multiple encryption or decryption rounds to improve security over regular DES.

10. **B.** The best encryption key to have is one that is long and random, to reduce the predictability of the key.

11. **D.** A shift cipher works by shifting the letter of plaintext to a different letter, based upon a numeric shift in the alphabet.

12. **A.** Digital signatures use hashing and asymmetric encryption.

13. **B.** Differential cryptanalysis requires large amounts of plaintext and ciphertext.

14. **C.** Brute forcing is the attempt to use every possible key to find the correct one.

15. **D.** Rijndael was chosen as the new Advanced Encryption Standard.

Public Key Infrastructure

In this chapter, you will

- Learn the basics of public key infrastructures
- Understand certificate authorities
- Understand registration authorities
- Know certificate repositories
- Know trust and certificate verification
- Be able to use digital certificates
- Understand centralized or decentralized infrastructures
- Explore private key protection
- Learn public certificate authorities
- Understand in-house certificate authorities
- Understand outsourced certificate authorities
- Check out tying different PKIs together

Public key infrastructures (PKIs) are becoming a central security foundation for more and more companies. The technology was developed more than a decade ago, but only within the last few years has it really started to bloom and be integrated into diverse environments around the world. It can provide the underlying mechanisms that offer confidentiality, integrity, authentication, and nonrepudiation. It does this by offering an infrastructure that uses symmetric and asymmetric cryptographic technologies that can be used by e-mail clients, virtual private network products, web server components, and domain controllers to authenticate users for network participation and resource access. The important point here is that it offers an infrastructure or a framework that provides a foundation based on which different products and technologies can integrate with each other to supply various security services. The other approach, without PKIs, is to implement many different security solutions and hope for interoperability and equal levels of protection.

The Basics of Public Key Infrastructures

A PKI is a structure that provides all of the necessary components for different types of users and entities to be able to communicate securely and in a predictable manner. A PKI is made up of hardware, applications, policies, services, programming interfaces, cryptographic algorithms, protocols, users, and utilities. These components work together to allow communication to take place using public key cryptography and symmetric keys for digital signatures, data encryption, and integrity. (Please refer to Chapter 10 if you need a refresher on these concepts.) Many different applications and protocols can provide the same type of functionality, so why would anyone need to go through the trouble of constructing and implementing a PKI if applications and protocols can already do this? It all comes down to a level of trust.

If John and Diane want to communicate securely, John can generate his own public/private key pair and send his public key to Diane or place his public key in a directory that is available to everyone. If Diane receives John's public key, either from him or from a public directory, how does she know it really came from John? Maybe another individual is masquerading as John and replaced John's public key with her own, as shown in Figure 11-1. If this took place, Diane would believe that her messages could only be read by John and that the replies were actually from him. However, she would really be communicating with Katie. What is needed is a way to verify an individual's identity, to ensure that a person's public key is bound to their identity, and thus ensure that the previous scenario (and others) cannot take place.

In PKI environments, entities called *registration authorities* and *certificate authorities* will provide a service similar to that of the Department of Motor Vehicles (DMV). When

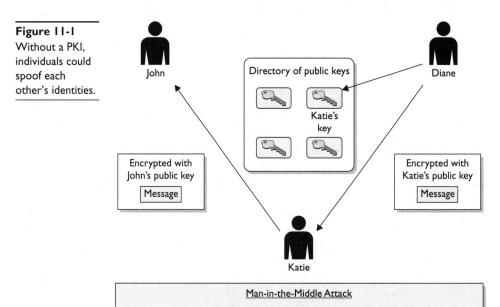

Figure 11-1
Without a PKI, individuals could spoof each other's identities.

Man-in-the-Middle Attack

1. Katie replaces John's public key with her key in the publicly accessible directory.
2. Diane extracts what she thinks is John's key, but it is in fact Katie's key.
3. Katie can now read messages Diane encrypts and sends to John.
4. After Katie decrypts and reads Diane's message, she encrypts it with John's public key and sends it on to him so he will not be the wiser.

John goes to register for a driver's license, he has to prove his identity to the DMV by providing his passport, birth certificate, or other identification documentation. If the DMV is satisfied with the proof John provides (and John passes a driving test), the DMV will create a driver's license that can then be used by John to prove his identity. If John is stopped by a police officer a few months later, the officer will ask for this license. The officer will not fully trust John, but the officer does trust the DMV and will be more willing to trust John and his identity claim if it matches what is stated on the license.

In the PKI context, while some variations exist in specific products, the registration authority will require proof of identity from the individual requesting a certificate and will validate this information. The registration authority will then advise the certificate authority to generate a certificate, which is analogous to a driver's license. The certificate authority will digitally sign the certificate using its private key. When Diane receives John's certificate and verifies that it was actually digitally signed by a certificate authority that she trusts, she will believe that the certificate is actually John's—not because she trusts John, but because she trusts the entity that is vouching for his identity (the certificate authority).

This is commonly referred to as a third-party trust model. Public keys are components of digital certificates, so when Diane verifies the certificate authority's digital signature, this verifies that the certificate is truly John's and that the public key the certificate contains is also John's. This is how John's identity is bound to his public key.

This process allows John to authenticate himself to Diane and communicate with her through encryption without prior communication or a preexisting relationship. Once Diane is convinced of the legitimacy of John's public key, she can use it to encrypt and decrypt messages between herself and John, as illustrated in Figure 11-2.

Figure 11-2
Public keys are components of digital certificates.

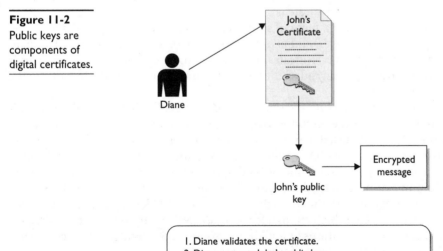

1. Diane validates the certificate.
2. Diane extracts John's public key.
3. Diane uses John's public key for encryption purposes.

There are several applications and protocols that can generate public/private key pairs and provide functionality similar to what a PKI provides, but there is no third party that the two communicating parties both trust. For two entities to choose to communicate this way without a third party vouching for each other's identity, they must choose to trust each other and the communication channel they are using. In many situations, it is impractical and dangerous to arbitrarily trust an individual you do not know, and this is when the components of a PKI must fall into place—to provide the necessary level of trust you cannot, or choose not to, provide on your own.

What does the "infrastructure" in "public key infrastructure" really mean? An infrastructure provides a sustaining groundwork for other things to be built upon. For example, network topology and data-link technologies (Ethernet, Token Ring, and the like) provide us with a foundation for a network, but without the operating systems, applications, and users, nothing very interesting can take place. On the other hand, without this network foundation (topology and data-link technologies) the operating systems, applications, and users could not communicate or participate in a network. So an infrastructure works at a low level to provide a predictable and uniform environment that allows other higher level technologies to work together through uniform access points. The environment that the infrastructure provides allows these higher level applications to communicate with each other and gives them the underlying tools to carry out their tasks.

Certificate Authorities

The *certificate authority (CA)* is the trusted authority for certifying individuals' identities and creating an electronic document indicating that individuals are who they say they are. That electronic document is referred to as a *digital certificate*, and it establishes an association between the subject's identity and a public key. The private key that is paired with the public key in the certificate is stored separately.

The CA is more than just a piece of software; it is actually made up of the software, hardware, procedures, policies, and people who are involved in validating individuals' identities and generating the certificates. This means that if one of these components is compromised, it can negatively affect the CA overall and can threaten the integrity of the certificates it produces.

Every CA should have a *certification practices statement (CPS)* that outlines how identities are verified, the steps the CA follows to generate, maintain, and transmit certificates, and why the CA can be trusted to fulfill its responsibilities. It describes how keys are secured, what data is placed within a digital certificate, and how revocations will be handled. If a company is going to use and depend upon a public CA, the company's security officers, administrators, and legal department should review the CA's entire CPS to ensure that it will properly meet the company's needs, and to make sure that the level of security claimed by the CA is high enough for their use and environment. A critical aspect of a PKI is the trust between the users and the CA, so the CPS should be reviewed and understood to ensure that this level of trust is warranted.

The *certificate server* is the actual service that issues certificates based on the data provided during the initial registration process. The server constructs and populates the

How Do We Know We Can Actually Trust a CA?

This question is part of the continuing debate on how much security PKIs actually provide. Overall, people put a lot of faith in a CA. The companies that provide CA services understand this and also understand that their business is based on their reputation. If a CA was compromised or did not follow through on its various responsibilities, word would get out and they would quickly lose customers and business. CAs work to ensure the reputation of their product and services by implementing very secure facilities, methods, procedures, and personnel. But it is up to the company or individual to determine what degree of trust can actually be given and what level of risk is acceptable.

digital certificate with the necessary information and combines the user's public key with the resulting certificate. The certificate is then digitally signed with CA's private key. (To learn more about how digital signatures are created and verified, review Chapter 10.)

Registration Authorities

The *registration authority (RA)* is the component that accepts a request for a digital certificate and performs the necessary steps of registering and authenticating the person requesting the certificate. The authentication requirements differ depending on the type of certificate being requested.

The types of certificates available can vary between different CAs, but there are usually at least three different types, and they are referred to as classes.

- **Class 1** A Class 1 certificate is usually used to verify an individual's identity through e-mail. A person who receives a Class 1 certificate can use their public/private key pair to digitally sign e-mail and encrypt message contents.

- **Class 2** A Class 2 certificate may be used for software signing. A software vendor would register for this type of certificate so they could digitally sign their software. This will provide integrity for the software after it is developed and released, and it will allow the receiver of the software to verify where the software actually came from.

- **Class 3** A Class 3 certificate may be used by a company to set up its own certificate authority, which will allow it to carry out its own identification verification and generate certificates internally.

Each higher class of certificate can carry out more powerful and critical tasks than the one before it. This is why the different classes have different requirements for proof of identity. If you want to receive a Class 1 certificate, you may only be asked to provide your name, e-mail address, and physical address. For a Class 2 certification, you may need to give the RA more data, such as your driver's license, passport, and company information that can be verified. To obtain a Class 3 certificate, you will be asked to provide even more information and most likely will need to go to the RA's office for a face-to-face meeting. Each CA will outline the certification classes it provides and the identification requirements that must be met to acquire each type of certificate.

In most situations, when a user requests a Class 1 certificate, the registration process will require the user to enter specific information into a Web-based form. The web page will have a section that will step the user through creating a public/private key pair, which will allow the user to choose the size of the keys to be created. Once all the data is inserted into the form, the browser initiates the key generation process. It will often require random input values, which may be acquired through random mouse movements or keystrokes, or by extracting specific information from within the system itself. These random values are inserted into a cryptographic algorithm that is used to generate the keys, and the resulting keys are saved to a local key store. If the key store is being created for the first time, the application should request a password from the user that will be used to access and use the keys held within that particular key store.

Once these steps have been completed, the public key is attached to the certificate registration form and both are forwarded to the RA for processing. The RA is responsible only for the registration process and cannot actually generate a certificate. Once the RA is finished processing the request and verifying the individual's identity, the request will be sent to the CA. The certificate server (CS), which is a component of the CA, will generate the digital certificate, integrate the necessary data into the certificate fields (user identification information, public key, validity dates, proper use for the key and certificate, and so on), and send a copy of the certificate to the user. These steps are shown in Figure 11-3. The certificate may also be posted to a publicly accessible directory so that others can have access to it.

In the previous description, a web browser generated the cryptographic key pair, but other applications can have this capability too. A user can also have more than one private/public key pair for different applications and for different purposes. In most implementations, different applications will create and maintain their own key store and not share it with other programs unless the different applications were created by the same vendor. If a user has two or more applications that were developed by the same software vendor, they might, but might not, share the same key pair and store.

The keys and certificates within the stores can be accessed through specific interfaces. If application A created its own key pair and key store, and application B knows how to make a request to this store's interface to use the keys and certificate, then it can use these items instead of having to generate its own. However, if applications A and B have created individual certificates and generated their own key pairs, they will most likely also have created their own key stores.

If an application creates a key store that can be accessed by other applications, it will provide a standardized interface, referred to as an application programming interface (API). In Netscape and UNIX systems, this interface is usually PKCS #11, and in

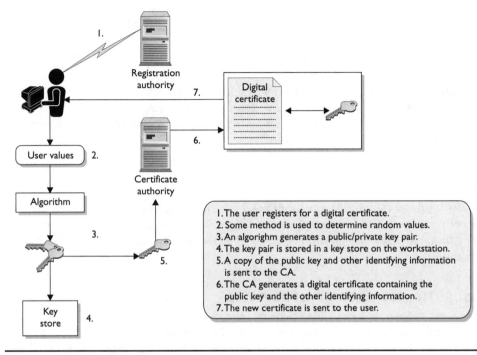

Figure II-3   Steps for obtaining a digital certificate

Microsoft applications the interface is Crypto API (CAPI). As an example, Figure 11-4 shows that application A went through the process of registering a certificate and generating a key pair. It created a key store that provides an interface to allow other applications to communicate with it and use the items held within the store.

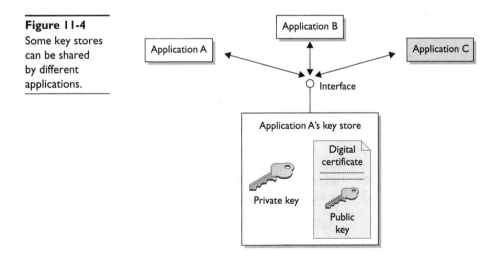

Figure II-4
Some key stores
can be shared
by different
applications.

PART V

> ### Sharing Stores
> Different applications from the same vendor may share key stores. Microsoft applications keep a user's keys and certificates in a Registry entry within that particular user's profile. The applications save and retrieve them from this single location, or key store.

The local key store is just one location where these items can be held. Often the digital certificate and public key are also stored in a certificate repository (as discussed in the "Certificate Repositories" section of this chapter) so that it is available to a subset of individuals.

Local Registration Authorities

A *local registration authority (LRA)* performs the same functions as an RA, but the LRA is closer to the end users. This component is usually implemented in companies that have their own internal PKI and have distributed sites. Each site has users that need RA services, so instead of requiring them to communicate with one central RA, each site can have their own LRA. This reduces the amount of traffic that would be created by several users making requests across WAN lines.

The LRA will perform identification, verification, and registration functions. It will then send the request, along with the user's public key, to a centralized CA so that the certificate can be generated. It acts as an interface between the users and the CA.

Certificate Repositories

Once the certificate is registered, identity proven, and a key pair generated, the certificate must be put somewhere. Public keys need to be available to whomever requires them to communicate within a PKI environment. These keys, and their corresponding certificates, are usually held in a publicly available repository. *Repository* is a general term that describes a centralized directory that can be accessed by a subset of individuals. The directories are usually LDAP-compliant, meaning that they can be accessed and searched via the Lightweight Directory Access Protocol (LDAP).

When an individual initializes communication with another person, the sender can send their certificate and public key to the receiver, which will allow the receiver to communicate with the sender using encryption or digital signatures (or both) without needing to track down the necessary public key in a certificate repository. This is equivalent to the sender saying, "If you would like to encrypt any future messages you send to me, or if you would like the ability to verify my digital signature, here are the necessary components." But if a person wants to encrypt the first message sent to the receiver, the sender will need to find the receiver's public key in a certificate repository. (For a refresher on how public and private keys come into play with encryption and digital signatures, please refer to Chapter 10.)

Since the certificates are to be available and used by the public, or by a wide range of people, special emphasis should be put into looking at the specific information included within the certificates. For example, some certificates allow the CA to insert an individual's address and phone number into specific fields within the certificate. This may be more information than a company wants to release about its employees. Similarly all certificates must contain a distinguished name, and this might give outsiders some insight into the naming conventions used by the company. Before these items are actually inserted into certificates and released, a company needs to ensure that it does not provide too much information and possibly open the door to a security compromise. The company can review the CA's CPS to find out exactly what type of data will and will not be included within the certificates the CA creates.

A *certificate repository* is a holding place for individuals' certificates and public keys that are participating in a particular PKI environment. The security requirements for repositories themselves are not as high as is needed for actual CAs and for the equipment and software used to carry out CA functions. Since each certificate is digitally signed by the CA, if a certificate stored in the certificate repository is modified, the recipient would be able to detect this change and not accept the certificate as valid.

Trust and Certificate Verification

We have explored the reason that we would need a PKI—we do not automatically trust individuals we do not know. Security is all about being suspicious and being safe, so we need a third party that we *do* trust to vouch for the other individual before confidence can be instilled and sensitive communication can take place. But what does it mean that we trust a CA, and how can we use this to our advantage?

Distinguished Names

A distinguished name is a label that follows the X.500 standard. This standard defines a naming convention that can be employed so that each subject within an organization has a unique name. An example is {Country = US, Organization = Real Secure, Organizational Unit = R&D, Location = Washington}.

CAs use distinguished names to identify the owners of specific certificates.

When a user chooses to trust a CA, they will download that CA's digital certificate and public key, which will be stored on their local computer. Most browsers have a list of CAs configured to be trusted by default, so when a user installs a new web browser several of the most well-known and most trusted CAs will be trusted without any change of settings. An example of this listing is shown in Figure 11-5.

In the Microsoft CAPI environment, the user can add and remove CAs from this list as needed. In production environments that require a higher degree of protection, this list will be pruned, and possibly the only CAs listed will be the company's internal CAs. This ensures that digitally signed software will only be automatically installed if it was signed by the company's CA. Other products, like Entrust, use centrally controlled policies to determine which CAs are to be trusted instead of expecting the user to make these critical decisions.

There are a number of steps involved in checking the validity of a message. Suppose Maynard receives a digitally signed message from Joyce, who he does not know or trust. Joyce has also included her digital certificate with her message, which has her public key embedded within it. Before Maynard can be sure of the authenticity of this message, he has some work to do. The steps are illustrated in Figure 11-6.

First, Maynard will see which CA signed Joyce's certificate and compare it to the list of CAs he has configured within his computer. He trusts the CAs in his list and no others. (If the certificate was signed by a CA he does not have in the list, he would not accept the certificate as being valid, and thus he could not be sure that this message was actually sent from Joyce or that the attached key was actually her public key.)

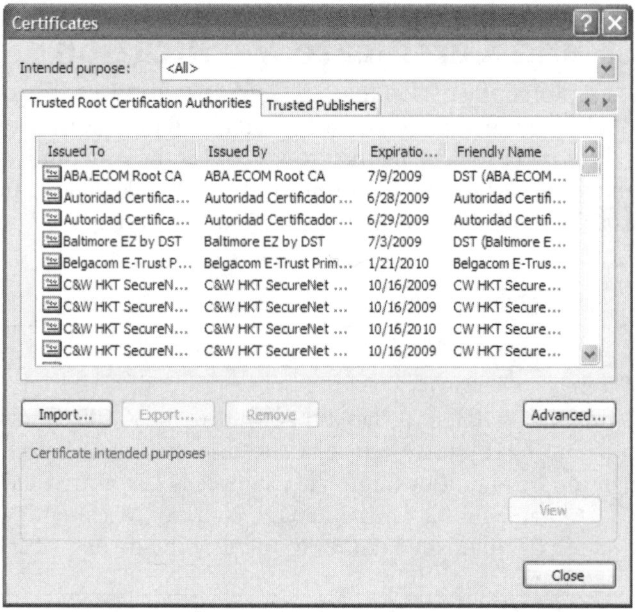

Figure 11-5

Browsers have a long list of CAs configured to be trusted by default.

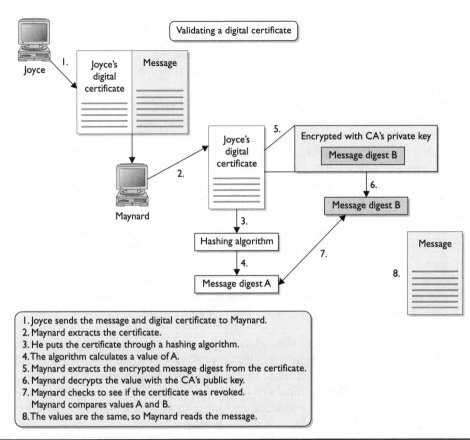

Figure 11-6 Steps for verifying the authenticity and integrity of a certificate

Key Concept

Maynard sees that the CA that signed Joyce's certificate is indeed in his list of trusted CAs, so he will pass Joyce's certificate through a hashing algorithm (such as MD5 or SHA1), which will result in a message digest—call the resulting message digest A.

Every certificate has a different encrypted message digest value embedded within it, which is the digital signature. The embedded message digest value is encrypted with the CA's private key, which is what digitally signing means—to encrypt a message digest with a private key. Maynard takes the CA's public key and decrypts the embedded digital signature value—call the decrypted digital signature value B.

If values A and B match, then Maynard can be assured that this CA did actually create the certificate, so he can now trust the origin of Joyce's certificate. But he is not done yet. Maynard needs to be sure that the issuing CA has not revoked this certificate.

The use of digital signatures allows certificates to be saved in public directories without the concern of them being accidentally or intentionally altered. If a user extracts a certificate from a repository and creates a message digest value that does not match the digital signature embedded within the certificate itself, that user will know that the certificate has been modified by someone other than the CA, and they will know not to accept the validity of the corresponding public key. Similarly, an attacker could not create a new message digest, encrypt it, and embed it within the certificate because they would not have access to the CA's private key.

Although Maynard trusts the CA that created this digital certificate for Joyce, and he trusts the integrity of the certificate (because the message digest values match), he still has a few steps to complete.

As stated earlier, the CA generates the certificate and inserts the requester's identification information within it. For a simple function, such as proving one's identity through e-mail, the information that the requester of the certificate has to provide is pretty minimal, but may include the user's e-mail address. Once Maynard goes through the previous steps, he will also compare the e-mail address the CA inserted in the certificate with the address that sent this message. If these values are the same, he can be assured that it came from the e-mail address that was provided during the registration process of this certificate.

The certificate also has start and stop dates, indicating a time during which the certificate is valid. If the start date hasn't happened yet, or the stop date has been passed, the certificate is not valid. Maynard reviews these dates to make sure the certificate is still deemed valid.

Another step Maynard may go through is to check whether this certificate has been revoked for any reason, so he will refer to a list of revoked certificates to see if Joyce's certificate is listed. The revocation list could be checked directly with the CA that issued the certificate or via a specialized online service that supports the Online Certificate Status Protocol (OCSP). (Certificate revocation and list distribution will be explained in the "Certificate Lifecycles" section, later in this chapter.)

To recap, here are the steps for validating a certificate:

1. Compare the CA that digitally signed the certificate to a list of CAs that have already been loaded into the receiver's computer.

2. Calculate a message digest for the certificate.

3. Use the CA's public key to decrypt the digital signature and recover what is claimed to be the original message digest embedded within the certificate (validating the digital signature).

4. Compare the two resulting message digest values to ensure the integrity of the certificate.

5. Review the identification information within the certificate, such as the e-mail address.

6. Review the validity dates.

7. Check a revocation list to see if the certificate has been revoked.

Maynard now trusts that this certificate is legitimate and that it belongs to Joyce. Now what does he need to do? The certificate holds Joyce's public key, which he needs to validate the digital signature she appended to her message, so Maynard extracts Joyce's public key from her certificate, runs her message through a hashing algorithm, and calculates a message digest value of X. He then uses Joyce's public key to decrypt her digital signature (remember that a digital signature is just a message digest encrypted with a private key). This decryption process provides him with another message digest of value Y. Maynard compares values X and Y, and if they are the same, he is assured that the message has not been modified during transmission. Thus he has confidence in the integrity of the message. But, how does Maynard know that the message actually came from Joyce? Because he can decrypt the digital signature using her public key. The public key can only decrypt something that was encrypted with the related private key, and only the owner of the private key is supposed to have access to it. Maynard can be sure that this message came from Joyce.

After all of this he reads her message, which says, "Hi. How are you?" All of that work just for this message? Maynard's blood pressure would surely go through the roof if he had to do all of this work only to end up with short and not very useful messages. Fortunately, it all happens behind the scenes. Maynard didn't have to exert any energy. He simply replies, "Fine. How are you?"

Digital Certificates

A digital certificate binds an individual's identity to a public key, and it contains all the information a receiver needs to be assured of the identity of the public key owner. After an RA verifies an individual's identity, the CA generates the digital certificate, but how does the CA know what type of data to insert into the certificate? The certificates are created and formatted based on the X.509 standard, which outlines the necessary fields of a certificate and the possible values that can be inserted into the fields. As of this writing, X.509 version 3 is the most current version of the standard. X.509 is a standard of the International Telecommunication Union (http://www.itu.int).

The different fields within a digital certificate are as follows:

Version number Identifies the version of the X.509 standard that was followed to create the certificate. The version number indicates the format and fields that can be used.

Subject Specifies the owner of the certificate.

Public key Contains the public key being bound to the certified subject. The public key also identifies the algorithm that was used to create the private/public key pair.

Issuer Identifies the CA that generated and digitally signed the certificate.

Serial number Contains a unique number identifying this one specific certificate issued by a particular CA.

PART V

Validity   Specifies the dates through which the certificate is valid for use.

Certificate usage   Specifies the approved use of certificate, which dictates what the user can use this public key for.

Signature algorithm   Identifies the hashing algorithm and digital signature algorithm used to digitally sign the certificate.

Extensions   Allow additional data to be encoded into the certificate to expand the functionality of the certificate. Companies can customize the use of certificates within their environment by using these extensions. X.509 version 3 has extended the extension possibilities.

Figure 11-7 shows the actual values of these different certificate fields for a particular certificate in Internet Explorer. The version of this certificate is V3 (X.509 v3) and the serial number is also listed—this number is unique for each certificate that is created by a specific CA. The CA used the MD5 hashing algorithm to create the message digest value, and it then signed (or encrypted this value) with its private key using the RSA algorithm. The actual CA that issued the certificate is Root SGC Authority, and the Valid dates indicate how long this certificate is valid. The subject is MS SGC Authority, which is the entity that registered for this certificate and is the entity that is bound to the embedded public key. The actual public key is shown in the lower window and is represented in hexadecimal.

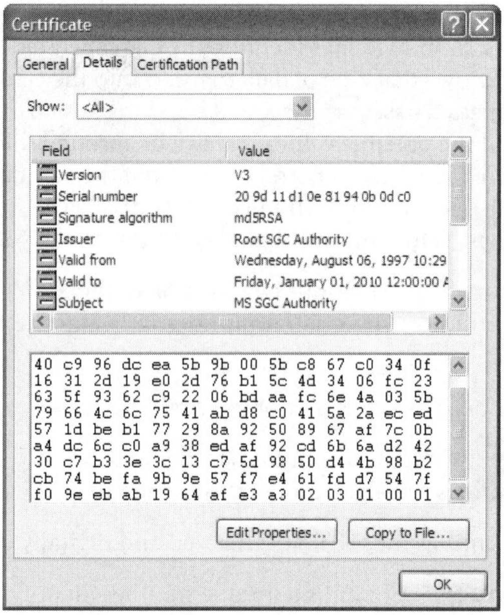

Figure 11-7
Fields within a digital certificate

The subject of a certificate is commonly a person, but it does not have to be. The subject can be a network device (router, web server, firewall, and so on), an application, a department, a company, or a person. Each has its own identity that needs to be verified and proven to another entity before secure, trusted communication can be initiated. If a network device is using a certificate for authentication, the certificate may contain the network address of that device. This means that if the certificate has a network address of 10.0.0.1, the receiver will compare this to the address from which it received the certificate to make sure a man-in-the-middle attack is not being attempted.

Certificate Attributes

There are four main types of certificates used:

- End-entity certificates
- CA certificates
- Cross-certification certificates
- Policy certificates

End-entity certificates are issued by a CA to a specific subject, such as Joyce, the Accounting department, or a firewall, as illustrated in Figure 11-8.

Figure 11-8
End-entity and
CA certificates

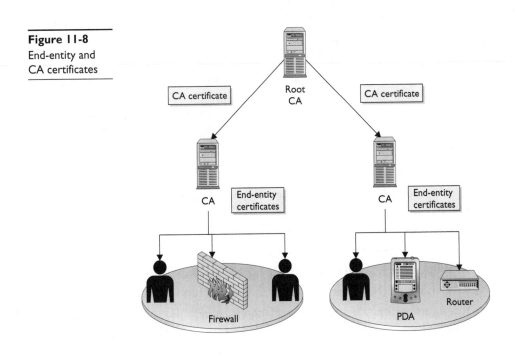

A *CA certificate* may be self-signed, in the case of a standalone or root CA, or it may be issued by a superior CA within a hierarchical model. In the model in Figure 11-8, the superior CA gives the authority and allows the subordinate CA to accept certificate requests and generate the individual certificates itself. This may be necessary when a company needs to have multiple internal CAs, and different departments within an organization need to have their own CA servicing their specific end-entities in their section. In these situations, a representative from each department requiring a CA registers with the higher trusted CA and requests a Certificate Authority certificate. (Public and private CAs are discussed in the "Public Certificate Authorities" and "In-House Certificate Authorities" sections later in this chapter, as are the different trust models that are available for companies.)

Cross-certificates, or *cross-certification certificates*, are used when independent CAs establish peer-to-peer trust relationships. Simply put, they are a mechanism through which one CA can issue a certificate allowing its users to trust another CA.

Within sophisticated CAs used for high-security applications, a mechanism is required to provide centrally controlled policy information to PKI clients. This is often done by placing the policy information in a *policy certificate*.

Certificate Extensions

Certificate extensions allow for further information to be inserted within the certificate, which can be used to provide more functionality in a PKI implementation. Certificate extensions can be standard or private. *Standard certificate extensions* are implemented for every PKI implementation. *Private certificate extensions* are defined for specific organizations (or domains within one organization), and they allow companies to further define different, specific uses for digital certificates to best fit their business needs.

There are several different extensions that can be implemented, one being key usage extensions. *Key usage extensions* dictate how the public key that is held within the certificate can be used. Remember that public keys can be used for different functions: symmetric key encryption, data encryption, verifying digital signatures, and more. The following are some key examples of certificate extension:

- **DigitalSignature**   The key is to be used to verify a digital signature.
- **KeyEncipherment**   The key is to be used to encrypt other keys used for secure key distribution.
- **DataEncipherment**   The key is to be used to encrypt data and cannot be used to encrypt other keys.
- **CRLSign**   The key is used to verify a CA signature on a revocation list.
- **KeyCertSign**   The key is used to verify CA signatures on certificates.
- **NonRepudiation**   The key is used when a nonrepudiation service is being provided.

A nonrepudiation service can be provided by a third-party notary. In this situation, the sender's digital signature is verified and then signed by the notary so that the sender cannot later deny signing and sending the message. This is basically the same function performed by a traditional notary using paper—validate the sender's identity and validate the time and date of an item being signed and sent. This is required when the receiver needs to *really* be sure of the sender's identity and wants to be legally protected against possible fraud or forgery.

If a company needs to be sure that accountable nonrepudiation services will be provided, a trusted time source needs to be used. This trusted time source can be a trusted third party, referred to as a time stamp authority. Using a trusted time source allows users to have a higher level of confidence as to *when* specific messages were digitally signed. For example, suppose Barry sends Ron a message and digitally signs it, and Ron later civilly sues Barry over a dispute. This digitally signed message may be submitted by Ron as evidence pertaining to an earlier agreement that Barry now is not fulfilling. If a trusted time source was not used in their PKI environment, Barry could claim that his private key had been compromised before that message was sent. If a trusted time source was implemented, then it could be shown that the message was signed *before* the date on which Barry claims his key was compromised. If a trusted time source is not used, no activity that was carried out within a PKI environment can be truly proven because it is so easy to change system and software time settings.

Critical and Non-Critical Extensions

Certificate extensions are considered either *critical* or *non-critical*, which is indicated by a specific flag within the certificate itself. When this flag is set to critical, it means that the extension *must* be understood and processed by the receiver. If the receiver is not configured to understand a particular extension marked as critical, and thus cannot process it properly, the certificate cannot be used for its proposed purpose. If the flag does not indicate that the extension is critical, then the certificate can be used for the intended purpose, even if the receiver does not process the appended extension.

So how does this work? When an extension is marked as critical, it means that the CA is certifying the key for only that specific purpose. If Joe receives a certificate with a DigitalSignature key usage extension and the critical flag is set, Joe can only use the public key within that certificate to validate digital signatures, and no more. If the extension was marked as non-critical, the key can be used for purposes outside of those listed in the extensions, so in this case it is up to Joe (and his applications) to decide how the key will be used.

Certificate Lifecycles

Keys and certificates should have lifetimes set, which will force the user to register for a new certificate after a certain amount of time. The proper length of these lifetimes is a trade-off. Shorter lifetimes limit the ability of attackers to crack them, but longer lifetimes lower system overhead. More sophisticated PKI implementations perform automated and often transparent key updates to avoid the time and expense of having users register for new certificates when old ones expire.

This means that the certificate and key pair has a lifecycle that must be managed. Certificate management involves administrating and managing each of these phases, including registration, certificate and key generation, renewal, and revocation.

Registration and Generation

A key pair (public and private keys) can be generated locally by an application and stored in a local key store on the user's workstation. The key pair may also be created by a central key-generation server, which will require secure transmission of the keys to the user. The key pair that is created on the centralized server can be stored on the user's workstation or on the user's smart card, which will allow for more flexibility and mobility.

In most modern PKI implementations, users have two key pairs. One key pair is often generated by a central server and used for encryption and key transfers. This allows the corporate PKI to retain a copy of the encryption key pair for recovery, if necessary. The second key pair, a digital signature key pair, is usually generated by the user to make sure that user is the only one with a copy of the private key. Nonrepudiation can be challenged if there is any doubt about someone else obtaining a copy of an individual's signature private key. If the key pair was created on a centralized server, that could weaken the case that the individual was the only one who had a copy of their private key. If a copy of a user's signature private key is stored anywhere other than in their possession, or if there is a possibility of someone obtaining the user's key, then true nonrepudiation may not be provided.

The act of verifying that an individual indeed has the corresponding private key for a given public key is referred to as *proof of possession*. Not all public/private key pairs can be used for digital signatures, so asking the individual to sign a message and return it to prove that they have the necessary private key will not always work. If a key pair is used for encryption, the RA can send a challenge value to the individual, who, in turn, can use their private key to encrypt that value and return it to the RA. If the RA can successfully decrypt this value with the public key that was provided earlier, the RA can be confident that the individual has the necessary private key and can continue through the rest of the registration phase.

When the key pair is first generated, the administrator (or the individual user) chooses the algorithm that is to be used to generate the key pair and the key size. (Who actually chooses the algorithm type depends upon the configuration of the PKI implementation.) The specific algorithm will be chosen for its strength and interoperability with other algorithms that will most likely be used by other end-entities. The key size will depend upon the sensitivity of the data that is being protected. The RSA algorithm is the de facto standard for asymmetric key generation, and if the data you will be protecting with these keys is not considered sensitive, you may choose a key size of 128 bits. The estimated time necessary to break this cryptosystem is less than five minutes, if the hacker could dedicate at least 105 computers just to this task. If you choose a key size of 1,024 bits, the time estimated to break it would increase to three million years if the hacker has at least 114 computers dedicated to this task, with 170GB of memory, and that much time to kill.

So if it could take an attacker up to three million years to break the cryptosystem, why would you ever need to change the key pair? Surely the attackers won't have that type of time on their hands. Unfortunately, most encryption key compromises do not come from brute-force attacks but from improper key management processes, poor software implementations, and human error. A key can be shown in clear text or shared with another user, the key store may not be protected with a password, or a user may fall victim to a social engineering ploy. These types of attacks can be performed with the end goal of obtaining a cryptographic key, and they are usually much easier to carry out than a full brute-force attack on an algorithm.

Key regeneration and replacement is usually done to protect against these types of threats, although as computers increase in processing power and our knowledge of cryptography and new possible cryptanalysis attacks, key lifetimes may drastically decrease. As with everything within the security field, it is better to be safe than surprised later and sorry.

The PKI administrator usually configures the minimum required key size that users must use to have a key generated for the first time, and then for each renewal. In most applications, there is a drop-down list of possible algorithms to choose from, and possible key sizes. The key size should provide the necessary level of security for the current environment. The lifetime of the key should be long enough that continual renewal will not negatively affect productivity, but short enough to ensure that the key cannot be successfully compromised.

Renewal

The certificate itself has its own lifetime, which can be different than the key pair's lifetime. The certificate's lifetime is specified by the validity dates inserted into the digital certificate. These are beginning and ending dates indicating the time period during which the certificate is valid. The certificate cannot be used before the start date, and once the end date is met, the certificate is expired and a new certificate will need to be issued.

A renewal process is different than the registration phase in that the RA assumes that the individual has already successfully completed one registration round. If the certificate has not actually been revoked, the original keys and certificate can be used to provide the necessary authentication information and proof of identity for the renewal phase.

PART V

Approaches to Protection
Good key management and proper key replacement intervals protect keys from being compromised through human error. Choosing a large key size makes a brute-force attack more difficult.

The certificate may or may not need to change during the renewal process; it usually depends on why the renewal is taking place. If the certificate just expired and the keys will still be used for the same purpose, a new certificate can be generated with new validity dates. If, however, the key pair functionality needs to be expanded or restricted, new attributes and extensions may need to be integrated into the new certificate. These new functionalities may require more information to be gathered from the individual renewing the certificate, especially if the class changes or the new key uses allow for more powerful abilities.

This renewal process is required when the certificate has fulfilled its lifetime and its end validity date has been met. This is different than if a certificate is revoked.

Revocation

Certificates are revoked when the certificate's validity needs to be ended before its actual expiration date is met. There are several reasons why a certificate may need to be revoked: a user may have lost a laptop or a smart card that stored a private key, an improper software implementation may have been uncovered that directly affected the security of a private key, a user may have fallen victim to a social engineering attack and inadvertently given up a private key, data held within the certificate may no longer apply to the specified individual, or perhaps an employee left a company and should not be identified as a member of an in-house PKI any longer. In the last instance, the certificate, which was bound to the user's key pair, identified the user as an employee of the company, and the administrator would want to ensure that the key pair could not be used in the future to validate this person's affiliation with the company. Revoking the certificate does this.

If any of these things happen, a user's private key has been compromised or should no longer be mapped to the owner's identity. A different individual may have access to that user's private key and could use it to impersonate and authenticate as the original user. If the impersonator used the key to digitally sign a message, the receiver would verify the authenticity of the sender by verifying the signature by using the original user's public key, and the verification would go through perfectly—the receiver would believe it came from the proper sender and not the impersonator. If receivers could look at a list of certificates that have been revoked before verifying the digital signature, they could find out that the certificate had been revoked, and they would know not to trust the digital signature.

For example, if Joe stole Mike's laptop, which held, among other things, Mike's private key, Joe might be able to use it to impersonate Mike. Suppose Joe writes a message, digitally signs it with Mike's private key, and sends it to Stacy. Stacy communicates with Mike periodically and has his public key, so she uses it to verify the digital signature. It computes properly, so Stacy is assured that this message did indeed come from Mike, but in truth it did not. If, before validating any certificate or digital signature, Stacy could check a list of revoked certificates, she might not fall victim to Joe's false message.

The CA can provide this type of protection by maintaining a *certificate revocation list (CRL)*, which is a list of serial numbers of certificates that have been revoked. The CRL also contains a statement indicating why the individual certificates were revoked and a date when the revocation took place. The list usually contains all certificates that have been revoked within the lifetime of the CA. Certificates that have expired are not the same as ones that have been revoked. If a certificate has expired, it means that its end validity date has been reached.

The CA is the entity that is responsible for the status of the certificates it generates, and it is who needs to be told of a revocation, and it must be the one to provide this information to others. The CA is responsible for maintaining the revocation list and posting it in a publicly available directory.

What if Stacy wants to get back at Joe for trying to trick her earlier, and she attempts to revoke Joe's certificate herself? If she is successful, then Joe's participation in the PKI can be negatively affected because others will not trust his public key. Although we might think Joe may deserve this, we need to have some system in place to make sure people cannot arbitrarily have others' certificates revoked, whether for revenge or for malicious purposes.

When a revocation request is submitted, the individual submitting the request must be authenticated. Otherwise this could permit a type of denial of service attack, where someone has another person's certificate revoked. The authentication can involve an agreed upon password that was created during the registration process, but authentication should not be based on the individual proving that they have the corresponding private key, because it may have been stolen, and the CA would be authenticating an imposter.

The CRL's integrity needs to be protected to ensure that attackers cannot modify data pertaining to a revoked certification from the list. If this were allowed to take place, anyone who stole a private key could just delete that key from the CRL and continue to use the private key fraudulently. The integrity of the list also needs to be protected to ensure that bogus data is not added to it. Otherwise anyone could add another person's certificate to the list and effectively revoke that person's certificate. The only entity that should be able to modify any information on the CRL is the CA.

The mechanism used to protect the integrity of a CRL is a digital signature. The CA's revocation service creates a digital signature for the CRL as shown in Figure 11-9. To validate a certificate, the user goes to the directory where the CRL is posted, downloads the list, and verifies the CA's digital signature to ensure that the proper authority signed the list and to ensure that the list was not modified in an unauthorized manner. The user then looks through the list to see if the serial number of the certificate that they are trying to validate is listed. If the serial number is on the list, the private key should no longer be trusted, and the public key should no longer be used. This may sound like a cumbersome process, so it has been automated in several ways that are described in the next section.

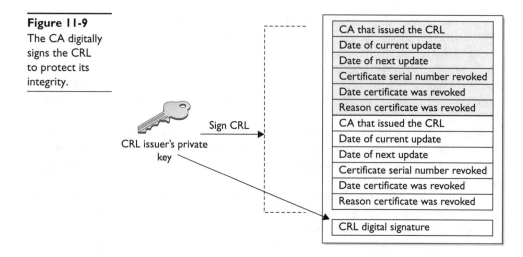

Figure 11-9
The CA digitally signs the CRL to protect its integrity.

One concern is how up-to-date the CRL is—how often is it updated and does it actually reflect *all* the certificates currently revoked? The actual frequency with which the list is updated depends upon the CA and its certification practices statement (CPS). It is important that the list is updated in a timely manner so that anyone using the list has the most current information.

CRL Distribution

CRL files can be requested by individuals who need to verify and validate a newly received certificate, or the files can be periodically pushed down to all users participating within a specific PKI. This means the CRL can be pulled (downloaded) by individual users when needed, or the CRL can be pushed down (sent) to all users within the PKI on a timed interval.

The actual CRL file can grow substantially, and transmitting this file and requiring PKI client software on each workstation to save and maintain it can use a lot of resources, so the smaller the CRL is, the better. It is also possible to first push down the full CRL, and after that initial load, the following CRLs pushed down to the users are delta CRLs, meaning that they only contain the changes to the original or base CRL. This can greatly reduce the amount of bandwidth consumed when updating CRLs.

In implementations where the CRLs are not pushed down to individual systems, the users' PKI software needs to know where to look for the posted CRL that relates to the certificate it is trying to validate. The certificate itself may have an extension that points the validating user to the necessary *CRL distribution point*. The network administrator sets up the distribution points, and there may be just one point for a particular PKI or there may be more than one. The distribution point holds one or more lists containing the serial numbers of revoked certificates, and the user's PKI software scans the list for the serial number of the certificate the user is attempting to validate. If the serial number is not present, the user is assured that it has not been revoked. This approach helps point users to the right resource and also reduces the amount of information that needs to be scanned when checking that a certificate has not been revoked.

One last option for checking distributed CRLs is an online service. When a client needs to validate a certificate and ensure that it has not been revoked, they can communicate with an online service that will query the necessary CRLs available within the environment. This service can query the lists for the client instead of pushing down the full CRL to each and every system. So if Joe receives a certificate from Stacy, he can contact an online service and send it the serial number listed in the certificate Stacy sent. The online service would query the necessary revocation lists and respond to Joe indicating whether that serial number was listed as being revoked or not.

Online services are newer technologies, and there are different protocols being developed and used for these purposes. Figuring out how to get information from within the CRL to the different clients is one of the harder obstacles to be overcome in many PKI implementations. In many cases, clients do not even check with any lists, and they would never know if a certificate was revoked or not. This, of course, is not the optimal approach, and solutions and technologies to ensure that CRL data gets properly populated and reviewed is continually being improved upon.

One of the protocols used for online revocation services is *Online Certificate Status Protocol (OCSP)*. It is a request and response protocol that obtains the serial number of the certificate that is being validated and reviews revocation lists for the client. The protocol has a responder service that reports the status of the certificate back to the client, indicating whether it has been revoked, it is valid, or its status is unknown. This protocol and service saves the client from having to find the right lists, download, and process them.

Suspension

Instead of being revoked, a certificate may sometimes need to be *suspended*, meaning it is temporarily put on hold. If, for example, Bob is taking an extended vacation and wants to ensure that his certificate will not be compromised or used during that time, a suspension request can be made to the CA. The CRL would list this certificate and its serial number, and in the field that describes why a certificate was revoked, it would instead indicate a hold state. Once Bob returns to work, he can make a request to the CA to remove his certificate from the list.

Authority Revocation Lists

In some PKI implementations, a separate revocation list is maintained for CA keys that have been compromised or should no longer be trusted. This list is known as an *authority revocation list (ARL)*. In the event that a CA's private key is compromised or a cross certification is cancelled, the relevant certificate's serial number is included in the ARL. A client can review an ARL to make sure the CA's public key can still be trusted.

Another reason to suspend a certificate is if the administrator is suspicious that a private key may have been compromised. While the issue is under investigation, the certificate can be put on hold to ensure that it cannot be used.

Key Destruction

Key pairs and certificates have set lifetimes, meaning that they will expire at some specified time. It is important that the certificates and keys are properly destroyed when that time comes, wherever the keys are stored (on users' workstations, centralized key servers, USB token devices, smart cards, and so on).

The goal is to make sure that no one can gain access to a key after its lifetime has ended and use this key for malicious purposes. The attacker might use the key to digitally sign or encrypt a message with the hopes of tricking someone else about their identity (this would be an example of a man-in-the-middle attack). Also, if the attacker is performing some type of brute-force attack on your cryptosystem, trying to figure out specific keys that were used for encryption processes, obtaining an old key may give them more insight into how your cryptosystem generates keys. The less information you supply to potential hackers, the better.

The level of protection that is required within the environment will dictate the actual key destruction procedures that must be followed. In most environments, just allowing the applications that created the keys in the first place to delete the keys is enough. In environments that require higher levels of protection (such as government and military agencies) the media that holds the keys may need to go through a "zeroization" process. This means that a specialized tool is used to overwrite the media that held the cryptographic key, and the overwriting process that is usually carried out by this tool continually writes NULL values to the sectors until that media holds no remnants of the original key.

Note that in modern PKIs, encryption key pairs usually must be retained long after they expire so that users can decrypt information that was encrypted with the old keys. For example, if Bob encrypts a document using his current key and the keys are updated three months later, Bob's software must maintain a copy of the old key so he can still decrypt the document. In the PKI world, this issue is referred to as *key history maintenance.*

Centralized or Decentralized Infrastructures

Keys used for authentication and encryption within a PKI environment can be generated in a centralized or decentralized manner. In a *decentralized* approach, software on individual computers generates and stores cryptographic keys local to the systems themselves. In a *centralized* infrastructure, the keys are generated and stored on a central server, and the keys are transmitted to the individual systems as needed. There are several reasons to choose one type or the other.

If a company uses an asymmetric algorithm that is resource intensive to generate the public/private key pair, and if the key sizes that are needed are large (which is also resource intensive), then the individual computers may not have the necessary processing power to produce the keys in an acceptable fashion. In this situation, the company can choose a centralized approach where a very high-end server with powerful processing capabilities is used, probably along with a hardware-based random number generator.

To create cryptographic keys, the more randomness that is introduced, the better, because the resulting keys will be more indiscriminate and harder to brute force. The random number generator creates numbers that work as seed values, or starting values, for the algorithm to work from. The algorithm uses the seed value as a starting place to create a key, and if the algorithm used the same seed values over and over again, it would generate the same or similar keys over and over, which would make it easier for attackers to uncover the key. The more random the seed values, the better, which is why a random number generator is used.

Central key generation and storage has other benefits. For example, it is much easier to back the keys up and implement key recovery procedures, when compared to a decentralized approach. Implementing a key recovery procedure on each and every computer holding one or more key pairs is difficult, and many applications that generate their own key pairs do not usually interface well with a centralized archive system. This means that if a company chooses to allow their individual users to create and maintain their own key pairs on their separate workstations, no real key recovery procedure can be put in place. This puts the company at risk. If an employee leaves the organization or is unavailable for one reason or another, the company may not be able to access its own business information encrypted by that employee.

So a centralized approach seems like the best approach, right? Well, the centralized method has some drawbacks to consider too. If the keys will be generated on a server, they need to be securely transmitted to the individual clients that require them. This can be harder than it sounds. A technology needs to be employed that will send the keys in an encrypted manner, ensure the keys' integrity, and make sure that only the intended user is actually receiving the key.

Also, the server that centrally stores the keys needs to be highly available and can provide a single point of failure, so some type of fault tolerance or redundancy mechanism may need to be put into place. If that one server goes down, no one could access their keys, which might prevent them from properly authenticating to the network, resources, and applications. Also, since all the keys are in one place, it is a prime target for an attacker—if the central key server is compromised, the whole environment is compromised.

Random Number Generators

In most cases, software- and hardware-based generators are actually considered *pseudo-random number generators* because they have a finite number of values to work from. They usually extract these values from their surroundings, which are predictable in nature—the values can come from the system's time or from CPU cycles. If the starting values are predictable, the numbers they generate cannot be truly random. An example of a true random number generator would be a system that collects radiation from a radioactive item. The elements that escape from the radioactive item do so in an unpredictable manner, and the results are used as seed values for key generation.

One other issue pertains to how the keys will actually be used. If a public/private key pair is being generated for digital signatures, and if the company wants to ensure that it can be used to provide *true* authenticity and nonrepudiation, the keys should not be generated at a centralized server. This would introduce doubt that only the one person had access to a specific private key.

If a company uses smart cards to hold users' private keys, the private key often has to be generated on the card itself and cannot be copied for archiving purposes. This is a disadvantage of the centralized approach. There are also some types of applications that have been developed to create their own public/private key pairs and do not allow other keys to be imported and used. This means the keys would have to be created locally by these applications, and keys from a central server could not be used. These are just some of the considerations that need to be evaluated before any decision is made and implementation begins.

Hardware Storage Devices

PKIs can be constructed in software without special cryptographic hardware, and this is perfectly suitable for many environments. But software can be vulnerable to viruses, hackers, and hacking. If a company requires a higher level of protection than a purely software-based solution can provide there are several hardware-based solutions available.

In most situations, hardware key-storage solutions are only used for the most critical and sensitive keys, which are the root and possibly the intermediate CA private keys. If those keys are compromised, the whole security of the PKI is gravely threatened. If a person obtained a root CA private key, they could digitally sign any certificate, and that certificate would be quickly accepted by all entities within the environment. Such an attacker might be able to create a certificate that has extremely high privileges, perhaps allowing them to modify bank account information in a financial institution, and no alerts or warnings would be initiated because the ultimate supreme being (the root CA) signed it.

There are other hardware components that can be implemented within a PKI to hold users' private key information. These include smart cards, USB tokens, and Fortezza cards. These items can be used to securely hold a user's private key and can be inserted into a reader attached to a workstation or server when the user needs to present their private key for authentication purposes. These devices usually provide a higher level of protection compared to holding the keys in software because they are more tamper-proof in nature. These items were covered further in Chapter 7.

Private Key Protection

Although a PKI implementation can be complex, with many different components and options, there is a critical concept common to all PKIs that must be understood and enforced: the private key needs to stay private. A digital signature is created solely for the purpose of proving who sent a particular message by using a private key. This rests on the assumption that only one person has access to this private key. If an imposter obtains a person's private key, authenticity and nonrepudiation can no longer be claimed or proven.

When a private key is generated for the first time, it must be stored somewhere for future use. This storage area is referred to as a key store, and it is usually created by the application registering for a certificate, such as a web browser, smart card software, or other application. In most implementations, the application will prompt the user for a password, which will be used to create an encryption key that protects the key store. So if Cheryl used her web browser to register for a certificate, her private key would be generated and stored in the key store. Cheryl would then be prompted for a password, which the software would use to create a key that will encrypt the key store. When Cheryl needs to access this private key later that day, she will be prompted for the same password, which will decrypt the key store and allow her access to her private key.

Unfortunately, many applications do not require that a strong password must be chosen to protect the key store, and in some implementations the user can choose to not provide a password at all. The user still has a private key available, and it is bound to the user's identity, so what do we care if a password must be entered or not? If, for example, Cheryl decided to not use a password, another person could sit down at her computer, use her web browser and her private key and digitally sign a message. If Cliff received this message, he would think it came from Cheryl and not necessarily think that someone else could have sent it.

The moral to this story is that users should be required to provide some type of authentication information (password, smart card, PIN, or the like) before being able to use private keys. Otherwise, the keys could be used by other individuals or imposters, and authentication and nonrepudiation would be of no use.

A private key is a crucial component of any PKI implementation, so the key itself should contain the necessary characteristics and be protected at each stage of its life. The following list sums up the characteristics and requirements of proper private key use:

- The key size should provide the necessary level of protection for the environment.
- The lifetime of the key should correspond with how often it is used and the sensitivity of the data it is protecting.
- The key should be changed and not used past its allowed lifetime.
- Where appropriate, the key should be properly destroyed at the end of its lifetime.
- The key should never be exposed in clear text.
- No copies of the private key should be made if it is being used for digital signatures.
- The key should not be shared.
- The key should be stored securely.
- Authentication should be required before it can be used.

- The key should be transported securely.
- Software implementations that store and use the key should be evaluated to ensure they provide the necessary level of protection.

If digital signatures will be used for legal purposes, these points and others may need to be audited to ensure that true authenticity and nonrepudiation are provided.

Key Recovery

One individual may have one, two, or many key pairs that are tied to their identity. That is because users can have different needs and requirements for public/private key pairs. As mentioned earlier, certificates can have specific attributes and usage requirements dictating what their corresponding keys can and cannot be used for. For example, David can have one key pair he uses to encrypt and transmit symmetric keys. He can also have one key pair that allows him to encrypt data and another key pair to perform digital signatures. David can also have a digital signature key pair for his work-related activities and another pair for personal activities, as in e-mailing his friends. These key pairs need to be used only for their intended purposes, and this is enforced through certificate attributes and usage values.

If a company is going to perform and maintain a key recovery system, they will generally only back up the key pair used to encrypt data, not the key pairs that are used to generate digital signatures. The reason that a company archives keys is to ensure that if a person leaves the company, falls off a cliff, or for some reason is unavailable to decrypt important company information, the company can still get to its company-owned data. This is just a matter of the organization protecting itself. A company would not need to be able to recover a key pair that is used for digital signatures, since those keys are only to be used to prove the authenticity of the individual who sent a message. A company would not benefit from having access to those keys and really should not have access to them, since they are tied to one individual for a specific purpose.

CA Private Key

The most sensitive and critical public/private key pairs are those used by CAs to digitally sign certificates. These need to be highly protected because if they were compromised, the trust relationship between the CA and all of the end-entities would be threatened. In high security environments, these keys are often kept in a tamper-proof hardware encryption store, only accessible to individuals with a need to know.

There are two elements to backing up and restoring cryptographic keys: key archiving and key recovery. The *key archiving system* is a way of backing up keys and securely storing them in a repository; *key recovery* is the process of restoring lost keys to the users or the company.

If keys are backed up and stored in a centralized computer, this system must be tightly controlled, because if it were compromised, the attacker could then have access to all keys for the entire infrastructure. Also, it is usually not a good idea to have only one person who can recover all the keys within the environment, because that one person could use this power for evil purposes instead of just recovering keys when they are needed for legitimate purposes. In security systems, it is wise not to fully trust anyone.

Dual control can be used as part of a system to back up and archive data encryption keys. PKI systems can be configured to allow multiple individuals to be involved in any key recovery process. When a key recovery is required, at least two people can be required to authenticate by the key recovery software before the recovery procedure is performed. This enforces *separation of duties*, which means that one person cannot complete a critical task by themselves. Requiring two individuals to together recover a lost key is called *dual control*, which simply means that two people have to be present to carry out a specific task.

This approach to key recovery is referred to as the *"m of n" authentication*, where *n* number of people can be involved in the key recovery process, but at least *m* (which is a smaller number than *n*) *must* be involved before the task can be completed. The goal is to minimize fraudulent or improper use of access and permissions. A company would not require all possible individuals to be involved in the recovery process because getting all the people together at the same time could be impossible with meetings, vacations, sick time, and travel. At least some of all possible individuals must be available to participate, and this is the subset *m* of the number *n*.

All key recovery procedures should be highly audited. The audit logs should capture at least what keys were recovered, who was involved in the process, and the time and date. Keys are an integral piece of any encryption cryptosystem and are critical to a PKI environment, so you need to track who does what with them.

Key Escrow

Key recovery and *key escrow* are terms that are often used interchangeably, but they are terms that actually describe two different things. *You* should not use them interchangeably after you have read this section.

Key recovery is a process that allows for lost keys to be recovered. *Key escrow* is a process of giving keys to a third party so that they can decrypt and read sensitive information when this need arises. Key escrow almost always pertains to handing over encryption keys to the government so that they can use them to collect evidence during investigations.

There have been several movements, supported by parts of the U.S. government, that would require all or many people residing in the United States to hand over copies of the keys they use to encrypt communication channels. The movement behind the Clipper Chip is the most well-known effort to put this requirement and procedure in place. It was suggested that all American-made communication devices should have a hardware encryption chip within them. The chip could be used to encrypt data going back and forth between two individuals, but if a government agency uncovered a reason that they should be able to eavesdrop on this dialog, they would just need to obtain a court order. If the court order was approved, the law enforcement agent would take the order to two escrow agencies, each of which would have a piece of the key that was necessary to decrypt this communication information. The agent would obtain both pieces of the key and combine them, which would allow the agent to listen in on the encrypted communication outlined in the court order.

This was a standard that never saw the light of day because it seemed too "Big Brother" to many American citizens. But the idea was that the encryption keys would be escrowed to two agencies, meaning that each agency would hold one piece of the key. One agency could not hold the whole key, because they could then use this key to wiretap people's conversations illegally. Splitting up the key is an example of separation of duties, put into place to try and prevent fraudulent activities.

Public Certificate Authorities

An individual or company may decide to rely on a CA that is already established and being used by many other individuals and companies—this would be a *public CA*. A company, on the other hand, may decide that they need their own CA for internal use, which gives them more control over the certificate registration and generation process and allows them to configure items specifically for their own needs. This second type of CA is referred to as a *private CA* (or *in-house CA*).

A public CA is a company that specializes in verifying individual identities and creating and maintaining their certificates. These companies issue certificates that are not bound to specific companies or inter-company departments. Instead, their services are to be used by a larger and more diversified group of people and organizations. If a company uses a public CA, that means that it will be paying this other company for individual certificates and for the service of maintaining these certificates. Some examples of public CAs are VeriSign, Entrust, and Baltimore.

One advantage of using a public CA is that they are usually well known and easily accessible to many people. Most web browsers have a list of public CAs installed and configured by default, along with their corresponding root certificates. This means that if you install a web browser onto your computer, it is already configured to trust a list of CAs, even though you may have never heard of them before. So, if you receive a certificate from Bob, and his certificate was digitally signed by a CA listed in your browser, you will automatically trust the CA and can easily walk through the process of verifying Bob's certificate. This has raised some eyebrows among security professionals, since trust is installed by default, but the industry has deemed this is a necessary approach that provides users with transparency and increased functionality. Users can remove these CAs from their browser list if they want to have more control over who their system trusts and who it doesn't.

Earlier in the chapter, the different certificate classes and their uses were explained. There is no global standard defining these classes, the exact requirements for obtaining these different certificates, or their uses. There are standards in place, usually for a particular country or industry, but this means that public CAs can define their own certificate classifications. This is not necessarily a good thing for companies that depend upon public CAs, because it does not give enough control to the company over how the company should interpret certificate classifications and how they should be used.

This means another component needed to be carefully developed for companies that use and depend upon public CAs, and this component is referred to as the *certificate policy (CP)*. This policy allows the company to decide what certification classes are acceptable and how they will be used within the organization. This is different from the CPS, which is what explains how the CA verifies entities, generates certificates, and maintains these certificates. The CP is generated and owned by an individual company that uses an external CA, and it allows the company to enforce *its* security decisions and control how certificates are used with its applications.

In-House Certificate Authorities

A CA that is considered to be an in-house CA is implemented, maintained, and controlled by the company that implemented it. This type of CA can be used to create certificates for internal employees, devices, applications, partners, and customers. This approach allows the company to completely control how individuals are identified, what certification classifications are created, who can and cannot have access to the CA, and how the certifications can be used.

In-house CAs also provide more flexibility for companies, which often integrate them into current infrastructures and into applications for authentication, encryption, and nonrepudiation purposes. If the CA is going to be used over an extended period of time, this can be a cheaper method of generating and using certificates than having to purchase them through a public CA. However, when the decision between an in-house and public CA is made, various factors need to be identified and accounted for. Many companies have embarked upon implementing an in-house PKI environment, which they estimated would be implemented within x number of months and would cost approximately y amount in dollars. If the proper homework is not done, the current environment is not clearly understood, the intended purpose of the PKI is not completely hammered out, and there is not enough skilled staff supporting the project, time estimates can double or triple and the required funds and resources can become unacceptable. Several companies have started on a PKI implementation, only to quit halfway through, resulting in wasted time and money, with nothing to show for it except heaps of frustration and many ulcers.

In some situations, it is better for a company to use a public CA, since public CAs already have the necessary equipment, skills, and technologies. In other situations, companies may feel it is a better business decision to take on these efforts themselves. This is not always a strictly monetary decision—a specific level of security may be a requirement. Some companies do not feel that they can trust an outside authority to generate and maintain their users' and company's certificates. In this situation, the scale may tip towards an in-house CA.

PART V

Each company is different, with various goals, security requirements, functionality needs, budgetary restraints, and ideologies. The decision to use a private or in-house CA depends upon the expansiveness of the PKI within the organization, how integrated it will be with different business needs and goals, its interoperability with a company's current technologies, the number of individuals who will be participating, and how it will work with outside entities. This could be quite a large undertaking that ties up staff, resources, and funds, so a lot of strategic planning should be done, and a full understanding of what will and won't be gained from a PKI should be carried out before the first dollar is spent on the implementation.

Outsourced Certificate Authorities

The last available option for using PKI components within a company is to outsource different parts of it to a specific service provider. Usually the more complex parts are outsourced, such as the CA, RA, CRL, and key recovery mechanisms. This is done if a company does not have the necessary skills to implement and carry out a full PKI environment.

An *outsourced CA* is different than a public CA in that it provides dedicated services, and possibly equipment, to an individual company. A public CA, in contrast, can be used by hundreds or thousands of companies—they don't maintain specific servers and infrastructures for individual companies.

Although outsourced services may be easier for the individual company to implement, several factors need to be reviewed before making this type of commitment. The company needs to determine what level of trust it is willing to give to the service provider and what level of risk it is willing to accept. Often a PKI and its components serve as large security components within a company's enterprise, and allowing a third party to maintain the PKI may introduce too many risks and liabilities the company is not willing to undertake. The liabilities the service provider is willing to accept, security precautions and procedures the outsourced CAs provide, and the surrounding legal issues need to be examined before this type of agreement is made.

Some large vertical markets have their own outsourced PKI environments set up because they share similar needs and usually have the same requirements for certification types and uses. This allows several companies within the same market to split the costs of the necessary equipment, and it allows for industry-specific standards to be drawn up and followed. For example, although many medical facilities work differently and have different environments, they have a lot of the same functionality and security needs. If several of them came together, purchased the necessary equipment to provide CA, RA, and CRL functionality, employed one staff to maintain it, and each connected their different sites to the centralized components, they could save a lot of money and resources. In this case, not every facility would need to strategically plan their own full PKI, and they would not need to purchase redundant equipment or employ redundant staff members. Figure 11-10 illustrates how one outsourced service provider can offer different PKI components and services to different companies, and how companies within one vertical market can share the same resources.

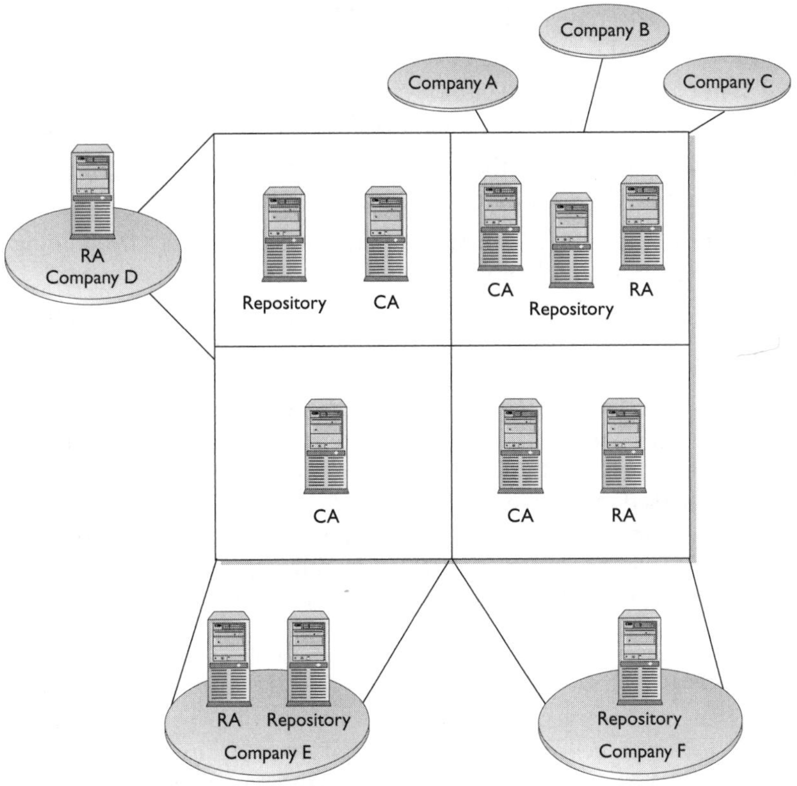

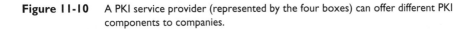

Figure 11-10   A PKI service provider (represented by the four boxes) can offer different PKI components to companies.

A set of standards can be drawn up about how different facilities should integrate their own infrastructures and how they should integrate with the centralized PKI components. This also allows for less complicated intercommunication to take place between the different medical facilities, which will ease information-sharing attempts.

Tying Different PKIs Together

There are several reasons that more than one CA may be needed for a specific PKI to work properly, and there may be a requirement for different PKIs to intercommunicate. Here are some examples of where this may be required:

- A company wants to be able to communicate seamlessly with their suppliers, customers, or business partners via PKI.

- One department within a company may have higher security requirements than all other departments, and thus needs to configure and control their own CA.

- One department may need to have specially constructed certificates with unique fields and usages.

- Different parts of an organization want to control their own piece of the network and the CA that is encompassed within it.

- The number of certificates that need to be generated and maintained would overwhelm one CA, so multiple CAs may need to be deployed.

- The political culture of a company inhibits one department from being able to control elements of another department.

- Enterprises are partitioned geographically, and different sites need their own local CA.

These situations can add much more complexity to the overall infrastructure, inter-communication capabilities, and procedures for certificate generation and validation. To properly control this complexity from the beginning, these requirements need to be understood, addressed, and planned for. Then the necessary trust model needs to be chosen and molded for the company to build upon. Selecting the right trust model will give the company a solid foundation from the beginning, instead of trying to add structure to an inaccurate and inadequate plan later on.

Trust Models

There is more involved in the previously listed scenarios than just having more than one CA—each of the companies or each department of an enterprise can actually represent a trust domain itself. A *trust domain* is a construct of systems, personnel, applications, protocols, technologies, and policies that work together to provide a certain level of protection. All of these components can work together seamlessly within the same trust domain because they are known to the other components within the domain and are trusted to some degree. Different trust domains are usually managed by different groups of administrators, have different security policies, and restrict outsiders from privileged access.

Most trust domains (whether individual companies or departments) are not usually islands cut off from the world—they need to communicate with other less trusted domains. The trick is to figure out how much two different domains should trust each other, and how to implement and configure an infrastructure that would allow these two domains to communicate in a way that will not allow security compromises or breaches. This can be harder than it sounds.

In the non-digital world, it is hard to figure out who to trust, how to carry out legitimate business functions, and how to ensure that one is not being taken advantage of or lied to. Jump into the digital world and add protocols, services, encryption, CAs, RAs, CRLs, differing technologies and applications, and the business risks can become overwhelming and confusing. So start with a basic question: What is the criteria we will use to determine who we trust and to what degree?

One example of trust that we considered earlier in the chapter was the driver's license issued by the DMV. Suppose Bob is buying a lamp from Carol and he wants to pay by check. Since Carol does not know Bob, she does not know if she can trust him or have much faith in his check. But if Bob shows Carol his driver's license, she can compare the name to what is on the check, and she can choose to accept it. The *trust anchor* (the agreed-upon trusted third party) in this scenario is the DMV, since both Carol and Bob trust it more than they trust each other. Since Bob had to provide documentation to prove his identity to the DMV, and they trusted him enough to generate a license, and Carol trusts the DMV, she decides to trust Bob's check.

Consider another example of a trust anchor. If Joe and Stacy need to communicate through e-mail and would like to use encryption and digital signatures, they will not trust each other's certificate all by itself. But when they receive each other's certificate and see that they have been digitally signed by an entity they both do trust—the CA—then they have a deeper level of trust in each other. The trust anchor here is the CA. This is easy enough, but when we need to establish trust anchors between different CAs and PKI environments, it gets a little more complicated.

When two companies need to communicate using their individual PKIs, or if two departments within the same company each have their own CA, there are two separate trust domains to contend with. The users and devices from these different trust domains will need to communicate with each other, and they will need to exchange certificates and public keys. This means that trust anchors need to be identified, and a communication channel must be constructed and maintained.

A trust relationship must be established between two issuing authorities (CAs). This happens when one or both of the CAs issue a certificate for the other CA's public key, as shown in Figure 11-11. This means that each CA registers for a certificate and public key from the other CA. Each CA validates the other CA's identification information and generates a certificate containing a public key for that CA to use. This establishes a trust path between the two entities that can then be used when users need to verify other users' certificates that fall within the different trust domains. The trust path can be unidirectional or bidirectional, so either the two CAs trust each other (bidirectional) or only one trusts the other (unidirectional).

As illustrated in Figure 11-11, all the users and devices in trust domain 1 trust their own CA 1, which is their trust anchor. All users and devices in trust domain 2 have their own trust anchor, CA 2. The two CAs have exchanged certificates and trust each other, but they do not have a common trust anchor between them.

The trust models describe and outline the trust relationships between the different CAs and different environments, which will indicate where the trust paths reside. The trust models and paths need to be thought out before implementation to properly restrict and control access and to ensure that there are as few trust paths as possible. There are several different trust models: the hierarchical, peer-to-peer, and hybrid models will be discussed in the following sections.

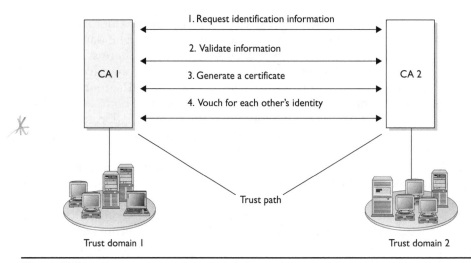

1. Request identification information

2. Validate information

3. Generate a certificate

4. Vouch for each other's identity

CA 1

CA 2

Trust path

Trust domain 1

Trust domain 2

Figure 11-11 A trust relationship can be built between two trust domains to set up a communication channel.

Hierarchical Trust Model

The first type of trust model to look at is a basic hierarchical structure that contains a root CA, intermediate CAs, leaf CAs, and end-entities. The configuration is that of an inverted tree, as shown in Figure 11-12. The root CA is the ultimate trust anchor for all other entities in this infrastructure, and it generates certificates for the intermediate CAs, which in turn generate certificates for the leaf CAs, and the leaf CAs generate certificates for the end-entities (users, network devices, applications).

As shown in Figure 11-12, there are no bidirectional trusts—they are all unidirectional trusts as indicated by the one-way arrows. Since no other entity can certify and generate certificates for the root CA, it creates a *self-signed certificate*. This means that the certificate's issuer and subject fields hold the same information, both representing the root CA, and the root CA's public key is what will be used to verify this certificate when that time comes. This root CA certificate and public key is distributed to all entities within this trust model.

Root CA

If the root CA's private key was ever compromised, all entities within the hierarchical trust model would be drastically affected, because this is their sole trust anchor. The root CA usually has a small amount of interaction with the intermediate CAs and end-entities, and can therefore be taken offline much of the time. This provides a greater degree of protection for the root CA, because when it is offline it is basically inaccessible.

Figure II-I2
The hierarchical trust model outlines trust paths.

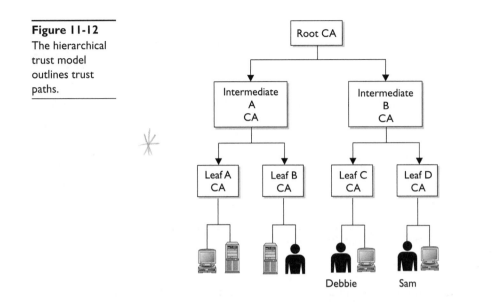

Walking the Certificate Path   When a user in one trust domain needs to communicate with another user in another trust domain, one user will need to validate the other's certificate. This sounds simple enough, but what it really means is that each certificate for each CA, all the way up to a shared trusted anchor, needs to be validated also. If Debbie needs to validate Sam's certificate, as shown in Figure 11-12, she actually also needs to validate the Leaf D CA and Intermediate B CA certificates, as well as Sam's.

So in Figure 11-12, we have a user, Sam, who digitally signs a message and sends it and his certificate to Debbie. Debbie needs to validate this certificate before she can trust Sam's digital signature. In Sam's certificate, there is an issuer field, which indicates that the certificate was issued by Leaf D CA. Debbie has to obtain Leaf D CA's digital certificate and public key to validate Sam's certificate. Remember that Debbie validates the certificate by verifying its digital signature. The digital signature was created by the certificate issuer using its private key, so Debbie needs to verify it using the issuer's public key.

Debbie tracks down Leaf D CA's certificate and public key, but now needs to verify this CA's certificate, so she looks at the issuer field, which indicates that Leaf D CA's certificate was issued by Intermediate B CA. Debbie now needs to get Intermediate B CA's certificate and public key.

Debbie's client software tracks this down and sees that the issuer for the Intermediate B CA is the Root CA, which she already has a certificate and public key for. So Debbie's client software had to follow the *certificate path*, meaning it had to continue to track down and collect certificates until it came upon a self-signed certificate. A self-signed certificate indicates that it was signed by a root CA, and Debbie's software has been configured to trust this entity as her trust anchor, so she can stop there. Figure 11-13 illustrates the steps Debbie's software had to carry out just to be able to verify Sam's certificate.

PART V

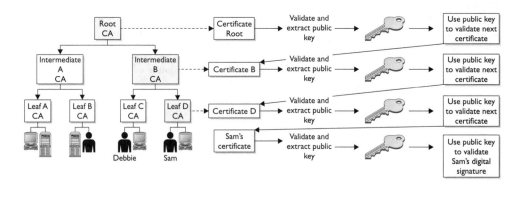

Figure 11-13   Verifying each certificate in a certificate path

This type of simplistic trust model works well within an enterprise that easily follows a hierarchical organizational chart, but many companies cannot use this type of trust model because different departments or offices may require their own trust anchors. These demands can be derived from direct business needs or from inter-organizational politics. This hierarchical model may also not be possible when two or more companies need to communicate with each other. Neither company will let the other's CA be the root CA, because they do not necessarily trust the other entity to that degree. In these situations, the CAs will need to work in a peer-to-peer relationship instead of in a hierarchical relationship.

Peer-to-Peer Model

In a *peer-to-peer* trust model, one CA is not subordinate to another CA, and there is no established trusted anchor between the CAs involved. The end-entities will look to their issuing CA as their trusted anchor, but the different CAs will not have an agreed-upon anchor.

Figure 11-14 illustrates this type of trust model. The two different CAs will certify the public key for each other, which creates a bidirectional trust. This is referred to as *cross certification*, since the CAs are not receiving their certificates and public keys from a superior CA, but instead they are creating them for each other.

One of the main drawbacks to this model is scalability. Each CA must certify every other CA that is participating, and a bidirectional trust path must be implemented, as shown in Figure 11-15. If there was one root CA certifying all the intermediate CAs, scalability would not be as much of an issue.

Figure 11-15 represents a fully connected *mesh architecture,* meaning that each CA is directly connected to and has a bidirectional trust relationship with every other CA. As you can see in this illustration, the complexity of this setup can become overwhelming.

Figure 11-14
Cross
certification
creates a
peer-to-peer
PKI model.

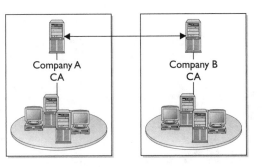

Figure 11-15
Scalability is a
drawback in
cross-certification
models.

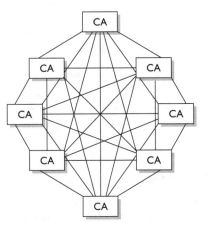

Hybrid Trust Model

Companies can be complex within themselves, and when the need arises to properly communicate with outside partners, suppliers, and customers in an authorized and secured manner, it can make sticking to either the hierarchical or peer-to-peer trust model difficult, if not impossible. In many implementations, the different model types have to be combined to provide the necessary communication lines and levels of trust. In a *hybrid* trust model, the two companies have their own internal hierarchical models and are connected through a peer-to-peer model using cross certification.

Another option in this hybrid configuration is to implement a *bridge CA*. Figure 11-16 illustrates the role that a bridge CA could play—it is responsible for issuing cross-certificates for all connected CAs and trust domains. The bridge is not considered a root or trust anchor, but just the entity that generates and maintains the cross certification for the connected environments.

PART V

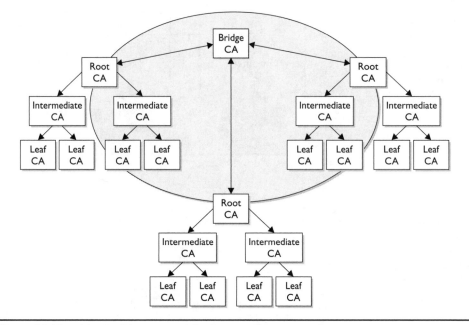

Figure 11-16 A bridge CA can control the cross-certification procedures.

Chapter Review

Public key infrastructures can be complex beasts, as this chapter has shown. They have many different components that must work together seamlessly to provide the expected protection and functionality. The reason a PKI is implemented is to provide users and devices with the ability to communicate securely and to provide them with trust anchors, since they do not directly trust each other.

Certificate registration requests are validated by a registration authority (RA), and the certificate is then generated by a certificate authority (CA). The digital certificate binds an individual's identity to the public key that is within the certificate.

Certificates can expire, be revoked, or be suspended. When a user receives a certificate from another user, they must validate it, which means that the CA's digital signature that is embedded within the certificate itself must be validated. This may require the user to validate a whole string of certificates and digital signatures, referred to as a certificate path. This path must be followed until a self-signed trusted root certificate is reached.

Certificate authorities can be public, private (in-house), or outsourced, depending upon a company's needs. Internal PKIs can follow different trust models, which will dictate their trust paths and anchors.

PKIs have been waiting in the wings for several years—waiting for the time when they would finally be accepted and implemented. That time has come, and more and more companies are putting them into place. This also means more and more companies have experienced the pain of implementing such a complex framework into a preexisting working environment. All the aspects of a PKI must be understood before filling out the first purchase order, which also means determining exactly what a PKI will do for you and what it won't. In any security activity, understanding the reality of any protection mechanism is necessary, but this is especially true for a PKI because it can drastically affect the whole production environment in both good and bad ways.

Finally, it is important to understand that a majority of these authentication activities take place behind the scenes for the users—the technology and intelligence have been programmed into the software itself. So, in this chapter, when we said that users need to see if their system has been configured to trust a specific CA, or that they need to validate a digital signature or obtain a higher-level CA certificate, the user's client software is actually carrying out these tasks. A majority of what was discussed in this chapter happens transparently to the users.

Questions

1. When a user wants to participate in a PKI, what is the component they need to obtain, and how does that happen?

   A. The user submits a certification request to the CA.

   B. The user submits a key pair request to the CRL.

   C. The user submits a certification request to the RA.

   D. The user submits proof of identification to the CA.

2. How does a user validate a digital certificate that is received from another user?

   A. The user will first see if their system has been configured to trust the CA that digitally signed the other user's certificate, and then will validate that CA's digital signature.

   B. The user will calculate a message digest and compare it to the one attached to the message.

   C. The user will first see if their system has been configured to trust the CA that digitally signed the certificate, and then will validate the public key that is embedded within the certificate.

   D. The user will validate the sender's digital signature on the message.

3. What is the purpose of a digital certificate?

   A. It binds a CA to a user's identity.

   B. It binds a CA's identity to the correct RA.

   C. It binds an individual to an RA.

   D. It binds an individual to a public key.

4. What steps does a user take to validate a CA's digital signature on a digital certificate?

A. The user's software creates a message digest for the digital certificate and decrypts the encrypted message digest included within the digital certificate. If the decryption performs properly and the message digest values are the same, the certificate is validated.

B. The user's software creates a message digest for the digital signature and encrypts the message digest included within the digital certificate. If the encryption performs properly and the message digest values are the same, the certificate is validated.

C. The user's software creates a message digest for the digital certificate and decrypts the encrypted message digest included within the digital certificate. If the user can encrypt the message digest properly with the CA's private key and the message digest values are the same, the certificate is validated.

D. The user's software creates a message digest for the digital signature and encrypts the message digest with its private key. If the decryption performs properly and the message digest values are the same, the certificate is validated.

5. What is a bridge CA, and what is its function?

A. It is a hierarchical trust model that establishes a root CA, which is the trust anchor for all other CAs.

B. It is an entity that creates and maintains the CRL for several CAs at one time.

C. It is a CA that handles the cross-certification certificates for two or more CAs in a peer-to-peer relationship.

D. It is an entity that validates the user's identity information for the RA before the request goes to the CA.

6. Why would a company implement a key archiving and recovery system within their organization?

A. To make sure all data encryption keys are available for the company if and when it needs them

B. To make sure all digital signature keys are available for the company if and when it needs them

C. To create session keys for users to be able to access when they need to encrypt bulk data

D. To back up the RA's private key for retrieval purposes

7. Within a PKI environment, where does the majority of the trust actually lie?

A. All users and devices within an environment trust the RA, which allows them to indirectly trust each other.

    B. All users and devices within an environment trust the CA, which allows them to indirectly trust each other.

    C. All users and devices within an environment trust the CRL, which allows them to indirectly trust each other.

    D. All users and devices within an environment trust the CPS, which allows them to indirectly trust each other.

8. Which of the following properly explains the *"m of n"* control?

    A. This is the process a user must go through to properly register for a certificate through the RA.

    B. This ensures that a certificate has to be fully validated by a user before they can extract the public key and use it.

    C. This is a control in key recovery to enforce separation of duties.

    D. This is a control in key recovery to ensure that the company cannot recover a user's key without the user's consent.

9. Which of the following is not a valid field that could be present in an X.509 version 3 digital certificate?

    A. Validity dates

    B. Serial number

    C. Extensions

    D. Symmetric key

10. What does a certificate path pertain to?

    A. All of the digital certificates that need to be validated before a received certificate can be fully validated and trusted

    B. All of the digital certificates that need to be validated before a sent certificate can be properly encrypted

    C. All of the digital certificates that need to be validated before a user trusts their own trust anchor

    D. All of the digital certificates that need to be validated before a received certificate can be destroyed

11. Which of the following certificate characteristics was expanded upon with version 3 of the X.509 standard?

    A. Subject

    B. Extensions

    C. Digital signature

    D. Serial number

12. What is a certification practices statement (CPS), and what is its purpose?

   A. A CPS outlines the steps a CA goes through to validate identities and generate certificates. Companies should review this document to ensure that the CA follows the necessary steps the company requires and provides the necessary level of protection.

   B. A CPS outlines the steps a CA goes through to communicate with other CAs in other states. Companies should review this document to ensure that the CA follows the necessary steps the company requires and provides the necessary level of protection.

   C. A CPS outlines the steps a CA goes through to set up an RA at a company's site. Companies should review this document to ensure that the CA follows the necessary steps the company requires and provides the necessary level of protection.

   D. A CPS outlines the steps a CA goes through to become a business within a vertical market. Companies should review this document to ensure that the CA follows the necessary steps the company requires and provides the necessary level of protection.

13. Which of the following properly describes what a public key infrastructure (PKI) actually is?

   A. A protocol written to work with a large subset of algorithms, applications, and protocols

   B. An algorithm that creates public/private key pairs

   C. A framework that outlines specific technologies and algorithms that must be used

   D. A framework that does not specify any technologies, but provides a foundation for confidentiality, integrity, and availability services

14. Once an individual validates another individual's certificate, what is the use of the public key that is extracted from this digital certificate?

   A. The public key is now available to use to create digital signatures.

   B. The user can now encrypt session keys and messages with this public key and can validate the sender's digital signatures.

   C. The public key is now available to encrypt future digital certificates that need to be validated.

   D. The user can now encrypt private keys that need to be transmitted securely.

15. Why would a digital certificate be added to a certificate revocation list (CRL)?

   A. If the public key had become compromised in a public repository

   B. If the private key had become compromised

   C. If a new employee joined the company and received a new certificate

   D. If the certificate expired

16. What is an online CRL service?

    A. End-entities can send a request containing a serial number of a specific certificate to an online CRL service. The online service will query several CRL distribution points and respond with information about whether the certificate is still valid or not.

    B. CAs can send a request containing the expiration date of a specific certificate to an online CRL service. The online service will query several other RAs and respond with information about whether the certificate is still valid or not.

    C. End-entities can send a request containing a public key of a specific certificate to an online CRL service. The online service will query several end-entities and respond with information about whether the certificate is still valid or not.

    D. End-entities can send a request containing a public key of a specific CA to an online CRL service. The online service will query several RA distribution points and respond with information about whether the CA is still trustworthy or not.

17. If an extension is marked as critical, what does this indicate?

    A. If the CA is not programmed to understand and process this extension, the certificate and corresponding keys can be used for their intended purpose.

    B. If the end-entity is programmed to understand and process this extension, the certificate and corresponding keys cannot be used.

    C. If the RA is not programmed to understand and process this extension, communication with the CA is not allowed.

    D. If the end-entity is not programmed to understand and process this extension, the certificate and corresponding keys cannot be used.

18. How can users have faith that the CRL was not modified to present incorrect information?

    A. The CRL is digitally signed by the CA.

    B. The CRL is encrypted by the CA.

    C. The CRL is open for anyone to post certificate information to.

    D. The CRL is only accessible to the CA.

19. When would a certificate be suspended, and where is that information posted?

    A. It would be suspended when an employee leaves the company. It is posted on the CRL.

    B. It would be suspended when an employee changes their last name. It is posted on the CA.

    C. It would be suspended when an employee goes on vacation. It is posted on the CRL.

    D. It would be suspended when a private key is compromised. It is posted on the CRL.

20. What does cross certification pertain to in a PKI environment?

    A. When a company uses an outsourced service provider, it needs to modify its CPS to allow for cross certification to take place between the RA and CA.

    B. When two end-entities need to communicate in a PKI, they need to exchange certificates.

    C. When two or more CAs need to trust each other so that their end-entities can communicate, they will create certificates for each other.

    D. A RA needs to perform a cross certification with a user before the certificate registration is terminated.

Answers

1. **C.** The user must submit identification data and a certification request to the registration authority (RA). The RA validates this information and sends the certification request to the certificate authority (CA).

2. **A.** A digital certificate is validated by the receiver by first seeing if their system has been configured to trust the CA that digitally signed the certificate. If this has been configured, the user's software takes the CA's public key and validates the CA's digital signature that is embedded within the certificate.

3. **D.** A digital certificate vouches for an individual's identity and binds that identity to the public key that is embedded within the certificate.

4. **A.** The user's software calculates a message digest for the digital certificate and decrypts the encrypted message digest value included with the certificate, which is the digital signature. The message digest is decrypted using the CA's public key. If the two message digest values match, the user knows that the certificate has not been modified in an unauthorized manner, and since the encrypted message digest can be decrypted properly with the CA's public key, the user is assured that this CA created the certificate.

5. **C.** A bridge CA is a CA that is set up to handle all of the cross-certification certificates and traffic between different CAs and trust domains. A bridge CA is used instead of requiring all of the CAs to authenticate to each other and create certificates with one another, which would end up in a full mesh configuration.

6. **A.** To protect itself, the company will make backups of the data encryption keys its employees use for encrypting company information. If an employee is no longer available, the company must make sure that it still has access to its own business data. Companies should not need to back up digital signature keys, since they are not used to encrypt data.

7. **B.** The trust anchor for a PKI environment is the CA. All users and devices trust the CA, which allows them to indirectly trust each other. The CA verifies and vouches for each user's and device's identity, so these different entities can have confidence that they are communicating with specific individuals.

8. **C.** The "*m of n*" control is the part of the key recovery software that allows a certain number of people to be involved with recovering and reconstructing a lost or corrupted key. A certain number of people (n) are allowed to authenticate to the software, which will allow them to participate in the key recovery process. Not all of those people may be available at one time, however, so a larger number of people (m) need to be involved with the process. The system should not allow only one person to carry out key recovery because that person could then use the keys for fraudulent purposes.

9. **D.** The first three values are valid fields that are used in digital certificates. Validity dates indicate how long the certificate is good for, the serial number is a unique value used to identify individual certificates, and extensions allow companies to expand the use of their certificates. A public key is included in the certificate, which is an asymmetric key, not a symmetric key.

10. **A.** The certificate path is all of the certificates that must be validated before the receiver of a certificate can validate and trust the newly received certificate. When a user receives a certificate, they must obtain the certificate and public key of all of the CAs until they come to a self-signed certificate, which is the trusted anchor. So, the user must validate each of these certificates until the trusted anchor is reached. The path between the receiver and a trusted anchor is referred to as the certificate path. This is a hierarchical model of trust, and each rung of the trust model must be verified before the end user's certificate can be validated and trusted.

11. **B.** The X.509 standard is currently at version 3. Version 3 added more extension capabilities to digital certificates, which added more flexibility for companies using PKIs. Companies can define many of these extensions to mean specific things that are necessary for their proprietary or customized environment and software.

12. **A.** The CPS outlines the certificate classes the CA uses and the CA's procedures for verifying end-entity identities, generating certificates, and maintaining the certificates throughout their lifetimes. Any company that will be using a specific CA needs to make sure it is going through these procedures with the level of protection the company would require of itself. The company will be putting a lot of trust in the CA, and so should do some homework and investigate how the CA actually accomplishes its tasks.

13. **D.** A PKI is a framework that allows several different types of technologies, applications, algorithms, and protocols to be plugged into it. The goal is to provide a foundation that can provide a hierarchical trust model, which will

allow end-entities to indirectly trust each other and allow for secure and trusted communications.

14. **B.** Once a receiver validates a digital certificate, the embedded public key can be extracted and used to encrypt symmetric session keys, encrypt messages, and validate the sender's digital signatures.

15. **B.** Certificates are added to a CRL if there is a reason that the public/private key pair should no longer be bound to a specific person's identity. This can happen if a private key is compromised, meaning that it was stolen or captured—this would mean someone else could be using the private key instead of the original user, so the CRL is a protection mechanism that will alert others in the PKI of this incident. Certificates can be added to the CRL if an employee leaves the company or is no longer affiliated with the company for one reason or another. Expired certificates are not added to CRLs.

16. **A.** Actually getting the data on the CRLs to end-entities is a huge barrier for many PKI implementations. The environment can have distribution points set up, which provides a centralized place that allows the users' systems to query to see if a certificate has been revoked or not. Another approach is to push down the CRLs to each end-entity or to use an online service. The online service will do the busy work for the end-entity by querying all the available CRLs and returning a response to the end-entity indicating whether the certificate has been revoked or not.

17. **D.** Digital certificates have extensions that allow companies to expand the use of certificates within their environments. When a CA creates a certificate, it is certifying the key pair to be used for a specific purpose (for digital signatures, data encryption, validating a CA's digital signature, and so on). If a CA adds a critical flag to an extension, it is stating that the key pair can only be used for the reason stated in the extension. If an end-entity receives a certificate with this critical flag set and cannot understand and process the marked extension, the key pair cannot be used at all. The CA is stating, "I will only allow the key pair to be used for this purpose and under these circumstances." If an extension is marked non-critical, the end-entity does not have to be able to understand and process that extension.

18. **A.** The CRL contains all of the certificates that have been revoked. Only the CA can post information to this list. The CA then digitally signs the list to ensure that any modifications will be detected. When an end-entity receives a CRL, they verify the CA's digital signature, which will tell them if the list has been modified in an unauthorized manner and guarantees the correct CA signed the list.

19. **C.** A certificate can be suspended if it needs to be temporarily taken out of production for a period of time. If an employee goes on vacation and wants to make sure no one can use their certificate, they can make a suspension request to the CA, which will post the information to the CRL. The other answers in

this question would require the certificate to be revoked, not suspended, and a new certificate would need to be created for the user.

20. **C.** Cross certification means that two or more CAs create certificates for each other. This takes place when two trust domains, each with their own CA, need to be able to communicate—a trusted path needs to be established between these domains. Once the first CA validates the other CA's identity and creates a certificate, it then trusts this other CA, which creates a trusted path between the different PKI environments. The trust can be bidirectional or unidirectional.

Standards and Protocols

In this chapter, you will

- Learn about the standards involved in establishing an interoperable Internet PKI
- Understand interoperability issues with PKI standards
- Discover how the common Internet protocols use and implement the PKI standards

One of the biggest growth industries in the 1990s was the commercial use of the Internet. While the early 2000s haven't seen explosive growth, due to other factors, none of the still steadily growing Internet commerce would be possible without the use of standards and protocols to provide a common, interoperable environment for securely exchanging information. Due to the wide distribution of users and businesses, the most practical solution to date has been the commercial implementation of public key infrastructures (PKIs).

This chapter examines the standards and protocols involved in secure Internet transactions and e-business using a PKI. Though you may only use a portion of the related standards and protocols on a daily basis, you should understand how they interact to provide the services that are critical for security: confidentiality, integrity, authentication, and nonrepudiation.

Chapter 11 introduced the algorithms and techniques used to implement a PKI, but as you probably noticed, there is a lot of room for interpretation. Various organizations have developed and implemented standards and protocols that have been accepted as the basis for secure interaction in a PKI environment. These standards fall into three general categories:

- **Standards that define the PKI** These standards define the data and data structures exchanged and the means for managing that data to provide the functions of the PKI (certificate issuance, storage, revocation, registration, and management).
- **Standards that define the interface between applications and the underlying PKI** These use the PKI to establish the services required by applications.
- **Standards that provide bits and pieces that glue everything together and may address not only the PKI structure and the methods and protocols**

for using it, but that may also provide an overarching business process environment for PKI implementation (for example, ISO 17799 and the FIPS PUBS)   These standards don't neatly fit in either of the previous two categories.

Figure 12-1 shows the relationships between these standards and protocols.

Figure 12-1 conveys the interdependence of the standards and protocols discussed in this chapter. The Internet PKI relies on three main standards for establishing interoperable PKI services: Public Key Infrastructure X.509 (PKIX), Public Key Cryptography Standards (PKCS), and X.509. There are other protocols and standards that help define the management and operation of the PKI and related services— Internet Security Association and Key Management Protocol (ISAKMP) and XML Key Management Specification (XKMS) are both key management protocols, while Certificate Management Protocol (CMP) is for managing certificates. Wired Equivalent Privacy (WEP) is used to encrypt wireless communications in an 802.11 environment to support some of the more application-oriented standards and protocols: Secure/Multipurpose Internet Mail Extensions (S/MIME) for e-mail; Secure Sockets Layer (SSL), Transport Layer Security (TLS), and Wireless Transport Layer Security (WTLS) for secure packet transmission; and IP Security (IPsec) and Point-to-Point Tunneling Protocol (PPTP) to support virtual private networks. ISO 17799, Common Criteria, and Federal Information Processing Standards Publications (FIPS) each address security at the business process, application, protocol, and PKI implementation levels. Finally, Pretty Good Privacy (PGP) provides an alternative method spanning the protocol and application levels.

We'll be examining each standard from the bottom up, starting with building an infrastructure through protocols and applications, and finishing with some of the inherent weaknesses of and potential attacks on a PKI.

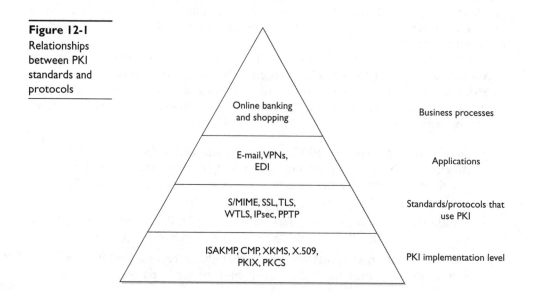

Figure 12-1
Relationships between PKI standards and protocols

Online banking and shopping — Business processes

E-mail, VPNs, EDI — Applications

S/MIME, SSL, TLS, WTLS, IPsec, PPTP — Standards/protocols that use PKI

ISAKMP, CMP, XKMS, X.509, PKIX, PKCS — PKI implementation level

PKIX/PKCS

Two main standards have evolved over time to implement PKI on a practical level on the Internet. Both are based on the X.509 certificate standard (discussed shortly in the "X.509" section) and establish complimentary standards for implementing PKI. Public Key Infrastructure X.509 (PKIX) and Public Key Cryptography Standards (PKCS) intertwine to define the most commonly used set of standards.

PKIX was produced by the Internet Engineering Task Force (IETF) and defines standards for interactions and operations for four component types: the user (end-entity), certificate authority (CA), registration authority (RA), and the repository for certificates and certificate revocation lists (CRLs). PKCS defines many of the lower-level standards for message syntax, cryptographic algorithms, and the like. The PKCS set of standards is a product of RSA Security.

The PKIX working group was formed in 1995 to develop the standards necessary to support PKIs. At the time, the X.509 Public Key Certificate (PKC) format was proposed as the basis for a PKI. X.509 includes information regarding data formats and procedures used for CA-signed PKCs, but it doesn't specify values or formats for many of the fields within the PKC. X.509 v1 (version 1) was originally defined in 1988 as part of the X.500 Directory standard. After being co-opted by the Internet community for implementing certificates for secure Internet communications, it became apparent that there were several shortcomings. The current version, X.509 v3 was adopted in 1996. X.509 is very complex, allowing a great deal of flexibility in implementing certificate features. PKIX provides standards for extending and using X.509 v3 certificates and for managing them, enabling interoperability between PKIs following the standards.

PKIX uses the model in Figure 12-2 for representing the components and users of a PKI. The user, called an *end-entity*, is not part of the PKI, but they are either users of the PKI certificates, the subject of a certificate (an entity identified by it), or both. The certificate authority (CA) is responsible for issuing, storing, and revoking certificates—both Public Key Certificates (PKCs) and Attribute Certificates (ACs). The registration authority (RA) is responsible for management activities designated by the CA. The RA may, in

PART V

Figure 12-2
The PKIX model

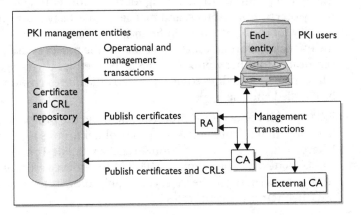

fact, be a component of the CA rather than a separate component. The final component of the PKIX model is the repository, a system or group of distributed systems that provide certificates and certificate revocation lists to the end-entities.

PKIX Standards

Now that we have looked at how PKIX views the world, let's take a look at what PKIX does. Using X.509 v3, there are five major areas that the PKIX working group addresses:

- PKIX outlines certificate extensions and content not covered by X.509 v3 and the format of version 2 CRLs thus providing compatibility standards for sharing certificates and CRLs between CAs and end-entities in different PKIs. The PKIX profile of the X.509 v3 PKC describes the contents, required extensions, optional extensions, and extensions that need not be implemented. The PKIX profile suggests a range of values for many extensions. In addition, PKIX provides a profile for version 2 CRLs, allowing different PKIs to share revocation information. (For more information on PKIX see "Internet X.509 Public Key Infrastructure Certificate and CRL Profile" [RFC 3280].)

- PKIX provides certificate management message formats and protocols, defining the data structures, management messages, and management functions for PKIs. The working group also addresses the assumptions and restrictions of their protocols. This standard identifies the protocols necessary to support online interactions between entities in the PKIX model. The management protocols support functions for entity registration, initialization of the certificate (possibly key pair generation), issuance of the certificate, key pair update, certificate revocation, cross-certification (between CAs), and key pair recovery if available.

- PKIX outlines certificate policies and certification practices statements (CPSs), establishing the relationship between policies and CPSs. A policy is a set of rules that help determine the applicability of a certificate to an end-entity. For example, a certificate for handling routine information would probably have a policy on creation, storage, and management of key pairs quite different from a policy for certificates used in financial transactions, due to the sensitivity of the financial information. A CPS explains the practices used by a CA to issue certificates. In other words, the CPS is the method used to get the certificate, while the policy defines some characteristics of the certificate and how it will be handled and used.

- PKIX specifies operational protocols, defining the protocols for certificate handling. In particular, there are protocol definitions for using Lightweight Directory Access Protocol version 2 (LDAP v2), File Transfer Protocol (FTP), and Hypertext Transfer Protocol (HTTP) to retrieve certificates from repositories. These are the most common protocols for applications to use when retrieving certificates.

- PKIX includes time-stamping and data certification and validation services, which are areas of interest to the PKIX working group, and which will probably grow in use over time. A time stamp authority (TSA) certifies that a particular entity existed at a particular time. A Data Validation and Certification Server certifies the validity of signed documents, PKCs, and the possession or existence of data. These capabilities support nonrepudiation requirements and are considered building blocks for a nonrepudiation service.

PKCs are the most commonly used certificates, but the PKIX working group has been working on two other types of certificates: Attribute Certificates and Qualified Certificates.

An Attribute Certificate (AC) is used to grant permissions using rule-based, role-based, and rank-based access controls. ACs are used to implement a privilege management infrastructure (PMI). In a PMI, an entity (user, program, system, and so on) is typically identified as a client to a server using a PKC. There are then two possibilities: either the identified client pushes an AC to the server, or the server can query a trusted repository to retrieve the attributes of the client. This situation is modeled in Figure 12-3.

The client push of the AC has the effect of improving performance, but there is no independent verification by the server of the client's permissions. The alternative is to have the server pull the information from an AC issuer or a repository. This method is preferable from a security standpoint, because the server or server's domain determines the client's access rights. The pull method has the added benefit of requiring no changes to the client software.

The QC is based on the term used within the European Commission to identify certificates with specific legislative uses. This concept is generalized in the PKIX QC profile to indicate a certificate used to identify a specific individual (a single human rather than the *entity* of the PKC) with a high level of assurance in a nonrepudiation service.

Table 12-1 summarizes the Internet Requests For Comment (RFCs) that have been produced by the PKIX working group for each of these five areas.

There are other documents produced by the Internet Engineering Task Force PKIX working group, but the ones listed in Table 12-1 cover the major implementation details for PKIX. For a complete list of current and pending documents, see the Internet Draft for the PKIX working group roadmap.

PART V

Figure 12-3
The PKIX PMI model

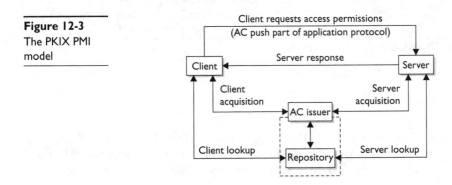

Subject	RFCs
Certificate and CRL profiles	—RFC 3280 (replaces RFC 2459): Internet X.509 Public Key Infrastructure Certificate and CRL Profile —RFC 3039: Internet X.509 Public Key Infrastructure Qualified Certificates Profile —RFC 3280: Internet X.509 Public Key Infrastructure Certificate and Certificate Revocation List (CRL) Profile —RFC 3281: An Internet Attribute Certificate Profile for Authorization
Certificate management protocols	—RFC 2510: Internet X.509 Public Key Infrastructure Certificate Management Protocols —RFC 2511: Internet X.509 Certificate Request Message Format —RFC 2560: X.509 Internet Public Key Infrastructure Online Certificate Status Protocol—OCSP —RFC 2797: Certificate Management Messages over CMS
Certificate policies and CPSs	—RFC 2527: Internet X.509 Public Key Infrastructure Certificate Policy and Certification Practices Framework
Operational protocols	—RFC 2528: Internet X.509 Public Key Infrastructure Representation of Key Exchange Algorithm (KEA) Keys in Internet X.509 Public Key Infrastructure Certificates —RFC 2559: Internet X.509 Public Key Infrastructure Operational Protocols—LDAP v2 —RFC 2585: Internet X.509 Public Key Infrastructure Operational Protocols: FTP and HTTP —RFC 2587: Internet X.509 Public Key Infrastructure LDAP v2 Schema
Time-stamp and data validation	—RFC 2875: Diffie-Hellman Proof-of-Possession Algorithms —RFC 3029: Internet X.509 Public Key Infrastructure Data Validation and Certification Server Protocols —RFC 3161: Internet X.509 Public Key Infrastructure Time-Stamp Protocol (TSP)
Other PKIX topics	—RFC 3279: Algorithms and Identifiers for the Internet X.509 Public Key Infrastructure Certificate and Certificate Revocation List (CRL) Profile —RFC 3379: Delegated Path Validation and Delegated Path Discovery Protocol Requirements

Table 12-1   PKIX Subjects and Related RFCs

PKCS

RSA Laboratories created the Public Key Cryptography Standards (PKCS) to fill some of the gaps in the standards that existed in PKI implementation. Just as with the PKIX standards, PKI developers have adopted many of these standards as a basis for achieving interoperability between different certificate authorities. PKCS is composed of a set of (currently) 13 active standards, with 2 other standards that are no longer active. The standards are referred to as PKCS #1 through PKCS #15, as listed in Table 12-2. The standards combine to establish a common base for services required in a PKI.

Standard	Title and Description
PKCS #1	RSA Cryptography Standard: Definition of the RSA encryption standard.
PKCS #2	No longer active; it covered RSA encryption of message digests and was incorporated into PKCS #1.
PKCS #3	Diffie-Hellman Key Agreement Standard: Definition of the Diffie-Hellman key-agreement protocol.
PKCS #4	No longer active; it covered RSA key syntax and was incorporated into PKCS #1.
PKCS #5	Password-Based Cryptography Standard: Definition of a password-based encryption (PBE) method for generating a secret key.
PKCS #6	Extended-Certificate Syntax Standard: Definition of an extended certificate syntax that is being replaced by X.509 v3.
PKCS #7	Cryptographic Message Syntax Standard: Definition of the cryptographic message standard for encoded messages, regardless of encryption algorithm. Commonly replaced with PKIX Cryptographic Message Syntax.
PKCS #8	Private-Key Information Syntax Standard: Definition of a private key information format, used to store private key information.
PKCS #9	Selected Attribute Types: Definition of attribute types used in other PKCS standards.
PKCS #10	Certification Request Syntax Standard: Definition of a syntax for certification requests.
PKCS #11	Cryptographic Token Interface Standard: Definition of a technology-independent programming interface for cryptographic devices (such as smart cards).
PKCS #12	Personal Information Exchange Syntax Standard: Definition of a format for storage and transport of user private keys, certificates, and other personal information.
PKCS #13	Elliptic Curve Cryptography Standard: Description of methods for encrypting and signing messages using elliptic curve cryptography.
PKCS #14	A standard for pseudo-random number generation.
PKCS #15	Cryptographic Token Information Format Standard: Definition of a format for storing cryptographic information in cryptographic tokens.

Table 12-2 PKCS Standards

Though adopted early in the development of PKIs, some of these standards are being phased out. For example, PKCS #6 is being replaced by X.509 v3 (covered shortly in the "X.509" section) and PKCS #7 and PKCS #10 are used less, as their PKIX counterparts are being adopted.

Why You Need to Know

If you or your company are simply planning to use one of the existing certificate servers to support e-commerce, you may not need to know the specifics of these standards (except perhaps for your exam). However, if you plan to implement a private PKI to support secure services within your organization, you will need to understand what standards are out there and how the decision to use a particular PKI implementation (either home grown or commercial) may lead to incompatibilities with other certificate-issuing entities. Your business-to-business requirements must be taken into account when deciding how to implement a PKI within your organization.

X.509

So what is a certificate? In the late 1980s, the X.500 OSI Directory Standard was defined by ISO and the ITU. It was developed for implementing a network directory system, and part of this directory standard was the concept of authentication of entities within the directory. X.509 is the portion of the X.500 standard that addresses the structure of certificates used for authentication.

There have been several versions of the certificates, with version 3 being the current version (as this is being written). Each version has extended the contents of the certificates to include additional information necessary to use certificates in a PKI. The original ITU X.509 definition was published in 1988 and was formerly referred to as CCITT X.509 and is sometimes referred to as ISO/IEC/ITU 9594-8. The 1988 certificate format, version 1, was revised in 1993 as the ITU-T X.509 definition when two more fields were added to support directory access control. ITU-T is the Standards Section of the ITU created in 1992.

The 1993, version 2 specification was revised following lessons learned from implementing Internet Privacy Enhanced Mail (PEM). Version 3 added additional optional extensions for more subject identification information, key attribute information, policy information, and certification path constraints. In addition, version 3 allows additional extensions to be defined in standards or to be defined and registered by organizations or communities. Table 12-3 gives a description of the fields in a X.509 certificate.

Certificates are used to encapsulate the information needed to authenticate an entity. The X.509 specification defines a hierarchical certification structure that relies on a root certification authority that is *self-certifying* (meaning it issues its own certificate). All other certificates can be traced back to such a root through a *path*. A certificate authority issues a certificate to a uniquely identifiable entity (person, corporation, computer, and so on)—issuing a certificate to "John Smith" would cause some real problems if that were all the information you had when issuing the certificate. We are saved somewhat by the requirement that the CA determines what identifier is unique (the distinguished name), but when certificates and trust are extended between CAs, the unique identification becomes critical.

Field Name	Field Description
Certificate Signature	X.509 version used for this certificate: Version 1 = 0 Version 2 = 1 Version 3 = 2
Serial Number	A nonnegative integer assigned by the certificate issuer that must be unique to the certificate.

Signature Algorithm
  Algorithm
  Parameters (optional)
	The algorithm identifier for the algorithm used by the CA to sign the certificate. The optional "parameters" field is used to provide the cryptographic algorithm parameters used in generating the signature.

Issuer	Identification for the entity that signed and issued the certificate. This must be a distinguished name within the hierarchy of certificate authorities.

Validity
  Not valid before time
  Not valid after time
	Validity specifies a period of time during which the certificate is valid using a "not valid before" time and a "not valid after" time (expressed in UTC or in a generalized time).

Subject	The name for the certificate owner.
Subject Public Key Info	This field consists of an encryption algorithm identifier followed by a bit string for the public key.
Issuer Unique ID	Optional for versions 2 and 3—a unique bit-string identifier for the CA that issued the certificate.
Subject Unique ID	Optional for versions 2 and 3—a unique bit-string identifier for the subject of the certificate.

Extensions
  Extension ID
  Critical
  Extension Value
	Optional for version 3—the extension area consists of a sequence of extension fields containing an extension identifier, a Boolean field indicating whether the extension is critical, and an octet string representing the value of the extension. Extensions can be defined in standards or defined and registered by organizations or communities.

Thumbprint Algorithm
  Algorithm
  Parameters (optional)
	This field identifies the algorithm used by the CA to sign this certificate. This field must match the algorithm identified above.

Thumbprint	The signature is the bit-string hash value obtained when the CA signed the certificate. The signature certifies the contents of the certificate, binding the public key to the subject.

Certificate Contents (rows 1–11) | *Certificate Signature* (rows 12–13)

Table 12-3 X.509 Certificate Fields

PART V

Some other extensions to the X.509 certificate have been proposed for use in implementing a PKI. For example, PKIX identified several extensions for use in the certificate policy framework (see RFC 2427). It is essential to ensure that your PKI ignores extensions that it is not prepared to handle.

SSL/TLS

Secure Sockets Layer (SSL) and Transport Layer Security (TLS) provide the most common means of interacting with a PKI and certificates. The older SSL protocol was introduced by Netscape as a means of providing secure connections for web transfers using encryption. These two protocols provide secure connections between the client and server for exchanging information. They also provide server authentication (and optionally, client authentication) and confidentiality of information transfers.

The IETF established the TLS Working Group in 1996 to develop a standard transport layer security protocol. The working group began with SSL version 3.0 as its basis and released RFC 2246, TLS Protocol Version 1.0, in 1999 as a proposed standard. The working group also published RFC 2712, "Addition of Kerberos Cipher Suites to Transport Layer Security (TLS)," as a proposed standard, and two RFCs on the use of TLS with HTTP. Like its predecessor, TLS is a protocol that ensures privacy between communicating applications and their users on the Internet. When a server and client communicate, TLS ensures that no third party may eavesdrop or tamper with any message.

TLS is composed of two parts: the TLS Record Protocol and the TLS Handshake Protocol. The TLS Record Protocol provides connection security by using supported encryption methods, such as the Data Encryption Standard (DES). The TLS Record Protocol can also be used without encryption. The TLS Handshake Protocol allows the server and client to authenticate each other and to negotiate a session encryption algorithm and cryptographic keys before data is exchanged (http://searchVB.techtarget.com/sDefinition/0,,sid8_gci211545,00.html).

Though TLS is based on SSL and is sometimes referred to as SSL, they are not interoperable. However, the TLS protocol does contain a mechanism that allows a TLS implementation to back down to SSL 3.0. The difference between the two is in the way they perform key expansion and message authentication computations. TLS uses the MD5 and SHA1 hashing algorithms XORed together to determine the session key. The most recent browser versions support TLS. Though SSL also uses both hashing algorithms, SSL is considered less secure because the way it uses them forces a reliance on MD5 rather than SHA1.

The TLS Record Protocol is a layered protocol. At each layer, messages may include fields for length, description, and content. The Record Protocol takes messages to be transmitted, fragments the data into manageable blocks, optionally compresses the data, applies a message authentication code (MAC) to the data, encrypts it, and transmits the result. Received data is decrypted, verified, decompressed, and reassembled, and then delivered to higher-level clients.

The TLS Handshake Protocol involves the following steps, which are summarized in Figure 12-4:

1. Exchange hello messages to agree on algorithms, exchange random values, and check for session resumption.

2. Exchange the necessary cryptographic parameters to allow the client and server to agree on a pre-master secret.

3. Exchange certificates and cryptographic information to allow the client and server to authenticate themselves.

4. Generate a master secret from the pre-master secret and exchanged random values.

5. Provide security parameters to the record layer.

6. Allow the client and server to verify that their peer has calculated the same security parameters and that the handshake occurred without tampering by an attacker.

Though it has been designed to minimize this risk, TLS still has potential vulnerabilities to a man-in-the-middle attack. A highly skilled and well-placed attacker can force TLS to operate at lower security levels. Regardless, through the use of validated and trusted certificates, a secure cipher suite can be selected for the exchange of data.

Once established, a TLS session remains active as long as data is being exchanged. If sufficient inactive time has elapsed for the secure connection to time out, it can be reinitiated.

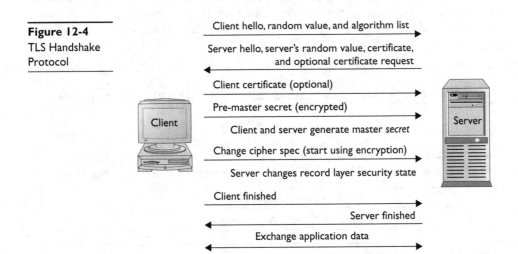

Figure 12-4
TLS Handshake Protocol

Client hello, random value, and algorithm list

Server hello, server's random value, certificate, and optional certificate request

Client certificate (optional)

Pre-master secret (encrypted)

Client and server generate master secret

Change cipher spec (start using encryption)

Server changes record layer security state

Client finished

Server finished

Exchange application data

Client

Server

PART V

ISAKMP

The Internet Security Association and Key Management Protocol (ISAKMP) provides a method for implementing a key exchange protocol and for negotiating a security policy. It defines procedures and packet formats to negotiate, establish, modify, and delete security associates. Because it is a framework, it doesn't define implementation-specific protocols, such as the key exchange protocol or hash functions. An example of ISAKMP is the Internet Key Exchange (IKE) protocol.

An important definition for understanding ISAKMP is the term *security association*. A security association (SA) is a relationship where two or more entities define how they will communicate securely. ISAKMP is intended to support security associations at all layers of the network stack. For this reason, it can be implemented on the transport level using TCP or UDP, or it can be implemented on IP directly.

Negotiation of a security association between servers occurs in two stages. First, the entities agree on how to secure negotiation messages (the ISAKMP SA). Once the entities have secured their negotiation traffic, they then determine the security associations for the protocols used for the remainder of their communications. Figure 12-5 shows the structure of the ISAKMP header. This header is used during both parts of the ISAKMP negotiation.

The initiator cookie is set by the entity requesting the SA, and the responder sets the responder cookie. The payload byte indicates the type of the first payload. Payload types include security associations, proposals, key transforms, key exchanges, vendor identities, and other things. The major and minor revision fields refer to the major version number and minor version number for the ISAKMP protocol. The exchange type helps determine the order of messages and payloads. The flag bits indicate options for the ISAKMP exchange, including whether the payload is encrypted, whether the initiator and responder have "committed" to the SA, and whether the packet is to be authenticated only (and is not encrypted). The final fields of the ISAKMP header indicate the

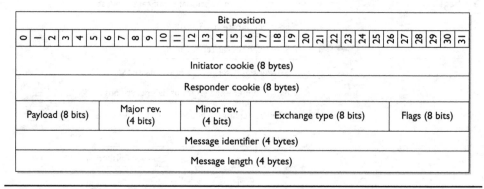

Figure 12-5   ISAKMP header format

message identifier and a message length. Payloads encapsulated within ISAKMP use a generic header, and each payload has its own header format.

Once the ISAKMP SA is established, multiple protocol SAs can be established using the single ISAKMP SA. This feature is valuable due to the overhead associated with the two-stage negotiation. SAs are valid for specific periods of time, and once the time expires, the SA must be renegotiated. For more information on the ISAKMP protocol, see Internet RFC 2408. There are also many resources for specific implementations of ISAKMP within the IPsec protocol.

CMP

The PKIX Certificate Management Protocol (CMP) is specified in RFC 2510. This protocol defines the messages and operations required to provide certificate management services within the PKIX model. Though part of the IETF PKIX effort, CMP provides a framework that works well with other standards, such as PKCS #7 and PKCS #10. CMP provides for the following certificate operations:

- CA establishment, including creation of the initial CRL and export of the public key for the CA
- Certification of an end-entity, including the following:
  - Initial registration and certification of the end-entity (registration, certificate issuance, and placement of the certificate in a repository)
  - Updates to the key pair for end-entities, required periodically and when a key pair is compromised or keys cannot be recovered
  - End-entity certificate updates, required when a certificate expires
  - Periodic CA key pair update, similar to end-entity key pair updates
  - Cross-certification requests, placed by other CAs
  - Certificate and CRL publication, performed under the appropriate conditions of certificate issuance and certificate revocation
  - Key pair recovery, a service to restore key pair information for an end-entity; for example, if a certificate password is lost or the certificate file is lost
  - Revocation requests, supporting requests by authorized entities to revoke a certificate

CMP also defines mechanisms for performing these operations, either online or offline using files, e-mail, tokens, or web operations.

PART V

XKMS

The XML Key Management Specification defines services to manage PKI operations within the Extensible Markup Language (XML) environment. These services are provided for handling PKI keys and certificates automatically. Developed by the W3C, it is intended to simplify integration of PKIs and management of certificates in applications. As well as responding to problems of authentication and verification of electronic signatures, it also allows certificates to be managed, registered, or revoked.

XKMS services reside on a separate server that interacts with an established PKI. The services are accessible via a simple XML protocol. Developers can rely on the XKMS services, making it less complex to interface with the PKI. The services provide for retrieving key information (owner, key value, key issuer, and the like) and key registration and management (such as key registration and revocation).

Retrieval operations rely on the XML signature for the necessary information. There are three tiers of service based on the client requests and application requirements.

Tier 0 provides a means of retrieving key information by embedding references to the key within the XML signature. The signature contains an element called a RetrievalMethod that indicates ways to resolve the key. In this case, the client sends a request, using the retrieval method, to obtain the desired key information. For example, if the verification key contained a long chain of X.509 v3 certificates, a retrieval method could be included to avoid sending the certificates with the document. The client would use the retrieval method to obtain the chain of certificates. For tier 0, the server indicated in the retrieval method responds directly to the request for the key, possibly bypassing the XKMS server. The tier 0 process is shown in Figure 12-6.

With tier 1 operations, the client forwards the key information portions of the XML signature to the XKMS server, relying on the server to perform the retrieval of the desired key information. The desired information may be local to the XKMS sever or it may reside on an external PKI system. The XKMS server provides no additional validation of the key information, such as checking to see if the certificate has been revoked and is still valid. Just as in tier 0, the client performs final validation of the document. Tier 1 is called the *locate service* because it locates the appropriate key information for the client, as shown in Figure 12-7.

Tier 2 is called the *validate service*, and it is illustrated in Figure 12-8. In this case, just as in tier 1, the client relies on the XKMS service to retrieve the relevant key information

Figure 12-6
Tier 0 XKMS
retrieval

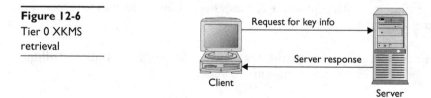

Request for key info

Server response

Client

Server

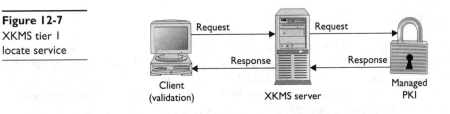

Figure 12-7
XKMS tier 1
locate service

Request ——→ Request ——→

←—— Response ←—— Response

Client
(validation)   XKMS server   Managed
PKI

from the external PKI. The XKMS server also performs a data validation on a portion of the key information provided by the client for this purpose. This validation verifies the binding of the key information with the data indicated by the key information contained in the XML signature.

The primary difference between tier 1 and tier 2 is the level of involvement of the XKMS server. In tier 1, it may serve only as a relay or gateway between the client and the PKI. In tier 2, the XKMS server is actively involved in verifying the relation between the PKI information and the document containing the XML signature.

XKMS relies on the client or underlying communications mechanism to provide for the security of the communications with the XKMS server. The specification suggests using one of three methods for ensuring server authentication, response integrity, and relevance of the response to the request. The three methods are digitally signed correspondence, a transport layer security protocol (such as SSL, TLS, or WTLS), or a packet layer security protocol (such as IPsec). Obviously, digitally signed correspondence introduces its own issues regarding validation of the signature, which is the purpose of XKMS.

It is possible to define other tiers of service. Tiers 3 and 4, an *assertion service* and an *assertion status service*, respectively, are mentioned in the defining XKMS specification, but are not defined. The specification states they "could" be defined in other documents.

XKMS also provides services for key registration, key revocation, and key recovery. Authentication for these actions is based on a password or passphrase, which is provided when the keys are registered and when they must be recovered.

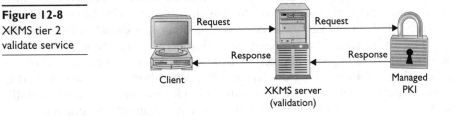

Figure 12-8
XKMS tier 2
validate service

Request ——→ Request ——→

←—— Response ←—— Response

Client
XKMS server
(validation)   Managed
PKI

S/MIME

The Secure/Multipurpose Internet Mail Extensions (S/MIME) message specification is an extension to the MIME standard that provides a way to send and receive signed and encrypted MIME data. RSA Security created the first version of the S/MIME standard, using the RSA encryption algorithm and the PKCS series of standards. The second version dates from 1998 but had a number of serious restrictions, including the restriction to 40-bit DES. The current version of the IETF standard is dated August 2002.

The changes in the S/MIME standard have been so frequent that the standard has become difficult to implement. Far from having a stable standard for several years that product manufacturers could have time to gain experience with, there have been changes to the encryption algorithms being used. Just as importantly, and not immediately clear from the IETF documents, the standard places reliance upon more than one other standard for it to function. Key amongst these is the format of a public key certificate as expressed in the X.509 standard.

The S/MIME v2 specifications outline a basic strategy to provide security services for electronic mail, but lack many security features required by the Department of Defense (DoD) for use by the military. In early 1996, the Internet Mail Consortium (IMC) was formed as a technical trade association pursuing cooperative use and enhancement of Internet electronic mail and messaging. An early goal of the IMC was to bring together the DoD (along with its vendor community) and commercial industry in order to devise a standard security protocol acceptable to both. Several existing security protocols were considered, including: MIME Object Security Services (MOSS); Pretty Good Privacy (PGP); and S/MIME v2. After examining these protocols, it was determined that none met the requirements of both the military and commercial communities. Instead of launching into a development of an entirely new set of specifications, however, the group decided that with certain enhancements the S/MIME set of specifications could be used. It was also decided that, since the discussion was about a common set of specifications to be used throughout the Internet community, it would be best if this resulting specification were brought under the control of the IETF.

Shortly after the decision was made to revise the S/MIME version 2 specifications, the DoD, its vendor community, and commercial industry met to begin development of the enhanced specifications. The new enhanced specifications would be known as S/MIME Version 3. It was quickly agreed upon by the participants that backward compatibility between the S/MIME v3 and v2 should be preserved, otherwise S/MIME v3-compatible applications would not be able to work with older S/MIME v2-compatible applications.

In order for different implementations of the new S/MIME v3 set of specifications to be interoperable, a minimum set of cryptographic algorithms were mandated. This minimum set must be implemented in an application for it to be considered S/MIME-compliant. Applications can implement additional cryptographic algorithms in order to meet their customer's needs, but the minimum set must also be present in the application for interoperability with other S/MIME applications. Thus, users are not forced to use S/MIME specified algorithms, they can choose their own, but if the application is to be considered S/MIME compliant the standard algorithms must also be present.

IETF S/MIME v3 Specifications

Building upon the original work by the IMC organized group, the IETF has worked hard to enhance the S/MIME v3 specifications. The ultimate goal is to have the S/MIME v3 specifications receive recognition as an Internet standard. The current IETF S/MIME v3 set of specifications includes:

- Cryptographic Message Syntax (CMS)
- S/MIME version 3 message specification
- S/MIME version 3 certificate handling specification
- Enhanced security services (ESS) for S/MIME

The Cryptographic Message Syntax (CMS) defines a standard syntax for transmitting cryptographic information about contents of a protected message. Originally based on the PKCS #7 version 1.5 specification the IETF S/MIME Working Group enhanced the specification to include optional security components. Just as the S/MIME version 3 provides backward compatibility with version 2, CMS provides backward compatibility with PKCS #7 so applications will be interoperable even if the new components are not implemented in a specific application.

Integrity, authentication, and nonrepudiation security features are provided by using digital signatures utilizing the SignedData syntax described by the CMS. CMS also describes what is known as the EnvelopedData syntax in order to provide confidentiality of the message's content through the use of encryption. The PKCS #7 specification supports key encryption algorithms, such as RSA. Algorithm independence is promoted through the addition of several fields to the EnvelopedData syntax in CMS which is the major difference between the PKCS #7 and CMS specifications. The goal was to be able to support specific algorithms such as Diffie-Hellman and the Key Exchange Algorithm (KEA) which is implemented on the Fortezza Crypto Card developed for the DoD. One final significant change to the original specifications is the capability to include X.509 Attribute Certificates in the SignedData and EnvelopedData syntaxes for CMS.

CMS Triple Encapsulated Message

An interesting feature of CMS is the ability to nest security envelopes to provide a combination of security features. As an example, a CMS triple-encapsulated message can be created in which the original content and associated attributes are signed and encapsulated within the inner SignedData object. The inner SignedData is in turn encrypted and encapsulated within an EnvelopedData object. The resulting EnvelopedData object is then also signed and finally encapsulated within a second SignedData object, the outer SignedData object. Usually the inner SignedData object is signed by the original user and the outer SignedData is signed by another entity such as a firewall or a mail list agent providing an additional level of security. It should be mentioned that this triple-encapsulation is not required of every CMS object. All that is required is a single SignedData object created by the user in order to sign a message or an EnvelopedData object if the user desired to encrypt a message.

PGP

Pretty Good Privacy (PGP) is a popular program that has been around for several years to encrypt and decrypt e-mail and files. It also provides the ability to digitally sign a message so the receiver can be certain of the sender's identity. Taken together, encrypting and signing a message, the receiver can be positive of who sent it and can be assured that it was not modified during transmission. Public domain versions of PGP have been available for years as well as inexpensive commercial versions. It is one of the most widely used programs and is frequently used by both individuals and businesses to ensure data and e-mail privacy. It was developed by Philip R. Zimmermann in 1991 and quickly became a de facto standard for e-mail security.

How It Works

PGP uses a variation of the standard public key encryption process. In public key encryption, the user (utilizing the encryption program) creates a pair of keys. One key is known as the public key and is designed to be given freely to others. The other key is called the private key and is designed to be known only by the creator. Individuals wishing to send a private message to the user will encrypt the message using the user's public key. The algorithm is designed such that only the private key can decrypt the message so only the user will be able to decrypt it. The method, known as public key or asymmetric encryption, is time consuming. Symmetric encryption which uses only a single key is generally faster. It is because of this that PGP is designed the way it is. PGP uses a symmetric encryption algorithm to encrypt the message to be sent. It then encrypts the symmetric key used to encrypt this message with the public key of the intended recipient. Both the encrypted key and message is then sent. The receiver's version of PGP will first decrypt the symmetric key with the private key supplied by the recipient and then uses the resulting decrypted key to decrypt the rest of the message.

PGP can utilize two different public key algorithms—Rivest-Shamir-Adleman (RSA) or Diffie-Hellman. The RSA version uses the IDEA algorithm to generate a short symmetric key to be used to encrypt the message and RSA to encrypt the short IDEA key. The Diffie-Hellman version uses the CAST algorithm to encrypt the message and the Diffie-Hellman algorithm to encrypt the CAST key.

In order to generate a digital signature, PGP takes advantage of another property of public key encryption schemes. Normally the sender will encrypt using the receiver's public key and the message will be decrypted at the other end using the receiver's private key. The process can be reversed such that the sender encrypts with his own private key. The receiver then decrypts the message with the sender's public key. Since the sender is the only individual who has a key that will correctly be decrypted with the sender's public key, the receiver knows that the message was created by the sender who claims to have sent it. The way PGP accomplishes this task is to generate a hash value from the user's name and other signature information. This hash value is then encrypted with the sender's private key known only by the sender. The receiver uses the sender's public key, which is available to everyone, to decrypt the hash value. If the decrypted hash value matches the hash value sent as the digital signature for the message, then the receiver is assured that the message was sent by the sender who claims to have sent it.

Typically, versions of PGP will contain a user interface that works with common e-mail programs such as Outlook. If you want others to be able to send you an encrypted message, you will need to register your public key that was generated by your PGP program with a PGP public-key server. Alternatively you will have to send your public key to all those who want to send you an encrypted message or post your key to some location they can download it from such as your web page. Note that using a public-key server is the better method for all of the reasons of trust described in the discussions of PKIs found in Chapter 11. In order to help promote the use of public-key encryption, Network Associates maintains an LDAP/HTTP public-key server with hundreds of thousands of registered public keys.

Where Can You Use PGP?

For many years the U.S. government raged a fight over the exportation of PGP technology and for many years its exportation was illegal. Today, however, PGP encrypted e-mail can be exchanged with most users outside the U.S. and many versions of PGP are available from numerous sites overseas. Of course, being able to exchange PGP encrypted e-mail requires the individuals on both sides of the communication to have valid versions of PGP. Interestingly, international versions of PGP are just as secure as domestic versions—a feature that is not true of other encryption products. It should be noted that the freeware versions of PGP are not licensed for commercial purposes.

HTTPS

Most web activity occurs using the Hypertext Transfer Protocol (HTTP), but it is also prone to interception. HTTPS uses the Secure Sockets Layer (SSL) to transfer information. Originally developed by Netscape Communications and implemented in their browser, HTTPS has since been incorporated into most common browsers. It uses the open standard SSL to encrypt data at the application layer. In addition, HTTPS uses the standard port 443 for TCP/IP communications rather than the standard port 80 used for HTTP. HTTPS makes use of the 40-bit RC4 encryption algorithm in most cases. A 128-bit version is also implemented.

IPsec

IPsec (Internet Protocol Security) is a collection of IP security features designed to introduce security at the network or packet-processing layer in network communication. Other approaches have attempted to incorporate security at higher levels of the TCP/IP protocol suite such as at the level where applications reside. IPsec is designed to be used to provide secure virtual private network capability over the Internet. In essence, what IPsec does is provide a secure version of the Internet Protocol by introducing authentication and encryption at the packet level. IPsec is optional for the current version of the IP protocol (IPv4) but is required for the next release (IPv6). Obviously both ends of the communication need to use IPsec for the encryption/decryption process to occur.

IPsec provides two types of security service to ensure authentication and confidentiality for either the data alone (referred to as IPsec transport mode) or for both the data and header (referred to as tunnel mode). IPsec introduces several new protocols including the Authentication Header (AH), which basically provides authentication of the sender, and the Encapsulating Security Payload (ESP), which adds encryption of the data to ensure confidentiality. IPsec also provides for payload compression before encryption using IPcomp. Frequently encryption negatively impacts the ability to fully compress data for transmission. By providing the ability to compress the data before encryption, IPsec addresses this issue.

CEP

Certificate Enrollment Protocol (CEP) was originally developed by VeriSign for Cisco Systems. It was designed to support certificate issuance, distribution, and revocation using existing technologies. Its use has grown in client and CA applications. The operations supported include CA and RA public key distribution, certificate enrollment, certificate revocation, certificate query, and CRL query.

One of the key goals of CEP was to use existing technology where possible. It uses both PKCS #7 (Cryptographic Message Syntax Standard) and PKCS #10 (Certification Request Syntax Standard) to define a common message syntax. It supports access to certificates and CRLs using either LDAP or the CEP-defined certificate query.

FIPS

The Federal Information Processing Standards Publications (FIPS PUBS or simply FIPS) describe various standards for data communication issues. These documents are issued by the U.S. government through the National Institute of Standards and Technology (NIST) who is tasked with their development. NIST develops these publications when there is a compelling government need for a standard for use in areas such as security or system interoperability when there is no recognized industry standard. There are three categories of FIPS PUBS currently maintained by NIST. These categories are:

- Hardware and Software Standards/Guidelines
- Data standards/guidelines
- Computer security standards/guidelines

It is obviously this last category that we are most interested in. One way that these documents are used is to require products sold to the U.S. government to comply with one (or more) of the FIPS standards. The standards can be obtained from http://www.itl.nist.gov/fipspubs.

Common Criteria (CC)

The Common Criteria (CC) are the result of an effort to develop a joint set of security processes and standards that could be used by the international community. The major contributors to the CC are the governments of the U.S., Canada, France, Germany, the Netherlands, and the United Kingdom. The CC also provides a listing of laboratories that apply the criteria in the testing of security products. Products that are evaluated by one of the approved laboratories receive an Evaluation Assurance Level of EAL1 through EAL7 (EAL7 is the highest level) with EAL4, for example, designed for environments requiring a moderate to high level of independently assured security, and EAL1 being designed for environments in which some confidence in the correct operation of the system is required but where the threats to the system are not seen as serious. The Common Criteria also provide a listing of products by function that have performed at a specific Evaluation Assurance Level.

WTLS

The Wireless Transport Layer Security (WTLS) protocol is based on the Transport Layer Security (TLS) protocol. WTLS provides reliability and security for wireless communications using the Wireless Application Protocol (WAP). WTLS is necessary due to the limited memory and processing capabilities of WAP-enabled phones.

WTLS can be implemented in one of three classes. Class 1 is called anonymous authentication but is not designed for practical use. Class 2 is called server authentication and is the most common model. The clients and server may authenticate using different means. Class 3 is server and client authentication. In Class 3 authentication, the client and server's WTLS certificates are authenticated. Class 3 is the strongest form of authentication and encryption.

WEP

The Wired Equivalent Privacy (WEP) algorithm is part of the 802.11 standard and is used to protect wireless communications from interception. A secondary function is to prevent access to a wireless network from unauthorized access. WEP relies on a secret key that is shared between a mobile station and an access point. In most installations, a single key is used by all of the mobile stations and access points.

WEP Security Issues

In modern corporate environments it is not uncommon to have wireless networks created in which systems with 802.11 network interface cards communicate with wireless access points which connect the computer to the corporations network. WEP is an optional security protocol specified in the 802.11 standard designed to address the security needs in this wireless environment. It uses a 24-bit initialization vector as a seed value to begin the security association. This, in itself, is a potential security problem as there are only just over sixteen million possible vectors with 24 bits. At the speeds modern networks operate, it does not take long before initialization vectors will repeat. The secret key is only 40 to 64 bits in length, another problem since it does not take too long to brute-force break encryption schemes utilizing key lengths this short. Some vendors are providing 128-bit WEP 2 keys in their products to overcome the short encryption key length. In addition, the WEP keys are static. It is up to the system administrator to manually change WEP keys. One final problem with WEP is that many wireless network implementations do not even come with WEP enabled.

ISO 17799

ISO 17799 is a very popular and detailed standard for creating and implementing security policies. ISO 17799 is based on Version 2 of the British Standard 7799 (BS7799) published in May 1999. With the increased emphasis placed on security in both the government and industry over the last few years, many organizations are now training their audit personnel to evaluate their organization against the ISO 17799 standard. The standard is divided into ten sections, each containing more detailed statements describing what is involved for that topic. The ten major sections, as originally detailed in BS7799, are:

- Business continuity planning
- System access control
- System development and maintenance
- Physical and environmental security
- Compliance
- Personnel security
- Security organization
- Computer and network management
- Asset classification and control
- Security policy

Chapter Review

Chapter 11 discussed the various components of a public key infrastructure (PKI). This chapter continued the discussion with the many different standards and protocols that have been implemented to support PKI. Standards and protocols are important because they define the basis for how communication will take place. Without these protocols, two entities may independently develop their own method to implement the various components for a PKI, as described in Chapter 11, and the two will not be compatible. On the Internet, not being compatible and not being able to communicate is not an option.

Three main standards have evolved over time to implement PKI on the Internet. Both are based on a third standard, the X.509 standard, and establish complimentary standards for implementing PKI. These two standards are Public Key Infrastructure X.509 (PKIX) and Public Key Cryptography Standards (PKCS). PKIX defines standards for interactions and operations for four component types: the user (end-entity), certificate authority (CA), registration authority (RA), and the repository for certificates and certificate revocation lists (CRLs). PKCS defines many of the lower-level standards for message syntax, cryptographic algorithms, and the like.

There are other protocols and standards that help define the management and operation of the PKI and related services, such as ISAKMP, XKMS, and CMP. WEP is used to encrypt wireless communications in an 802.11 environment and S/MIME for e-mail; SSL, TLS, and WTLS are used for secure packet transmission; and IPsec and PPTP are used to support virtual private networks.

The Common Criteria establishes a series of criteria from which security products can be evaluated. The ISO 17799 standard provides a point from which security policies and practices can be developed in ten areas. Various types of publications are available from NIST such as those found in the FIPS series.

Questions

1. Which organization created PKCS?

   A. RSA

   B. IEEE

   C. OSI

   D. ISO

2. Which of the following is not part of a public key infrastructure?

   A. Certificates

   B. Certificate revocation list (CRL)

    C. Substitution cipher

    D. Certificate authority (CA)

3. Which of the following is used to grant permissions using rule-based, role-based, and rank-based access controls?

    A. Attribute Certificate

    B. Qualified Certificate

    C. Control Certificate

    D. Operational Certificate

4. Transport Layer Security consists of which two protocols?

    A. TLS Record Protocol and TLS Certificate Protocol

    B. TLS Certificate Protocol and TLS Handshake Protocol

    C. TLS Key Protocol and TLS Handshake Protocol

    D. TLS Record Protocol and TLS Handshake Protocol

5. Which of the following provides connection security by using common encryption methods?

    A. TLS Certificate Protocol

    B. TLS Record Protocol and TLS Handshake Protocol

    C. TLS Handshake Protocol

    D. TLS Key Protocol

6. Which of the following provides a method for implementing a key exchange protocol?

    A. EISA

    B. ISA

    C. ISAKMP

    D. ISAKEY

7. A relationship where two or more entities define how they will communicate securely is known as what?

    A. Security association

    B. Security agreement

    C. Three-way agreement

    D. Three-way handshake

8. The entity requesting an SA sets what?

   A. Initiator cookie

   B. Process ID

   C. Session number

   D. Session ID

9. What protocol is used to establish a CA?

   A. Certificate Management Protocol

   B. Internet Key Exchange Protocol

   C. Secure Sockets Layer

   D. Public Key Infrastructure

10. What is the purpose of XKMS?

   A. Encapsulates session associations over TCP/IP

   B. Extends session associations over many transport protocols

   C. Designed to replace SSL

   D. Defines services to manage heterogeneous PKI operations via XML

11. Which of the following is a secure e-mail standard?

   A. POP3

   B. IMAP

   C. S/MIME

   D. SMTP

12. Secure Sockets Layer uses what port to communicate?

   A. 143

   B. 80

   C. 443

   D. 53

Answers

1. A. RSA Laboratories created Public Key Cryptography Standards (PKCS).

2. C. The substitution cipher is not a component of PKI. The substitution cipher is an elementary alphabet-based cipher.

3. A.

4. **D.** Transport Layer Security consists of the TLS Record Protocol, which provides security, and the TLS Handshake Protocol, which allows the server and client to authenticate each other.

5. **B.** The TLS Record Protocol provides connection security by using common encryption methods, such as DES.

6. **C.** The Internet Security Association and Key Management Protocol (ISAKMP) provides a method for implementing a key exchange protocol and for negotiating a security policy.

7. **A.** During a security association, the client and the server will list the types of encryption they are capable of and will choose the most secure encryption standard that they have in common.

8. **A.** The entity requesting a security association will request an initiator cookie.

9. **A.** The Certificate Management Protocol is used to establish a CA.

10. **D.** XML Key Management Specification (XKMS) allows services to manage PKI via XML, which is interoperable across different vendor platforms.

11. **C.** Secure/Multipurpose Internet Mail Extensions (S/MIME) is a secure e-mail standard. Other popular standards include Pretty Good Privacy (PGP) and OpenPGP.

12. **C.** SSL's well-known port is 443. SSL was developed by Netscape.

PART VI

Operational Security

Operational/ Organizational Security

13

In this chapter, you will

- Learn about the various operational aspects to security in your organization
- See what physical security components can protect your computers and network
- Confront social engineering as a means to gain access to computers and networks and how your organization should deal with it
- Consider the growing use of wireless cellular technology for data transmission and how factors such as location affect our ability to secure it
- Explore the use of shielding technology to prevent disclosure through electronic emanations
- Learn about the different types of fires and the various fire suppression systems designed to limit the damage caused by fires

Recall from Chapter 1 the operational model of computer security. The model described the various components in computer and network security. Specifically, the operational model of computer security stated that:

Protection = Prevention + (Detection + Response)

Security Operations in Your Organization

Prevention technologies are designed to keep individuals from being able to gain access to systems or data they are not authorized to use. Originally, this was the sole approach to security. Eventually we learned that in an operational environment, prevention was extremely difficult and relying on prevention technologies alone was not sufficient. This led to the rise of technologies to detect and respond to events that occur when prevention failed. Together, these form the operational model for computer security.

Prevention technologies are static. They are put in place and generally left alone. Detection and response technologies, on the other hand, are dynamic in the sense that they acknowledge that security is an ongoing process. Systems and networks are constantly changing. They therefore need to be constantly monitored. Monitoring the operation of the various components that make up your security perimeter is an essential part of any organization's security program.

Policies, Procedures, Standards, and Guidelines

An important part of any organization's approach to implementing security are the policies, procedures, standards, and guidelines that are established to detail what users and administrators should be doing to maintain the security of the systems and network. Collectively, these documents provide the guidance needed to determine how security will be implemented in the organization. Given this guidance, the specific technology and security mechanisms required can be planned for.

Policies are high-level, broad statements of what the organization wants to accomplish. Standards are mandatory elements regarding the implementation of a policy. Some standards may be externally driven. Regulations for banking and financial institutions, for example, may require certain security measures be taken by law. Other standards may be set by the organization for its own goals. Guidelines are recommendations relating to a policy. The key term in this case is recommendation—guidelines are not mandatory steps. Procedures are the step-by-step instructions on how to implement policies in the organization.

Just as the network itself constantly changes, the policies, procedures, and guidelines should be living documents that are periodically evaluated and changed if necessary. The constant monitoring of the network and the periodic review of the relevant documents are part of the process that is the operational model. This operational process roughly consists of four steps:

1. Plan (adjust)
2. Implement
3. Monitor
4. Evaluate

The first step is to plan for security in your organization. In this step, you develop the policies, procedures, and guidelines that will be implemented and design the security components that will protect your network. Once these are designed and developed, you can implement the plans. Next you monitor to ensure that both the hardware and the software as well as the policies, procedures, and guidelines are effective in securing your systems. Finally, you evaluate the effectiveness of the security measures you have in place. This step may include a vulnerability assessment and penetration test of your system to ensure the security is adequate. After evaluating your security posture, you begin again with step one, this time adjusting the security mechanisms you have in place, and then continue with this cyclical process.

The Security Perimeter

The discussion to this point has not included any mention of the specific technology used to enforce operational and organizational security or a description of the various components that constitute the organization's security perimeter. If the average administrator were asked to draw a diagram depicting the various components of their network, the diagram would probably look something like Figure 13-1.

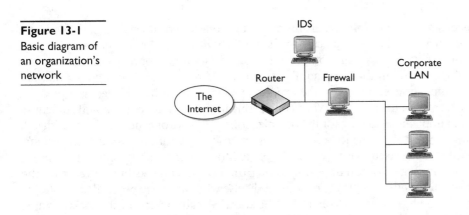

Figure 13-1
Basic diagram of an organization's network

This diagram includes the major components typically found in a network. There is some connection to the Internet. This connection will generally have some sort of protection attached to it such as a firewall. An intrusion detection system will also often be part of the security perimeter for the organization. This may be on the inside of the firewall, or the outside, or it may in fact be on both sides, the specific location depending on the company and what they are more concerned with preventing (i.e., the insider threat or external threats). Beyond this security perimeter is the corporate network. This is obviously a very simple depiction—an actual network may have numerous subnets and extranets—but the basic components are present. Unfortunately, if this were the diagram provided by the administrator to show the organization's basic network structure, the administrator would have missed a very important component. A more astute administrator would provide a diagram more like Figure 13-2.

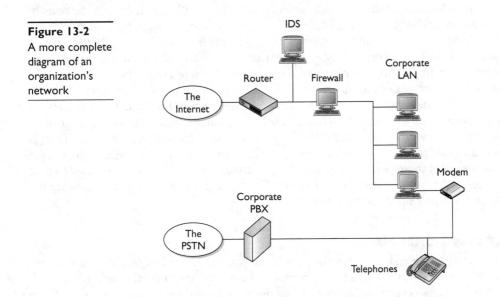

Figure 13-2
A more complete diagram of an organization's network

This diagram includes the other important network found in every organization, the telephone network that is connected to the public switched telephone network (PSTN), otherwise known as the phone company. The organization may or may not have any authorized modems, but the savvy administrator would realize that because the potential exists for unauthorized modems, the telephone network must be included as a possible source of access for the network. When considering the policies, procedures, and guidelines needed to implement security for the organization, both networks need to be considered.

While Figure 13-2 provides a more comprehensive view of the various components that need to be protected, it is still incomplete. Most experts will agree that the biggest danger to any organization does not come from external attacks but rather from the insider—a disgruntled employee or somebody else who may have physical access to the facility. Given physical access to an office, the knowledgeable attacker will quickly be able to find the information needed to gain access to the organization's computer systems and network. Consequently, every organization also needs security policies, procedures, and guidelines that cover physical security, and every security administrator should be concerned with these as well. While physical security will probably not fall under the purview of the security administrator, the operational state of the organization's physical security measures is just as important as many of the other network-centric measures.

Physical Security

Physical security consists of all mechanisms used to ensure that physical access to the computer systems and networks is restricted to only authorized users. Additional physical security mechanisms may be used to provide increased security for especially sensitive systems such as servers and devices such as routers, firewalls, and intrusion detection systems. When considering physical security, access from all six sides should be considered. Not only should the security of obvious points of entry be examined, such as doors and windows, but the walls themselves as well as the floor and ceiling should also be considered. Is there a false ceiling with tiles that can be easily removed? Do the walls extend to the actual ceiling or only to this false ceiling? Is there a raised floor? Do the walls extend to the actual floor, or do they stop at the raised floor? How are important systems situated? Do the monitors face away from windows, or could the activity of somebody at a system be monitored? Who has access to the facility? What type of access control is there, and are there any guards? Who is allowed unsupervised access to the facility? Is there an alarm system or security camera that covers the area? What procedures govern the monitoring of these and the response should unauthorized activity be detected? These are just some of the numerous questions that need to be asked when examining the physical security surrounding a system.

Access Controls

The purpose of physical access controls is the same as that of computer and network access controls—you want to restrict access to those who are authorized to have it. Similarly, physical access controls can be based on something the individual has, something they know, or something they are.

The most common physical access control device, which has been around in some form for centuries, is a lock. Combination locks represent an access control device that depends on something the individual knows (the combination). Locks with keys depend on something the individual has (the key). Each of these has certain advantages and disadvantages. Combinations don't require any extra hardware, but they must be remembered (which means individuals may write them down—a security vulnerability in itself) and are hard to control. Anybody who knows the combination may provide it to somebody else. Key locks are simple and easy to use, but the key may be lost, which means another has to be made or the lock rekeyed. Keys may also be copied and can be hard to control the dissemination of. Newer locks replace the traditional key with a card that must be passed through a reader or placed against it. The individual may also have to provide a personal access code, thus making this form of access both a something-you-know and something-you-have method. In addition to locks on doors, other common physical security devices include video surveillance and even simpler access control logs (sign-in logs). While sign-in logs don't provide an actual barrier, they do provide a record of access, and when used in conjunction with a guard who verifies an individual's identity, they can dissuade potential adversaries from attempting to gain access to a facility.

Another common access control mechanism is a human security guard. Many organizations employ a guard to provide an extra level of examination of individuals wanting to gain access. Other devices are limited to their designed function. A human guard can apply common sense to situations that might have been unexpected. Having security guards also addresses the common practice of piggybacking, where an individual follows another person closely to avoid having to go through the access control procedures. For example, if one employee enters the combination to a door and then opens it, another individual might follow quickly behind before the door closes to avoid having to enter the combination. A security guard checking each individual's identification would eliminate this problem.

Biometrics

Access controls that utilize something you know (e.g., combinations) or something you have (e.g., keys) are not the only methods to limit facility access to authorized individuals. A third approach is to utilize something unique about the individual, their fingerprints, for example, to identify them. Unlike the other two methods, the something you are, known as biometrics, does not rely on the individual to either remember something or to have something in their possession. Biometrics is a more sophisticated access control approach and is also more expensive. Other methods to accomplish biometrics include handwriting analysis, retinal scans, iris scans, voiceprints, hand geometry, and facial geometry.

Biometrics can be used to control access to computer systems and networks as well as to serve as a physical access control device. Used for physical access control, however, this approach allows for methods that are not generally used in biometric access control for computer systems and networks. Hand geometry, for example, requires a fairly large device. This can easily be placed outside of a door to control access to the room but would not be as convenient to control access to a computer system, since a reader would need to be placed with each computer or at least with groups of computers. In a mobile environment where laptops are being used, a device such as a hand geometry reader would be unrealistic.

PART VI

To add an additional layer of security, biometrics are normally used in conjunction with another method. An individual might, for example, be required to also provide a personal access code or to pass a card through a reader, and thus the individual would also need something you have and something you know. While it may seem at first that nothing else should be needed besides a biometric access control, the biometric devices currently in use are not 100 percent accurate and have been known to allow access to individuals who were not authorized. This is the reason for the additional something you know or something you have method to supplement the biometric device.

It should be pointed out that all forms of authentication have weaknesses that can be exploited. It is for this reason that "strong authentication" or "two-factor authentication" is often used. These methods use two of the three different types of authentication (something you have, know, or are) to provide two levels of security. Which two are used in combination depends on a number of factors, including user acceptance, budget, and the exact level of security the organization is trying to obtain.

Physical Barriers

An even more common security feature than locks (using the term device to describe them is unusual) is a physical barrier. Physical barriers help implement the physical-world equivalent of layered security. The outermost layer of physical security should contain the more public activities. A guard at a gate in a fence, for example, would be visible by all who happen to pass by. As you progress through the layers, the barriers and security mechanisms should become less public to make it more difficult for observers to determine what mechanisms are in place. Signs are also an important element in security, as they announce to the public what areas are public and which are private. In addition to walls and fences, open space can also serve as a barrier. While this may at first seem to be an odd statement, consider the use of large areas of open space. For an intruder to cross this open space takes time—time in which they are vulnerable and their presence may be discovered. In today's environment in which terrorist attacks have become more common, areas that may be considered a possible target for terrorist activity should take additional precautions. In addition to open space, which is necessary to lessen the effect of explosions, concrete barriers that will stop vehicles from getting too close to facilities should also be used. It is not necessary for these to be unsightly concrete walls; many facilities have placed large, round concrete circles, filled them with dirt, and then planted flowers and other plants to construct a large, immovable, planter.

Social Engineering

Social engineering is the process of convincing an authorized individual to provide confidential information or access to an unauthorized individual. Social engineering takes advantage of what continually turns out to be the weakest point in our security perimeter—the humans. Kevin Mitnick, a convicted cybercriminal turned security consultant, once stated "Don't rely on network safeguards and firewalls to protect your information. Look to your most vulnerable spot. You'll usually find that vulnerability lies in your people." In 2000 after being released from jail, Mitnick testified before Congress and spoke on several other occasions about social engineering and how effective it is. He stated that he "rarely had to resort to a technical attack" because of how easily information and access could be obtained through social engineering.

Individuals who are attempting to social-engineer some piece of information generally rely on two aspects of human nature. First, most people generally want to help somebody who is requesting help. Second, people generally want to avoid confrontation. The knowledgeable social engineer may call a help desk pretending to be a new employee needing help to log on to the organization's network. By doing so, valuable information may be obtained as to the type of system or network that is being employed. After making this call, a second call may be made that uses the information from the first call to provide background for the second call so that the next individual the attacker attempts to obtain information from will not suspect it is an unauthorized individual asking the questions. This works because people generally will assume that somebody is who they claim to be, especially if they have information that would be known by the individual they claim to be.

If the pleasant approach doesn't work, a more aggressive approach may be attempted. People will normally want to avoid unpleasant confrontations and will also not want to get into trouble with their superiors. An attacker, knowing this, may attempt to obtain information by threatening to go to the individual's supervisor or by claiming that they are working for somebody who is high up in the organization's management structure. Because employees want to avoid both a confrontation and a possible reprimand, they may provide the information requested even though they may realize that it is against the organization's policies or procedures.

The goal of social engineering is to gradually obtain the pieces of information necessary to make it to the next step. This is done repeatedly until the ultimate goal is reached. If social engineering is such an effective means of gaining unauthorized access to data and information, how can it be stopped? The most effective means is through the training and education of users, administrators, and security personnel. All employees should be instructed in the techniques that attackers might use and trained to recognize when a social engineering attack is being attempted. One important aspect of this training is for employees to recognize the type of information that should be protected and also how seemingly unimportant information may be combined with other pieces of information to potentially divulge sensitive information. This is known as *data aggregation*.

Environment

Environmental issues may not at first seem to be of a security concern, but when considering the availability of a computer system or network, they must be taken into consideration. Environmental issues include items such as heating, ventilation, and air conditioning (HVAC) systems, electrical power, and the "environments of nature." HVAC systems are used to maintain the comfort of an office environment. A few years back, they were also critical for the smooth operation of computer systems that had low tolerances for humidity and heat. Today's systems are much more tolerant, and the limiting factor is now often the human user. One interesting aspect of HVAC systems is that they themselves are often computer controlled and frequently provide remote access via telephone connections. These connections should be protected in a similar manner to computer modems, or else attackers may locate them and change the HVAC settings for an office or building.

Electrical power is obviously an essential requirement for computer systems and networks. Electrical power is subject to momentary surges and disruption. Surge protectors are needed to protect sensitive electronic equipment from fluctuations in voltage. Uninterruptible power supplies (UPSs) should be considered for critical systems so that a loss of power will not halt processing. The size of the batteries associated with a UPS will determine the amount of time that it can operate before it too loses power. Many sites ensure sufficient power to provide administrators the opportunity to cleanly bring the system or network down. For installations that require continual operations, even in the event of a power outage, electric generators may be purchased that can automatically start when a loss of power is detected. These systems may take a few seconds to start before they reach full operation, so a UPS should also be considered to smooth the transition between normal and backup power.

The frequency of natural disasters is a contributing factor that must be considered when making contingency processing plans for an installation. In an area that experiences frequent electric storms, for example, power surge protectors and UPSs are an absolute must. Frequent storms and floods may require devices that can sense water building up in a facility to warn of pending problems. Frequent hurricanes, earthquakes, and tornadoes in an area may require reinforced facilities to protect important processing equipment. All of these provide reasons for not only having an active program to ensure frequent backup of critical data, but off-site storage as well. Off-site storage limits the chance that a natural disaster affecting one area will result in the total loss of the organization's critical data. When considering backup and contingency plans, it is also important to consider a backup processing location in case a disaster not only destroys the data at the organization's primary site but all processing equipment as well.

Fire Suppression

According to the Fire Suppression Systems Association, 43 percent of businesses closed as a result of a fire never reopen. An additional 29 percent will fail within three years of the event. The ability to respond to a fire quickly and effectively is thus critical to the long-term success of any organization. Addressing potential fire hazards and vulnerabilities has long been a concern of organizations in their risk analysis process. The goal should obviously be never to have a fire, but in the event that one does occur, it is important that mechanisms are in place to limit the damage the fire can cause.

Water-Based Fire Suppression Systems

Water-based fire suppression systems have long been, and still are today, the primary tool to address and control structural fires. With the amount of electrical equipment found in today's office environment and since, for obvious reasons, this equipment does not react well to large applications of water, it is important to know what to do with equipment if it does become subjected to a water-based sprinkler system. The 1992 National Fire Protection Association Standard 75 on Electronic Computer/Data Processing Equipment outlines measures that can be taken to minimize the damage to electronic equipment exposed to water. This guidance includes these suggestions:

- Open cabinet doors, remove side panels and covers, and pull out chassis drawers to allow water to run out of equipment.

- Set up fans to move room-temperature air through the equipment for general drying. Move portable equipment to dry air-conditioned areas.

- Use compressed air at no higher than 50 psi to blow out trapped water.

- Use hand-held dryers on lowest setting to dry connectors, backplane wirewraps, and printed circuit cards.

CAUTION   Keep the dryer well away from components and wires. Overheating of electrical components can cause permanent damage.

- Use cotton-tipped swabs for hard-to-reach places. Lightly dab the surfaces to remove residual moisture. Do not use cotton-tipped swabs on wirewrap terminals.

- Water-displacement aerosol sprays containing Freon-alcohol mixtures are effective as a first step in drying critical components. Follow up with professional restoration as soon as possible.

NOTE   The preceding list provides useful, albeit somewhat dated, guidance. Users will probably not see wirewrap terminals, and other compounds are now available to replace the Freon-alcohol mixture described. Overall, however, the guidance is still sound and provides a useful starting point to begin cleanup operations from.

Even if these guidelines are followed, damage to the systems may have already occurred. Since water is so destructive to electronic equipment, not only because of the immediate problems of electronic shorts to the system but also because of longer-term corrosive damage water can cause, alternative fire suppression methods have been sought. One of the more common alternative methods used was Halon-based systems.

Halon-Based Fire Suppression Systems

A fire needs fuel, oxygen, and high temperatures for the chemical combustion to occur. If you remove any of these, the fire will not continue. Halon interferes with the chemical combustion present in a fire. Even though Halon production was banned in 1994, a number of these systems still exist today. They were originally popular because Halon will mix quickly with the air in a room and will not cause harm to computer systems. Halon is also dangerous to humans, especially when subjected to extremely hot temperatures (such as might be found during a fire), when it can degrade into other toxic chemicals.

PART VI

As a result of these dangers, and also because Halon has been linked with the issue of ozone depletion, Halon is no longer allowed to be used in new fire suppression systems. It is important to note that under the Environmental Protection Agency (EPA) rules that mandated no further production of Halon, existing systems were not required to be destroyed. Replacing the Halon in a discharged system, however, will be a problem, since only existing stockpiles of Halon may be used and the cost is becoming prohibitive. For this reason, many organizations are switching to alternative solutions. These alternatives are known as Clean Agent Fire Suppression Systems, since they not only provide fire suppression capabilities but also protect the contents of the room including people, documents, and electronic equipment. Examples of clean agents include carbon dioxide, Argon, Inergen, and FM200 (heptafluoropropane).

Clean-Agent Fire Suppression Systems

The use of Carbon Dioxide (CO_2) as a fire suppression agent have been known for a long time. The Bell Telephone Company used portable CO_2 extinguishers in the early part of the twentieth century. Carbon Dioxide extinguishers attack all three necessary elements for a fire to occur. CO_2 will displace oxygen so that the amount of oxygen remaining is insufficient to sustain the fire. It also provides some cooling in the fire zone and will also reduce the concentration of "gasified" fuel. Argon extinguishes fire by lowering the oxygen concentration below the 15 percent level required for combustible items to burn. Argon systems are designed to reduce the oxygen content to about 12.5 percent, which is below the 15 percent needed for the fire but is still above the 10 percent required by the EPA for human safety. INERGEN is composed of three gases: 52 percent nitrogen, 40 percent argon, and 8 percent carbon dioxide. In a manner similar to pure Argon systems, INERGEN systems reduce the level of oxygen to about 12.5 percent, which is sufficient for human safety but not sufficient to sustain a fire. Another chemical used to phase out Halon is FE-13, or trifluoromethane. This chemical was originally developed as a chemical refrigerant and works to suppress fires by raising the total heat capacity of the environment. FE-13 is gaseous and leaves behind no residue that would harm equipment and is considered safe to use in occupied areas.

Handheld Fire Extinguishers

Automatic fire suppression systems designed to discharge when a fire is detected are not the only systems you should be aware of. If a fire can be caught and contained before the automatic systems discharge, it can mean significant savings to the organization in terms of both time and equipment costs (including the recharging of the automatic system). Handheld extinguishers are common in offices, but the correct use of them must be understood or disaster can occur. There are four different types of fire, as shown in Table 13-1. Each type of fire has its own fuel source and method for extinguishing it. Type A systems, for example, are designed to extinguish fires with normal combustible material as the fire's source. Water can be used in an extinguisher of this sort, since it is effective against fires of this type. Water, as we've discussed, is not appropriate for fires involving wiring or electrical equipment. Using a type A extinguisher against an electrical fire will not only be ineffective but can result in additional damage. Some extinguishers are designed to be effective against more

Class of Fire	Type of Fire	Examples of Combustible Material	Examples of Suppression Methods
A	Common Combustibles	Wood, paper, cloth, plastics	Water or dry chemical
B	Combustible Liquids	Petroleum products, organic solvents	CO_2 or dry chemical
C	Electrical	Electrical wiring and equipment, power tools	CO_2 or dry chemical
D	Flammable Metals	magnesium, titanium	Copper metal or sodium chloride

Table 13-1   Types of Fire and Suppression Methods

than one type of fire, such as the common ABC fire extinguishers. This is probably the best type of system to have in a data processing facility. All fire extinguishers should be easily accessible and should be clearly marked. Before anybody uses an extinguisher, they should know what type of extinguisher it is and what the source of the fire is. When in doubt, get out and let the fire department handle the situation.

Fire Detection Devices

Going hand-in-hand with fire suppression are fire detection devices (fire detectors). Detectors can be useful because some may be able to detect a fire in its very early stages before a fire suppression system is activated, and they can potentially sound a warning. This warning could provide employees the opportunity to address the fire before it becomes serious enough for the fire suppression equipment to kick in.

There are several different types of fire detectors. One type, of which there are two varieties, is activated by smoke. The two forms smoke detectors come in are ionization and photoelectric. A photoelectric detector is good for potentially providing advance warning of a smoldering fire. This type of device monitors an internal beam of light. If something degrades the light, for example by obstructing it, the detector assumes it is something like smoke and the alarm sounds. An ionization style of detector uses an ionization chamber and a small radioactive source to detect fast-burning fires. Shown in Figure 3-3, the chamber consists of two plates, one with a positive charge and one with a negative charge. Oxygen and nitrogen particles in the air become "ionized" (an ion is freed from the molecule). The freed ion, which will have a negative charge, will be attracted to the positive plate, and the remaining part of the molecule, now with a positive charge, will be attracted to the

PART VI

Figure 13-3

An ionization chamber for an ionization type of smoke detector

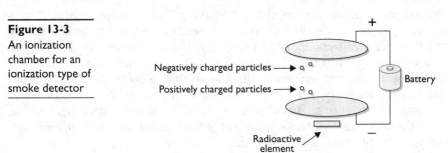

negative plate. This movement of particles creates a very small electric current that the device measures. Smoke will inhibit this process, and the resulting drop in current will be detected and an alarm sounded. Both of these devices are often referred to as smoke detectors, and combinations of both varieties are possible. For more information on smoke detectors see http://home.howstuffworks.com/smoke2.htm.

Another type of fire detector is activated by heat. These devices come in two varieties. Fixed-temperature or fixed-point devices activate if the temperature in the area ever exceeds some predefined level. Rate-of-rise or rate-of-increase temperature devices activate when there is a sudden increase in local temperature that may indicate the beginning stages of a fire. Rate-of-rise sensors can provide an earlier warning but are also responsible for more false warnings.

A third type of detector is flame activated. This type of device relies on the flames from the fire to provide a change in the infrared energy that can be detected. Flame-activated devices are generally more expensive than the other two types but can frequently detect a fire sooner.

Wireless

When someone talks about wireless communication, they generally are referring to cellular phones. These devices have become ubiquitous in today's modern office environment. A cell phone network consists of the phones themselves, the cells with their accompanying base stations that they are used in, and the hardware and software that allow them to communicate. The base stations are made up of antennas, receivers, transmitters, and amplifiers. The base stations will communicate with those phones that are currently in the geographical area that is serviced by that station. As a person travels across town, they may exit and enter multiple cells. The stations must conduct a handoff to ensure continuous operation for the phone. As the individual moves toward the edge of a cell, a mobile switching center will notice the power of the signal beginning to drop. It will check to see if another cell has a stronger signal for your phone (cells frequently overlap) and if so, it can switch operation to this new cell and base station. All of this is done without the user ever knowing that they have moved from one cell to another.

Cellular telephones are a tremendous technology providing a great service to modern businesses and individuals. Cell phone technology is advancing, and more and more phones are being used for more than just voice communication. Phones can also provide messaging capability, some even provide Internet connectivity, and some can be used as digital cameras.

Wireless technology can also be used for networking. There are two main standards for wireless network technology. Bluetooth is designed as a short range (approximately 10 meters) Personal Area Network (PAN) cable replacement technology that may be built into a variety of devices such as mobile phones, PDAs, and laptop computers. The idea is to create low-cost wireless technology so that many different devices can communicate with each other. Bluetooth is also interesting because, unlike other wireless technology, it is designed so that devices can talk directly with each other without having to go through a central device (such as the base station described previously). This is known as peer-to-peer communication.

The other major wireless standard is the IEEE 802.11 set of standards, which is well suited for the local area network environment. 802.11 networks can operate in either an ad hoc peer-to-peer fashion or an infrastructure mode, which is more common. In this mode, computers with 802.11 network cards will communicate with a wireless access point. This access point connects to the network so that the computers communicating with it are essentially also connected to the network.

In an office environment, wireless networks are tremendously useful, as they free the user to take their computer anywhere in the building (as long as an access point is nearby). If a new employee joins the company, wire cable does not need to be strung in order to connect them; instead, they simply need to be within transmission distance to an access point.

While wireless networks are very useful in today's modern office (and home), they are not without their security problems. Access points are generally placed throughout a building so that all employees can access the corporate network. The transmission and reception areas covered by access points are not easily controlled. Consequently, many publicly accessible areas might fall into the range of one of the organization's access points, and thus the corporate network may become vulnerable to attack. Wireless networks are designed to incorporate some security measures, but all too often the networks are set up without security enabled, and serious security flaws exist in the 802.11 design.

Electromagnetic Eavesdropping

In 1985, a paper by Wim van Eck of the Netherlands described what became known as the van Eck phenomenon. In the paper van Eck described how eavesdropping on what was being displayed on monitors could be accomplished by picking up and then decoding the electromagnetic interference produced by the monitors. With the appropriate equipment, the exact image of what is being displayed can be re-created some distance away. While the original paper discussed emanations as they applied to video display units (monitors), the same phenomenon applies to other devices such as printers and computers as well.

This phenomenon had actually been known about for quite some time before van Eck published his paper. The U.S. Department of Defense used the term TEMPEST (Transient Electromagnetic Pulse Emanation Standard) as both a description for a program in the military to control these electronic emanations from electrical equipment and the actual process for controlling the emanations. One of the simplest ways to protect against equipment being monitored in this fashion is to put enough distance between the target and the attacker. The emanations can be picked up from only a limited distance. If the physical security for the facility is sufficient to put enough space between the equipment and publicly accessible areas that the signals cannot be picked up, then the organization doesn't have to take any additional measures to ensure security.

A natural question to ask is, how prevalent is this form of attack? The equipment needed to perform electromagnetic eavesdropping is not readily available, but it would not cost an inordinate amount of money to produce it. The cost could certainly be afforded by any large corporation, and industrial espionage using such a device is a possibility. While there are no public records of this sort of activity being conducted, it is reasonable to assume that it can and may be taking place in large corporations and the government, especially in foreign countries.

Shielding

Distance is not the only way to protect against eavesdropping on electronic emanations. Devices can be shielded so that their emanations are blocked. In fact, there are three basic ways to prevent these emanations from being picked up by an attacker:

- Put the equipment beyond the point that the emanations can be picked up.
- Provide shielding for the equipment itself.
- Provide a shielded enclosure (such as a room) to put the equipment in.

All of these solutions can be costly. Acquiring enough property to provide the necessary distance needed to protect against an eavesdropper may be possible if the facility is in the country with lots of available land surrounding it. If, however, the organization is in the middle of a city, then purchasing additional property may be prohibitive. Indeed, for smaller organizations that occupy only a few offices or floors in a large office building, it would be impossible to acquire enough space.

In this case, the organization may resort to purchasing shielded equipment. A "TEMPEST approved" computer will cost at least double what a normal computer would cost. Shielding a room (in what is known as a Faraday cage) is also an extremely expensive endeavor. The cost of shielding is so substantial that in most cases it probably cannot be justified. It may be a better idea to carefully select the location you put your most sensitive equipment—maybe it is possible to protect these computers by putting them in the center of your organization and leaving the less-sensitive equipment in the areas closest to public areas.

Location

On several occasions, the careful placement of equipment has come up as a possible means to provide security. It has been said that the three most important factors in the success of most businesses are location, location, and location. While the same is not exactly true of security (location is not the most important element in this case), it certainly can play a contributing role. In the case of a wireless network, the location one picks to place the wireless access points can make it easier or harder for an attacker to access the network from a publicly accessible area. For electromagnetic emanations, location is also a contributing factor. By placing the most sensitive equipment deep inside the organization, enough space may be obtained to protect the equipment from eavesdropping. Location also plays a significant role in physical security, since some facilities will be easier to protect than others, depending on their proximity to other buildings and roads.

Chapter Review

In this chapter, the operational model of computer security was reviewed along with the role that policies, procedures, standards, and guidelines play in it. Taken together, these documents outline the security plan for the organization. The various components of the security perimeter for organizations were outlined, including the connections to the telephone network, which are often overlooked when considering connections to the outside world. Various factors that affect the security of the organization were discussed, including physical security measures such as barriers and access control, as well as the environment and natural disasters. Biometrics, which are a useful mechanism to enhance access control for electronic access to computers and networks, were described. There are in fact more opportunities to use biometrics for physical access control, since size limitations are not as severe and one access device can be used to cover access to an area used by many individuals. Another common physical hazard that can affect security is fire suppression. There are a number of methods to suppress fires, some more damaging to electronic equipment or hazardous to humans than others. Knowing what type of device to use on a fire, based on what is providing the fuel for the fire, is critical to being able to effectively contain and suppress the fire.

Questions

1. Which type of fire extinguisher can be used for electrical fires?

   A. Type A

   B. Type AB

   C. Type C

   D. Type D

2. Social engineering attacks work so well because the individual who is the target of the attack/attempt:

   A. Is often not very intelligent and can't recognize the fact that a social engineering attempt is being tried on them.

   B. Often either genuinely wants to help or is trying to avoid a confrontation, depending on the specific tack the attacker is taking.

   C. Is new to the organization and can't tell that the story they are being fed is bogus.

   D. Knows the attacker.

3. The most common physical access control device is a

   A. Lock

   B. Card reader

   C. Hand geometry reader

   D. Security guard

4. In what way does the location of an organization affect the security?

   A. There may be sufficient controlled space to eliminate or reduce threats such as those posed by electronic emanations and wireless access.

   B. The location will have a bearing on the environment and the specific threats posed by natural means.

   C. The location, a high-crime area, for instance, may contribute to the chance that a crime may occur.

   D. All of the above.

5. Which of the following would be considered a clean-agent fire suppression component?

   A. Freon

   B. Water

   C. Argon

   D. Compressed air

6. Why is Halon being replaced as a fire suppression agent in computer and networking facilities?

   A. Halon production has been banned and use regulated because it is considered an ozone-depletion agent.

   B. Halon will cause electrical shorts when discharged, thus ruining electronic equipment.

   C. Halon is a corrosive agent and will destroy sensitive electronic equipment.

   D. Halon was found to not be effective in combating fires caused by electrical equipment.

7. What technique can be used to protect against electromagnetic eavesdropping (known as the van Eck phenomenon)?

   A. Provide sufficient distance (too far for the signal to travel) between the potential target and the nearest location an attacker could get to.

   B. Put the equipment that you are trying to protect inside a shielded room.

   C. Purchase specially shielded equipment.

   D. All of the above.

8. Which fire detection device relies on sudden changes in temperature to activate?

   A. Smoke detectors

   B. Rate-of-rise fire detectors

   C. Fixed-temperature fire detectors

   D. Flame-activated fire detectors

9. When should a human security guard be used for physical access control?

   A. When the organization's budget can afford it

   B. To avoid piggybacking

   C. When other access controls are unavailable

   D. When the organization wants to enhance its image

10. What device should be used only for organizations where continuous operations are essential?

    A. Surge protector

    B. Uninterruptible power supply

    C. Backup power generator

    D. Redundant array of in-line batteries (RAIB)

11. In the event of a fire, what is the most important priority?

    A. Protect expensive electronic equipment.

    B. Protect the critical data that your organization relies on for operations.

    C. Extinguish the fire.

    D. Ensure that all personnel are safe.

12. Which statement is most accurate when describing the prevalence of electromagnetic eavesdropping?

    A. It is so difficult that it is not likely to be occurring at any level.

    B. It requires technical equipment that only governments and large corporations would likely purchase or develop. It is therefore possible but how extensive it is, is unknown.

    C. The equipment required to perform it is easy to assemble and inexpensive. Examples of this sort of activity has been seen at all levels of corporate and government organizations.

    D. It is extremely common; the equipment can be assembled by hobbyists who can easily re-create the signals from any organization that they can get close enough to.

13. Environmental issues should be considered when planning for security because:

    A. They may affect the availability of the system and data.

    B. Environmental activists may attempt to breach the physical security perimeter in protest of various environmental issues.

    C. Nobody else will be worried about them, so the job will fall to the network security administrator.

    D. They really don't need to be considered.

PART VI

14. What common network access point is often forgotten when considering network electronic perimeter defenses?

    A. The Internet

    B. An organization's web site

    C. The Public Switched Telephone Network and modems

    D. Extranets connected to corporate partners

15. Which of the following is a high-level, broad statement of what the organization wants to accomplish?

    A. Policy

    B. Procedure

    C. Guideline

    D. Standard

Answers

1. **C.** An electrical fire requires an extinguisher that is designed to suppress Type C fires, which are electrical fires. It is very important to not use the wrong type of extinguisher on a fire, as not only will it fail to extinguish the fire, but it may cause additional damage as well. A type A extinguisher is used for fires involving paper, wood, cloth, or plastic materials. A type AB extinguisher is useful against type A fires as well as type B fires, which involve petroleum chemicals. A type D extinguisher is a special device designed to be used for fires involving combustible metals such as magnesium.

2. **B.** Social engineering works because people generally truly want to help an individual asking for assistance or because they are trying to avoid a confrontation. They also work because people generally want to believe that the individual really is who they claim to be. Intelligence doesn't matter for the target; anybody can fall prey to a really good social engineer. Being new to an organization can certainly make it easier for an attacker to convince a target they are entitled to the information requested but it is not a requirement. Long-time employees can just as easily provide sensitive information to a talented social engineer. The target and attacker generally do not know each other in a social engineering attack, so **D** is not a good answer.

3. **A.** The lock is the most common security access control device. They are ubiquitous. We use them in our homes as well as our places of employment. Biometrics are becoming more common but are not currently widespread. Card readers are also becoming more common, and they may someday replace locks (that use keys and combos) in the workplace, but that is still many years away. Security guards are also a common access control technique but are still not as common as the simple lock and key or combo lock.

4. **D.** All of these are true. If sufficient space can be controlled, the ability of an attacker to get close enough to try to catch a signal from electronic emanations or from a wireless network will be significantly reduced. Where an organization is also plays a role in the type of natural disaster (e.g., tornado, hurricane, earthquake), that must be planned for. Whether the organization is located in a high-crime area also would be a factor in its ability to remain secure.

5. **C.** Argon is a clean-agent fire suppression chemical. While water may be considered clean, it is not discussed in the category of clean agents because the goal is actually to move away from water as a fire suppression agent—it has too many problems associated with it. Freon is used in refrigeration, not fire suppression. Generally, you want to reduce the amount of oxygen, not increase the amount of oxygen, available to a fire, so compressed air would not be a correct answer.

6. **A.** Halon is associated with ozone depletion and its production has been banned and its use regulated. It was, however, an effective fire suppression agent. Halon had originally been used in computer rooms because it did not cause the damage that water caused when it was discharged, subsequently saturating the equipment in the room.

7. **D.** All of these are effective measures to take against possible electromagnetic eavesdropping.

8. **B.** Rate-of-rise or rate-of-increase detection devices are keyed into rapid changes in local temperatures such as might occur when a fire starts. Fixed-rate detectors must wait until a specific temperature is reached. Smoke detectors rely on the presence of smoke to warn of a fire (or potential fire). Flame-activated detectors rely on changes in the infrared energy.

9. **B.** Human security guards should be used when judgment is necessary and to avoid occurrences of things such as piggybacking. Guards are often going to be more expensive than other widely available mechanisms. Use of them should not be considered simply because the organization can afford them or because the organization wants to enhance their image.

10. **C.** While a surge protector and UPS should both be used in a facility where continuous operations are important, they are also both useful for other facilities as well. The only time a backup generator is required is when continuous operations are essential.

11. **D.** While the equipment is important and valuable, insurance can cover a large portion of the expense to replace it. The data too is valuable, but if your organization has an effective backup policy, then only a minimal amount of data would be lost in the event of a fire. Putting the fire out would certainly solve the problem, but unless it is a small fire that can be easily handled by a handheld extinguisher (of the right type for the fire), then it is better to let professional firefighters extinguish the fire. The most important priority should be the protection of the personnel in the area and building. This is always the top priority.

12. **B.** The equipment is specialized but not so expensive that larger organizations and governments could reasonably be expected to acquire it. There is no current example, however, of this being performed by corporations against other corporations. The equipment is not believed to be in the hands of hobbyists.

13. **A.** Items such as heating, air conditioning, and electrical power can affect the operation of the computer systems and networks and ultimately their availability. As such, environmental issues should be considered as part of any security plan for an organization's computer systems and network.

14. **C.** One of the most often overlooked ways to access a network is through modems and the ordinary telephone system. The problem of unauthorized modems is a frequent security issue for any organization. The Internet and corporate web sites (which go hand-in-hand) are certainly a possible method to access a system inside your network, but this is understood and most security plans are designed to address these points of access. Extranets are also a problem, but not everybody has a connection to another organization that circumvents the rest of their security devices, so the best answer is **C**.

15. **A.** This is the definition of what a policy is.

Disaster Recovery, Business Continuity, and Organizational Policies

In this chapter, you will

- Learn about the various ways backups are conducted and stored
- Discover different strategies for alternative site processing
- Understand the various components of a business continuity plan.
- Understand how policies and procedures play a daily role in addressing the security needs of an organization

Much of this book focuses on avoiding the loss of confidentiality or integrity due to a security breach. The issue of availability is also discussed in terms of specific events, such as denial of service and distributed denial of service attacks. In reality, however, there are many things that can disrupt the operations of your organization.

Disaster Recovery

Many types of disasters, whether natural or caused by people, can stop your organization's operations for some length of time. Such disasters are unlike the previously discussed threats to your computer systems and networks because the events that cause the disruption are not specifically aimed at your organization. This is not to say that those other threats won't disrupt operations—they may, and industrial espionage, hacking, disgruntled employees, and insider threats all must be considered. The purpose of this chapter is to point out additional events that may not have been previously considered. How long your organization's operations are disrupted depends in part on how prepared it is for a disaster and what plans are in place to mitigate the effects of a disaster. Any of these events could cause a disruption in operations:

fire	flood	tornado	hurricane
electrical storm	earthquake	political unrest/riot	blizzard
gas leak/explosion	chemical spill	terrorism	war

Fortunately these types of events do not happen too often. It is more likely that business operations will be interrupted due to employee error (such as accidental corruption of a database, or unplugging a system in order to plug in a vacuum cleaner—an event that has actually occurred to more than one organization). A good disaster recovery plan will prepare your organization for any type of organizational disruption.

Disaster Recovery Plans/Process

No matter what the event is that you are worried about—whether natural or not, targeted at your organization or not—there are certain preparations you can make to lessen the impact on your organization and the length of time that your organization will be out of operation. A *disaster recovery plan (DRP)* is critical for effective disaster recovery efforts. A DRP defines the data and resources necessary and the steps to take in order to restore critical organizational processes.

Put another way, what is it that is needed by your organization to perform its mission? Answer this question, and you have the beginning of a DRP, since you now know what needs to be quickly restored. When speaking of the resources, don't forget to include both the physical resources (such as computer hardware and software) and the personnel (you need somebody who knows how to run the systems that process your critical data).

A common way to begin creating your DRP is to answer the following questions for all critical functions:

- Who is responsible for the operation of this function?
- What do these individuals need to perform the function?
- When should this function be accomplished in relation to other functions?
- Where will this function be performed?
- How is this function performed (what is the process)?
- Why is this function so important or critical to the organization?

By answering these questions, you can create an initial draft of your organization's DRP. The name often used to describe the document created by addressing these questions is a *business impact assessment (BIA)*. This plan, of course, will need to be approved by management, and it is essential that they buy into the plan—otherwise your efforts will more than likely fail. That old adage, "those who fail to plan, plan to fail" certainly applies in this situation.

It is important in a good DRP to include the processes and procedures needed to restore your organization so that it is functioning again and ensure continued operation. What specific steps will be required to restore operations? These processes should be documented and, where possible and feasible, they should be reviewed and exercised on a periodic basis. Having a plan with step-by-step procedures that nobody knows how to follow does nothing to ensure the continued operation of the organization. Exercising your disaster recovery plans and processes before a disaster occurs provides you with the opportunity to discover flaws or weaknesses in the plan when there is still time to modify and correct them.

Categories of Business Functions

It may be useful in developing your BIA and DRP to categorize the various functions your organization performs. This categorization is based on how critical or important the function is to your business operation. Those functions that are the most critical will be the ones that you want to restore first, and your DRP should reflect this. One possible categorization scheme might be to divide functions into the following categories:

- **Critical** The function is absolutely essential for operations. Without the function, the basic mission of the organization cannot occur.

- **Necessary for normal processing** The function is required for normal processing, but the organization can live without it for a short period of time (such as for less than 30 days).

- **Desirable** The function is not needed for normal processing but enhances the organization's ability to conduct its mission efficiently.

- **Optional** The function is nice to have but does not affect the operation of the organization.

An important aspect of this categorization scheme is understanding how long the organization can survive without the specific function. Asking yourself "how long can my organization operate without this function" will enable you to correctly place the function in the correct category. If the function is needed immediately, it is *critical*. If you can live without it for at most 30 days before severely impacting your organization, it falls into the *necessary for normal processing* category. If you can live without the function for more than 30 days, but it is a function that will eventually need to be accomplished when normal operations are restored, it falls into the *desirable* category (this implies some subsequent catch-up processing will need to be accomplished). If the function is not needed, and no subsequent processing will be required to restore this function, it falls into the *optional* category. If the function doesn't fall into any of these categories because it doesn't really affect the operation of your organization, it falls into a category not mentioned yet—*get rid of it*. You may want to consider eliminating this function, since it may not really be providing any useful purpose.

Business Continuity Plans

Another term that is often used when discussing the issue of continued organizational operations is *business continuity plan (BCP)*. You might wonder what the difference is between a DRP and a BCP—after all, isn't the purpose of the DRP the continued operation of the organization or business? In reality, these two terms are sometimes used synonymously, and for many organizations there may be no major difference in the two. There are, however, slight differences between a BCP and a DRP, one of which is the focus.

The focus of business continuity planning is the continued operation of the business or organization. The focus of a disaster recovery plan is also on continued operation, but that is in the face of a disaster. In a DRP, the protection of human life should be addressed and is a major focus of the document. Evacuation plans and system shutdown

PART VI

procedures should be addressed. The safety of employees should be a theme throughout a DRP. In a BCP, on the other hand, you may not see the same level of emphasis placed on protection of employees. In a BCP, you will often see a more significant emphasis placed on the critical systems the organization needs to operate.

The difference between a DRP and BCP can be illustrated by imagining a disaster hitting an organization. The organization quickly assesses the situation and the amount of damage sustained. If systems can be restored within a maximum tolerable downtime, the DRP is executed. If not, both the DRP and BCP are executed. In cases where there are two separate plans, the DRP may be executed first, to ensure the safety of personnel, then the BCP is employed to bring operations back up.

However you view these two plans, an organization that is not able to quickly restore business functions after an operational interruption is an organization that will most likely suffer an unrecoverable loss and may cease to exist.

Backups

A key element in any BCP or DRP is backups. This is true not only because of the possibility of a disaster but also because hardware and storage media will periodically fail, resulting in loss or corruption of critical data. Data backup is thus a critical element in DRPs and BCPs, as well as in normal operation. There are several factors to consider in an organization's data backup strategy:

- How frequently should backups be conducted?
- How extensive do the backups need to be?
- What is the process for conducting backups?
- Who is responsible for ensuring backups are created?
- Where will the backups be stored?
- How long will backups be kept?
- How many copies will be maintained?

Keep in mind that the purpose of a backup is to provide valid, uncorrupted data in the event of corruption or loss of the original file or the media where the data was stored. Depending on the type of organization you are part of, there may be legal requirements for conducting backups that will affect the factors mentioned previously.

What Needs to Be Backed Up

Backups are commonly thought of in terms of the data that an organization relies on to conduct its daily operations. While this is certainly true, a good backup plan will consider more than just the data; it will include any application programs needed to process the data, and the operating system and utilities that the hardware platform requires to run the applications. Obviously the application programs and operating system will change much less frequently than the data itself, so the frequency with which these items need to be backed up is considerably different. This should be reflected in the organization's backup plan and strategy.

The DRP should also address other items related to backups. Personnel, equipment, and electrical power must also be part of the plan. Somebody needs to have an understanding of the operation of the critical hardware and software used by the organization. If the disaster that destroyed the original copy of the data and the original systems also results in the loss of the only personnel that know how to process the data, having backup data will not be enough to restore normal operations for the organization. Similarly, if the data requires specific software to be run on a very specific hardware platform, then having the data without the application program or required hardware will also not be sufficient. As you can see, a DRP or BCP is an involved document that must consider many different factors and take into account many different possibilities.

Strategies for Backups

The process for actually creating a backup copy of data and software requires more thought than simply stating "copy all required files." The size of the resulting backup must be considered, as well as the time required to conduct the backup. Both of these will affect details such as how frequently the backup will occur and the type of storage media that will be used for the backup. Other considerations for backup strategies include who will be responsible for conducting the backup, where the backups will be stored, and how long they should be maintained. Short-term storage for those occasional accidentally deleted files that users need to have restored should probably be close at hand. Longer-term storage for backups that may be several months or even years old should occur in a different facility. It should be evident by now that even something that sounds as simple as maintaining backup copies of essential data requires careful consideration and planning.

Types of Backups   The amount of data that will be backed up, and the time it takes to accomplish this, has a direct bearing on the type of backup that will be performed. There are four basic types of backups that can be conducted, and the amount of space required for each, and the ease of restoration using each strategy, is outlined in Table 14-1.

The values for each of the strategies in the table are highly variable depending on your specific environment. The more files are changed between backups the more these strategies will look alike. What each strategy entails bears further explanation.

The easiest type of backup to understand is the *full backup*. In a full backup, all files and software are copied onto the storage media. Restoration from a full backup is similarly straightforward—you must copy all of the files back onto the system. While this is easy to understand, it may take a considerable amount of time. Consider the size of even the average home PC today, where storage is measured in tens and hundreds of gigabytes. Copying this amount of data takes time.

	Full	Differential	Incremental	Delta
Amount of Space	Large	Medium	Medium	Small
Restoration	Simple	Simple	Involved	Complex

Table 14-1   Characteristics of Different Backup Types

In a *differential backup*, only the files and software that have changed since the last full backup was completed need to be stored. This also implies that periodically a full backup needs to be accomplished. The frequency of the full backup versus the interim differential backups depends on your organization and is part of your defined strategy. Restoration from a differential backup requires two steps: the last full backup first needs to be loaded, and then the differential backup can be applied to update the files that have been changed since the full backup was conducted. Again, this is not a difficult process, but it does take some time. The amount of time to accomplish the actual periodic differential backup, however, is much less than a full backup, and this is one of the advantages of this method. Obviously if the period of time between differential backups is long, or if your environment results in most files changing frequently, then the differential backup does not differ much from a full backup. It should also be obvious that in order to accomplish the differential backup, the system has to have a method to determine which files have been changed since some given point in time.

With *incremental backups*, even less information will be stored in each backup. The incremental backup is actually a variation on a differential backup, and the difference is that instead of copying all files that have changed since the last full backup, as in the case of the differential, the incremental backup will only copy files that have changed since the last full or incremental backup occurred. Just as in the case of the differential backup, the incremental backup relies on the occasional full backup being accomplished. After that, you only back up files that have changed since the last backup of any sort was conducted. To restore a system using this type of backup method requires quite a bit more work. You first need to go back to the last full backup and reload the system with this data. Then you have to update the system with every incremental backup that has occurred since then. The advantage of this type of backup is that it requires less storage and time to accomplish. The disadvantage is that the restoration process is more involved. Assuming that you don't frequently have to conduct a complete restoration of your system, however, the incremental type of backup is a very valid technique.

The final type of backup that can be accomplished is the *delta backup*. The goal with the delta backup is to save as little information as possible each time you conduct a backup. As in the other strategies, an occasional full backup must be accomplished. After that, when a delta backup is conducted at specific intervals, only the portions of the files that have been changed will be stored. The advantage of this is easy to illustrate. If your organization maintains a large database with thousands of records that is several hundred megabytes in size, the entire database would be copied in the previous backup types even if only one record is changed. For a delta backup, only the actual record that changed would be stored. The disadvantage of this method should also be readily apparent—restoration is a complex process since it requires more than just loading a file (or several files). It requires application software be run to update the records in the files that have been changed.

There are advantages and disadvantages to each of the backup types described. Which type is best for your organization depends on a number of things, including the amount of data you routinely process and store, how frequently it changes, how often you expect to have to restore from a backup, and a number of other factors. The type you select, however, will greatly affect your overall backup strategy, plans, and processes.

Backup Frequency and Retention   What type of backup strategy an organization employs is often affected by how frequently the organization conducts the backup activity. The usefulness of a backup is directly related to how many changes have occurred since the backup was created, and this is obviously affected by how often backups are created. The longer it has been since the backup was created, the more changes will likely have occurred. There is no easy answer, however, to how frequently an organization should perform backups. Every organization should consider how long it can survive without current data from which to operate. It can then determine how long it will take to restore from backups, using various methods, and decide how frequently backups need to occur. This sounds simple, but it is actually a serious, complex decision to make.

Related to the frequency question is the issue of how long backups should be maintained. Is it sufficient to simply maintain a single backup from which to restore data? Security professionals will tell you the answer to this is easy—"no." Multiple backups should be maintained for a variety of reasons. If the reason for restoring from the backup is the discovery of an intruder in the system, it is important to restore the system to its pre-intrusion state. If the intruder has been in the system for several months before being discovered, and backups are taken weekly, it will not be possible to restore to a pre-intrusion state if only one backup is maintained. This would mean that all data and system files would be suspect and may not be reliable. If multiple backups were maintained, at various intervals, then it is easier to return to a point before the intrusion (or before the security or operational event that is necessitating the restoration) occurred.

There are several strategies or approaches to backup retention. One common and easy to remember one is the "rule of three." This entails simply keeping the three most recent backups. When a new backup is created, the oldest copy is overwritten. Another strategy is to keep the most recent copy of backups for various time intervals. For example, you might keep the latest daily, weekly, monthly, quarterly, and yearly backups. It should be noted that in certain environments, regulatory issues may prescribe a specific frequency and retention period, so it is important to know your organization and its requirements when determining how often you will create a backup and how long you will keep it for.

If you are not in an environment where regulatory issues dictate the frequency and retention for backups, your goal will be to optimize the frequency. In determining the optimal backup frequency, there are two major costs that need to be considered. The first is the cost of the backup strategy you choose. The second is the cost of recovery if you do not implement this backup strategy (meaning if there were no backups created). Into this equation must also be factored the probability that the backup will be needed on any given day. The two figures to consider then are:

(probability the backup is needed) × (cost of restoring with no backup)

(probability the backup isn't needed) × (cost of the backup strategy)

The first of these two figures can be considered the probable loss you can expect if your organization has no backup. The second figure can be considered the price you are willing to pay (lose) to ensure that you can restore, should a problem occur (think of this as backup insurance—the cost of an insurance policy that may never be used but that you are willing to pay, just in case).

In order to optimize your backup strategy, you need to determine the correct balance between these two figures. Obviously you do not want to spend more in your backup strategy than you face losing should you not have a backup plan at all. When working with these two calculations, you have to remember that this is a cost-avoidance exercise. The organization is not going to increase revenues with their backup strategy. All that you are trying to do is minimize the potential loss due to some catastrophic event by creating a backup strategy that will address your organization's needs.

When calculating the cost of the backup strategy, there are several elements that must be taken into consideration. These include

- The cost of the backup media required for a single backup
- The storage costs for the backup media and the retention policy
- The labor costs associated with performing a single backup
- The frequency with which backups are created

All of these considerations can be used to arrive at an annual cost for implementing your chosen backup strategy, and this figure can then be used as previously described.

Storage of Backups   One of the elements to be factored into the cost of the backup strategy is the expense of storing the backups. Backup storage is an important issue to consider. A simple strategy might be to store all of your backups together for quick and easy recovery actions. This is not, however, a good idea. Suppose the catastrophic event that made the restoration of backed-up data necessary was something like a fire that destroyed the computer system the data was processed on. In this case, any backups that were stored in the same facility might also be lost in the same fire.

The solution is to obviously keep copies of backups in separate locations. The most recent copy could be stored locally, as it is the most likely to be needed. Other copies can be kept at other locations. Depending on the level of security desired, the storage facility itself could be reinforced against possible threats in your area (such as tornados or floods). Another more recent advance is online backup services. There are a number of third-party companies that now offer high-speed connections for storing data in a separate facility on a frequent basis. Transmitting the backup data via network connections alleviates some other concerns with physical movement of more traditional storage media—concerns such as the care during transportation (tapes do not fare well in direct sunlight, for example) or the time that it takes to transport the tape data.

Alternative Sites   An issue related to the location of backup storage is where the restoration services will be conducted. If the organization has suffered physical damage to a facility, having offsite storage of data is only part of the solution. This data will need to be processed somewhere, which means that computing facilities similar to those used in normal operations must be found. There are a number of ways to approach this problem, including hot sites, warm sites, cold sites, and mobile backup sites.

A *hot site* is a fully configured environment similar to the normal operating environment that can be operational within a few hours. A *warm site* is partially configured, usually having the peripherals and software but perhaps not the more expensive main processing computer. It is designed to be operational within a few days. A *cold site* will have the basic environmental controls necessary to operate but will have few of the computing components necessary for processing. Getting a cold site operational may take weeks. Mobile backup sites are generally trailers with the required computers and electrical power that can be driven to a location within hours of a disaster and set up to commence processing immediately.

All of these options can come with a considerable price tag, which makes another option, *mutual aid agreements*, a possible alternative. With mutual aid agreements, similar organizations agree to assume the processing for the other party in the event that a disaster occurs. The obvious assumption here is that both organizations will not be hit by the same disaster and that both have similar processing environments. If these two assumptions are correct, then a mutual aid agreement should be considered.

Issues with Long-Term Storage of Backups   Depending on the media used for an organization's backups, degradation of the media is a distinct possibility and needs to be considered. Magnetic media degrade over time (measured in years). In addition, tapes can only be used a limited number of times before the surface begins to flake off.

Another consideration is advances in technology. The media you used to store your data two years ago may now be considered obsolete (5.25-inch floppy drives, for example). Software applications also evolve, and the media may be present but may not be compatible with current versions of the software.

Another issue is security related. If the file you stored was encrypted for security purposes, is there anybody remaining in the company who remembers the password to decrypt the file in order to restore the data?

Utilities

The interruption of power is a common issue during a disaster. Computers and networks obviously require power to operate, so emergency power must be planned for in the event of any disruption of operations. For short-term interruptions, such as what might occur as the result of an electrical storm, uninterruptible power supplies (UPSs) may suffice. These devices contain a battery that provides steady power for short periods of time—enough to keep a system running should power only be lost for a few minutes, or enough to allow administrators to gracefully halt the system or network. For continued operations that extend beyond a few minutes, another source of power will be required. Generally this is provided by a backup emergency generator.

While backup generators are frequently used to provide power during an emergency, they are not a simple, maintenance-free solution. Generators need to be tested on a regular basis, and they can easily become strained if they are required to power too much equipment. If your organization is going to rely on an emergency generator for backup power, you must ensure that the system has reserve capacity beyond the anticipated load for the unanticipated loads that will undoubtedly be placed on it.

There are a number of other issues with generators. They take time to start up, so power will most likely be lost, even if only for a brief second, while they come on. This means that a UPS should also be used to allow for a smooth transition to backup power. Generators are also expensive and require fuel—when looking for a place to locate your generator, don't forget the need to deliver fuel to it or you may find yourself hauling cans of fuel up a number of stairs.

When determining the need for backup power, don't forget to factor in environmental conditions. Power to computer systems in a room with no air conditioning in the middle of the summer in the Southwest will result in an extremely uncomfortable environment for all to work in. Mobile backup sites, generally utilizing trailers, often rely on generators for their power but also factor in the requirement for environmental controls.

Power is not the only essential utility for operations. The most obvious other one is communications. Depending on the type of disaster that has occurred, telephone and Internet communication may also be lost. Wireless services may also not be available. Planning for redundant means of communication (such as using both land lines and wireless) can help with most outages, but for large disasters, your backup plans should include the option to continue operations from a completely different location while waiting for communications in your area to be restored. Telecommunication carriers have their own emergency equipment and are fairly efficient at restoring communications, but it may take a few days.

Secure Recovery

Several companies offer recovery services, including power, communications, and technical support that may be needed in the event that your organization's operations are disrupted. These companies advertise secure recovery sites or offices from which your organization can again begin to operate in a secure environment. Secure recovery is also advertised by other organizations that provide services that can remotely (over the Internet, for example) provide restoration services for critical files and data.

In both cases—the actual physical suites and the remote service—security is an important element. During a disaster, your data does not become any less important, and you will want to make sure that you maintain the security (in terms of confidentiality and integrity, for example) of your data.

High Availability and Fault Tolerance

Some other terms that may be used in discussions of continuity of operations in the face of a disruption of some sort are *high availability* and *fault tolerance*.

High availability is exactly what it seems. We earlier defined one of the objectives of security as the availability of data and processing power when an authorized user desires it. High availability refers to the ability to maintain availability of data and operational processing despite a disrupting event of some sort. Generally this requires redundant systems, both in terms of power and processing, so that should one system fail, the other can take over operations without any break in service.

Fault tolerance basically refers to the same situation and is accomplished by the mirroring of data and systems. Should a "fault" occur, causing disruption in a device such as a disk controller, the mirrored system provides the requested data with no apparent interruption in service to the user.

Obviously, providing redundant systems and equipment comes with a price, and the need to provide this level of continuous, uninterrupted operation needs to be carefully evaluated.

Policies and Procedures

Disaster recovery and business continuity plans are designed to address the needs of an organization in the event of a disruption of operations. What, however, governs the organization's operations on a daily basis? *Policies* are high-level statements made by management laying out the organization's position on some issue. Policies are mandatory but are not specific in their details. Policies are focused on the result, not the methods for achieving that result.

Standards are accepted specifications providing specific details on how a policy is to be enforced. *Procedures* are generally step-by-step instructions that prescribe exactly how employees are expected to act in a given situation or to accomplish a specific task. While there are standard policies that can be described in general terms that will be applicable to all organizations, standards and procedures are often more organizational specific and driven by specific organizational policies. This chapter will therefore concentrate on the higher-level general policy statements that every organization should have and will leave specific implementations to the individual organizations.

In security, there are several common policies that every organization should have in place. These policies include acceptable use policies, due care, separation of duties, and password management, and they will be addressed in the following sections. Other important policy-related issues that will also be covered include privacy, service level agreements, human resources policies, code of ethics, and policies governing incident response.

Security Policies

In keeping with the high-level nature of policies, the *security policy* is a high-level statement produced by senior management that outlines what security means to the organization and what the organization's goals are for security. Statements like "this organization will exercise the principle of least access in its handling of client information" would be an example of a security policy. The security policy may also describe how security is to be handled from an organizational point of view (it may describe which office and which corporate officer or manager oversees the organization's security program).

The security policy should include the other more specific policies just mentioned and spelled out next, and should be reviewed on a regular basis and updated as needed. Generally, policies will need to be updated less frequently than the procedures that implement them, since the high-level goals will not change as often as the environment in which they must be implemented. All policies should also be reviewed by the organization's legal counsel, and a plan should be outlined describing how the organization will ensure that employees will all be made aware of the policies. Policies can also be made stronger by including references to the authority who made the policy (for example, whether this policy comes from the CEO, or whether it is a department-level policy) and also refer to any laws or regulations that are applicable to the specific policy and environment.

Acceptable Use

An *acceptable use policy (AUP)* outlines what the organization considers to be the appropriate use of company resources, such as computer systems and networks. Organizations should be concerned with the personal use of organizational assets which does not benefit the company.

The goal of the policy is to ensure employee productivity while limiting organizational liability through inappropriate use of the organization's assets. The policy should clearly delineate what activities are not allowed. Issues such as the use of resources to conduct personal business, installation of hardware or software, remote access to systems and networks, the copying of company-owned software, and the responsibility of users to protect company assets, including data, software, and hardware should be addressed. Statements regarding possible penalties for ignoring any of the policies (such as termination) should also be included.

Related to appropriate use of the organization's computer systems and networks by employees is the appropriate use by the organization. The most important of such issues is whether the organization will consider it appropriate to monitor the employee's use of the systems and network. If monitoring is considered appropriate, the organization will want to include a statement to this effect in the banner seen at login. This repeatedly warns employees, and possible intruders, that their actions are subject to monitoring and that any misuse of the system will not be tolerated. Should the organization have to use any information gathered during monitoring in a civil or criminal case, the issue of whether the employee had an expectation of privacy, or whether it was even legal for the organization to be monitoring, is simplified if the organization can point to a statement that is always displayed, stating that use of the system constitutes consent to monitoring. Before any monitoring is conducted, or the actual wording on the warning message is created, the organization's legal counsel should be consulted to determine the appropriate way to address this issue in the particular location.

Internet Usage Policy   In today's highly connected environment, employee use of access to the Internet is of particular concern. The goal for the *Internet usage policy* is to ensure maximum employee productivity and to limit potential liability to the organization from inappropriate use of the Internet in a workplace. The Internet provides a tremendous temptation for employees to waste hours as they surf the Web for the scores of the important games from the previous night, or conduct some quick online stock transactions, or read the review of the latest blockbuster movie everyone is talking about. Obviously, every minute they spend conducting this sort of activity is time they are not productively engaged in the organization's business, and their job. In addition, allowing employees to visit sites that may be considered offensive to others (such as pornographic or hate sites) may open the company up to accusations of condoning a hostile work environment and may result in legal liability.

The Internet usage policy needs to address what sites employees are allowed to visit, and what sites they are not. If the company will allow them to surf the Web during non-work hours, the policy needs to clearly spell out what the acceptable parameters are, in terms of when they are allowed to do this and what sites they are still prohibited from visiting (such as the potentially offensive ones mentioned before). The policy should also describe under what circumstances an employee would be allowed to post something from the organization's network on the Web. A necessary addition to this policy would be the procedure for an employee to follow to obtain permission to post the object or message.

E-Mail Usage Policy   Related to the Internet usage policy is the *e-mail usage policy*, which deals with what the company will allow employees to send in terms of e-mail. This policy should spell out whether non-work e-mail traffic is allowed at all or is at least severely restricted. It needs to cover the type of message that would be considered inappropriate to send to other employees (for example, no offensive language, no sex-related or ethnic jokes, no harassment, and so on). The policy should also specify any disclaimers that must be attached to an employee's message sent to an individual outside of the company.

Due Care

Due care and *due diligence* are terms used in the legal and business community to address issues where one party's actions may have caused loss or injury to another's. Basically, the law recognizes the responsibility of an individual or organization to act reasonably in relation to another. Reasonable precautions need to be taken that indicate that the organization is being responsible. In terms of security, it is expected that organizations will take reasonable precautions to protect the information that it maintains on other individuals. Should a person suffer a loss as a result of negligence on the part of an organization in terms of its security, a legal suit may be brought against the organization.

The standard applied—reasonableness—is extremely subjective and will often be determined by a jury. The organization will need to show how it had taken reasonable precautions to protect the information, and despite these precautions, an unforeseen security event occurred that caused the injury to the other party. Since this is so subjective, it is hard to describe what would be considered reasonable, but many sectors have "security best practices" for their industry, which provides a basis for organizations in that sector to start from. If the organization decides to not follow any of the best practices the industry agrees on, it needs to be prepared to justify its reasons in court should an incident occur.

Another element which can help establish due care from a security standpoint is developing and implementing the security policies discussed in this chapter.

Separation of Duties

Separation of duties is a principle employed in many organizations to ensure that no single individual has the ability to conduct transactions alone. This means that the level of trust in any one individual is lessened, and the ability for any individual to do catastrophic damage to the organization is also lessened. An example might be an organization where one person has the ability to order equipment, but it will be another individual who makes the payment. This would mean that an individual who wants to make an unauthorized purchase for their own personal gain would have to convince another person to go along with the transaction.

Separating duties as a security tool is a good practice, but it is possible to go overboard with this and break transactions up into too many pieces or require too much oversight. This results in inefficiency and may actually be less secure, since individuals may not scrutinize transactions as thoroughly, since they know others will also be reviewing them. The temptation is to hurry something along and assume that somebody else will or has examined it.

Another aspect of the separation of duties principle is that it spreads responsibilities out over an organization so no single individual becomes the indispensable individual with all of the "keys to the kingdom" or unique knowledge about how to make everything work. If there are enough tasks that have been distributed, having a primary and a backup person for each will ensure that the loss of any one individual will not have a disastrous impact on the organization.

Need to Know

Another common security principle is that of *need to know* and *least privilege*. The guiding factor here is that each individual in the organization is only supplied with the absolute minimum amount of information and privileges they need in order to perform their tasks. In order to obtain access to any piece of information, they must have a justified "need to know" it. In addition, they will only be granted the bare minimum number of privileges that are needed to perform their jobs.

A policy spelling out these two principles as guiding philosophies for the organization should be created. The policy should also address who in the organization can grant access to information or may assign privileges to employees.

Password Management

Since passwords are the most common authentication mechanism, it is imperative that organizations have a policy addressing them. The *password management policy* should address the procedures used for selecting user passwords (specifying what is considered an acceptable password in the organization in terms of the character set and length, for example), the frequency with which they must be changed, and how they will be distributed. Procedures for creating new passwords should an employee forget their old password also need to be addressed, as well as the acceptable handling of passwords (for example, they should not be shared with anybody else, they should not be written down, and so on). It might also be useful to have the policy address the issue of password cracking by administrators, in order to discover weak passwords that may have been selected by employees.

It should be noted that it is possible for the developer of the password management policy and procedure to go overboard and create an environment that leads to poorer security not better, and that negatively impacts employee productivity. If, for example, the frequency with which passwords are changed is too great, users will have a tendency to write them down or forget them. Neither of these is a desirable outcome, as the one makes it possible for an intruder to find a password and gain access to the system, and the other leads to too many people losing productivity as they have to wait for a new password to be created to allow them access again.

Disposal and Destruction

Many potential intruders have learned the value of "dumpster diving." This entails the potential intruder rummaging through the target organization's trash in order to find valuable information that may be used to penetrate the organization's security. The type of information that may be found includes documents, letters, scratch paper, old removable storage media, and even old equipment. Several government organizations have been embarrassed when old computers they had sold to salvagers proved to still contain sensitive documents on the hard drives. Other "dumpster diving" successes include finding e-mail or yellow sticky notes that contained passwords and userids. It is critical for the organization to have a strong *disposal and destruction policy* and related procedures.

Important papers should be shredded, and important, in this case, means anything that may be useful to a potential intruder. It is amazing what intruders can do with what appear to be the most innocent pieces of information.

Magnetic storage media need to have all files deleted, and then the media should be overwritten at least three times with all ones, all zeros, and then random characters. There are commercial products available to destroy files using this process. It is not sufficient to simply delete all files and leave it at that, since the deletion process only affects the pointers to where the files are stored and doesn't actually get rid of all of the bits in the file. This is why it is possible to "undelete" files and recover them after they have been deleted. A safer method for destroying files from a storage device is to magnetically destroy the data by using a strong magnetic field to degauss the media. This effectively destroys all data on the media, and there are several commercial degaussers that can be purchased for this purpose. Another method that can be used on hard drives is to take a file to them (the sort of file you'd find in a hardware store) and actually file off the magnetic material from the surface of the platter. Shredding floppy media is normally sufficient, but simply cutting a floppy into a few pieces is not enough—data has been successfully recovered from floppies that were cut into only a couple of pieces.

Privacy

Customers place an enormous amount of trust in organizations when they provide personal information to them. These customers expect their information to be kept secure so that unauthorized individuals will not gain access to it and so that authorized users will not use the information in unintended ways. Organizations should have a *privacy policy* that explains what their guiding principles will be in guarding personal data that they are given access to. In many locations, customers have a legal right to expect that their information is kept private, and organizations that violate this trust may find themselves involved in a lawsuit. In certain sectors, such as health care, federal regulations have been created that prescribe stringent security controls on private information.

It is a general practice today in most organizations to have a policy that describes very explicitly how information provided to the organization will be used (for example, it will not be sold to other organizations). Watchdog organizations have sprung up that monitor the use of individual information by organizations, and businesses can subscribe to services that will vouch for the organization to consumers, stating that the company has agreed to protect and keep private any information supplied to them. The organization is then granted permission to display a seal or certification on their web site where customers can see it. Organizations that then misuse the information they promised to protect will find themselves subject to penalties from the watchdog organization.

Service Level Agreements

Service level agreements (SLAs) are contractual agreements between entities describing specified levels of service that the servicing entity agrees to guarantee for the customer. These agreements not only clearly lay out what the expectations are in terms of the service provided and support expected, but also generally include penalties should the described level of service or support not be provided. An organization contracting with a service provider should remember to include in the agreement a section describing the service provider's responsibility in terms of business continuity and disaster recovery. The provider's backup plans and processes for restoring lost data should also be clearly described.

Human Resources Policies

It has been said that the weakest links in the security chain are the humans. Consequently, it is important to examine the policies that organizations have in place in relation to these employees. The first policies to be concerned with are those that relate to the hiring of individuals. You want to make sure that you hire individuals that you can trust with your organization's data and that of its clients. Once you've hired employees, you want to keep them from slipping into the category of "disgruntled employee." Finally, you need policies to address the inevitable point in the future when your employees leave the organization—either on their own or with the "encouragement" of the organization itself. There are security issues that must be considered at each of these points.

Employee Hiring and Promotions

It has increasingly become common for organizations to run background checks on prospective employees and check the references they supply. Drug tests, possible criminal activity in the past, claimed educational background, and reported work history are all elements that are frequently checked today. For highly sensitive environments, security background checks may also be required. You want to make sure that you hire the most capable and trustworthy employees, and your policies should be designed to ensure this.

Once you have made your selection and hired an individual, your organization needs to minimize the risk that the employee will "turn against you." Periodic reviews by supervisory personnel, additional drug checks, and monitoring of activity during work may all be considered by the organization. If there is an intent to accomplish any of these, they need to be specified in the organization's policies, and prospective employees should be made aware of these policies before being hired. What an organization can do in terms of monitoring and requiring of additional drug tests, for example, can be severely restricted if not spelled out in advance as terms of employment. New hires should be made aware of all pertinent policies, especially those applying to security, and documents should be signed by them indicating that they have read them and that they understand them.

Occasionally an employee's status will change within the company. If the change can be construed as a negative personnel action (such as a demotion), supervisors should be alerted to watch for changes in behavior that might indicate unauthorized activity is being contemplated or conducted. It is likely that the employee will be upset, and whether they act on this to the detriment of the company is something that needs to be guarded against. In the case of a demotion, the individual may also lose certain privileges or access rights, and these changes should be made quickly so as to lessen the likelihood that the employee can destroy previously accessible data if they become disgruntled and decide to take revenge on the organization. On the other hand, if the employee is promoted, privileges may still change, but the need to make the change to access privileges may not be as urgent, though it should still be accomplished as quickly as possible. If the move is a lateral one, there may still be changes that need to take place, and again they should be accomplished as quickly as possible. The organization's goals in terms of making changes to access privileges should be clearly spelled out in their policies.

Retirement, Separation, or Termination of an Employee

An employee leaving an organization can be either a positive or a negative action. Employees who are retiring by their own choice may announce their planned retirement weeks or even months in advance. Limiting their access to sensitive documents the moment they announce their intention may be the safest thing to do, but it may not be necessary. Each situation should be evaluated individually. Should the situation be a forced retirement, the organization must determine the risk to its data if the employee becomes disgruntled as a result of the action. In this situation, it may be the wisest choice to quickly cut off their access and simply provide them with some additional vacation time. This may seem like an expensive proposition, but the danger to the company of having a disgruntled employee may justify it. Again, each case should be evaluated individually.

When an employee decides to leave a company, generally as a result of a new job offer, continued access to sensitive information should be carefully considered. If the employee is leaving as a result of hard feelings for the company, it may be the wise choice to quickly revoke their access privileges. If they are leaving as a result of a better job offer, you may decide to allow them to gracefully transfer their projects to other employees, but the decision should be considered very carefully, especially if the new company can be considered a competitor.

If the employee is leaving the organization because they are being terminated, you have to plan on their becoming disgruntled. While it may not seem the friendliest thing to do, an employee in this situation should immediately have their access privileges to sensitive information and facilities revoked. Access cards, keys, and badges should be collected, the employee should be escorted to their desk and watched as they pack their personal belongings and then should be escorted from the building. It is better to give somebody several weeks of paid vacation rather than have a disgruntled employee trash sensitive files they have access to. Combinations should also be quickly changed once they have been informed of their termination.

No matter what the situation, the organization should have policies that describe the intended goals, and there should be procedures that detail the process to be followed for each of the described situations.

Code of Ethics

Numerous professional organizations have established codes of ethics for their members. Each of these describe the expected behavior of their members from a high-level standpoint. Organizations can adopt this idea as well. For organizations, a code of ethics can set the tone for how employees will be expected to act and to conduct business. The code should demand honesty from employees, and should require that they perform all activities in a professional manner. The code could also address principles of privacy and confidentiality and state how employees should treat client and organizational data. Conflicts of interest can often cause problems, so this could also be another item covered in the code of ethics.

By outlining a code of ethics, the organization can encourage an environment that will be conducive to integrity and high ethical standards. For additional ideas on possible codes of ethics, check professional organizations such as the Institute for Electrical and Electronics Engineers (IEEE), the Association for Computing Machinery (ACM), or the Information Systems Security Association (ISSA).

Incident Response Policies

No matter how careful an organization is, eventually a security incident of some sort will occur. When it happens, how effectively the organization deals with it will depend greatly on how prepared they are to handle incidents. An *incident response policy* and associated procedures should be developed to outline how the organization will deal with security incidents when they occur. Waiting until an incident happens is not the right time to establish your policies—they need to be designed in advance.

There are several phases that should be covered in an incident response policy: preparation, detection, containment and eradication, recovery, and any follow-on actions.

Preparation

Preparing for an incident is the first phase. Steps to be taken when an incident is discovered (or suspected) should be established. Points of contact should be determined. All employees should be trained so they understand the steps to take and who to call. An incident response team should be established, the equipment necessary to detect, contain, and recover from an incident should be acquired, and those who will use the equipment will need to be trained. Any additional training in areas such as computer forensics that are determined to be necessary should also be accomplished.

The incident response team is a critical part of the incident response plan. Team membership will vary depending on the type of incident or suspected incident, but there are some general points to think about. The team will need a leader, preferably a higher-level manager who will have the ability to obtain the cooperation from employees as needed. A computer or network security analyst will be useful to have as a member, since the assumption is that a security incident may have occurred. Specialists may be added to the team for specific hardware or software platforms as needed. The organization's legal counsel should be part of the team on at least a part-time or as-needed basis. The public affairs office should also be available on an as-needed basis, because it will be their responsibility to formulate the public response should the event become public. The organization's security office should also be kept informed, and there should be a point of contact for the team in case criminal activity is suspected. In this case, care must be taken to preserve evidence, should the organization decide to push for prosecution of the individuals.

This is by no means a complete list, as each organization is different and each will need to evaluate what the best mixture is for their own response team. Whatever the decision, the composition of the team, and how and when it will be formed, need to be clearly addressed in the incident response policy.

Detection

It goes without saying that before an incident response team can begin the investigation of an incident, there needs to be a suspected incident, which in turn implies that somebody needs to have detected what they believe may be an incident. Security incidents can take a variety of forms, and who discovers it will vary as well.

One of the most likely group of individuals to discover an incident will be the network and security administrators. These are the people who run devices such as the organization's firewalls and intrusion detection systems. So that this is not an ad hoc, hit-or-miss proposition, procedures need to be established that describe the process the administrators should use to check for possible security events. The tools for accomplishing this need to be identified during the preparation phase described previously, and any required training to operate the equipment should also be acquired.

Another common incident is a virus. There are several packages available that can help an organization discover potential virus activity or other malicious code. Administrators will often be the ones to notice something is amiss, but so might an average user who has been hit by the virus. Again, the appropriate hardware, software, and training needs to be acquired during the preparation phase.

A common technique used by potential intruders to acquire information that may be useful in gaining access to computer systems, networks, or the physical facilities that house them is social engineering. Anybody in the organization can be the target of a social engineering attack, so all employees need to know what to be looking for regarding this type of attack. In fact, it may not even be one of your organization's actual employees that is the target—it may be an "extended employee" of the company, such as somebody on the custodial staff or a night watchman. To thwart social engineering attacks, training is essential, and the organization should have a policy on who will be required to receive this type of training and how frequently they should receive it.

Whatever the type of security incident suspected, and no matter who suspects it, a reporting procedure needs to be in place for the employees to use. Everybody needs to know who to call should they suspect something, and everybody needs to know what to do. A common technique is to develop a reporting template that can be supplied to an individual suspecting an incident so that the necessary information is gathered in a timely manner.

One final word on detection remains. One of the first jobs of the incident response team will be to determine whether an actual incident has occurred. Many things can happen that may be interpreted as a possible incident but that may not be. A software bug in an application may cause a user to lose a file, and the user may blame this on a virus or similar malicious software. Each reported incident must be investigated and treated as a possible incident until it can be determined whether it is or isn't. This may mean that your organization may want to respond initially with a limited response team before wasting a lot of time having the full team respond.

Containment and Eradication

Once the determination has been made that an incident most likely has occurred, the team is going to want to quickly contain the problem. At this point, or very soon after containment begins, a decision will need to be made by management as to whether the organization will want to prosecute the individual who has caused the incident, or whether it is more important to simply restore operations. In certain circumstances there may not be a choice, such as if there are specific regulations or laws that require incidents in certain sectors to be reported. If the decision to prosecute has been made, specific procedures will need to be followed in handling potential evidence. Individuals trained in forensics should be used in this case.

Another decision that will need to be made quickly is how to address containment. If an intruder is on your system, one response is to disconnect from the Internet until the system can be restored and vulnerabilities patched. This, however, means that your organization may not be accessible to customers over the Internet anymore, and it may result in lost revenue. A decision will need to be made as to which is more important for your organization.

Other possible containment activities might include adding additional filtering rules or modifying existing rules on firewalls, routers, or intrusion detection systems, updating antivirus software, or removing specific pieces of hardware or halting specific software applications. If an intruder has gained access through a specific account, disabling that account or removing it may also be necessary.

Once the immediate problems have been contained, the cause of the incident needs to be addressed. If the incident is the result of a vulnerability that was not patched, the patch should be obtained, tested, and applied. Accounts may need to be deleted or passwords changed. It may also be necessary to completely reload the entire operating system if the intruder has been in the system for an unknown length of time or has been seen to have modified system files. Determining when an intruder first gained access to your system or network is critical in determining how far back to go in restoring the system or network.

Recovery

The major thrust of this chapter has been on business continuity and the quick recovery of operations. After the incident has been contained, and any malicious software or vulnerabilities have been taken care of, it is time to put the procedures described earlier into action. Again, the goal here is to quickly have the organization back to normal processing.

Follow-On Actions

Once the excitement of the incident is over and operations have been restored to their pre-incident state, it is time to take care of a few last items. Senior-level management will need and want to be informed of what occurred and what was done to address it. An after-action report should be created to outline what happened and how it was addressed. Recommendations will most likely be made to improve processes and policies so that a repeat incident will not occur. If prosecution of the individual responsible is desired, there will be additional time that will be spent in helping law enforcement agencies and possibly testifying in court. Training material may also need to be developed or modified as part of the new, modified policies and procedures.

Chapter Review

Each organization should have a plan to address the interruption of the organization's normal operations. The first step in developing such a plan is creating a business impact assessment, which helps the organization determine the critical systems and processes needed for the organization to function. A disaster recovery plan must also be created to outline how the organization will address various disasters that may affect operations. A business continuity plan should be created to address long-term disruptions of the organization's operations, and it is focused on reestablishing those functions essential for the continued operation of the organization.

There are also a number of policies that an organization should consider adopting. Policies are high-level statements, approved by corporate management, that state the organization's position on key issues. Policies don't describe the mechanics of how these positions will be implemented; instead they are focused on the result, not the method. Example issues that organizations should consider addressing in policies are human resource issues, acceptable use of company assets, and whether employee use of assets will be subject to monitoring.

Questions

1. A business impact assessment is designed to do which of the following?

    A. Determine the impact your business has on other organizations

    B. Determine the impact your business has on local, regional, and national economies

    C. Determine the effect your corporate security strategy has on the way you conduct your operations

    D. Determine which processes, systems, and people are critical to the operation of your organization

2. A good backup plan will include which of the following?

    A. The critical data needed for the organization to operate

    B. Any software that is required to process the organization's data

    C. Specific hardware to run the software or to process the data

    D. All of the above

3. In which backup strategy are only the files and software that have changed since the last full backup saved?

    A. Full

    B. Differential

    C. Incremental

    D. Delta

4. Which of the following is *not* a consideration in calculating the cost of a backup strategy?

    A. The cost of the backup media

    B. The storage costs for the backup media

    C. The probability that the backup will be needed

    D. The frequency with which backups are created

5. Which of the following is the name for a fully configured environment similar to the normal operating environment that can be operational within a few hours?

    A. Hot site

    B. Warm site

    C. Online storage system

    D. Backup storage facility

6. Which of the following is considered an issue with long-term storage of magnetic media, as discussed in the chapter?

    A. Tape media can only be used a limited number of times before it degrades.

    B. Software and hardware evolve, and the media stored may no longer be compatible with current technology.

    C. Both of the above.

    D. None of the above.

7. The best approach to take for potential short-term loss of electrical power is

   A. Don't worry about it. If it is short term, then the systems will be back up in at most a few minutes, and processing can resume.

   B. Install an uninterruptible power supply to allow processing to continue while you wait for power to be restored. If it will take longer than a few minutes, the supply will allow you to gracefully bring the system down so no loss of information is suffered.

   C. Install a backup power generator and maintain a supply of fuel for it.

   D. Have the power company install a backup power line into your facility.

8. What other common utility is it important to consider when developing your recovery plans?

   A. Water

   B. Gas

   C. Communications

   D. Television/cable

9. Policies are

   A. High-level statements made by management

   B. Statements that lay out the organization's position on some issue

   C. Mandatory but not specific in their details

   D. All of the above

   E. None of the above

10. A policy that outlines what the organization considers to be the appropriate use of company resources is known as

    A. A security policy

    B. An acceptable use policy

    C. A due care policy

    D. A need to know policy

11. Which of the following is true concerning an organization's ability to monitor employee use of resources?

    A. It can generally be done, but a policy stating that it will be conducted should be created, and a warning message should be displayed when employees use the organization's resources (such as the network).

    B. It can be done without any policy or warning message since the corporation owns the resources in the first place.

    C. It cannot be done under any circumstances.

    D. It cannot be done except under extreme circumstances, such as when a person's life is in danger.

12. Due care and due diligence refer to

    A. The situation in which one party's actions may have caused loss or injury to another's as a result of reasonable cautions not being taken

    B. The requirement to post safety notices about potentially hazardous situations

    C. The practice of determining what precautions should be taken by an organization to avoid financial responsibility for hazardous activities required of employees

    D. The responsibility placed on management to ensure that no corporate assets are lost as a result of a computer intrusion

13. What is the term for the principle employed by an organization to ensure that no single individual has the ability to conduct transactions alone?

    A. Need to know

    B. Due care/diligence

    C. Separation of duties

    D. No-lone-zone processing

14. The activity in which a potential intruder rummages through an organization's trash in order to try and discover valuable information that may be useful in attempting to penetrate the organization's security is known as

    A. Incremental information discovery

    B. Dumpster diving

    C. Disposal container investigation

    D. Social engineering

15. In which of the following situations is it imperative that badges and other access control devices be *immediately* confiscated from an employee?

    A. Termination of the employee

    B. Announced retirement of the employee

    C. Announced separation of the employee

    D. All of the above

Answers

1. **D.** This is the description of what a business impact assessment is supposed to accomplish. It is important to emphasize that the BIA not only includes the systems (hardware and software) needed by the organization, but any supplies or specific individuals that are critical for the operation of the organization.

2. **D.** All of these are important. Having copies of your data will not be useful if specialized software is required to process it and if specialized hardware is

needed to run the special software. You must consider all of these in your backup plan.

3. **B.** This is the definition of a differential backup. In an incremental backup, the data and software that has changed since the last full or incremental backup is saved. A delta backup only saves those portions of the files that have changed, instead of the entire file.

4. **C.** This was a trickier question. The probability that the backup will be needed is a factor in determining the optimal backup frequency, but it was not discussed as part of the cost of the backup strategy. It is also a figure that may be used in a risk analysis to determine the optimum strategy.

5. **A.** This is the definition of a hot site.

6. **C.** Both A and B were identified as issues that must be considered when planning your long-term storage strategy.

7. **B.** Purchasing and using a UPS is the best strategy to address short-term power loss. It allows for continued operation if the loss is brief or lets you bring the system down without loss of data. Generators are expensive to purchase and maintain and are not appropriate for short-term power loss. They may be essential for long-term loss of power in installations where this is likely and processing is critical. Ignoring the issue (answer **A**) is not a good approach as even a brief loss in power can disrupt processing and cause loss of data. Installing a second power line is also not a reasonable answer.

8. **C.** Communications (whether telephone or wireless) is critical for organizations today. Water and gas may be important, especially for long-term utility interruption, but they are generally not considered as important as communications, where even a short-term loss can be disastrous. While loss of television or cable may result in you missing your favorite show, it generally is not considered as crucial to business (unless the cable also supplies your Internet connectivity and is relied on for business operations).

9. **D.** The first three answers describe what a policy is.

10. **B.** This is the definition of an acceptable use policy. There are several different items that should be considered in this policy, and they may be addressed separately or as a whole. These items include the use of the Internet and e-mail.

11. **A.** Though local laws should be checked, generally it is important to have a policy and to let the employees (and potential intruders) know that monitoring is being conducted.

12. **A.** This is the best answer (as it is the definition presented in the chapter). Posting of safety notices may be considered part of an organization's responsibility for due care and diligence, but the responsibility is much broader. Trying to avoid financial responsibility may be at the heart of the issue, as far as corporate officers are concerned, but it is also just part of what due care and diligence is all about. The last answer, again, may be a consideration, but it is not the only reason for considering due care and diligence.

PART VI

13. **C.** This is the definition of separation of duties.

14. **B.** This is the definition of dumpster diving.

15. **A.** The only one that absolutely requires the immediate confiscation is the termination of the employee. An announced separation or retirement may prompt you to do the same, but only under unusual circumstances (such as the employee leaving or retiring as a result of a major disagreement). The announcement of a normal retirement or separation under friendly circumstances will normally not require the immediate confiscation of access control devices—especially since a retirement may be announced months in advance of the actual date.

PART VII

Administrative Controls

Security and Law

In this chapter, you will

- Learn about the laws and rules concerning importing and exporting encryption software
- Know the laws that govern computer access and trespass
- Understand the laws that govern encryption and digital rights management
- Learn about the laws that govern digital signatures
- Know the laws that govern privacy in various industries with relation to computer security

Computer security is no different than any other subject in our society; as it changes our lives, laws will be enacted to enable desired behaviors and prohibit undesired behaviors. The one substantial difference between this aspect of our society and others is that the speed of advancement in the information systems world as driven by business, computer network connectivity, and the Internet is much greater than in the legal system of compromise and law-making. In some cases, laws have been overly restrictive, limiting business options, such as in the area of importing and exporting encryption technology. In other cases, legislation has been slow in coming and this fact has stymied business initiatives, such as in digital signatures. And in some areas, it has been both too fast and too slow, as in the case of privacy laws. One thing is certain—you will never satisfy everyone with a law, but it does delineate the rules of the game.

Import/Export Encryption Restrictions

Encryption technology has been controlled by governments for a variety of reasons. The level of control varies from outright banning to little or no regulation. The reasons behind the control vary as well, and control over import and export is a vital method of maintaining a level of control over encryption technology in general. The majority of the laws and restrictions are centered around the use of cryptography, which was until recently mainly a military issue. The advent of commercial transactions and network communications over public networks such as the Internet has expanded the use of cryptographic methods to include securing of network communications. As is the case in most rapidly changing technologies, the practice moves faster than law. Many countries still have laws that are outmoded in terms of e-commerce and the Internet. Over time, these laws will be changed to serve these new uses in a way consistent with each country's needs.

United States Law

Export controls on commercial encryption products are administered by the Bureau of Industry and Security (BIS) in the U.S. Department of Commerce. The responsibility for export control and jurisdiction was transferred from the State Department to the Commerce Department in 1996 and most recently updated on June 6, 2002. Rules governing exports of encryption are found in the Export Administration Regulations (EAR), 15 C.F.R. Parts 730–774. Sections 740.13, 740.17, and 742.15 are the principal references for the export of encryption items.

Needless to say, violation of encryption export regulations is a serious matter and is not an issue to take lightly. Until recently, encryption protection was accorded the same level of attention as the export of weapons for war. With the rise of the Internet, widespread personal computing, and the need for secure connections for e-commerce, this position has relaxed somewhat. The United States updated its encryption export regulations to provide treatment consistent with regulations adopted by the European Union (EU), easing export and re-export restrictions among the 15 EU member states and Australia, the Czech Republic, Hungary, Japan, New Zealand, Norway, Poland, and Switzerland. The member nations of the Wassenaar Arrangement agreed to remove key length restrictions on encryption hardware and software that is subject to the certain reasonable levels of encryption strength. This action effectively removed "mass market" encryption products from the list of dual-use items controlled by the Wassenaar Arrangement.

The U.S. encryption export control policy continues to rest on three principles: review of encryption products prior to sale, streamlined post-export reporting, and license review of certain exports of strong encryption to foreign government end users. The current set of U.S. rules require notification to the BIS for export in all cases, but the restrictions are significantly lessened for "Mass Market" products as defined by all of the following:

- They are generally available to the public by being sold, without restriction, from stock at retail selling points by any of these means:
  - Over-the-counter transactions
  - Mail-order transactions
  - Electronic transactions
  - Telephone call transactions
- The cryptographic functionality cannot easily be changed by the user.
- They are designed for installation by the user without further substantial support by the supplier.
- When necessary, details of the items are accessible and will be provided, upon request, to the appropriate authority in the exporter's country in order to ascertain compliance with export regulations.

Mass-market commodities and software employing a key length greater than 64 bits for the symmetric algorithm must be reviewed in accordance with BIS regulations. Restrictions on exports by U.S. persons to terrorist-supporting states (Cuba, Iran, Iraq,

Libya, North Korea, Sudan, or Syria), their nationals, and other sanctioned entities are not changed by this rule.

As you can see, this is a very technical area, with significant rules and significant penalties for infractions. The best rule is that whenever you are faced with a situation involving the export of encryption-containing software, consult an expert and get the appropriate permission, or else a statement that permission is not required, first. This is one case where it is better to be safe than sorry; if in doubt, read the associated sidebar.

For Immediate Release
January 7, 2003

Silicon Graphics Settles Criminal and Civil Charges that Computer Shipments Violated U.S. Export Controls

The Department of Commerce's Bureau of Industry and Security (BIS) announced that Silicon Graphics, Inc. (SGI) of Mountain View, California pled guilty to two felony charges that the company violated Commerce Department regulations by illegally exporting high performance computers to a Russian nuclear laboratory in 1996. SGI agreed to pay $1 million in criminal fines to resolve the charges. In a related administrative case, SGI agreed to pay $182,000, the maximum penalty authorized by the Export Administration Regulations (EAR), to settle civil charges arising from the same exports to the Russian nuclear laboratory, as well as additional charges relating to illegal computer exports to Israel and for failure to meet reporting requirements for exports to China, Qatar, and the United Arab Emirates.

As part of the settlement of criminal charges, SGI admitted that, on two occasions in 1996, the company exported four Challenge L computer systems, upgrades, and peripheral equipment to the All-Russian Institute for Technical Physics (Chelyabinsk-70) in violation of U.S. export control regulations. Chelyabinsk-70, located in Snezhinsk, Russia, is a nuclear laboratory operated by Russia's Ministry of Atomic Energy and is engaged in research, development, testing, and maintenance of nuclear devices.

In addition to the monetary penalties, the civil settlement agreement provided that SGI's exporting privileges to Russia will be denied for a period of three years. The denial of export privileges will be suspended provided that SGI does not commit any export control violations involving Russia during the suspension period. SGI also agreed, for a period of three years, not to exercise its eligibility to use License Exception CTP for exports and re-exports to Russia, or to engage in any activity, such as repair or maintenance of computers, involving any military or nuclear end-user, or end-user in Russia without the prior written consent of BIS. Finally, SGI agreed to report to BIS, within 45 days, all of its exports to certain countries of concern during the last six months.

In announcing the settlement, Acting Assistant Secretary of Commerce for Export Enforcement Lisa Prager stated that this case demonstrates the Bureau's determination to rigorously enforce its controls over items that can be used in the proliferation of weapons of mass destruction. The Department of Commerce, through BIS, administers and enforces export controls for reasons of national security, foreign policy, anti-terrorism, nonproliferation, and short supply. Criminal penalties and administrative sanctions can be imposed for violations of the EAR.

http://www.bxa.doc.gov/press/2003/SiliconGraphics1_7.html

Non-U.S. Laws

Export control rules for encryption technologies fall under the Wassenaar Arrangement, an international arrangement on export controls for conventional arms and dual-use goods and technologies. The Wassenaar Arrangement has been established in order to contribute to regional and international security and stability, by promoting transparency and greater responsibility in transfers of conventional arms and dual-use goods and technologies, thus preventing destabilizing accumulations. Participating states, of which the United States is one of 33, will seek, through their own national policies and laws, to ensure that transfers of these items do not contribute to the development or enhancement of military capabilities that undermine these goals, and are not diverted to support such capabilities.

Many nations have more restrictive policies than those agreed upon as part of the Wassenaar Arrangement. Australia, New Zealand, the U.S.A., France, and Russia go further than is required under Wassenaar and restrict general-purpose cryptographic software as dual-use goods through national laws. The Wassenaar Arrangement has had a significant impact on cryptography export controls, and there seems little doubt that some of the nations represented will seek to use the next round to move toward a more repressive cryptography export control regime based on their own national laws. There are ongoing campaigns to attempt to influence other members of the agreement toward less restrictive rules, and in some cases no rules. These lobbying efforts are based on e-commerce and privacy arguments.

Digital Signature Laws

On October 1, 2000, the Electronic Signatures in Global and National Commerce Act (commonly called the E-Sign law) went into effect in the United States. This law implements a simple principle: a signature, contract, or other record may not be denied legal effect, validity, or enforceability solely because it is in electronic form. Another source of law on digital signatures is the National Conference of Commissioners on Uniform State Laws' Uniform Electronic Transactions Act (UETA), which has been adopted in over 20 states. A number of the states have adopted a nonuniform version of UETA, and the precise relationship between the Federal E-Sign law and UETA has yet to be resolved and will most likely be worked out through litigation in the courts over complex technical issues.

Many states have adopted digital signature laws, the first being Utah in 1995. The Utah law, which has been used as a model by several other states, confirms the legal status of digital signatures as valid signatures, provides for use of state-licensed certification authorities, endorses the use of public key encryption technology, and authorizes online databases called repositories, where public keys would be available. The Utah act specifies a negligence standard regarding private encryption keys and places no limit on liability. Thus, if a criminal uses a consumer's private key to commit fraud, the consumer is financially responsible for that fraud, unless the consumer can prove that they used reasonable care in safeguarding their private key. Consumers assume a duty of care when they adopt the use of digital signatures for their transactions, not unlike the care required for PINs on debit cards.

From a practical standpoint, the existence of the E-Sign law and UETA have enabled e-commerce transactions to proceed, and the resolution of the technical details via court actions will probably have little effect on consumers. It is worthy to note that consumers will have to exercise reasonable care over their signature keys, much as they must over PINs and other private numbers. For the most part, software will handle these issues for the typical user.

Non-U.S. Laws

The United Nations has a mandate to further harmonize international trade. With this in mind, the UN General Assembly adopted the United Nations Commission on International Trade Law (UNCITRAL) Model Law on E-Commerce. To implement specific technical aspects of this model law, further work on electronic signatures was needed. The UN General Assembly then adopted the United Nations Commission on International Trade Law (UNCITRAL) Model Law on Electronic Signatures. These model laws have become the basis for many national and international efforts in this area.

Canada

Canada was an early leader in the use of digital signatures. Singapore, Canada, and the U.S. State of Pennsylvania were the first governments to have digitally signed an interstate contract. This contract, digitally signed in 1998, concerned the establishment of a Global Learning Consortium between the three governments (source: *Krypto-Digest* Vol. 1 No. 749, June 11, 1998). Canada went on to adopt a national model bill for electronic signatures to promote e-commerce. This bill, the Uniform Electronic Commerce Act (UECA), allows the use of electronic signatures in communications with the government. The law contains general provisions for the equivalence between traditional and electronic signatures (source: *BNA ECLR*, May 27, 1998, p. 700) and is modeled after the UNCITRAL Model Law on E-Commerce (source: *BNA ECLR*, September 13, 2000, p. 918). The UECA is similar to Bill C-54 in authorizing governments to use electronic technology to deliver services and communicate with citizens.

Individual Canadian provinces have passed similar legislation defining digital signature provisions for e-commerce and government use. These laws are modeled after the UNCITRAL Model Law on E-Commerce to enable widespread use of e-commerce transactions. These laws have also modified the methods of interactions between the citizens and the government, enabling electronic communication in addition to previous forms.

PART VII

The EU

The European Commission adopted a Communication on Digital Signatures and Encryption: "Towards a European Framework for Digital Signatures and Encryption." This communication states that a common framework at the EU level is urgently needed in order to stimulate "the free circulation of digital signature related products and services within the Internal market" and "the development of new economic activities linked to electronic commerce" as well as "to facilitate the use of digital signatures across national borders." Community legislation should address (1) common legal requirements for CAs, (2) legal recognition of digital signatures, and (3) international cooperation. This communication was debated, and a common position was presented to the member nations for incorporation into national laws.

On May 4, 2000, the European Parliament and Council approved the common position adopted by the Council. In June 2000, the final version of the directive, Directive 2000/31/EC, was adopted. The directive is now being implemented by member states. To implement the articles contained in the directive, member states will have to remove barriers, such as legal form requirements, to electronic contracting, leading to uniform digital signature laws across the EU.

Digital Rights Management

The ability to make flawless copies of digital media has led to another 'new' legal issue. For years, the music and video industry has relied on technology to protect its rights with respect to intellectual property. It has been illegal for decades to copy information protected by copyright. This has included items such as music and videos. Even with the law, people have for years made copies of music and videos to share, violating the basic copyright law. This has not had a significant economic impact in the eyes of the industry, as the copies were of lesser quality and that people would pay for original quality in sufficient numbers to keep the economics of the industry healthy. As such, legal action against piracy was typically limited to large scale duplication and sale efforts, commonly performed overseas and subsequently shipped to the U.S. as 'counterfeit' items.

The ability of anyone with a PC to make a perfect copy of digital media has led to industry fears that individual piracy actions could lead to major economic issues in the recording industry. To protect the rights of the recording artists and the economic health of the industry as a whole, the music and video recording industry lobbied the U.S. Congress for protection, which was granted under the Digital Millennium Copyright Act (DMCA) on October 20, 1998. This law was stated, "To amend title 17, United States Code, to implement the World Intellectual Property Organization Copyright Treaty and Performances and Phonograms Treaty, and for other purposes." The majority of this law was well crafted, but one section has drawn considerable comment and criticism. A section of the law makes it illegal to develop, produce, and trade any device or mechanism designed to circumvent technological controls used in copy protection.

Although on the surface, this seems to be reasonable. The methods used in most cases are cryptographic in nature, and this provision had the ability to eliminate and/or severely limit research into encryption, and the strengths and weaknesses of specific methods. A provision, Section 1201(g) of the Digital Millennium Copyright Act, was included to provide for specific relief and allow exemptions for legitimate research. With this section, the law garnered industry support from several organizations such as the Software & Information Industry Association (SIIA), Recording Industry Association of America (RIAA), and Motion Picture Association of America (MPAA). Based on these inputs, the U. S. Copyright Office issued a report supporting the DMCA in a required report to the Congress. This seemed to settle the issues until the RIAA threatened to sue an academic research team headed by Professor Felten from Princeton. The issue behind the suit was the potential publication of results demonstrating that several copy protection methods were flawed in their application. This research came in response to an industry-sponsored challenge to break the methods. After breaking the methods developed and published by the industry, Professor Felten and his team prepared to publish their findings. The RIAA objected and threatened a suit under provisions of DMCA . After several years of litigation and support of Professor Felten by the Electronic Freedom Foundation (EFF), the case was eventually resolved in the academic team's favor, although no case law to prevent further industry-led threats was developed.

This may seem a remote issue; however, industries have been subsequently using the DMCA to protect their technologically inspired copy protection schemes in such industries as laser-toner cartridges and garage-door openers. It is doubtful that the U.S. Congress intended the law to have such effects, yet until they are resolved in court, the DMCA may have wide-reaching implications. The act has specific exemptions for research provided four elements are satisfied:

"(A) the person lawfully obtained the encrypted copy, phonorecord, performance, or display of the published work;

(B) such act is necessary to conduct such encryption research;

(C) the person made a good faith effort to obtain authorization before the circumvention; and

(D) such act does not constitute infringement under this title or a violation of applicable law other than this section, including section 1030 of title 18 and those provisions of title 18 amended by the Computer Fraud and Abuse Act of 1986."*

Additional exemptions are scattered through the law, although many were pasted in during various deliberations on the act and do not make sense when the act is viewed in whole. The effect of these exemptions upon people in the software and technology industry is not clear, and until restrained by case law, the DMCA gives large firms with deep legal pockets a potent weapon to use against parties who disclose flaws in encryption technologies used in various products. Actions have already been initiated against individuals and organizations who have reported security holes in products. This will be an active area of legal contention as the real issues behind digital rights management have yet to be truly resolved.

PART VII

---

* Section 1201(g)(2) of DCMA

Privacy Laws

The advent of interconnected computer systems has enabled businesses and governments to share and integrate information. This has lead to a resurgence in the importance of privacy laws worldwide. Governments in Europe and the United States have taken different approaches in attempts to control privacy via legislation. There are many social and philosophical differences that have lead to these differences, but as the world becomes interconnected, understanding and resolving these differences will be important.

United States Laws

The Electronic Communications Privacy Act (ECPA) of 1986 was passed by Congress and signed by President Ronald Reagan to address a myriad of legal privacy issues that were resulting from the increasing use of computers and other technology specific to telecommunications. Sections of this law addressed e-mail, cellular communications, workplace privacy, and a whole host of other issues related to communicating electronically. A major provision was the prohibition against an employer's monitoring an employee's computer usage, including e-mail, unless consent is obtained. Other legal provisions protect electronic communications from wiretap and outside eavesdropping, as users were assumed to have a reasonable expectation of privacy and afforded protection under the Fourth Amendment to the Constitution.

A common practice with respect to computer access today is the use of a warning banner. These banners are typically displayed whenever a network connection occurs and serve four main purposes. First, from a legal standpoint, they establish the level of expected privacy (usually none on a business system) and serve as consent to real-time monitoring from a business standpoint. Real-time monitoring can be for security reasons, business reasons, or technical network performance reasons. The key is that the banner tells the user that their connection to the network signals their consent to monitoring. Consent can also be obtained to look at files and records. In the case of government systems, consent is needed to prevent direct application of the Fourth Amendment. And the last reason is that the warning banner can establish the system or network administrator's common authority to consent to a law enforcement search.

The Patriot Act of 2001, passed in response to the September 11 terrorist attack on the World Trade Center buildings in New York, substantially changed the levels of checks and balances in laws related to privacy in the United States. This law extended the tap and trace provisions of existing wiretap statutes to the Internet and mandated certain technological modifications at ISPs to facilitate electronic wiretaps on the Internet. The Act also permits the Justice Department to proceed with its rollout of the Carnivore program, an eavesdropping program for the Internet. There has been much stated on both sides of the controversy over Carnivore, but until changed, the Patriot Act mandates that ISPs cooperate and facilitate monitoring. The Patriot Act also permits federal law enforcement personnel to investigate computer trespass (intrusions) and enacts civil penalties for trespassers.

In November 1999, President Clinton signed the Gramm-Leach-Bliley Act, a major piece of legislation affecting the financial industry, and also one with significant privacy provisions for individuals. The key privacy tenets enacted in GLB included the establishment of an opt-out method for individuals to maintain some control over the use of the information provided in a business transaction with a member of the financial community. GLB is enacted through a series of rules governed by state law, federal law, securities law, and federal rules. These rules cover a wider range of financial institutions, from banks and thrifts, to insurance companies, to securities dealers. Some internal information sharing is required under the Fair Credit Reporting Act (FCRA) between affiliated companies, but GLB ended sharing to external third-party firms.

Identity privacy and the establishment of identity theft crimes is governed by the Identity Theft and Assumption Deterrence Act, which makes it a violation of federal law to knowingly use another's identity—identity theft. The collection of information necessary to do this is also governed by GLB, which makes it illegal for someone to gather identity information on another under false pretenses. Student records have even further protections under the Family Education Records and Privacy Act of 1974.

Medical and health information also has privacy implications, which is why the U.S. Congress enacted the Health Insurance Portability & Accountability Act (HIPAA) of 1996. HIPAA calls for sweeping changes in the way health and medical data is stored, exchanged, and used. From a privacy perspective, significant restrictions of data transfers to ensure privacy are included in HIPAA, including security standards and electronic signature provisions. HIPAA security standards mandate a uniform level of protections regarding all health information that pertains to an individual and is housed or transmitted electronically. The standard mandates safeguards for physical storage, maintenance, transmission, and access to individuals' health information. HIPAA mandates that organizations that use electronic signatures will have to meet standards ensuring information integrity, signer authentication, and nonrepudiation. These standards leave to industry the task of specifying the specific technical solutions and only mandate compliance to significant levels of protection as provided by the rules being released by industry.

European Laws

The governments of Europe have developed a comprehensive concept of privacy administered via a set of statutes known as data protection laws. These privacy statutes cover all personal data, whether collected and used by government or private firms. These laws are administered by state and national data protection agencies in each country. With the advent of the European Union (EU), this common comprehensiveness stands in distinct contrast to the patchwork of laws in the United States.

Privacy laws in Europe are built around the concept that privacy is a fundamental human right that demands protection through government administration. When the EU was formed, many laws were harmonized across the fifteen member nations, and data privacy was among those standardized. One important aspect of this harmonization is the Data Protection Directive, adopted by EU members, which has a provision allowing the European Commission to block transfers of personal data to any country outside the EU that has been determined to lack adequate data protection policies. The differences in approach between the U.S. and the EU with respect to data protection lead to the EU issuing expressions of concern about the adequacy of data protection in the U.S., a move that could pave the way to the blocking of data transfers. After negotiation, it was determined that U.S. organizations that voluntarily joined an arrangement known as Safe Harbor would be considered adequate in terms of data protection.

Safe Harbor is a mechanism for self-regulation that can be enforced through trade practice law via the Federal Trade Commission. A business joining the Safe Harbor Consortium must make commitments to abide by specific guidelines concerning privacy. Safe Harbor members also agree to be governed by certain self-enforced regulatory mechanisms, backed ultimately by FTC action.

Another major difference between U.S. and European regulation lies in where the right of control is exercised. In European directives, the right of control over privacy is balanced in such a way as to favor consumers. Rather than having to pay to opt out, as in unlisted phone numbers, consumers have such services for free. Rather than having to opt out at all, consumers get the option to opt in. The default privacy setting is deemed to be the highest level of data privacy, and users have to opt in to share information. This default setting is a cornerstone of the EU Data Protection Directive and is enforced through national laws in all member nations.

Computer Trespass

With the advent of global network connections and the rise of the Internet as a method of connecting computers between homes, businesses, and governments across the globe, a new type of criminal trespass can now be committed. Computer trespass is the unauthorized entry into a computer system via any means, including remote network connections. This has led to a new area of law, one that has both national and international consequences. For crimes that are committed within a country's borders, national laws apply. For cross-border crimes, international laws and international treaties are the norm.

Computer trespass is treated as a crime in many countries. National laws exist in many countries, including the EU, Canada, and the United States. These laws vary by state, but they all have similar provisions defining the unauthorized entry into and use of computer resources as a crime. Whether called computer mischief as in Canada, or computer trespass as in the U.S., unauthorized entry and use of computer resources can be a crime with significant punishments under any of these laws. With the globalization of the computer network infrastructure, or Internet, issues that cross national boundaries have arisen and will continue to grow in prominence. Some of these issues are dealt with through the application of national laws upon request of another government. In the future, an international treaty may pave the way for closer cooperation.

Convention on Cybercrime

The Convention on Cybercrime is the first international treaty on crimes committed via the Internet and other computer networks. The Convention is the product of four years of work by Council of Europe experts, but also by the United States, Canada, Japan, and other countries that are not members of the organization of the member states of the European Council. The current status of the convention is as a draft treaty, ratified by only two members. A total of five members must ratify it for it to become law.

The main objective of the convention, set out in the preamble, is to pursue a common criminal policy aimed at the protection of society against cybercrime, especially by adopting appropriate legislation and fostering international cooperation. This has become increasingly an issue with the globalization of network communication. The ability to write a virus anywhere in the world and escape prosecution because of lack of local laws has become a global concern.

The convention deals particularly with infringements of copyright, computer-related fraud, child pornography, and violations of network security. It also contains a series of powers and procedures covering, for instance, searches of computer networks and interception. It will be supplemented by an additional protocol making any publication of racist and xenophobic propaganda via computer networks a criminal offence.

Chapter Review

From a system administrator's position, these privacy laws are actually fairly easy to comply with. Put warning banners in place on all of your systems that enable consent to monitoring as a condition of access. This will protect you and the firm during normal routine operation of the system. Safeguard all personal information obtained in the course of your duties and do not obtain unnecessary information merely because you can get it. With respect to the various privacy statutes that are industry specific—GLB, FCRA, ECPA, FERPA, HIPAA—refer to your own institution's guidelines and policies. When confronted with aspects of the USA Patriot Act, refer to your company's general counsel, for although the act may absolve you and the firm of responsibility, this act's implications with respect to existing law are still unknown. And in the event that your system is trespassed upon (hacked), you now have the ability to get federal law enforcement assistance in investigating and prosecuting the perpetrators.

Questions

1. The VP of IS desires to monitor user actions on the company's intranet. What is the best method to obtain the proper permissions?

   A. A consent banner displayed upon login

   B. Written permission from a company officer

   C. Nothing, the system belongs to the company

   D. Written permission from the user

2. Your Social Security number and other associated facts kept by your bank are protected by what law against disclosure?

   A. The Social Security Act of 1934

   B. The Patriot Act of 2001

   C. The Gramm-Leach-Bliley Act

   D. HIPAA

3. Breaking into another computer system in the U.S., even if you do not cause any damage, is regulated by what laws?

   A. State law, as the damage is minimal

   B. Federal law under the Identity Theft and Assumption Deterrence Act

   C. Federal law under Electronic Communications Privacy Act (ECPA) of 1986

   D. Federal law under the Patriot Act of 2001

4. Export of encryption programs is regulated by the

   A. U.S. State Department

   B. U.S. Commerce Department

   C. U.S. Department of Defense

   D. National Security Agency

5. For the FBI to install and operate Carnivore on an ISP's network, what is required?

   A. A court order specifying specific items being searched for

   B. An official request from the FBI

   C. An impact statement to assess recoverable costs to the ISP

   D. A written request from an ISP to investigate a computer trespass incident

6. True or false: Digital signatures are equivalent to notarized signatures for all transactions in the United States.

   A. True for all transactions in which both parties agree to use digital signatures

   B. True only for non–real property transactions

   C. True only where governed by specific state statute

   D. False, as the necessary law has not yet passed as of 2002

7. The primary factor(s) behind data sharing compliance between U.S. and European companies is/are

   A. Safe Harbor Provision

   B. European Data Privacy Laws

   C. U.S. FTC enforcement actions

   D. All of the above

8. True or false: Writing viruses and releasing them across the Internet is a violation of law.

   A. Always True: All countries have reciprocal agreements under international law.

   B. Partially True: Depends upon laws in country of origin.

   C. False: Computer security laws do not cross international boundaries.

   D. Partially True: Depends upon the specific countries involved, for the author of the virus and the recipient.

9. Publication of flaws in encryption used for copy protection is a potential violation of

   A. HIPAA

   B. U.S. Commerce Department regulations

   C. DMCA

   D. National Security Agency regulations

10. Violation of DMCA can result in

    A. Civil fine

    B. Jail time

    C. Activity subject to legal injunctions

    D. All of the above

Answers

1. **A.** A consent banner consenting to monitoring resolves issues of monitoring with respect to the Electronic Communications Privacy Act (ECPA) of 1986.

2. **C.** The Gramm-Leach-Bliley Act governs the sharing of privacy information with respect to financial institutions.

3. **D.** The Patriot Act of 2001 made computer trespass a federal felony.

4. **B.** Export controls on commercial encryption products are administered by the Bureau of Industry and Security (BIS) in the U.S. Department of Commerce.

5. **B.** The Patriot Act of 2001 mandated ISP compliance with the FBI Carnivore program.

6. **A.** Electronic digital signatures are considered valid for transactions in the U.S. since the passing of the Electronic Signatures in Global and National Commerce Act (E-Sign) in 2001.

7. **D.** All of the above. The primary driver is European Data protection laws as enforced on U.S firms by FTC enforcement through the Safe Harbor provision mechanism.

8. **D.** This is partially true, for not all countries share reciprocal laws. Some common laws and reciprocity issues exist in certain international communities, for example, European Union, so some cross-border legal issues have been resolved.

9. **C.** This is a potential violation of the Digital Millennium Copyright Act of 1998 unless an exemption provision is met.

10. **D.** All of the above have been attributed to DMCA, including the jailing of a Russian programmer who came to the U.S. to speak at a security conference. See www.eff.org/IP/DRM/DMCA/20010830_eff_dmca_op-ed.html.

Privilege Management

In this chapter, you will

- Learn the differences between user, group, and role management
- Discover the advantage of single sign-ons
- Understand the pros and cons of centralized vs. decentralized privilege management
- Learn about different auditing types (privilege, usage, and escalation)
- Explore methods of managing access (MAC, DAC, and RBAC)

Computer systems are in such wide use now that they touch almost every facet of our lives: they process credit card transactions, they handle airline reservations, they store a vast amount of personal information, and they manage car engines to ensure optimal fuel efficiency. Most of the time, computers—particularly the more complicated systems, such as PCs, servers and mainframes—require interaction from a human user. The user interacts with the applications and operating system of the computer to complete tasks and perform specific functions.

On single-user systems, such as PCs, the individual user typically has access to most of the system's resources, processing capability, and stored data. On multiuser systems, such as servers and mainframes, an individual user may have very limited access to the system and the data stored on that system. An administrator responsible for managing and maintaining the multiuser system may have much greater access. So how does the computer system know which users should have access to what data? How does the operating system know what applications a user is allowed to use?

On early computer systems, anyone with physical access had fairly significant rights to the system and could typically access any file or execute any application. As computers became more popular and it became obvious that some way of separating and restricting users was needed, the concept of users, groups, and privileges came into being. These concepts continue to be developed and refined and are now part of what we call *privilege management*.

Though privilege management has become a crucial part of modern operating systems and computer operations, it's really quite a simple concept. *Privilege management* is the process of restricting a user's ability to interact with the computer system. A user's interaction with a computer system covers a fairly broad area and includes items such as viewing, modifying and deleting data, running applications, stopping and starting processes, and controlling computer resources. Essentially, everything a user can do to or with a computer system falls into the realm of privilege management.

Privilege management occurs at many different points within an operating system or even within applications running on a particular operating system. While UNIX and Windows operating systems have a slightly different approach to privilege management, there are some similar approaches and concepts that we will cover in this chapter.

User, Group, and Role Management

In order to effectively manage the privileges of many different people on the same system, you must have a mechanism for separating people into distinct entities (users) so you can control things on an individual level. At the same time, it's convenient and efficient to be able to lump users together when granting many different people (groups) access to something at the same time. At other times, it's useful to be able to grant or restrict access based upon a person's job or function within the organization (role). While you can manage privileges on the basis of users alone, it is far more convenient and efficient to manage using the users, group, and role capabilities together.

User

The term "user" generally applies to any person accessing a computer system. In privilege management, a *user* is a single individual, such as "John Forthright" or "Sally Jenkins." This is generally the lowest level addressed by privilege management and the most common area for addressing things like access, rights, and capabilities. When accessing a computer system, each user is generally given a *userid*—a unique alphanumeric identifier they will use to identify themselves when logging in or accessing the system. Userids are usually based on some combination of the user's first, middle, and last name and will often include numbers. When developing a scheme for selecting userids, it is important to keep in mind that userids must be unique to each user, but must also be fairly easy for the user to remember and use.

Though there are some notable exceptions, in general a user wishing to access a computer system must first have a userid created for them on the system they wish to use. This is usually done by a system administrator, security administrator, or other privileged user, and this is the first step in privilege management—a user should not be allowed to create their own account.

Once the account is created and a userid is selected, the administrator may assign specific permissions to that user. *Permissions* control what the user is allowed to do on the system—which files they may access, which programs they may execute, and so on. While PCs typically only have one or two user accounts, larger systems such as servers and mainframes may have hundreds of accounts on the same system. Figure 16-1 shows the Users and Passwords screen from a Windows 2000 Professional system. Note that there are several user accounts on this system, each identified by a unique userid.

There are a few "special" user accounts that don't typically match up one-to-one with a real person. These accounts are reserved for special functions and typically have much more access and control over the computer system than the average user does. Two such accounts are the "administrator" account under Windows and the "root" account under

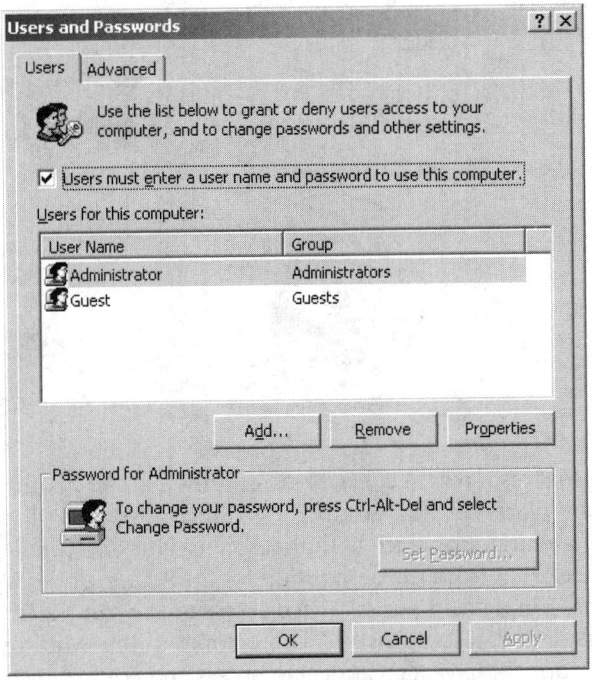

Figure 16-1

Windows 2000's
Users and
Passwords utility

UNIX. The "administrator" and "root" accounts are known as *superusers*—if something can be done on the system, the superuser has the power to do it. These accounts are not typically assigned to a specific individual and are often shared, only being accessed when the full capabilities of that account are needed.

Due to the power these accounts possess, and the few, if any, restrictions placed on these accounts, they must be protected with strong passwords that are not easily guessed or obtained. These accounts are also the most common targets of attackers—if the attacker can become root or assume the privilege level associated with the root account, they can bypass most access controls and accomplish anything they want to on that system.

Groups

Under privilege management, a *group* is pretty much what you think it would be. A group is a collection of users with some common criteria, such as a need for access to a particular dataset or group of applications. A group can have one user or hundreds of users, and each user can belong to one or more groups. Figure 16-2 shows a common approach to grouping users—building groups based on job function.

By assigning a user membership in a specific group, it becomes much easier to control that user's access and privileges. For example, if every member of the Engineering department needs access to product development documents, administrators can place all the users in the Engineering department in a single group and then allow that group to access the necessary documents. Once a group is assigned permissions to access a particular resource, adding a new user to that group will automatically allow that user

PART VII

Figure 16-2
Logical
representation
of groups

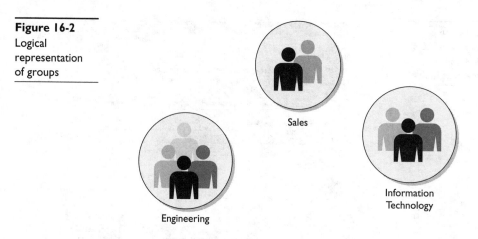

Sales

Information
Technology

Engineering

to access that resource. In effect, the user "inherits" the permissions of the group as soon as they are placed in that group. As Figure 16-3 shows, a computer system can have many different groups, each with their own rights and privileges.

As you can see from the description for the Administrators group in Figure 16-3, this group has complete and unrestricted access to the computer. This includes all files, applications, and datasets. Anyone who belongs to the Administrators group or is placed in this group will have a great deal of access and control over the system.

Role

The other common method of managing access and privileges is by roles. A *role* is usually synonymous with a job or set of functions. For example, the role of "backup operator" may be applied to someone who is responsible for making sure that the system and any data residing on the system is regularly and successfully saved (usually to some sort of removable media, such as tapes). Backup operators need to accomplish specific functions

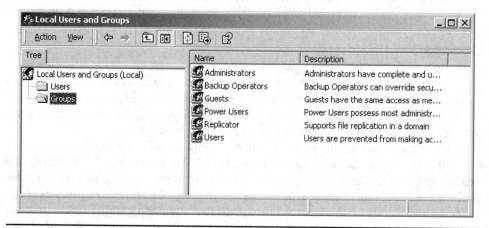

Figure 16-3   Group management screen from a Windows 2000 system

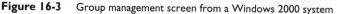

and will need access to certain resources; for example, they may need the ability to read files on the system and save them to tape. In general, anyone serving in the role of backup operator will need the same rights and privileges as every other backup operator. For simplicity and efficiency, rights and privileges can be assigned to the role "backup operator," and anyone assigned to fulfill that role will automatically have the correct rights and privileges to perform their tasks.

Single Sign-On

In order to use a system, users must be able to access it, which they usually do by supplying their userid and corresponding password. As any security administrator knows, the more systems a particular user has access to, the more passwords that user must have and remember. The natural tendency for users is to select passwords that are easy to remember, or even the same password for use on the multiple systems they access. Invariably, users will forget the passwords they chose for infrequently accessed systems, which creates more work for system administrators who must assist users with password changes or password recovery efforts. Wouldn't it be easier for the user to just log in once and only have to remember a single, good password? This is made possible with a technology called *single sign-on*.

Single sign-on, often called SSO, is an authentication process where the user can enter a single userid and password and then be able to move from application to application or resource to resource without having to supply further authentication information. Put simply, you supply the right userid and password once and you have access to all the applications and data you're supposed to, without having to log in multiple times and remember many different passwords. From a user standpoint, single sign-on is much easier—you only need to remember one userid and one password. From an administration standpoint, single sign-on can be easier to manage and maintain. From a security standpoint, single sign-on may even be more secure, as the user who needs to remember only one password is less likely to pick something that is simple and easy or to write it down. Figure 16-4 shows a logical depiction of the single sign-on process:

1. The user signs in once, providing their userid and password to the single sign-on server.

2. The single sign-on server then provides authentication information to any resource the user accesses during that session. The server interfaces with the other applications and systems—the user does not need to log in to each system individually.

In reality, single sign-on is usually a little more difficult to implement than vendors would lead you to believe. To be effective and useful, all your applications need to be able to access and use the authentication provided by the single sign-on process. The more diverse your network is, the less likely this is to be the case. If your network, like most, contains multiple operating systems, custom applications, and a diverse user base, single sign-on may not even be a viable option.

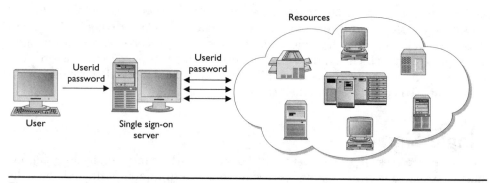

Figure 16-4 Single sign-on process

Centralized vs. Decentralized Management

In the world of telecommunications and computers, there is almost always more than one way to accomplish the same goal. Coincidentally, there are usually several schools of thought as to why one method is better than the other. This is especially true of security and privilege management. Regardless of how vast or minute your computer deployment is, you will have to manage the rights and privileges of the users and processes using those systems, and the two main approaches to rights and privilege management are centralized and decentralized.

Centralized Management

Centralized management brings the authority and responsibility for managing and maintaining rights and privileges into a single group, location, or area. To illustrate, consider the employees of a bank. In a bank, the bank teller has certain rights and privileges: they can process withdrawals and deposits, count money, and process a specific set of transactions. But a bank teller can't approve your car loan, and they don't have unrestricted access to the bank vault. Even if they wanted to, the bank teller can't expand their privileges or give additional access to other tellers. In a bank, the bank manager is the central management authority—they decide who can approve loans, access the vault, and give away free toasters. In order to get elevated rights and privileges, the teller must go through the central authority, the bank manager. In a similar fashion, when it comes to managing and maintaining rights and privileges under the centralized model, there is a single group or person that creates and manages users, assigns rights and privileges, and controls access to information systems for the entire organization.

The centralized model has certain advantages and disadvantages.

Advantages

- It can be more efficient, especially for large organizations, to have a specialized central capability for privilege management.
- Fewer people must be trained on tasks associated with privilege management.

- It is easier to implement new capabilities and processes centrally.
- Central control makes systems easier to audit and manage.
- A more consistent approach is ensured, as everyone "does it the same way."

Disadvantages

- Central management makes it more difficult to implement changes quickly.
- Functions at remote offices may be slowed down.
- It adds bureaucracy and is less flexible.
- Central control usually requires dedicated personnel and resources.

Most large corporations will use some form of centralized management, particularly at the local office level. For example, if a company has offices in Dallas, New York, and Seattle, each city may have its own centralized privilege management functions that perform all of the appropriate tasks for that location. In general, when dealing with a large number of users, it is better to use a centralized approach to privilege management.

Decentralized Management

Decentralized management spreads out the authority and capability to manage privileges and rights. While this may sound like a recipe for anarchy to some, it can be an effective model for the right organization. To illustrate, consider a police department. As a group, police officers are working toward a common goal—the "protect and serve" type of approach that makes our cities safer. Yet each individual police officer has a wide amount of latitude and authority: they can decide when to issue tickets and traffic citations, when to perform an arrest, what sort of activity is considered suspicious, and so on. In essence, individual police officers are constantly modifying their behavior and actions to fit the situation around them, sometimes using more authority and sometimes using less authority. With regard to computer systems, this is similar to each user or department controlling their own access to information systems and associated resources.

The decentralized model has certain advantages and disadvantages.

Advantages

- The decentralized model is highly flexible, as changes can be made whenever they are needed.
- It does not require a dedicated set of personnel and resources.
- Bureaucracy is reduced.

Disadvantages

- It produces very different approaches in each department and office.
- It is more difficult to manage, audit, and maintain.

- There is an increased risk of security breach and corruption.
- More users must be trained on the same tasks.

A decentralized model works well for rapidly changing environments where the tasks are constantly changing and the personnel are highly skilled and motivated. An academic research lab is a good example—in this environment, each researcher may need the capability to modify, manage, and maintain their own information systems without having to rely on a centralized authority.

The Decentralized, Centralized Model

In reality, most companies, and particularly the larger ones, use a combination approach. Imagine a company with 100,000 employees and offices in 52 locations around the world. It's not feasible to have a single person or group manage the rights and privileges of every user in an organization that large. It's much more efficient to decentralize control away from the main corporate office and let each office location handle their own privilege management tasks. Within each office, privilege management is usually centralized to a specific group of individuals (often the system administrators or security personnel). On a macro scale, the company as a whole is decentralized, while on a micro scale each office is centralized—it just depends on the level at which you're examining the organization.

Auditing (Privilege, Usage, and Escalation)

If you go through the trouble and effort to restrict access to certain resources and datasets, you will likely want to make sure only authorized individuals are able to gain access to those resources. Chances are, you'll also want to know who accessed what resources, when they accessed the resources, and what they did. When dealing with privilege management, *auditing* is the name given to any actions or processes used to verify the assigned privileges and rights of a user, as well as any capabilities used to create and maintain a record showing who accessed a particular system and what actions they performed. Records showing which users accessed a computer system and what actions they performed are called *audit trails*. In this section, we will discuss auditing as it pertains to three specific areas: privilege, usage, and escalation.

Privilege Auditing

Privilege auditing is the process of checking the rights and privileges assigned to a specific account or group of accounts. Each user account, group, and role is checked to see what rights and privileges are assigned to them. These results are then compared to the "expected" results to see where the actual results and expected results differ. Privilege auditing helps to find accounts with more privileges than they should have, as well as accounts that have fewer privileges than they should have. By comparing expected to actual results, the auditor can then determine which changes need to be made (like the removal of certain accounts, putting users into new groups or taking them out of other groups, and so on) and which rights and privileges need to be adjusted. Most organizations will perform some type of privilege auditing, either formally or informally, on a regular basis.

How does privilege auditing enhance security? Privilege auditing helps ensure that users have the correct privileges and rights to perform their jobs—not too much access and not too little access. Privilege auditing follows the "trust but verify" philosophy of double-checking each account, group, and role to ensure administrators have performed their jobs correctly. This is particularly important in large corporations or positions where there is a high rate of turnover or employee movement. As an employee leaves or changes positions, their privileges and rights must be revoked or modified to ensure their account is properly disabled (if they are leaving) or their account has been adjusted to reflect their new position (if they are changing positions).

Usage Auditing

Usage auditing is the process of recording who did what and when. Usage auditing creates a record showing who has accessed specific computer systems and what actions that user performed during a given period of time. Usage auditing can also be applied to datasets, specific applications, or databases, and it is very commonly used in accounting systems, transaction-based systems, and database management systems.

Usage auditing is usually performed by a process that records actions and stores them in a file for later analysis. These files can be in plain text or custom formats or can even be encrypted to prevent unauthorized access. Figure 16-5 shows an example of the usage-auditing process on a Red Hat Linux system.

In this example you can see various processes starting, a user logging in, and actions being performed. Each of these pieces of information can help a system administrator determine what happened on that system during that given period of time. In this example, we see an entry indicating the root user logged in on January 3 at 16:21:48 (4:21 P.M.). This tells us several things:

- Someone with knowledge of the password for the root account has accessed the system.

- The login from 127.0.0.1 tells us that the user logged in on the system's console, so they had physical access to the system.

- The time of 4:21 P.M. tells us it was during business hours.

```
Jan  3 15:48:03 donald sshd[729]: Server listening on 0.0.0.0 port 22.
Jan  3 16:20:22 donald webmin[4086]: Webmin starting
Jan  3 16:20:40 donald xinetd[743]: START: sgi_fam pid=4142 from=<no address>
Jan  3 16:21:48 donald webmin[4212]: Successful login as root from 127.0.0.1
Jan  3 16:29:19 donald useradd[4323]: new group: name=mysql, gid=101
Jan  3 16:29:19 donald useradd[4323]: new user: name=mysql, uid=100, gid=101,
home=/var/lib/mysql, shell=/bin/bash
Jan  3 16:57:02 donald sshd[729]: Received signal 15; terminating.
Jan  3 16:58:03 donald sshd[728]: Server listening on 0.0.0.0 port 22.
Jan  3 16:58:14 donald webmin[917]: Webmin starting
Jan  3 16:58:40 donald xinetd[742]: START: sgi_fam pid=1024 from=<no address>
Jan  3 17:08:52 donald sshd[728]: Received signal 15; terminating.
```

Figure 16-5   Sample of a usage-auditing log from a Red Hat Linux system

PART VII

Usage auditing is very common in both UNIX and Windows operating systems. Depending on the operating system and logging utility, the administrator can have a great deal of flexibility in what types of information are logged. Figure 16-6 shows the Audit Policy options available in the Windows 2000 operating system. As you can see, there are several audit policies that can be enabled with success and failure criteria. For example, you can audit the successful access to a particular file, or you can audit a logon failure. This type of customizable auditing allows the administrator to adjust the auditing process to suit their particular concerns and environment.

As you can see, this sort of information can be very useful when performing any sort of security investigation or incident response activities. With usage-auditing information, if there is a security incident, you can attempt to re-create the event: which accounts were compromised, what actions were performed, and so on. Having this type of information may enable you to spot the incident, correct any problems, address any issues, and return the machine to operational status. Without this type of information, you might be forced to completely rebuild the system as you would have no way of knowing what the attacker did or what they had access to on the system.

Escalation Auditing

Escalation auditing is the process of looking for an increase in privileges—a normal user suddenly switches to the administrator or root account or obtains admin-level access. Administrators normally operate using their own accounts and switch to the administrator or root account only when they need to perform specific operations that require that level of privilege. So, in the normal course of operations, you will see certain users elevating their privilege level, and this is acceptable behavior. However, this is usually a

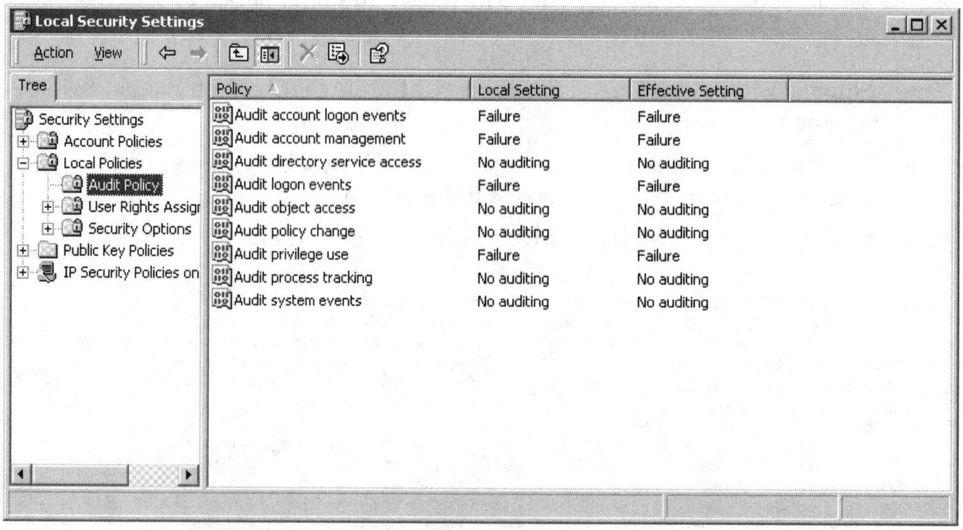

Figure 16-6   Audit Policy settings under Windows 2000

small subset of the overall user community, and any privilege escalation by someone outside the administrator group is likely a security breach. Escalation auditing looks for those unexpected or unauthorized increases in rights or privileges and can help security administrators determine when they have happened.

Figure 16-7 shows a good example of escalation auditing. In this section of the auditing log file, you see the user "zack" log in to the system and attempt to switch to the root account. Zack fails once and then succeeds, becoming root and assuming all the rights and privileges associated with that account. As a security administrator, you would need to make sure Zack had legitimate access to the root account and is authorized to elevate his privileges accordingly.

Handling Access Control (MAC, DAC, and RBAC)

The last area of privilege management we will discuss deals with three methods for handling access control:

- **MAC**   Mandatory access control
- **DAC**   Discretionary access control
- **RBAC**   Role-based access control

Mandatory Access Control (MAC)

Mandatory access control is the process of controlling access to information based on the sensitivity of that information and whether or not the user is operating at the appropriate sensitivity level and has the authority to access that information. Under a MAC system, each piece of information and every system resource (files, devices, networks, and so on) is labeled with its sensitivity level (such as Public, Engineering Private, Jones Secret). Users are assigned a clearance level that sets the upper boundary of the information and devices that they are allowed to access. For example, if the administrator defines a file as having an "Engineering Private" sensitivity level, then only the members of the engineering group with access to private information currently operating at a Private sensitivity level can access that file and its contents. A file with a Public sensitivity label would be available to anyone on the system.

The access control and sensitivity labels are required in a MAC system. Administrators define the labels and assign them to users and resources. Users must then operate within their assigned sensitivity and clearance levels—they don't have the option to

```
Jan 26 15:17:21 donald (pam_unix)[16605]: session opened for user zack
Jan 26 15:17:45 donald su(pam_unix)[16650]: authentication failure; logname=
uid=500 euid=0 tty= ruser=zack rhost=  user=root
Jan 26 15:17:51 donald su(pam_unix)[16651]: session opened for user root by
(uid=500)
Jan 26 15:17:53 donald su(pam_unix)[16651]: session closed for user root
Jan 26 15:17:54 donald su(pam_unix)[16605]: session closed for user zack
```

Figure 16-7   Escalation auditing example

modify their own sensitivity levels or the levels of the information resources they create. Due to the complexity involved, MAC is typically only run on systems and operating systems such as Trusted Solaris and OpenBSD where security is a top priority.

Figure 16-8 illustrates MAC in operation. The information resource on the right has been labeled "Engineering Secret," meaning only users in the Engineering group operating at the Secret sensitivity level or above can access that resource. The top user is operating at the Secret level but is not a member of Engineering and is denied access to the resource. The middle user is a member of Engineering, but is operating at a Public sensitivity level and is therefore denied access to the resource. The bottom user is a member of Engineering, is operating at a Secret sensitivity level, and is allowed to access the information resource.

Discretionary Access Control (DAC)

Discretionary access control is the process of using file permissions and optional access control lists to restrict access to information based on a user's identity or group membership. DAC is the most common access control system and is commonly used in both UNIX and Windows operating systems. The "discretionary" part of DAC means that a file or resource owner has the ability to change the permissions on that file or resource.

Under UNIX operating systems, file permissions consist of three distinct parts:

- Owner permissions (read, write, and execute)
- Group permissions (read, write, and execute)
- World permissions (read, write, and execute)

In a simplified view, a file's permissions are usually displayed as a series of nine characters with the first three characters representing the owner's permissions, the second three characters representing the group permissions, and the last three characters representing the permissions for everyone else, or for the "world." This concept is illustrated in Figure 16-9.

Figure 16-8
Logical representation of mandatory access control

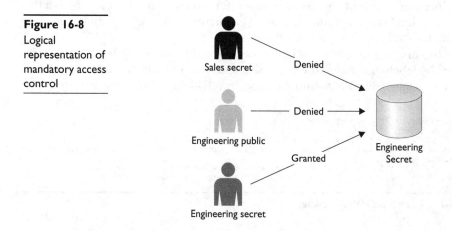

Figure 16-9
Discretionary file
permissions in
the UNIX
environment

Owner	Group	World
rwx	**rw-**	**---**

For example, if you have a file called "design one" owned by Bob, group permissions for Engineering, and the permissions on that file are "rwx rw- ---" as in Figure 16-9, then

- Bob can read, write, and execute the file (rwx)
- Members of the Engineering group can read and write the file but not execute it (rw-)
- The world has no access to the file and can't read, write, or execute the file

Remember that under the discretionary model, the file's owner, Bob, can change the file's permissions anytime he wants.

Role-Based Access Control (RBAC)

Role-based access control is the process of managing access and privileges based on the user's assigned roles. RBAC is the access control model that most closely resembles an organization's structure. Under RBAC, you must first determine the activities that must be performed and the resources that must be accessed by specific roles. For example, the role of "backup operator" must be able to mount and write to removable media and must be able to read every file (in order to save it to tape). Once all the roles are created and the rights and privileges associated with those roles are determined, users can then be assigned one or more roles based on their job functions. When a role is assigned to a specific user, the user gets all the rights and privileges assigned to that role.

Chapter Review

Privilege management is the process of restricting a user's ability to interact with the computer system. Privilege management can be performed on an individual user basis, on membership in a specific group or groups, or on a function/role basis. Regardless of the method chosen, the key concepts are the ability to restrict and control access to information and information systems. One of the methods used to simplify privilege management is single sign-on. Single sign-on requires a user to authenticate successfully once. The validated credentials and associated rights and privileges are then automatically carried forward when the user accesses other systems or applications.

Privilege management can be performed in a centralized or decentralized mode. In a centralized mode, control, along with modifications, updates, and maintenance, is performed from a central entity. In a decentralized mode, control is pushed down to a much lower and more distributed level. Tracking the effectiveness of privilege management

PART VII

and any suspected violations can be done through the use of auditing. *Auditing* is the process of tracking things such as logons, logoffs, file access, and process start or stop events. Auditing can be performed on a privilege level, usage, or escalation basis.

Access control is a specific part of privilege management, more specifically the part that deals with user access. The three main models of access control are mandatory access control, discretionary access control, and role-based access control. Mandatory access control is based on the sensitivity of the information or process itself. Discretionary access control uses file permissions and access lists to restrict access based on a user's identity or group membership. Role-based access control restricts access based on the user's assigned role or roles.

Questions

1. Privilege management applies to

   A. Files, resources, and users

   B. Users, physical locations, and resources

   C. Users, physical locations, and processes

   D. Applications, systems, and security

2. A userid is

   A. A unique identifier assigned to each user

   B. A form of privilege management

   C. A unique identifier given to each process

   D. A type of system command

3. Role management is based on

   A. The userid

   B. The group a user is assigned to

   C. A job or function

   D. The rights associated with the root user

4. Single sign-on

   A. Only works for one user

   B. Requires only one userid and password

   C. Groups like users together

   D. Requires the user to log in to each resource one time

5. Compared to decentralized management, centralized management

   A. Typically requires less training and fewer resources

   B. Brings control into a central location

    C. Is easier to audit and manage

    D. All of the above

6. Records showing what users accessed a computer system and what actions they performed are called

    A. User rights

    B. System and event logs

    C. Audit trails

    D. Permissions

7. The three types of auditing are

    A. Privilege, usage, and escalation

    B. User, system, and application

    C. File, process, and media

    D. None of the above

8. In the context of privilege management, MAC stands for

    A. Media access control

    B. Monetary audit control

    C. Mandatory access control

    D. None of the above

9. Under discretionary access control

    A. File access is controlled by permissions

    B. Owners can change permissions of their own files

    C. File permissions may consist of owner, group, and world

    D. All of the above

10. In role-based access control

    A. Resources are assigned to individual userids

    B. Access is granted based on job function

    C. Files are labeled with sensitivity levels

    D. Users are divided into groups

Answers

1. **A.** Privilege management is the process of restricting a user's ability to interact with the computer system, including files and resources.

2. **A.** A userid is a unique identifier assigned to each user of a computer system. This allows the system to distinguish one user from another as well as determine what information, applications, and resources a particular user has access to.

3. **C.** Role management is based on jobs and functions, not specific groups or users.

4. **B.** Single sign-on only requires one userid and password. The user logs on to the single sign-on server once, and the SSO server then performs any additional authentication tasks for the user.

5. **D.** When compared to decentralized management, centralized management typically requires less training and fewer resources, brings control to a central location, and is easier to audit and manage.

6. **C.** Records showing what users accessed a computer system and what actions they performed are called audit trails.

7. **A.** The three main types of auditing discussed were privilege, usage, and escalation.

8. **C.** MAC stands for mandatory access control, which is the process of controlling access to information based on the sensitivity of that information and whether or not the user is operating at the appropriate sensitivity level and has the authority to access that information.

9. **D.** Under discretionary access control, owners can change their files' permissions when they want to, file access is controlled by permissions, and file permissions in UNIX operating systems consist of different privileges for owner, group, and world.

10. **B.** In role-based access control, access to files and resources is usually assigned by job function. For example, a person with a "backup operator" role would be assigned the rights and privileges needed to perform that function.

Computer Forensics

In this chapter, you will

- Learn the rules and types of evidence
- Review the collection of evidence
- Study the preservation of evidence
- Discover the importance of a viable chain of custody
- Explore the steps to investigating a computer crime or policy violation

Computer forensics is certainly one of the popular buzzwords in computer security. This chapter will address the key aspects of computer forensics in preparation for the Security+ certification. It is not intended to be a legal tutorial regarding the presentation of evidence in a court of law. The principles are of value in conducting any investigative processes, including internal or external audit procedures, but there are many nuances of handling legal cases that are far beyond the scope of this text.

The term *forensics* relates to the application of scientific knowledge to legal problems. Specifically, computer forensics involves the preservation, identification, documentation, and interpretation of computer data, as explained in Warren G. Kruse and Jay Heiser's *Computer Forensics: Incident Response Essentials* (Boston: Addison-Wesley, 2002). In today's practice, computer forensics can be performed for three purposes:

- Investigating and analyzing computer systems as related to a violation of laws
- Investigating and analyzing computer systems for compliance with an organization's policies
- Investigating computer systems that have been remotely attacked

This last point is often referred to as *incident response* and can be a subset of the first two points. If an unauthorized person is remotely attacking a system, laws may indeed have been violated. However, a company employee performing similar acts may or may not violate laws and may or may not violate corporate policies. So, any of these three purposes could ultimately result in legal actions. Therefore, it is important to note that computer forensics actions may, at some point in time, deal with legal violations, and investigations could go to court proceedings. It is extremely important to understand this concept, because even minor procedural missteps can have significant legal consequences.

Evidence

Evidence consists of the documents, verbal statements, and material objects admissible in a court of law. Evidence is critical to convincing management, juries, judges, or other authorities that some kind of violation has occurred. The submission of evidence is challenging, but it is even more challenging when computers are used because the people involved may not be technically educated and thus may not fully understand what's happened.

Computer evidence presents yet more challenges because the data itself cannot be sensed with the physical senses. You can see printed characters, but you can't see the bits where that data is stored—it is a magnetic pulse on a disk or some other storage technology. Therefore, it must always be evaluated through some kind of "filter" rather than sensed directly by human senses. This is often of concern to auditors, because good auditing techniques recommend accessing the original data or a version as close as possible to the original data.

Standards for Evidence

To be credible, especially if it will be used in court proceedings or in corporate disciplinary actions which could be challenged legally, evidence must meet these three standards:

- **Sufficient**   The evidence must be convincing or measure up without question.
- **Competent**   The evidence must be legally qualified and reliable.
- **Relevant**   The evidence must be material to the case or have a bearing on the matter at hand.

Types of Evidence

All evidence is not created equal. Some evidence is stronger and better than other, weaker evidence. There are several types of evidence:

- **Direct evidence**   Oral testimony that proves a specific fact (such as an eyewitness's statement). The knowledge of the facts is obtained through the five senses of the witness. There are no inferences or presumptions.
- **Real evidence** (also known as associative or physical evidence)   Tangible objects that prove or disprove a fact. Physical evidence links the suspect to the scene of a crime.
- **Documentary evidence**   Evidence in the form of business records, printouts, manuals, and the like. Much of the evidence relating to computer crimes is documentary evidence.
- **Demonstrative evidence**   Used to aid the jury and may be in the form of a model, experiment, chart, and so on, offered to prove that an event occurred.

For more information on the types of evidence, see Harold F. Tipton and Micki Krause's *Information Security Management Handbook*, 4th edition (Boca Raton: Auerbach Publications, 2000), p. 607.

Three Rules Regarding Evidence

There are some rules that guide the use of evidence, especially if they could result in court proceedings:

- **Best evidence rule**   Courts prefer original evidence rather than a copy to ensure that no alteration of the evidence (whether intentional or unintentional) has occurred. There are instances when a duplicate can be accepted, such as when the original is lost or destroyed by acts of God or in the normal course of business. A duplicate is also acceptable when a third party beyond the court's subpoena power possesses the original.

- **Exclusionary rule**   The Fourth Amendment to the United States Constitution precludes illegal search and seizure. Therefore, any evidence collected in violation of the Fourth Amendment is not admissible as evidence. Additionally, if evidence is collected in violation of the Electronic Communications Privacy Act (ECPA) or other related violations of the United States Code, it may not be admissible to a court. For example, if there is no policy regarding the company's intent to electronically monitor network traffic or systems, and the employee has not acknowledged this policy by signing an agreement, sniffing network traffic could be a violation of the ECPA.

- **Hearsay rule**   Hearsay is second-hand evidence—evidence not gathered from the personal knowledge of the witness. Computer-generated evidence is considered hearsay evidence—see Tipton and Krause's *Information Security Management Handbook*, p. 608–609.

 NOTE   The laws just mentioned are U.S. laws. Other countries and jurisdictions may have other laws that are similar and would need to be considered in a similar manner.

Collecting Evidence

When information or objects are presented to management or admitted to court to support a claim, that information or those objects can be considered as evidence or documentation supporting your investigative efforts. Senior management will always ask a lot of questions—second- and third-order questions that you need to be able to answer quickly. Likewise, in a court, credibility is critical. Therefore, evidence must be properly acquired, identified, protected against tampering, transported, and stored.

Acquiring Evidence

When an incident occurs, you will need to collect data and information to facilitate your investigation. If someone is committing a crime or intentionally violating a company policy, they will likely try to hide the fact that they were involved. Therefore, collect as much information as soon as you can. Obviously, as time passes, evidence can be tampered with or destroyed. Look around on the desk, on the Rolodex, under the keyboard, in desktop storage areas, and on cubicle bulletin boards for any information that might be relevant. Secure floppy disks, CDs, flash memory cards, USB drives, tapes, and other removable media. Request copies of logs as soon as possible. Most Internet service providers (ISPs) will protect logs that could be subpoenaed. Take photos (some localities require use of Polaroid photos, as they are harder to modify without obvious tampering) or video tapes. Include photos of operating computer screens and hardware components from multiple angles. Be sure to photograph internal components before removing them for analysis.

When an incident occurs and the computer being used is going to be secured, there are two facts to consider: should it be turned off, and should it be disconnected from the network? There has been much discussion concerning the reasons for turning a computer on or turning it off. Some forensics professionals state that the plug should be pulled in order to freeze the current state of the computer. However, this results in the loss of any data associated with an attack in progress from the machine. Any data in RAM will also be lost. Further, it may corrupt the computer's file system and could call into question the validity of your findings.

On the other hand, it is possible for the computer criminal to leave behind a software bomb that you don't know about, and any commands you execute, including shutting down or restarting the system, could destroy or modify files, information, or evidence. The criminal may have anticipated such an investigation and altered some of the system's binary files. This is trivial to do in UNIX systems and is now becoming common in Windows systems. Dr. Larry Leibrock at University of Texas, Austin, led a research project to quantify how many files are changed when turning a Windows workstation off and on. Their research documents that approximately 0.6 percent of the operating system files are changed each time a Windows XP system is shut down and restarted (http://praetor.bus.utexas.edu/leibrock/xpforensics/).

Further, if the computer being analyzed is a server, it is unlikely management will support taking it offline and shutting it down for investigation. So, from an investigative perspective, either course may be correct and either course may be incorrect, depending on the circumstances surrounding the incident. What is most important is that you are deliberate in your work, you document your actions, and you can explain why you took the actions you did.

 STUDY TIP For Security+ testing purposes, the memory should be dumped, the system powered down, and an image should be made and worked from.

There are many investigative methods. Figure 17-1 shows the continuum of investigative methods from simple to more rigorous.

Examine suspect system using its software without verification	Verify software on suspect system and use that software for investigation	Examine suspect system using external media with verified software	Build a new system that completely images suspect system	Boot suspect system with verified floppy, CD, kernel and tools	Use dedicated forensic workstation

Simple ◀————————————————————————————————————▶ Rigorous

Figure 17-1   Investigative method rigor

Figure 17-2 shows the relationship between the complexity of your investigation and both the reliability of your forensic data and the difficulty of investigation.

 CAUTION   You should never examine a system with the utilities provided by that system. You should always use utilities that have been verified as correct and uncorrupted. Do not open any files, or start any applications. If possible, document the current memory and swap files, running processes, and open files. Unplug the system from the network and immediately contact senior management. If your organization has Computer Incidence Response Team (CIRT) procedures, follow them. Capture and secure mail, Domain Name Service (DNS), and other network service logs on supporting hosts. Unless you have appropriate forensic training and experience, consider calling in a professional.

Identifying Evidence

Evidence must be properly marked as it is collected so that it can be identified as the particular piece of evidence gathered at the scene. Properly label and store evidence. Be sure the labels can't be easily removed. Keep a log book identifying each piece of evidence (in case the label is removed), the persons who discovered it, the case number, the date, time, and location discovered, and the reason for collection. This information should be specific enough for recollection later in court. Log other identifying marks, such as device make, model, serial number, cable configuration or type, and so on. Note any type of damage to the piece of evidence.

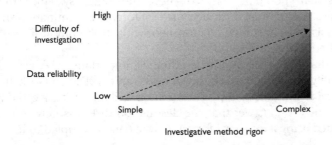

Figure 17-2   Rigor of the investigative method versus both data reliability and the difficulty of investigation

Being methodical is extremely important while identifying evidence. Do not collect evidence by yourself—have a second person who can serve as a witness to your actions. A sample log is shown here:

Item Description	Investigator	Case #	Date	Time	Location	Reason
Dell Latitude laptop computer, C600, Serial number: 62H5J25	Smith	C-25	30 Jan 2003	1325	Room 312 safe	Safekeeping

Protecting Evidence

Protect evidence from electromagnetic or mechanical damage. Ensure that evidence is not tampered with, damaged, or compromised by the procedures used during the investigation. Be careful not to damage the evidence to avoid potential liability problems later. Protect evidence from extremes in heat and cold, humidity, water, magnetic fields, and vibration. Use static-free evidence protection gloves as opposed to standard latex gloves. Seal the evidence in a proper container with evidence tape, and mark it with your initials, date, and case number.

Transporting Evidence

Properly log all evidence in and out of controlled storage. Use proper packing techniques, such as placing components in static-free bags, using foam packing material, and using cardboard boxes. Be especially cautious during transport of evidence to ensure custody of evidence is maintained and it isn't damaged or tampered with.

Storing Evidence

Store the evidence in an evidence room that has low traffic, restricted access, camera monitoring, and entry logging capabilities. Store components in static-free bags, foam packing material, and cardboard boxes.

Conducting the Investigation

When analyzing computer storage components, it is important to use extreme caution. A copy of the system should be analyzed—never the original system, as that will have to serve as evidence. A system specially designed for forensics examination should be used. Conduct analysis in a controlled environment with strong physical security, minimal traffic, controlled access, and so on.

Remember that witness credibility is extremely important. It is easy to imagine how quickly credibility can be damaged if the witness is asked, "Did you lock the file system?" and can't answer affirmatively. Or, "When you imaged this disk drive, did you use a new system?" and one can't answer that the destination disk was new or had been completely formatted using a low-level format before data was copied to it.

Unless you have tools specifically designed to take forensic images under Windows, your imaging process should use DOS instead of standard Windows. Boot it from a floppy disk or CD, and have only the minimal amount of software installed to preclude propagation of a virus or the inadvertent execution of a Trojan horse or other malicious program. Windows can then be used when examining copies of the system.

Although each investigation will be different, the following image backup process is a good example of a comprehensive investigation (see Tipton and Krause's *Information Security Management Handbook*, p. 634):

1. Remove or image only one component at a time.

2. Remove the hard disk and label it. Be sure to use an anti-static or static-dissipative wristband and mat before conducting forensic analysis.

3. Identify the disk type (IDE, SCSI, or other type). Log the disk capacity, cylinders, heads, and sectors.

4. Image the disk by using a bit-level copy, sector by sector. This will retain deleted files, unallocated clusters, and slack space.

5. Make either three or four copies of the drive: one replaces the drive removed if the system is to be returned to its owner and you don't want to divulge that the drive has been exchanged; one is marked, sealed, logged, and stored with the original, unmodified disk as evidence; one will be used for file authentication; the last is for analysis.

6. Check the disk image to make sure there were no errors during the imaging process.

7. Before analyzing the suspect disk, generate a message digest for all system directories, files, disk sectors, and partitions. MD5 and SHA are suitable and are superior to the older CRC32 or weaker hashing algorithms. Remember that even creating the message digest can change file access times, so it is important to have the files locked and to use the image, not the original evidence. Keep a good log of the hash values.

8. Inventory all files on the system.

9. Document the system date and time.

TIP   You should note that although this text describes the process and provides specific steps to be performed, they are to be used as guidelines. Any notes or record of results you make can end up being evidence in a court. Therefore, using a checklist and making notes on it could result in those lists and notes becoming evidence. Your credibility could be damaged if you have specific checklists and you skip a step or two because they aren't applicable—remember that you may need to explain why you skipped certain steps. While following the checklist, keep a log of all commands you issued on the system between the time you identified the incident and the time you imaged the disk. That way, if you are questioned in court about whether you changed anything on the disk, you can say, in effect, "Yes, but here is exactly what I did and here is how it would have changed things."

Chain of Custody

Evidence, once collected, must be properly controlled to prevent tampering. The chain of custody accounts for all persons who handled or had access to the evidence. The chain of custody shows who obtained the evidence, when and where it was obtained, where it was stored, and who had control or possession of the evidence.

The following is a list of the critical steps in a chain of custody:

- Record each item collected as evidence.

- Record who collected the evidence along with the date and time.

- Write a description of the evidence in the documentation.

- Put the evidence in containers and tag the containers with the case number, the name of the person who collected it, and the date and time.

- Record all message digest (hash) values in the documentation.

- Securely transport the evidence to a protected storage facility.

- Obtain a signature from the person who accepts the evidence at this storage facility.

- Provide controls to prevent access to and compromise of the evidence while it is being stored.

- Securely transport it to court for proceedings.

Free Space vs. Slack Space

When a user deletes a file, the file is not actually deleted. Instead, a pointer in a file allocation table is deleted. This pointer was used by the operating system to track down the file when it was referenced, and the act of "deleting" the file merely removes the pointer and marks the sector(s) holding the file as available for the operating system to use. The actual data originally stored on the disk remains on the disk (until that space is used again); it just isn't recognized as a coherent file by the operating system.

Free Space

Since the "deleted" file is not actually completely erased or overwritten, it just sits there until the operating system needs to use that space for another file or application. Sometimes the second file that is saved in the same area does not occupy as many sectors as the first file, so there will still be a fragment of the original file.

The sector that holds the fragment of this file is referred to as *free space* because the operating system has marked it as usable when needed. As soon as the operating system stores something else in this sector, it is referred to as *allocated*. The unallocated sectors still contain the original data until the operating system overwrites those unallocated sectors. Looking at the free space might reveal information left over from files the user thought were deleted from the drive.

Slack Space

Another place that should be reviewed is *slack space*, which is different from free space. When a file is saved to a storage media, such as a hard drive, the operating system allocates space in blocks of a predefined size, called *sectors*. The size of all sectors is the same on a given system or hard drive. Even if your file contains only 10 characters, the operating system will allocate a full sector of, say 1,024 bytes—there will be space left over in the sector. This is slack space.

It is possible for a user to hide malicious code, tools, or clues in slack space, as well as in the free space. You may also find information in slack space from files that previously occupied that same physical sector on the drive. Therefore, an investigator should review slack space using utilities that can display the information stored in these areas.

What's This Message Digest and Hash?

If files, logs, and other information are going to be captured and used for evidence, you need to ensure that the data isn't modified. In most cases, a tool that implements a hashing algorithm to create message digests is used.

 NOTE The mathematics behind these hashing algorithms has been researched extensively, and although it is possible that two different data streams could produce the same message digest, it is very, very improbable. This is an area of cryptography that has been rigorously reviewed, and the mathematics behind Message Digest 5 (MD5) and Secure Hash Algorithm (SHA) are very sound. (For more information about hashing and algorithms, see Chapter 10.)

A hashing algorithm performs a function similar to the familiar parity bits, checksum, or cyclical redundancy check (CRC). It applies mathematical operations to a data stream (or file) to calculate some number that is unique based on the information contained in the data stream (or file). If a subsequent analysis on the same data stream produces a different result, there is a very high probability that the data stream was changed.

The hash tool is applied to each file or log and the message digest value is noted in the investigation documentation. When the case actually goes to trial, the investigator may need to run the tool on the files or logs again to show that they have not been altered in any way. The logs may also need to be written to a write-once media, such as a CD-ROM.

 NOTE The number of files stored on today's hard drives can be very large, literally tens of thousands. Obviously this is far too many for the investigator to analyze. However, if it were possible to know the message digests for most of the files installed by the most popular software products, and those message digests matched the message digests of the files on the drive being analyzed, approximately 90 percent of the files would not need to be analyzed by the investigator because they can be assumed to be unmodified. (See Dan Mares' "Using File Hashes to Reduce Forensic Analysis" in SC Online, May 2002, www.scmagazine.com/scmagazine/sc-online/2002/article/24/article.html. Also see www.nsrl.nist.gov.)

PART VII

Analysis

After successfully imaging the drives to be analyzed and calculating and storing the message digests, the investigator will now begin the analysis. The details of the investigation will depend on the particulars of the incident being investigated. However, in general, the following steps will be involved:

- Check the Recycle Bin for deleted files.

- Check the web browser history files and address bar histories.

- Check the web browser cookie files. Each web browser stores cookies in different places. Some examples are provided. Browsers not listed here will require individual research. Netscape 7.0 for Windows stores them in a file called cookies.txt (click Tools | Cookie Manager, or search for files named cookies.txt). In Netscape 7.0 for Mac, click Netscape | Preferences | Privacy & Security | Cookies. Netscape for UNIX stores them in $HOME/netscape. Internet Explorer stores cookies in the Temporary Internet Files folder with all the other temporary Internet files. (Each cookie is stored in a separate file with the format "Cookie: <username>@URL", where <username> is the user who is logged into the Windows machine, and the URL is the address of the web server that set the cookie. Opening each cookie file will give you the details about that specific cookie. A handy tool for viewing Internet Explorer cookies is IECookiesView found at www.simtel.net/pub/dl/59299.shtml.)

- Check the Temporary Internet Files folders. Usually these are found in the Windows directory C:\Documents and Settings\<username>\Local Settings\ Temporary Internet Files. This location can be changed, so be sure to check where Internet Explorer is storing those files. In Internet Explorer, click Tools | Internet Options | General | Settings | View Files.

- Search files for suspect character strings. To conserve valuable time, be wise in the choice of words you search for, choosing "confidential," "sensitive," "sex" or other explicit words and phrases related to your investigation.

- Search the slack and free space for suspect character strings as described previously.

Chapter Review

This chapter has provided information essential to understanding the role of forensic analysis. The topics covered help you understand that certain rules must be followed when dealing with evidence and why evidence must be properly collected, protected, and controlled to be of value during court or disciplinary activities. The terms discussed and concepts presented are essential to understand in your preparation for the Security+ certification. Understanding the process of conducting an investigation will not only assist the reader during Security+ exam preparations but will also help in the discovery of potential violations of laws or corporate policies.

Chapter 17: Computer Forensics

473

Questions

1. Which of the following correctly defines evidence as being sufficient?

   A. The evidence is material to the case or has a bearing to the matter at hand.

   B. The evidence is presented in the form of business records, printouts, and so on.

   C. The evidence is convincing or measures up without question.

   D. The evidence is legally qualified and reliable.

2. Which of the following correctly defines direct evidence?

   A. The knowledge of the facts is obtained through the five senses of the witness.

   B. The evidence consists of tangible objects that prove or disprove a fact.

   C. The evidence is used to aid the jury and may be in the form of a model, experiment, chart, or the like, offered to prove an event occurred.

   D. It is physical evidence that links the suspect to the scene of a crime.

3. Which of the following correctly defines demonstrative evidence?

   A. The evidence is legally qualified and reliable.

   B. The evidence consists of tangible objects that prove or disprove a fact.

   C. The evidence is used to aid the jury and may be in the form of a model, experiment, chart, or the like, offered to prove an event occurred.

   D. The evidence is in the form of business records, printouts, manuals, and so on.

4. Which of the following correctly defines the best evidence rule?

   A. The evidence is legally qualified and reliable.

   B. Courts prefer original evidence rather than a copy to ensure that no alteration of the evidence (intentional or unintentional) has occurred.

   C. The evidence is used to aid the jury and may be in the form of a model, experiment, chart, or the like, offered to prove an event occurred.

   D. Physical evidence that links the suspect to the scene of a crime.

5. Which of the following correctly defines the exclusionary rule?

   A. The knowledge of the facts is obtained through the five senses of the witness.

   B. The evidence consists of tangible objects that prove or disprove a fact.

   C. The evidence is used to aid the jury and may be in the form of a model, experiment, chart, or the like, offered to prove an event occurred.

   D. Any evidence collected in violation of the Fourth Amendment is not admissible as evidence.

6. Which of the following is the *most* rigorous investigative method?

   A. Build a new system that completely images the suspect system.

   B. Verify software on the suspect system and use that software for investigation.

   C. Examine the suspect system using its software without verification.

   D. Use a dedicated forensic workstation.

7. Which of the following correctly defines slack space?

   A. The space on a disk drive that is occupied by the boot sector.

   B. The space located at the beginning of a partition.

   C. The remaining sectors of a previously allocated file that are available for the operating system to use.

   D. The unused space on a disk drive when a file is smaller than the allocated unit of storage (such as a sector).

8. Which of the following correctly defines the process of acquiring evidence?

   A. Dump the memory, power down the system, create an image of the system, and analyze the image.

   B. Power down the system, dump the memory, create an image of the system, and analyze the image.

   C. Create an image of the system, analyze the image, dump the memory, and power down the system.

   D. Dump the memory, analyze the image, power down the system, and create an image of the system.

9. If you are investigating a computer incident, and you need to remove the disk drive from a computer and replace it with a copy so the user doesn't know it has been exchanged, how many copies of the disk should you make, and how should they be used?

   A. Three copies. One to replace the drive removed, one to be used for file authentication, and one for analysis.

   B. Four copies. One to replace the drive removed; one is marked, sealed, logged, and stored with the original, unmodified disk as evidence; one is for file authentication; and one is for analysis.

   C. Five copies. One to replace the drive removed; one is marked, sealed, logged, and stored with the original, unmodified disk as evidence; one is for file authentication; one is for analysis; and one is for holding message digests.

   D. Four copies. One to replace the drive removed; one is marked, sealed, logged, and stored with the original, unmodified disk as evidence; one is for file authentication; and one is for holding message digests.

10. Which of the following correctly describes the hashing concept?

    A. A method of verifying that data has been completely deleted from a disk.

    B. A method of overwriting data with a specified pattern of 1s and 0s on a disk.

    C. An algorithm that applies mathematical operations to a data stream to calculate a unique number based on the information contained in the data stream.

    D. A method used to keep an index of all files on a disk.

Answers

1. **C**, by definition. Answer A is the definition of relevant evidence. Answer B is the definition of documentary evidence. Answer D is the definition of competent evidence.

2. **A**, by definition. Answer B is the definition of real evidence. Answer C is the definition of demonstrative evidence. Answer D is the definition of real evidence.

3. **C**, by definition. Answer A is the definition of competent evidence. Answer B is the definition of real evidence. Answer D is the definition of documentary evidence.

4. **B**, by definition. Answer A is the definition of competent evidence. Answer C is the definition of demonstrative evidence. Answer D is the definition of real evidence.

5. **D**, by definition. Answer A is the definition of direct evidence. Answer B is the definition of real evidence. Answer C is the definition of demonstrative evidence.

6. **D**. Answers A and B are other methods on the rigor spectrum. Answer C is the least rigorous method.

7. **D**. Answers A and B are contrived definitions. Answer C is the definition of free space.

8. **A**. The other answers are not in the correct order.

9. **B**. The other answers are contrived responses.

10. **C**, by definition. The other answers are contrived responses.

CHAPTER 18

Risk Management

In this chapter, you will

- Discover the purpose of risk management and an approach to effectively manage risk
- Learn the differences between qualitative and quantitative risk assessment
- See, by example, how both approaches are necessary to effectively manage risk
- Review important definitions and tools

Risk management can best be described as a decision-making process. In the simplest terms, when you manage risk, you determine what could happen to your business, you assess the impact if it were to happen, and you decide what you could do to control that impact as much as you or your management deems necessary. You then decide to act or not to act and, finally, evaluate the results of your decision. The process may then iterate. Industry best practices clearly indicate that an important aspect of effectively managing risk is to consider it an ongoing process.

An Overview of Risk Management

Risk management is an essential element of management from the enterprise level down to the individual project. Risk management encompasses all the actions taken to reduce complexity, increase objectivity, and identify important decision factors. There has been, and will continue to be, discussion as to how complex risk management can be, and whether or not it should be done. Businesses must take risks to retain their competitive edge, and as a result, risk management must be done as part of managing any business, any program, or any project.

Risk management is both a skill and a task that all managers do, either deliberately or intuitively. It can be simple or complex, depending on the size of the project or business and the amount of risk inherent in an activity. Every manager, at all levels, must learn to manage risk. The required skills can be learned.

STUDY TIP This chapter contains several bulleted lists. These are designed for easy memorization in preparation for taking the Security+ exam.

Example of Risk Management at the International Banking Level

The Basel Committee on Banking Supervision is composed of government central-bank governors from around the world. This body created a basic, global risk management framework for market and credit risk. They implemented internationally a flat 8 percent capital charge to banks to manage bank risks. In layman's terms, this means that for every $100 a bank makes in loans, it must possess $8 in reserve to be used in the event of financial difficulties. However, if banks can show they have very strong risk mitigation procedures and controls in place, that capital charge can be reduced to as low as $0.37 (0.37 percent). If a bank has poor procedures and controls, that capital charge can be as high as $45 (45 percent).

This example shows that risk management can be and is used at very high levels—the remainder of this chapter will focus on smaller implementations. It will be shown that risk management is used in many aspects of business conduct.

Key Terms Essential to Understanding Risk Management

There are a number of key terms that should be understood to manage risk. Some of these terms will be defined here because they are used throughout the remainder of the chapter. This listing is somewhat ordered according to the organization of this chapter. More comprehensive definitions and other pertinent terms are listed alphabetically in the glossary at the end of this book.

Risk The possibility of suffering harm or loss.

Risk management The overall decision-making process of identifying threats and vulnerabilities and their potential impacts, determining the costs to mitigate such events, and deciding what actions are cost effective for controlling these risks.

Risk assessment (or risk analysis) The process of analyzing an environment to identify the threats, vulnerabilities, and mitigating actions to determine (either quantitatively or qualitatively) the impact of an event that would affect a project, program, or business.

Asset Resource or information an organization needs to conduct its business.

Threat Any circumstance or event with the potential to cause harm to an asset.

Vulnerability Characteristic of an asset that can be exploited by a threat to cause harm.

Impact The loss resulting when a vulnerability is exploited by a threat.

Control (also called countermeasure or safeguard) A measure taken to detect, prevent, or mitigate the risk associated with a threat.

Qualitative risk assessment The process of subjectively determining the impact of an event that affects a project, program, or business. Qualitative risk assessment usually involves the use of expert judgment, experience, or group consensus to complete the assessment.

Quantitative risk assessment   The process of objectively determining the impact of an event that affects a project, program, or business. Quantitative risk assessment usually involves the use of metrics and models to complete the assessment.

Mitigate   To reduce the likelihood of a threat occurring.

Single loss expectancy (SLE)   The monetary loss or impact of each occurrence of a threat.

Exposure factor   A measure of the magnitude of loss of an asset. Used in the calculation of single loss expectancy.

Annualized rate of occurrence (ARO)   On an annualized basis, the frequency with which an event is expected to occur.

Annualized loss expectancy (ALE)   How much an event is expected to cost per year.

What Is Risk Management?

Three definitions relating to risk management show why it is sometimes considered difficult to understand. (See Figure 18-1.)

- The dictionary defines *risk* as the possibility of suffering harm or loss.
- Carnegie Mellon University's Software Engineering Institute (SEI) defines *continuous risk management* as "processes, methods, and tools for managing risks

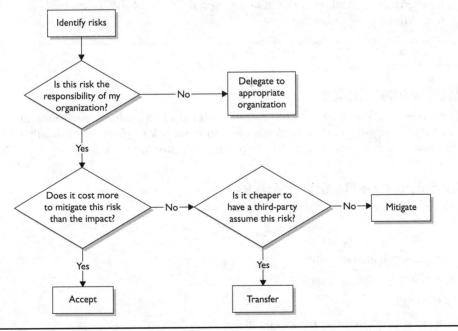

Figure 18-1   A planning decision flowchart for risk management

in a project. It provides a disciplined environment for proactive decision-making to 1) assess continuously what could go wrong (risks); 2) determine which risks are important to deal with; and 3) implement strategies to deal with those risks" (SEI, *Continuous Risk Management Guidebook* [Pittsburgh, PA: Carnegie Mellon University, 1996], 22).

- The Information Systems Audit and Control Association (ISACA) says, "In modern business terms, risk management is the process of identifying vulnerabilities and threats to an organization's resources and assets and deciding what countermeasures, if any, to take to reduce the level of risk to an acceptable level based on the value of the asset to the organization" (ISACA, *Certified Information Systems Auditor (CISA) Review Manual, 2002* [Rolling Meadows, IL:ISACA, 2002], 344).

These three definitions show that risk management is based upon what can go wrong and what action should be taken, if any. Figure 18-1, provides a macro-level view of how to manage risk.

Transferring Risk

One possible action to manage risk is to transfer that risk. The most common method of transferring risk is to purchase insurance. Insurance allows risk to be transferred to a third party that manages specific types of risk for multiple parties, thus reducing the individual cost.

Business Risks

There is no comprehensive identification of all risks in a business environment. In today's technology-dependent business environment, risk is often simplistically divided into two areas: business risk and a major subset, technology risk.

Examples of Business Risks

The most common business risks include

- Treasury management
- Revenue management
- Contract management
- Fraud
- Environmental risk management
- Regulatory risk management

- Business continuity management
- Technology

 NOTE It is important to understand that technology, itself, is a business risk. Hence, it must be managed along with other risks. Today, technology risks are so important they should be considered separately.

Examples of Technology Risks

The most common technology risks include

- Security and privacy
- Information technology operations
- Business systems control and effectiveness
- Business continuity management
- Information systems testing
- Reliability and performance management
- Information technology asset management
- Project risk management
- Change management

Risk According to the Basel Committee

The Basel Committee referenced at the beginning of this chapter defined three types of risk specifically to address international banking:

- **Market Risk** Risk of losses due to fluctuation of market prices
- **Credit Risk** Risk of default of outstanding loans
- **Operational Risk** Risk from disruption by people, systems, processes, or disasters

Risk Management Models

Risk management concepts are fundamentally the same despite their definitions, requiring similar skills, tools, and methodologies. There are several models for managing risk through its various phases. Two models will be presented: the first can be applied to managing risks in general, the second is tailored for managing risk in software projects.

General Risk Management Model

The following steps can be used in virtually any risk management process. Following these steps will lead to an orderly process of analyzing and mitigating risks.

Asset Identification   Identify and classify the assets, systems, and processes that need protection because they are vulnerable to threats. This classification leads to the ability to prioritize assets, systems, and processes and to evaluate the costs of addressing the associated risks. Assets can include

- Inventory
- Buildings
- Cash
- Information and data
- Hardware
- Software
- Services
- Documents
- Personnel
- Brand recognition
- Organization reputation
- Goodwill

Threat Assessment   Identify the possible threats and vulnerabilities associated with each asset and the likelihood of their occurrence. Threats can be defined as any circumstance or event with the potential to cause harm to an asset. Common classes of threats include

- Natural disasters
- Man-made disasters
- Terrorism
- Errors
- Malicious damage or attacks
- Fraud
- Theft
- Equipment or software failure

Vulnerabilities are characteristics of resources that can be exploited by a threat to cause harm. Examples of vulnerabilities include

- Unprotected facilities
- Unprotected computer systems

- Unprotected data
- Insufficient procedures and controls
- Insufficient or unqualified personnel

Impact Definition and Quantification   An impact is the loss created when a threat exploits a vulnerability. When a threat is realized, it turns risk into impact. Impacts can be either tangible or intangible. For example, in a manufacturing facility, storing and using flammable chemicals creates a risk of fire to the facility. The vulnerability is that there are flammable chemicals stored there. The threat would be that a person could cause a fire by mishandling the chemicals (either intentionally or unintentionally). The impact would be the loss incurred (say $500,000) if a person ignites the chemicals and fire then destroys part of the facility.

Tangible impacts include

- Direct loss of money
- Endangerment of staff or customers
- Loss of business opportunity
- Reduction in operational efficiency or performance
- Interruption of a business activity

Intangible impacts include

- Breach of legislation or regulatory requirements
- Loss of reputation or goodwill (brand damage)
- Breach of confidence

Control Design and Evaluation   Controls (also called countermeasures or safeguards) are designed to control risk by reducing vulnerabilities to an acceptable

Business Dependencies

An area often overlooked in risk assessment is the need to address business dependencies—each organization must assess risks caused by other organizations with which it interacts. This occurs when the organization is either a consumer of, or a supplier to, other organizations (or both). For example, if a company is dependent on products produced by a laboratory, then the company must determine the impacts that could be caused if that laboratory could not deliver the product when needed. Likewise, an organization must assess risks that can occur when it is considered a supplier to some other company dependent on its products.

Can All Risks Be Identified?

It is important to note that not all risks need to be mitigated or controlled; however, as many risks as possible should be identified and reviewed. Those deemed to have potential impacts should be mitigated by controls or countermeasures.

level. For use in this text, the terms *control*, *countermeasure*, and *safeguard* will be considered synonymous and will be used interchangeably.

Controls, countermeasures, or safeguards can be actions, devices, or procedures. They can be preventive or detective. *Preventive controls* are designed to prevent the vulnerability from causing an impact. *Detective controls* are those that detect a vulnerability that has been exploited so that action can be taken.

Residual Risk Management   It is important to understand that risk cannot be completely eliminated. Any risks that remain after implementing controls are termed *residual risks*. Residual risks can be further evaluated to identify where additional controls are required to reduce risk even more. This leads us to the earlier statement that the risk management process is iterative.

Software Engineering Institute Model

In an approach tailored for managing risk in software projects, SEI uses the following paradigm (SEI, *Continuous Risk Management Guidebook* [Pittsburgh, PA: Carnegie Mellon University, 1996], 23). Although the terminology varies slightly from the previous model, the relationships are apparent, and either model can be applied wherever risk management is used.

1. **Identify**   Look for risks before they become problems.

2. **Analyze**   Convert the data gathered into information that can be used to make decisions. Evaluate the impact, probability, and timeframe of the risks. Classify and prioritize each of the risks.

3. **Plan**   Review and evaluate the risks and decide what actions to take to mitigate them. Implement those mitigating actions.

4. **Track**   Monitor the risks and the mitigation plans. Trends may provide information to activate plans and contingencies. Review periodically to measure progress and identify new risks.

5. **Control**   Make corrections for deviations from the risk mitigation plans. Correct products and processes as required. Changes in business procedures may require adjustments in plans or actions, as do faulty plans and risks that become problems.

These two example models define steps that can be used in any general or software risk management process. These risk management principles can be applied to any

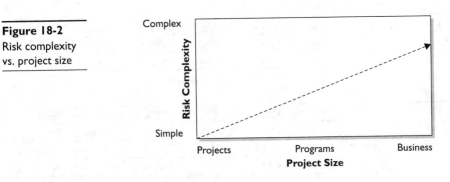

Figure 18-2
Risk complexity
vs. project size

project, program, or business activity, no matter how simple or complex. Figure 18-2 shows how risk management can be applied across the continuum and that the complexity of risk management generally increases with the size of the project, program, or business to be managed.

Qualitatively Assessing Risk

Qualitative risk analysis allows expert judgment and experience to assume a prominent role. To qualitatively assess risk, you compare the impact of the threat with the probability of occurrence. For example, if a threat has a high impact and a high probability of occurring, the risk exposure is high and probably requires some action to reduce this threat (see darkest box in Figure 18-3). Conversely, if the impact is low with a low probability, the risk exposure is low and no action may be required to reduce this threat (see white box in Figure 18-3). Figure 18-3 shows an example of a *binary assessment*. There are only two possible outcomes each for impact and probability. Either it will have an impact or it will not (or it will have a low or high impact). And it can occur or it will not (or it will have a high probability of occurring or a low probability of occurring).

In reality, there are usually a few threats that can be identified as presenting high-risk exposure and a few threats that present low-risk exposure. The threats that fall somewhere between (see light gray boxes in Figure 18-3) tend to be those that will have to be evaluated by judgment and management experience.

If the analysis is more complex, requiring three levels of analysis, such as low- medium-high or red-green-yellow, there are nine possible combinations as shown in Figure 18-4. Again, the darkest boxes probably require action, the white boxes may not require action, and the gray boxes require judgment. (Note that for brevity, in Figures 18-4 and 18-5, the first term in each box refers to the magnitude of the impact, the second term refers to the probability of the threat occurring.)

Figure 18-3
Binary assessment

Impact	High Impact/Low Probability	High Impact/High Probability
	Low Impact/Low Probability	Low Impact/High Probability

Probability

Figure 18-4

Three levels of analysis

Impact

High	Low	High	Medium	High	High
Medium	Low	Medium	Medium	Medium	High
Low	Low	Low	Medium	Low	High

Probability

Figure 18-5

A 3 by 5 level analysis

Impact

Very high	Low	Very high	Medium	Very high	High
High	Low	High	Medium	High	High
Medium	Low	Medium	Medium	Medium	High
Low	Low	Low	Medium	Low	High
Very low	Low	Very low	Medium	Very low	High

Probability

Other levels of complexity are possible. If there are five levels of analysis, there will be 25 possible values of risk exposure. In this case, the possible values of impact and probability could take on the values: very low, low, medium, high, or very high. Also, note that the matrix does not have to be symmetrical. For example, if the probability is assessed with three values (low, medium, high) and the impact has five values (very low, low, medium, high, very high), the analysis would be as shown in Figure 18-5. (Again, note that the first term in each box refers to the impact, the second term in each box refers to the probability of occurrence.)

So far, the examples have focused on assessing probability versus impact. Qualitative risk assessment can be adapted to a variety of attributes and situations in combination with each other. For example, Figure 18-6 shows the comparison of some specific risks that have been identified during a security assessment. The assessment identified the risk areas listed in the first column (weak intranet security, high number of modems,

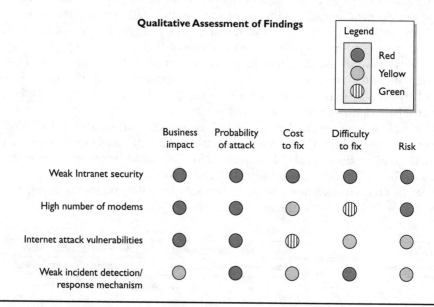

Figure 18-6   Example of a combination assessment

Internet attack vulnerabilities, and weak incident detection and response mechanisms). The assessment also identified various potential impacts listed across the top (business impact, probability of attack, cost to fix, and difficulty to fix). Each of the impacts has been assessed as low, moderate, or high (depicted using green (G), yellow (Y), and red (R), respectively). Each of the risk areas has been assessed with respect to each of the potential impacts, and an overall risk assessment has been determined in the last column.

Quantitatively Assessing Risk

Whereas qualitative risk assessment relies on judgment and experience, quantitative risk assessment applies historical information and trends to attempt to predict future performance. This type of risk assessment is highly dependent on the historical data, and gathering such data can be difficult. Quantitative risk assessment may also rely heavily on models. These models provide decision-making information in the form of quantitative metrics, which attempt to measure risk levels across a common scale.

It is important to understand that key assumptions underlie any model, and different models will produce different results even when given the same input data. Although significant research and development have been invested in improving and refining the various risk analysis models, expert judgment and experience must still be considered an essential part of any risk assessment process. Models can never replace judgment and experience, but they can significantly enhance the decision-making process.

Adding Objectivity to a Qualitative Assessment

Quantitative assessment can be as simple as just assigning numeric values to one of the tables shown in Figures 18-3 through 18-6. For example, the impacts listed in Figure 18-6 can be prioritized from highest to lowest and then weighted as shown in Table 18-1 with Business Impact weighted the most and Difficulty to Fix weighted least.

Next, values can be assigned to reflect how each risk was assessed. Figure 18-6 can thus be made more objective by assigning a value to each color that represents an assessment. For example, a 'red' assessment means there are many critical, unresolved issues and this will be given an assessment value of 3. Likewise, 'green' means there are few unresolved issues, so it is given a value of 1. Table 18-2 shows values that can be assigned for an assessment using green, yellow, and red.

Table 18-1	Impact	Explanation	Weight
Adding Weights and Definitions to the Potential Impacts	Business impact	If exploited, would this have a material business impact?	4
	Probability of attack	How likely is a potential attacker to try this technique or attack?	3
	Cost to fix	How much will it cost in dollars and resources to correct this vulnerability?	2
	Difficulty to fix	How hard is this to fix from a technical standpoint?	1

Table 18-2	Assessment	Explanation	Value
Adding Values to Assessments	Red	Many critical, unresolved issues	3
	Yellow	Some critical, unresolved issues	2
	Green	Few unresolved issues	1

The last step will be to calculate an overall risk value for each risk area (each row in Figure 18-6) by multiplying the weights depicted in Table 18-1 times the assessed values from Table 18-2 and summing the products:

$$\text{Risk} = W_1 * V_1 + W_2 * V_2 + \ldots W_4 * V_4$$

The risk calculation and final risk value for each risk area listed in Figure 18-6 have been incorporated into Figure 18-7. The assessed areas can then be ordered from highest to lowest based on the calculated risk value to aid management in focusing on the risk areas with the greatest potential impact.

A Common Objective Approach

More complex models permit a variety of analyses based on statistical and mathematical models. A common method is the calculation of the annualized loss expectancy (ALE). This calculation begins by calculating a single-loss expectancy (SLE) with the following formula:

SLE = asset value * exposure factor

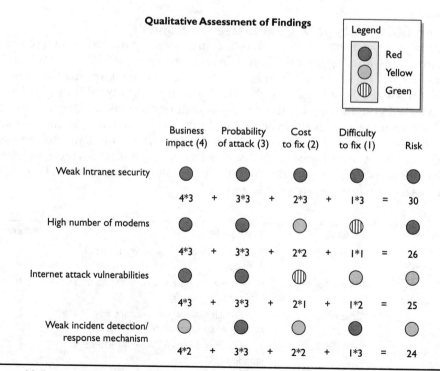

Figure 18-7   Final quantitative assessment of the findings

By example, to calculate the exposure factor, assume the asset value of a small office building and its contents is $2 million. Also assume that this building houses the call center for a business, and the complete loss of the center would take away about half of the capability of the company. Therefore, the exposure factor is 50 percent. The SLE is

$2 million * 0.5 = $1 million

The ALE is then calculated simply by multiplying the SLE by the number of times the event is expected to occur in a year, which is called the annualized rate of occurrence (ARO):

ALE = SLE * ARO

If the event is expected to occur once in 20 years, then the annualized rate of occurrence is 1/20. Typically the ARO is defined by historical data, either from a company's own experience or from industry surveys. Continuing our example, assume that a fire where this business is located is expected to occur about once in 20 years. Given this information, the ALE is

$1 million * 1/20 = $50,000

The ALE determines a threshold for evaluating the cost/benefit ratio of a given countermeasure. Therefore, a countermeasure to protect this business adequately should cost no more than the calculated ALE of $50,000 per year.

STUDY TIP It is always advisable to memorize these fundamental equations for certifications such as Security+.

The examples in this chapter have been simplistic, but they demonstrate the concepts of both quantitative and qualitative risk analysis. There are more complex algorithms and software packages for accomplishing risk analysis, but these examples suffice for the purposes of this text.

Qualitative vs. Quantitative Risk Assessment

It is recognized throughout industry that it is *impossible* to conduct risk management that is purely *quantitative*. Usually risk management includes both qualitative and quantitative elements, requiring both analysis and judgment or experience. It is important to note that in contrast to quantitative assessment, it is *possible* to accomplish purely *qualitative* risk management.

It is easy to see that it is impossible to define and quantitatively measure all factors that exist in a given risk assessment. It is also easy to see that a risk assessment that measures no factors quantitatively but measures them all qualitatively is possible.

The decision of whether to use qualitative versus quantitative risk management depends on the criticality of the project, the resources available, and the management style. The decision will be influenced by the degree to which the fundamental risk management metrics, such as asset value, exposure factor, and threat frequency can be quantitatively defined.

Accepting Risk

In addition to mitigating risk or transferring risk, it may be acceptable for a manager to *accept* risk in that despite the potential cost of a given risk and its associated probability, the manager of the organization will accept responsibility for the risk if it does happen. For example, a manager may choose to allow a programmer to make "emergency" changes to a production system (in violation of good segregation of duties) because the system cannot go down during a given period of time. The manager accepts the risk that the programmer could possibly make unauthorized changes because of the high-availability requirement of that system. However, there should always be some additional controls such as management review or a standardized approval process to ensure the assumed risk is adequately managed.

Tools

Many tools can be used to enhance the risk management process. The following tools can be used during the various phases of risk assessment to add objectivity and structure to the process. Understanding the details of each of these tools is not necessary for the Security+ exam, but understanding what they can be used for is important. More information on these tools can be found in any good project-management text.

Affinity grouping   A method of identifying items that are related and then identifying the principle that ties them together into a group.

Baseline identification and analysis   The process of establishing a baseline set of risks. It produces a "snapshot" of all the identified risks at a given point in time.

Cause and effect analysis   Identifying relationships between a risk and the factors that can cause it. This is usually accomplished using *fishbone diagrams* developed by Dr. Kaoru Ishikawa, former Professor of Engineering at the Science University of Tokyo.

Cost/benefit analysis   A straightforward method for comparing cost estimates with the benefits of a mitigation strategy.

Gantt charts   A management tool for diagramming schedules, events, and activity duration.

Interrelationship digraphs   A method for identifying cause-and-effect relationships by clearly defining the problem to be solved, identifying the key elements of the problem, and then describing the relationships between each of the key elements.

Pareto charts   A histogram that ranks the categories in a chart from most frequent to least frequent, thus facilitating risk prioritization.

Risks Really Don't Change, But They Can Be Mitigated

One final thought to keep in mind is that the risk itself doesn't really change, no matter what actions are taken to mitigate that risk. A high risk will always be a high risk. However, actions can be taken to reduce the impact of that risk if it occurs.

PERT (program evaluation and review technique) charts   A diagram depicting interdependencies between project activities, showing the sequence and duration of each activity. When complete, the chart shows the time necessary to complete the project and the activities that determine that time (the critical path). The earliest and latest start and stop times for each activity and available slack times can also be shown.

Risk management plan   A comprehensive plan documenting how risks will be managed on a given project. It contains processes, activities, milestones, organizations, responsibilities, and details of each major risk management activity and how it is to be accomplished. It is an integral part of the project management plan.

Chapter Review

Risk management is a key management process that must be used at every level, whether managing a project, a program, or an enterprise. Managing risk is key to keeping a business competitive and must be done by managers at all levels. Both qualitative and quantitative risk assessment approaches must be used to effectively manage risk, and a number of approaches were presented in this chapter. It is important to understand that it is impossible to conduct a purely quantitative risk assessment, but it is possible to conduct a purely qualitative risk assessment.

Questions

1. Which of the following correctly defines qualitative risk management?

   A. The loss resulting when a vulnerability is exploited by a threat.

   B. To reduce the likelihood of a threat occurring.

   C. The process of subjectively determining the impact of an event that affects a project, program, or business.

   D. The process of objectively determining the impact of an event that affects a project, program, or business.

2. Which of the following correctly defines risk?

  A. The risks still remaining after an iteration of risk management.

  B. The possibility of suffering harm or loss.

  C. The loss resulting when a vulnerability is exploited by a threat.

  D. Any circumstance or event with the potential to cause harm to an asset.

3. Single loss expectancy (SLE) can best be defined by which of the following equations?

  A. SLE = asset value * exposure factor

  B. SLE = annualized loss expectancy * annualized rate of occurrence

  C. SLE = asset value * annualized rate of occurrence

  D. SLE = annualized loss expectancy * exposure factor

4. Which of the following correctly defines annualized rate of occurrence?

  A. On an annualized basis, the frequency with which an event is expected to occur.

  B. How much an event is expected to cost per year.

  C. A measure of the magnitude of loss of an asset.

  D. Resources or information an organization needs to conduct its business.

5. Which of the following are business risks?

  A. Business continuity management

  B. Fraud

  C. Contract management

  D. Treasury management

  E. All of the above

  F. None of the above

6. The Basel Committee defines operational risk as which of the following?

  A. Risk of default of outstanding loans

  B. Risk of losses due to fluctuations of market prices

  C. The possibility of suffering harm or loss

  D. Risk from disruption by people, systems, processes, or disasters

7. Which of the following are *not* assets?

  A. Hardware

  B. Inventory

  C. Equipment or software failure

  D. Cash

E. All of the above

F. None of the above

For questions 8 and 9, assume the following: The asset value of a small distribution warehouse is $5 million, and this warehouse serves as backup capability. Its complete destruction by a disaster would take away about 1/5 of the capability of the business. Also assume that this sort of disaster is expected to occur about once every 50 years.

8. Which of the following is the calculated single loss expectancy (SLE)?

   A. SLE = $25 million

   B. SLE = $1 million

   C. SLE = $2.5 million

   D. SLE = $5 million

9. Which of the following is the calculated annualized loss expectancy (ALE)?

   A. ALE = $50,000

   B. ALE = $20,000

   C. ALE = $1 million

   D. ALE = $50 million

10. When discussing qualitative risk assessment versus quantitative risk assessment, which of the following is true?

   A. It is impossible to conduct a purely quantitative risk assessment, and it is impossible to conduct a purely qualitative risk assessment.

   B. It is possible to conduct a purely quantitative risk assessment, but it is impossible to conduct a purely qualitative risk assessment.

   C. It is possible to conduct a purely quantitative risk assessment, and it is possible to conduct a purely qualitative risk assessment.

   D. It is impossible to conduct a purely quantitative risk assessment, but it is possible to conduct a purely qualitative risk assessment.

Answers

1. **C,** by definition. Answer A is the definition of impact. Answer B is the definition of mitigate. Answer D is the definition of quantitative risk assessment.

2. **B,** by definition. Answer A is the definition of residual risk. Answer C is the definition of impact. Answer D is the definition of threat.

3. **A,** by definition.

4. **A.** Answer B is the definition of annualized loss expectancy. Answer C is the definition of exposure factor. Answer D is the definition of asset.

5. E.

6. D. Answer A is the definition of credit risk. Answer B is the definition of market risk. Answer C is the definition of risk.

7. C. Equipment or software failure is a threat. All other answers are examples of assets.

8. C. SLE = asset value ($5 million) * exposure factor (1/5) = $1 million.

9. B. ALE = SLE ($1 million) * annualized rate of occurrence (1/50) = $20,000.

10. D.

Change Management

In this chapter, you will
- Learn why change management is an important enterprise management tool
- Understand the key concept of segregation of duties
- Review the essential elements of change management
- Learn a process for implementing change management
- Study the concepts of the Capability Maturity Model

It is well recognized that today's software systems are extremely complex. It is obvious that inventory management systems for large international enterprises like Wal-Mart or Home Depot are probably as complex as an aircraft or skyscraper. Prominent operating systems like Windows or UNIX are very complex, as are computer processors on a chip. Even a Web-based shopping cart application is relatively complex.

It would be absurd to think of constructing an aircraft, large building, computer chip, or automobile in the informal manner we sometimes use to develop and operate software of equal complexity. Software systems have grown to be so complex and mission-critical that enterprises cannot afford to develop and maintain software in an ad hoc manner.

Change management procedures are one way to add structure and control to the development of large software systems as they move from development to operation. Change management, as discussed in this chapter, refers to a standard methodology for performing and recording changes during software development and operation. The methodology defines steps that ensure that system changes are required by the organization, and are properly authorized, documented, tested, and approved by management. In this chapter, the term *software configuration management* is considered synonymous with *software change management* and, in a more limited manner, *version control*.

The term *change management* is often applied to the management of changes in the business environment, typically as a result of business process reengineering or quality enhancement efforts. The term *change management* as used in this chapter is directly related to managing and controlling software development, maintenance, and operation.

Why Change Management?

In Chapter 18, risk management was presented as an essential decision-making process. In much the same way, change management is an essential practice for managing software

495

during its entire lifecycle, from development, through deployment and operation, until it is taken out of service. In order to effectively manage the software development and maintenance processes, discipline and structure can help conserve resources and enhance effectiveness. Software change management, like risk management, is often considered expensive, non-productive, unnecessary, and confusing—an impediment to progress. However, like risk management, it can be scaled to properly control and manage the development and maintenance of software effectively.

Change management should be used in all phases of software's life: development, testing, quality assurance (QA), and production. Short development cycles have not changed the need for an appropriate amount of management control over software development, maintenance, and operation. In fact, short turnaround times make change management more necessary because once a system goes active in today's Web-based environment, often it cannot be taken offline to correct errors—it must stay up and online or business will be lost and brand recognition damaged. In today's volatile stock market, even small indicators of lagging performance can have dramatic impacts on a company's stock value.

The following scenarios exemplify the need for appropriate change management policy and for procedures over software and data:

- The developers can't find the latest version of the production source code.
- A bug corrected a few months ago mysteriously reappeared.
- Fielded software was working fine yesterday but does not work properly today.
- Development team members overwrote each other's changes.
- A programmer spent several hours changing the wrong version of the software.
- A customer record corrected by the call center yesterday, shows the old, incorrect information today.
- New tax rates stored in a table have been overwritten with last year's tax rates.
- An application runs fine at some overseas locations but not at other locations.

Just about anyone with more than a year's experience in software development can relate to at least one of the preceding scenarios. However, each of these scenarios can be controlled, and impacts mitigated, through proper change management procedures.

NOTE All software can be placed under an appropriate software change management process, including:
Web pages
Service packs
Security patches
Third-party software releases
Test data and test scripts
Parameter files
Scripts, stored procedures, or job control language–type programs
Customized vendor code
Source code of any kind

The Key Concept: Segregation of Duties

A key foundation for software change management is the recognition that involving more than one individual in a process may reduce risk. Good business control practices require that duties be assigned to individuals in such a way that no one individual can control all phases of a process or the processing and recording of a transaction. This is called *segregation of duties* (sometimes called *separation of duties*). It is an important means by which errors and fraudulent or malicious acts can be discouraged and prevented. Segregation of duties can be applied in many organizational scenarios because it establishes a basis for accountability and control. Proper segregation of duties can safeguard enterprise assets and protect against risks. They should be documented, monitored, and enforced.

Information technology (IT) organizations should design, implement, monitor, and enforce appropriate segregation of duties for the enterprise's information systems and processes. Today's computer systems are rapidly evolving into an increasingly decentralized and networked computer infrastructure. In the absence of adequate IT controls, such rapid growth may allow exploitation of large amounts of enterprise information in a short time. Further, the knowledge of computer operations held by IT staff is significantly greater than that of an average user, and this knowledge could be abused for malicious purposes.

Some of the best practices for ensuring proper segregation of duties in an IT organization are as follows:

- Segregation of duties between development, testing, quality assurance, and production should be documented in written procedures and implemented by software or manual processes.

- Program developers' and program testers' activities should be conducted on "test" data only. They should be restricted from accessing "live" production data. This will assist in ensuring an independent and objective testing environment without jeopardizing the confidentiality and integrity of production data.

- End users or computer operations personnel should not have direct access to program source code. This control helps lessen the opportunity of exploiting software weaknesses or introducing malicious code (or code that has not been properly tested) into the production environment either intentionally or unintentionally.

- Functions of creating, installing, and administrating software programs should be assigned to different individuals. For example, since developers create and enhance programs, they should not be able to install it on the production system. Likewise, database administrators should not be program developers on database systems they administer.

- All accesses and privileges to systems, software, or data should be granted based on the principle of least privilege, which gives users no more privileges than are necessary to perform their jobs. Access privileges should be reviewed regularly to ensure that individuals who no longer require access have had their privileges removed.

- Formal software change management policy and procedures should be enforced throughout the enterprise. The number of changes in software components (including emergency changes) that are implemented after the product has been placed into production and that do not go through the approved formal change management mechanism should be minimized.

Managers at all levels should review existing and planned processes and systems to ensure proper segregation of duties. Smaller business entities may not have the resources to fully implement all of the preceding practices, but other control mechanisms, including hiring qualified personnel, bonding contractors, and using training, monitoring, and evaluation practices, can reduce any organization's exposure to risk. The establishment of such practices can ensure enterprise assets are properly safeguarded and can also greatly reduce error and the potential for fraudulent or malicious activities.

Change management practices implement and enforce segregation of duties by adding structure and management oversight to the software development process. Change management techniques can ensure that only correct and authorized changes, as approved by management or other authorities, are allowed to be made, following a defined process.

Elements of Change Management

Change management has its roots in system engineering, where it is commonly referred to as *configuration management*. For example, auto makers know that a certain amount of configuration management is necessary to efficiently and effectively build safe cars. Bolts and screws with proper strengths and qualities are used on every car, in specific places—employees don't just reach into a barrel of bolts, pull one out that looks about right, and bolt it on. The same applies to aircraft—for an aircraft to fly safely, it must be built of parts of the right size, shape, strength, and so on. Computer hardware and software development have also evolved over the last few decades. Proper management structure and controls must exist to ensure the products operate as planned.

Change management and configuration management have different terms for their various phases, but they can all fit into the four general phases defined under configuration management: configuration identification, configuration control, configuration status accounting, and configuration auditing.

Configuration identification is the process of identifying which assets need to be managed and controlled. These assets could be software modules, test cases or scripts, table or parameter values, major subsystems, or entire systems. The idea is that, depending on the size and complexity of the software project, an appropriate set of data and software (or other assets) must be identified and properly managed. These identified assets are called *configuration items* or *computer software configuration items*.

Related to configuration identification, and the result of it, is the definition of a baseline. A *baseline* serves as a foundation for comparison or measurement. It provides the necessary visibility to control change. In our case, a software baseline defines the software system as it is built and running at a point in time. As another example, network security best practices clearly state that any large organization should build their servers to a standard build configuration to enhance overall network security. The servers are the configuration items, and the standard build is the server baseline.

Configuration control is the process of controlling changes to items that have been baselined. Configuration control ensures that only approved changes to a baseline are allowed to be implemented. It is easy to understand why a software system, such as a Web-based order entry system, should not be changed without proper testing and control—otherwise the system might stop functioning at a critical time. Configuration control is a key step that provides valuable insight to managers. If a system is being changed, and configuration control is being observed, managers and others concerned will be better informed. This ensures proper use of assets and avoids unnecessary downtime due to the installation of unapproved changes.

Configuration status accounting consists of the procedures for tracking and maintaining data relative to each configuration item in the baseline. It is closely related to configuration control. Status accounting involves gathering and maintaining information relative to each configuration item. For example, it documents what changes have been requested; what changes have been made, when, and for what reason; who authorized the change; who performed the change; and what other configuration items or systems were affected by the change.

Returning to our example of servers being baselined, if the operating system of those servers is found to have a security flaw, then the baseline can be consulted to determine which servers are vulnerable to this particular security flaw. Those systems with this weakness can be updated (and only those that need to be updated). Configuration control and configuration status accounting help ensure systems are more consistently managed and, ultimately in this case, the organization's network security is maintained. It is easy to imagine the state of an organization that has not built all servers to a common baseline and has not properly controlled their systems' configurations. It would be very difficult to know the configuration of individual servers, and security could quickly become weak.

NOTE It is important to understand that even though all servers may be initially configured to the same baseline, individual applications might require a system-specific configuration to run properly. Change management actually facilitates system-specific configuration in that all exceptions from the standard configuration are documented. All people involved in managing and operating these systems will have documentation to help quickly understand why a particular system is configured in this unique way.

Configuration auditing is the process of verifying that the configuration items are built and maintained according to the requirements, standards, or contractual agreements. It is similar to how audits in the financial world are used to ensure that generally accepted accounting principles and practices are adhered to and that financial statements properly reflect the financial status of the enterprise. Configuration audits ensure that policies and procedures are being followed, that all configuration items (including hardware and software) are being properly maintained, and that existing documentation accurately reflects the status of the systems in operation.

Configuration auditing takes on two forms: functional and physical. A *functional configuration audit* verifies that the configuration item performs as defined by the documentation of the software requirements. A *physical configuration audit* confirms that all configuration items to be included in a release, change, or upgrade are actually included and that no additional items are included—no more, no less.

Implementing Change Management

Change management requires some structure and discipline in order to be effective. The change management function is scalable from small to enterprise-level projects. Figure 19-1 illustrates a sample change management flow appropriate for medium to large projects. It can be adapted to small organizations, by having the developer only perform work on his/her workstation (never on the production system) and having the system administrator serve in the buildmaster function. The buildmaster is usually an independent person responsible for compiling and incorporating changed software into an executable image.

Figure 19-1 shows that developers never have access to the production system or data. It also demonstrates proper segregation of duties between developers, QA and test people, and production. It implies that there is a distinct separation between development, testing and QA, and production environments. This workflow is for major changes that have a major impact on production or the customer's business process. For changes that are minor or have minimal risk or impact on business processes, some of the steps may be omitted.

The change management workflow proceeds as follows:

1. The developer checks out source code from the code-control tool archive to the development system.

2. The developer modifies the code and conducts unit testing.

3. The developer checks the modified code into the code-control tool archive.

4. The developer notifies the buildmaster of changes and that they are ready for a new build and testing/QA.

5. The buildmaster creates a build incorporating the modified code and compiles the code.

6. The buildmaster notifies the system administrator that the executable image is ready for testing/QA.

7. The system administrator moves the executables to the test/QA system.

8. QA tests the new executables. If tests are passed, test/QA notifies the manager. If tests fail, the process starts over.

9. Upon manager approval, the system administrator moves the executable to the production system.

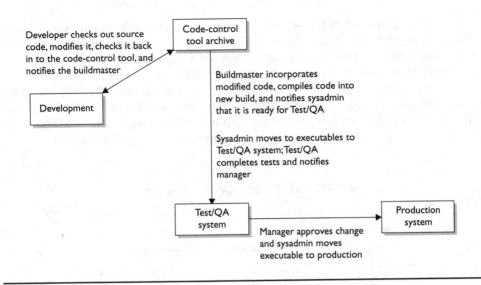

Figure 19-1 Software change control workflow

NOTE Observe the segregation of duties between development, test/QA, and production. The functions of creating, installing, and administrating are assigned to different individuals. Note also appropriate management review and approval. This implementation also ensures that no compiler exists on the production system.

The Purpose of a Change Control Board

To oversee the change management process, most organizations establish a change control board (CCB). In practice, a change control board not only facilitates adequate management oversight, it also facilitates better coordination between projects. The CCB convenes on a regular basis, usually weekly or monthly, and can be convened on an emergency or as-needed basis. Figure 19-2 shows the process for implementing and properly controlling software during changes.

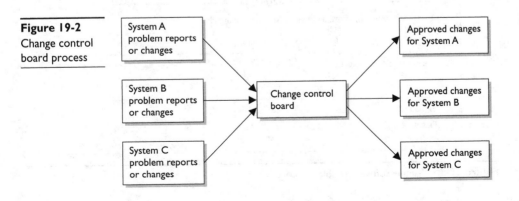

Figure 19-2 Change control board process

The CCB's membership should consist of development project managers, network administrators, system administrators, test/QA managers, an information security manager, an operations center manager, and a help desk manager. Others can be added as necessary, depending on the size and complexity of the organization.

A software problem report (SPR) is used to track changes through the CCB. The SPR is used to document changes or corrections to a software system. It reflects who requested the change and why, what analysis must be done and by whom, and how it was corrected or implemented. Figure 19-3 shows a sample software problem report.

SOFTWARE PROBLEM REPORT (SPR)

❏ Error   SPR Number:_____

❏ Improvement   Originator:_____

----------------------------------- **Problem** -----------------------------------

System Affected:_____

Related Systems:_____

Classification: Problem Description:_____

❏ Software   _____

❏ Hardware   _____

❏ Documentation   _____

❏ Comment   _____

Analysis Assigned to:_____

----------------------------------- **Analysis** -----------------------------------

(Prepared by responsible software design organization)   Date Received:_____

Classification: Explanation:

❏ Design   _____

❏ Coding   _____

❏ Documentation   _____

❏ Environment   _____

Signatures

Analyst:_____ Date:_____ Originator:_____ Date:_____

----------------------------------- **Correction** -----------------------------------

Brief Description of Work and List of Modules Changed:

_____
_____

Documentation Changed:

_____
_____

Signatures

Developer:_____ Date:_____ Manager:_____ Date:_____

Figure 19-3   Sample software problem report

Code Integrity

One key benefit of adequate change management is the assurance of code consistency and integrity. Whenever a modified program is moved to the production source-code library, the executable version should also be moved to the production system. Automated change management systems greatly simplify this process and, hence, are better controls for ensuring executable and source-code integrity. Again, at no time should the user or application developer have access to production source and executable code libraries in the production environment.

Finally, in today's networked environment, the integrity of the executable code is critical. It is a common hacking technique to replace key system executable code with modified code that may contain backdoors, allowing unauthorized access or functions to be performed. Executable code integrity can be verified using a variety of host-based intrusion detection systems. These systems create and maintain a database of the size and content of executable modules. This is usually done by performing some kind of hashing or sophisticated checksum operation on the executable modules and storing the results in a database. The operation is performed on a regular schedule against the executable modules, and the results are compared to the database to identify any unauthorized changes that may have occurred to the executable modules.

The Capability Maturity Model

One area that is likely to be covered on the Security+ test is the Capability Maturity Model (CMM) for software developed at Carnegie Mellon University's Software Engineering Institute (SEI). The CMM relies on configuration or change management as one of its fundamental concepts. It provides organizations with the capability to improve their software processes by providing an evolutionary path from ad hoc processes to disciplined software management processes.

The SEI's web page defines the five maturity levels:

- **Initial** The software process is ad hoc.

- **Repeatable** The software process is structured enough that success with one project can be repeated for another similar project.

- **Defined** The software process is standardized and documented.

- **Managed** Various aspects of the software process and products are measured and evaluated.

- **Optimizing** Key business processes and their supporting software projects are continuously improved based on measurements and testing new ideas.

STUDY TIP To complete your preparations for the Security+ exam, it is recommended that you consult SEI's Web site (www.sei.cmu.edu/cmm/cmm.sum.html) for specific CMM definitions.

Change management is a key process to implementing the CMM in an organization. For example, if an organization is at CMM level 1, then it probably has no formal change management processes in place. At level 3, an organization has a defined change management process that is followed. At level 5, the change management process is a routine part of improving software products and implementing new ideas. In order for an organization to effectively manage software development, operation, and maintenance, then it should be using the CMM and must have effective change management processes in place.

Chapter Review

Change management is an essential management tool and control mechanism. The key concept of segregation of duties ensures that no single individual or organization possesses too much control in a process. Therefore, it helps prevent errors and fraudulent or malicious acts. The elements of change management (configuration identification, configuration control, configuration status accounting, and configuration auditing), coupled with a defined process and a change control board, will provide management with proper oversight of the software lifecycle. Once such a process and management oversight exists, the company will be able to use the Capability Maturity Model to help the organization move from ad hoc activities to a disciplined software management process.

Questions

1. An upgrade to a software package resulted in errors that had been corrected in the previously released upgrade. This type of problem could have been prevented by

   A. The system administrator making the changes instead of the developer

   B. Proper change management procedures over the object code

   C. The use of an object-oriented design approach rather than a rapid prototyping design approach

   D. Proper change management procedures over the source code

2. Software change management procedures are established to

   A. Ensure continuity of business operations in the event of a major disruption

   B. Ensure changes in business operations caused by a major disruption are properly controlled

   C. Add structure and control to the development of software systems

   D. Identify threats, vulnerabilities, and mitigating actions that could impact an organization

3. Which of the following is *not* a principle of segregation of duties?

    A. Software development, testing, quality assurance, and production should be assigned to different individuals.

    B. Software developers should have access to production data and source-code files.

    C. Software developers and testers should be restricted from accessing "live" production data.

    D. The functions of creating, installing, and administrating software programs should be assigned to different individuals.

4. Why should end users not be given access to program source codes?

    A. It could allow an end user to implement the principle of least privilege.

    B. It helps lessen the opportunity of exploiting software weaknesses.

    C. It assists in ensuring an independent and objective testing environment.

    D. It ensures testing and quality assurance perform their proper functions.

5. Configuration status accounting consists of

    A. The process of controlling changes to items that have been baselined

    B. The process of identifying which assets need to be managed and controlled

    C. The process of verifying that the configuration items are built and maintained properly

    D. The procedures for tracking and maintaining data relative to each configuration item in the baseline

6. Configuration identification consists of

    A. The process of controlling changes to items that have been baselined

    B. The process of identifying which assets need to be managed and controlled

    C. The process of verifying that the configuration items are built and maintained properly

    D. The procedures for tracking and maintaining data relative to each configuration item in the baseline

7. Which position is responsible for moving executable code to the test/QA or production systems?

    A. System administrator

    B. Developer

    C. Manager

    D. Quality assurance

8. Which computer security technology is used to ensure the integrity of executable code?

A. Host-based intrusion detection systems

B. Firewalls

C. Gateways

D. Network-based intrusion detection systems

9. In the Software Engineering Institute's Capability Maturity Model (CMM), which of the following correctly defines Level 3, Defined?

A. Various aspects of the software process and products are measured and evaluated.

B. Key business processes and their supporting software projects are continuously improved based on measurements and testing new ideas.

C. The software process is standardized and documented.

D. The software process is structured enough that success with one project can be repeated for another similar project.

10. In the Software Engineering Institute's Capability Maturity Model (CMM), which of the following correctly defines Level 2, Repeatable?

A. Various aspects of the software process and products are measured and evaluated.

B. Key business processes and their supporting software projects are continuously improved based on measurements and testing new ideas.

C. The software process is standardized and documented.

D. The software process is structured enough that success with one project can be repeated for another similar project.

Answers

1. **D.** When errors reappear, it is likely caused by a developer not using the most recent version of the source code. Answer A is wrong because proper segregation of duties states that the developer is responsible for changing software programs, not the system administrator. Answer B is wrong because the source code will be recompiled, not the object code. Answer C is wrong because the design approach would not have caused this problem.

2. **C.** The fundamental purpose of software change management is to add structure and control to the software development process. Answers A and B are incorrect because software change management does not apply directly to ensuring business continuity. Answer D is incorrect; this is the definition of risk management.

3. **B.** Programmers should not be given direct access to production data or files. All the other answers are principles of segregation of duties, as outlined in the chapter.

4. **B.** End users having access to source code allows them to possibly view and identify errors or weaknesses in the source code. Answer A is incorrect because the principle of least privilege does not directly apply here. Answer C is incorrect because end user access to program source code is not directly related to the testing environment. Answer D is incorrect because end user access to program source code is not directly related to the testing and quality assurance functions.

5. **D.** Answers A, B, and C are the definitions of configuration control, configuration identification, and configuration auditing, respectively.

6. **B.** Answers A, C, and D are the definitions of configuration control, configuration auditing, and configuration status accounting, respectively.

7. **A.** The system administrator is the only person allowed to move executables. The developer modifies the source code, the manager approves moving the executable to the production system, and quality assurance tests the executables.

8. **A.** Host-based intrusion detection systems create and maintain a database of the size and content of executable modules. Firewalls filter IP traffic; gateways also filter traffic, and network-based intrusion detection systems monitor IP traffic.

9. **C.** Answers A, B, and D are the definitions of Level 4, Managed; Level 5, Optimizing; and Level 2, Repeatable.

10. **D.** Answers A, B, and C are the definitions of Level 4, Managed; Level 5, Optimizing; and Level 3, Defined.

PART VIII

Appendixes

About the CD-ROM

The CD-ROM included with this book comes complete with MasterExam, the electronic version of the book, and Session 1 of LearnKey's on-line training. The software is easy to install on any Windows 98/NT/2000 computer and must be installed to access MasterExam. You may, however, browse the electronic book directly from the CD-ROM without installation. To register for LearnKey's online training and a second bonus MasterExam, simply click the Online Training link on the Main Page and follow the directions to the free online registration.

System Requirements

The software requires Windows 98 or higher and Internet Explorer 5.0 or above and 20MB of hard disk space for full installation. The Electronic book requires Adobe Acrobat Reader. To access the Online Training from LearnKey you must have RealPlayer Basic 8 or Real1 Plugin, which will be automatically installed when you launch the on-line training.

LearnKey Online Training

The LearnKey Online Training link will allow you to access online training from Osborne.Onlineexpert.com. The first session of this course is provided at no charge. Additional sessions for this course and other courses may be purchased directly from www.LearnKey.com or by calling 800 865-0165.

The first time that you run the Training, you will be required to Register with the on-line product. Follow the instructions for a first time user. Please make sure to use a valid e-mail address.

Prior to running the Online Training you will need to add the Real Plugin and the RealCBT plugin to your system. This will automatically be facilitated to your system when you run the training the first time.

Installing and Running MasterExam

If your computer CD-ROM drive is configured to auto run, the CD-ROM will automatically start up upon inserting the disk. From the opening screen you may install MasterExam by pressing the *MasterExam* button. This will begin the installation process and create a program group named "LearnKey." To run MasterExam use Start | Programs | LearnKey. If the auto run feature did not launch your CD, browse to the CD and Click on the "RunInstall" icon.

MasterExam

MasterExam provides you with a simulation of the actual exam. The number of questions, the type of questions, and the time allowed are intended to be an accurate representation of the exam environment. You have the option to take an open book exam, including hints, references, and answers, a closed book exam, or the timed MasterExam simulation.

When you launch MasterExam, a digital clock display will appear in the upper left-hand corner of your screen. The clock will continue to count down to zero unless you choose to end the exam before the time expires.

Electronic Book

The entire contents of the *Security+ Certification All-in-One Exam Guide* are provided in PDF format. Adobe's Acrobat Reader has been included on the CD.

Help

A help file is provided through the help button on the main page in the lower left hand corner. Individual help features are also available through MasterExam and LearnKey's Online Training.

Removing Installation(s)

MasterExam is installed to your hard drive. For *best* results for removal of programs use the Start | Programs | LearnKey | Uninstall options to remove MasterExam.

If you desire to remove the Real Player use the Add/Remove Programs Icon from your Control Panel. You may also remove the LearnKey training program from this location.

Technical Support

For questions regarding the technical content of the electronic book or MasterExam please visit www.Osborne.com <http://www.Osborne.com> or you may e-mail customer.service@mcgraw-hill.com <mailto:customer.service@mcgraw-hill.com>. For customers outside the 50 United States, e-mail: international_cs@mcgraw-hill.com <mailto: international_cs@mcgraw-hill.com>.

LearnKey Technical Support

For technical problems with the software (installation, operation, removing installations), and for questions regarding LearnKey Online Training content, please visit www.learnkey.com <http://www.learnkey.com> or you may e-mail techsupport@ learnkey.com <mailto:techsupport@learnkey.com>.

OSI Model and Internet Protocols

In this appendix, you will

- Learn about the OSI model
- Review the network protocols associated with the Internet

Networks are interconnected groups of computers and specialty hardware designed to facilitate the transmission of data from one device to another. The basic function of the network is to allow machines and devices to communicate with each other in an orderly fashion.

Networking Frameworks and Protocols

For effective and efficient transfer of information between devices, agreements have to be made as to how this will happen. Today's networks consist of a wide variety of types and sizes of equipment from multiple vendors, so these agreements need to be multi-vendor in nature.

The term *protocol* refers to a standard set of rules that has been developed to communicate the rules to facilitate a specific level of functionality. In networking, a wide range of protocols have been developed, some proprietary and some public, to facilitate communication between machines. Just as two speakers have to agree on a common language, or at least must understand each other's language, computers and networks must agree as well. If a speaker is speaking in English, and the audience only understands Italian, there will be difficulties in communicating.

For two speakers to discuss an item, they need to have a common understanding of the object under discussion. If the object is intangible or not present, they each need some method of referencing items in such a way that the other person understands what they are talking about. A *model* is a tool used as a framework to give people common points of reference when discussing items. Mathematical models are common in science, for they give people the ability to compare answers and results. In much the same way, models are used in many disciplines to facilitate communication. Network models have been developed by many companies as ways to communicate among engineers what specific functionality is occurring when and where in a network. To facilitate cross-vendor and multi-company communication, in 1984 the International Organization for Standardization (ISO) created the Open Systems Interconnection (OSI) model for networking.

As the Internet took shape, a series of protocols was needed to ensure interoperability across this universal network structure. The Transmission Control Protocol (TCP), User Datagram Protocol (UDP), and Internet Protocol (IP) are three of the commonly used protocols that enable data movement across the Internet. As these protocols work in concert with each other, you typically see TCP/IP or UDP/IP as the pairs that are used. The Internet also has resulted in a variant of the OSI model, referred to as the Internet model. A basic understanding of the terms and of the usage of these protocols and models is essential to discuss networking functionality, for it provides the necessary points of reference to understand what is happening where and when in the complex stream of operations that are involved in networking.

OSI Model

The OSI model is probably the most referenced and talked about model in networking. Although it never fully caught on in North America, portions of it have been adopted as reference points, even to the extent of being incorporated into company names. Layer 2, layer 3, network layer, level 3—these are all references to portions of the model. These references allow people to communicate in a clear and unambiguous fashion when speaking of abstract issues and issues out of context. These references give context to detail in the complex arena of networking. The terms *level* and *layer* have been used interchangeably to describe the sections of the OSI model, although *layer* is the more common term.

The OSI model is composed of seven layers stacked in a linear fashion. These layers are, from top to bottom, application, presentation, session, transport, network, data-link, and physical. A way to remember them is: All People Seem To Need Data Processing. Each layer has defined functionality and separation designed to allow multiple protocols to work together in a coordinated fashion.

Although the OSI model is probably the most referenced, standardized network model, a more common model, the Internet model, has risen to dominate the Internet. The OSI model enjoys the status of being a formal, defined international standard, while the Internet model has never been formally defined. The Internet model is basically the same as the OSI model, with the top three OSI layers combined into a single application layer, leaving a total of five layers in the Internet model. Both models are shown in Figure B-1.

One aspect of these models is that they allow specific levels of functionality to be broken apart and performed in sequence. This delineation also determines which layers can communicate with others. At each layer, specific data forms and protocols can exist, which makes them compatible with similar protocols and data forms on other machines at the same layer. This makes it seem as if each layer is communicating with its counterpart on the same layer in another computer, although this is just a virtual connection. The only real connection between boxes is at the physical layer of these models. All other connections are virtual—although they appear real to a user, they do not actually exist in reality.

Figure B-1
OSI and Internet
network models

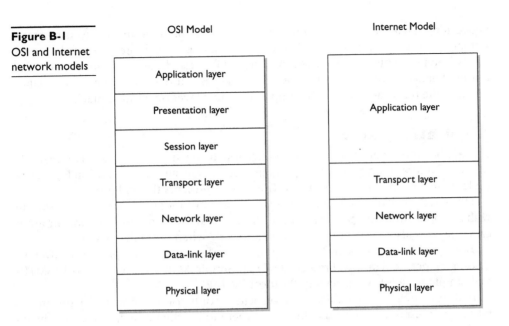

The true communication between layers is up and down—each layer can only communicate with its immediate neighbor above and below itself. In Figure B-2, the direct communication path is shown as a bold line between the two physical layers. All data

Figure B-2   Network model communication paths

PART VIII

between the boxes traverses this line. The dotted lines between higher layers represent virtual connections, and the associated activities and protocols are also listed for most layers (the protocols are also listed in Table B-1). These dotted lines are virtual—data does not actually cross them, although it appears as if it does. The true path of data is down to the physical layer and back up to the same layer on another machine.

Application Layer

The application layer is the actual application being used by a user. For example, Internet Explorer is an application program that operates in the application layer using HTTP to move data between systems. This layer represents the end user's access to the system and the network. While it appears that the application is communicating directly with an application on another machine, this is actually a virtual connection. The application layer is also sometimes referred to as layer 7 when using the OSI model.

There are several protocols that can be commonly found in the application layer, including Hypertext Transfer Protocol (HTTP), Simple Mail Transfer Protocol (SMTP), and Simple Network Management Protocol (SNMP).

In the OSI model, the application layer actually only communicates with the presentation layer on its own machine. In the Internet model, the immediate level below the application layer is the transport layer, and this is the only layer directly called by the application layer in the Internet model. As a result of the "missing" presentation and session layers in the Internet model, the functionality of these OSI layers is performed by the application layer in this model.

The session layer functionality present in the Internet model's application layer includes the initiation, maintenance, and termination of logical sessions between endpoints in the network communication. The session layer functionality also includes session level accounting and encryption services. The presentation layer functionality of the OSI model is also included in the Internet model's application layer, specifically functionality to format the display parameters of the data being received. Any other functions not specifically included in the lower layers of the Internet model are also specifically included in the application layer.

Layer	Commonly Used Protocols
Application	HTTP, SNMP, SMTP, FTP, Telnet
Presentation	XDR
Session	SSL, TLS
Transport	TCP, UDP
Network	IP, ICMP
Data-link	IEEE 802.3 (Ethernet), IEEE 802.5 (Token Ring), ARP, RARP
Physical	IEEE 802.3 (Ethernet) hardware, IEEE 802.5 (Token Ring) Hardware

Table B-1   Common Protocols by OSI Layer

Presentation Layer

The presentation layer gets its name from its primary function: preparing for the presentation of data. It has the responsibility of preparing the data for different interfaces on different types of terminals or displays so the application does not have to worry about this task. Data compression, character set translation, and encryption are all functions that can be found in this layer.

The presentation layer communicates with only two layers—the application layer above it and the session layer below it. The presentation layer is also known as layer 6 of the OSI model.

Session Layer

The primary responsibility of the session layer is the managing of communication sessions between machines. The management functions include initiating, maintaining, and terminating sessions. Managing a session can be compared to making an ordinary phone call. When you dial, you initiate a session. The session must be maintained in an open state during the call. At the completion of the call, you hang up and the circuit must be terminated. As each session can have its own parameters, the session layer is responsible for setting them up, including security, encryption, and billing or accounting functions.

The session layer communicates exclusively with the presentation layer above it and the transport layer below it. The session layer is also known as layer 5 of the OSI model.

Transport Layer

The transport layer has the primary functionality of dealing with the end-to-end transport of data across the network connection. To perform this task, the transport layer handles data entering and leaving the network through logical connections. It can add and use address-specific information, such as ports, to accomplish this task. A *port* is an address-specific extension to enable multiple simultaneous communications between machines. Should the data transmission be too large for a single-packet transport, the transport layer manages the breaking of the data stream into chunks and reassembling it. It is responsible for ensuring that all packets are transmitted and received, and it has the ability to request lost packets and eliminate duplicate packets. Error checking can also be performed at this level, although this function is usually performed at the data-link layer.

The transport layer communicates exclusively with the session layer above it and the network layer below it. The transport layer is also known as layer 4 of the OSI model.

Network Layer

The network layer is responsible for routing packets across the network. Routing functions determine the next best destination for a packet and will determine the full address of the target computer if necessary. Common protocols at this level include IP and Internet Control Message Protocol (ICMP).

The network layer communicates exclusively with the transport layer above it and the data-link layer below it. The network layer is also known as layer 3 of the OSI model.

Data-Link Layer

The data-link layer is responsible for the delivery and receipt of data from the hardware in layer 1, the physical layer. Layer 1 only manipulates a stream of bits, so the data-link layer must convert the packets from the network layer into bit streams in a form that can be understood by the physical layer. To ensure accurate transmission, the data-link layer adds end-of-message markers onto each packet and also manages error detection, correction, and retransmission functions. This layer also performs the media-access function, determining when to send and receive data based on network traffic. At this layer, the data packets are technically known as *frames*, although many practitioners use *packet* in a generic sense.

The data-link layer communicates exclusively with the network layer above it and the physical layer below it. The data-link layer is also known as layer 2 of the OSI model, and it is where LAN switching based on machine address functionality occurs.

Physical Layer

The physical layer is the realm of communication hardware and software, where 1's and 0's become waves of light, voltage levels, phase shifts, and other physical entities as defined by the particular transmission standard. This layer defines the physical method of signal transmission between machines in terms of electrical and optical characteristics. The physical layer is the point of connection to the outside world via standard connectors, again determined by signal type and protocol.

The physical layer communicates with the physical layer on other machines via wire, fiber optics, or radio waves. The physical layer also communicates with the data-link layer above it. The physical layer is also referred to as OSI layer 1.

Internet Protocols

To facilitate cross-vendor product communication, protocols have been adopted to standardize methods. The Internet brought several new protocols into existence, a few of which are commonly seen in routing of information. Two protocols used at the transport layer are TCP and UDP, whereas IP is used at the network layer. In each session, one transport layer protocol and one network layer protocol is used, making the pairs TCP/IP and UDP/IP.

TCP

TCP is the primary transport protocol used on the Internet today, accounting for over 80 percent of packets on the Internet.

TCP begins by establishing a virtual connection through a mechanism known as the TCP handshake. This handshake involves three signals: a SYN signal sent to the target, a SYN/ACK returned in response, and then an ACK sent back to the target to complete the circuit. This establishes a virtual connection between machines over which the data will be transported, and that is why TCP is referred to as being connection oriented.

TCP is classified as a reliable protocol and will ensure that packets are sent, received, and ordered using sequence numbers. There is overhead associated with the sequencing of packets and maintaining this order, but for many communications, this is essential, such as in Domain Name Service (DNS) requests and the like.

TCP has facilities to perform all the required functions of the transport layer. TCP has congestion- and flow-control mechanisms to report congestion and other traffic-related information back to the sender to assist in traffic-level management. Multiple TCP connections can be established between machines through a mechanism known as ports. TCP ports are numbered from 0 up to 65,535, although ports below 1,024 are typically reserved for specific functions. TCP ports are separate entities from UDP ports and can be used at the same time.

UDP

UDP is a simpler form of transport protocol than TCP. UDP performs all of the required functionality of the transport layer, but it does not perform the maintenance and checking functions of TCP. UDP does not establish a connection and does not use sequence numbers. UDP packets are sent via the "best effort" method, and this is often referred to as "fire and forget," for the packets either reach their destination or they are lost forever. There is no retransmission mechanism, which is why UDP is called an unreliable protocol.

UDP does not have traffic-management or flow-control functions as TCP does. This results in much lower overhead and makes UDP ideal for streaming data sources, such as audio and video traffic, where latency between packets can be an issue.

Multiple UDP connections can be established between machines through a mechanism known as ports. UDP ports are numbered from 0 up to 65,535, although ports below 1,024 are typically reserved for specific functionality. UDP ports are separate entities from TCP ports and can be used at the same time.

IP

IP is a connectionless protocol used for routing messages across the Internet. The primary purpose of IP is to address packets with IP addresses, both destination and source, and to use these addresses to determine the next hop to transmit the packet to. As IP is connectionless, IP packets can take different routes at different times between the same hosts, depending on traffic conditions. IP also maintains some traffic-management information, such as time to live (a function to give packets a limited lifetime) and fragmentation control (a mechanism to split packets en route if necessary).

The current version of IP is version 4, referred to as IPv4, and it uses a 32-bit address space. The newer IPv6 protocol adds significant levels of functionality, such as security, improved address space, 128 bits, and a whole host of sophisticated traffic-management options. IPv4 addresses are written as four sets of numbers in the form v.x.y.z, with each of these values ranging from 0 to 255. As this would be difficult to remember, a naming system for hosts was developed around domains, and DNS servers convert the host names, such as www.ietf.org, to IP addresses, such as 4.17.168.6.

Message Encapsulation

As a message traverses a network from one application on one host, down through the OSI model, out through the physical layer, and up another machine's OSI model, the data is encapsulated at each layer. This can be viewed as an envelope inside an envelope scheme. As only specific envelopes are handled at each layer, only the necessary information for that layer is presented on the envelope. At each layer, the information inside the envelope is not relevant and previous envelopes have been discarded—only the information on the current envelope is used. This offers efficient separation of functionality between layers. This concept is illustrated in Figure B-3.

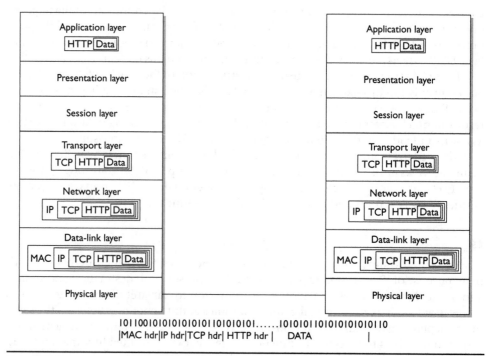

Figure B-3   OSI message encapsulation

As a message traverses the OSI model from the application layer to the physical layer, envelopes are placed inside bigger envelopes. This increases the packet size, but this increase is known and taken into account by the higher-level protocols. At each level, a header is added to the front end, and it acts to encapsulate the previous layer as data. At the physical level, the bits are turned into the physical signal and are transmitted to the next station.

At the receiving station, the bits are turned into one large packet, which represents the original envelope-within-envelope concept. Then each envelope is handled at the appropriate level. This encapsulation exists at the transport layer and lower, as this is the domain of a packet within a session.

Review

To understand the functions performed in network communication, a common framework is necessary. This framework is provided by the OSI and Internet network models. These models specify which functions occur, and in what order, in the transmission of data from one application to another across a network.

An understanding of the OSI model and thus the state in which the data exists as it transits a network enables a deeper understanding of issues related to security. Understanding that SSL occurs before TCP and IP allows you to understand how SSL protects TCP and IP from outside sniffing. Understanding the different protocols and what happens with data loss enables a better understanding of how certain types of attacks are performed.

The essence of a framework is to allow enhanced understanding of relationships, and these network models perform this function for network professionals.

3DES   An abbreviation for Triple DES encryption.

802.11   A family of standards that describe network protocols for wireless devices.

802.1X   An IETF standard for performing authentication over networks.

Access   A subject's (user's) ability to perform specific operations on an object, such as a file. Typical access levels include read, write, execute, and delete.

Access control   Mechanisms or methods used to determine what access permissions subjects (such as users) have for specific objects (such as files).

Access control list (ACL)   A list associated with an object (such as a file) that identifies what level of access each subject (such as a user) has—what they can do to the object (such as read, write, or execute).

Algorithm   A step-by-step procedure—typically an established computation for solving a problem within a set number of steps.

Annualized loss expectancy (ALE)   How much an incident is expected to cost the business per year, given the dollar cost of the loss and how often it is likely to occur. ALE = single loss expectancy * annualized rate of occurrence.

Annualized rate of occurrence (ARO)   The frequency with which an event is expected to occur on an annualized basis.

Anomaly   Something that does not fit into an expected pattern.

Application   A program or group of programs designed to provide specific end-user functions, such as a word processor or web server.

Asset   Resources and information an organization needs to conduct its business.

Asymmetric encryption   This is also called public key cryptography. It is a system for encrypting data that uses two mathematically derived keys to encrypt and

523

decrypt a message—a public key, available to everyone, and a private key, only available to the owner of the key.

Auditing   The name given to any actions or processes used to verify the assigned privileges and rights of a user, as well as any capabilities used to create and maintain a record showing who accessed a particular system and what actions they performed.

Audit trail   A set of records or events, generally organized chronologically, that record what activity has occurred on a system. These records (often computer files) are often used in an attempt to re-create what took place when an incident occurs. They can also be used to detect possible intruders.

Authentication   The process by which a subject's (such as a user's) identity is verified.

Authentication, authorization, and accounting (AAA)   AAA is short-hand for three common functions performed upon system login. Authentication and authorization are almost always done, with accounting being somewhat less common.

Authentication Header (AH)   A portion of the IPsec security protocol that provides authentication services and replay-detection ability. AH can be used either by itself or with Encapsulating Security Payload (ESP). Refer to RFC 2402.

Availability   Part of the CIA of security. Availability applies to hardware, software, and data. All of these should be present and accessible when the subject (the user) wants to access or use them.

Backdoor   A hidden method to gain access to a computer system, network, or application. Often used by software developers to ensure unrestricted access to the systems they create. Synonymous with trapdoor.

Backup   Generally used to refer to copying and storing data in a secondary location, separate from the original, in order to preserve the data in the event that the original is lost, corrupted, or destroyed.

Baseline   Describes a system or software as it is built and functioning at a point in time. Serves as a foundation for comparison or measurement, providing the necessary visibility to control change.

Biometrics   Used to verify an individual's identity to the system or network. This approach uses something unique about the individual for the verification process. Examples include fingerprints, retinal scans, hand and facial geometry, and voice analysis.

BIS   Bureau of Industry and Security in the U.S. Department of Commerce, the department responsible for Export Administration Regulations which cover encryption technology in the United States.

Blowfish   A free implementation of a symmetric block cipher developed by Bruce Schneier as a drop-in replacement for DES and IDEA. It has a variable bit length scheme from 32 to 448 bits, resulting in varying levels of security.

Capability Maturity Model (CMM)   A structured methodology helping organizations improve the maturity of their software processes by providing an evolutionary path from ad hoc processes to disciplined software management processes. Developed at Carnegie Mellon University's Software Engineering Institute.

Centralized management   A type of privilege management that brings the authority and responsibility for managing and maintaining rights and privileges into a single group, location, or area.

Certificate   A cryptographically signed object that contains an identity and a public key associated with this identity. The certificate can be used to establish identity, analogous to a notarized written document.

Certificate revocation list (CRL)   A digitally signed object that lists all of the current but revoked certificates issued by a given CA. This allows users to verify whether a certificate is currently valid even if the expiration date hasn't passed. This is analogous to a list of stolen charge card numbers that allows stores to reject bad credit cards.

Certification authority (CA)   An entity that is responsible for issuing and revoking certificates. CAs are typically third parties, although they exist for internal company use as well. This term is also applied to server software that provides these services.

Chain of custody   Rules for documenting, handling, and safeguarding evidence to ensure no unanticipated changes are made to the evidence.

Challenge Handshake Authentication Protocol (CHAP)   Used to provide authentication across point-to-point links using the Point-to-Point Protocol (PPP).

Change (configuration) management   A standard methodology for performing and recording changes during software development and operation.

Change control board (CCB)   A body that oversees the change management process. Enables management to oversee and coordinate projects.

CHAP   *See* Challenge Handshake Authentication Protocol.

CIA   The CIA of security refers to Confidentiality, Integrity and Authorization, basic functions of any security system.

Cipher   A cryptographic system that accepts plaintext input and then outputs ciphertext according to its internal algorithm and key.

Ciphertext-encrypted data   Used to denote the output of an encryption algorithm.

Collisions   Used in the analysis of hashing cryptography, it is the property by which an algorithm will produce the same hash from two different sets of data.

Computer security   In general terms, the methods, techniques, and tools used to ensure that a computer system is secure.

Computer software configuration item   *See* configuration item.

Confidentiality   Part of the CIA of security. Refers to the security principle that states that information should not be disclosed to unauthorized individuals.

Configuration auditing   The process of verifying that configuration items are built and maintained according to requirements, standards, or contractual agreements.

Configuration control   The process of controlling changes to items that have been baselined.

Configuration identification   The process of identifying which assets need to be managed and controlled.

Configuration item (or computer software configuration item)
Data and software (or other assets) that are identified and managed as part of the software change management process.

Configuration status accounting   Procedures for tracking and maintaining data relative to each configuration item in the baseline.

Control   A measure taken to detect, prevent, or mitigate the risk associated with a threat.

Cookie   Information stored on a user's computer by a web server to maintain the state of the connection to the web server. Used primarily so preferences or previously used information can be recalled on future requests to the server.

Countermeasure   *See* control.

Cracking   A term used by some to refer to malicious hacking in which individuals attempt to gain unauthorized access to computer systems or networks. *See also* hacking.

Cryptanalysis   The process of attempting to break a cryptographic system.

Cryptography   The art of secret writing that enables an individual to hide the contents of a message or file from all but the intended recipient.

Data Encryption Standard (DES)   A private key encryption algorithm adopted by the government as a standard for the protection of sensitive but unclassified information.

Decision tree   A data structure where each element in the structure is attached to one or more structures directly beneath it.

Denial of service (DOS) attack   An attack in which actions are taken to deprive authorized individuals access to a system, its resources, the data it stores or processes, or the network it is connected to.

DES   *See* Data Encryption Standard.

DIAMETER   The DIAMETER base protocol is intended to provide an authentication, authorization, and accounting (AAA) framework for applications such as network access or IP mobility. DIAMETER is a draft IETF proposal.

Diffie-Hellman   A cryptographic method of establishing a shared key over an insecure medium in a secure fashion.

Direct-sequence spread spectrum (DSSS)   A method of distributing a communication over multiple frequencies to avoid interference and detection.

Disaster recovery plan (DRP)   A written plan developed to address how an organization will react to a natural or man-made disaster in order to ensure business continuity. Related to the concept of a business continuity plan (BCP).

Discretionary access control (DAC)   An access control mechanism in which the owner of an object (such as a file) can decide which other subjects (such as other users) may have access to the object, and what access (read, write, execute) these objects may have.

Distributed denial of service (DDOS) attack   A special type of denial of service attack in which the attacker elicits the generally unwilling support of other systems to launch a many-against-one attack.

Diversity of defense   The approach of creating dissimilar security layers so that an intruder who is able to breach one layer will be faced with an entirely different set of defenses at the next layer.

Domain Name Service (DNS)   Domain Name Service.

DSSS   *See* Direct-sequence spread spectrum.

Encapsulating Security Payload (ESP)   ESP is a portion of the IPsec implementation that provides for data confidentiality with optional authentication and replay-detection services. ESP completely encapsulates user data in the datagram. ESP can be used either by itself or in conjunction with Authentication Headers for varying degrees of IPsec services.

Escalation auditing   The process of looking for an increase in privileges, such as when an ordinary user obtains administrator-level privileges.

Evidence   The documents, verbal statements, and material objects admissible in a court of law.

Exposure factor   A measure of the magnitude of loss of an asset. Used in the calculation of single loss expectancy (SLE).

False positive   Term used when a security system makes an error and incorrectly reports the existence of a searched-for object. Examples include when an intrusion detection system misidentifies benign traffic as hostile, an antivirus program reports the existence of a virus in software that actually is not infected, or a biometric system allows access to a system to an unauthorized individual.

FHSS   *See* frequency-hopping spread spectrum.

File Transfer Protocol (FTP)   File Transfer Protocol is an application level protocol used to transfer files over a network connection.

Forensics (or computer forensics)   The preservation, identification, documentation, and interpretation of computer data for use in legal proceedings.

Free space   Sectors on a storage medium that are available for the operating system to use.

Frequency-hopping spread spectrum (FHSS)   A method of distributing a communication over multiple frequencies over time to avoid interference and detection.

Hacking   The term used by the media to refer to the process of gaining unauthorized access to computer systems and networks. The term has also been used to refer to the process of delving deep into the code and protocols used in computer systems and networks. *See also* cracking.

Hash   Form of encryption that creates a digest of the data put into the algorithm. These algorithms are referred to as *one-way* algorithms because there is no feasible way to decrypt what has been encrypted.

Hash value   *See* message digest.

Honeypot   A computer system or portion of a network that has been set up to attract potential intruders to it, in the hope that they will leave the other systems alone. Since there is no legitimate user of this system, any attempt to access it is an indication of unauthorized activity and provides an easy mechanism to spot attacks.

Host-based intrusion detection system (HIDS)   A system that looks for computer intrusions by monitoring activity on one or more individual PCs or servers.

IDEA   *See* International Data Encryption Algorithm.

IEEE   *See* Institute for Electrical and Electronics Engineers.

IETF   *See* Internet Engineering Task Force.

IKE   *See* Internet Key Exchange.

Impact The result of a vulnerability being exploited by a threat, resulting in a loss.

Incident response The process of responding to, containing, analyzing, and recovering from a computer-related incident.

Information security Often used synonymously with computer security but places the emphasis on the protection of the information that the system processes and stores, as opposed to the hardware and software that constitute the system.

Institute for Electrical and Electronics Engineers A non-profit, technical, professional institute associated with computer research, standards, and conferences.

Intangible asset An asset for which a monetary equivalent cannot be determined. Examples are brand recognition and goodwill.

Integrity Part of the CIA of security, the security principle that requires that information is not modified except by individuals authorized to do so.

International Data Encryption Algorithm (IDEA) IDEA is a symmetric encryption algorithm used in a variety of systems for bulk encryption services.

Internet Assigned Numbers Authority (IANA) The central coordinator for the assignment of unique parameter values for Internet protocols. The IANA is chartered by the Internet Society (ISOC) to act as the clearinghouse to assign and coordinate the use of numerous Internet protocol parameters.

Internet Engineering Task Force (IETF) A large international community of network designers, operators, vendors, and researchers, open to any interested individual concerned with the evolution of the Internet architecture and the smooth operation of the Internet. The actual technical work of the IETF is done in its working groups, which are organized by topic into several areas (such as routing, transport, and security). Much of the work is handled via mailing lists, with meetings held three times per year.

Internet Key Exchange (IKE) The protocol formerly known as ISAKMP/Oakley, defined in RFC 2409. A hybrid protocol that uses part Oakley and part of SKEME protocol suites inside the Internet Security Association and Key Management Protocol (ISAKMP) framework. IKE is used to establish a shared security policy and authenticated keys for services that require keys (such as IPsec).

Internet Protocol (IP) The network layer protocol used by the Internet for routing packets across a network.

Internet Security Association and Key Management Protocol (ISAKMP) A protocol framework that defines the mechanics of implementing a key exchange protocol and negotiation of a security policy.

Internet service provider (ISP) Internet service provider, the term associated with a telecommunications firm that provides access to the Internet.

Intrusion detection system (IDS)　A system to identify suspicious, malicious, or undesirable activity that indicates a breach in computer security.

IPsec　IP Security, a protocol used to secure IP packets during transmission across a network. IPsec offers authentication, integrity, and confidentiality services. It uses Authentication Headers (AHs) and Encapsulating Security Payload (ESP) to accomplish this functionality.

ISAKMP/Oakley　*See* Internet Key Exchange.

Kerberos　A network authentication protocol designed by MIT for client/server environments.

Key　In cryptography, a sequence of characters or bits used by an algorithm to encrypt or decrypt a message.

Keyspace　The entire set of all possible keys for a specific encryption algorithm.

Least privilege　A security principle in which a subject is provided with the minimum set of rights and privileges that the subject needs in order to perform its function. The goal is to limit the potential damage that any subject can cause.

Layer Two Tunneling Protocol (L2TP)　L2TP is a Cisco switching protocol that operates at the data-link layer.

Local area network (LAN)　A LAN is a grouping of computers in a network structure confined to a limited area and using specific protocols, such as Ethernet for OSI Layer Two traffic addressing.

Logic bomb　A form of malicious code or software that is triggered by a specific event or condition. *See also* time bomb.

Mandatory access control (MAC)　An access control mechanism in which the security mechanism controls access to all objects (files), and individual subjects (processes or users) cannot change that access.

Man-in-the-middle attack　Any attack that attempts to use a network node as the intermediary between two other nodes. Each of the endpoint nodes think they are talking directly to each other, but they are actually talking to the intermediary.

Message digest　The result of applying a hash function to data. Sometimes also called a hash value. *See also* hash value.

Metropolitan area network (MAN)　A collection of networks interconnected in a metropolitan area and usually connected to the Internet.

Mitigate　Action taken to reduce the likelihood of a threat occurring.

Network-based intrusion detection system (NIDS)　A system for examining network traffic to identify suspicious, malicious, or undesirable behavior.

Network operating system (NOS)   An operating system that includes additional functions and capabilities to assist in connecting computers and devices, such as printers, to a local area network.

Nonrepudiation   The ability to verify that a message has been sent and received. This is a property of a system that prevents the parties to a transaction from subsequently denying involvement in the transaction.

Oakley   A key exchange protocol that defines how to acquire authenticated keying material based on the Diffie-Hellman key exchange algorithm.

Object reuse   Assignment of a previously used medium to a subject. The security implication is that before it is provided to the subject, any data present from a previous user must be cleared.

One-time pad   An unbreakable encryption scheme where a series of nonrepeating, random bits are used once as a key to encrypt a message. Since each pad is used only once, no pattern can be established and traditional cryptanalysis techniques are not effective.

Operating system (OS)   The basic software that handles things such as input, output, display, memory management, and all the other highly detailed tasks required to support the user environment and associated applications.

Orange Book   The name commonly used to refer to the now outdated Department of Defense Trusted Computer System Evaluation Criteria (TCSEC).

Password   A string of characters that are used to prove an individual's identity to a system or object. Used in conjunction with a userid, it is the most common method of authentication. The password should be kept secret by the individual who owns the password.

Patch   A replacement set of code designed to correct problems or vulnerabilities in existing software.

Penetration testing   A security test in which an attempt is made to circumvent security controls in order to discover vulnerabilities and weaknesses. This is also called a pen test.

Permissions   Authorized actions a subject can perform on an object. *See also* access control.

Phreaking   Used in the media to refer to the hacking of computer systems and networks associated with the phone company. *See also* cracking.

Plaintext   In cryptography, a piece of data that is not encrypted. It can also mean the data input into an encryption algorithm that would output ciphertext.

Point-to-Point Protocol (PPP)   PPP is the Internet standard for transmission of IP packets over a serial line, as in a dial-up connection to an ISP.

Point-to-Point Protocol Extensible Authentication Protocol (PPP EAP)   EAP is a PPP extension that provides support for additional authentication methods within PPP.

Point-to-Point Protocol Password Authentication Protocol (PPP PAP)   PAP is a PPP extension that provides support for password authentication methods over PPP.

Pretty Good Privacy (PGP)   A popular encryption program. It has the ability to encrypt and digitally sign e-mail and files.

Preventative intrusion detection   A system that detects hostile actions or network activity and prevents them from impacting information systems.

Privacy   Protecting an individual's personal information from those not authorized to see it.

Privilege auditing   The process of checking the rights and privileges assigned to a specific account or group of accounts.

Privilege management   The process of restricting a user's ability to interact with the computer system.

Public key cryptography   *See* asymmetric encryption.

Public Key Infrastructure (PKI)   Infrastructure for binding a public key to a known user through a trusted intermediary, typically a certificate authority.

Qualitative risk assessment   The process of subjectively determining the impact of an event that affects a project, program, or business. It involves the use of expert judgment, experience, or group consensus to complete the assessment.

Quantitative risk assessment   The process of objectively determining the impact of an event that affects a project, program, or business. It usually involves the use of metrics and models to complete the assessment.

RADIUS   Remote Authentication Dial-In User Service is a standard protocol for providing authentication services. It is commonly used in dial-up, wireless, and PPP environments.

Repudiation   The act of denying that a message was either sent or received.

Residual risk   Risks remaining after an iteration of risk management.

Risk   The possibility of suffering a loss.

Risk assessment or risk analysis   The process of analyzing an environment to identify the threats, vulnerabilities, and mitigating actions to determine (either quantitatively or qualitatively) the impact of an event affecting a project, program, or business.

Risk management   Overall decision-making process of identifying threats and vulnerabilities and their potential impacts, determining the costs to mitigate such events, and deciding what actions are cost effective to take to control these risks.

Role-based access control (RBAC)   An access control mechanism in which, instead of the users being assigned specific access permissions for the objects associated with the computer system or network, a set of roles that the user may perform will be assigned to each user.

Safeguard   *See* control.

Secure Shell (SSH)   SSH is a set of protocols for establishing a secure remote connection to a computer. This protocol requires a client on each end of the connection and can use a variety of encryption protocols.

Secure Sockets Layer (SSL)   SSL is an encrypting layer between the session and transport layer of the OSI model designed to encrypt above the transport layer, enabling secure sessions between hosts.

Security association (SA)   An instance of security policy and keying material applied to a specific data flow. Both IKE and IPsec use SAs, although these SAs are independent of one another. IPsec SAs are *unidirectional* and they are unique in each security protocol, whereas IKE SAs are bidirectional. A set of SAs are needed for a protected data pipe, one per direction per protocol. SAs are uniquely identified by destination (IPsec endpoint) address, security protocol (AH or ESP), and security parameter index (SPI).

Security baseline   The end result of the process of establishing an information system's security state. It is a known good configuration resistant to attacks and information theft.

Segregation or separation of duties   A basic control that prevents or detects errors and irregularities by assigning responsibilities to different individuals such that no single individual can commit fraudulent or malicious actions.

Service set identifier (SSID)   Identifies a specific 802.11 wireless network. It transmits information about the access point that the wireless client is connecting to.

Signature database   Collection of predefined activity patterns that have already been identified and categorized—activity patterns that typically indicate suspicious or malicious activity.

Single loss expectancy (SLE)   Monetary loss or impact of each occurrence of a threat. SLE = asset value * exposure factor.

Single sign-on (SSO)   An authentication process where the user can enter a single userid and password and then be able to move from application to application or resource to resource without having to supply further authentication information.

Slack space   Unused space on a disk drive created when a file is smaller than the allocated unit of storage (such as a sector).

S/MIME   Secure/Multipurpose Internet Mail Extensions is an encrypted implementation of the MIME (Multipurpose Internet Mail Extensions) protocol specification.

SMTP   Simple Mail Transfer Protocol, the standard Internet protocol used to transfer e-mail between hosts.

Sniffer   A software or hardware device used to observe network traffic as it passes through a network on a shared broadcast media.

Social engineering   The art of deceiving another individual so that they reveal confidential information. This is often accomplished by posing as an individual who should be entitled to have access to the information.

Spam   E-mail that is not requested by the recipient and is typically of a commercial nature. Also known as unsolicited commercial e-mail (UCE).

Spoofing   Making data appear to have originated from another source so as to hide the true origin from the recipient.

Symmetric encryption   Encryption that needs all parties to have a copy of the key, sometimes called a *shared secret*. The single key is used for both encryption and decryption.

Tangible asset   An asset for which a monetary equivalent can be determined. Examples are inventory, buildings, cash, hardware, software, and so on.

Tempest   The military's name for the field associated with electromagnetic eavesdropping on signals emitted by electronic equipment. *See also* Van Eck phenomenon.

Threat   Any circumstance or event with the potential to cause harm to an asset.

Time bomb   A form of logic bomb in which the triggering event is a date or specific time. *See also* logic bomb.

Token   A hardware device that can be used in a challenge-response authentication process.

Transport Control Protocol (TCP)   TCP is the transport layer protocol for use on the Internet and allows packet-level tracking of a conversation.

Transport layer security (TLS)   A newer form of SSL being proposed as an Internet standard.

Trapdoor   *See* backdoor.

Trojan horse   A form of malicious code that appears to provide one service (and may indeed provide that service) but that also hides another purpose. This hidden purpose often has a malicious intent. This code may also be referred to as simply a Trojan.

Uninterruptible power supply (UPS)   A source of power (generally a battery) designed to provide uninterrupted power to a computer system in the event of a temporary loss of power.

Usage auditing   The process of recording who did what and when on an information system.

User Datagram Protocol (UDP)   An Internet standard protocol for the transport layer that does not sequence packets—it is fire and forget in nature.

Userid   A unique alphanumeric identifier that identifies individuals when logging in or accessing a system.

Van Eck phenomenon   Electromagnetic eavesdropping through the interception of electronic signals emitted by electrical equipment. *See also* Tempest.

Virtual local area network (VLAN)   A broadcast domain inside a switched system.

Virtual private network (VPN)   An encrypted network connection across another network, offering a private communication channel across a public medium.

Virus   A form of malicious code or software that attaches itself to other pieces of code in order to replicate. Viruses may contain a payload, which is a portion of the code that is designed to execute when a certain condition is met (such as on a certain date). This payload is often malicious in nature.

Vulnerability   A weakness in an asset that can be exploited by a threat to cause harm.

WAP   *See* Wireless Application Protocol.

War-dialing   An attacker's attempt to gain unauthorized access to a computer system or network by discovering unprotected connections to the system through the telephone system and modems.

War-driving   The attempt by an attacker to discover unprotected wireless networks by wandering (or driving) around with a wireless device, looking for available wireless access points.

WEP   *See* Wired Equivalent Privacy.

Wide area network (WAN)   A network across a large geographic region.

Wired Equivalent Privacy (WEP)   The encryption scheme used to attempt to provide confidentiality and data integrity on 802.11 networks.

Wireless Application Protocol (WAP)   A protocol for transmitting data to small handheld devices like cellular phones.

Wireless Transport Layer Security (WTLS)   The encryption protocol that is used on WAP networks.

Worm   A independent piece of malicious code or software. Unlike a virus, it does not need to be attached to another piece of code. A worm replicates by breaking into another system and making a copy of itself on this new system. A worm may contain a destructive payload but does not have to.

X.509   The standard format for digital certificates.

XOR   Bitwise exclusive OR, an operation commonly used in cryptography.

INDEX

INTERNATIONAL CONTACT INFORMATION

AUSTRALIA
McGraw-Hill Book Company Australia Pty. Ltd.
TEL +61-2-9900-1800
FAX +61-2-9878-8881
http://www.mcgraw-hill.com.au
books-it_sydney@mcgraw-hill.com

CANADA
McGraw-Hill Ryerson Ltd.
TEL +905-430-5000
FAX +905-430-5020
http://www.mcgraw-hill.ca

GREECE, MIDDLE EAST, & AFRICA
(Excluding South Africa)
McGraw-Hill Hellas
TEL +30-210-6560-990
TEL +30-210-6560-993
TEL +30-210-6560-994
FAX +30-210-6545-525

MEXICO (Also serving Latin America)
McGraw-Hill Interamericana Editores S.A. de C.V.
TEL +525-117-1583
FAX +525-117-1589
http://www.mcgraw-hill.com.mx
fernando_castellanos@mcgraw-hill.com

SINGAPORE (Serving Asia)
McGraw-Hill Book Company
TEL +65-6863-1580
FAX +65-6862-3354
http://www.mcgraw-hill.com.sg
mghasia@mcgraw-hill.com

SOUTH AFRICA
McGraw-Hill South Africa
TEL +27-11-622-7512
FAX +27-11-622-9045
robyn_swanepoel@mcgraw-hill.com

SPAIN
McGraw-Hill/Interamericana de España, S.A.U.
TEL +34-91-180-3000
FAX +34-91-372-8513
http://www.mcgraw-hill.es
professional@mcgraw-hill.es

UNITED KINGDOM, NORTHERN,
EASTERN, & CENTRAL EUROPE
McGraw-Hill Education Europe
TEL +44-1-628-502500
FAX +44-1-628-770224
http://www.mcgraw-hill.co.uk
computing_europe@mcgraw-hill.com

ALL OTHER INQUIRIES Contact:
McGraw-Hill/Osborne
TEL +1-510-420-7700
FAX +1-510-420-7703
http://www.osborne.com
omg_international@mcgraw-hill.com